Bond's Minority Franchise Guide

2000 Edition

1st Annual Edition

Robert E. Bond, Publisher

Nicole Thompson, Editor

Amy Lau, Editorial Assistant
Steve Schiller, Senior Writer
Alex Wedemeyer, Editorial Assistant

Source Book Publications
Serving the Franchising Industry
P.O. Box 12488, Oakland, CA 94604
(510) 839-5471

ISBN 1-887137-16-5

DISCLAIMER

BOND'S MINORITY FRANCHISE GUIDE is based on data submitted by the franchisors themselves. Every effort has been made to obtain up-to-date and reliable information. As the information returned has not been independently verified, we assume no responsibility for errors or omissions and reserve the right to include or eliminate listings and otherwise edit and present the data based on our discretion and judgment as to what is useful to the readers of this directory. Inclusion in the publication does not imply endorsement by the editors or the publisher. Errors brought to the attention of the publisher and verified to the satisfaction of the publisher will be corrected in future editions. The publisher specifically disclaims all warranties, including the implied warranties of merchantability and fitness for a specific purpose.

This publication is designed to provide its readers with accurate and authoritative information with regard to the subject matter covered. It is sold with the understanding that neither the author nor the publisher is engaged in rendering legal, accounting or other professional services. If legal advice or other expert assistance is required, the services of a competent professional person should be sought.

From a Declaration of Principles jointly adopted by a Committee of the American Bar Association and a Committee of Publishers.

Cover Design by Joyce Coffland, Artistic Concepts, Oakland, CA.

ISBN 1-887137-16-5

Printed in the United States of America.
10 9 8 7 6 5 4 3 2 1

BOND'S MINORITY FRANCHISE GUIDE is available at special discounts for bulk purchase. Special editions or book excerpts can also be created to specifications. For details, contact **Source Book Publications**, P.O. Box 12488, Oakland, CA 94604. Phone: (510) 839-5471; FAX: (510) 839-2104.

BK
1995

To Terrian Barnes —

Who has done more to
promote and foster minority franchising
than any other person or organization.
We are deeply indebted to your
leadership and commitment.

Preface

Franchising touches virtually every aspect of our lives — from fast food to tax services to child development to printing services. It encompasses roughly 13% of retail sales and directly employs millions. Most importantly, franchising represents a unique opportunity to take advantage of a proven operating system that significantly reduces the risks generally associated with entrepreneurship.

Although there are no hard statistics, most would agree that minority ownership is poorly represented within the franchising community. Conversely, most franchisors have come to realize that minority franchising is a ripe market that should be tapped. To this end, forward-looking franchisors are aggressively trying to attract minorities into their systems. Many have developed creative programs that focus specifically on minority recruitment, training and financing. Many have made the financing part of the equation (the major stumbling block for many prospective franchisees) significantly less of a chore. Today's under-representation clearly presents a real window of opportunity for minorities, but only for someone who is otherwise qualified and who has already done his or her homework. If you meet these constraints, then you are prepared to approach the supportive franchisors listed below about becoming a part of their system. We hope that you will take advantage of this opportunity and, in so doing, create a lifestyle for yourself that meets your goals and ambitions.

The U.S. population currently stands at 273 million. Ethnic minorities make up roughly 29.2%. These include 34.9 million (12.8%) African-Americans, 31.4 million (11.5%) Hispanics, 10.9 million (4.0%) Asian-Americans and 2.5 million (0.9%) Native Americans. Unfortunately, the representation of minorities within the franchising community bears little relation to the total population. Based on the most definitive questionnaire (see Appendix B) yet sent to the franchising community regarding minority participation, our best guess is that minorities collectively make up only 6–9% of the total franchisees currently in operation. This represents a short-fall of 20–23% of the U.S. population. Lots of ground to make up!

To bridge this unacceptable gap, the National Minority Franchising Initiative was conceived in late Spring 1999. The primary objectives were 1) to educate prospective minority franchisees about the realistic pros and cons of franchising and 2) to expose them to those franchise systems that truly encourage and support the inclusion of minorities within their systems.

The Initiative has been completely underwritten by those forward-looking companies that are noted on the cover of the book — 7-Eleven, AAMCO, Bass Hotels & Resorts, Coverall Cleaning Concepts, FastSigns, General Nutrition Centers, Meineke Discount Mufflers, New York Burrito Gourmet Wraps, PostNet Postal & Business Services, RadioShack, Star Mart and the 3 Tricon companies (KFC, Pizza Hut and Taco Bell). In addition, we received the support of Black Enterprise Magazine, the Department of Commerce (Minority Business Development Agency), HispanicBusiness.com and the National Franchise Council. These companies are not only leaders within the franchising industry, but exemplary corporate citizens when it comes to creating a level playing field.

There are 3 primary facets to the Initiative: 1) *Bond's Minority Franchising Guide*; 2) an easy-to-use, comprehensive and searchable (5 custom sorts) Website — **www.minorityfranchising.com** — that will include all of the franchisor profiles in the book, as well as all relevant resource materials (the information on the Website will be periodically updated); and 3) a series of rigorous, yet affordable, 2-day seminars that will be held in San Francisco (March 4–5), Atlanta (April 15–16), Los Angeles (May 20–21), Boston (June 24–25), Detroit (August 26–27), Chicago (September 23–24), and Philadelphia (October 21–22). More information about the seminars is available on page 11 or on the Website at **www.minorityfranchising.com.**

Although only a starting point, these efforts should go a long way towards jump-starting minority participation in the field of franchising. It is also hoped that this Initiative will provide an incentive for those franchisors not listed below to focus on aggressively recruiting minorities into their system. While there is clearly a long way to go, this is a promising start. To ensure continued progress, the National Minority Franchising Initiative will be an annual program.

❋

At its best, purchasing a franchise is a time-tested, paint-by-the-numbers method of starting a new business. It avoids many of the myriad pitfalls normally encountered by someone starting anew and vastly improves the odds of success. It represents an exceptional blend of operating independence with a proven system that includes a detailed blueprint on starting and managing the business, as well as the all-important on-going support.

But purchasing a franchise is clearly not a foolproof investment that somehow guarantees the investor financial independence.

At its worst, if the evaluation and investment decision is sloppy or haphazard, franchising can be a nightmare. You can lose your original investment plus any assets used to personally secure your debt, not to mention your marriage and your self-confidence.

Your ultimate success as a franchisee will be determined by two factors:

1. The homework you do at the front-end to ensure that you are selecting the optimal franchise for your particular needs, experience and financial resources.

2. Your commitment to work hard and play by the rules once you have signed a binding, long-term franchise agreement. A franchise system is only as good as you make it. In most cases, this involves working 60+ hours per week until you can justify delegating some of the day-to-day responsibilities. It also requires being a team player within the system — not acting as an entrepreneur who does his or her own thing without regard for the system as a whole.

The motivation for writing this annual directory has been to better assist the minority community in the evaluation phase of the equation: to provide accurate, in-depth data on the many legitimate companies actively selling franchises. The book is written for the sophisticated businessperson seriously interested in the process of selecting an optimal franchise opportunity: someone willing to commit the time and resources necessary to find the best franchise for his or her particular needs; someone with the wisdom to know that the franchise selection process is exceedingly difficult and filled with potholes; someone keenly aware of the risks — including missed opportunities — of going through the process in a half-hearted way.

We hope we can facilitate the evaluation process by ensuring that the potential franchisee is exposed to the full range of options open to him or her and that he or she goes about the selection process in a logical and systematic manner.

�֍

Over 400 franchising opportunities are listed on the following pages. All of the companies listed support the objectives of the National Minority Franchising Initiative and actively encourage the inclusion of minorities within their systems.

No doubt you will be familiar with a large number of the listings. Many are household names. That, incidentally, is one of the primary benefits of franchising. Most people would agree that AAMCO Transmissions has a better ring to it than Jimmy's Transmission Shop. Apart from the proven systems and procedures, you are buying a recognized name and the reputation that the name enjoys in the marketplace.

✖

After you have decided which of the 39 industry groups provide the most interest, contact **all** of the companies listed in a particular category(ies) and request a marketing brochure. Thoroughly read their literature and pick out the companies that interest you and that represent a natural fit with your talents and financial resources. You should be able to narrow your choices down to a manageable list of 6 or 8 franchises that fit these criteria. Initiate an in-depth analysis of and dialogue with each of these franchisors. Concurrently, develop a thorough knowledge of the business and/or services that you are considering. Seek the advice of professionals, even if you are experienced in various elements of the evaluation process. Don't leave any stone unturned.

✖

Remember, this is not a game! You are quite literally betting the ranch on your ability to pick a well-managed, market-oriented franchise. You want one that will take advantage of your unique talents and experience and not take advantage of you in the process! Don't take short-cuts. Listen to what the franchisor and your advisors tell you. Don't think you are so clever or independent that you

can't benefit from the advice of outside professionals. Don't assume that the franchisor's guidelines regarding the amount of investment, experience, temperament, etc., somehow don't apply to you. Don't accept any promises or "understandings" from the franchisor that are not committed in writing to the franchise agreement. Spend the extra money to talk to and/or meet with other franchisees in the system. The additional front-end investment you make, both in time and money, will pay off handsomely if it saves you from making a marginal, or poor, investment decision. This is one of the few times in business when second chances are rare. Make the extra effort to do it right the first time.

✖

Good luck and Godspeed.

Table of Contents

Section Four — Appendices

Section Five — Index

Minority Franchising Seminar Schedule

March 4 and 5	San Francisco, California
April 15 and 16	Atlanta, Georgia
May 20 and 21	Los Angeles, California
June 24 and 25	Boston, Massachusetts
August 26 and 27	Detroit, Michigan
September 23 and 24	Chicago, Illinois
October 21 and 22	Philadelphia, Pennsylvania

A rigorous, yet affordable, 2-day seminar series that will be held from 9:30 until 5:00 each day. The cost of attendance is $35. Free copies of the *Bond's Minority Franchise Guide* will be provided to all seminar attendees. The in-depth and "even-handed" seminars will cover all facets of franchising, including benefits and areas of concern, evaluation, financing, the negotiation process, legal considerations, etc.

Contact Source Book Publications at (800) 841-0873 or (510) 839-5471 for more information, or by e-mail at sourcebook@earthlink.net.

In presenting this data, we have made some unilateral assumptions about our readers. The first is that you purchased the book because of the depth and accuracy of the data provided — not as a how-to manual. Chapter 3, Recommended Reading, lists several resources for anyone requiring additional background information on the franchising industry and on the process of evaluating a company. Clearly, dedication to hard work, adequate financing, commitment, good business sense and access to trusted professional counsel will determine your ultimate success as a franchisee. A strong working knowledge of the industry, however, will help ensure that you have made the best choice of franchise opportunities. I advise you to acquaint yourself with the dynamics of the industry before you initiate the evaluation and negotiation phases of selecting a franchise.

The second assumption is that you have already devoted the time necessary to conduct a detailed personal inventory. This self-assessment should result in a clear understanding of your skills, aptitudes, weaknesses, long-term personal goals, commitment to succeed and financial capabilities. Most of the books in the Recommended Reading Chapter provide worksheets to accomplish this important step.

There are 3 primary stages to the franchise selection process: 1) the investigation stage, 2) the evaluation stage and 3) and the negotiation stage. This book is intended primarily to assist the reader in the investigation stage by providing a thorough list of the options available. Chapters 1 and 2 include various observations based on my 15 or so years of involvement with the franchising industry. Hopefully, they will provide some insights that you will find of value.

Understand at the outset that the entire process will take many months and involve a great deal of frustration. I suggest that you set up a realistic time-line for signing a franchise agreement and that you stick with that schedule. There will be a lot of pressure on you to prematurely complete the selection and negotiation phases. Resist the temptation. The penalties are too severe for a seat-of-the-pants attitude. A decision of this magnitude clearly deserves your full attention. Do your homework!

Before starting the selection process, you would be well advised to briefly review the areas that follow.

Franchise Industry Structure

The franchising industry is made up of two distinct types of franchises. The first, and by far the larger, encompasses product and trade name franchising. Automotive and truck dealers, soft drink bottlers and gasoline service stations are included in this group. For the most part, these are essentially distributorships.

The second group encompasses business format franchisors. This book only includes information on this latter category.

Layman's Definition of Franchising

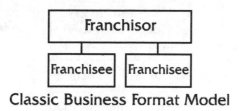

Classic Business Format Model

Business format franchising is a method of market expansion by which one business entity expands the distribution of its products and/or services through independent, third-party operators. Franchising occurs when the operator of a concept or system (the **franchisor**) grants an independent businessperson (the **franchisee**) the right to duplicate its entire business format at a particular location and for a specified period, under terms and conditions set forth in the contract (**franchise agreement**). The franchisee has full access to all of the trademarks, logos, marketing techniques, controls and systems that have made the franchisor successful. In effect, the franchisee acts as a surrogate for a company-owned store in the distribution of the franchisor's goods and/or services. It is important to keep in mind that the franchisor and the franchisee are separate legal entities.

In return for a front-end **franchise fee** — which usually ranges from $15,000–$35,000 — the franchisor is obligated to "set up" the franchisee in business. This generally includes assistance in selecting a location, negotiating a lease, obtaining financing, building and equipping a site and providing the necessary training, operating manuals, etc. Once the training is completed and the store is open, the new franchisee should have a carbon copy of other units in the system and enjoy the same benefits they do, whether they are company-owned or not.

Business format franchising is unique because it is a long-term relationship characterized by an on-going, mutually beneficial partnership. On-going services include research and development, market-

ing strategies, advertising campaigns, group buying, periodic field visits, training updates, and whatever else is required to make the franchisee competitive and profitable. In effect, the franchisor acts as the franchisee's "back office" support organization. To reimburse the franchisor for this support, the franchisee pays the franchisor an on-going **royalty fee**, generally 4–8% of gross sales or income. In many cases, franchisees also contribute an **advertising fee** to reimburse the franchisor for expenses incurred in maintaining a national or regional advertising campaign.

For the maximum advantage, both the franchisor and the franchisees should share common objectives and goals. Both parties must accept the premise that their fortunes are mutually intertwined and that they are each better off working in a co-operative effort, rather than toward any self-serving goals. Unlike the parent/child relationship that has dominated franchising over the past 30 years, franchising is now becoming a true and productive relationship of partners.

Legal Definition of Franchising

The Federal Trade Commission (FTC) has its own definition of franchising. So do each of the 16 states that have separate franchise registration statutes. The State of California's definition, which is the model for the FTC's definition, follows:

Franchise means a contract or agreement, express or implied, whether oral or written, between two or more persons by which:

> *A franchisee is granted the right to engage in the business of offering, selling, or distributing goods or services under a marketing plan or system prescribed in substantial part by a franchisor;*

> *The operation of the franchisee's business pursuant to that plan or system as substantially associated with the franchisor's trademark, service mark, trade name, logotype, advertising, or other commercial symbol designating the franchisor or its affiliates; and*

> *The franchisee is required to pay, directly or indirectly, a franchise fee.*

Multi-Level Franchising

With franchisors continually exploring new ways to expand their distribution, the classic business format model shown above has evolved over the years. Modifications have allowed franchisors to grow more rapidly and at less cost than might have otherwise been possible.

If a franchisor wishes to expand at a faster rate than its financial resources or staff levels allow, it might choose to sell development rights in an area (state, national or international) and let the new entity do the development work. No matter which development method is chosen, the franchisee should still receive the same benefits and support provided under the standard model. The major difference is that the entity providing the training and on-going support and receiving the franchise and royalty fees changes.

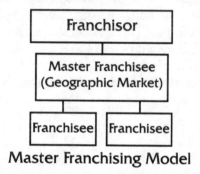

Master Franchising Model

Three variations of the master franchising model include: 1) master (or regional) franchising, 2) sub-franchising and 3) area development franchising.

In **master (or regional) franchising**, the franchisor sells the development rights in a particular market to a master franchisee who, in turn, sells individual franchises within the territory. In return for a front-end master franchise fee, the master franchisee has sole responsibility for developing that area under a mutually agreed upon schedule. This includes attracting, screening, signing and training all new franchisees within the territory. Once established, on-going support is generally provided by the parent franchisor.

The master franchisee is rewarded by sharing in the franchise fees and the on-going royalties paid

to the parent franchisor by the franchisees within the territory.

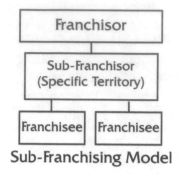

Sub-Franchising Model

Sub-franchising is similar to master franchising in that the franchisor grants development rights in a specified territory to a sub-franchisor. After the agreement is signed, however, the parent franchisor has no on-going involvement with the individual franchisees in the territory. Instead, the sub-franchisor becomes the focal point. All fees and royalties are paid directly to the sub-franchisor. It is solely responsible for all recruiting, training and on-going support, and passes on an agreed upon percentage of all incoming fees and royalties to the parent franchisor.

In a sub-franchising relationship, the potential franchisee has to be doubly careful in his or her investigation. He or she must first make sure that the sub-franchisor has the necessary financial, managerial and marketing skills to make the program work. Secondarily, the potential franchisee has to feel comfortable that the parent franchisor can be relied upon to come to his or her rescue if the sub-franchisor should fail.

The third variation is an **area development agreement**. Here again, the franchisor grants exclusive development rights for a particular geographic area to an area development investment group. Within its territory, the area developer may either develop individual franchise units for its own account or find independent franchisees to develop units. In the latter case, the area developer has a residual equity position in the profits of its "area franchisees."

In return for the rights to an exclusive territory, the area developer pays the franchisor a front-end development fee and commits to develop a certain number of units within a specified time period. (The front-end fee is generally significantly less than the sum of the individual unit fees.) Individual franchisees within the territory pay all contractual franchise, royalty and advertising fees directly to the parent franchisor. The area developer shares in neither the franchise fee nor in on-going royalty or advertising fees. Instead, the area developer shares only in the profitability of the individual franchises that it "owns." In essence, the area developer is buying multiple locations over time at a discount, since the franchise fee and (frequently) the royalty fee are less than the per unit rate.

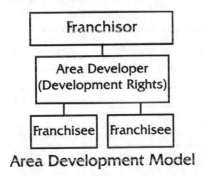

Area Development Model

Franchise Industry Statistics

In their most recent industry survey, the International Franchise Association (IFA) estimated that product and trade name franchising accounted for $554 billion in sales in 1992. This represents roughly 28% of all retail sales.

Business format franchising produced total sales of $249 billion in 1992, roughly 13% of all retail sales. In layman's language, this means that for every $1.00 spent at the retail level, more than $0.13 went to franchised establishments. There is no question that franchising has had a profound impact on the way business is conducted in the U.S. Most analysts anticipate that the overall numbers and market share of retail business will continue to grow well into the foreseeable future and at a faster rate than the economy in general.

According to the IFA's 1997 "Profile of Franchising (Statistical Profile of the 1997 Uniform Franchise Offering Circular Data)," 18% of the industry was concentrated in fast-food and 11% in retail, while only 1% of the concentration was in travel or printing. In terms of system size, about half of the systems analyzed had more than 50 units, with 27% (the largest concentration) having between 11 and 50 franchised units and 75% having 10 or fewer company-owned units. 60% of the companies had been in business 12 or more years, but only 44% had been franchising for more than 8 years. Only 4% of the franchisors had an initial franchise fee of over $50,000; fast-food, which was the largest category, had an average fee of $19,999. The average total investment for most companies was under $250,000, and most had renewable franchise contracts. Although royalties varied greatly from franchise to franchise, most based it on sales/revenue and ranged from 3–6% monthly. 48% of franchisors had an advertising fee based on percentage, usually ranging between .01–2%. Franchisor-sponsored financing was offered by 37% of the companies. Data for 1998 is expected to be available in February, 2000.

Exhibits 1–5, noted below, are the result of querying our proprietary franchisor database (which has some 30 fields of information on 2,300 franchisors) and the database of some 1,050 detailed questionnaires that were returned as a result of our 1999 industry survey for Bond's Franchise Guide. You should spend some time reviewing the various Exhibits below to get a better idea of the relative size, fees and investment levels required in various industry categories. If the size of the franchise fee, total investment or royalty fee fall far outside the averages noted, the franchisor should have a ready explanation as to why.

The Players

Franchisors

Over 400 U.S. and Canadian franchisors are shown on the following pages. Although questionnaires were sent to all 2,300 North American franchisors, these are the companies that made the commitment to actively recruit minorities. Given the fact that the other 1,900 franchisors failed to respond to 2 separate mailings, my sense is that you should limit your search to the companies profiled below.

Exhibit 1

CATEGORY	# of Fran- chisors	Fran- chised Units	Company- Owned Units	Total Operating Units
Automotive Products & Services	133	23,046	3,317	26,363
Auto/Truck/Trailer Rental	22	7,233	1,010	8,243
Building & Remodeling/Furniture/Appliance Repair	79	5,600	137	5,737
Business: Financial Services	26	9,813	5,937	15,750
Business: Advertising & Promotion	29	1,715	71	1,786
Business: Telecommunications/Miscellaneous	49	3,026	629	3,655
Child Development/Education/Products	57	4,441	196	4,637
Education/Personal Development/Training	52	23,044	756	23,800
Employment & Personnel	65	3,993	1,900	5,893
Food: Donuts/Cookies/Bagels	62	10,913	889	11,802
Food: Coffee	24	1,269	196	1,465
Food: Ice Cream/Yogurt	38	14,708	1,092	15,800
Food: Quick Service/Take-out	294	94,810	21,538	116,348
Food: Restaurant/Family-Style	155	14,969	11,120	26,089
Food: Specialty Foods	83	5,464	664	6,128
Hairstyling Salons	26	5,512	851	6,363
Health/Fitness/Beauty	45	9,076	1,162	10,238
Laundry & Dry Cleaning	16	1,787	44	1,831
Lawn and Garden	20	1,314	136	1,450
Lodging	55	21,506	2,570	24,076
Maid Service & Home Cleaning	24	3,306	72	3,378
Maintenance/Cleaning/Sanitation	100	32,298	582	32,880
Medical/Optical/Dental Products & Services	20	2,495	791	3,286
Packaging & Mailing	19	7,868	28	7,896
Printing & Graphics	25	5,414	75	5,489
Publications	19	859	38	897
Real Estate Inspection Services	20	1,905	62	1,967
Real Estate Services	41	20,697	84	20,781
Recreation & Entertainment	31	2,196	141	2,337
Rental Services	11	2,449	325	2,774

CATEGORY	# of Franchisors	Franchised Units	Company-Owned Units	Total Operating Units
Retail: Art, Art Supplies & Framing	9	673	29	702
Retail: Athletic Wear/Sporting Goods	25	2,255	529	2,784
Retail: Clothing/Shoes/Accessories	9	151	427	578
Retail: Convenience Stores/Supermarkets/Drugs	27	27,477	5,595	33,072
Retail: Home Furnishings	38	2,933	127	3,060
Retail: Home Improvement & Hardware	15	12,643	485	13,128
Retail: Pet Products & Services	12	625	143	768
Retail: Photographic Products & Services	13	953	94	1,047
Retail: Specialty	103	6,146	3,293	9,439
Retail: Video/Audio/Electronics	17	4,776	10,860	15,636
Retail: Miscellaneous	16	1,678	132	1,810
Security & Safety Systems	18	888	103	991
Signs	14	1,531	9	1,540
Travel	19	4,940	438	5,378
Miscellaneous	62	4,528	517	5,045
Industry Total	2,037	414,923	79,194	494,117
% of Total		83.97%	16.03%	

Exhibit 2

Relative Size - By Number of Total Operating Units.	#	%
> 5,000 Total Operating Units	16	0.8%
1,000 - 4,999 Total Operating Units	61	3.0%
500 - 999 Total Operating Units	84	4.1%
250 - 499 Total Operating Units	149	7.3%
100 - 249 Total Operating Units	294	14.4%
50 - 99 Total Operating Units	294	14.4%
25 - 49 Total Operating Units	311	15.3%
15 - 24 Total Operating Units	227	11.1%
Less Than 15 Total Operating Units	601	29.5%
Total	2,037	100.0%

Exhibit 3

Country of Origin:	#
United States	1,719
Canada	318
Total	2,037

All of the data in Exhibits 1 - 3 are proprietary and should not be used or quoted without specifically acknowledging Bond's Franchise Guide as the source.

Exhibit 4

CATEGORY	Average Franchise Fee	Average Total Investment	Average Royalty Fee	# Survey Partici- pants	% of Industry Represent.
Automotive Products & Services	22,159	190,881	5.5%	77	57.9%
Auto / Trunk / Trailer Rental	41,620	257,143	5.2%	12	54.6%
Building & Remodeling/Furniture/Appliance Repair	21,266	76,176	5.0%	47	59.5%
Business: Financial Services	18,655	131,200	6.0%	11	42.3%
Business: Advertising & Promotion	24,600	42,509	1.8%	11	37.9%
Business: Telecommunications/Miscellaneous	23,530	118,219	5.8%	28	57.1%
Child Development/Education/Products	22,981	156,661	6.3%	36	63.2%
Education/Personal Development/Training	29,943	111,743	6.3%	24	46.2%
Employment & Personnel	19,034	106,346	6.3%	30	46.2%
Food: Donuts/Cookies/Bagels	24,843	263,657	4.9%	37	59.7%
Food: Coffee	21,269	199,492	5.7%	13	54.2%
Food: Ice Cream/Yogurt	18,781	182,719	4.2%	21	55.3%
Food: Quick Service/Take-out	19,998	305,250	4.8%	145	49.3%
Food: Restaurant/Family-Style	32,403	837,427	4.5%	62	40.0%
Food: Specialty Foods	22,130	183,373	4.8%	33	39.8%
Hairstyling Salons	17,154	100,169	5.9%	13	50.0%
Health/Fitness/Beauty	13,718	122,046	4.3%	24	53.3%
Laundry & Dry Cleaning	21,118	176,467	5.3%	12	75.0%
Lawn and Garden	21,773	67,136	7.1%	12	60.0%
Lodging	31,577	3.6MM	4.7%	13	23.6%
Maid Service & Home Cleaning	15,754	48,123	5.3%	13	54.2%
Maintenance/Cleaning/Sanitation	18,988	71,903	7.4%	61	61.0%
Medical/Optical/Dental Products & Services	21,533	311,862	5.9%	9	45.0%
Packaging & Mailing	23,723	86,192	5.5%	13	68.4%
Printing & Graphics	24,141	241,900	5.5%	17	68.0%
Publications	9,160	14,500	5.8%	6	31.6%
Real Estate Inspection Services	19,885	32,808	6.9%	13	65.0%
Real Estate Services	15,890	61,156	5.5%	21	51.2%
Recreation & Entertainment	17,155	333,386	8.1%	14	45.2%
Rental Services	14,929	216,886	3.9%	7	63.6%

CATEGORY	Average Franchise Fee	Average Total Investment	Average Royalty Fee	# Survey Partici-pants	% of Industry Represent.
Retail: Art, Art Supplies & Framing	24,083	142,050	6.1%	6	66.7%
Retail: Athletic Wear/Sporting Goods	29,833	260,772	3.8%	18	72.0%
Retail: Clothing/Shoes/Accessories	12,500	51,300	2.0%	2	22.2%
Retail: Convenience Stores/Supermarkets/Drugs	18,255	504,413	7.6%	11	40.7%
Retail: Home Furnishings	20,626	147,105	4.2%	19	50.0%
Retail: Home Improvement & Hardware	20,167	304,917	3.8%	6	40.0%
Retail: Pet Products & Services	17,857	151,757	4.4%	7	58.3%
Retail: Photographic Products & Services	28,112	102,625	4.3%	8	61.5%
Retail: Specialty	24,957	179,386	4.6%	44	42.7%
Retail: Video/Audio/Electronics	24,286	152,771	4.4%	7	41.2%
Retail: Miscellaneous	23,700	140,825	4.1%	8	50.0%
Security & Safety Systems	17,043	96,443	2.8%	7	38.9%
Signs	21,787	110,462	5.8%	8	57.1%
Travel	16,183	58,771	1.2%	7	36.8%
Miscellaneous	37,158	141,726	8.3%	20	32.3%

Exhibit 5

	Average Franchise Fee	Average Total Investment	Average Royalty Fee	# Survey Partici-pants	% of Industry Represent.
Categories with Lowest Franchise Fee:					
Publications	9,160	14,500	5.8%	6	31.6%
Retail: Clothing/Shoes/Accessories	12,500	51,300	2.0%	2	22.2%
Health/Fitness/Beauty	13,718	122,046	4.3%	24	53.3%
Categories with Lowest Total Investment:					
Publications	9,160	14,500	5.8%	6	31.6%
Real Estate Inspection Services	19,885	32,808	6.9%	13	65.0%
Business: Advertising & Promotion	24,600	42,509	1.8%	11	37.9%
Categories with Lowest Royalty Fee:					
Travel	16,183	58,771	1.2%	7	36.8%
Business: Advertising & Promotion	24,600	42,509	1.8%	11	37.9%
Retail: Clothing/Shoes/Accessories	12,500	51,300	2.0%	2	22.2%

All of the data in Exhibits 4 - 5 are proprietary and should not be used or quoted without specifically acknowledging Bond's Franchise Guide as the source.

The Regulatory Agencies

The offer and sale of franchises are regulated at both the federal and state levels. Federal requirements cover all 50 states. In addition, certain states have adopted their own requirements.

In 1979, after many years of debate, the Federal Trade Commission (FTC) implemented Rule 436. This Rule requires that franchisors provide prospective franchisees with a disclosure statement (called an offering circular) containing specific information about a company's franchise offering. The Rule has two objectives: to ensure that the potential franchisee has sufficient background information to make an educated investment decision and to provide him or her with adequate time to do so.

Certain "registration states" require additional safeguards to protect potential franchisees. Their requirements are generally more stringent than the FTC's requirements. These states include California, Florida, Hawaii, Illinois, Indiana, Maryland, Michigan, Minnesota, New York, North Dakota, Oregon, Rhode Island, South Dakota, Virginia, Washington and Wisconsin. Separate registration is also required in the province of Alberta, Canada.

For the most part, registration states require a disclosure format know as the Uniform Franchise Offering Circular (UFOC). As a matter of convenience and because the state requirements are more demanding, most franchisors have adopted the UFOC format. This format requires that the franchisor provides a prospective franchisee with the required information at their first face-to-face meeting or at least 10 business days prior to the signing of the franchise agreement, whichever is earlier. Required information includes:

1. The Franchisor and Any Predecessors.
2. Identity and Business Experience of Persons Affiliated with the Franchisor.
3. Litigation.
4. Bankruptcy.
5. Franchisee's Initial Fee/Other Initial Payments.
6. Other Fees.
7. Franchisee's Initial Investment.

8. Obligations of Franchisee to Purchase or Lease from Designated Sources.
9. Obligations of Franchisee to Purchase or Lease in Accordance with Specifications or from Approved Suppliers.
10. Financing Arrangements.
11. Obligations of the Franchisor; Other Supervision, Assistance or Services.
12. Exclusive Area of Territory.
13. Trademarks, Service Marks, Trade Names, Logotypes and Commercial Symbols.
14. Patents and Copyrights.
15. Obligations of the Franchisee to Participate in the Actual Operation of the Franchise Business.
16. Restrictions on Goods and Services Offered by Franchisee.
17. Renewal, Termination, Repurchase, Modification and Assignment of the Franchise Agreement and Related Information.
18. Arrangements with Public Figures.
19. Actual, Average, Projected or Forecasted Franchise Sales, Profits or Earnings.
20. Information Regarding Franchises of the Franchisor.
21. Financial Statements.
22. Contracts.
23. Acknowledgment of Receipt by Respective Franchisee.

If you live in a registration state, make sure that the franchisor you are evaluating is, in fact, registered to sell franchises there. If not, and the franchisor has no near-term plans to register in your state, you should consider other options.

Keep in mind that neither the FTC nor any of the states has reviewed the offering circular to determine whether the information submitted is true or not. They merely require that the franchisor make representations based upon a prescribed format. If the information provided is false, franchisors are subject to civil penalties. That may not help a franchisee, however, who cannot undo a very expensive mistake.

It is up to you to read and thoroughly understand all elements of the offering circular. There is no question that it is tedious reading. Know exactly what you can expect from the franchisor and what your own obligations are. Under what circumstances can the relationship be unilaterally terminated by the franchisor? What is your protected territory? Specifically, what front-end assistance will the franchisor provide? You should have a professional review the UFOC. Shame on you if you don't take full advantage of the documentation that is available to you. The penalties are severe, and you will have no one to blame but yourself.

The Trade Associations

The **International Franchise Association** (IFA) was established as a non-profit trade association to promote franchising as a responsible method of doing business. The IFA currently represents over 650 franchisors in the U.S. and around the world. It is recognized as the leading spokesperson for responsible franchising. For most of its 30+ years, the IFA has represented the interests of franchisors only. In recent years, however, it has initiated an aggressive campaign to recruit franchisees into its membership and represent their interests as well. The IFA's address is 1350 New York Avenue, NW, Suite 900, Washington, DC 20005. (202) 628-8000; FAX (202) 628-0812.

The **Canadian Franchise Association** (CFA), which has some 250+ members, is the Canadian equivalent of the IFA. Information on the CFA can be obtained from its offices at 5045 Orbit Dr., Bldg. 12, Unit 201, Mississauga, ON L4W 4Y4 Canada. (416) 625-2896; FAX (416) 625-9076.

The **American Association of Franchisees & Dealers** (AAFD) represents the rights and interests of franchisees and independent dealers. Formed in 1992 with the mission of "Bringing Fairness to Franchising," the AAFD represents thousands of franchised businesses, representing over 250 different franchise systems. It provides a broad range of services designed to help franchisees build market power, create legislative support, provide legal and financial support and provide a wide range of general member benefits. P.O. Box 81887, San Diego, CA 92138. (800) 733-9858, (619) 209-3775; FAX: (619) 209-3777.

Franchise Survival/Failure Rate

In order to promote the industry's attractiveness, most literature on the subject of franchising includes the same often-quoted, but very misleading, statistics that leave the impression that franchising is a near risk-free investment.

In the 1970's, the Small Business Administration produced a poorly documented report that 38% of all small businesses fail within their first year of operation and 77% fail within their first five years. With franchising, however, comparative failure rates miraculously drop to only 3% after the first year and 8% after five years. No effort was made to define failure. Instead, "success" was defined as an operating unit still in business under the same name at the same location.

While most people would agree that the failure rates for franchised businesses are substantially lower than the failure rates for independent businesses, that assumption is not substantiated by reliable statistics. Part of the problem is definitional. Part is the fact that the industry has a vested interest in perpetuating the myth rather than debunking it.

FRANDATA, a Washington, DC-based franchise research firm, recently conducted a review of franchise terminations and renewals. It found that 4.4% of all franchisees left their franchise system each year for a variety of reasons. This figure does not include sales to third parties, however. To be fully meaningful, the data should include sales to third parties and the underlying reasons behind a sale.

The critical issue is to properly define failure and success, and then require franchisors to report changes in ownership based on these universally accepted definitions. A logical starting point in defining success should be whether the franchisee can "make an honest living" as a franchisee. A "success" would occur when the franchisee prefers to continue as a franchisee rather than sell the business. A "failure" would occur when the franchisee is forced to sell his or her business at a loss.

A reasonable measure of franchise success would be to ask franchisees "would you do it again?" If a legitimate survey were conducted of all franchisees of all systems, my guess is that the answer to this question would indicate a "success rate" well under 70% after a 5-year period. Alternatively, one could ask the question "has the franchise investment met your expectations?" I estimate that fewer than 50% would say "yes" after a 5-year period. These are just educated guesses. Like the franchising industry, I have no basis in fact for these estimates.

The failure rate is unquestionably lower for larger, more mature companies in the industry that have proven their systems and carefully chosen their franchisees. It is substantially higher for smaller, newer companies that have unproven products and are less demanding in whom they accept as a franchisee.

As it now stands, the Uniform Franchise Offering Circular (UFOC) only requires the franchisor to provide the potential franchisee with the names of owners who have left the system within the past 12 months. In my opinion, this is a severe shortcoming of the regulatory process. Unless required, franchisors will not willingly provide information about failures to prospective franchisees. There is no question in my mind, however, that franchisors are fully aware of when and why past failures have occurred.

It is patently unfair that a potential investor should not have access to this critical information. To ensure its availability, I propose that the UFOC be amended to require that franchisors provide franchisee turn-over information for the most recent 5-year period. Underlying reasons for a change in ownership would be provided by a departing franchisee on a universal, industry-approved questionnaire filled out during an "exit" interview. The questionnaire would then be returned to some central clearing house.

The only way to make up for this lack of information is to aggressively seek out as many previous and current franchisees as possible. Request past UFOC's to get the names of previous owners, and then contact them. Whether successful or not, these owners are an invaluable resource. Try to determine the reason for their failure and/or disenchantment. Most failures are the result of poor management or inadequate finances on the part of the departing franchisee. But people give up franchises for other reasons.

Current franchisees are the best source of meaningful information. For systems with under 25 units, I strongly encourage your to talk to all franchisees. For those having between 25 and 100 units, I recommend talking to at least half. And for all others, interview a minimum of 50.

What Makes a Winning Franchise

Virtually every writer on the subject of franchising has his or her own idea of what determines a winning franchise. I maintain that there are five primary factors.

1. **A product or service with a clear advantage over the competition.** The advantage may be in brand recognition, a unique, proprietary product or 30 years of proven experience.

2. **A standardized franchise system that has been time-tested.** Look for a company in which most of the bugs in the system have been worked out through the cumulative experience of both company-owned and franchised units. By the time a system has 30 or more operating units, it should be thoroughly tested.

3. **Exceptional franchisor support.** This includes not only the initial training program, but the on-going support (R&D, refresher training, [800] help-lines, field representatives and on-site training, annual meetings, advertising and promotion, central purchasing, etc.).

4. **The financial wherewithal and management experience** to carry out any announced growth plans without short-changing its franchisees. Sufficient depth of management is often lacking in high-growth franchises.

5. **A strong mutuality of interest between franchisor and franchisees.** Unless both parties realize that their relationship is one of long-term

partners, it is unlikely that the system will ever achieve its full potential. Whether they have the necessary rapport is easily determined by a few telephone calls to existing franchisees.

Financial Projections

The single most important factor in buying a franchise — or any business for that matter — is having a realistic projection of sales, expenses and profits. Specifically, how much can you expect to make after working 65 hours a week for 52 weeks a year? No one is in a better position to supply accurate information (subject to caveats) about a franchise opportunity than the franchisor itself. A potential franchisee often does not have the experience to sit down and project what his or her sales and profits will be over the next five years. This is especially true if he or she has no applied experience in that particular business.

Earnings claim statements (Item 19 of the Uniform Franchise Offering Circular) present franchisor-supplied sales, expense and/or profit summaries based on actual operating results for company-owned and/or franchised units. Since no format is prescribed, however, the data may be cursory or detailed. The only constraint is that the franchisor must be able to substantiate the data presented. Further complicating the process is the fact that providing an earnings claim statement is strictly optional. Accordingly, only 20% of franchisors provide one.

Virtually everyone agrees that the information included in an earnings claim statement can be exceedingly helpful to a potential franchisee. Unfortunately, there are many reasons why franchisors might not willingly choose to make their actual results available to the public. Many franchisors feel that a prospective investor would be turned off if he or she had access to actual operating results. Others may not want to go to the trouble and expense of collecting the data.

Other franchisors are legitimately afraid of being sued for "misrepresentation." There is considerable risk to a franchisor if a published earnings claim statement is interpreted in any way as a "guarantee" of sales or income for new units. Given today's highly litigious society, and the propensity of courts to award large settlements to the "little guy," it's not surprising that so few franchisors provide the information.

As an assist to prospective franchisees, Source Book Publications has recently published the third edition of *"How Much Can I Make?"* It includes 150 earnings claim statements covering a diverse group of industries. It is the only publication that contains current earnings claim statements submitted by the franchisors. Given the scarcity of industry projections, this is an invaluable resource for potential franchisees or investors in determining what he or she might make by investing in a franchise or similar business. The book is $29.95, plus $4.00 shipping. See the inside rear cover of the book for additional details on the book and the companies that have submitted earnings claim statements. The book can be obtained from Source Book Publications, P.O. Box 12488, Oakland, CA 94604 or by calling (510) 839-5471 or faxing a request to (510) 839-2104.

New vs. Used

As a potential franchisee, you have the option of becoming a franchisee in a new facility at a new location or purchasing an existing franchise. It is not an easy decision. Your success in making that choice will depend upon your business acumen and your insights into people.

Purchasing a new franchise unit will mean that everything is current, clean and under warranty. Purchasing an existing franchise will probably involve a smaller investment and allow greater financial leverage. However, you will have to assess the seller's reason for selling. Is the business not performing to expectations because of poor management, poor location, poor support from the franchisor, an indifferent staff, obsolete equipment and/or facilities, etc.? The decision is further clouded because you may be working through a business broker who may or may not be giving you good information. Regardless of the obstacles, evaluating a "used" franchise merits your consideration. Apply the same analytical tools you would to a new franchise. Do your homework. Be thorough. Be unrelenting.

The Negotiation Process

Once you have narrowed your options down to your top two or three choices, you must negotiate the best deal you can with the franchisor. In most cases, the franchisor will tell you that the franchise agreement cannot be changed. If you accept this explanation, shame on you. Notwithstanding the legal requirement that all of a franchisor's agreements be **substantially** the same at any point in time, there are usually a number of variables in the equation. If the franchisor truly wants you as a franchisee, it may be willing to make concessions not available to the next applicant.

Will the franchisor take a short-term note for all or part of the franchise fee? Can you expand from your initial unit after you have proven yourself? If so, can the franchise fee be eliminated or reduced on a second unit? Can you get a right of first refusal on adjacent territories? Can the term of the agreement be extended from 10 to 15 years? Can you include a franchise cancellation right if the training and/or initial support don't meet your expectations or the franchisor's promises? The list goes on ad infinitum.

To successfully negotiate, you must have a thorough knowledge of the industry, the franchise agreement you are negotiating (and agreements of competitive franchise opportunities) and access to experienced professional advice. This can be a lawyer, an accountant or a franchise consultant. Above all else, they should have proven experience in negotiating franchise agreements. Franchising is a unique method of doing business. Don't pay someone $100+ per hour to learn the industry. Make them demonstrate that they have been through the process several times before. Negotiating a long-term agreement of this type is extremely tricky and fraught with pitfalls. The risks are extremely high. Don't be so smug as to think that you can handle the negotiations yourself. Don't be so frugal as to think you can't afford outside counsel. In point of fact, you can't afford not to employ an experienced professional advisor.

The 4 R's of Franchising

We are told as children that the three R's of reading, 'riting, and 'rithmetic are critical to our scholastic success. Success in franchising depends on four R's — realism, research, reserves and resolve.

Realism

At the outset of your investigation, it is important that you be realistic about your strengths and weaknesses, your goals and your capabilities. I strongly recommend that you take the time necessary to do a personal audit — possibly with the help of outside professionals — before risking your life's savings in a franchise.

Franchising is not a money machine. It involves hard work, dedication, set-backs and long hours. Be realistic about the nature of the business you are buying. What traits will ultimately determine your success? Do you have them? If it is a service-oriented business, will you be able to keep smiling when you know the client is a fool? If it is a fast-food business, will you be able to properly manage a minimum-wage staff? How well will you handle the uncertainties that will invariably arise? Can you make day-to-day decisions based on imperfect information? Can you count on your spouse's support after you have gone through all of your working capital reserves, and the future looks cloudy and uncertain?

Be equally realistic about your franchise selection process. Have you thoroughly evaluated all of the alternatives? Have you talked with everyone you can to ensure that you have left no stone unturned? Have you carefully and realistically assessed the advantages and disadvantages of the system offered, the unique demographics of your territory, near-term market trends, the financial projections, etc.? The selection process is tiring. It is easy to convince yourself that the franchise opportunity in your hand is really the best one for you. The penalties for doing so, however, are extreme.

Research

There is no substitute for exhaustive research!

Bond's Minority Franchise Guide contains over 400 franchise listings, broken into 39 distinct business categories. Each of these companies has expressed its commitment to recruiting minority franchisees. This represents a substantial number of options from which to choose. It is up to you to spend the time required to come up with an optimal selection. At a minimum, you will probably be in that business for five years. More likely, you will be in it 10 years or more. Given the long-term commitment, allow yourself the necessary time to ensure you don't regret having made a hasty decision. Research is a tedious, boring process. But doing it carefully and thoroughly can greatly reduce your risk and exposure. The benefits are measurable.

I suggest you first determine which industry groups hold your interest. Don't arbitrarily limit yourself to a particular industry in which you have first-hand experience. Next, request information from all of the companies that are listed in those industries. The incremental cost of mailing (or calling) requests to an additional 15 or 20 companies is insignificant in the larger picture. Based on personal experience, you may feel you already know the best franchise. Step back. Assume there is a competing franchise out there with a comparable product or service, comparable management, etc., that charges a royalty fee 2% of sales less than your intuitive choice. Over a 10-year period, that could add up to a great deal of money. It certainly justifies your requesting initial information.

A thorough analysis of the literature you receive should allow you to reduce the list of prime candidates down to 6–8 companies. Aggressively evaluate each firm. Talking with current and former franchisees is the single best source of information you can get. Where possible, site visits are invaluable. My experience is that franchisees tend to be candid in their level of satisfaction with the franchisor. However, since they don't know you, they may be less candid about their sales, expenses and income. Go to the library and get studies that forecast industry growth, market saturation, industry problems, technical break-throughs, etc. Don't find out a year after becoming a franchisee of a coffee company that earlier reports suggested that the coffee market was over-saturated or that coffee was linked to some form of colon cancer.

Reserves

As a new business, franchising is replete with uncertainty, uneven cash flows and unforeseen problems. It is an imperfect world that might not bear any relation to the clean pro formas you prepared to justify getting into the business. Any one of these unforeseen contingencies could cause a severe drain on your cash reserves. At the same time, you will have fixed and/or contractual payments that must be met on a current basis regardless of sales: rent, employee salaries, insurance, etc. Adequate back-up reserves may be in the form of savings, commitments from relatives, bank loans, etc. Just make certain that the funds are available when, and if, you need them. To be absolutely safe, I suggest you double the level of reserves recommended by the franchisor.

Keep in mind that the most common cause of business failure is inadequate working capital. Plan properly so you don't become a statistic.

Resolve

Let's assume for the time being that you have demonstrated exceptional levels of realism, research and reserves. You have picked an optimal franchise that takes full advantage of your strengths. You are in business and bringing in enough money to achieve a positive cash flow. The future looks bright. Now the fourth R — resolve — comes into play. Remember why you chose franchising in the first place: to take full advantage of a system that has been time-tested in the marketplace. Remember also what makes franchising work so well: the franchisor and franchisees maximize their respective success by working within the system for the common good. Invariably, two obstacles arise.

The first is the physical pain associated with writing that monthly royalty check. Annual sales of $250,000 and a 6% royalty fee result in a monthly royalty check of $1,250 that must be sent to the franchisor. Every month. As a franchisee, you may look for any justification to reduce this sizable monthly outflow. Resist the temptation. Accept the fact that royalty fees are simply another cost of doing business. They are also a legal obligation that you willingly agreed to pay when you signed the franchise agreement. They are the dues you agreed to pay when you joined the club.

Although there may be an incentive, don't look for loopholes in the contract that might allow you to sue the franchisor or get out of the relationship. Don't report lower sales than actual in an effort to reduce royalties. If you have received the support that you were promised, continue to play by the rules. Honor your commitment. Let the franchisor enjoy the rewards it has earned from your success.

The second obstacle is the desire to change the system. You need to honor your commitment to be a "franchisee" and to live within the franchise system. What makes franchising successful as far as your customers are concerned is uniformity and consistency of appearance, product/service quality and corporate image. The most damaging thing an individual franchisee can do is to suddenly and unilaterally introduce changes to the proven system. While these modifications may work in one market, they only serve to diminish the value of the system as a whole. Imagine what would happen to the national perception of your franchise if every franchisee had the latitude to make unilateral changes in his or her operations. Accordingly, any ideas you have on improving the system should be submitted directly to the franchisor for its evaluation. Accept the franchisor's decision on whether or not to pursue an idea.

If you suspect that you may be a closet entrepreneur, for unrestrained experimenting and tinkering, you are probably not cut out to be a franchisee. Seriously consider this question before you get into a relationship, instead of waiting until you are locked into an untenable situation.

Summary

I hope that I have been clear in suggesting that the selection of an optimal franchise is both time- and energy-consuming. Done properly, the process may take 6–9 months and may involve the expenditure of several thousand dollars. The difference between a hasty, gut-feel investigation and an exhaustive, well-thought out investigation may mean the difference between finding a poorly-conceived, or even fraudulent, franchise and an exceptional one.

My sense is that there is a strong correlation between the efforts you put into the investigative process and the ultimate degree of success you enjoy as a franchisee. The process is to investigate, evaluate and negotiate. Don't try to bypass any one of these critical elements.

How to use the data

The appendix includes the original questionnaire sent to some 2,200 U.S. and Canadian franchisors in the Fall of 1999. Franchisors who did not respond to the original mailing received a follow-up package roughly one month later. The end result was that roughly 20% of the contacted franchisors returned a completed questionnaire.

The data returned has been condensed into the profiles shown on the following pages. In some cases, an answer has been abbreviated to conserve room and to make the profiles more directly comparable. All of the data is displayed with the objective of providing as much background data as possible. In those cases where no answer was provided to a particular question within the questionnaire, an "NR" is used to signify "No Response."

Please take 20 minutes to acquaint yourself with the composition of the sample profile. Supplementary comments have been added where some interpretation of the franchisor's response is required.

Keep in mind that all of the profile data is based on questionnaires returned by the franchisors themselves, with no effort on our part to independently verify its accuracy. There is no doubt that franchisors had some latitude to exaggerate their responses in order to make themselves appear bigger, more mature and/or more franchisee-oriented than they really are. I am confident some small percentage did just that. The vast majority,

however, would see any such deception as dishonest, counter-productive and a general waste of everyone's time.

AAMCO, a household name in the automotive repair industry, has been selected to illustrate how this book uses the collected data.

AAMCO TRANSMISSIONS
One Presidential Blvd.
Bala Cynwyd, PA 19004
Tel: (800) 523-0402 (610) 668-2900
Fax: (610) 617-9532
E-Mail: rcastellani@aamco.com
Web Site: www.aamcotransmissions.com
Mr. Bob Castellani, Director Franchise Development

AAMCO is the world's largest chain of transmission specialists with 35 years' experience as the undisputed industry leader. An American icon, AAMCO's trademark is recognized by 90% of the driving public. Transmission repair is a $2.9 billion business in the United States and is projected to be a $3.6 billion business by the year 2001.

Background:

Established: 1963;	1st Franchised: 1963
Franchised Units:	712
Company-Owned Units:	2
Total Units:	714
Minority-Owned Units:	
African-American:	3%
Asian-American:	10%
Hispanic:	0%
Native American:	0%
Other:	
North America:	48 States, 3 Provinces
Density:	109 in CA, 62 in FL, 45 NY

Financial/Terms:

Cash Investment:	$60K
Total Investment:	$175K
Minimum Net Worth:	$250K
Fees: Franchise —	$30K
Royalty — 7%;	Ad. — 4-5%
Earnings Claim Statement:	No
Term of Contract (Years):	15/15
Avg. # Of Employees:	4 FT, 1 PT
Passive Ownership:	Not Allowed
Area Develop. Agreements:	No
Sub-Franchising Contracts:	No
Expand In Territory:	Yes
Space Needs: 4,000 SF; FS, SF, Automall	

Support & Training Provided:

Site Selection Assistance:	Yes
Lease Negotiation Assistance:	Yes
Co-Operative Advertising:	No
Franchisee Assoc./Member:	Yes/No
Size Of Corporate Staff:	245
On-Going Support:	A,B,C,D,E,G,H,I

Training: 5 Weeks Home Office, Philadelphia, PA.
Minority-Specific Programs: Although we support the objectives of the NMFI, we do not have any specific programs in place at this time.

Specific Expansion Plans:

US: NE, Great Lakes Region

Address/Contact:

1. **Company name, address, telephone and fax numbers.**

Comment: All of the data published in the book was current at the time the completed questionnaire was received or upon subsequent verification by phone. Over a 12-month period between annual publications, 10–15% of the addresses and/or telephone numbers become obsolete for various reasons. If you are unable to contact a franchisor at the address/telephone number listed, please give us a call at (510) 839-5471 (or fax [510] 839-2104) and we will provide you with the current address and telephone number.

2. **(800) 523-0402 (610) 668-2900.** In many cases, you may find that you cannot access the (800) number from your area. Do not conclude that the company has gone out of business. Simply call the local number.

Comment: An (800) number serves two important functions. The first is to provide an efficient, no-cost way for potential franchisees to contact the franchisor. Making the prospective franchisee foot the bill artificially limits the number of people who might otherwise make the initial contact. The second function is to demonstrate to existing franchisees that the franchisor is doing everything it can to efficiently respond to problems in the field as they occur. Many companies have a restricted (800) line for their franchisees that the general public cannot access. Since you will undoubtedly be talking with the franchisor's staff on a periodic basis, determine whether an (800) line is available to franchisees.

More than half of the companies listed in the book have (800) numbers. Extreme competition among telephone companies today makes the incremental cost of an (800) number relatively minor. My feeling is that it is an expense a franchisor should incur if it wants to stay competitive.

3. **Contact.** You should honor the wishes of the franchisor and address all initial correspondence to the contact listed. It would be counter-productive

to try to reach the president directly if the designated contact is the director of franchising.

Comment: The president is the designated contact in approximately half of the profiles noted below. The reason for this varies among franchisors. The president is the best spokesperson for his or her operation. It flatters the franchisee to talk directly with the president. There is no one else around. Regardless of the justification, it is important to determine if the operation is a one-man show in which the president does everything or if the president merely feels that having an open line to potential franchisees is the best way for him or her to sense the "pulse" of the company and the market. Convinced that the president can only do so many things well, I would want assurances that, by taking all incoming calls, he or she is not neglecting the day-to-day responsibilities of managing the business.

Description of Business:

4. **Description of Business:** The questionnaire provides franchisors with adequate room to differentiate their franchise from the competition. In a minor number of cases, some editing was required.

Comment: In instances where franchisors show no initiative or imagination in describing their operations, you must decide whether this is symptomatic of the company or simply a reflection on the individual who responded to the questionnaire.

Background:

5. **Established: 1963.** AAMCO was founded in 1963, and, accordingly, has 37 years of experience in its primary business. It should be intuitively obvious that a firm that has been in existence for over 10 years has a greater likelihood of being around 5 years from now than a firm that was founded only last year.

6. **1st Franchised: 1963.** 1963 was also the year that AAMCO's first franchised unit(s) were established.

Comment: Over 10 years of continuous operation, both as an operator and as a franchisor, is

compelling evidence that a firm has staying power. The number of years a franchisor has been in business is one of the key variables to consider in choosing a franchise. This is not to say that a new franchise should not receive your full attention. Every company has to start from scratch. Ultimately, a prospective franchisee has to be convinced that the franchise has 1) been in operation long enough, or 2) its key management personnel have adequate industry experience to have worked out the bugs normally associated with a new business. In most cases, this experience can only be gained through on-the-job training. Don't be the guinea pig that provides the franchisor with the experience it needs to develop a smoothly running operation.

7. **Franchised Units: 712.** As of 12/31/1999, AAMCO had 712 franchisee-owned and operated units.

8. **Company-Owned Units: 2.** As of 12/31/1999, AAMCO had 2 Company-owned and operated units.

Comment: A younger franchise should prove that its concept has worked successfully in several company-owned units before it markets its "system" to an inexperienced franchisee. Without company-owned prototype stores, the new franchisee may well end up being the "testing kitchen" for the franchise concept itself.

If a franchise concept is truly exceptional, why doesn't the franchisor commit some of its resources to take advantage of the investment opportunity? While this is clearly a financial decision on the part of the franchisor, the absence of company-owned units should not be a negative in and of itself. This is especially true of proven franchises, which may have previously sold their company-owned operations to franchisees.

Try to determine if there is a noticeable trend in the percentage of company-owned units. If the franchisor is buying back units from franchisees, it may be doing so to preclude litigation. Some firms also "churn" their operating units with some regularity. If the sales pitch is compelling, but the follow-through is not competitive, a franchisor may sell a unit to a new franchisee, wait for him or her to fail, buy it back for $0.60 cents on the dollar, and then sell that same unit to the next unsuspecting franchisee. Each time the unit is resold, the franchisor collects a franchise fee, plus the negotiated discount from the previous franchisee.

Alternatively, an increasing or high percentage of company-owned units may well mean the company is convinced of the long-term profitability of such an approach. The key is to determine whether a franchisor is building new units from scratch or buying them from failing and/or unhappy franchisees.

9. **Total Units: 714.** As of 12/31/1999, AAMCO had a total of 714 franchisee-owned and company-owned units.

Comment: Like a franchisor's longevity, its experience in operating multiple units offers considerable comfort. Those franchisors with over 15–25 operating units have proven that their system works and have probably encountered and overcome most of the problems that plague a new operation. Alternatively, the management of franchises with less than 15 operating units may have gained considerable industry experience before joining the current franchise. It is up to the franchisor to convince you that it is providing you with as risk-free an operation as possible. You don't want to be providing a company with its basic experience in the business.

10. **Minority-Owned Units: African-American: 3%; Asian-American: 10%; Hispanic: 0%; Native American: 0%; Other: NR.** As of 12/31/1999, 3% (12 units) of AAMCO's 712 franchised units were owned by African-Americans: 10% (71 units) were owned by Asian-Americans; 0% (0 units) were owned by Hispanics; and 0% (0 units) were owned by Native Americans.

Comment: As you review the franchisor profiles, you will note that the specific number of minority-owned units has not been filled out in some cases. Many of the companies said that they were truly unable to accurately identify the ethnic ownership of their franchisees. Some said that they didn't

keep records. Others said that they thought it might be against the law to keep records. Some may have been reluctant to answer because of a concern that an under-representation (compared with the general population) might somehow be used against them. Others may have no actual minority franchisees at this time and were embarrassed to acknowledge this.

Whatever the reason, each of the companies listed below actively supports the inclusion of minorities into their system now. The fact that some companies may not currently have any minorities in their ranks may augur well for you. Realizing that they are under-represented, they may create special programs to "level the playing field." If so, and you are qualified, you could be the beneficiary. My suggestion is that you not agonize about any current under-representation and instead focus on the opportunities that are presented and how your unique talents could build upon the system.

11. **Distribution: North America: 48 States, 3 Provinces.** As of 12/31/1999, AAMCO had operations in 48 states and 3 provinces in Canada.

Comment: It should go without saying that the wider the geographic distribution, the greater the franchisor's level of success. For the most part, such distribution can only come from a large number of operating units. If, however, the franchisor has operations in 15 states but only 18 total operating units, it is unlikely that it can efficiently service these accounts because of geographic constraints. Other things being equal, a prospective franchisee would vastly prefer a franchisor with 15 units in New York to one with 15 units scattered throughout the U.S., Canada and overseas.

12. **Distribution: Density: 109 in CA, 62 in FL, 45 in NY.** The franchisor was asked "what 3 states/provinces have the largest number of operating units." (No distinction was made between company-owned and franchisee-owned units.) As of 12/31/1999, AAMCO had 109 units in California, 62 units in Florida and 45 units in New York.

Comment: For smaller, regional franchises, geographic distribution could be a key variable in deciding whether to buy. If the franchisor has a concentration of units in your immediate geographic area, it is likely you will be well-served.

For those far removed geographically from the franchisor's current areas of operation, however, there can be problems. It is both time consuming and expensive to support a franchisee 2,000 miles away from company headquarters. To the extent that a franchisor can visit four franchisees in one area on one trip, there is no problem. If, however, your operation is the only one west of the Mississippi, you may not receive the on-site assistance you would like. Don't be a missionary who has to rely on his or her own devices to survive. Don't accept a franchisor's idle promises of support. If on-site assistance is important to your ultimate success, get assurances in writing that the necessary support will be forthcoming. Remember, you are buying into a system, and the availability of day-to-day support is one of the key ingredients of any successful franchise system.

Capital Requirements/Rights:

13. **Cash Investment: $60K.** On average, an AAMCO franchisee will have made a cash investment of $60,000 by the time he or she finally opens the initial operating unit.

Comment: It is important that you be realistic about the amount of cash you can comfortably invest in a business. Stretching beyond your means can have grave and far-reaching consequences. Assume that you will encounter periodic set-backs and that you will have to draw on your reserves. The demands of starting a new business are harsh enough without adding the uncertainties associated with inadequate working capital. Trust the franchisor's recommendations regarding the suggested minimum cash investment. If anything, there is an incentive for setting the recommended level of investment too low, rather than too high. The franchisor will want to qualify you to the extent that you have adequate financing. No legitimate franchisor wants you to invest if there is a chance that you might fail because of a shortage of funds.

Keep in mind that you will probably not achieve a positive cash flow from the business before 6

months or more. In your discussions with the franchisor, be absolutely certain that its calculations include an adequate working capital reserve.

14. **Total Investment: $175K.** On average, AAMCO franchisees will invest a total of $175,000, including both cash and debt, by the time the franchise opens its doors.

Comment: The total investment should be the cash investment noted above plus any debt that you will incur in starting up the new business. Debt could be a note to the franchisor for all or part of the franchise fee, an equipment lease, building and facilities leases, etc. Make sure that the total includes all of the obligations that you assume, especially any long-term lease obligations.

Be conservative in assessing what your real exposure is. If you are leasing highly specialized equipment or if you are leasing a single-purpose building, it is naive to think that you will recoup your investment if you have to sell or sub-lease those assets in a buyer's market. If there is any specialized equipment that may have been manufac tured to the franchisor's specifications, determine if the franchisor has a buy-back provision.

15. **Minimum Net Worth: $250K.** In this case, AAMCO feels that a potential franchisee should have a minimum net worth of $250,000. Although net worth can be defined in vastly different ways, the franchisor's response should suggest a minimum level of equity that the prospective franchisee should possess. Net worth is the combination of both liquid and illiquid assets. Again, don't think that franchisor-determined guidelines somehow don't apply to you.

16. **Fees (Franchise): $30K.** AAMCO requires a front-end, one-time-only payment of $30,000 to grant a franchise for a single location. As noted in Chapter 1, the franchise fee is a payment to reimburse the franchisor for the costs incurred in setting the franchisee up in business — from recruiting through training and manuals. The fee usually ranges from $15,000–30,000. It is a function of competitive franchise fees and the actual out-of-pocket costs incurred by the franchisor.

Depending upon the franchisee's particular circumstances and how well the franchisor thinks he or she might fit into the system, the franchisor may finance all or part of the franchise fee.

The franchise fee is one area in which the franchisor frequently provides either direct or indirect financial support.

Comment: Ideally, the franchisor should do no more than recover its costs on the initial franchise fee. Profits come later in the form of royalty fees, which are a function of the franchisee's sales. Whether the franchise fee is $5,000 or $35,000, the total should be carefully evaluated. What are competitive fees and are they financed? How much training will you actually receive? Are the fees reflective of the franchisor's expenses? If the fees appear to be non-competitive, address your concerns with the franchisor.

Realize that a $5,000 differential in the one-time franchise fee is a secondary consideration in the overall scheme of things. You are in the relationship for the long-term.

By the same token, don't get suckered in by an extremely low fee if there is any doubt about the franchisor's ability to follow through. Franchisors need to collect reasonable fees to cover their actual costs. If they don't recoup these costs, they cannot recruit and train new franchisees on whom your own future success partially depends.

17. **Fees (Royalty): 7%** means that 7% of gross sales (or other measure, as defined in the franchise agreement) must be periodically paid directly to the franchisor in the form of royalties. This on-going expense is your cost for being part of the larger franchise system and for all of the "back-office" support you will receive. In a few cases, the amount of the royalty fee is fixed rather than variable. In others, the fee decreases as the volume of sales (or other measure) increases (i.e., 6% on the first $200,000 of sales, 5% on the next $100,000 and so on). In others, the fee is held at artificially low levels during the start-up phase of the franchisee's business, then increases once the franchisee is better able to afford it.

Comment: Royalty fees represent the mechanism by which the franchisor finally recoups the costs it has incurred in developing its business. It may take many years and many operating units before the franchisor is able to make a true operating profit.

Consider a typical franchisor who might have been in business for three years. With a staff of five, rent, travel, operating expenses, etc., assume it has annual operating costs of $300,000 (including reasonable owner's salaries). Assume also that there are 25 franchised units with average annual sales of $250,000. Each franchise is required to pay a 6% royalty fee. Total annual royalties under this scenario would total only $375,000. The franchisor is making a $75,000 profit. Then consider the personal risk the franchisor took in developing a new business and the initial years of negative cash flows. Alternatively, evaluate what it would cost you, as a sole proprietor, to provide the myriad services included in the royalty payment.

In assessing various alternative investments, the amount of the royalty percentage is a major on-going expense. Assuming average annual sales of $250,000 per annum over a 15 year period, the total royalties at 5% would be $187,500. At 6%, the cumulative fees would be $225,000. You have to be fully convinced that the $37,500 differential is justified. While this is clearly a meaningful number, what you are really evaluating is the quality of management and the unique competitive advantages of the goods and/or services offered by the franchisor.

18. **Fees (Advertising): 4–5%.** Most national or regional franchisors require their franchisees to contribute a certain percentage of their sales (or other measure, as determined in the franchise agreement) into a corporate advertising fund. These individual advertising fees are pooled to develop a corporate advertising/marketing effort that produces great economies of scale. The end result is a national or regional advertising program that promotes the franchisor's products and services. Depending upon the nature of the business, this percentage usually ranges from 2–6% and is in addition to the royalty fee.

32

Comment: One of the greatest advantages of a franchised system is its ability to promote, on a national or regional basis, its products and services. The promotions may be through television, radio, print media or direct mail. The objective is name recognition and, over time, the assumption that the product and/or service has been "time-tested." An individual business owner could never justify the expense of mounting a major advertising program at the local level. For a smaller franchise that may not yet have an advertising program or fee, it is important to know when an advertising program will start, how it will be monitored and its expected cost.

19. **Earnings Claim Statement: No** means AAMCO does not provide an Earnings Claim state-ment to potential franchisees. Unfortunately, only 20% of franchisors provide an earnings claim statement in their Uniform Franchise Offering Cir-cular (UFOC). The franchising industry's failure to require earnings claim statements does a serious disservice to the potential franchisee. See Chapter 1 for comments on this important document.

20. **Term of Contract (Years): 15/15.** AAMCO's initial franchise period runs for 15 years. The first renewal period runs for an additional 15 years. Assuming that the franchisee operates within the terms of the franchise agreement, he or she has 30 years within which to develop and, ultimately, sell the business.

Comment: The potential (discounted) value of any business (or investment) is the sum of the operating income that is generated each year plus its value upon liquidation. Given this truth, the length of the franchise agreement and any renew-als are extremely important to the franchisee. It is essential that he or she has adequate time to develop the business to its full potential. At that time, he or she will have maximized the value of the business as an on-going concern. The value of the business to a potential buyer, however, is largely a function of how long the franchise agree-ment runs. If there are only two years remaining before the agreement expires, or if the terms of an extension(s) are vague, the business will be worth only a fraction of the value assigned to a business

with 15 years to go. For the most part, the longer the agreement and the subsequent extension, the better. (The same logic applies to a lease. If your sales are largely a function of your location and traffic count, then it is important that you have options to extend the lease under known terms. Your lease should never be longer than the remain-ing term of your franchise agreement, however.)

Assuming the length of the agreement is accept-able, be clear under what circumstances renewals might not be granted. Similarly, know the circum-stances under which a franchise agreement might be prematurely and unilaterally canceled by the franchisor. I strongly recommend you have an experienced lawyer review this section of the fran-chise agreement. It would be devastating if, after spending years developing your business, there were a loophole in the contract that allowed the franchisor to arbitrarily cancel the relationship.

21. **Avg. # of Employees: 4 FT, 1 PT.** The question was asked "Including the owner/operator, how many employees are recommended to prop-erly staff the average franchised unit?" In AAM-CO's case, 4 full-time employees and 1 part-time employee are required.

Comment: Most entrepreneurs start a new busi-ness based on their intuitive feel that it will be "fun" and that their talents and experience will be put to good use. They will be doing what they enjoy and what they are good at. Times change. Your business prospers. The number of employees increases. You are spending an increasing percent-age of your time taking care of personnel prob-lems and less and less on the fun parts of the business. In Chapter 1, the importance of conduct-ing a realistic self-appraisal was stressed. If you found that you really are not good at managing people, or you don't have the patience to manage a large minimum wage staff, cut your losses before you are locked into doing just that.

22. **Passive Ownership: Not Allowed.** Depend-ing on the nature of the business, many franchisors are indifferent as to whether you manage the busi-ness directly or hire a full-time manager to run it. Others are insistent that, at least for the initial fran-

chise, the franchisee be a full-time owner/operator. AAMCO does not allow franchisees to hire full-time managers to run their retail outlets.

Comment: Unless you have a great deal of experience in the business you have chosen or in managing similar businesses, I feel strongly that you should initially commit your personal time and energies to make the system work. After you have developed a full understanding of the business and have competent, trusted staff members who can assume day-to-day operations, then consider delegating these responsibilities. Running the business through a manager can be fraught with peril unless you have mastered all aspects of the business and there are strong economic incentives and sufficient safeguards to ensure the manager will perform as desired.

23. **Area Development Agreements: No.** Area development agreements are more fully described in Chapter 1. Essentially, they allow an investor or investment group to develop an entire area or region. The schedule for development is clearly spelled out in the area development agreement. (Note: "Var." means varies and "Neg." means negotiable.) AAMCO does not allow area development agreements.

Comment: Area development agreements represent an opportunity for the franchisor to choose a single franchisee or investment group to develop an entire area. The franchisee's qualifications should be strong and include proven business experience and the financial depth to pull it off. An area development agreement represents a great opportunity for an investor to tie up a large geographical area and develop a concept that may not have proven itself on a national basis. Keep in mind that this is a quantum leap from making an investment in a single franchise and is relevant only to those with development experience and deep pockets.

24. **Sub-Franchising Agreements: No.** AAMCO does not grant sub-franchising agreements. (See Chapter 1 for a more thorough explanation.) Like area development agreements, sub-franchising also allows an investor or investment group to develop

an entire area or region. The difference is that the sub-franchisor becomes a self-contained business, responsible for all relations with franchisees within its area, from initial training to on-going support. Franchisees pay their royalties to the sub-franchisor, who in turn pays a portion to the master franchisor.

Comment: Sub-franchising is used primarily by smaller franchisors who have a relatively easy concept and who are prepared to sell a portion of the future growth of their business to someone for some front-end cash and a percentage of the future royalties they receive from their franchisees.

25. **Expand in Territory: Yes.** Under conditions spelled out in the franchise agreement, AAMCO will allow its franchisees to expand within their exclusive territory.

Comment: Some franchisors define the franchisee's exclusive territory so tightly that there would never be room to open additional outlets within an area. Others provide a larger area in the hopes that the franchisee will do well and have the incentive to open additional units.

There are clearly economic benefits to both parties from having franchisees with multiple units. There is no question that it is in your best interest to have the option to expand once you have proven to both yourself and the franchisor that you can manage the business successfully. Most would concur that the real profits in franchising come from managing multiple units rather than being locked into a single franchise in a single location. Additional fees may or may not be required with these additional units.

26. **Space Needs: 4,000 SF; FS, SF, Automall.** The average AAMCO retail outlet will require 4,000 square feet in a Free-Standing (FS) building, Storefront (SF) location or Automall. Other types of leased space might be Strip Center (SC), Regional Mall (RM), Home Based location (HB), Executive Suite (ES), Industrial Park (IP), Kiosk (KI), Office Building (OB), Power Center (PC) or Warehouse (WH).

Comment: Armed with the rough space requirements, you can better project your annual occupancy costs. It should be relatively easy to get comparable rental rates for the type of space required. As annual rent and related expenses can be as high as 15% of your annual sales, be as accurate as possible in your projections.

Franchisor Support and Training Provided:

27. **Assistance with Site Selection: Yes** means that AAMCO will assist the franchisee in selecting a site location. While the phrase "location, location, location" may be hackneyed, its importance should not be discounted, especially when a business depends upon retail traffic counts and accessibility. If a business is home- or warehouse-based, assistance in this area is of negligible or minor importance.

Comment: Since you will be locked into a lease for a minimum of three, and probably five, years, optimal site selection is absolutely essential. Even if you were somehow able to sub-lease and extricate yourself from a bad lease or bad location, the franchise agreement may not allow you to move to another location. Accordingly, it is imperative that you get it right the first time.

If a franchisor is truly interested in your success, it should treat your choice of a site with the same care it would use in choosing a company-owned site. Keep in mind that many consulting firms provide excellent demographic data on existing locations at a very reasonable cost.

28. **Assistance with Lease Negotiations: Yes.** Once a site is selected, AAMCO will be actively involved in negotiating the terms of the lease.

Comment: Given the complexity of negotiating a lease, an increasing number of franchisors are taking an active role in lease negotiations. There are far too many trade-offs that must be considered — terms, percentage rents, tenant improvements, pass-throughs, kick-out clauses, etc. This responsibility is best left to the professionals. If the franchisor doesn't have the capacity to support you directly, enlist the help of a well-recommended broker. The penalties for signing a bad long-term lease are very severe.

29. **Co-operative Advertising: No** refers to the existence of a joint advertising program in which the franchisor and franchisees each contribute to promote the company's products and/or services (usually within the franchisee's specific territory).
Comment: Co-op advertising is a common and mutually-beneficial effort. By agreeing to split part of the advertising costs, whether for television, radio or direct mail, the franchisor is not only supporting the franchisee, but guaranteeing itself royalties from the incremental sales. A franchisor that is not intimately involved with the advertising campaign — particularly when it is an important part of the business — may not be fully committed to your overall success.

30. **Franchisee Assoc./Member: Yes/No.** This response notes that the AAMCO system does include an active association made up of AAMCO franchisees. A Yes/No response indicates that AAMCO has an association, but is not itself a member of the franchisee association.

Comment: The empowerment of franchisees has become a major rallying cry within the industry over the past 3 years. Various states have recently passed laws favoring franchisee rights, and the subject has been widely discussed in congressional staff hearings. Political groups even represent franchisee rights on a national basis. Similarly, the IFA is now actively courting franchisees to become active members. Whether they are equal members remains to be seen.

Franchisees have also significantly increased their clout with respect with the franchisor. If a franchise is to grow and be successful in the long term, it is critical that the franchisor and its franchisees mutually agree they are partners rather than adversaries.

31. **Size of Corporate Staff: 245.** AAMCO has 245 full-time employees on its staff to support its 714 operating units.

Comment: There are no magic ratios that tell you whether the franchisor has enough staff to provide the proper level of support. It would appear, however, that AAMCO's staff of 245 is adequate to support 714 operating units. Less clear is whether a staff of 3, including the company president and his wife, can adequately support 15 fledgling franchisees in the field.

Many younger franchises may be managed by a skeleton staff, assisted by outside consultants who are performing various management functions during the start-up phase. From the perspective of the franchisee, it is essential that the franchisor have actual in-house franchising experience, and that the franchisee not be forced to rely on outside consultants to make the system work. Whereas a full-time, salaried employee will probably have the franchisee's objectives in mind, an outside consultant may not have the same priorities. Franchising is a unique form of business that requires specific skills and experience — skills and experience that are markedly different from those required to manage a non-franchised business. If you are thinking about establishing a long-term relationship with a firm just starting out in franchising, you should insist that the franchisor prove that it has an experienced, professional team on board and in place to provide the necessary levels of support to all concerned.

32. On-Going Support: A,B,C,D,E,G,H,I.
Like initial training, the on-going support services provided by the franchisor are of paramount importance. Having a solid and responsive team behind you can certainly make your life much easier and allow you to concentrate your energies on other areas. As is noted below, the franchisors were asked to indicate their support for 9 separate on-going services:

Service Provided	Included in Fees	At Add'l. Cost	NA
Central Data Processing	A	a	NA
Central Purchasing	B	b	NA
Field Operations Evaluation	C	c	NA
Field Training	D	d	NA
Initial Store Opening	E	e	NA
Inventory Control	F	f	NA
Franchisee Newsletter	G	g	NA
Regional or National Meetings	H	h	NA
800 Telephone Hotline	I	i	NA

If the franchisor provides the service at no additional cost to the franchisee (as indicated by letters A–I), a capital letter was used to indicate this. If the service is provided, but only at an additional cost, a lower case letter was used. If the franchisor responded with a NA, or failed to note an answer for a particular service, the corresponding letter was omitted from the data sheet.

33. Training: 5 Weeks Home Office, Philadelphia, PA.

Comment: Assuming that the underlying business concept is sound and competitive, adequate training and on-going support are among the most important determinants of your success as a franchisee. The initial training should be as lengthy and as "hands-on" as necessary to allow the franchisee to operate alone and with confidence. Obviously, every potential situation cannot be covered in any training program. But the franchisee should come away with a basic understanding of how the business operates and where to go to resolve problems when they come up. Depending on the business, there should be operating manuals, procedures manuals, company policies, training videos, (800) help-lines, etc. It may be helpful at the outset to determine how satisfied recent franchisees are with a company's training. I would also have a clear understanding about how often the company updates its manuals and training programs, the cost of sending additional employees through training, etc.

Remember, you are part of an organization that you are paying (in the form of a franchise fee and on-going royalties) to support you. Training is the first step. On-going support is the second step.

34. Minority-Specific Programs: Although we support the objectives of the National Minority Franchising Initiative, we do not have any specific programs in place at this time.
Franchisors were asked to identify any programs specifically geared to recruit and/or assist potential

minority franchisees (see Question 33 in the questionnaire in Appendix B). While some franchisors were readily able to identify specific programs available to minorities, the majority do not have specific programs in place. In conducting the initial market research to develop the questionnaire, many franchisors questioned whether or not it was legal for them to favor any specific group, whether women or minorities or veterans. My sense is that many franchisors that in fact might have such programs in place (if not in writing) were reluctant to publicize them for fear of somehow being criticized for reverse discrimination. Accordingly, they reverted to the boilerplate answer.

Comment: The development of specific programs directed to the minority market is just beginning to take place. As franchisors become aware of the economic potential that the minority community holds, they will aggressively pursue qualified franchisees to take advantage of these markets. As a prospective franchisee, I would not hesitate to raise the question of minority-specific programs. Quite possibly, even though there are no publicized programs, the franchisor may have "non-published" programs that you can take advantage of at this time.

Specific Expansion Plans:

35. **U.S.: NE, Great Lakes Region.** AAMCO is currently focusing its growth on the Northeast and the Great Lakes Region. Alternatively, the franchisor could have listed particular states or regions into which it wished to expand.

If you have not already done so, I would strongly encourage you to invest the modest time required to read Chapter 1 — 30 Minute Overview.

My strong sense is that every potential franchisee should be well-versed in the underlying fundamentals of the franchising industry before he or she commits to the way of life it involves. The better you understand the industry, the better prepared you will be to take maximum advantage of the relationship with your franchisor. There is no doubt that it will also place you in a better position to negotiate the franchise agreement — the conditions of which will dictate every facet of your life as a franchisee for the term of the agreement. The few extra dollars spent on educating yourself could well translate into tens of thousand of dollars to the bottom line in the years ahead.

With the 2000 Edition, we have taken the liberty of limiting the number of franchising-only books included in the bibliography. In addition to general franchising publications, we have included several special interest books that relate to specific, but critical, parts of the start-up and on-going management process — site selection, hiring and managing minimum wage employees, preparing accurate cash flow projections, developing comprehensive business and/or marketing plans, etc. Also included are several audio tapes and software packages that we feel represent good values.

We have also attempted to make the purchasing process easier by allowing readers to purchase the books directly from Source Book Publications, either via our 800-line or our website. All of the books are currently available in inventory and are generally sent the same day an order is received. A 15% discount is available on all orders over $100.00. See page 41 for an order form. Your complete satisfaction is 100% guaranteed on all books.

Background/Evaluation

Buying a Franchise: How To Make the Right Choice, Kezios, Women in Franchising. 1996. Audio cassettes. $49.95. *Item #4.*

Buying A Franchise: How To Make The Right Choice

Dynamic advice on selecting a franchisor, the advantages and potential pitfalls of owning a franchise and protecting your investment. Includes legal and financial considerations, as well as insider's tips about franchising. Two audio cassettes and companion workbook are well-presented and packed with nuts-and-bolts information. Excellent industry overview.

Franchise Bible: A Comprehensive Guide, 3rd Edit., Keup, Oasis Press. 1996. 314 pp. $24.95. *Item #6.*

This recently updated classic is equally useful for prospective franchisees and franchisors alike. The comprehensive guide and workbook explain in

detail what the franchise system entails and the precise benefits it offers. The book features the new franchise laws that became effective January, 1995. To assist the prospective franchisee in rating a potential franchisor, Keup provides necessary checklists and forms. Also noted are the franchisor's contractual obligations to the franchisee and what the franchisee should expect from the franchisor in the way of services and support.

How to Buy and Manage a Franchise, Mancuso and Boroian, Simon & Schuster. 1993. 287 pp. $11.00. *Item #12.* If your objective is to either be your own boss or to expand a business you already own, you should seriously consider franchising. The authors share their expert advice on purchasing, owning and operating a franchise. Keen insights into the mechanics and advantages of franchising. Good starter book.

Tips & Traps When Buying a Franchise, Revised 2nd Edition, Tomzack, Source Book Publications. 1999. 236 pp. $19.95. *Item #19.*

Many a green franchisee is shocked to discover that the road to success in franchising is full of hidden costs, inflated revenue promises, reneged marketing support and worse. In this candid, hard-hitting book, Tomzack steers potential franchisees around the pitfalls and guides them in making a smart, lucrative purchase. Topics include: matching a franchise with personal finances and lifestyle, avoiding the 5 most common pitfalls, choosing a prime location, asking the right questions, etc.

Franchising 101. Dugan, Upstart Publishing Company. 1998. 267 pp. $22.95. *Item #10.* A thoughtful, thorough guide that offers indispensable advice on everything you need to know about evaluating, buying and growing a franchise — from choosing the right franchise to handling taxes and banks to keep records. It will help you evaluate your needs and your personality in order to determine the type of franchise that will make you happy — and prosperous — for the long term. You'll also learn how to scout for a franchise company that is a leader within the strong, vibrant and growing franchise industry. This book offers valuable guidance and support from respected professionals in the franchising industry.

Understanding an Offering Circular and Negotiating a Franchise Agreement, Kanouse, Professional Press. 1995. 159 pp. $21.95. *Item #20.*

Allows you to better understand and evaluate the information in the franchisor's Uniform Franchise Offering Circular (UFOC). Discusses 62 legal and business issues which should be "negotiated" in a franchise agreement to make it fairer from a franchisee's standpoint. With an understanding of the key underlying issues, you will be better able to communicate with your own franchise attorney.

Databases

Franchisor Database, Source Book Publications. (800) 841-0873/(510) 839-5471. *Item #21.*

Listing of over 2,500 active North American franchisors. 23 fields of information per company: full address, telephone/800/fax numbers, Internet address, contact/title/salutation, president/title/salutation, # of franchised units, # of company-owned units, # total units, IFA/CFA Member, etc. 54 industry categories. Unlimited use. Guaranteed deliverability — $0.50 rebate for any returned mail. $550 for initial database, $75 per quarter for updates. See page 186 for details.

Directories

Bond's Franchise Guide — 1999 Edition, Bond, Source Book Publications, 1999. 496 pp. $29.95. *Item #1.*

The definitive and most comprehensive franchising directory available. Over 2,150 listings, including over 1,050 detailed franchisor profiles resulting from an exhaustive 40-point questionnaire. 51 distinct business categories. Excellent industry overview.

Earnings Claim

"How Much Can I Make?" Bond, Source Book Publications. 2000. 448 pp. $29.95. *Item #2.*

The single most important task for a prospective investor is to prepare a realistic cash flow statement that accurately reflects the economic potential of that business. *"How Much Can I Make?"* is an invaluable "insider's guide" that details historical sales, expense and/or profit data on actual franchise operations, **as provided by the franchisors themselves.** Whether you plan to buy a franchise or start your own business, these actual performance statistics will ensure that you have a realistic starting point in determining how much you can expect to make in a similar business. 167 current Earnings Claim Statements, in their entirety, are included for 46 major industry categories. Unfortunately, less than 15% of franchisors provide such projections/guidelines to prospective franchisees. *"How Much Can I Make?"* includes roughly half of the total universe of earnings claim statements available. The list of companies included runs from the McDonalds and Burger Kings of the world to newer, smaller franchises with only a few operat-

ing units. See page 272 for a full listing of companies included. Any serious investor would be short-sighted not to take full advantage of this extraordinary resource.

Financing Your Franchise

Financing Your Franchise, Whittemore/Sherman/Hotch, McGraw-Hill. 1993. 275 pp. $16.95. *Item #5.*

This book is an easy-to-understand guide on how to locate money for a franchise. It offers information on steps and techniques for raising capital, including how to write a loan proposal, how to deal with bankers, what is in a purchasing agreement, financing tips for women and minorities, interpreting disclosure documents and how to cut through the sales hype. In addition, the book provides directories of franchise lenders, sample forms, checklists and business plans. Lists of franchisors who offer financing assistance, those who target women and minorities and helpful federal agencies are also included.

General

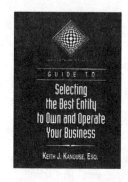

Guide to Selecting the Best Entity to Own and Operate Your Business, Kanouse, Professional Press. 1995. 139 pp. $15.95. *Item #17.*

Clearly explains the differences between joint ventures, sole proprietorships, general partnerships, "C" corps, "S" corps, etc. Learn the advantages and disadvantages of these and many more organizational forms from a formation, tax, liability adn management perspective. Understand complex financial, business and legal words and phrases. Extremely valuable in forming your business.

How to Really Create a Successful Marketing Plan, Gumpert, Inc., Business Resources. 319 pp. $19.95. *Item #14.*

By examining the actual marketing plans of many "hot" companies, you'll learn practical steps for developing a winning plan, including the wisdom of: targeting the right market, staying current with your competition, communicating with your market, developing and executing your budget, linking your marketing plan to your business plan and maximizing your marketing efforts. Real experience-based advice.

How to Really Start Your Own Business, Gumpert, Inc., Business Resources. 278 pp. $19.95. *Item #15.*

Takes you step-by-step through the launch process, exploring questions like: where do the best, most viable launch ideas come from; what kind of legal protection do entrepreneurs need; how to attract the best employees on start-up budgets; and how to create cash flow projections that are on target. Packed with eye-opening detailed worksheets that allow you to assess launch ideas, evaluate market potential, determine needs, projections, financing. Includes worksheets/forms.

International Franchising

The International Herald Tribune International Franchise Guide, Bond/Thompson, Source Book Publications. 1999. 192 pp. $34.95. *Item #3.*

This annual publication, sponsored by the International Herald Tribune, is the definitive guide to international franchising. It lists comprehensive, in-depth profiles of major franchisors who are committed (not just the usual lip service) to promote and support overseas expansion. Details specific geographic areas of desired expansion for each company, country by country — as well as the number of units in each foreign country as of the date of publication. Geared specifically to the needs and requirements of prospective international area developers, master franchisees and investors. Investors must be prepared to assume responsibility for the development of large geographic areas. Also listed are international franchise consultants, attorneys and service providers. Covers 32 distinct business categories.

Legal

Franchising Law & Practice Forms, Fern, Costello, Asbill & Scott, STP Specialty Technical Publishers. 3 volumes in loose-leaf manual. Individual volumes are $275. $480 for full set. Annual subscription includes quarterly updates at no extra cost. *Not eligible for 15% volume discount. Item #11.*

The definitive word on franchising law for franchisors, franchisees and legal counsel. This definitive 3-volume set, fully updated, is an essential resource containing practical legal advice about every facet of franchising. Separate sections on *The Franchisor; The Franchisee/Source Materials;* and *Forms.* The work provides quick-reference, practical advice on the legal and business aspects of franchising, with clause-by-clause analysis of agreements, precedent cases and advice on how to minimize potentially devastating disputes (and liabilities), as well as the significant costs of complying with federal and state regulations. 30-day risk-free trial. Choose any combination of the 3 volumes.

Site Selection

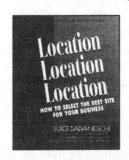

Location, Location, Location: How to Select the Best Site for Your Business, Salvaneschi, Oasis Press. 1996. 280 pp. $19.95. *Item #16.*

Whether you are searching for a new business site or relocating an existing business, you have the power to dramatically increase your profits by choosing the right location. For any business that depends on a customer's ability to find it, location is the most important ingredient for success. Learn how to: spot the essential characteristics of the best location; understand why and how people move from one point to another; analyze and learn from your competitor's business; and learn about the retail trading zone and how to use it to capture the most customers.

Other Franchise Publications

Franchise Times, Restaurant Finance Corp., 2500 Cleveland Ave., North, # D-South, Roseville, MN 55113; (651) 631-3132; FAX (651) 633-8749.

Published 10 times per year, *Franchise Times* magazine focuses on the issues multi-unit franchisees and franchisors need to take their businesses to the next level. Issues such as financing (where is it; who's doing it), real estate (tips for site selection, leases, etc.) and legal issues are tackled. The magazine also highlights successful franchisees and franchisors. In these profiles, the reveal how they have grown their companies to be large franchise businesses and discuss the problems they have conquered along the way. Along with those profiles, *Franchise Times* covers the constantly changing relationship between franchisors and franchisees; how they offer support to each other and conversely the never-ending legal battles that sometimes ensue. The franchise owner survey and the top 200 franchise businesses are eagerly anticipated issues.

The Franchise Bookstore
Order Form

Call (800) 841-0873 or (510) 839-5471; or FAX (510) 839-2104

Item #	Title	Price	Qty.	Total

	Total
Basic postage (1 Book)	$4.00
Each additional book add $3.00	
California tax @ 8.25% (if CA resident)	
Total due in U.S. dollars	
Deduct 15% if total due is over $100.00	
Net amount due in U.S. dollars	

Please include credit card number and expiration date for all charge card orders! Checks should be made payable to Source Book Publications. All prices are in U.S. dollars.

Mailing Information: All books shipped by USPS Priority Mail (2nd Day Air). Please print clearly and include your phone number in case we need to contact you. Postage and handling rates are for shipping within the U.S. Please call for international rates.

Name: _____

Company: _____

Address: _____

City: _____

❑ Check enclosed or

Charge my:
❑ MasterCard   ❑ VISA

Card #: _____

Expiration Date: _____

Signature: _____

Title: _____

Telephone No.: (____) _____

State/Prov.: _____ Zip: _____

Special Offer — Save 15%

If your total order above exceeds $100.00, deduct 15% from your bill.

Please send order to:
Source Book Publications
P.O. Box 12488, Oakland, CA 94604
Satisfaction Guaranteed. If not fully satisfied, return for a prompt, 100% refund.

7-Eleven: making franchising convenient for entrepreneurs

The 7-Eleven® store chain was born in 1927 when an innovative employee of the Southland Ice Company began selling milk, eggs and bread from his Dallas, Texas, ice dock as a convenience to customers. Over the years, that humble ice dock has grown, and today, independent retailers are using the 7-Eleven system to serve time-pressed consumers at 18,000 7-Eleven stores in 19 countries, including almost 6,000 U.S. stores.

7-Eleven joined the world of franchising in 1963. Today, approximately 3,000 U.S. stores are operated by franchisees, and about 35% of 7-Eleven's franchisees operate more than one store.

The grass always looks greener on the other side — and sometimes it actually is. Just ask James Ellis, who worked for 7-Eleven, Inc. for 10 years before franchising the first of his 3 stores in Detroit. Ellis, an African-American, recently acquired 2 additional stores each with a gas island, giving him a total of 5 stores.

During his decade as a 7-Eleven employee, Ellis held a number of operations positions, including division sales manager and assistant market manager.

"I figured that if I had the ability to run an operation for 7-Eleven, I could run one for myself," says Ellis, who advises prospective franchisees to research any business well before they take the plunge. "Some people think they're going to be an owner and not work, but ultimately, the responsibility for the business all comes back to you. When I work, I work really hard, and when I'm away on vacation, I play really hard."

Ellis believes a major key to any franchisee's success is the ability to handle the challenges of dealing with employees.

"Without a great staff, I could only run one store," according to Ellis. "I'm fortunate I can get good employees in Detroit with such a low unemployment rate. I have good managers, and I'm working now with one employee who wants to franchise his own 7-Eleven. I'll do whatever is necessary to help him do that."

A 7-Eleven franchise is a reasonably priced turn-key franchise. Support for franchisees includes initial training, on-going merchandising and operations assistance, record keeping and auditing services, and weekly visits from a field consultant. Up to 100% financing may be available through 7-Eleven for qualified applicants. Franchisees have 180 days to try the system. If it isn't what they expected, they can receive a refund of their down payment and franchise fee with no further obligation.

This year, the company plans to open over 100 new stores in major markets throughout the country. Like older 7-Eleven locations that were remodeled during a recent nationwide refurbishing effort, these new stores will feature wider aisles, brighter lighting, new layouts and high-tech security systems. Many will offer gasoline pumps and pay-at-the-pump credit card readers.

As customers' demands and tastes change, so does the variety of products available at 7-Eleven. Thanks to a growing system of combined distribution centers and proprietary commissaries/bakeries located around the country, many 7-Eleven stores now offer customers fresh products, such as sandwiches, entrees and baked goods, on a daily basis.

In addition, the company is installing a proprietary retail information system that will allow each franchisee to make more timely and informed merchandising decisions on every item and stay in stock on the fast-moving items that customers want and need.

Presently, 7-Eleven franchises are available on the West Coast and in parts of the Midwest, Northeast and Southwest.

For the past 5 years, 7-Eleven has been ranked among the top 5 of Entrepreneur Magazine's Top 500 franchisors and is looking for prospective franchisees who are motivated to succeed and who are willing to work within a proven system.

For information about franchise opportunities, contact the 7-Eleven Franchise Department, P.O. Box 711, Dallas, TX 75221-0711, or call (800) 255-0711 or visit the franchising section at www.7-eleven.com.

Bass Hotels & Resorts: the industry's most global hotel company offers investors a world of franchising opportunities

Every year, more than 150 million travelers find a warm welcome at a hotel or resort bearing one of Bass Hotels & Resorts' internationally recognized lodging brands: Holiday Inn, Holiday Inn Express, Staybridge Suites by Holiday Inn, Inter-Continental and Crowne Plaza. Bass Hotels & Resorts is the hotel business of Bass PLC of the United Kingdom.

With more than 2,700 hotels and 450,000 guest rooms in more than 90 countries and territories, Bass Hotels & Resorts truly is the world's most global hotel company. The company's targeted brands offer a variety of services, amenities and lodging experiences catering to virtually every travel occasion and guest need. For investors, that translates into a wealth of franchising opportunities.

Currently, Bass Hotels & Resorts offers franchising opportunities with the following targeted brands:

- Holiday Inn — An American icon for travelers for nearly five decades, Holiday Inn is one of the hospitality industry's most successful and well-known full-service brands. Today's business and leisure travelers turn to Holiday Inn for dependability, friendly service and attractive, modern facilities at an excellent value. And Bass Hotels & Resorts is taking the brand to the next level, conducting an on-going quality

initiative that is rapidly positioning Holiday Inn for the year 2000 and beyond.

- Holiday Inn Express — Recognized as the fastest-growing brand in the midscale hotel segment, Holiday Inn Express is the modern hotel for value-oriented travelers. Launched in 1991, Holiday Inn Express has already opened 1,000 hotels worldwide and reached over $1 billion in sales. Express has quickly struck a chord with travelers who appreciate the brand's straightforward, no-frills approach. Guests who stay at Express properties enjoy comfortable, reasonably priced rooms; a free breakfast bar; and free local phone calls (U.S. only).

- Staybridge Suites by Holiday Inn — Bass Hotels & Resorts' newest brand, Staybridge Suites was launched in 1997 and represents the company's entry into the extended-stay segment. Staybridge properties offer studios and one- and two-bedroom layouts, all with functional work areas that feature high-speed Internet access, two phone lines with voice mail and direct-dial access, and fully equipped kitchens. Guests enjoy a complimentary breakfast buffet, on-site 24-hour convenience store, free self-service laundry, exercise room, business center and library.

Our Resources are Behind You

As an individual Bass Hotels & Resorts entrepreneur, you're in business for yourself, but you're not alone. You can count on Bass Hotels & Resorts to provide extensive resources, from technology to marketing, advertising and training support, that will help your investment grow.

Leading the way in technology is the company's Property Based System (PBS), an integrated hardware and software system designed to promote competitiveness and profitability through applied technology. It combines the power of three tremendous resources:

- The Holiday Inn Reservation Optimizer (HIRO) system, an automated tool that maximizes hotel room revenues by instantly reacting to shifts in demand conditions, accurately forecasting future business, and keeping close tabs on room inventory levels.

- The Property Management System, the company's front-desk system that provides basic hotel management functions, as well as a two-way interface with the company's reservations system.

- HOLIDEX, an advanced computer reservation system, which manages calls to the company's toll-free reservation number, 1-800-HOLIDAY. HOLIDEX books and delivers approximately 30% of the total annual occupancy of the Bass Hotels & Resorts system — more than 20 million room nights per year, and over $1 billion in yearly revenues. It also connects Bass directly to travel intermediaries.

Marketing and Advertising Support

Bass Hotels & Resorts helps drive guest awareness and loyalty through national and local advertising, targeted promotions and its frequent-stay program, Priority Club Worldwide. Franchisees receive hands-on support to help implement those marketing programs at the local level.

The company currently commits approximately $200 million annually on a worldwide basis to keep its brand names in the public eye. The result? Bass Hotels & Resorts enjoys a top-of-mind awareness level three times greater than any other chain.

What can franchisees expect from this major advertising effort? A lot. Staff expertise and direct-marketing know-how; advanced technology tools plus extensive research and analysis experience and capabilities; the largest global frequency program in the industry; local, hands-on support to help you plan and execute marketing and advertising programs; city and regional cooperative marketing and national programs; strong relationships with tour operators all over the world; and a Worldwide Sales force that calls on the top 500 global business and leisure accounts.

The Priority Club Worldwide frequent-guest program is a highly successful business-building tool for Bass Hotels & Resorts. Introduced in 1983, it was among the first customer loyalty programs in the hotel industry. Today, it has more than 8 million members, who generate approximately 15% of our brands' yearly occupancy. Bass assists franchisees in targeting Priority Club members through direct marketing.

Think Global, Act Local

Bass Hotels & Resorts works closely with franchisees to ensure they have the right tools to create local advertising and marketing programs. Every franchise receives the Admaker Plus, a specific advertising resource designed to assist with advertising, public relations and promotional efforts.

Additionally, a Marketing Resource Guide is published twice a year to help franchisees choose the marketing programs best suited to their specific hotel. They also receive the management and training tools necessary to help them take advantage of marketing support and programs available through Bass Hotels & Resorts.

Part of a Winning Team

From the moment you contact Bass Hotels & Resorts about a franchise, the company's powerful resources come together with a comprehensive hotel support team — a team dedicated to supporting your project.

Every hotel that enters the Bass Hotels & Resorts system is assigned a Field Manager, located at the regional level, who functions as an on-site consultant in revenue issues, service considerations, marketing analysis, training tools, operational policies and other strategic essentials. The Field Manager typically provides management training at the hotel level, and conducts follow-up on all action plans developed for the hotel.

Each hotel also has its own Atlanta-based Franchise Service Manager (FSM), who can be reached 24 hours a day by calling a special toll-free number. The FSM can quickly answer questions regarding procedures, systems and services. In short, the FSM functions as an in-house liaison between the franchisee and corporate headquarters. Together, the FSM and Field Manager provide around-the-clock-response to any issue that arises in the day-to-day operation of the hotels.

Franchisees also benefit from Bass Hotels & Resorts' Guest Satisfaction Tracking System, which measures and tracks key product and service attributes directly related to guest satisfaction and retention at your hotel.

Finally, BHR Capital can assist you in finding a source for your financing needs. Our subsidiary offers programs to qualified franchisees for new development, refurbishment and leasing packages that are tailored to your specific situation, a task made simpler by the fact that financing is more easily obtained with a well-known company like Bass Hotels & Resorts.

For more information on franchise opportunities, contact: Brown Kessler, vice president, Franchise Sales and Development, Bass Hotels & Resorts, 3 Ravinia Dr., # 2900, Atlanta, GA 30346; (770) 604-2000.

Information is also available on-line at the following websites: www.basshotels.com for company information, www.holiday-inn.com for Holiday Inn Hotels and Resorts, www.hiexpress.com for Holiday Inn Express hotels, www.crowneplaza.com for Crowne Plaza Hotels and Resorts, www.interconti.com for Inter-Continental Hotels and Resorts, and www.staybridge.com for the company's newest brand, Staybridge Suites by Holiday Inn.

Coverall North America, Inc.: minority franchising opportunities

The Coverall® Story

Coverall® began in 1985 with one goal in mind, to revolutionize the commercial cleaning industry. Today, **Coverall Cleaning Concepts®** is one of the world's largest commercial cleaning franchise companies. The company's reputation has been nationally acknowledged by some of the most prestigious business publications. It has been listed by *Inc.* magazine for 4 consecutive years as one of the 500 fastest growing private companies in the United States, and *Entrepreneur* ranked Coverall as the #1 commercial cleaning franchise company in 1996. *Black Enterprise* magazine has also recognized Coverall as a leader in minority franchising by naming the company one of the "15 Great Franchises."

In 1998, system-wide sales for the company exceeded $150 million. Truly a global company, Coverall has 70 regional offices in the United States, along with offices in Australia, Asia — Japan, Thailand and Singapore — Canada and South America — Chile — with more always on the way.

Recent studies by the federal government have projected continued growth in the commercial cleaning industry. This growth pattern combined with an increasing demand for higher quality commercial cleaning services helps to create a solid customer base for Coverall® franchise owners.

Coverall's Franchise Program: The Best in the Industry

Coverall® is a company of owners and business people working together as a team toward one common goal — success. The September 1998 article in *Black Enterprise Magazine* cited Coverall® as a recognized leader of minority participation when it comes to franchise ownership, as demonstrated by the fact that a majority of its franchises are owned by minorities. Coverall has attained this position in part by encouraging its regional offices to become aware of and take advantage of special programs and services available to minority entrepreneurs interested in the commercial cleaning industry.

Franchisee Edwin Ross summed up Coverall's commitment to minority entrepreneurs, "It was more than just investing in a business. After speaking with friends who had already invested in Coverall franchises, I knew Coverall viewed African-Americans as key players in their system. And when I spoke with the regional office here in Cincinnati, they were extremely helpful. They worked very hard to help me secure the financial help I needed to get my business started. I always felt welcome and part of the Coverall team."

Becoming part of the Coverall team is not made complicated by a rigorous application process and unrealistic financial requirements. With an initial franchise fee as low as $5,000, an individual can become involved in an industry that has experienced unparalleled growth.

The Coverall® Model for Success

By analyzing successful business prototypes and modifying them to fit the unique needs of the commercial cleaning industry, Coverall® has developed an unrivaled model for promoting entrepreneurial success. This formula, which fosters success, is a combination of business programs and support systems that focus on meeting the needs of franchisees and customers alike. Divided into three distinct components, the programs consist of the Start-Up Phase, Operating Phase and Growth Phase.

The Start-Up Phase includes a comprehensive 10-step training program, covering virtually all aspects of the commercial cleaning business. This training program introduces franchisees to innovative cleaning techniques and the latest technology. The program also teaches them to manage a business and to follow environmental, safety and security procedures. Included in the Start-Up Phase is a beginning equipment package, an initial customer base, financing options and national membership opportunities.

The Operating Phase continues to build on the solid relationship between Coverall and its franchisees. It is during this operating period that Coverall's guidance and support really benefit franchisees. With Coverall providing customer relations, billing and collection and cash flow protection services, franchisees are able to focus their attention on the customer by providing top-quality, superior work, while avoiding many of the pitfalls that can plague independent small business owners. As an added bonus, Coverall's vast resources allow franchisees to take advantage of the cost savings obtained through volume buying.

Jesse Rodriguez, a San Diego, California franchisee, appreciates firsthand how Coverall's business programs help. "With the guidance of Coverall's management team, we were able to really get things moving. Coverall® has proven that there is no limit to one's own personal success. The business is doing very well. Coverall® has given me all the tools I need to train my employees to be effective providers of commercial cleaning services. My staff and I work as a team, and we all benefit."

Once a Coverall franchise is up and running, the growth potential is virtually limitless. Franchisees can again utilize the strength and reputation of Coverall to grow their business. It is during the Growth Phase of the Coverall program that franchisees are provided with options and information to foster their company's growth. National marketing support is available to enhance and augment local initiatives. Also provided are regular and ongoing, advanced and specialized training for unique services and niche markets such as facilities in the health care and biotech industries.

Coverall® — A View from the Top

Coverall's commitment to supporting franchise owners is evidenced by the keen insight and experience of Phil Kubec, President and CEO of Coverall. "Over 13 years ago, I became the first master franchise owner in the Coverall system, so I understand the fear, frustration and excitement you may feel about becoming a business owner. I suggest you discuss your various options with your family, friends and business advisors. Consider the commercial cleaning industry: Is it a fad? Can it maintain steady growth? Will it stay technically state-of-the-art? Does the company have a good reputation, integrity and long-term direction? I saw these qualities in Coverall in 1986, and they are still the qualities that can make Coverall a sound investment in virtually any economic situation.

"Today, Coverall's team is moving ahead with accelerated growth and outstanding potential, because it is the best in the industry. The dynamic combination of our successful franchise owners and an experienced supporting staff has positioned Coverall to dominate the commercial cleaning industry. Coverall's proven system will help you be in business for yourself, not by yourself. Coverall North America, Inc., a worldwide leader in the commercial cleaning industry, will be your partner."

Contact Coverall® for a Franchise Application Kit

To receive a Coverall® Franchise Application Kit without obligation, and to learn more about the unique opportunities available to minority franchisees, call (800) 537-3371, or visit Coverall on the World Wide Web at www.coverall.com.

The dream of owning your own business — being your own boss — is the dream of thousands of men and women across North America who have entrepreneurial spirit and drive. They want to feel the sense of accomplishment and pride that comes from successfully owning a business. Business ownership has many advantages; most notably the ability to create equity and value in their own business rather than someone else's business.

Franchising offers business professionals the opportunity to be in business *for* themselves, but not *by* themselves. Owning a business, like many of life's opportunities, has many potential pitfalls along the way. Fortunately, business professionals can significantly reduce the likelihood of falling prey to these risks if they buy a credible franchise, and commit the time and energy necessary to make it prosper. Buying a franchise means buying time tested systems — operational and marketing systems — that have been tried and found true by a large number of operators

When you go into a new business on your own, you are solely responsible for establishing the concept, evaluating the market and developing the marketing plan and systems that your business will utilize in the short- and long-term. Independence allows you to shape your business as you wish, and alter any element, at any time.

When you buy a credible, well-developed franchise, however, all of these elements are already in place. This "head start" allows you to focus on building sales by executing a program that has already been tested by other owners in the franchise. Depending on the franchise you choose, you may also enjoy the benefits of an established name and presence in the marketplace — an advantage that could otherwise take many years to build on your own.

According to a 1991 study by Arthur Andersen & Company, which looked at 366 franchise companies in 60 different industries, nearly 86% of all franchised store operations that had opened in the previous 5 years were still under the same ownership. In fact, only 3% of those businesses were out of business. On the other hand, according to statistics from the U.S. Small Business Administration from 1978 to 1988, 62.2% of all new non-franchised businesses closed or terminated within the first 6 years of their operation due to operational failure, bankruptcy, retirement or other reasons.

Statistics show that franchises have a far greater chance of success than a stand-alone new business. Keep in mind, however, that your personal aptitudes and resources, the nature of your marketplace and many other factors also play crucial roles in the success of any business — franchised or independent.

"I know what it's like to open a non-franchised business," explains Gary Salomon, President and founder of American Fastsigns, Inc. "When my partner and I got the idea to open the first FAST-SIGNS®, we had to figure everything out for ourselves. It seemed that no matter how much we learned, there was something new to figure out every day. It was like trying to herd cats!"

While franchising offers many benefits and opportunities, it may not be right for everyone. While it takes a strongly motivated person to own his or her own business, the individual must conform to the recommended — or even required — systems, so it's important to take a hard look at yourself to make sure you are a good match for franchising.

Success in franchising is a result of both hard work and smart work. Individuals who carefully learn about franchising, research various franchise concepts, and then work hard and smart can find great success as franchise owners.

In our 14 years of franchising, we've found great diversity in successful franchisees within the FAST-SIGNS network. This diversity is found in both the cultural, ethnic and racial aspects of their background, as well as in their business experience prior to joining FASTSIGNS. We have franchisees within our system who are Hispanic, African-American, Caucasian, Asian and Middle Eastern. Since FASTSIGNS provides custom sign products, communication between various parties is critical. Therefore, a great deal of communication, knowledge and comfort with the English language is critical. That appears to be the only clear qualification one must possess.

We also have great diversity in the professional backgrounds of franchisees. The spectrum includes professional salespeople and managers, engineers, lawyers, accountants, education administrators — even ex-race car drivers and tennis instructors populate the FASTSIGNS network.

To give a flavor of the type of success various minorities have experienced, we've spotlighted three individuals, each of whom has become a profitable, successful and enthusiastic FASTSIGNS

franchisee. Ed Yang and Linda Fong are each of Asian-American heritage, and Wendell Haynes is African-American.

Ed Yang opened his Sunnyvale, California FAST-SIGNS store in 1992, and has done extremely well with his business. His store ranked #21 out of 356 domestic FASTSIGNS stores last year for total gross sales. He explains his experience in choosing to purchase a FASTSIGNS center. "I wanted to own my own business, not only for the financial independence and rewards, but also for the challenges. I wanted to prove myself. Franchising was attractive to me because of the support and proven systems it offered. I felt my risks would be significantly reduced. I looked at different franchises and chose FASTSIGNS because I thought it was a good investment. The computer-aided retail sign industry was a growth industry, plus I was very impressed with the management team at the FASTSIGNS corporate office. Once I bought the business, I attended training, learned from the experiences of other FASTSIGNS owners, and then committed to working very hard to succeed. I'm very pleased with my choice."

Salomon and the management team at American Fastsigns, Inc. feel it is critical to offer prospective franchisees as much information as possible. "When choosing a business to own, an individual is making an important decision — a decision that will affect that person and his or her family for years to come, so we encourage our prospects to weigh all of their options carefully."

Among the first criteria to consider is the management team stability and integrity of the franchisor — you should not consider a franchise whose reputation is questionable. Another issue is the nature of the business itself. Does the type of work you would be doing appeal to you? Can you see yourself in that business for years to come? How does the franchise fit into current trends? How will it be affected by rapidly changing technologies? You should also consider the "personality" of the franchise. Do you feel the leaders in the company share your business philosophies? Are you comfortable with the mood and style of their operation?

Linda Fong, a FASTSIGNS owner in Oakland, CA, was previously employed in the marketing department of a local utility company, and first became interested in FASTSIGNS because it was a business-to-business opportunity. "I'd worked in the corporate arena and I felt like I could better reach my full potential with a business of my own. I was climbing the corporate ladder, and while I enjoy politics on an even playing field, I did not enjoy corporate politics. I joined my husband in the field of hairdressing for about six years. I enjoyed that experience, but decided that, while I had not cared for being in the corporate world, I missed the business world environment. I looked for a business-to-business opportunity that would allow me to interact with corporate America without having to deal with the politics." Linda was interested in a franchise for the same reasons as many others. "I was swayed with the success rate and proven systems that franchises can offer," she explains. "As I investigated FASTSIGNS, I was impressed. Their communication and follow-up from the corporate office were very professional and helpful. The staff members that I met were consistent in answering similar questions and concerns. The structure appeared sound, and as I spoke with various FASTSIGNS franchisees, I knew this was a network that I wanted to be a part of." Linda continues to explain that the first few years were very challenging. "Even though my husband and I had owned businesses before, I had forgotten how hard it is to learn a new industry. It was a real challenge. While I still work very hard, I can say with confidence that I am very happy to be a FASTSIGNS owner." Linda's store has been open since 1995. She has consistently exceeded her sales forecast each year since.

"When prospective franchisees are considering the purchase of a FASTSIGNS, we are committed to helping them get all the information they need about FASTSIGNS in order for them to make the best decision for their future," explains Salomon. "We also feel an obligation to look for those characteristics that we feel identify prospects who will be successful in this business. We aren't doing anyone any favors if we approve them to buy a FASTSIGNS and accept their franchise fee if we aren't fully confident they will be successful."

Some of the many factors that are looked at when considering potential franchisees are work experience, personality traits and financial stability.

"While a background in the sign industry is helpful, it is not required. Experience in sales, marketing and management, however, can be very valuable," Salomon continues. "It's infinitely easier to teach a person how to make a sign than it is to teach him or her how to be a good manager or salesperson."

There are distinct personal skills and traits that are common among the FASTSIGNS owners who are most successful. "We have created a profile of these characteristics. Prospective franchisees are compared against this profile to determine the likelihood of their success in this industry," Salomon continues. "While we would never deny someone the opportunity to own a FASTSIGNS based solely on this comparison, we use this information to identify ways to increase each person's potential for success in this business. We might recommend that their first employee be someone with strong sales skills if we feel they are weak in that area. In other cases, we might recommend training in management skills that supplements our in-house training."

The third factor that is considered is the individual's financial stability. "After opening over 425 stores in the past 13 years, we have a pretty good idea of how much money it takes to operate and market a new FASTSIGNS store until it is generating profits. We want to make sure that we communicate this clearly and unequivocally to our prospective franchisees and that they have the financial backing and foundation necessary to support those expectations," explains Salomon.

At FASTSIGNS, we have just one goal," explains Salomon. "That is to help our franchisees succeed in building and maintaining high sales volumes and maximizing their profit potential. That process begins the day we meet the franchisee and continues as long as they are FASTSIGNS owners. Our owners are backed by the industry's most respected name, the most thoroughly researched and proven operating system, and the most all-encompassing program of professional training and marketing support in the computer-aided retail sign industry."

Wendell Haynes had extensive experience in selling investment services. In 1998, he made the decision to buy a FASTSIGNS. In his second year of operation, he is showing triple digit increases in sales revenue. "I had worked for large corporations and sold services to large institutions, but wanted the opportunity to have a little more control over the direction of my business," Haynes explains. "I first considered buying an existing business, but then decided to look into franchising. A franchise could offer the security of existing systems that I wanted, but I could also feel I had control of the business from the beginning without having to 'undo' any existing problems." Haynes looked for a business in which he could leverage both his computer skills and sales experience. He also had a somewhat unique factor to consider. "I knew I wanted my business to be in Manhattan. It's a special market and I had to look at each business concept in relation to the characteristics of this dense business market. I also was looking for a business for which there was a clear demand — and a demand that would not go away in the future. I was intrigued by the fact that FASTSIGNS uses state-of-the-art technology to create a product that has been around in some form or fashion for centuries. People will always need signs, and I liked the idea of using modern technology to offer them better

signs." Haynes also advises new franchise owners not to be frightened by the competition. "If you choose a product for which there is sufficient demand, the competition should not be a problem," he explains. "This doesn't mean that you can just show up at work everyday and that the customers will somehow find you. You have to be willing to go out and get your own customers — or hire someone who will." Haynes offers more advice to those considering the purchase of a franchise. "Know your market, find a good location and don't rush. Take your time and do your homework. Talk to lots of the other franchisees in the system. They can give you a great picture of what the business is really like, what kind of support you can expect from the franchisor, and how much you can reasonably expect to make. If you like what you hear from the franchisees, and you feel good about your visit to the corporate headquarters, you probably have found a winner."

As these three people have indicated, success in any franchise depends on the following characteristics; doing the homework to find out which franchise best meets your needs, knowing the market in your area for such a product, and your willingness to commit yourself to success.

These traits and abilities are common to all ethnic groups. FASTSIGNS is committed to the success of all its franchise owners.

GNC *franchising opens doors to business world success*

Chapter 8

When Joyce Patterson became the first 10-year franchisee in the history of GNC earlier this year, it marked an important milestone for the company that is consistently ranked one of America's top franchising opportunities.

For Patterson — an African-American woman — much of GNC Franchising's success can be traced to the company's philosophy of creating an atmosphere where franchise operators know they can achieve business world success if they work hard and have initiative.

"I worked at a number of GNC stores before becoming one of the company's first franchisees and I have always been impressed at GNC's approach of teaching employees and franchise operators the formula for success and supporting them at every step along the way. I think my career at GNC and tenure as a GNC store operator attests to that," said Patterson.

GNC Franchising, Inc., a subsidiary of General Nutrition Companies, Inc., is regularly ranked as one of America's top franchise opportunities by leading franchising industry magazines. It is the only nationwide specialty retailer of vitamin and mineral supplements, sports nutrition products and herbs.

According to Russell L. Cooper, senior vice president and general manager of GNC Franchising, Inc., the company's strong franchisee training and support programs are what have allowed the company to grow and prosper.

"Any prospective franchise operator is concerned about the level of training and support they receive. GNC is known throughout the franchising world for the importance we place on having store operators that are knowledgeable about running a business in general and our products in particular," said Cooper.

Cooper said that successful franchise operators also share several common traits, the most important being good business sense.

"We look at what's inside a person when awarding a franchise. We look for individuals with strong people skills and an ability to understand how a business operates. People that are willing to work hard at learning the business, follow our proven operating system and provide an exceptional shopping experience. Those are the qualities that we believe are important and I believe they are reflected in all our store operators," said Cooper.

Patterson is one of many minority GNC store operators who have been attracted to GNC franchising opportunities by the company's no-nonsense approach to preparing franchisees for running a business. Nearly 28% of all GNC franchise stores — or more than 350 individual units — are run by minority operators.

While Patterson is GNC's longest-termed franchise operator, among the most recent are Ray and Angela Hendricks — an African-American husband-and-wife team who opened their GNC franchise store in Dunedin, Florida, in early 1999. Patterson and the Hendricks took different paths to becoming GNC franchise operators. Joyce Patterson's road to operating a GNC franchise actually began as a nursing major in college.

"I always had wanted to be in the health profession, but realized that nursing wasn't for me after three years in the nursing program in college. I looked at a number of opportunities in the business world and found GNC of interest because of its health connection. It's along the same lines of what I wanted to do — help people stay healthy — only on the preventive side," said Patterson. Joining GNC in its pre-franchising days as an assistant manager, Patterson was promoted to a store manager position within one month. Quickly proving herself as a 'turnaround' specialist, she was assigned to a series of underperforming company-owned stores, dramatically improving sluggish sales at each store to which she was sent.

"I always hoped that GNC would offer franchises, and when they began franchising corporate stores in 1988, management encouraged me to 'go for it'," she said.

Patterson became GNC's first franchise operator, taking over the Greenwood Park Mall store in Greenwood, Indiana, in 1989. She franchised a second store in Indianapolis 3 years later and added a third store in Mooresville, Indiana, in early 1999.

The Hendricks, on the other hand, had been in business for themselves, owning a computer portrait business operating out of a kiosk in a Miami, Florida shopping mall.

"Ray and I had been operating our business for 3½ years, and saw a lot of franchised retail stores opening up in the mall. We also saw the kind of company support that they received. That's when we got the idea to explore opportunities in franchising. We had no idea about franchising in the beginning, but we wanted a business that was more than a single kiosk in a mall," said Angela Hendricks.

After spending a year of researching franchises for availability, costs and support, the Hendricks selected GNC.

"Basically, we felt that GNC had the best package in terms of financing, had an excellent training program and offered a great opportunity for growth," said Angela Hendricks.

Cooper said GNC's generous financing package is one of the best in the franchising industry. "Many of our franchise operators are going into business for themselves for the first time. We offer would-be franchisees an attractive financing program that includes direct financing to qualified candidates, deferred fees, special terms and grand-opening assistance," he said.

GNC Franchising is also a strong promoter of minority assistance programs, including the Local Initiative Support Corporation and programs associated with the International Franchise Association. Minorities also have the opportunity to utilize GNC's special Expansion Market financing that offers a reduced loan rate for first-time franchisees who increase their initial cash down payment.

"I've looked at other franchising programs and nothing matches it or even comes close. The amount of return on your investment is outstanding," said Patterson.
General Nutrition Companies, Inc. also supports its more than 4,000 stores with national advertising campaigns, which will exceed $75 million in 1999, with approximately 85% corporate-sponsored and 15% franchise-sponsored.

As part of an aggressive, 5-year expansion program, GNC Franchising has identified nearly 600 markets across the U.S. that have no GNC presence.

Angela Hendricks and Joyce Patterson encourage like-minded entrepreneurs to consider the path they took. Both stress, however, that prospective franchise operators must be prepared to work hard and have a commitment to excellence.

"If you have the desire and commitment, GNC Franchising provides an excellent training program and on-going support that will help you succeed," said Patterson.

Angela Hendricks adds that franchise operators must go beyond the existing company support system.

"You can't be totally dependent on your franchise company. You have to do a lot of work on your own, reading magazines and such, to stay on top of what's new in the industry. It's not location-location-location, it's research-research-research," said Angela Hendricks.

She also suggested prospective franchisees talk to current franchise operators before making any decision.

"Talk to as many franchise store operators as possible. Follow them around if you can. It's important to learn what it's like before you leap into the business," said Hendricks.

General Nutrition Companies, Inc., which is based in Pittsburgh, Pennsylvania, is the only nationwide specialty retailer of vitamin and mineral supplements, sports nutrition and herbal products, and is also a leading provider of personal care and other health-related products. The Company's products are sold through a network of 4,277 retail stores operating under the General Nutrition Centers, Health & Diet Centre and GNC Live Well names, of which 2,767 are Company-owned and 1,510 are franchised. GNC stores are located in all 50 states, Puerto Rico and 25 international markets.

For more information regarding GNC Franchising, Inc., call (800) 766-7099; write to: 300 6th Ave., Pittsburgh, PA 15222 ; or visit: www.gncfranchising.com.

In July, 1993, after operating as independent small business consultants for more than 10 years in the mail and parcel industry, the founders of PostNet International Franchise Corporation took a leap of faith into franchising. That leap of faith, as described by PostNet's President and Chief Executive Officer Steven Greenbaum, was "logical and consistent with our evolution as a company and industry."

PostNet's early vision of the industry was illustrated in its first franchise brochure entitled *Experience the Evolution of an Industry*. Greenbaum said, "In 1993, we likened the mail and parcel business to the Pony Express and the general store. Mail and parcel centers essentially are the general stores of today and tomorrow. They are places where people go to send and receive items, purchase products, communicate and build long and trusting relationships with the shopkeeper, who is typically well entrenched and respected in the community." Greenbaum went on to explain, "We utilized a timeline in our initial brochure which illustrated every significant invention or achievement in postal, business and communication technology up to the inception of PostNet. The message positioned PostNet as the conduit to the customer for the providers of this technology. PostNet's convenient retail locations provided the bricks-and-mortar, relationship-based interface that offered value to the service and product vendors that needed to reach the local and community markets." It was this early vision that fueled PostNet's growth and continually placed the company as an industry leader, both in terms of franchise system growth and technology.

Leap ahead to October, 1994, when PostNet's Director of Information Systems, Rick Greenbaum, conceived the original idea that became the foundation for PostNet's Internet and E-commerce initiatives. "I was always intrigued with the concept of being able to communicate with other computers to send and receive information and do it with a personal computer from the privacy of your own home," Rick Greenbaum explained. "We introduced PostNet's first web site to the 'Net' in early 1995. At that time, Mosaic was the beta version of Netscape. Other industry standards at that time included the use of 14.4 modems (prior to the release of 28.8), which have been replaced by ISDN, cable modems and DSL.

PostNet's initial web site was among the first on the Internet from the industry of franchising. The original concept was that of an on-line franchise sales brochure with the added value of user-friendly features, including a searchable database of franchise locations. From an efficiency standpoint, PostNet also felt that it could deliver franchise information faster and cheaper than its competitors via the web site, which translated into more sales and significant saving in mailing costs.

"We were operating on 'Internet time' long before it was fashionable," said Steven Greenbaum.

"When someone is researching franchise opportunities, it is typically an event driven decision. Once the decision is made to go into business for himself or herself, the prospect wants to start the investigation process immediately. The Internet, coupled with PostNet's response time of 4 business hours or less, provides an excellent vehicle for prospective franchisees to get the information they need fast." As companies like Yahoo developed, PostNet positioned itself at the top of search engine listings, making it easy to find PostNet on the web and easier for customers to do business with PostNet. The company also included its web site and E-mail addresses in all its printed materials and throughout its franchised locations, with the intent to drive people to the PostNet web site.

Over the past few years, PostNet has updated the image and content of its site regularly and added detailed content, including information about the company, its corporate goals and objectives, vision, core values and commitment to its franchisees. The site also takes you into a PostNet franchise to fully explain the full line of products and services and its unique delivery of sensational customer service coupled with neighborhood convenience. Consistent with PostNet's early vision of using the Internet as a franchise sales tool, you can also find a description of the company's multitude of franchise opportunities, as well as request franchise information on-line or submit an application for consideration. Another differentiating factor about PostNet is that it publishes a complete list of E-mail addresses for its managers and senior executives on its web site. They are always available to respond to prospective franchisees, vendors or customers, consistent with the company leadership's open door policy and commitment to accessibility. In 1997, PostNet introduced its Franchisee Web, a password-protected Intranet site that can be accessed from PostNet's home page. The Franchisee Web was developed solely for the purpose of bringing value to its franchisees.

PostNet's Franchisee Web is the culmination of focus group meetings with franchisees and PostNet's National Franchisees Advisory Council. The meetings determined where and how to add value to the system. According to Brian Spindel, Post-Net's Executive Vice President and key contributor in the Franchisee Web's development, it is "a continual work in progress. We were intent on utilizing the Internet to support our mission statement and our commitment to our franchisees by utilizing the latest technology to cost-effectively connect our stores and enable them to communicate and interface in real time." To support that commitment, PostNet provides a Message Board utility for franchisees to post and respond to day-to-day issues on topics from hiring personnel to customer service policies. Participation is open and encouraged by all members of the PostNet family from the executive management team at PostNet headquarters to international franchise owners and partners around the world. PostNet also provides a Chat Area on its Franchisee Web for real-time discussions covering a wide variety of subjects. According to Spindel, "These tools provide us with an opportunity to stay connected to our franchisees and their issues on a day-to-day basis."

PostNet's Franchisee Web also includes various industry-specific tools like an Address Resource, which assists PostNet franchisees in making business easier at the point of sale. PostNet also provides access to its approved vendors with on-line ordering and account servicing, regularly scheduled chat sessions and a download section, which includes everything from logos, marketing materials and press releases to PostNet's current national television and radio commercials. According to Ron Bradley, a PostNet franchisee in Asheville, North Carolina, "The Franchisee Web is an asset not only to the franchisee, but also to the customer. It allows for many opinions that could ultimately maximize the profit margins for the owner, and optimize the customer's satisfaction through a 'team of opinions and advice.' It's like having an extended family all over the country and world."

PostNet's Intranet site also includes a Franchisee Profiles area. It was developed and administered by franchisees, so they could better know and understand each other's unique attributes and challenges. Franchisees can post their store information and share experiences, including unique products or services, as well as contact information and photos. Unlike other franchise systems, PostNet provides a certain level of flexibility in terms of product and service offerings due to the unique convenience-oriented nature of the business. This flexibility is carefully managed to ensure that the PostNet system and standards remain intact; however, it provides an excellent opportunity for franchisees to carve out competitive niche markets in their local communities. For example, you will find Karen Hehn of Hilo, Hawaii, the Franchisee Profiles creator, illustrating her use of technology (including large format picture imaging and high speed color copying) and sharing her secret to carving out her niche on the Islands.

The National Database utility, another breakthrough technology initiated by PostNet enables franchisees to upload their customer records for inclusion in a national mail management system. This allows for regular, seamless promotional mailings to their customers. PostNet's National Database utility enables PostNet to support the re-marketing efforts to its franchisees' current customers, while franchisees focus on bringing in new customers. "It's all quite simple," explains Spindel. "We wanted to create a vehicle for our franchisees to add value to their customers shopping experience and, at the same time, make it easier for our franchisees to grow their businesses." There are presently over 200,000 PostNet customers across America benefitting from this utility. All costs associated with the direct marketing efforts are funded by PostNet's National Ad Fund at the recommendation of PostNet's National Franchisees Advisory Council.

PostNet franchises can also download current and past copies of *PostNet News*, PostNet's monthly newsletter, as well as past bulletins. They are able to communicate with their respective National Franchisees Advisory Council respresentatives at the click of a mouse button. Franchisees can link directly to PostNet's franchise support department, just as easily. From there, franchisees can order supplies or customized marketing materials, reserve professional displays for local or community trade and business shows, and check PostNet's activity calendar for upcoming local and national events. PostNet franchisees, Jim and Diane Hutkin of Fort Collins, Colorado, comment, "Being connected to

the Franchisee Web is like having 500 knowledgeable consultants on your staff. It allows us all to grow our businesses utilizing ideas from all over the country."

One more leap ahead takes us to February, 1999, with the launching of PostNetonline.com, Post-Net's E-commerce site. Spindel describes it as "what really puts the 'Net' in PostNet." PostNetonline provides small business owners and the general consumer with the opportunity to purchase a wide variety of fully customized products and services, such as business cards and stationery, rubber stamps, labels and stickers, logo merchandise and advertising specialties, all from the convenience of their own homes or businesses. PostNetonline has a unique graphic interface that allows consumers to either fully create or customize their printing orders using pre-developed templates. They can also build their own style or appearance, as well as insert photos or graphics. The same holds true for PostNetonline's web page design area, where consumers can place their own customized web sites on the Internet, or create on-line product offerings and participate in the E-commerce revolution. What's even more revolutionary is that each time a consumer makes a purchase on PostNetonline.com, he or she enters his or her ZIP Code and selects the nearest PostNet center, the on-line sale is fully credited to the selected PostNet center. PostNet proclaims that "this is another way of adding value to our franchise owners' investment in the business and system."

If you are in need of a business address in a far away land, through PostNetonline.com, you can rent a private mailbox at any participating PostNet center in the world. Also, you can purchase flowers, gift baskets and executive gifts for even the most discerning clients. When it comes time for a business or personal relocation, PostNetonline provides an easy to use utility for selecting and ordering the right amount of moving boxes, packaging materials and supplies, which are then shipped direct to your home or office. When it comes to service, the nearest participating PostNet center can be accessed through the Internet or PostNet's toll-free telephone number, in order to obtain a price quote for the moving or shipment of your boxes or furniture, removing the hassle of preparing for and completing a move.

When asked where PostNet goes from here, Brian Spindel says, "PostNet Postal and Business Centers and PostNetonline.com will continue to evolve in meeting consumer needs and using technology as the Internet continues to evolve. We see PostNet as a convenient resource for small business owners, small office/home office workers and general consumers with the added value of providing totally outrageous service. We are committed to the philosophy and culture of 360-degree marketing and providing our franchisees, suppliers and customers with 24/7/365 access to PostNet's products, services and resources."

It's no wonder that in just over 6 years PostNet has grown to more than 650 licensed locations worldwide. Currently, PostNet is operating in 17 countries with options signed in an additional 28 countries. When we asked Steven Greenbaum what PostNet's long terms plans were, he smiled and replied, "world dominance, at least in the postal and business services industry!"

AAMCO TRANSMISSIONS

One Presidential Blvd.
Bala Cynwyd, PA 19004
Tel: (800) 523-0402 (610) 668-2900
Fax: (610) 617-9532
E-Mail: rcastellani@aamco.com
Web Site: www.aamcotransmissions.com
Mr. Bob Castellani, Director Franchise
Development

AAMCO is the world's largest chain of transmission specialists with 35 years' experience as the undisputed industry leader. An American icon, AAMCO's trademark is recognized by 90% of the driving public. Transmission repair is a $2.9 billion business in the United States and is projected to be a $3.6 billion business by the year 2001.

Background:
Established: 1963;   1st Franchised: 1963
Franchised Units: 712
Company-Owned Units: 2
Total Units: 714
Minority-Owned Units:
    African-American: 3%
    Asian-American: 10%
    Hispanic: 0%
    Native American: 0%
North America: 48 States, 3 Provinces
Density: 109 in CA, 62 in FL, 45 NY

Financial/Terms:
Cash Investment: $60K
Total Investment: $175K
Minimum Net Worth: $250K
Fees: Franchise — $30K
    Royalty — 7%;   Ad. — 4-5%
Earnings Claim Statement: No
Term of Contract (Years):   15/15
Avg. # Of Employees: 4 FT, 1 PT
Passive Ownership: Not Allowed
Area Develop. Agreements: No
Sub-Franchising Contracts: No
Expand In Territory: Yes
Space Needs: 4,000 SF; FS, SF, Automall

Support & Training Provided:
Site Selection Assistance: Yes
Lease Negotiation Assistance: Yes
Co-Operative Advertising: No
Franchisee Assoc./Member: Yes/No
Size Of Corporate Staff: 245
On-Going Support: A,B,C,D,E,G,H,I
Training: 5 Weeks Home Office,
Philadelphia, PA.
Minority-Specific Programs: Although we support the objectives of the NMFI, we do not have any specific programs in place at this time.

Specific Expansion Plans:
US: NE, Great Lakes Region

AERO-COLOURS

6971 Washington Ave. S., # 102
Minneapolis, MN 55439-1508
Tel: (800) 696-2376 (612) 277-0309
Fax: (612) 942-0628
E-Mail: jspellmire@aerocolours.com
Web Site: www.aerocolours.com
Mr. James F. Spellmire, President

AERO-COLOURS is an exclusive mobile automotive paint repair process, providing service to dealerships, fleet operations and individual vehicle owners. Our solid support system, complemented by our industry-leading training, allows our franchisees to provide unmatched service. We will show you how to operate, market and grow your own business.

Background:
Established: 1985;   1st Franchised: 1993
Franchised Units: 62
Company-Owned Units: 14
Total Units: 76
Minority-Owned Units:
    African-American: 0
    Asian-American: 1
    Hispanic: 0
    Native American: 0
    Other: 0
North America: 27 States
Density: 15 in CA, 5 in TX

Financial/Terms:
Cash Investment: $5-30K
Total Investment: $5-60K
Minimum Net Worth: $100K
Fees: Franchise — $25K
    Royalty — 7-4%/Sliding;   Ad. — 0%
Earnings Claim Statement: No
Term of Contract (Years):   10/10

Avg. # Of Employees:	4-5 FT
Passive Ownership:	Allowed
Area Develop. Agreements:	No
Sub-Franchising Contracts:	Yes
Expand In Territory:	Yes
Space Needs: 2,000 SF; Warehouse	

Support & Training Provided:

Site Selection Assistance:	Yes
Lease Negotiation Assistance:	Yes
Co-Operative Advertising:	No
Franchisee Assoc./Member:	Yes/Yes
Size Of Corporate Staff:	14
On-Going Support:	A,B,C,D,E,G,H,I
Training: 2 Weeks Tampa, FL; 2 Weeks Territory.	

Minority-Specific Programs: Although we support the objectives of the NMFI, we do not have any specific programs in place at this time.

Specific Expansion Plans:

US:	All United States

The Choice Is Clear.

ALTA MERE COMPLETE AUTO IMAGING

4444 W. 147th St.
Midlothian, IL 60445
Tel: (800) 377-9247 (708) 389-5922
Fax: (708) 389-9882
E-Mail: vsmithson@moranindustries.com
Web Site: www.moranindustries.com
Ms. Virginia Smithson, Qualification Specialist

ALTA MERE offers complete auto imaging; window tinting, auto security, cellular phones, beepers and auto accessories. This specialty division of Moran Industries franchises complete auto imaging service centers throughout the US. We offer our franchisees a superior business system, strong brand name, customized marketing and a service that is in strong demand. Our exclusive business system, along with the skills of our franchisees, create customer experiences that result in satisfaction and loyalty.

Background:

Established: 1993;	1st Franchised: 1993
Franchised Units:	36
Company-Owned Units:	1

Total Units:	37
Minority-Owned Units:	
African-American:	
Asian-American:	
Hispanic:	
Native American:	
Other:	
North America:	9 States
Density:	15 in TX, 7 in OK, 4 in AK

Financial/Terms:

Cash Investment:	$35-40K
Total Investment:	$93K
Minimum Net Worth:	$90K
Fees: Franchise —	$27.5K
Royalty — 7%;	Ad. — $100/Mo.
Earnings Claim Statement:	Yes
Term of Contract (Years):	20/20
Avg. # Of Employees:	3 FT
Passive Ownership:	Discouraged
Area Develop. Agreements:	Yes
Sub-Franchising Contracts:	No
Expand In Territory:	Yes
Space Needs: 2,500 SF; FS, SF, SC, RM	

Support & Training Provided:

Site Selection Assistance:	Yes
Lease Negotiation Assistance:	Yes
Co-Operative Advertising:	Yes
Franchisee Assoc./Member:	Yes/Yes
Size Of Corporate Staff:	55
On-Going Support:	A,C,D,E,G,H,I
Training: Training is provided.	

Minority-Specific Programs: Although we support the objectives of the NMFI, we do not have any specific programs in place at this time.

Specific Expansion Plans:

US:	All United States

AUTO-LAB DIAGNOSTIC & TUNE-UP CENTERS

1050 W. Columbia Ave.
Battle Creek, MI 49015
Tel: (877) 349-4968 (616) 966-0500
Fax: (616) 966-0520
E-Mail:
Web Site: www.AutoLabusa.com
Mr. Daniel J. Kiefer, President

Full service automotive repair facility, performing all aspects of auto service and repair. Our specialty is in the diagnostics and repair of computerized and electrical systems. Our goal is to be a professional alternative to auto dealer repair shops.

Background:

Established: 1984;	1st Franchised: 1989
Franchised Units:	25
Company-Owned Units:	1
Total Units:	26
Minority-Owned Units:	
African-American:	1
Asian-American:	
Hispanic:	
Native American:	
Other:	
North America:	2 States
Density:	25 in MI, 1 in OH

Financial/Terms:

Cash Investment:	$35-75K
Total Investment:	$110-175K
Minimum Net Worth:	$250K
Fees: Franchise —	$19.5K
Royalty — 6%;	Ad. — 3%
Earnings Claim Statement:	No
Term of Contract (Years):	15/15
Avg. # Of Employees:	5 FT, 1 PT
Passive Ownership:	Discouraged
Area Develop. Agreements:	Yes/15
Sub-Franchising Contracts:	No
Expand In Territory:	Yes
Space Needs: 3,000+ SF; FS	

Support & Training Provided:

Site Selection Assistance:	Yes
Lease Negotiation Assistance:	Yes
Co-Operative Advertising:	Yes
Franchisee Assoc./Member:	No
Size Of Corporate Staff:	10
On-Going Support:	a,b,C,D,E,G,H,I
Training: 2 Weeks Grand Rapids, MI; 2-4 Week Battle Creek, MI.	

Minority-Specific Programs: Although we support the objectives of the NMFI, we do not have any specific programs in place at this time.

Specific Expansion Plans:

US:	MW & E to Gulf of Mexico

BIG O TIRES

12650 E. Briarwood Ave. # 2D
Englewood, CO 80112
Tel: (800) 622-2446 (303) 728-5500
Fax: (303) 728-5700
Web Site: www.bigotires.com
Mr. Troy Benson, Franchise Qual. Specialist

BIG O TIRES is the fastest-growing retail tire and under-car service center franchisor in North America. We offer over 30 years' experience and proven success, site selection assistance, comprehensive training and on-going field support, protected territory, exclusive product lines, consistent product supply, unique marketing programs, contemporary building designs, effective advertising support, and proven business systems.

Background:

Established: 1962;	1st Franchised: 1967
Franchised Units:	438
Company-Owned Units:	16
Total Units:	464
Minority-Owned Units:	
African-American:	
Asian-American:	
Hispanic:	
Native American:	
North America:	19 States, 1 Province
Density:	153 in CA, 52 in AZ, 42 CO

Financial/Terms:

Cash Investment:	$100K
Total Investment:	$300K
Minimum Net Worth:	$300K
Fees: Franchise —	$25K
Royalty — 2%;	Ad. — 2-4%
Earnings Claim Statement:	No
Term of Contract (Years):	10
Avg. # Of Employees:	6
Passive Ownership:	Discouraged
Area Develop. Agreements:	Yes/Varies
Sub-Franchising Contracts:	Yes
Expand In Territory:	Yes
Space Needs: NR SF; FS	

Support & Training Provided:

Site Selection Assistance:	Yes
Lease Negotiation Assistance:	Yes
Co-Operative Advertising:	Yes
Franchisee Assoc./Member:	NR
Size Of Corporate Staff:	100
On-Going Support:	A,B,C,d,E,F,G,h,I
Training: 5 Weeks Denver, CO.	

Minority-Specific Programs: Although we support the objectives of the NMFI, we do not have any specific programs in place at this time.

Specific Expansion Plans:

US:	All United States

BRAKE CENTERS OF AMERICA
35 Old Battery Rd.
Bridgeport, CT 06605
Tel: (203) 336-1995
Fax: (203) 336-1995
E-Mail: brakesusa@aol.com
Web Site: www.infonews.com/franchise/bcoa
Mr. Bill Pelletier, President

True brakes only brake specialist. Eliminate the headaches of operating a "we do everything shop." Do one thing right. This is a great opportunity for the right person cooking for a business in the Northeast.

Background:

Established: 1989;	1st Franchised: 1992
Franchised Units:	0
Company-Owned Units:	8
Total Units:	8
Minority-Owned Units:	
African-American:	0
Asian-American:	0
Hispanic:	0
Native American:	0
Other:	0
North America:	1 State
Density:	8 in CT

Financial/Terms:

Cash Investment:	$50-90K
Total Investment:	$50-100K
Minimum Net Worth:	$Open
Fees: Franchise —	$12K
Royalty — 6%;	Ad. — 4%
Earnings Claim Statement:	No
Term of Contract (Years):	17/10
Avg. # Of Employees:	3 FT, 1 PT
Passive Ownership:	Not Allowed
Area Develop. Agreements:	No
Sub-Franchising Contracts:	No
Expand In Territory:	Yes
Space Needs: 2,500 SF; FS, SC	

Support & Training Provided:

Site Selection Assistance:	Yes
Lease Negotiation Assistance:	Yes
Co-Operative Advertising:	Yes
Franchisee Assoc./Member:	No
Size Of Corporate Staff:	3
On-Going Support:	a,B,c,d,e,F
Training: 80 Hours in Norwalk, CT.	

Minority-Specific Programs: No minority or other programs inplace. Will work with prospect on a one to one basis to open store. Would be proud to have minority owners.

Specific Expansion Plans:

US:	Northeast

BRAKE MASTERS
6179 E. Broadway Blvd.
Tucson, AZ 85711
Tel: (800) 888-5545 (520) 512-0000
Fax: (520) 512-1000
E-Mail: franchisee@brakemasters.com
Web Site: www.brakemasters.com
Mr. Richard A. Beuzekom, Director of Franchising

Brake repair, brake-related services and lubrication.

Background:

Established: 1983;	1st Franchised: 1994
Franchised Units:	31
Company-Owned Units:	24
Total Units:	55
Minority-Owned Units:	
African-American:	
Asian-American:	9.6%
Hispanic:	19.4%
Native American:	
North America:	4 States
Density:	24 in CA, 23 in AZ, 7 in NM

Financial/Terms:

Cash Investment:	$50K
Total Investment:	$125-150K
Minimum Net Worth:	$NR
Fees: Franchise —	$19.5K
Royalty — 5%;	Ad. — 1%
Earnings Claim Statement:	No
Term of Contract (Years):	20
Avg. # Of Employees:	6 FT, 2 PT
Passive Ownership:	Discouraged
Area Develop. Agreements:	Yes/20
Sub-Franchising Contracts:	Yes
Expand In Territory:	Yes
Space Needs: 4,000 SF; FS	

Support & Training Provided:

Site Selection Assistance:	Yes
Lease Negotiation Assistance:	Yes
Co-Operative Advertising:	Yes
Franchisee Assoc./Member:	NR
Size Of Corporate Staff:	16
On-Going Support:	B,C,D,E,F,I
Training: 2 Weeks Tucson, AZ; 2 Weeks	

Location Near Franchisee.
Minority-Specific Programs: Financing available for all related franchisees, regardless of race, creed or color.

Specific Expansion Plans:
US: West, Southwest, Midwest

BRAKE SHOP, THE

31900 Utica Rd.
Fraser, MI 48026
Tel: (800) 747-2113 (810) 415-2800
Fax: (810) 415-2813
Web Site: www.thebrakeshop.com
Mr. Ken Rempel, Director of Franchising

Automotive business that specializes in the service and repair of automobile braking systems, as well as other under body repair such as shocks, struts, etc. No automotive skills necessary. People skills a plus.

Background:
Established: 1988; 1st Franchised: 1990
Franchised Units: 82
Company-Owned Units: 18
Total Units: 100
Minority-Owned Units:
  African-American:
  Asian-American:
  Hispanic:
  Native American:
North America: 16 States
Density: 36 in MI, 8 in OH, 7 in NY

Financial/Terms:
Cash Investment: $50K
Total Investment: $75K
Minimum Net Worth: $50K
Fees: Franchise — $20K
  Royalty — 8% Brakes; Ad. — 0%
Earnings Claim Statement: No
Term of Contract (Years): 20/20
Avg. # Of Employees: 2 FT
Passive Ownership: Discouraged
Area Develop. Agreements: Yes/20
Sub-Franchising Contracts: Yes
Expand In Territory: Yes
Space Needs: 2,000 SF; FS

Support & Training Provided:
Site Selection Assistance: Yes
Lease Negotiation Assistance: Yes
Co-Operative Advertising: N/A
Franchisee Assoc./Member: No
Size Of Corporate Staff: 17
On-Going Support: C,D,E,F,G,H,I
Training: 1 Week Detroit, MI.
Minority-Specific Programs: Financing assistance through third party financing. Reduced franchise fee. Royalty abatement program.

Specific Expansion Plans:
US: All United States

CAR-X MUFFLER & BRAKE

8430 W. Bryn Mawr Ave., # 400
Chicago, IL 60631
Tel: (800) 359-2359 (773) 693-1000
Fax: (773) 693-0309
E-Mail: dmaltzma@carx.com
Web Site: www.carx.com.
Mr. David Maltzman, Franchise Development Manager

Retail automotive specialists providing service in brakes, exhaust, road handling, steering systems, air conditioning, and oil changes for all makes of cars and light trucks.

Background:
Established: 1971; 1st Franchised: 1973
Franchised Units: 132
Company-Owned Units: 53
Total Units: 185
Minority-Owned Units:
  African-American: 6%
  Asian-American: 0%
  Hispanic: 0%
  Native American: 0%
  Other: 18%
North America: 11 States
Density: 59 in IL, 25 in MN, 21 in MO

Financial/Terms:
Cash Investment: $65-90K
Total Investment: $225-285K
Minimum Net Worth: $200K
Fees: Franchise — $20K
  Royalty — 5%; Ad. — 5-7%

Earnings Claim Statement: Yes
Term of Contract (Years): 15/5
Avg. # Of Employees: 3-6 FT
Passive Ownership: Discouraged
Area Develop. Agreements: Yes
Sub-Franchising Contracts: No
Expand In Territory: Yes
Space Needs: 4,000 SF; FS

Support & Training Provided:
Site Selection Assistance: Yes
Lease Negotiation Assistance: Yes
Co-Operative Advertising: No
Franchisee Assoc./Member: Yes/No
Size Of Corporate Staff: 20
On-Going Support: B,C,D,E,G,h,I
Training: 5 Weeks Headquarters; 2 Weeks at Franchisee's Shop.
Minority-Specific Programs: No specific programs. Third party financing available to all qualified applicants.

Specific Expansion Plans:
US: MW, SW, and South

CARTEX LIMITED

42816 Mound Rd.
Sterling Heights, MI 48314
Tel: (800) 421-7328 (810) 739-4339
Fax: (810) 739-4331
E-Mail: crismar@aol.com
Ms. Diana Klukowski, Secretary

CARTEX LIMITED, better known as Fabrion, is a mobile service business, specializing in automotive interior repair. The Fabrion repair process electrostatically repairs auto cloth, velour and carpet. Due to our specialization, we have revolutionized auto upholstery repair. Updating on current (OEM) original equipment materials and providing the tools to match all current patterns being used in auto interiors are our strong points.

Background:
Established: 1980; 1st Franchised: 1988

Franchised Units:	85
Company-Owned Units:	1
Total Units:	86
Minority-Owned Units:	
African-American:	1
Asian-American:	
Hispanic:	2
Native American:	1
Other:	
North America:	32 States
Density:	15 in CA, 14 in FL, 8 in OH

Financial/Terms:

Cash Investment:	$23.5K
Total Investment:	$25K
Minimum Net Worth:	$N/A
Fees: Franchise —	$15/18.5/23.5K
Royalty — $160-300/Mo.;	Ad. — 0%
Earnings Claim Statement:	No
Term of Contract (Years):	5/5
Avg. # Of Employees:	6 FT, 1 PT
Passive Ownership:	Discouraged
Area Develop. Agreements:	No
Sub-Franchising Contracts:	No
Expand In Territory:	Yes
Space Needs: N/A SF; N/A	

Support & Training Provided:

Site Selection Assistance:	N/A
Lease Negotiation Assistance:	N/A
Co-Operative Advertising:	N/A
Franchisee Assoc./Member:	No
Size Of Corporate Staff:	6
On-Going Support:	B,C,D,G,H,I

Training: 3 Weeks On-Site Under Development.

Minority-Specific Programs: Although we support the objectives of the NMFI, we do not have any specific programs in place at this time.

Specific Expansion Plans:

US:	All United States

COLORS ON PARADE

5201 Brook Hollow Pkwy. # A
Norcross, GA 30071
Tel: (800) 929-3363 (678) 243-2000
Fax: (678) 243-2016
E-Mail: wilson@colorsfranchise.com
Web Site: www.colorsfranchise.com
Mr. Bill Wilson, Director of Franchising

America's premier paint and body automotive restoration franchise, COLORS ON PARADE was voted # 1 for franchisee financial satisfaction in Success magazine's 1999 survey.

Background:

Established: 1988;	1st Franchised: 1991	
Franchised Units:		348
Company-Owned Units:		0
Total Units:		348
Minority-Owned Units:		
African-American:		6
Asian-American:		4
Hispanic:		7
Native American:		0
Other:		
North America:		26 States
Density:	50 in CA, 44 in FL, 32 in GA	

Financial/Terms:

Cash Investment:	$7.5-45K
Total Investment:	$46.6-147.4K
Minimum Net Worth:	$50-400K
Fees: Franchise —	$5-30K
Royalty — 7-15%;	Ad. — 0%
Earnings Claim Statement:	No
Term of Contract (Years):	10/5
Avg. # Of Employees:	2 FT
Passive Ownership:	Discouraged
Area Develop. Agreements:	Yes/5
Sub-Franchising Contracts:	No
Expand In Territory:	Yes
Space Needs: N/A SF; Mobile	

Support & Training Provided:

Site Selection Assistance:	N/A
Lease Negotiation Assistance:	N/A
Co-Operative Advertising:	N/A
Franchisee Assoc./Member:	No
Size Of Corporate Staff:	19
On-Going Support:	B,C,D,G,H,I

Training: 3 Weeks Conway, SC.

Minority-Specific Programs: Although we support the objectives of the NMFI, we do not have any specific programs in place at this time.

Specific Expansion Plans:

US:	All United States

COTTMAN TRANSMISSION

240 New York Dr.
Fort Washington, PA 19034
Tel: (888) 4COTTMAN (215) 643-5885
Fax: (215) 643-2519
E-Mail:

Web Site: www.cottman.com
Mr. Barry Auchenbach, Manager Franchise Development

Automotive transmission service franchise with centers nationwide. A market leader with new opportunities available in major markets as a result of our expansion plans. A highly-supportive company that offers intensive training, outstanding advertising and on-site support.

Background:

Established: 1962;	1st Franchised: 1964	
Franchised Units:		260
Company-Owned Units:		4
Total Units:		264
Minority-Owned Units:		
African-American:		3%
Asian-American:		3%
Hispanic:		3%
Native American:		0%
North America:	33 States, 2 Province	
Density:	43 in PA, 22 in NJ, 18 in CA	

Financial/Terms:

Cash Investment:	$40K
Total Investment:	$130-160K
Minimum Net Worth:	$100K
Fees: Franchise —	$25K
Royalty — 7.5%;	Ad. — $605/Wk.
Earnings Claim Statement:	Yes
Term of Contract (Years):	15/15
Avg. # Of Employees:	3-4 FT, 1 PT
Passive Ownership:	Not Allowed
Area Develop. Agreements:	Yes/6
Sub-Franchising Contracts:	No
Expand In Territory:	Yes
Space Needs: 3,000-4,000 SF; FS, SC, Auto	

Support & Training Provided:

Site Selection Assistance:	Yes
Lease Negotiation Assistance:	Yes
Co-Operative Advertising:	No
Franchisee Assoc./Member:	No
Size Of Corporate Staff:	50
On-Going Support:	C,D,E,F,G,H,I

Training: 3 Weeks Ft. Washington, PA; 1 Week On-Site.

Minority-Specific Programs: Although we support the objectives of the NMFI, we do not have any specific programs in place at this time.

Specific Expansion Plans:

US:	All United States

ESTRELLA INSURANCE

7480 NW 186th St.
Miami, Fl 33015
Tel: (888) 511-7722 (305) 828-2444

Fax: (305) 556-7788
E-Mail: estrella@sunnyweb.com
Web Site: www.estrellainsurance.net
Mr. Jose E. Merille, President

ESTRELLA INSURANCE is the leader in the state of Florida in the auto insurance agency field and currently insures close to 100,000 autos in Dade and Broward county alone. Future expansion plans are to West Palm, Tampa, Orlando and other large cities. We offer outstanding support and advertising (TV, radio, outdoor, direct mail, etc.).

Background:

Established: 1980;	1st Franchised: 1997
Franchised Units:	5
Company-Owned Units:	35
Total Units:	40
Minority-Owned Units:	
African-American:	
Asian-American:	
Hispanic:	
Native American:	
Other:	
North America:	1 State
Density:	40 in FL

Financial/Terms:

Cash Investment:	$20-30K
Total Investment:	$79.5-99.5K
Minimum Net Worth:	$75-100K
Fees: Franchise —	$39.5K
Royalty — 2-4%;	Ad. — 1%
Earnings Claim Statement:	Yes
Term of Contract (Years):	7/7
Avg. # Of Employees:	3 FT, 1 PT
Passive Ownership:	Discouraged
Area Develop. Agreements:	Yes/10
Sub-Franchising Contracts:	No
Expand In Territory:	No
Space Needs: 800 SF; FS, SF, SC, RM	

Support & Training Provided:

Site Selection Assistance:	Yes
Lease Negotiation Assistance:	Yes
Co-Operative Advertising:	Yes
Franchisee Assoc./Member:	Yes/Yes

Size Of Corporate Staff:	30
On-Going Support:	A,B,C,D,E,H
Training: 8 Weeks Miami, FL.	

Minority-Specific Programs: Although we support the objectives of the NMFI, we do not have any specific programs in place at this time.

Specific Expansion Plans:

US:	Florida

KING BEAR AUTO SERVICE CENTERS

130 - 29 Merrick Blvd.
Springfield Gardens, NY 11434
Tel: (800) 311-KING (718) 527-1252
Fax: (718) 527-4985
E-Mail: kingbear32@aol.com
Web Site:
www.KingBearAutoFranchise.com
Mr. Melvin D. Messinger, Director of Franchising

KING BEAR AUTO SERVICE CENTER was the first organized automotive franchise in the state of New York. Founded in 1973, it has been a household name known for quality auto service at a reasonable cost. KING BEAR has retained its status as a complete one-stop auto service center.

Background:

Established: 1973;	1st Franchised: 1973
Franchised Units:	33
Company-Owned Units:	0
Total Units:	33
Minority-Owned Units:	
African-American:	2
Asian-American:	0
Hispanic:	2
Native American:	0
Other:	4
North America:	1 State
Density:	33 in NY

Financial/Terms:

Cash Investment:	$65-90K
Total Investment:	$159-294K
Minimum Net Worth:	$50K
Fees: Franchise —	$29.5K
Royalty — 5% or Fee;	Ad. — 7% or Fee
Earnings Claim Statement:	No
Term of Contract (Years):	25/25
Avg. # Of Employees:	3 FT
Passive Ownership:	Allowed

Area Develop. Agreements:	Yes/25
Sub-Franchising Contracts:	No
Expand In Territory:	Yes
Space Needs: 2,000-6,000 SF; FS, SC	

Support & Training Provided:

Site Selection Assistance:	Yes
Lease Negotiation Assistance:	Yes
Co-Operative Advertising:	Yes
Franchisee Assoc./Member:	No
Size Of Corporate Staff:	6
On-Going Support:	B,C,D,E,F,H,I
Training: 2 Weeks at Corporate Office; On-Site as Needed.	

Minority-Specific Programs: Advertising, assistance with obtaining financing and assistance in preparing loan documents.

Specific Expansion Plans:

US:	All United States

LINE-X SPRAY-ON TRUCK BEDLINERS

2525-A S. Birch St.
Santa Ana, CA 92707
Tel: (800) 831-3232 (714) 850 1662
Fax: (714) 850-8759
E-Mail: linexcor@pacbell.net
Web Site: www.linexcorp.com
Mr. Scott Jewett, General Manager

A LINE-X franchisee operates a retail/industrial location that applies sprayed on coatings. LINE-X has a number of applications from flooring to industrial applications. LINE-X is in a growing, new and unsaturated market with extraordinary opportunities for minority entrepreneurs.

Background:

Established: 1993;	1st Franchised: 1999
Franchised Units:	360
Company-Owned Units:	1
Total Units:	361
Minority-Owned Units:	
African-American:	
Asian-American:	
Hispanic:	
Native American:	
Other:	
North America:	50 States
Density:	20 in CA, 15 in WA, 10 in GA

Financial/Terms:

Cash Investment:	$25K
Total Investment:	$68-147K

Minimum Net Worth:	$20K
Fees: Franchise —	$20K
Royalty — 0%;	Ad. — 1.5%
Earnings Claim Statement:	No
Term of Contract (Years):	5/15
Avg. # Of Employees:	2 FT
Passive Ownership:	Discouraged
Area Develop. Agreements:	Yes
Sub-Franchising Contracts:	Yes
Expand In Territory:	Yes
Space Needs: 2,500 SF; Industrial/ Commercial	

Support & Training Provided:

Site Selection Assistance:	Yes
Lease Negotiation Assistance:	Yes
Co-Operative Advertising:	No
Franchisee Assoc./Member:	No
Size Of Corporate Staff:	14
On-Going Support:	C,D,E,G,H,I

Training: Up to 5 Days at our Location; up to 7 Days at Franchisee's Location.

Minority-Specific Programs: Although we support the objectives of the NMFI, we do not have any specific programs in place at this time.

Specific Expansion Plans:

US:	All United States

MEINEKE DISCOUNT MUFFLERS

128 S. Tryon St., # 900
Charlotte, NC 28202
Tel: (800) 275-5200 (704) 377-8855
Fax: (704) 358-4706
E-Mail: Alice_Griffin@meineke.com
Web Site: www.meineke.com
Ms. Alice Griffin, Franchise Develop. Coord.

MEINEKE DISCOUNT MUFFLERS is the nation's largest discount muffler and brake repair specialist with more than 860 shops across the nation. They have been offering great service at discount prices for more than 25 years. Their franchisees come from all walks of life and represent many nationalities.

Background:

Established: 1972;	1st Franchised: 1973
Franchised Units:	859
Company-Owned Units:	8
Total Units:	867

Minority-Owned Units:	
African-American:	
Asian-American:	
Hispanic:	
Native American:	
Other:	
North America:	46 States
Density:	77 in NY, 64 in PA, 58 in NJ

Financial/Terms:

Cash Investment:	$40-50K
Total Investment:	$140-250K
Minimum Net Worth:	$100K
Fees: Franchise —	$25K
Royalty — 2.5-7%;	Ad. — 1.5-10%
Earnings Claim Statement:	Yes
Term of Contract (Years):	15/15
Avg. # Of Employees:	3 FT
Passive Ownership:	Not Allowed
Area Develop. Agreements:	Yes/Varies
Sub-Franchising Contracts:	No
Expand In Territory:	Yes
Space Needs: 2,880 SF; FS, SC	

Support & Training Provided:

Site Selection Assistance:	No
Lease Negotiation Assistance:	Yes
Co-Operative Advertising:	No
Franchisee Assoc./Member:	Yes/No
Size Of Corporate Staff:	134
On-Going Support:	C,D,E,G,H,I

Training: 4 Weeks Charlotte, NC.

Minority-Specific Programs: Although we support the objectives of the NMFI, we do not have any specific programs in place at this time.

Specific Expansion Plans:

US:	All United States

MERLIN'S MUFFLER & BRAKE

1 N. River Ln., # 206
Geneva, IL 60134
Tel: (800) 652-9900 (630) 208-9900
Fax: (630) 208-8601
E-Mail: Merlins-undercar@worldnet.att.net
Web Site: www.merlins.com
Mr. Mark M. Hameister, Director Franchise Development

MERLIN'S is an up-scale automotive service business, specializing in brakes, exhaust, suspension, oil/lubrication and related services. Automotive experience is not always necessary, but candidates must have significant experience in managing employees and serving customers honestly. MERLIN'S is expanding in Illinois, Michigan, Georgia, Texas and Wisconsin.

Background:

Established: 1975;	1st Franchised: 1975
Franchised Units:	59
Company-Owned Units:	3
Total Units:	62
Minority-Owned Units:	
African-American:	1
Asian-American:	1
Hispanic:	1
Native American:	0
Other:	3
North America:	5 States
Density:	47 in IL, 5 in TX, 5 in GA

Financial/Terms:

Cash Investment:	$45-60K
Total Investment:	$160-185K
Minimum Net Worth:	$75K
Fees: Franchise —	$26-30K
Royalty — 4.9%;	Ad. — 5%
Earnings Claim Statement:	Yes
Term of Contract (Years):	20/20
Avg. # Of Employees:	3-4 FT, 1 PT
Passive Ownership:	Not Allowed
Area Develop. Agreements:	No
Sub-Franchising Contracts:	No
Expand In Territory:	Yes
Space Needs: 3,850 SF; FS, SC, RM, Other Center	

Support & Training Provided:

Site Selection Assistance:	Yes
Lease Negotiation Assistance:	Yes
Co-Operative Advertising:	Yes
Franchisee Assoc./Member:	Yes/Yes
Size Of Corporate Staff:	20
On-Going Support:	B,C,D,E,F,G,H,I

Training: 6 Weeks Corporate Headquarters; In-Shop as Needed.

Minority-Specific Programs: Although we support the objectives of the NMFI, we do not have any specific programs in place at this time.

Specific Expansion Plans:

US:	IL, MI, GA, TX and WI

MIGHTY DISTRIBUTING SYSTEM OF AMERICA

650 Engineering Dr.
Norcross, GA 30092
Tel: (800) 829-3900 (770) 448-3900
Fax: (770) 446-8627

E-Mail: tracy.brown@mightyautoparts.com
Web Site: www.mightyautoparts.com
Ms. Tracy Brown, Franchise Marketing
Manager

Wholesale distribution of original equipment-quality, MIGHTY-branded auto parts. Franchisees operate in exclusive territories, supplying automotive maintenance and repair facilities with undercar and underhood products, such as filters, belts, tune-up and brake parts.

Background:

Established: 1963;	1st Franchised: 1970
Franchised Units:	142
Company-Owned Units:	5
Total Units:	147
Minority-Owned Units:	
African-American:	0
Asian-American:	0
Hispanic:	0
Native American:	0
Other:	
North America:	45 States
Density:	12 in PA, 10 in FL, 9 in CA

Financial/Terms:

Cash Investment:	$42-95K
Total Investment:	$84-190K
Minimum Net Worth:	$200K
Fees: Franchise —	$5K+ $.035/Vcl
Royalty — 5%;	Ad. — 0.5%
Earnings Claim Statement:	Yes
Term of Contract (Years):	10
Avg. # Of Employees:	4 FT
Passive Ownership:	Not Allowed
Area Develop. Agreements:	No
Sub-Franchising Contracts:	No
Expand In Territory:	N/A
Space Needs: 2,500 SF; Warehouse	

Support & Training Provided:

Site Selection Assistance:	No
Lease Negotiation Assistance:	No
Co-Operative Advertising:	Yes
Franchisee Assoc./Member:	Yes/No
Size Of Corporate Staff:	50
On-Going Support:	C,D,F,G,h

Training: 1 Week Home Office; 1 Week On-The-Job Training.
Minority-Specific Programs: Although we support the objectives of the NMFI, we do not have any specific programs in place at this time.

Specific Expansion Plans:

US:	All United States

MILEX

4444 W. 147th St.
Midlothian, IL 60445
Tel: (800) 377-9247 (708) 389-5922
Fax: (708) 389-9882
E-Mail: vsmithson@moranindustries.com
Web Site: www.moranindustries.com
Ms. Virginia Smithson, Qualification Specialist

MILEX TUNE-UPS, BRAKES AND AIR CONDITIONING is a division of Moran Industries that franchises service centers throughout the US. We offer our franchisees a superior business system, strong brand name, customized marketing and a service that is in strong demand. Comprehensive training and continuous support ensure our franchisee's potential. Our exclusive business system, along with the skills of our franchisees, create customer experiences that result in satisfaction and loyalty.

Background:

Established: 1967;	1st Franchised: 1967
Franchised Units:	9
Company-Owned Units:	0
Total Units:	9
Minority-Owned Units:	
African-American:	
Asian-American:	
Hispanic:	
Native American:	
Other:	
North America:	2 States
Density:	8 in IL, 1 in CT

Financial/Terms:

Cash Investment:	$60K
Total Investment:	$144K
Minimum Net Worth:	$120K
Fees: Franchise —	$27.5K
Royalty — 7%;	Ad. — $100/Mo.
Earnings Claim Statement:	Yes
Term of Contract (Years):	20/20

Avg. # Of Employees:	4-6 FT
Passive Ownership:	Discouraged
Area Develop. Agreements:	Yes/Varies
Sub-Franchising Contracts:	No
Expand In Territory:	Yes
Space Needs: 3,500 SF; FS	

Support & Training Provided:

Site Selection Assistance:	Yes
Lease Negotiation Assistance:	Yes
Co-Operative Advertising:	Yes
Franchisee Assoc./Member:	Yes/Yes
Size Of Corporate Staff:	55
On-Going Support:	C,D,E,G,H,I

Training: 3 Weeks at Various Locations.
Minority-Specific Programs: Although we support the objectives of the NMFI, we do not have any specific programs in place at this time.

Specific Expansion Plans:

US:	Midwest

MOTORWORKS

4210 Salem St.
Philadelphia, PA 19124
Tel: (800) 327-9905 (215) 533-4456
Fax: (215) 533-7801
E-Mail: motorworks@motorworksinc.com
Web Site: www.motorworksinc.com
Mr. Dennis J. Prendergast, Director Franchise Sales

The nation's leading chain of remanufactured engine installation centers franchise.

Background:

Established: 1969;	1st Franchised: 1987
Franchised Units:	68
Company-Owned Units:	2
Total Units:	70
Minority-Owned Units:	
African-American:	2
Asian-American:	9
Hispanic:	
Native American:	
North America:	25 States
Density:	15 in PA, 10 uin VA, 6 in NJ

Financial/Terms:

Cash Investment:	$52K
Total Investment:	$73-97K
Minimum Net Worth:	$250K
Fees: Franchise —	$23.5K
Royalty — 5%;	Ad. — 1
Earnings Claim Statement:	Yes
Term of Contract (Years):	10/5
Avg. # Of Employees:	3 FT, 1 PT
Passive Ownership:	Discouraged
Area Develop. Agreements:	Yes/10
Sub-Franchising Contracts:	No

Expand In Territory: No
Space Needs: NR SF; FS, SF, SC, 2-Bay Garage

Support & Training Provided:
Site Selection Assistance: Yes
Lease Negotiation Assistance: Yes
Co-Operative Advertising: Yes
Franchisee Assoc./Member: No
Size Of Corporate Staff: 17
On-Going Support: C,D,E,F,G,I
Training: 1 Week Philadelphia, PA; 1 Week On-Site.
Minority-Specific Programs: Although we support the objectives of the NMFI, we do not have any specific programs in place at this time.

Specific Expansion Plans:
US: All United States

MR. TRANSMISSION

4444 W. 147th St.
Midlothian, IL 60445
Tel: (800) 377-9247 (708) 389-5922
Fax: (708) 389-9882
E-Mail: vsmithson@moranindustries.com
Web Site: www.moranindustries.com
Ms. Virginia Smithson, Qualifications Specialist

MR. TRANSMISSION, a division of Moran Industries, franchises transmission service centers throughout the US. We offer our franchisees a superior business system, strong brand name, customized marketing and a service that is in strong demand. In addition, comprehensive training and continuous support help to ensure our franchisees maximaize their potential. Our exclusive business system, along with the skills of our franchisees, create customer experiences that result in satisfaction and loyalty.

Background:
Established: 1956; 1st Franchised: 1990
Franchised Units: 86
Company-Owned Units: 1
Total Units: 87
Minority-Owned Units:
  African-American:
  Asian-American:
  Hispanic:
  Native American:
North America: 14 States
Density: 21 in GA, 12 in IN, 12 in FL

Financial/Terms:
Cash Investment: $50K
Total Investment: $149K
Minimum Net Worth: $100K
Fees: Franchise — $27.5K
  Royalty — 7%; Ad. — $100/Mo.
Earnings Claim Statement: Yes
Term of Contract (Years): 20/20
Avg. # Of Employees: 3-5 FT
Passive Ownership: Discouraged
Area Develop. Agreements: Yes/Varies
Sub-Franchising Contracts: No
Expand In Territory: Yes
Space Needs: 4,000 SF; FS, SC, Automotive Use

Support & Training Provided:
Site Selection Assistance: Yes
Lease Negotiation Assistance: Yes
Co-Operative Advertising: No
Franchisee Assoc./Member: Yes
Size Of Corporate Staff: 55
On-Going Support: A,C,D,E,F,G,H,I
Training: Yes
Minority-Specific Programs: Although we support the objectives of the NMFI, we do not have any specific programs in place at this time.

Specific Expansion Plans:
US: All United States

SAF-T AUTO CENTERS

121 N. Plains Industrial Rd., Unit H
Wallingford, CT 06492
Tel: (800) 382-7238 (203) 294-1094
Fax: (203) 269-2532
E-Mail: saft@snet.net
Web Site: www.saftauto.com
Mr. Richard Biladeau, President

SAF-T AUTO CENTERS is an owner-operated, auto repair shop offering steering, suspension, brakes, muffler, lubrication and minor repair. Our main effort is to put good mechanics in a business opportunity, where they can capitalize on their trade.

Background:
Established: 1978; 1st Franchised: 1985
Franchised Units: 8
Company-Owned Units: 1
Total Units: 9
Minority-Owned Units:
  African-American: 0
  Asian-American: 0
  Hispanic: 0
  Native American: 0
  Other:

North America: 1 State
Density: 9 in CT

Financial/Terms:
Cash Investment: $25K
Total Investment: $32-65K
Minimum Net Worth: $50K
Fees: Franchise — $15K
  Royalty — $500/Mo.; Ad. — 1%
Earnings Claim Statement: No
Term of Contract (Years): 10/10
Avg. # Of Employees: 2 FT
Passive Ownership: Discouraged
Area Develop. Agreements: Yes
Sub-Franchising Contracts: No
Expand In Territory: Yes
Space Needs: 2,000 SF; FS, SC

Support & Training Provided:
Site Selection Assistance: Yes
Lease Negotiation Assistance: Yes
Co-Operative Advertising: Yes
Franchisee Assoc./Member: No
Size Of Corporate Staff: 3
On-Going Support: A,B,C,E,F,G,H,I
Training: 1 Month On-Site.
Minority-Specific Programs: Although we support the objectives of the NMFI, we do not have any specific programs in place at this time.

Specific Expansion Plans:
US: Connecticut

SPEEDY TRANSMISSION CENTERS

902 Clint Moore Rd., # 216
Boca Raton, FL 33487
Tel: (800) 336-0310 (561) 995-8282
Fax: (561) 995-8005
E-Mail: speedy216@earthlink.net
Web Site: www.speedytransmission.com
Mr. D'Arcy J. Williams, President

Centers repair, rebuild and recondition automatic and standard transmissions. Other drive train repair services also available. Training, marketing and operational assistance. Warranties are honored throughout the U. S. and Canada.

Background:
Established: 1974; 1st Franchised: 1974

Franchised Units: 28
Company-Owned Units: 0
Total Units: 28
Minority-Owned Units:
   African-American:
   Asian-American:
   Hispanic:
   Native American:
North America: 6 States
Density: 18 in FL, 7 in GA, 2 in CA

Financial/Terms:
Cash Investment: $40K
Total Investment: $80-100K
Minimum Net Worth: $NR
Fees: Franchise — $14.5K
   Royalty — 7%; Ad. — $100/Mo.
Earnings Claim Statement: No
Term of Contract (Years): 20/10
Avg. # Of Employees: 4 FT, 1 PT
Passive Ownership: Discouraged
Area Develop. Agreements: Yes/10
Sub-Franchising Contracts: Yes
Expand In Territory: Yes
Space Needs: 2,400 SF; FS, SC

Support & Training Provided:
Site Selection Assistance: Yes
Lease Negotiation Assistance: Yes
Co-Operative Advertising: No
Franchisee Assoc./Member: Yes/Yes
Size Of Corporate Staff: 4
On-Going Support: C,D,E,F,G,H,I
Training: 2 Weeks Home Office; 1 Week On-Site.

Minority-Specific Programs: The SPEEDY TRANSMISSION Program offers a deferred payment of a major portion of the initial franchise fee. Outside suppliers also finance a major part of our equipment package. With financing in place, it represents a great percentage of the total expenditure. If the candidate is experienced in the transmission repair industry, more adjustments are available in the area of the franchise fee. The SPEEDY TRANSMISSION Program is designed to assist all candidates.

Specific Expansion Plans:
US: Southeast and Northeast

TILDEN CAR CARE CENTERS
1325 Franklin Ave., # 165
Garden City, NY 11530

Tel: (800) TILDENS (516) 746-7911
Fax: (516) 746-1288
E-Mail: info@tildencarcare.com
Web Site: www.tildencarcare.com
Mr. Jason Baskind, Dir. of Franchise Development

We're not just brakes. The total care concept allows you to offer a full menu of automotive services for maximum customer procurement — rather than a limited niche market. You benefit from a management team whose concept system and training were proven and perfected before we even considered offering franchises.

Background:
Established: 1923; 1st Franchised: 1996
Franchised Units: 60
Company-Owned Units: 0
Total Units: 60
Minority-Owned Units:
   African-American:
   Asian-American:
   Hispanic:
   Native American:
North America: 13 States
Density: 24 in FL, 15 in NY, 5 in GA

Financial/Terms:
Cash Investment: $50-60K
Total Investment: $131-171.5K
Minimum Net Worth: $150K
Fees: Franchise — $25K
   Royalty — 6%/$350/Wk.;Ad. — 3%/$175/Wk.
Earnings Claim Statement: No
Term of Contract (Years): 10/5/5
Avg. # Of Employees: 4 FT, 2 PT
Passive Ownership: Discouraged
Area Develop. Agreements: Yes/10
Sub-Franchising Contracts: No
Expand In Territory: Yes
Space Needs: 3,500+ SF; FS, Auto Mall

Support & Training Provided:
Site Selection Assistance: Yes
Lease Negotiation Assistance: Yes
Co-Operative Advertising: Yes
Franchisee Assoc./Member: Yes/Yes
Size Of Corporate Staff: 6
On-Going Support: A,B,C,D,E,F,G,H,I
Training: 2 Weeks Home Office.
Minority-Specific Programs: Although we support the objectives of the NMFI, we do not have any specific programs in place at this time.

Specific Expansion Plans:
US: All United States

TOP VALUE MUFFLER AND BRAKE SHOPS
36887 Schoolcraft
Livonia, MI 48150
Tel: (800) 860-8258 (734) 462-3633 x.16
Fax: (734) 462-1088
E-Mail: franchiseinfo@top_value.com
Web Site: www.top_value.com
Mr. Richard E. Zimmer, Dir. of Franchise Development

Our reputation of high quality, courteous service and competitive prices sets us apart. Our motto: Top Quality + Service + Price = TOP VALUE. We are the 'Undercar Specialist.' TOP VALUE is offering franchise opportunities in MI, OH, IN, and N. KY. As an owner of a TOP VALUE MUFFLER & BRAKE SHOP, you can start enjoying the benefits of a franchise while keeping the freedom of private ownership. Plus, you get one of the best-recognized logos in the undercar industry.

Background:
Established: 1977; 1st Franchised: 1980
Franchised Units: 31
Company-Owned Units: 5
Total Units: 36
Minority-Owned Units:
   African American:
   Asian-American:
   Hispanic:
   Native American:
   Other:3 Women, 1 Indian, 1 Arab, 1 Italian-American
North America: 3 States
Density: 27 in MI, 3 in OH, 1 in IN

Financial/Terms:
Cash Investment: $25K
Total Investment: $125K
Minimum Net Worth: $Not Required
Fees: Franchise — $15K
   Royalty — 2-5%; Ad. — 3%
Earnings Claim Statement: Yes
Term of Contract (Years): 10/5
Avg. # Of Employees: 2-3 FT
Passive Ownership: Discouraged
Area Develop. Agreements: Yes

Sub-Franchising Contracts: No
Expand In Territory: Yes
Space Needs: 2,500-3,500 SF; FS

Support & Training Provided:
Site Selection Assistance: Yes
Lease Negotiation Assistance: Yes
Co-Operative Advertising: Yes
Franchisee Assoc./Member: No
Size Of Corporate Staff: 12
On-Going Support: B,C,D,E,F,G,H,I
Training: 3 Weeks in Livonia, MI; 1 Week On-Site.
Minority-Specific Programs: Financing of the franchise fee based upon individual circumstances.

Specific Expansion Plans:
US: MI, OH, IN, IL and N. KY

AUTOMOTIVE SPECIALISTS

TUNEX INTERNATIONAL
556 East 2100 S.
Salt Lake City, UT 84106
Tel: (800) 448-8639 (801) 486-8133
Fax: (801) 484-4740
E-Mail: info@tunex.com
Web Site: www.tunex.com
Mr. Frank Hauber, Franchise Sales

We offer diagnostic, engine performance, tune-up services and repairs of engine related systems, i.e. ignition, carburetion, fuel injection, emission controls, computer controls, cooling, air conditioning, emission inspections, used-car evaluations, and lubrication services. For maximum customer satisfaction, we always analyze systems for the problem and maintenance requirements, so the customer can make service and repair decisions.

Background:
Established: 1974; 1st Franchised: 1975
Franchised Units: 23
Company-Owned Units: 2
Total Units: 25
Minority-Owned Units:
    African-American:
    Asian-American: 3
    Hispanic: 1
    Native American:
    Other:
North America: 6 States
Density: 16 in UT, 4 in CO, 1 in AZ

Financial/Terms:
Cash Investment: $50-60K
Total Investment: $122.5-163.1K
Minimum Net Worth: $200K
Fees: Franchise — $19K
    Royalty — 5%; Ad. — $600/Mo.
Earnings Claim Statement: No
Term of Contract (Years): 10/10
Avg. # Of Employees: 4 FT
Passive Ownership: Discouraged
Area Develop. Agreements: Yes/10
Sub-Franchising Contracts: Yes
Expand In Territory: No
Space Needs: 2,750 SF; FS, SF, SC

Support & Training Provided:
Site Selection Assistance: Yes
Lease Negotiation Assistance: Yes
Co-Operative Advertising: Yes
Franchisee Assoc./Member: No
Size Of Corporate Staff: 7
On-Going Support: C,D,E,G,H,I
Training: 1 Week Corporate Headquarters; 1 Week On-Site.
Minority-Specific Programs: Although we support the objectives of the NMFI, we do not have any specific programs in place at this time.

Specific Expansion Plans:
US: Inter-Mountain, Southwest

CARS. WE KNOW 'EM. WE LOVE 'EM.

VALVOLINE INSTANT OIL CHANGE
3499 Blazer Pkwy.
Lexington, KY 40509
Tel: (800) 622-6846 (606) 357-7070
Fax: (606) 357-7049
E-Mail:
Web Site: www.vioc.com
Mr. Eric Little, Manager Franchise Sales/Dev.

Offers licenses and development agreements for the establishment and operation of a business which provides a quick oil change, chassis lubrication and routine maintenance checks on automobiles. The licensor and/or its affiliates will offer (to qualified prospects) leasing programs for equipment, signage, POS systems and mortgage based financing for land, building.

Background:
Established: 1988; 1st Franchised: 1988
Franchised Units: 217
Company-Owned Units: 357
Total Units: 596
Minority-Owned Units:
    African-American: 0
    Asian-American: 1
    Hispanic: 0
    Native American: 0
    Other: 1 Women-Owned
North America: 30 States
Density: 74 in OH, 61 in MI, 51 in MN

Financial/Terms:
Cash Investment: $150K
Total Investment: $81-193K
Minimum Net Worth: $200K
Fees: Franchise — $30K
    Royalty — 4,5,6%; Ad. — 2%
Earnings Claim Statement: Yes
Term of Contract (Years): 15/5/5
Avg. # Of Employees: 4 FT, 2 PT
Passive Ownership: Allowed
Area Develop. Agreements: No
Sub-Franchising Contracts: No
Expand In Territory: Yes
Space Needs: 15,000 SF; FS

Support & Training Provided:
Site Selection Assistance: Yes
Lease Negotiation Assistance: Yes
Co-Operative Advertising: Yes
Franchisee Assoc./Member: No
Size Of Corporate Staff: 84
On-Going Support: A,B,C,D,E,F,G,h,I
Training: 2 Days Real Estate and Construction Training in Lexington, KY; 4 Weeks Operational Train.
Minority-Specific Programs: We have 2 African-American franchisees in our system. One is under construction and the second is in the real estate procurement phase.

Specific Expansion Plans:
US: All United States

DOLLAR RENT A CAR

5330 E. 31st St.
Tulsa, OK 74135
Tel: (800) 555-9893 (918) 669-3103
Fax: (918) 669-3006
E-Mail: pfritz@dollar.com
Web Site: www.dollar.com
Mr. Peter Fritz, Director Franchise
Development

DOLLAR RENT A CAR operates and licenses others to operate daily car rental operations. Established over 30 years ago, DOLLAR RENT A CAR now serves the worldwide car rental market.

Background:
Established: 1965;   1st Franchised: 1966
Franchised Units: 827
Company-Owned Units: 69
Total Units: 896
Minority-Owned Units:
    African-American: 3
    Asian-American: 1
    Hispanic: 1
    Native American: 0
North America: NR
Density: CA, TX, FL

Financial/Terms:
Cash Investment: $100K-2MM
Total Investment: $100K-2MM
Minimum Net Worth: $250K
Fees: Franchise — $12.5K+

Royalty — 8%;   Ad. — Included
Earnings Claim Statement: No
Term of Contract (Years):   10/10
Avg. # Of Employees: Varies
Passive Ownership: Not Allowed
Area Develop. Agreements: No
Sub-Franchising Contracts: No
Expand In Territory: Yes
Space Needs: 2,000+ SF; FS, SF, SC.

Support & Training Provided:
Site Selection Assistance: No
Lease Negotiation Assistance: No
Co-Operative Advertising: Yes
Franchisee Assoc./Member: Yes/No
Size Of Corporate Staff: 400
On-Going Support: a,B,C,D,E,G,H,I
Training: 3 Days Headquarters Orientation;
2 Weeks On-Site Field Training; 1 Week
Automation.
Minority-Specific Programs: DOLLAR is
racial and gender neutral in its franchise
development.

Specific Expansion Plans:
US: Not FL,MA,VT,NH,NV,AR,UT,MT

PAYLESS CAR RENTAL SYSTEM, INC.

2350-N 34th St., N.
St. Petersburg, FL 33713
Tel: (800) 729-5255 (727) 321-6352
Fax: (727) 323-3529
E-Mail: FRANCHISE@800-payless.com

Web Site: www.800-PAYLESS.com
Mr. Robert C. Meyer, Senior Vice President

PAYLESS CAR RENTAL SYSTEM, Inc., has been a recognized leader in the car rental industry for over 25 years. Payless is well known with customers and travel agents. Car rental expertise and an experienced corporate office staff give each franchisee individual assistance and the competitive edge. We offer the tools to become successful in the car rental market.

Background:
Established: 1971;   1st Franchised: 1971
Franchised Units: 67
Company-Owned Units: 0
Total Units: 67
Minority-Owned Units:
    African-American: 3
    Asian-American: 4
    Hispanic: 8
    Native American: 0
    Other: 10
North America: 18 States
Density: 12 in FL, 6 in AK, 6 in CA

Financial/Terms:
Cash Investment: $100K (Varies)
Total Investment: $Varies
Minimum Net Worth: $250K (Varies)
Fees: Franchise — $25-200K
    Royalty — 5%;   Ad. — 3%
Earnings Claim Statement: No
Term of Contract (Years):   5/5
Avg. # Of Employees: Varies
Passive Ownership: Discouraged
Area Develop. Agreements: Yes/5
Sub-Franchising Contracts: No
Expand In Territory: Yes
Space Needs: NR SF; FS

Support & Training Provided:

Site Selection Assistance:	Yes
Lease Negotiation Assistance:	No
Co-Operative Advertising:	Yes
Franchisee Assoc./Member:	Yes/Yes
Size Of Corporate Staff:	39
On-Going Support:	A,B,C,D,E,G,h,I

Training: 3-4 Days Corporate Office; 3-5 Days Franchisee's Location
Minority-Specific Programs: MBE/DBE assistance for in-terminal counters at major U.S. airports.

Specific Expansion Plans:

US:	All United States

RENT-A-WRECK OF AMERICA

11460 Cronridge Dr., # 120
Owings Mills, MD 21117
Tel: (800) 421-7253 (410) 581-5755
Fax: (410) 581-1566
E-Mail: raw@rent-a-wreck.com
Web Site: www.rent-a-wreck.com
Mr. Alan Wagner, Sales Director

America's # 1 neighborhood car rental company, RENT-A-WRECK has attained the highest ratings in the franchising industry. For 5 successive years, Entrepreneur Magazine rated RENT-A-WRECK # 1 in its category for the prestigious Franchise 500 awards. The annual Success Magazine named RENT-A-WRECK 'one of the best-managed franchises in America.' Success surveyed over 2,800 franchise companies in all industries and ranked RENT-A-WRECK 4th.

Background:

Established: 1973;	1st Franchised: 1978
Franchised Units:	675
Company-Owned Units:	0
Total Units:	675
Minority-Owned Units:	
African-American:	15
Asian-American:	
Hispanic:	
Native American:	
Other:	
North America:	47 States
Density:	53 in CA, 33 in NY, 24 in NJ

Financial/Terms:

Cash Investment:	$32.8K
Total Investment:	$32.8-209K
Minimum Net Worth:	$50K

Fees: Franchise —	$2.5K+
Royalty — $20/Car;	Ad. — $7/Car
Earnings Claim Statement:	Yes
Term of Contract (Years):	10/5
Avg. # Of Employees:	1 FT
Passive Ownership:	Discouraged
Area Develop. Agreements:	No
Sub-Franchising Contracts:	No
Expand In Territory:	Yes
Space Needs: 1,500 SF; FS, SF, SC	

Support & Training Provided:

Site Selection Assistance:	No
Lease Negotiation Assistance:	Yes
Co-Operative Advertising:	Yes
Franchisee Assoc./Member:	Yes/Yes
Size Of Corporate Staff:	27
On-Going Support:	C,D,e,G,h,I

Training: 1 Week Baltimore, MD.
Minority-Specific Programs: Although we support the objectives of the NMFI, we do not have any specific programs in place at this time.

Specific Expansion Plans:

US:	All United States

SENSIBLE CAR RENTAL

96 Freneau Ave., # 2
Matawan, NJ 07747
Tel: (800) 367-5159 (732) 583-8500
Fax: (732) 290-8305
E-Mail: sensible96@aol.com
Web Site:
Mr. Charles A. Vitale, Vice President General Manager

We offer a rental car program which provides training, insurance and support. Majority of franchisee are used car dealers and other automotive related businesspersons.

Background:

Established: 1986;	1st Franchised: 1986
Franchised Units:	105
Company-Owned Units:	0
Total Units:	105
Minority-Owned Units:	
African-American:	3
Asian-American:	0
Hispanic:	3
Native American:	0
Other:	
North America:	22 States
Density:	25 in NY, 24 in NJ, 10 in MA

Financial/Terms:

Cash Investment:	$20-25K
Total Investment:	$25-30K
Minimum Net Worth:	$Varies

Fees: Franchise —	$4-7K
Royalty — $10-15/Car;	Ad. — 0%
Earnings Claim Statement:	No
Term of Contract (Years):	Perpetual
Avg. # Of Employees:	1 FT, 1 PT
Passive Ownership:	Not Allowed
Area Develop. Agreements:	No
Sub-Franchising Contracts:	No
Expand In Territory:	Yes
Space Needs: NR SF; FS	

Support & Training Provided:

Site Selection Assistance:	No
Lease Negotiation Assistance:	No
Co-Operative Advertising:	Yes
Franchisee Assoc./Member:	Yes/Yes
Size Of Corporate Staff:	10
On-Going Support:	C,d,F,G,H,I

Training: 2 Days in Matawan, NJ.
Minority-Specific Programs: Although we support the objectives of the NMFI, we do not have any specific programs in place at this time.

Specific Expansion Plans:

US:	All United States

THRIFTY CAR RENTAL

5310 E. 31st St.
Tulsa, OK 74135
Tel: (800) 532-3401 (918) 669-2219
Fax: (918) 669-2061
E-Mail: franchisesales@thrifty.com
Web Site: www.thrifty.com
Mr. Jeff Bevis, Staff VP, US Franchise Opport.

THRIFTY operates in over 65 countries and territories, with over 1,200 locations throughout North and South America, Europe, the Middle East, Caribbean, Asia and the Pacific, and is the fastest-growing car rental company in Canada and Australia. THRIFTY has a significant presence both in the airport and local car rental markets. Approximately 51% of its business is in the airport market, 49% in the local market.

Background:

Established: 1950;	1st Franchised: 1970
Franchised Units:	1226
Company-Owned Units:	3
Total Units:	1229
Minority-Owned Units:	
African-American:	2
Asian-American:	1
Hispanic:	9

Native American: 0
Other: 68 Women, 5 East Indian
North America: 48 States
Density: 54 in CA, 28 in TX, 28 in FL.

Financial/Terms:

Cash Investment: $150K+
Total Investment: $200-250K
Minimum Net Worth: $600K
Fees: Franchise — $Varies
   Royalty — 3%; Ad. — 2.5-5%
Earnings Claim Statement: No
Term of Contract (Years): 10/5
Avg. # Of Employees: 4-6 FT min.
Passive Ownership: Not Allowed
Area Develop. Agreements: No
Sub-Franchising Contracts: No
Expand In Territory: Yes
Space Needs: Varies SF; FS, SF, SC, RM

Support & Training Provided:

Site Selection Assistance: No
Lease Negotiation Assistance: Yes
Co-Operative Advertising: Yes
Franchisee Assoc./Member: No
Size Of Corporate Staff: 650
On-Going Support: A,B,C,D,E,F,G,h,I
Training: 3 Days + Mentor Program at Headquarters in Tulsa, OK.
Minority-Specific Programs: Minority Franchise Development Program: Reduced net worth level from standard minimums maintained in the first year of operation; guaranteed access to an additional source of working capital with reduced repayment requirements; reduction in franchise fee; operating credit for automation or imaging included in the reduced franchise fee structure.

Specific Expansion Plans:

US: Selected Markets Remaining

AIRE SERV HEATING & AIR CONDITIONING

1020 N. University Parks Dr.
Waco, TX 76707
Tel: (800) 583-2662 (254) 745-2440
Fax: (254) 745-2546
E-Mail: aireserv@dwyergroup.com
Web Site: www.aireserv.com
Mr. Roger D. Goertz, President

Serving the heating, cooling and air balancing needs of all residential and light commercial buildings, including the repair and installation of systems and "whole house" analysis involving infiltrometer testing, duct cleaning, etc.

Background:

Established: 1992;   1st Franchised: 1994
Franchised Units: 55
Company-Owned Units: 0
Total Units: 55
Minority-Owned Units:
    African-American:
    Asian-American:
    Hispanic:
    Native American:
North America: 28 States, 3 Provinces
Density: 5 in GA, 4 in TX, 2 in NC

Financial/Terms:

Cash Investment: $15-71K
Total Investment: $52-91K
Minimum Net Worth: $100K
Fees: Franchise — $25K

Royalty — 4.5-2.5%;   Ad. — 2%
Earnings Claim Statement: No
Term of Contract (Years):   10/5
Avg. # Of Employees: Varies
Passive Ownership: Discouraged
Area Develop. Agreements: No
Sub-Franchising Contracts: No
Expand In Territory: No
Space Needs: NR SF; N/A

Support & Training Provided:

Site Selection Assistance: N/A
Lease Negotiation Assistance: N/A
Co-Operative Advertising: No
Franchisee Assoc./Member: Yes
Size Of Corporate Staff: 7
On-Going Support: C,D,E,G,h,I
Training: 6 Days Corporate Office; 3 Days On-Site.

Minority-Specific Programs: Although we support the objectives of the NMFI, we do not have any specific programs in place at this time.

Specific Expansion Plans:

US: All United States

ARTHUR RUTENBERG HOMES

13922 58th St., N.
Clearwater, FL 33760
Tel: (800) 274-6637 (727) 536-5900
Fax: (727) 538-9089
E-Mail: rjaghab@arhomes.com

Web Site: www.arhomes.com
Mr. Raja Jaghab, Senior Vice President

Home building franchisor. Master working drawings provided. All necessary forms, manuals, purchasing systems, computer software training and business planning systems provided.

Background:

Established: 1980;   1st Franchised: 1980
Franchised Units: 25
Company-Owned Units: 3
Total Units: 28
Minority-Owned Units:
    African-American: 0
    Asian-American: 0
    Hispanic: 0
    Native American: 0
North America: 2 States
Density: 27 in FL, 1 in LA

Financial/Terms:

Cash Investment: $350K
Total Investment: $350-500K
Minimum Net Worth: $100K
Fees: Franchise — $60K
    Royalty — 4%;   Ad. — 0%
Earnings Claim Statement: No
Term of Contract (Years):   10
Avg. # Of Employees: Varies
Passive Ownership: Allowed
Area Develop. Agreements: No
Sub-Franchising Contracts: No
Expand In Territory: Yes
Space Needs: NR SF; N/A

Support & Training Provided:

Site Selection Assistance: Yes
Lease Negotiation Assistance: N/A
Co-Operative Advertising: N/A
Franchisee Assoc./Member: No
Size Of Corporate Staff: 75

On-Going Support: A,B,C,D,H,I
Training: Yes.
Minority-Specific Programs: The Franchisor is in the process of establishing a lending program with the Small Business Administration (SBA). Franchisors will help in the preparation of loan discussions and in the process of paperwork.

Specific Expansion Plans:
US: Florida

CREATIVE COLORS INTERNATIONAL

5550 W. 175th St.
Tinley Park, IL 60477
Tel: (800) 933-2656 (708) 614-7786
Fax: (708) 614-9685
E-Mail: mark@creativecolorsintl.com
Web Site: www.creativecolorsintl.com
Mr. Mark Bollman, Senior Vice President

Mobile units providing repair and restoration in all markets that have leather, vinyl, fabric, velour, plastics and fiberglass. These markets include car dealerships (new and used), furniture retailers and manufactures, hotels, airports, car rental agencies and company fleet cars.

Background:
Established: 1980; 1st Franchised: 1991
Franchised Units: 38
Company-Owned Units: 2
Total Units: 40
Minority-Owned Units:
   African-American: 1%
   Asian-American: 0%
   Hispanic: 0%
   Native American: 0%
   Other: 37% Women-Owned
North America: 20 States, 1 Province
Density: IL, FL, OH

Financial/Terms:
Cash Investment: $19.5K+
Total Investment: $19.5K+
Minimum Net Worth: $50K+
Fees: Franchise — $27.5K
   Royalty — 6%/$173.33/Mo.; Ad. — 0%

Earnings Claim Statement: Yes
Term of Contract (Years): 10
Avg. # Of Employees: 2 FT
Passive Ownership: Discouraged
Area Develop. Agreements: Yes/10
Sub-Franchising Contracts: No
Expand In Territory: Yes
Space Needs: N/A SF; HB

Support & Training Provided:
Site Selection Assistance: Yes
Lease Negotiation Assistance: N/A
Co-Operative Advertising: Yes
Franchisee Assoc./Member: Yes/Yes
Size Of Corporate Staff: 8
On-Going Support: A,B,C,D,E,F,G,H,I
Training: 3 Weeks Headquarters, Tinley Park, IL; 1 Week in Franchisee's Territory.
Minority-Specific Programs: Although we support the objectives of the NMFI, we do not have any specific programs in place at this time.

Specific Expansion Plans:
US: All United States

DECKARE SERVICES

1501 Raff Rd., SW
Canton, OH 44710
Tel: (800) 711-3325 (330) 478-3665
Fax: (330) 478-0311
E-Mail: deckcare1@aol.com
Web Site: www.deckcare.com
Mr. Joe McClellan, Vice President

Rejuvenating exterior wood surfaces such as decks, fences, docks, gazebos and bridges with a total commitment to being the first nationally-recognized franchise based on image and quality. Franchisees will receive complete business and field training with on-going support services.

Background:
Established: 1995; 1st Franchised: 1997
Franchised Units: 35
Company-Owned Units: 0
Total Units: 35
Minority-Owned Units:
   African-American: 0
   Asian-American: 0
   Hispanic: 0
   Native American: 0
North America: 16 States
Density: 4 in OH, 3 in MO, 3 in TN

Financial/Terms:
Cash Investment: $25K

Total Investment: $45K
Minimum Net Worth: $50K
Fees: Franchise — $14.5K
   Royalty — 5%; Ad. — N/A
Earnings Claim Statement: No
Term of Contract (Years): 5/5
Avg. # Of Employees: 1 FT, 1 PT
Passive Ownership: Allowed
Area Develop. Agreements: No
Sub-Franchising Contracts: No
Expand In Territory: Yes
Space Needs: NR SF; HB

Support & Training Provided:
Site Selection Assistance: N/A
Lease Negotiation Assistance: N/A
Co-Operative Advertising: N/A
Franchisee Assoc./Member: No
Size Of Corporate Staff: 5
On-Going Support: C,D,G,H,I
Training: 5 Days at Corporate Office; 4 Days Franchisee's Location.
Minority-Specific Programs: Although we support the objectives of the NMFI, we do not have any specific programs in place at this time.

Specific Expansion Plans:
US: All United States

DR. VINYL & ASSOC.

821 NW Commerce St.
Lee's Summit, MO 64086
Tel: (800) 531-6600 (816) 525-6060
Fax: (816) 525-6333
E-Mail: tbuckley@drvinylcom
Web Site: www.drvinyl.com
Mr. Tom Buckley, Jr., President

We offer vinyl, leather and velour fabric repair and coloring, auto windshield repair, dashboard and hard plastic repair, vinyl striping and protective molding to new and used car dealers.

Background:
Established: 1972; 1st Franchised: 1980
Franchised Units: 145
Company-Owned Units: 2
Total Units: 147
Minority-Owned Units:
   African-American:
   Asian-American:
   Hispanic:
   Native American:

North America: NR
Density: 18 in MO, 7 in OH, 6 in CA

Financial/Terms:
Cash Investment: $23.5K
Total Investment: $35-40K
Minimum Net Worth: $23.5K
Fees: Franchise — $19.5K
Royalty — 7%; Ad. — 1%
Earnings Claim Statement: Yes
Term of Contract (Years): 10/10
Avg. # Of Employees: 1 FT
Passive Ownership: Discouraged
Area Develop. Agreements: Yes/10
Sub-Franchising Contracts: Yes
Expand In Territory: Yes
Space Needs: N/A SF; N/A

Support & Training Provided:
Site Selection Assistance: N/A
Lease Negotiation Assistance: N/A
Co-Operative Advertising: No
Franchisee Assoc./Member: Yes/No
Size Of Corporate Staff: 15
On-Going Support: b,C,D,F,G,h,I
Training: 2 Weeks Corporate Office; 2 Weeks Field Training.
Minority-Specific Programs: Although we support the objectives of the NMFI, we do not have any specific programs in place at this time.

Specific Expansion Plans:
US: All United States

DREAMMAKER BATH & KITCHEN BY WORLDWIDE
1020 N. University Parks Dr.
Waco, TX 76707
Tel: (800) 583-9099 (254) 745-2477
Fax: (254) 745-2588
E-Mail: dreammaker@dwyergroup.com
Web Site: www.dreammaker-remodel.com
Ms. Brenda Payne, Exec. Assistant to President

Unique combination of bath and kitchen remodeling options, consisting of: cabinet refacing, tubliners, traditional remodeling and more. Delivering the style and value that today's consumer demands.

Background:
Established: 1970; 1st Franchised: 1971
Franchised Units: 408
Company-Owned Units: 0
Total Units: 408
Minority-Owned Units:
African-American: 1%
Asian-American: 1%
Hispanic: 1%
Native American: 0%
North America: 50 States, 3 Provinces
Density: 48 in NY, TX, and IL

Financial/Terms:
Cash Investment: $6K
Total Investment: $25-50K
Minimum Net Worth: $50K
Fees: Franchise — $12.5K
Royalty — 3-6%; Ad. — 2%
Earnings Claim Statement: No
Term of Contract (Years): 10/5
Avg. # Of Employees: Varies
Passive Ownership: Discouraged
Area Develop. Agreements: Yes
Sub-Franchising Contracts: No
Expand In Territory: Yes
Space Needs: NR SF; Case by Case

Support & Training Provided:
Site Selection Assistance: Yes
Lease Negotiation Assistance: Yes
Co-Operative Advertising: Yes
Franchisee Assoc./Member: Yes/Yes
Size Of Corporate Staff: 25
On-Going Support: B,C,D,G,H,I
Training: 3 Weeks Headquarters, Waco, TX.
Minority-Specific Programs: We don't have any specific minority programs set up. Everything is geared toward all our franchisees or prospects. Not to say we don't support this. Sounds like a good idea.

Specific Expansion Plans:
US: All United States

HANDYMAN CONNECTION
227 Northland Blvd.
Cincinnati, OH 45246
Tel: (800) 466-5530 (513) 771-3003
Fax: (513) 771-6439
E-Mail:
tom.gyuro@handymanconnection.com
Web Site: www.handymanconnection.com
Mr. Tom Gyuro, Vice President

HANDYMAN CONNECTION specializes in the small to medium size home repair and remodeling industry. We offer a turnkey package that includes marketing, advertising and a complete training program. 90% of our franchise partners had NO handyman experience.

Background:
Established: 1990; 1st Franchised: 1993
Franchised Units: 101
Company-Owned Units: 4
Total Units: 105
Minority-Owned Units:
African-American: 2
Asian-American:
Hispanic:
Native American:
North America: 35+ States
Density: 24 in CA, 7 in OH, 4 in TN

Financial/Terms:
Cash Investment: $50-150K
Total Investment: $50-250K
Minimum Net Worth: $50K+
Fees: Franchise — $Varies
Royalty — 5%; Ad. — 2%
Earnings Claim Statement: No
Term of Contract (Years): 10/10
Avg. # Of Employees: Varies
Passive Ownership: Allowed
Area Develop. Agreements: Yes/10
Sub-Franchising Contracts: No
Expand In Territory: Yes
Space Needs: 500-600 SF; FS, Industrial Warehouse

Support & Training Provided:
Site Selection Assistance: No
Lease Negotiation Assistance: Yes
Co-Operative Advertising: No
Franchisee Assoc./Member: Yes/Yes
Size Of Corporate Staff: 10
On-Going Support: B,C,D,E,G,h,I
Training: 2 Weeks Flagship (Cincinnati, OH); 1 Week Franchisee Location.
Minority-Specific Programs: We offer our franchise concept to all interested parties. We offer an internal finance package and assistance in securing necessary licenses and qualifications

Specific Expansion Plans:
US: All United States

KITCHEN SOLVERS
401 Jay St.
La Crosse, WI 54601
Tel: (800) 845-6779 (608) 791-5516
Fax: (608) 784-2917
E-Mail: dave@kitchensolvers.com
Web Site: www.kitchensolvers.com

Mr. David Woggon, Dir. of Franchise Operations

Specialize or diversify... It's your option. "10 in 1" business concept offered by the most experienced kitchen remodeling franchise system in the United States. Home-based business with no inventory required. Complete start-up and on-going marketing program, experienced technical support. Call for a FREE introductory video.

Background:

Established: 1982;	1st Franchised: 1984
Franchised Units:	106
Company-Owned Units:	1
Total Units:	107
Minority-Owned Units:	
African-American:	1
Asian-American:	0
Hispanic:	0
Native American:	0
North America:	29 States
Density:	17 in WI, 12 in IA, 11 in IL

Financial/Terms:

Cash Investment:	$25K
Total Investment:	$27.6-41.5K
Minimum Net Worth:	$NR
Fees: Franchise —	$14-16K
Royalty — 6%;	Ad. — 1%
Earnings Claim Statement:	No
Term of Contract (Years):	10/10
Avg. # Of Employees:	1 FT
Passive Ownership:	Not Allowed
Area Develop. Agreements:	No
Sub-Franchising Contracts:	No
Expand In Territory:	Yes
Space Needs: N/A SF; HB	

Support & Training Provided:

Site Selection Assistance:	N/A
Lease Negotiation Assistance:	No
Co-Operative Advertising:	No
Franchisee Assoc./Member:	Yes
Size Of Corporate Staff:	8
On-Going Support:	a,B,C,D,G,h,I

Training: 6 Days La Crosse, WI (Refacing); 3 Days Houston, TX (Recoloring). Pre-Training Program.
Minority-Specific Programs: Although we support the objectives of the NMFI, we do not have any specific programs in place at this time.

Specific Expansion Plans:

US:	All United States

KITCHEN TUNE-UP

813 Circle Dr.
Aberdeen, SD 57401-3349
Tel: (800) 333-6385 (605) 225-4049
Fax: (605) 225-1371
E-Mail: kltuneup@midco.net
Web Site: www.kitchentuneup.com
Mr. Craig Green, Fran. Acquisitions Dir.

America's #1 home improvement franchise. We offer 'Kitchen Solutions For Any Budget.' Cabinet restoration, cabinet refacing and custom cabinetry along with shelf lining, replacement hardware and cabinet organization systems. Excellent initial and on-going training and support. High residential and commercial potential. Home-based and retail locations available.

Background:

Established: 1975;	1st Franchised: 1988
Franchised Units:	321
Company-Owned Units:	1
Total Units:	322
Minority-Owned Units:	
African-American:	0
Asian-American:	2
Hispanic:	0
Native American:	0
North America:	35 States, 1 Province
Density:	14 in CA, 10 in IL, 7 in CO

Financial/Terms:

Cash Investment:	$18-25K
Total Investment:	$28-35K
Minimum Net Worth:	$N/A
Fees: Franchise —	$15K
Royalty — 4.5-7%;	Ad. — 0%
Earnings Claim Statement:	Yes
Term of Contract (Years):	10/10
Avg. # Of Employees:1-2 FT, PT as needed	
Passive Ownership:	Discouraged
Area Develop. Agreements:	Yes/10
Sub-Franchising Contracts:	No
Expand In Territory:	Yes
Space Needs: 500-2,500 SF; FS, SF, SC, HB	

Support & Training Provided:

Site Selection Assistance:	Yes
Lease Negotiation Assistance:	Yes
Co-Operative Advertising:	No
Franchisee Assoc./Member:	No
Size Of Corporate Staff:	8
On-Going Support:	A,B,C,D,E,G,H,I

Training: 2 Weeks Pre-training Home Study, 6-10 Days Corporate Office, 12 Wks. Home Study, On-Going.
Minority-Specific Programs: Franchising available to qualified individuals.

Specific Expansion Plans:

US:	All United States

MARBLE RENEWAL

P. O. Box 56349
Little Rock, AR 72215
Tel: (888) 664-7866 (501) 663-2080
Fax: (501) 663-2401
E-Mail: marble@marblerenewal.com
Web Site: www.marblerenewal.com
Ms. Klimberly Colclasure, Dir. Sales & Marketing

International franchise company specializing in the care and treatment of natural stones and hardwood. Advanced and innovative techniques to give back the value and beauty of marble, granite, terrazzo, slate, limestone, time and other natural stones, as well as hardwood.

Background:

Established: 1988;	1st Franchised: 1989
Franchised Units:	24
Company-Owned Units:	1
Total Units:	25
Minority-Owned Units:	
African-American:	0
Asian-American:	0
Hispanic:	0
Native American:	0
North America:	12 States, 2 Provinces
Density:	1 in GA, 1 in NJ, 1 in NC

Financial/Terms:

Cash Investment:	$10-35K
Total Investment:	$49-162K
Minimum Net Worth:	$Varies
Fees: Franchise —	$15-50K
Royalty — 5-8%;	Ad. — 0%
Earnings Claim Statement:	No
Term of Contract (Years):	10/10
Avg. # Of Employees:	2 FT
Passive Ownership:	Discouraged
Area Develop. Agreements:	No
Sub-Franchising Contracts:	Yes
Expand In Territory:	Yes
Space Needs: NR SF; HB	

Support & Training Provided:

Site Selection Assistance:	N/A
Lease Negotiation Assistance:	N/A
Co-Operative Advertising:	No
Franchisee Assoc./Member:	Yes
Size Of Corporate Staff:	13
On-Going Support:	C,D,E,F,G,H,I

Training: 2 Weeks in Little Rock, AK

Minority-Specific Programs: Although we support the objectives of the NMFI, we do not have any specific programs in place at this time.

Specific Expansion Plans:

US:	All United States

PERMA-GLAZE

1638 S. Research Loop Rd., # 160
Tucson, AZ 85710
Tel: (800) 332-7397 (520) 722-9718
Fax: (520) 296-4393
E-Mail: permaglaze@permaglaze.com
Web Site: www.permaglaze.com
Mr. Dale R. Young, President

PERMA GLAZE specializes in multi-surface restoration of bathtubs, sinks, countertops, appliances, porcelain, metal, acrylics, cultured marble and more. PERMA GLAZE licensed representatives provide valued services to hotels/motels, private residences, apartments, schools, hospitals, contractors, property managers and many others.

Background:

Established: 1978;	1st Franchised: 1981
Franchised Units:	177
Company-Owned Units:	1
Total Units:	178
Minority-Owned Units:	
African-American:	0
Asian-American:	6
Hispanic:	5
Native American:	0
North America:	36 States, 1 Province
Density:	15 in CA, 7 in AZ, 6 in PA

Financial/Terms:

Cash Investment:	$2.5-3K
Total Investment:	$22-25K+
Minimum Net Worth:	$21.5K
Fees: Franchise —	$19.5K+
Royalty — 6/5/4%/$200 Min.;Ad. — $1,800/Yr.	
Earnings Claim Statement:	Yes
Term of Contract (Years):	10/10
Avg. # Of Employees:	1 FT

Passive Ownership:	Not Allowed
Area Develop. Agreements:	Yes/10
Sub-Franchising Contracts:	No
Expand In Territory:	No
Space Needs: N/A SF; HB	

Support & Training Provided:

Site Selection Assistance:	Yes
Lease Negotiation Assistance:	N/A
Co-Operative Advertising:	N/A
Franchisee Assoc./Member:	No
Size Of Corporate Staff:	6
On-Going Support:	C,D,G,H,I

Training: 5 Days Tucson, AZ.

Minority-Specific Programs: PERMA-GLAZE has just recently become registered with the SBA (Small Business Administration) on-line system. One of the benefits of being registered with the SBA is that it will help expedite the loan process.

Specific Expansion Plans:

US:	All United States

RE-BATH

1055 S. Country Club Dr., Bldg. # 2
Mesa, AZ 85210-4613
Tel: (800) 426-4573 (480) 844-1575
Fax: (480) 833-7199
E-Mail: newfranchise@re-bath.com
Web Site: www.re-bath.com
Mr. David W. Andow, General Manager

The franchise sells and installs custom-molded, acrylic bathtub liners, shower base liners and wall surrounds for homes, apartments, condos and commercial establishments. RE-BATH has proven products and installation technology, plus over 750,000 installations during the past 20 years. Go with the leader in the bathtub liner industry.

Background:

Established: 1979;	1st Franchised: 1991
Franchised Units:	85
Company-Owned Units:	2
Total Units:	87
Minority-Owned Units:	
African-American:	3
Asian-American:	1
Hispanic:	3
Native American:	0
North America:	33 States, 1 Province
Density:	8 in NY, 7 in PA, 6 in CA,

Financial/Terms:

Cash Investment:	$15-30K

Total Investment:	$35-80K
Minimum Net Worth:	$100K
Fees: Franchise —	$15-30K
Royalty — $25/Unit;	Ad. — 0%
Earnings Claim Statement:	No
Term of Contract (Years):	7/7
Avg. # Of Employees:	3 FT, 1 PT
Passive Ownership:	Not Allowed
Area Develop. Agreements:	No
Sub-Franchising Contracts:	No
Expand In Territory:	Yes
Space Needs: 200 SF; FS, SF	

Support & Training Provided:

Site Selection Assistance:	Yes
Lease Negotiation Assistance:	Yes
Co-Operative Advertising:	Yes
Franchisee Assoc./Member:	Yes/No
Size Of Corporate Staff:	12
On-Going Support:	B,d,G,h,I

Training: 9 Days Corporate Training Facility.

Minority-Specific Programs: Although we support the objectives of the NMFI, we do not have any specific programs in place at this time.

Specific Expansion Plans:

US:	All United States

SCREEN MACHINE, THE

19636 8th St. e.
Sonoma, CA 95476
Tel: (707) 996-5551
Fax: (707) 996-0139
E-Mail: screens@screen-machine.com
Web Site: www.screen-machine.com
Mr. Wayne T. Wirick, Sr., President

A mobile service unit, specializing in new window and door screens, and the re-screening of same. Security and pet doors, and a full line of Hunter Douglas window coverings.

Background:

Established: 1986;	1st Franchised: 1988
Franchised Units:	23
Company-Owned Units:	1
Total Units:	24
Minority-Owned Units:	
African-American:	0
Asian-American:	1
Hispanic:	1
Native American:	0
North America:	1 State
Density:	24 in CA

Financial/Terms:

Cash Investment:	$25K
Total Investment:	$53-72.1K
Minimum Net Worth:	$53K
Fees: Franchise —	$25K
Royalty — 5%;	Ad. — 3%
Earnings Claim Statement:	No
Term of Contract (Years):	10/10
Avg. # Of Employees:	1 FT
Passive Ownership:	Discouraged
Area Develop. Agreements:	No
Sub-Franchising Contracts:	No
Expand In Territory:	Yes
Space Needs: N/A SF; HB	

Support & Training Provided:

Site Selection Assistance:	N/A
Lease Negotiation Assistance:	N/A
Co-Operative Advertising:	N/A
Franchisee Assoc./Member:	Yes/No
Size Of Corporate Staff:	2
On-Going Support:	A,C,D,G,H
Training: 6 Days Sonoma, CA.	

Minority-Specific Programs: Although we support the objectives of the NMFI, we do not have any specific programs in place at this time.

Specific Expansion Plans:

US:	West

SUPERIOR WALLS OF AMERICA

937 E. Earl Rd.
New Holland, PA 17557
Tel: (800) 452-9255 (717) 351-9255
Fax: (717) 351-9263
E-Mail: shuman@superiorwalls.com
Web Site: www.superiorwalls.com
Mr. Scott Shuman, Director of Sales

We provide license agreements to manufacturer, sell and install the patented SUPERIOR WALLS SYSTEM, a pre-cast, insulated, studded, waterproof concrete foundation wall for new residential and light commercial construction.

Background:

Established: 1981;	1st Franchised: 1985
Franchised Units:	20
Company-Owned Units:	0
Total Units:	20
Minority-Owned Units:	
African-American:	
Asian-American:	
Hispanic:	
Native American:	
North America:	10 States
Density:	6 in PA, 2 in MI, 2 in WI

Financial/Terms:

Cash Investment:	$500K
Total Investment:	$2-3MM
Minimum Net Worth:	$500K
Fees: Franchise —	$30K
Royalty — 4%;	Ad. — 0%
Earnings Claim Statement:	No
Term of Contract (Years):	10/10/10
Avg. # Of Employees:	8 FT, 2 PT
Passive Ownership:	Discouraged
Area Develop. Agreements:	No
Sub-Franchising Contracts:	No
Expand In Territory:	Yes
Space Needs: ~30,000 SF; 28' Ceilings, O/H Crane	

Support & Training Provided:

Site Selection Assistance:	Yes
Lease Negotiation Assistance:	N/A
Co-Operative Advertising:	Yes
Franchisee Assoc./Member:	No
Size Of Corporate Staff:	20+
On-Going Support:	B,c,D,G,H,I
Training: 2 Weeks Corporate Office; 3 Weeks Field Location.	

Minority-Specific Programs: Although we support the objectives of the NMFI, we do not have any specific programs in place at this time.

Specific Expansion Plans:

US:	All United States

U BUILD IT

12006 98th Ave., # 200
Kirkland, WA 98034
Tel: (800) 992-4357 (425) 821-6200

Fax: (425) 821-6876
E-Mail: franchiseinfo@ubuildit.com
Web Site: www.ubuildit.com
Mr. Mark Kruschwitz, VP Franchise Sales

For 10 years, the U BUILD IT system has been assisting homeowners to act as their own general contractor for both remodeling and new home construction. By teaming a homeowner with a construction professional, the project is efficiently completed while avoiding the common pitfalls and saving thousands. Providing subcontractors, bank financing, site visits, etc., U BUILD IT is a perfect complementary service for the building professional looking to expand or simplify his or her business.

Background:

Established: 1997;	1st Franchised: 1998
Franchised Units:	29
Company-Owned Units:	1
Total Units:	30
Minority-Owned Units:	
African-American:	0
Asian-American:	0
Hispanic:	0
Native American:	0
North America:	8 States
Density:	18 in WA

Financial/Terms:

Cash Investment:	$28-62K
Total Investment:	$28-62K
Minimum Net Worth:	$50K
Fees: Franchise —	$20K
Royalty — 8-12%/$300;Ad. — 2%/$50/Mo.	
Earnings Claim Statement:	No
Term of Contract (Years):	10/10
Avg. # Of Employees:	1 FT, 1 PT
Passive Ownership:	Not Allowed
Area Develop. Agreements:	No
Sub-Franchising Contracts:	No
Expand In Territory:	No
Space Needs: 400 SF; Class B Office Space	

Support & Training Provided:

Site Selection Assistance:	No
Lease Negotiation Assistance:	No
Co-Operative Advertising:	Yes
Franchisee Assoc./Member:	No
Size Of Corporate Staff:	13
On-Going Support:	C,D,E,H,I
Training: 1 Week Seattle, WA.	

Minority-Specific Programs: Although we support the objectives of the NMFI, we do not have any specific programs in place at this time.

Specific Expansion Plans:

US:	All United States

ELECTRONIC TAX FILERS

P. O. Box 2077
Cary, NC 27512-2077
Tel: (800) 945-9277 (919) 469-0651
Fax: (919) 460-5935
E-Mail:
Web Site:
Ms. Rachel Wishon, President

We do no tax preparation! Instead, we provide a local, reasonably-priced, walk-in retail location where the 51% of the taxpayers who prepare their own returns can obtain electronic filing without being pressured into tax preparation they do not need. We transmit the data from self-prepared returns to the IRS and states in order that the taxpayer may receive his refunds in days, not months, via direct deposit into his bank, mail or refund loan.

Background:

Established: 1990;	1st Franchised: 1990
Franchised Units:	39
Company-Owned Units:	3
Total Units:	42
Minority-Owned Units:	
African-American:	3
Asian-American:	0
Hispanic:	0
Native American:	0

North America:	15 States
Density:	11 in NC, 4 in GA, 3 in MI

Financial/Terms:

Cash Investment:	$22.5K
Total Investment:	$22.5K
Minimum Net Worth:	$25K
Fees: Franchise —	$7.5K
Royalty — 8%;	Ad. — 4%
Earnings Claim Statement:	No
Term of Contract (Years):	3/17
Avg. # Of Employees:	2 FT, 4 PT
Passive Ownership:	Discouraged
Area Develop. Agreements:	No
Sub-Franchising Contracts:	No
Expand In Territory:	Yes
Space Needs: 1,000 SF; FS, SF, SC, RM	

Support & Training Provided:

Site Selection Assistance:	Yes
Lease Negotiation Assistance:	Yes
Co-Operative Advertising:	Yes
Franchisee Assoc./Member:	No
Size Of Corporate Staff:	Varies
On-Going Support:	A,C,D,h,I
Training: 1 Week in Cary, NC; 2-3 Days On-Site.	

Minority-Specific Programs: Although we support the objectives of the NMFI, we do not have any specific programs in place at this time.

Specific Expansion Plans:

US:	Eastern United States

LEDGERPLUS

401 St. Francis St.
Tallahassee, FL 32301
Tel: (888) 643-1348 (850) 681-1941

Fax: (850) 561-1374
E-Mail: lpp@vistech.net
Web Site: www.ledgerplus.com
Mr. Ron Baker, Marketing Director

LedgerPlus®

Helping Small Businesses Succeed Financially.

Accounting and tax franchise, offering services to America's small business clients. Reports they can understand and use, professional services at affordable prices.

Background:

Established: 1989;	1st Franchised: 1990
Franchised Units:	205
Company-Owned Units:	2
Total Units:	207
Minority-Owned Units:	
African-American:	4
Asian-American:	4
Hispanic:	2
Native American:	0
Other:	
North America:	NR
Density:	Fl, NC, CA

Financial/Terms:

Cash Investment:	$16.4-29.4K
Total Investment:	$16.4-29.4K
Minimum Net Worth:	$NR
Fees: Franchise —	$16K
Royalty — 8%;	Ad. — 2%
Earnings Claim Statement:	No
Term of Contract (Years):	10/10
Avg. # Of Employees:	1 FT
Passive Ownership:	Allowed
Area Develop. Agreements:	No

Sub-Franchising Contracts:	No
Expand In Territory:	Yes

Space Needs: 400 SF; Office

Support & Training Provided:

Site Selection Assistance:	N/A
Lease Negotiation Assistance:	No
Co-Operative Advertising:	Yes
Franchisee Assoc./Member:	No
Size Of Corporate Staff:	7
On-Going Support:	b,C,D,G,H

Training: 3 Days Tallahassee, FL.

Minority-Specific Programs: Although we support the objectives of the NMFI, we do not have any specific programs in place at this time.

Specific Expansion Plans:

US:	All United States

PADGETT BUSINESS SERVICES
160 Hawthorne Park
Athens, GA 30606
Tel: (800) 323-7292 (706) 548-1040
Fax: (706) 543-8537
E-Mail: bgrimes@smallbizpros.com
Web Site: www.smallbizpros.com
Mr. Bob Grimes, Director Franchise
Development

America's top-rated and fastest-growing tax and accounting franchise - serving the fastest-growing segment of the economy - America's small business owners. Initial training. Specialized software. On-going support.

Background:

Established: 1966;	1st Franchised: 1975
Franchised Units:	430
Company-Owned Units:	0
Total Units:	430

Minority-Owned Units:

African-American:	7%
Asian-American:	2%
Hispanic:	3%
Native American:	0%
Other:	
North America:	45 States, 8 Provinces
Density:	67 in ON, 38 in QC, 26 in GA

Financial/Terms:

Cash Investment:	$15-35K
Total Investment:	$40-60K
Minimum Net Worth:	$60K
Fees: Franchise —	$34.5K
Royalty — 9-4.5%;	Ad. — 0%
Earnings Claim Statement:	No
Term of Contract (Years):	20/20
Avg. # Of Employees:	1 FT, 2 PT
Passive Ownership:	Discouraged
Area Develop. Agreements:	No
Sub-Franchising Contracts:	No
Expand In Territory:	Yes

Space Needs: 200-400 SF; HB, OB, ES

Support & Training Provided:

Site Selection Assistance:	N/A
Lease Negotiation Assistance:	N/A
Co-Operative Advertising:	N/A
Franchisee Assoc./Member:	Yes/No
Size Of Corporate Staff:	20
On-Going Support:	C,D,G,H,I

Training: 2.5 Weeks Athens, GA.

Minority-Specific Programs: Although we support the objectives of the NMFI, we do not have any specific programs in place at this time.

Specific Expansion Plans:

US:	All United States

PEOPLES INCOME TAX
4915 Radford Ave., #100A
Richmond, VA 23230
Tel: (800) 984-1040 (804) 204-1040
Fax: (804) 213-4248
E-Mail: peoplesinc@aol.com
Web Site: www.peoplestax.com
Mr. Charles E. McCabe, President/CEO

Professional income tax preparation service specializing in middle-income and upwardly-mobile individual and small business taxpayers. Proven marketing and operating methods. Income tax school. Business training and support provided. Minimal start-up cost.

Background:

Established: 1987;	1st Franchised: 1998
Franchised Units:	0
Company-Owned Units:	13
Total Units:	13

Minority-Owned Units:

African-American:	
Asian-American:	
Hispanic:	
Native American:	
Other:	
North America:	1 State
Density:	13 in VA

Financial/Terms:

Cash Investment:	$40-60K
Total Investment:	$51-86K
Minimum Net Worth:	$100K
Fees: Franchise —	$16K
Royalty — 9%;	Ad. — 6%
Earnings Claim Statement:	No
Term of Contract (Years):	5
Avg. # Of Employees: 1 Ft, 9 PT (seasonal)	
Passive Ownership:	Not Allowed
Area Develop. Agreements:	No
Sub-Franchising Contracts:	No
Expand In Territory:	Yes

Space Needs: 600-1,000 SF; SF, SC, RM

Support & Training Provided:

Site Selection Assistance:	Yes
Lease Negotiation Assistance:	Yes
Co-Operative Advertising:	No
Franchisee Assoc./Member:	No
Size Of Corporate Staff:	10
On-Going Support:	C,d,E,G,H,I

Training: 25 Hrs. Richmond, VA.

Minority-Specific Programs: Although we support the objectives of the NMFI, we do not have any specific programs in place at this time.

Specific Expansion Plans:

US:	Virginia only

EFFECTIVE MAILERS

28510 Hayes Rd.
Roseville, MI 48066-2314
Tel: (810) 777-3223
Fax: (810) 777-4141
E-Mail: jgupta@couponvalue.com
Web Site: www.couponvalue.com
Mr. Jai Gupta, President

Co-op direct mail coupons design, print, insert and mail. Training and on-going support in all aspects of business. Our clients get one of the best coupon redemptions when they advertise with us. Four color coupons. Cutting edge technology. Price competitive in envelope type direct mail.

Background:

Established: 1982;	1st Franchised: 1993
Franchised Units:	4
Company-Owned Units:	1
Total Units:	5
Minority-Owned Units:	
African-American:	0
Asian-American:	1
Hispanic:	0
Native American:	0
North America:	3 States
Density:	2 in MA, 2 in NJ, 1 in MI

Financial/Terms:

Cash Investment:	$25K+
Total Investment:	$25-50K
Minimum Net Worth:	$25K
Fees: Franchise —	$18K
Royalty — 0%;	Ad. — 0%
Earnings Claim Statement:	No
Term of Contract (Years):	10/10
Avg. # Of Employees:	1 FT
Passive Ownership:	Not Allowed
Area Develop. Agreements:	No
Sub-Franchising Contracts:	No
Expand In Territory:	No
Space Needs: NR SF; HB	

Support & Training Provided:

Site Selection Assistance:	N/A
Lease Negotiation Assistance:	N/A
Co-Operative Advertising:	N/A
Franchisee Assoc./Member:	No
Size Of Corporate Staff:	60
On-Going Support:	NR

Training: 1 Week at Headquarters.
Minority-Specific Programs: Although we support the objectives of the NMFI, we do not have any specific programs in place at this time.

Specific Expansion Plans:

US:	All United States

VAL-PAK DIRECT MARKETING

8605 Largo Lakes Dr.
Largo, FL 33773
Tel: (800) 237-6266 (727) 393-1270
Fax: (727) 392-0049
E-Mail: david_elmer@valpak.com
Web Site: www.valpak.com
Mr. David Elmer, Director, Franchise Sales

North America's oldest and largest local co-operative direct mail advertising franchisor, with distribution of over 490 million coupon envelopes annually to over 53 million unduplicated homes and businesses. Subsidiary of Cox Enterprises, Inc. VAL-PAK OF CANADA is the Canadian franchisor.

Background:

Established: 1968;	1st Franchised: 1989
Franchised Units:	240
Company-Owned Units:	6
Total Units:	246
Minority-Owned Units:	
African-American:	0
Asian-American:	0
Hispanic:	2
Native American:	0
Other:	0
North America:	49 States,10 Provinces
Density:	19 in ON, 15 in CA, 14 in NY

Financial/Terms:

Cash Investment:	$25K+
Total Investment:	$25-85K
Minimum Net Worth:	$Varies
Fees: Franchise —	$7K
Royalty — 0%;	Ad. — 0%
Earnings Claim Statement:	No
Term of Contract (Years):	10/5
Avg. # Of Employees:	Varies
Passive Ownership:	Discouraged

Area Develop. Agreements:	No
Sub-Franchising Contracts:	No
Expand In Territory:	No
Space Needs: N/A SF; HB	

Support & Training Provided:

Site Selection Assistance:	N/A
Lease Negotiation Assistance:	N/A
Co-Operative Advertising:	Yes
Franchisee Assoc./Member:	Yes/Yes
Size Of Corporate Staff:	1,100
On-Going Support:	C,D,G,h,I

Training: 5 Days Home Study with Trainer; 2 Weeks Corporate Headquarters; On-Going, On- and Off-Site

Minority-Specific Programs: We are currently putting together a minority recruitment program for the year 2000. We have engaged the services of a leading minority recruiter.

Specific Expansion Plans:

US: All US, Limited Areas Remain

WORLDSITES

5915 Airport Rd., # 300
Mississauga, ON L4V 1T1 CANADA
Tel: (888) 678-7588 (905) 678-7588
Fax: (416) 213-8025
E-Mail: dkunkel@worldsites.net
Web Site: www.worldsites.net
Mr. David Kunkel, Director of Franchising

WORLDSITES has been ranked the # 1 Internet franchise by Entrepreneur Magazine, providing specialized Internet marketing solutions in over 30 countries aroung the globe. The WORLDSITES network provides: results-oriented Website development, E-commerce solutions, Internet telephone solutions, advanced promotional programs, high-speed corporate hosting and full-service consulting and education.

Background:

Established: 1995; 1st Franchised: 1996

Franchised Units:	215
Company-Owned Units:	1
Total Units:	2156

Minority-Owned Units:
African-American:
Asian-American:

Hispanic:
Native American:
Other:

North America:	9 States
Density:	4 in TX, FL Mast. Fran, WA

Financial/Terms:

Cash Investment:	$20-30K
Total Investment:	$29.5K+
Minimum Net Worth:	$NR
Fees: Franchise —	$29.5K+
Royalty — 10%;	Ad. — NR
Earnings Claim Statement:	No
Term of Contract (Years):	5/5
Avg. # Of Employees:	1-2 FT
Passive Ownership:	Allowed
Area Develop. Agreements:	Yes/5
Sub-Franchising Contracts:	No
Expand In Territory:	Yes
Space Needs: N/A SF; HB	

Support & Training Provided:

Site Selection Assistance:	N/A
Lease Negotiation Assistance:	N/A
Co-Operative Advertising:	Yes
Franchisee Assoc./Member:	Yes/Yes
Size Of Corporate Staff:	42
On-Going Support:	b,c,G,H,I

Training: 1 Week Mississauga, ON.

Minority-Specific Programs: Although we support the objectives of the NMFI, we do not have any specific programs in place at this time.

Specific Expansion Plans:

US: All United States

AMERICAN INSTITUTE OF SMALL BUSINESS

7515 Wayzata Blvd., # 129
Minneapolis, MN 55426
Tel: (800) 328-2906 (612) 545-7001
Fax: (612) 545-7020
E-Mail: aisbofmn@aol.com
Web Site: www.aisbofmn.com
Mr. Max Fallek, President

THE AMERICAN INSTITUTE OF SMALL BUSINESS provides educational materials, including books, on small business and entrepreneurship. It also provides a seminar for training people on how to set up and operate their own small business. THE INSTITUTE also supplies business software sold by franchisees.

Background:

Established: 1985;	1st Franchised: 1988
Franchised Units:	5
Company-Owned Units:	1
Total Units:	6

Minority-Owned Units:
African-American:	
Asian-American:	
Hispanic:	
Native American:	
Other:	
North America:	7 States
Density:	1 in MN, 1 in CO, 1 in IL

Financial/Terms:

Cash Investment:	$5K
Total Investment:	$10K
Minimum Net Worth:	$NR
Fees: Franchise —	$5K
Royalty — 0%;	Ad. — 0%
Earnings Claim Statement:	NR
Term of Contract (Years):	2/Varies
Avg. # Of Employees:	1 PT
Passive Ownership:	Allowed
Area Develop. Agreements:	No
Sub-Franchising Contracts:	No
Expand In Territory:	Yes
Space Needs: 600 SF; NR	

Support & Training Provided:

Site Selection Assistance:	Yes
Lease Negotiation Assistance:	N/A
Co-Operative Advertising:	N/A
Franchisee Assoc./Member:	NR
Size Of Corporate Staff:	8
On-Going Support:	B,D,E,h,I
Training: 1 Day Headquarters.	

Minority-Specific Programs: Although we support the objectives of the NMFI, we do not have any specific programs in place at this time.

Specific Expansion Plans:

US:	All United States

CENTURY SMALL BUSINESS SOLUTIONS

26722 Plaza Dr.
Mission Viejo, CA 92691
Tel: (800) 323-9000 (949) 348-5100
Fax: (949) 348-5126
E-Mail: franchise@centurysmallbiz.com
Web Site: www.centurysmallbiz.com
Ms. Karen Cagle, Director Franchise Development

CENTURY SMALL BUSINESS SOLUTIONS is a business services franchise specializing in accounting, tax, payroll and business counseling to the small business owner. Package includes all software and materials to start a professional practice. If you have a business and accounting background, we can show you how to develop a CENTURY business. Full training and support.

Background:

Established: 1935;	1st Franchised: 1999
Franchised Units:	642
Company-Owned Units:	8
Total Units:	650

Minority-Owned Units:
African-American:	8
Asian-American:	2
Hispanic:	10
Native American:	2
North America:	48 States, 1 Province
Density:	60 in CA, 37 in TX, 34 FL

Financial/Terms:

Cash Investment:	$30K
Total Investment:	$50-75K
Minimum Net Worth:	$150K
Fees: Franchise —	$35K
Royalty — 8%-0%;	Ad. — 0%
Earnings Claim Statement:	No
Term of Contract (Years):	10/10
Avg. # Of Employees:	2 FT, 1 PT
Passive Ownership:	Not Allowed
Area Develop. Agreements:	No

Sub-Franchising Contracts: No
Expand In Territory: No
Space Needs: 600 SF; Office Bldg.

Support & Training Provided:
Site Selection Assistance: Yes
Lease Negotiation Assistance: No
Co-Operative Advertising: No
Franchisee Assoc./Member: Yes/Yes
Size Of Corporate Staff: 60
On-Going Support: a,b,C,D,G,H,I
Training: 2 Weeks Training Ctr., Baltimore; 4 Days Post Grad, Various; 4 Days Tax Train., Baltimore
Minority-Specific Programs: Although we support the objectives of the NMFI, we do not have any specific programs in place at this time.

Specific Expansion Plans:
US: All United States

EMPIRE BUSINESS BROKERS
336 Harris Hill Rd.
Buffalo, NY 14221
Tel: (716) 677-5229
Fax: (716) 677-0955
E-Mail:
Web Site: www.empirebusinessbrokers.com
Mr. Nicholas R. Gugliuzza, President

We sell existing businesses and business opportunities throughout the U. S. and the world. Other profit centers relating to this are: franchise sales and development, financial brokering, equipment leasing, business valuation, business plans and business consulting. A complete training program is held, and therefore previous experience is not required. Success Magazine has ranked us the #1 business brokerage in the U.S. for two consecutive years.

Background:
Established: 1981; 1st Franchised: 1989
Franchised Units: 49
Company-Owned Units: 2
Total Units: 51
Minority-Owned Units:
African-American:
Asian-American:
Hispanic:
Native American:
Other:

North America: 22 States, 1 Province
Density: 6 in GA, 4 in OH, 3 in NY

Financial/Terms:
Cash Investment: $10K
Total Investment: $10K
Minimum Net Worth: $NR
Fees: Franchise — $8.9K
Royalty — $150/Mo.; Ad. — 0%
Earnings Claim Statement: No
Term of Contract (Years): 20/10
Avg. # Of Employees: 1 FT
Passive Ownership: Allowed
Area Develop. Agreements: Yes/5
Sub-Franchising Contracts: Yes
Expand In Territory: Yes
Space Needs: 500 SF; HB, Office Building

Support & Training Provided:
Site Selection Assistance: Yes
Lease Negotiation Assistance: Yes
Co-Operative Advertising: Yes
Franchisee Assoc./Member: Yes/Yes
Size Of Corporate Staff: 5
On-Going Support: a,b,C,D,E,G,H,I
Training: 1 Week at Home Office.
Minority-Specific Programs: Although we support the objectives of the NMFI, we do not have any specific programs in place at this time.

Specific Expansion Plans:
US: All United States

ENTREPRENEUR'S SOURCE, THE
900 Main St. S., Bldg. # 2
Southbury, CT 06488
Tel: (800) 289-0086 (203) 264-2006
Fax: (203) 264-3516
E-Mail: joe@thesource.com
Web Site: www.FranchiseSearch.com
Mr. Joe Mathews, Chief Operating Officer

Franchise consulting, coaching, placement/selection and development firm providing services to prospective and existing franchisees and franchisors. THE ENTREPRENEUR'S SOURCE has helped hundreds of people choose the right franchise. We also assist companies seeking to expand through franchising. Our experienced staff can provide you with everything you need to successfully package, launch and maintain a successful and profitable franchise system.

Background:
Established: 1984; 1st Franchised: 1998
Franchised Units: 27
Company-Owned Units: 1
Total Units: 28
Minority-Owned Units:
African-American:
Asian-American:
Hispanic:
Native American:
Other:
North America: 16 States
Density: 5 in GA, 5 in FL, 3 in SC,

Financial/Terms:
Cash Investment: $25K
Total Investment: $35-50K
Minimum Net Worth: $100K
Fees: Franchise — $25K
Royalty — 0%; Ad. — $350/Mo.
Earnings Claim Statement: No
Term of Contract (Years): 10/10
Avg. # Of Employees: 1 FT
Passive Ownership: Not Allowed
Area Develop. Agreements: Yes/10
Sub-Franchising Contracts: Yes
Expand In Territory: Yes
Space Needs: NR SF; Office

Support & Training Provided:
Site Selection Assistance: Yes
Lease Negotiation Assistance: Yes
Co-Operative Advertising: Yes
Franchisee Assoc./Member: No
Size Of Corporate Staff: 5
On-Going Support: C,D,G,H,I
Training: 8 Days CT.
Minority-Specific Programs: Although we support the objectives of the NMFI, we do not have any specific programs in place at this time.

Specific Expansion Plans:
US: All United States

INTERFACE FINANCIAL GROUP, THE
4521 PGA Blvd., # 211
Palm Beach Gardens, FL 33418
Tel: (800) 387-0860 (905) 475-5701
Fax: (905) 475-8688
E-Mail: ifg@interfacefinancial.com

Web Site: www.interfacefinancial.com
Mr. David T. Banfield, President

Franchise buys quality accounts receivable from client companies at a discount to provide short-term working capital to expanding businesses.

Background:
Established: 1971; 1st Franchised: 1991
Franchised Units: 50
Company-Owned Units: 0
Total Units: 50
Minority-Owned Units:
African-American: 0
Asian-American: 0
Hispanic: 0
Native American: 0
Other:
North America: 8 States, 5 Provinces
Density: 7 in ON, 6 in CA

Financial/Terms:
Cash Investment: $50K
Total Investment: $50-100K
Minimum Net Worth: $50K
Fees: Franchise — $25K
Royalty — 8%; Ad. — 1%
Earnings Claim Statement: No
Term of Contract (Years): 10/10
Avg. # Of Employees: 1 PT
Passive Ownership: Discouraged
Area Develop. Agreements: Yes
Sub-Franchising Contracts: NR
Expand In Territory: Yes
Space Needs: N/A SF; HB

Support & Training Provided:
Site Selection Assistance: N/A
Lease Negotiation Assistance: N/A
Co-Operative Advertising: No
Franchisee Assoc./Member: No
Size Of Corporate Staff: NR
On-Going Support: D,E,I
Training: 2 Days + Minimum 3 Days On-Site.
Minority-Specific Programs: Although we support the objectives of the NMFI, we do not have any specific programs in place at this time.

Specific Expansion Plans:
US: All United States

MISTER MONEY - USA
238 Walnut St.
Fort Collins, CO 80524
Tel: (800) 827-7296 (970) 493-0574
Fax: (970) 490-2099
E-Mail: tim@mistermoney.com

Web Site: www.mistermoney.com
Mr. Don Ettinger, Franchise Sales Director

MISTER MONEY - USA franchises offer pawn loans, payday loans, check cashing, money orders, and other financial services. Franchisees operate full-service retail stores or loan only outlets. MISTER MONEY - USA stores are modern, customer friendly and located in solid blue collar areas.

Background:
Established: 1976; 1st Franchised: 1996
Franchised Units: 25
Company-Owned Units: 14
Total Units: 39
Minority-Owned Units:
African-American: 0
Asian-American: 0
Hispanic: 0
Native American: 0
North America: 9 States
Density: 13 in IA, 9 in CO, 4 in WI

Financial/Terms:
Cash Investment: $65-150K
Total Investment: $65-200K
Minimum Net Worth: $65K
Fees: Franchise — $21.5-24.5K
Royalty — 3-5%; Ad. — 3%
Earnings Claim Statement: Yes
Term of Contract (Years): 5/5
Avg. # Of Employees: 3 FT, 1 PT
Passive Ownership: Discouraged
Area Develop. Agreements: No
Sub-Franchising Contracts: Yes
Expand In Territory: Yes
Space Needs: 4,000-10,000 SF; FS, SF, SC

Support & Training Provided:
Site Selection Assistance: Yes
Lease Negotiation Assistance: Yes
Co-Operative Advertising: Yes
Franchisee Assoc./Member: Yes/Yes
Size Of Corporate Staff: 25
On-Going Support: a,B,C,D,E,F,G,I
Training: 10-14 Days Fort Collins, CO.
Minority-Specific Programs: We provide extra training, both initial and on-going. Special financing considerations for qualified applicants. Financial support for loan expansion.

Specific Expansion Plans:
US: All United States

SUNBELT® BUSINESS BROKERS

SUNBELT BUSINESS BROKERS
2 Amherst St.
Charleston, SC 29403
Tel: (800) 771-7866 (843) 853-4781
Fax: (843) 853-4135
E-Mail: sales@sunbeltnetwork.com
Web Site: www.sunbeltnetwork.com
Mr. Edward T. Pendarvis, President

We offer business brokerage/merger and acquisition franchises. SUNBELT is the largest and fastest-growing business brokerage firm in the world. Our success comes from our name recognition, quality training programs and hands-on assistance. We are the leaders in computerized office management, networking and Internet technology. We take no percentage fees. All of our services are covered in our low semi-annual fee.

Background:
Established: 1978; 1st Franchised: 1993
Franchised Units: 196
Company-Owned Units: 1
Total Units: 197
Minority-Owned Units:
African-American: 1
Asian-American: 0
Hispanic: 2
Native American: 0
Other:
North America: 36 States
Density: 16 in FL, 10 in NC, 10 in VA

Financial/Terms:
Cash Investment: $5-15K
Total Investment: $5-50K
Minimum Net Worth: $N/A
Fees: Franchise — $5-10K
Royalty — $3-6K/Yr.; Ad. — 0%
Earnings Claim Statement: No
Term of Contract (Years): On-going
Avg. # Of Employees: Independent Contrac.
Passive Ownership: Not Allowed
Area Develop. Agreements: No

Sub-Franchising Contracts: No
Expand In Territory: Yes
Space Needs: 1,000 SF; FS

Support & Training Provided:
Site Selection Assistance: N/A
Lease Negotiation Assistance: N/A
Co-Operative Advertising: N/A
Franchisee Assoc./Member: Yes/Yes
Size Of Corporate Staff: 9
On-Going Support: C,D,G,H,I
Training: 4 Days Various Regional Centers.
Minority-Specific Programs: Financing franchise fee.

Specific Expansion Plans:
US: All United States

Support & Training Provided:
Site Selection Assistance: Yes
Lease Negotiation Assistance: Yes
Co-Operative Advertising: Yes
Franchisee Assoc./Member: Yes/Yes
Size Of Corporate Staff: 10
On-Going Support: A,B,C,d,G,H,I
Training: 2 1/2 Weeks Greensboro, NC; 2 1/2 Weeks Ft. Lauderdale, FL.
Minority-Specific Programs: SBA financing. Corporate financing for minorities.

Specific Expansion Plans:
US: All United States

VR BUSINESS BROKERS

2601 E. Oakland Park Blvd., # 205
Ft. Lauderdale, FL 33306
Tel: (800) 377-8722 (954) 565-1555
Fax: (954) 565-6855
E-Mail: pking@vrbusinessbrokers.com
Web Site: www.vrbusinessbrokers.com
Mr. Peter King, Principal

Oldest established chain of franchised business brokers in the nation. We also publish 'Today's Business Owner Magazine' for exclusive use of franchisees at no additional cost.

Background:
Established: 1979; 1st Franchised: 1979
Franchised Units: 85
Company-Owned Units: 0
Total Units: 85
Minority-Owned Units:
    African-American:
    Asian-American: 5
    Hispanic:
    Native American:
    Other:
North America: 37 States
Density: 12 in FL, 10 in CA, 5 in NC

Financial/Terms:
Cash Investment: $40-75K
Total Investment: $40-75K
Minimum Net Worth: $150K
Fees: Franchise — $12K
    Royalty — 6%; Ad. — $150/Mo.
Earnings Claim Statement: No
Term of Contract (Years): 10/10
Avg. # Of Employees: 2 FT, 1 PT
Passive Ownership: Not Allowed
Area Develop. Agreements: No
Sub-Franchising Contracts: No
Expand In Territory: No
Space Needs: Varies SF; OB

Computer fun . . . for little ones

COMPUTERTOTS/COMPUTER EXPLORERS

10132 Colvin Run Rd.
Great Falls, VA 22066
Tel: (800) 531-5053 (703) 759-2556
Fax: (703) 759-1938
E-Mail: sgould@computertots.com
Web Site: www.computertots.com
Ms. Sandy Gould, Dir. Fran. Dev./Training

A network of computer education services for children 3 - 12. The program was established in 1984 and offers programs through outreach programs at private and public educational sites.

Background:
Established: 1984; 1st Franchised: 1988
Franchised Units: 190
Company-Owned Units: 2
Total Units: 192
Minority-Owned Units:
    African-American:
    Asian-American:
    Hispanic:
    Native American:
    Other:

North America: 38 States
Density: 12 in CA, 8 in TX, 7 in OH

Financial/Terms:
Cash Investment: $45K
Total Investment: $45K
Minimum Net Worth: $100K
Fees: Franchise — $10-29.9K
    Royalty — 8%/$350;   Ad. — 1%
Earnings Claim Statement: Yes
Term of Contract (Years):   10/10
Avg. # Of Employees: 1 FT, 5 PT
Passive Ownership: Discouraged
Area Develop. Agreements: No
Sub-Franchising Contracts: No
Expand In Territory: No
Space Needs: N/A SF; HB

Support & Training Provided:
Site Selection Assistance: N/A
Lease Negotiation Assistance: N/A
Co-Operative Advertising: N/A
Franchisee Assoc./Member: Yes/Yes
Size Of Corporate Staff: 10
On-Going Support: b,c,d,g,h,I
Training: 7 Days Great Falls, VA.
Minority-Specific Programs: Although we support the objectives of the NMFI, we do not have any specific programs in place at this time.

Specific Expansion Plans:
US: All United States

FASTRACKIDS INTERNATIONAL LTD.

6900 E. Belleview Ave.
Englewood, CO 80111
Tel: (888) 576-6888 (303) 224-0200

Fax: (303) 224-0222
E-Mail:
Web Site: www.fastrackids.com
Mr. Kevin Krause, Director Franchise Development

FASTRACKIDS(r) is a remarkable new,

"Enrichment Education for Tomorrow's Leaders"

technologically-advanced educational system designed to enrich the knowledge of young children. FASTRACKIDS(r) enrichment education encourages the development of a child's creativity, leadership, speaking and communication skills in a stimulating, high-participation learning environment.

Background:
Established: 1998;   1st Franchised: 1998
Franchised Units: 60
Company-Owned Units: 0
Total Units: 60
Minority-Owned Units:
    African-American:
    Asian-American:
    Hispanic:
    Native American:
    Other:
North America: 4 States
Density: NR

Financial/Terms:

Cash Investment:	$8.7-34.4K
Total Investment:	$8.7-34.4K
Minimum Net Worth:	$NR
Fees: Franchise —	$5-15K
Royalty — 1.5%;	Ad. — 5%
Earnings Claim Statement:	Yes
Term of Contract (Years):	5/5
Avg. # Of Employees:	1-5 FT
Passive Ownership:	Discouraged
Area Develop. Agreements:	Yes/5
Sub-Franchising Contracts:	No
Expand In Territory:	Yes
Space Needs: 500 SF; N/A	

Support & Training Provided:

Site Selection Assistance:	Yes
Lease Negotiation Assistance:	No
Co-Operative Advertising:	Yes
Franchisee Assoc./Member:	No
Size Of Corporate Staff:	12
On-Going Support:	C,G,h,I

Training: 3-4 Days in Denver, CO.
Minority-Specific Programs: We have advertised in 30 countries.

Specific Expansion Plans:

US:	All United States

FOURTH R, THE

1715 Market St., # 103
Kirkland, WA 98033
Tel: (800) 821-8653 (425) 828-0336
Fax: (425) 828-0192
E-Mail: fourthR@fourthR.com
Web Site: www.FourthR.com
Mr. Robert L. McCauley, Director of Franchising

Computers have changed virtually all aspects of our lives. As we move into the information age, many experts agree that computer literacy has become THE FOURTH R in education today. As an international leader in computer training for children and adults, THE FOURTH R is one of the fastest-growing companies in the computer training sector and has been highlighted in prominent national publications as one of the top franchisors both in the U. S. and abroad.

Background:

Established: 1991;	1st Franchised: 1992
Franchised Units:	217
Company-Owned Units:	0
Total Units:	217
Minority-Owned Units:	
African-American:	4
Asian-American:	
Hispanic:	
Native American:	
Other:	
North America:	21 States, 2 Provinces
Density:	10 in CA, 8 in WA, 6 in PA

Financial/Terms:

Cash Investment:	$N/A
Total Investment:	$19-54K
Minimum Net Worth:	$None
Fees: Franchise —	$9-16K
Royalty — +-$240/Mo+5%;	Ad. — 0%
Earnings Claim Statement:	No
Term of Contract (Years):	5/5
Avg. # Of Employees:	2 FT, 4 PT (Variable)
Passive Ownership:	Allowed
Area Develop. Agreements:	Yes/5
Sub-Franchising Contracts:	No
Expand In Territory:	Yes
Space Needs: 800+ SF; SF, SC, HB, Commercial	

Support & Training Provided:

Site Selection Assistance:	Yes
Lease Negotiation Assistance:	Yes
Co-Operative Advertising:	Yes
Franchisee Assoc./Member:	Yes/Yes
Size Of Corporate Staff:	7
On-Going Support:	B,C,G,H,I

Training: 5 Days Seattle, WA.
Minority-Specific Programs: Although we support the objectives of the NMFI, we do not have any specific programs in place at this time.

Specific Expansion Plans:

US:	All United States

GYMBOREE

700 Airport Blvd., # 200
Burlingame, CA 94010-1912
Tel: (800) 222-7758 (650) 579-0600
Fax: (650) 696-7452
E-Mail: eva_crosland@gymmail.com
Web Site: www.gymboree.com
Ms. Eva Crosland, Assistant Manager

GYMBOREE, the world's largest development play program, offers weekly classes to parents and their children, aged newborn through 4 years, on custom-designed equipment. The program is based on sensory integration theory, positive parenting, child development principles and the importance of play.

Background:

Established: 1976;	1st Franchised: 1978
Franchised Units:	390
Company-Owned Units:	23
Total Units:	413
Minority-Owned Units:	
African-American:	
Asian-American:	
Hispanic:	
Native American:	
Other:	
North America:	41 States, 3 Provinces
Density:	51 in CA, 32 in NY, 30 in NJ

Financial/Terms:

Cash Investment:	$80-120K
Total Investment:	$80-150K
Minimum Net Worth:	$150K
Fees: Franchise —	$35K
Royalty — 6%;	Ad. — 2.25%
Earnings Claim Statement:	No
Term of Contract (Years):	10/10
Avg. # Of Employees:	1 FT, 3 PT
Passive Ownership:	Not Allowed
Area Develop. Agreements:	No
Sub-Franchising Contracts:	No
Expand In Territory:	Yes
Space Needs: 1,800 SF; SF, SC, RM	

Support & Training Provided:

Site Selection Assistance:	Yes
Lease Negotiation Assistance:	Yes
Co-Operative Advertising:	Yes
Franchisee Assoc./Member:	Yes
Size Of Corporate Staff:	18
On-Going Support:	B,D,G,h,I

Training: 6 Days Headquarters.
Minority-Specific Programs: Although we support the objectives of the NMFI, we do not have any specific programs in place at this time.

Specific Expansion Plans:

US:	All United States

GYMSTERS

6111 Paseo Pueblo Dr.
San Jose, CA 95120-2741
Tel: (408) 997-6997
Fax: (408) 997-6087
Ms. Lonnie Coppock, President

The GYMSTERS(r) system brings physical education to children from two to twelve by providing the equipment, the staff and the program. Experts in education and health agree that learning through physical movement is the primary way that children develop. The children's fitness industry offers a vast and huge market place whose potential has become even greater, due to budget cuts, and GYMSTERS(r) is the answer.

Background:
Established: 1980;   1st Franchised: 1988
Franchised Units: 8
Company-Owned Units: 1
Total Units: 9
Minority-Owned Units:
  African-American:
  Asian-American:
  Hispanic:
  Native American:
  Other: 5 Women
North America: 3 States
Density: 7 in CA, 1 in OH

Financial/Terms:
Cash Investment: $19.8-24.5K
Total Investment: $19.8-24.5K
Minimum Net Worth: $NR
Fees: Franchise — $12K
  Royalty — 7%;   Ad. — 3%
Earnings Claim Statement: Yes
Term of Contract (Years):   5/5
Avg. # Of Employees: 1 PT
Passive Ownership: Discouraged
Area Develop. Agreements: No
Sub-Franchising Contracts: No
Expand In Territory: NR
Space Needs: NR SF; N/A

Support & Training Provided:
Site Selection Assistance: Yes
Lease Negotiation Assistance: N/A
Co-Operative Advertising: N/A
Franchisee Assoc./Member: No
Size Of Corporate Staff: 4
On-Going Support: b,C,D,f,G,h,I
Training: Initially 6 Days in San Jose, CA.
Minority-Specific Programs: Franchise owners are obligated to hire the most experienced teaching personnel for their business. African-Americans, Hispanics and Asian-Americans are represented by the teaching staff at many of the Franchise territories. GYMSTERS personnel specifically work closely with children from 2-12. In that age range, historically teachers are female. So, as a minority reversal, "men" are minorities in the young child arena. GYMSTERS has 2 male franchisees; also men are hired to represent our teaching staff.

Specific Expansion Plans:
US: All United States

HIGH TOUCH-HIGH TECH
12352 Wiles Rd.
Coral Springs, FL 33076
Tel: (800) 444-4968 (954) 755-2900
Fax: (954) 755-1242
E-Mail: info@hightouch-hightech.com
Web Site: www.hightouch-hightech.com
Mr. Daniel Shaw, President/CEO

Provides hands-on science experiences that go right into the classroom. We provide in-school field trips. We also provide fun, science-oriented birthday parties.

Background:
Established: 1992;   1st Franchised: 1994
Franchised Units: 24
Company-Owned Units: 2
Total Units: 26
Minority-Owned Units:
  African-American: 1
  Asian-American:
  Hispanic:
  Native American:
  Other:
North America: 12 States
Density: 5 in FL, 2 in NJ, 2 in IL

Financial/Terms:
Cash Investment: $5-8K
Total Investment: $28-42K
Minimum Net Worth: $NR
Fees: Franchise — $20-35K
  Royalty — 7%;   Ad. — 0%
Earnings Claim Statement: Yes
Term of Contract (Years):   10/10
Avg. # Of Employees: 2-3 PT
Passive Ownership: NR
Area Develop. Agreements: No
Sub-Franchising Contracts: Yes
Expand In Territory: Yes
Space Needs: NR SF; HB

Support & Training Provided:
Site Selection Assistance: Yes
Lease Negotiation Assistance: N/A
Co-Operative Advertising: N/A
Franchisee Assoc./Member: No
Size Of Corporate Staff: 6

On-Going Support: D,G,H,I
Training: 5 Full Days National Programming Offices.
Minority-Specific Programs: Although we support the objectives of the NMFI, we do not have any specific programs in place at this time.

Specific Expansion Plans:
US: All United States, Global

IMAGINE THAT DISCOVERY MUSEUMS
P. O. Box 493
New Vernon, NJ 07976
Tel: (800) 820-1145 (973) 267-2907
Fax: (973) 445-1917
E-Mail:
Web Site:
Ms. Deborah Bodnar, Founder

A children's interactive hands-on museum, with abilities to do birthday parties, field trips, general admission and drop service (day care). Cafe on premises, educational gift shop and enrichment programs.

Background:
Established: 1992;   1st Franchised: 1994
Franchised Units: 2
Company-Owned Units: 1
Total Units: 3
Minority-Owned Units:
  African-American: 0
  Asian-American: 0
  Hispanic: 0
  Native American: 0
  Other:
North America: 2 States
Density: 2 in NJ, 1 in MD

Financial/Terms:
Cash Investment: $200K
Total Investment: $425-525K
Minimum Net Worth: $200K
Fees: Franchise — $25K
  Royalty — 6%;   Ad. — 0%
Earnings Claim Statement: No
Term of Contract (Years):   10/10
Avg. # Of Employees: 3 FT, 15 PT
Passive Ownership: Discouraged
Area Develop. Agreements: No
Sub-Franchising Contracts: No
Expand In Territory: NR
Space Needs: 15,000 SF; FS, SC

Support & Training Provided:
Site Selection Assistance: Yes
Lease Negotiation Assistance: Yes
Co-Operative Advertising: Yes

Franchisee Assoc./Member: No
Size Of Corporate Staff: 3
On-Going Support: A,B,C,D,E,F,I
Training: 2 Weeks E. Hanover, NJ.
Minority-Specific Programs: Although we support the objectives of the NMFI, we do not have any specific programs in place at this time.

Specific Expansion Plans:
US: All United States

JACADI
72 Parkway E.
Mount Vernon, NY 10552
Tel: (914) 667-2183
Fax: (914) 665-0416
E-Mail: jacadi@juno.com
Web Site: www.jacadiusa.com
Mr. Bruce Pettibone, Chief Operations Officer

JACADI is a childrenswear retail company whose collections include clothing, shoes, accessories, furniture and nursery items in newborn through size 12 for both boys and girls. The merchandise is a European-style which adapts the latest trends to classic design and allows the customer to mix and match the various styles and color groups. JACADI also strives to give excellent customer service and the highest price/quality ratio.

Background:
Established: 1988; 1st Franchised: 1992
Franchised Units: 20
Company-Owned Units: 3
Total Units: 23
Minority-Owned Units:
African-American: 0
Asian-American: 9
Hispanic: 5
Native American: 0
Other: 1 Mid-eastern
North America: 10 States, 1 Province
Density: 8 in CA, 3 in NY, 2 in FL

Financial/Terms:
Cash Investment: $120-250K
Total Investment: $183-313K
Minimum Net Worth: $750K Liquid

Fees: Franchise — $20K
Royalty — 4%; Ad. — 1%
Earnings Claim Statement: No
Term of Contract (Years): 7/7
Avg. # Of Employees: 2-3 FT, 2-3 PT
Passive Ownership: Not Allowed
Area Develop. Agreements: Yes/7
Sub-Franchising Contracts: No
Expand In Territory: Yes
Space Needs: 1,100 SF; FS, SF, RM

Support & Training Provided:
Site Selection Assistance: Yes
Lease Negotiation Assistance: Yes
Co-Operative Advertising: No
Franchisee Assoc./Member: No
Size Of Corporate Staff: 4
On-Going Support: B,C,d,E,f,G,h
Training: 3-5 Days in Subsidiary Shop; 3 Days Franchisee's Shop Before Opening; On-Going Corporate.
Minority-Specific Programs: Although we support the objectives of the NMFI, we do not have any specific programs in place at this time.

Specific Expansion Plans:
US: All United States

KID TO KID
406 W. South Jordan Pkwy., # 160
South Jordan, UT 84095
Tel: (888) KID-2-KID (801) 553-8799
Fax: (801) 553-8793
E-Mail: k2kcorp@aol.com
Web Site: www.kidtokid.com
Mr. Brent Sloan, President

KID TO KID is an up-scale children's resale store based on the premise that 'kids grow faster than paychecks.' Parents buy and sell better-quality used children's clothing, toys, equipment and accessories. If you enjoy working with people and want to increase your financial security as you grow your own business, call KID TO KID today!

Background:
Established: 1992; 1st Franchised: 1994
Franchised Units: 31
Company-Owned Units: 1
Total Units: 32
Minority-Owned Units:
African-American:
Asian-American:
Hispanic:

Native American:
Other:
North America: 13 States, Puerto Rico
Density: 12 in UT, 5 in TX, 3 in PA

Financial/Terms:
Cash Investment: $25-35K
Total Investment: $88-116K
Minimum Net Worth: $150K
Fees: Franchise — $20K
Royalty — 4.75%; Ad. — .5%
Earnings Claim Statement: Yes
Term of Contract (Years): 10/5
Avg. # Of Employees: 3 FT, 2 PT
Passive Ownership: Discouraged
Area Develop. Agreements: Yes/Varies
Sub-Franchising Contracts: No
Expand In Territory: No
Space Needs: 2,400 SF; FS, SF, SC

Support & Training Provided:
Site Selection Assistance: Yes
Lease Negotiation Assistance: Yes
Co-Operative Advertising: Yes
Franchisee Assoc./Member: No
Size Of Corporate Staff: 4
On-Going Support: B,C,d,E,f,G,H
Training: 10 Days Salt Lake City UT.
Minority-Specific Programs: Although we support the objectives of the NMFI, we do not have any specific programs in place at this time.

Specific Expansion Plans:
US: All United States

KIDDIE KOBBLER
68 Robertson Rd., # 106
Nepean, ON K2H 8P5 CANADA
Tel: (800) 561-9762 (613) 820-0505
Fax: (613) 820-8250
E-Mail: kiddiekobblerltd@sprint.ca
Web Site: www.kiddiekobbler.com
Mr. Fred Norman, President

Children's shoe stores, located in major shopping malls and strip centers. The extensive marketing program is designed to develop new and repeat business through intensive customer service, selection and value.

Background:

Established: 1951;   1st Franchised: 1968
Franchised Units: 29
Company-Owned Units: 0
Total Units: 29
Minority-Owned Units:
    African-American: 0
    Asian-American: 3
    Hispanic: 0
    Native American: 0
    Other: 9 Italians, 2 Jews, 2 French
North America: 6 Provinces
Density: 25 in ON, 2 in NS, 2 in PQ

Financial/Terms:

Cash Investment: $50K
Total Investment: $100K
Minimum Net Worth: $150K
Fees: Franchise — $25K
    Royalty — 4%;   Ad. — 1%
Earnings Claim Statement: No
Term of Contract (Years): 10/5/5
Avg. # Of Employees: 2 FT, 2 PT
Passive Ownership: Not Allowed
Area Develop. Agreements: Yes
Sub-Franchising Contracts: Yes
Expand In Territory: Yes
Space Needs: 1,000-1,200 SF; SC, RM, SF

Support & Training Provided:

Site Selection Assistance: Yes
Lease Negotiation Assistance: Yes
Co-Operative Advertising: Yes
Franchisee Assoc./Member: Yes
Size Of Corporate Staff: 6
On-Going Support: b,C,D,E,f,G,H,I
Training: 4 Weeks On-Site; 6 Weeks Supervised Home Study.
Minority-Specific Programs: Although we support the objectives of the NMFI, we do not have any specific programs in place at this time.

Specific Expansion Plans:

US: Area & Master Franchise Terr

KINDERDANCE INTERNATIONAL

268 N. Babcock St.
Melbourne, FL 32935
Tel: (800) 554-2334 (321) 242-0590

Fax: (321) 254-3388
E-Mail: kindercorp@kinderdance.net
Web Site: www.kinderdance.net
Mr. Jerry M. Perch, VP Sales & Marketing

KINDERDANCE franchisees are trained to teach 4 developmentally-unique dance and motor development programs: KINDERDANCE, KINDERGYM, KINDERTOTS and KINDERCOMBO, which are designed for boys and girls ages 2-8. They learn the basics of ballet, tap, gymnastics and creative dance, as well as learning numbers, colors, shapes and words. No studio or dance experience required. Franchisee teaches at child care center sites.

Background:

Established: 1979;   1st Franchised: 1985
Franchised Units: 58
Company-Owned Units: 1
Total Units: 59
Minority-Owned Units:
    African-American: 1
    Asian-American:
    Hispanic: 2
    Native American:
    Other: 59 Women
North America: 23 States, 2 Provinces
Density: 9 in CA, 4 in NY, 4 in FL

Financial/Terms:

Cash Investment: $6-20.6K
Total Investment: $6-20.6K
Minimum Net Worth: $N/A
Fees: Franchise — $6.5-15K
    Royalty — 6-15%;   Ad. — 3%
Earnings Claim Statement: No
Term of Contract (Years): 10/10
Avg. # Of Employees: 1+ FT, 1 PT
Passive Ownership: Discouraged
Area Develop. Agreements: No
Sub-Franchising Contracts: No
Expand In Territory: Yes
Space Needs: NR SF; N/A

Support & Training Provided:

Site Selection Assistance: N/A
Lease Negotiation Assistance: N/A
Co-Operative Advertising: Yes
Franchisee Assoc./Member: Yes/No
Size Of Corporate Staff: 7
On-Going Support: A,B,C,D,E,F,G,H,I
Training: 6 Days in Melbourne, FL.
Minority-Specific Programs: Financing available. List of alternative finance sources.

Specific Expansion Plans:

US: All United States

LITTLE SCIENTISTS

200 Main St., 3rd Fl.
Ansonia, CT 06401
Tel: (800) FACT-FUN (203) 732-3522
Fax: (203) 736-2165
E-Mail: Dr_Heidi@little-scientists.com
Web Site: www.little-scientists.com
Ms. Ronda Margolis, VP Franchise Development

LITTLE SCIENTISTS is a leader in hands-on science education for children ages 3 to 9. Nearly 200 hands-on lessons make up a innovative science curriculum. The curriculum has been developed by renowned scientists and educators. The market is growing at a remarkable rate. Owning a LITTLE SCIENTIST franchise is a highly profitable endeavor yielding great community benefits.

Background:

Established: 1993;   1st Franchised: 1996
Franchised Units: 15
Company-Owned Units: 3
Total Units: 18
Minority-Owned Units:
    African-American:
    Asian-American:
    Hispanic:
    Native American:
North America: 7 States
Density: 5 in CT, 2 in NJ

Financial/Terms:

Cash Investment: $25K
Total Investment: $35K
Minimum Net Worth: $50K
Fees: Franchise — $20K
    Royalty — 6%/$250/Mo.;   Ad. — 1%
Earnings Claim Statement: No
Term of Contract (Years): 10/10
Avg. # Of Employees: 2 FT, 6-10 PT
Passive Ownership: Discouraged
Area Develop. Agreements: Yes/10
Sub-Franchising Contracts: Yes
Expand In Territory: Yes
Space Needs: 500 SF; HB

Support & Training Provided:

Site Selection Assistance: N/A
Lease Negotiation Assistance: N/A
Co-Operative Advertising: N/A
Franchisee Assoc./Member: Yes/Yes
Size Of Corporate Staff: 15

On-Going Support: A,B,C,D,G,H,I
Training: 1 Week at HQ; 1-3 Day Seminars/ Training 2 Times/Year at HQ; 2-4 Times/Year On Site

Minority-Specific Programs: Although we support the objectives of the NMFI, we do not have any specific programs in place at this time.

Specific Expansion Plans:
US: All United States

PRE-FIT

10926 S. Western Ave.
Chicago, IL 60643
Tel: (773) 233-7771
Fax: (773) 233-7121
E-Mail: prefit@ameritech.net
Web Site: www.pre-fit.com
Ms. Latrice Lee, Franchise Director

PRE-FIT, INC offers America's premier sports, exercise and health systems for children. These systems include: PRE-FIT, a mobile preschool fitness program; FITNESS IS ELEMENTARY, our mobile elementary physical education program; and CHEC, the Children's Health and Executive Club. All of these programs are offered through our success-oriented franchise system that provides marketing, administrative and instructional training, an exclusive territory, and continuous support.

Background:
Established: 1987; 1st Franchised: 1992
Franchised Units: 37
Company-Owned Units: 0
Total Units: 37
Minority-Owned Units:
African-American: 20
Asian-American:
Hispanic: 1
Native American:
North America: 13 States
Density: 19 in IL, 6 in PA, 2 in MI

Financial/Terms:
Cash Investment: $10-41K
Total Investment: $10-118.2K
Minimum Net Worth: $25K
Fees: Franchise — $8.5-24.5K
Royalty — 10-8%; Ad. — 2%
Earnings Claim Statement: No
Term of Contract (Years): 10/10
Avg. # Of Employees: 1-2 FT, 2-5 PT
Passive Ownership: Discouraged
Area Develop. Agreements: No
Sub-Franchising Contracts: No
Expand In Territory: Yes
Space Needs: 2,000-4,000 SF; SC, RM, HB

Support & Training Provided:
Site Selection Assistance: Yes
Lease Negotiation Assistance: Yes
Co-Operative Advertising: No
Franchisee Assoc./Member: No
Size Of Corporate Staff: 6
On-Going Support: D,E,G,h,I
Training: Chicago, IL.

Minority-Specific Programs: We provide assistance in preparing loan documents and have recommended prospective franchisees for loans at 2 separate banks where they were in fact approved for the business loans. The franchisor is African-American.

Specific Expansion Plans:
US: All United States

PRIMROSE SCHOOLS

199 S. Erwin St.
Cartersville, GA 30120
Tel: (800) 745-0677 (770) 606-9600
Fax: (770) 606-0020
E-Mail: psfcfranchise@mindspring.com
Web Site: www.primroseschools.com
Mr. Ray Orgera, VP Franchise Dev.

Educational child-care franchise, offering a traditional pre-school curriculum and programs while also providing quality childcare services. Site selection assistance, extensive training, operations manuals, building plans, marketing plans and on-going support.

Background:
Established: 1982; 1st Franchised: 1989
Franchised Units: 103
Company-Owned Units: 1
Total Units: 104
Minority-Owned Units:
African-American: 0%
Asian-American: 0%
Hispanic: 2%
Native American: 0%
North America: 10 States
Density: 33 in GA, 35 in TX, 9 in NC

Financial/Terms:
Cash Investment: $190-300K
Total Investment: $1.3-2MM
Minimum Net Worth: $250K
Fees: Franchise — $48.5K
Royalty — 7%; Ad. — 1%
Earnings Claim Statement: Yes
Term of Contract (Years): 11/10
Avg. # Of Employees: 25 FT, 5 PT
Passive Ownership: Not Allowed
Area Develop. Agreements: No
Sub Franchising Contracts: No
Expand In Territory: No
Space Needs: 6,500-8,500 SF; FS

Support & Training Provided:
Site Selection Assistance: Yes
Lease Negotiation Assistance: Yes
Co-Operative Advertising: Yes
Franchisee Assoc./Member: Yes/Yes
Size Of Corporate Staff: 21
On-Going Support: C,D,E,f,G,h,I
Training: 1 Week Home Office; 1 Week at Existing School; 1 Week at Franchisee's New School.

Minority-Specific Programs: Although we support the objectives of the NMFI, we do not have any specific programs in place at this time.

Specific Expansion Plans:
US: SW, SE, TX, OH, CO

TECHNOKIDS

2232 Sheridan Garden Dr.
Oakville, ON L6J 7T1 CANADA
Tel: (800) 221-7921 (905) 829-4171
Fax: (905) 829-4172
E-Mail: info@technokids.com
Web Site: www.technokids.com
Mr. Scott Gerard, President

TECHNOKIDS teaches computing and technology skills to children aged 4 to 17 using proprietary thematic-based curriculum. Our program is licensed and sold to schools and delivered thorugh stand-alone computer learning centers.

Background:

Established: 1993;	1st Franchised: 1994
Franchised Units:	250
Company-Owned Units:	1
Total Units:	251
Minority-Owned Units:	
African-American:	1
Asian-American:	0
Hispanic:	0
Native American:	0
North America:	3 States, 2 Provinces
Density:	1 in NM, 1 in VA, 1 in CA

Financial/Terms:

Cash Investment:	$25K
Total Investment:	$25-50K
Minimum Net Worth:	$100K
Fees: Franchise —	$15K+
Royalty — 7%;	Ad. — 0%
Earnings Claim Statement:	No
Term of Contract (Years):	10/10
Avg. # Of Employees:	1 FT, 1 PT
Passive Ownership:	Discouraged
Area Develop. Agreements:	Yes/15
Sub-Franchising Contracts:	Yes
Expand In Territory:	Yes
Space Needs: NR SF; HB	

Support & Training Provided:

Site Selection Assistance:	N/A
Lease Negotiation Assistance:	N/A
Co-Operative Advertising:	Yes
Franchisee Assoc./Member:	No
Size Of Corporate Staff:	6
On-Going Support:	D,G,H,I

Training: 5-10 Days at Head Office.
Minority-Specific Programs: Although we support the objectives of the NMFI, we do not have any specific programs in place at this time.

Specific Expansion Plans:

US:	All United States

TUTOR TIME LEARNING CENTERS

621 N W 53rd St., # 450
Boca Raton, FL 33487
Tel: (800) 275-1235 (561) 994-6226
Fax: (561) 994-2778

E-Mail: franchisesales@tutortime.com
Web Site: www.tutortime.com
Mr. Dennis G. Fuller, SVP Franchise Dev.

Our child care learning centers are serving children from the ages of 6 weeks to 5 years old. Our colorful state-of-the-art 10,000 square foot centers feature TUTOR TOWNE, a miniature play village, as well as computer labs, learning centers, innovative curriculum, high tech security systems, playgrounds and information management systems. No experience in child care or education is required. We are seeking franchisees domestically and internationally.

Background:

Established: 1980;	1st Franchised: 1990
Franchised Units:	127
Company-Owned Units:	67
Total Units:	194
Minority-Owned Units:	
African-American:	11
Asian-American:	5
Hispanic:	10
Native American:	0
North America:	28 States, 1 Province
Density:	23 in FL, 21 in CA, 19 in NY

Financial/Terms:

Cash Investment:	$100K
Total Investment:	$200-250K
Minimum Net Worth:	$300K+
Fees: Franchise —	$50K
Royalty — 6%;	Ad. — 1.25%
Earnings Claim Statement:	No
Term of Contract (Years):	10/10
Avg. # Of Employees:	12 FT, 10 PT
Passive Ownership:	Allowed
Area Develop. Agreements:	No
Sub-Franchising Contracts:	No
Expand In Territory:	Yes
Space Needs: 10,000 SF; FS, SC	

Support & Training Provided:

Site Selection Assistance:	Yes
Lease Negotiation Assistance:	Yes
Co-Operative Advertising:	Yes
Franchisee Assoc./Member:	Yes/Yes
Size Of Corporate Staff:	102
On-Going Support:	A,B,C,D,E,G,h,I

Training: 1 Week Headquarters; 2 Weeks On-Site; 2 Weeks Franchisee's Location
Minority-Specific Programs: Although we support the objectives of the NMFI, we do not have any specific programs in place at this time.

Specific Expansion Plans:

US:	All United States

WONDERS OF WISDOM CHILDREN'S CENTERS

3114 Golansky Blvd., # 201
Prince William, VA 22192-4200
Tel: (800) 424-0550 (703) 670-9344
Fax: (703) 670-2851
E-Mail: pandahq@erols.com
Web Site: www.wondersofwisdom.com
Ms. Domini Anderson, Director of Sales

WONDERS OF WISDOM is a child care center franchise offering a 4-year initial term contract. Our emphasis is on franchise training and staff training to meet the demands of the children you serve. Our curriculum is based on brain development and is the cutting edge in child development.

Background:

Established: 1989;	1st Franchised: 1991
Franchised Units:	3
Company-Owned Units:	2
Total Units:	5
Minority-Owned Units:	
African-American:	1
Asian-American:	
Hispanic:	
Native American:	
Other:	1 Arabic
North America:	3 States
Density:	4 in VA

Financial/Terms:

Cash Investment:	$40K
Total Investment:	$120K+
Minimum Net Worth:	$200K
Fees: Franchise —	$20K
Royalty — 6%;	Ad. — 0%
Earnings Claim Statement:	No
Term of Contract (Years):	4/2
Avg. # Of Employees:	Varies
Passive Ownership:	Discouraged
Area Develop. Agreements:	Yes/4
Sub-Franchising Contracts:	No
Expand In Territory:	Yes
Space Needs: 5,000 SF; FS, SC, HB	

Support & Training Provided:

Site Selection Assistance:	Yes
Lease Negotiation Assistance:	Yes
Co-Operative Advertising:	Yes
Franchisee Assoc./Member:	Yes/Yes
Size Of Corporate Staff:	6
On-Going Support:	C,D,E,F,G,H,I

Training: 1 Week Home Office; 1 Week Franchisee Center.
Minority-Specific Programs: We would help a minority the same as any other prospect. We do everything to ensure each franchisee is successful.

Specific Expansion Plans:

US:	East Coast

Education/personal development/training

Chapter 17

AMRON SCHOOL OF THE FINE ARTS

1315 Medlin Rd.
Monroe, NC 28112
Tel: (704) 283-4290
Fax: (704) 283-7290
E-Mail:
Web Site:
Ms. Norma W. Williams, President/CEO

(Educational) Teach modeling, acting, cosmetics and photography for portfolios. Agency to get clients jobs in acting and modeling.

Background:
Established: 1979;   1st Franchised: 1986
Franchised Units: 0
Company-Owned Units: 1
Total Units: 1
Minority-Owned Units:
   African-American: 0
   Asian-American: 0
   Hispanic: 0
   Native American: 0
   Other:
North America: 1 State
Density: 1 in NC

Financial/Terms:
Cash Investment: $15K
Total Investment: $Approx. 20K
Minimum Net Worth: $20K
Fees: Franchise — $15K
   Royalty — Sliding Scale;   Ad. — 1%
Earnings Claim Statement: Yes
Term of Contract (Years):   5/5
Avg. # Of Employees: 2 PT
Passive Ownership: Allowed
Area Develop. Agreements: No
Sub-Franchising Contracts: No

Expand In Territory: Yes
Space Needs: NR SF; FS, SF, SC, RM, HB

Support & Training Provided:
Site Selection Assistance: N/A
Lease Negotiation Assistance: N/A
Co-Operative Advertising: N/A
Franchisee Assoc./Member: No
Size Of Corporate Staff: 2
On-Going Support: A,B,D,d,E,F,G,H,h
Training: 1 Week at Home Office in Monroe, NC.
Minority-Specific Programs: Although we support the objectives of the NMFI, we do not have any specific programs in place at this time.

Specific Expansion Plans:
US: All United States

BOSTON BARTENDERS SCHOOL ASSOCIATES

P. O. Box 176
Wilbraham, MA 01095
Tel: (800) 357-3210 (413) 596-4600
Fax: (413) 596-4631
Mr. William Green, CEO

BBS offers a 35-hour course in Mixology and alcohol awareness to men and women ages 18 and up. College students, people in-between or changing jobs or those moving to a new area will be interested in a job bartending. It's easy, fun, quick and affordable. The program takes one or two weeks of evenings to complete. The program costs $400-600, paid up front.

Background:
Established: 1968;   1st Franchised: 1995

Franchised Units: 3
Company-Owned Units: 6
Total Units: 9
Minority-Owned Units:
   African-American: 0
   Asian-American: 0
   Hispanic: 0
   Native American: 0
North America: NR
Density: 4 in MA, 2 in CT, 2 in RI

Financial/Terms:
Cash Investment: $30K
Total Investment: $30K
Minimum Net Worth: $50K
Fees: Franchise — $6.9K
   Royalty — 10%;   Ad. — NR
Earnings Claim Statement: No
Term of Contract (Years):   10/10
Avg. # Of Employees: 2 FT, 1 PT
Passive Ownership: Discouraged
Area Develop. Agreements: No
Sub-Franchising Contracts: No
Expand In Territory: Yes
Space Needs: 1,000 SF; N/A

Support & Training Provided:
Site Selection Assistance: Yes
Lease Negotiation Assistance: Yes
Co-Operative Advertising: N/A
Franchisee Assoc./Member: No
Size Of Corporate Staff: 2
On-Going Support: A,E,F,H,I
Training: 2 Weeks in Springfield, MA.
Minority-Specific Programs: Although we support the objectives of the NMFI, we do not have any specific programs in place at this time.

Specific Expansion Plans:
US: All United States

CITIZENS AGAINST CRIME

2001 N. Collins, # 107
Richardson, TX 75080
Tel: (800) 466-1010 (972) 578-2287
Fax: (972) 509-0054
E-Mail: jerry@trainingexperience.com
Web Site: www.trainingexperience.com
Mr. Jerry Aris, Chief Executive Officer

CITIZENS AGAINST CRIME, INC. has reached over 6 million people with its premier safety education seminars and safety products. Their international safety education and products franchise has been in business since 1980. CAC has taught people how to avoid becoming victims of crime. Their dynamic educational programs have received acclaim from businesses, schools, hospitals and other organizations across the country.

Background:
Established: 1980;	1st Franchised: 1986
Franchised Units:	25
Company-Owned Units:	1
Total Units:	26
Minority-Owned Units:	
African-American:	
Asian-American:	
Hispanic:	
Native American:	
Other:	60% Owned By Women
North America:	16 States
Density:	TX, FL, VA

Financial/Terms:
Cash Investment:	$6K
Total Investment:	$12.5-25K
Minimum Net Worth:	$20K
Fees: Franchise —	$6-12.5K
Royalty — 0%;	Ad. — 3-6%
Earnings Claim Statement:	Yes
Term of Contract (Years):	10/10
Avg. # Of Employees:	1-5 FT
Passive Ownership:	Allowed
Area Develop. Agreements:	No
Sub-Franchising Contracts:	No
Expand In Territory:	No
Space Needs: N/A SF; HB, Office Space	

Support & Training Provided:
Site Selection Assistance:	Yes
Lease Negotiation Assistance:	Yes
Co-Operative Advertising:	No
Franchisee Assoc./Member:	No
Size Of Corporate Staff:	4
On-Going Support:	A,C,D,E,F,G,H,I
Training: 1 Week in Dallas, TX; 1 Week In Franchise.	

Minority-Specific Programs: Assist in recruiting, on-going training and partial financing.

Specific Expansion Plans:
US:	All United States

CPR SERVICES

22 Stoneybrook Dr.
Ashland, MA 01721
Tel: (800) 547-5107 (508) 881-5107
Fax: (508) 881-4718
E-Mail: info@cpr-services.com
Web Site: www.cpr-services.com
Mr. Steven H. Greenberg, Sales Manager

Health education and training for the public and health professionals. Affiliations with the American Heart Association and the National Safety Council.

Background:
Established: 1984;	1st Franchised: 1998
Franchised Units:	0
Company-Owned Units:	1
Total Units:	1
Minority-Owned Units:	
African-American:	
Asian-American:	
Hispanic:	
Native American:	
Other:	
North America:	1 State
Density:	1 in MA

Financial/Terms:
Cash Investment:	$16.9K
Total Investment:	$7.5-16.9K
Minimum Net Worth:	$N/A
Fees: Franchise —	$7.5K
Royalty — $3/Student;	Ad. — N/A
Earnings Claim Statement:	No
Term of Contract (Years):	10
Avg. # Of Employees:	1 FT
Passive Ownership:	Allowed
Area Develop. Agreements:	No
Sub-Franchising Contracts:	No
Expand In Territory:	Yes
Space Needs: NR SF; HB	

Support & Training Provided:
Site Selection Assistance:	No
Lease Negotiation Assistance:	No
Co-Operative Advertising:	Yes
Franchisee Assoc./Member:	No
Size Of Corporate Staff:	4
On-Going Support:	C,d,G,h,I
Training: 4-5 Days in Boston, MA.	

Minority-Specific Programs: Although we support the objectives of the NMFI, we do not have any specific programs in place at this time.

Specific Expansion Plans:
US:	All United States

CRESTCOM INTERNATIONAL, LTD.

6900 E. Belleview Ave.
Englewood, CO 80111
Tel: (888) CRESTCOM (303) 267-8200
Fax: (303) 267-8207
E-Mail:
Web Site: www.crestcom.com
Mr. Kelly Krause, Dir. International Marketing

CRESTCOM is rated the #1 management training company of 1999 by Entrepreneur and other magazines. CRESTCOM uses a unique combination of video instruction and live facilitation to teach management, sales and office personnel. Internationally-renowned business/management training personalities appear on CRESTCOM videos. The company is active in 50 countries and CRESTCOM's materials are translated into 20+ languages.

Background:
Established: 1987;	1st Franchised: 1992
Franchised Units:	117
Company-Owned Units:	0
Total Units:	117
Minority-Owned Units:	
African-American:	
Asian-American:	
Hispanic:	
Native American:	
Other:	
North America:	22 States, 3 Provinces
Density:	NR

Financial/Terms:
Cash Investment:	$35-52.5K
Total Investment:	$44.4-72K
Minimum Net Worth:	$NR

Fees: Franchise — $35-52.5K
   Royalty — 1.5%;   Ad. — N/A
Earnings Claim Statement: Yes
Term of Contract (Years):   7/7/7
Avg. # Of Employees: 2-5 FT
Passive Ownership: Discouraged
Area Develop. Agreements: No
Sub-Franchising Contracts: No
Expand In Territory: Yes
Space Needs: NR SF; SF, HB

Support & Training Provided:
Site Selection Assistance: N/A
Lease Negotiation Assistance: N/A
Co-Operative Advertising: Yes
Franchisee Assoc./Member: No
Size Of Corporate Staff: 15
On-Going Support: D,G,H
Training: 7-10 Days Denver, CO, Phoenix, AZ or Sacramento, CA.
Minority Specific Programs: We advertise in 35 countries each year.

Specific Expansion Plans:
US: All United States

HUNTINGTON LEARNING CENTER

496 Kinderkamack Rd.
Oradell, NJ 07649
Tel: (800) 653-8400 (201) 261-8400
Fax: (201) 261-3233
E-Mail: hlcorp@aol.com
Web Site: www.huntingtonlearning.com
Mr. Richard C. Pittius, VP Franchise

Offers services to 5-19 year-olds, and occasionally to adults, in reading, spelling, phonics, language development study skills and mathematics, as well as programs to prepare for standardized entrance exams. Instruction is offered in a tutorial setting and is predominately remedial in nature, although some enrichment is offered.

Background:
Established: 1977;   1st Franchised: 1985
Franchised Units: 151
Company-Owned Units: 54
Total Units: 205
Minority-Owned Units:
   African-American: 2%
   Asian-American:
   Hispanic:
   Native American:
North America: 31 States
Density: 25 in NY, 19 in NJ, 16 in FL

Financial/Terms:
Cash Investment: $100K
Total Investment: $136.8-188.6K
Minimum Net Worth: $300K
Fees: Franchise — $34K
   Royalty — 8%/$1.2K minimum;Ad. — 2%/$300 Min
Earnings Claim Statement: Yes
Term of Contract (Years):   10/10
Avg. # Of Employees: 2-4 FT
Passive Ownership: Not Allowed
Area Develop. Agreements: Yes
Sub-Franchising Contracts: No
Expand In Territory: No
Space Needs: 2,800 SF; SF, SC, RM

Support & Training Provided:
Site Selection Assistance: Yes
Lease Negotiation Assistance: Yes
Co-Operative Advertising: Yes
Franchisee Assoc./Member: Yes/Yes
Size Of Corporate Staff: 70
On-Going Support: B,C,D,E,F,G,h,I
Training: 2 1/2 Weeks at Oradell, NJ.
Minority-Specific Programs: Although we support the objectives of the NMFI, we do not have any specific programs in place at this time.

Specific Expansion Plans:
US: NW, SW, MW, South

PROFESSIONAL DYNAMETRIC PROGRAMS/PDP

750 E. Hwy. 24, Bldg. I
Woodland Park, CO 80863
Tel: (719) 687-6074
Fax: (719) 687-8587
E-Mail: jimf@pdpnet.com
Web Site: www.pdpnet.com
Mr. Jim Farmer, Executive Vice President

PDP is a business-to-business franchise and offers independence with lucrative opportunity in the executive management market. Sell, train, consult and service large and small businesses in highly-successful and proven programs for hiring, motivating,

stress managing and evaluating. There is automatic, repeat business, low overhead, no inventory and no leases.

Background:
Established: 1978;   1st Franchised: 1980
Franchised Units: 24
Company-Owned Units: 0
Total Units: 24
Minority-Owned Units:
   African-American:
   Asian-American:
   Hispanic:
   Native American:
   Other:
North America: 28 States, 3 Provinces
Density: 4 in TX, 3 in CO, 2 in CA.

Financial/Terms:
Cash Investment: $5K-19.5K
Total Investment: $31.5-49.5K
Minimum Net Worth: $250K
Fees: Franchise — $29.5K
   Royalty — 0%;   Ad. — 0%
Earnings Claim Statement: No
Term of Contract (Years):   7
Avg. # Of Employees: 1 FT
Passive Ownership: Discouraged
Area Develop. Agreements: No
Sub-Franchising Contracts: Yes
Expand In Territory: Yes
Space Needs: N/A SF; HB, ES, OB

Support & Training Provided:
Site Selection Assistance: N/A
Lease Negotiation Assistance: N/A
Co-Operative Advertising: N/A
Franchisee Assoc./Member: No
Size Of Corporate Staff: 5
On-Going Support: c,d,F,G,h,i,
Training: 1 Week Corporate; 2 Days Field; 3 Days Corporate.
Minority Specific Programs: Although we support the objectives of the NMFI, we do not have any specific programs in place at this time.

Specific Expansion Plans:
US: All United States

SYLVAN LEARNING CENTERS

1000 Lancaster St.
Baltimore, MD 21202
Tel: (800) 284-8214 (410) 843-8000
Fax: (410) 843-8717

E-Mail: irene.vavas@educate.com
Web Site: www.educate.com
Ms. Flo Schell, VP Franchise System Dev.

SYLVAN is the leading provider of educational services to families, schools and industry. It provides computer-based testing services internationally for academic admissions, professional licensure and certification programs. SYLVAN services kindergarten through adult-levels from more than 800 SYLVAN LEARNING CENTERS worldwide.

Background:
Established: 1979;	1st Franchised: 1980
Franchised Units:	720
Company-Owned Units:	80
Total Units:	800

Minority-Owned Units:
African-American:	5
Asian-American:	6
Hispanic:	2
Native American:	1
Other:	12
North America:	50 States
Density:	CA, TX, NY

Financial/Terms:
Cash Investment:	$82-117K
Total Investment:	$92-165K
Minimum Net Worth:	$N/A
Fees: Franchise —	$38-46K
Royalty — 8-9%;	Ad. — 1.5%
Earnings Claim Statement:	Yes
Term of Contract (Years):	10/10
Avg. # Of Employees:	2 FT, 5 PT
Passive Ownership:	Not Allowed
Area Develop. Agreements:	Yes/Varies
Sub-Franchising Contracts:	No
Expand In Territory:	Yes
Space Needs: 2,400-3,200 SF; FS, SF, SC	

Support & Training Provided:
Site Selection Assistance:	Yes
Lease Negotiation Assistance:	No
Co-Operative Advertising:	Yes
Franchisee Assoc./Member:	Yes
Size Of Corporate Staff:	500
On-Going Support:	B,C,D,E,G,H,I

Training: 6 Days Baltimore, MD; 5 Days in Various Other Locations.
Minority-Specific Programs: We support the overall objectives of the Initiative and provide a very high level of support to both franchise candidates and franchise owners.

Specific Expansion Plans:
US:	All United States

TRAINAMERICA COMPUTER LEARNING CENTER
4083 Main St.
Bridgeport, CT 06606-2347
Tel: (203) 372-4836
Fax: (203) 372-4853
E-Mail: franchise@trainamerica.net
Web Site: www.trainamerica.net
Mr. R. A. Swift, President

Computer training and related services.

Background:
Established: 1992;	1st Franchised: 1999
Franchised Units:	0
Company-Owned Units:	1
Total Units:	1

Minority-Owned Units:
African-American:	0
Asian-American:	0
Hispanic:	0
Native American:	0
North America:	1 State
Density:	1 in CT

Financial/Terms:
Cash Investment:	$75K
Total Investment:	$75-120K
Minimum Net Worth:	$100K
Fees: Franchise —	$25K
Royalty — 5%;	Ad. — 3%
Earnings Claim Statement:	No
Term of Contract (Years):	20/10
Avg. # Of Employees:	N/A
Passive Ownership:	Allowed
Area Develop. Agreements:	No
Sub-Franchising Contracts:	No
Expand In Territory:	Yes
Space Needs: N/A SF; N/A	

Support & Training Provided:
Site Selection Assistance:	Yes
Lease Negotiation Assistance:	Yes
Co-Operative Advertising:	Yes
Franchisee Assoc./Member:	No
Size Of Corporate Staff:	6
On-Going Support:	c,d,E,F,G

Training: 2 Weeks Bridgport, CT.
Minority-Specific Programs: Deferment of franchise fees; loan documentation preparation; financing; training.

Specific Expansion Plans:
US:	All United States

Dunhill.
Staffing Systems, Inc.

DUNHILL STAFFING SYSTEMS, INC.

150 Motor Pkwy.
Hauppauge, NY 11788
Tel: (800) 386-7823 (613) 952-3000
Fax: (613) 952-3500
E-Mail: jn@Dunhillstaff.com
Web Site: www.dunhillstaff.com
Ms. Joanne Naccarato, Director, New Business Devel.

DUNHILL offers Professional Search and Temporary Staffing franchises. Our franchisees provide permanent executives, mid-level management, professionals, technical staffing and temporaries. Professional search franchisees benefit from the industry's best interview-to-placement ratio and leading edge computerized placement matching system. All DUNHILL executives have 'front line' industry experience.

Background:

Established: 1952;	1st Franchised: 1961
Franchised Units:	125
Company-Owned Units:	30
Total Units:	155
Minority-Owned Units:	
African-American:	
Asian-American:	
Hispanic:	
Native American:	
North America:	50
Density:	9 in IN, 2 in TX, 2 in CT

Financial/Terms:

Cash Investment:	$15-38K
Total Investment:	$70-140K
Minimum Net Worth:	$200K
Fees: Franchise —	$15-38K
Royalty — 7% Perm./Varies;Ad. — 1% Perm.	
Earnings Claim Statement:	No
Term of Contract (Years):	10/10
Avg. # Of Employees:	2-3 FT
Passive Ownership:	Discouraged
Area Develop. Agreements:	No
Sub-Franchising Contracts:	No
Expand In Territory:	Yes
Space Needs: 700-1,500 SF; FS, SF, SC, RM, Suites	

Support & Training Provided:

Site Selection Assistance:	Yes
Lease Negotiation Assistance:	Yes
Co-Operative Advertising:	Yes
Franchisee Assoc./Member:	Yes
Size Of Corporate Staff:	45
On-Going Support:	A,B,C,D,E,G,h,I

Training: 1-2 Weeks Corporate; 2 Weeks Field.
Minority-Specific Programs: Although Dunhill doesn't presently have any specific programs in place, we are very enthusiastic about the inclusion of more minority owners amongst our family of companies. We don't have any minority group in excess of 50%.

Specific Expansion Plans:

US:	All United States

EXPRESS PERSONNEL SERVICES

6300 Northwest Expy.
Oklahoma City, OK 73132
Tel: (877) 652-6400 (405) 840-5000
Fax: (405) 773-6442
E-Mail:
Web Site: www.expresspersonnel.com
Mr. C. Thomas Gunderson, Vice President Franchising

Three divisions - permanent placement, temporary placement and executive search - offering full and complete coverage of the employment field.

Background:

Established: 1983;	1st Franchised: 1985
Franchised Units:	404
Company-Owned Units:	0
Total Units:	404
Minority-Owned Units:	
African-American:	5
Asian-American:	0
Hispanic:	2
Native American:	0
Other:	4
North America:	45 States
Density:	48 in TX, 32 in OK, 24 in WA

Financial/Terms:

Cash Investment:	$90-120K
Total Investment:	$100-150K
Minimum Net Worth:	$150K
Fees: Franchise —	$14.5-17.5K
Royalty — 6-9%;	Ad. — 0.6-2%
Earnings Claim Statement:	No
Term of Contract (Years):	5/5
Avg. # Of Employees:	2 FT, 1 PT
Passive Ownership:	Not Allowed
Area Develop. Agreements:	No

Sub-Franchising Contracts: No
Expand In Territory: Yes
Space Needs: 1,200 SF; SC, RM, SF

Support & Training Provided:

Site Selection Assistance: Yes
Lease Negotiation Assistance: Yes
Co-Operative Advertising: Yes
Franchisee Assoc./Member: No
Size Of Corporate Staff: 175
On-Going Support: A,C,D,E,G,H,I
Training: 3 Weeks Oklahoma City, OK; 1 Week On-Site.

Minority-Specific Programs: Although we support the objectives of the NMFI, we do not have any specific programs in place at this time.

Specific Expansion Plans:

US: All United States

F-O-R-T-U-N-E PERSONNEL CONSULTANTS

1155 Avenue of the Americas, 15th Floor
New York, NY 10036
Tel: (800) 886-7839 (212) 302-1141
Fax: (212) 302-2422
E-Mail: rich@pfcfind.com
Web Site: www.fpcweb.com
Mr. Richard A. Simeone, Dir. Franchise Development

As one of the largest and most successful executive recruiting firms in the world, F-O-R-T-U-N-E PERSONNEL CONSULTANTS has set a distinguished standard of leadership and integrity in the executive placement industry. Franchisees enjoy all of today's technologies, along with good old-fashioned service. Intensive training and unparalleled support by industry experienced professionals securely places qualified candidates in their own professional business. Extensive on-going training.

Background:

Established: 1959; 1st Franchised: 1973
Franchised Units: 100
Company-Owned Units: 1
Total Units: 101
Minority-Owned Units:
 African-American: 1
 Asian-American: 1
 Hispanic:
 Native American:
North America: 28 States
Density: 7 in FL, 7 in MA, 7 in NJ

Financial/Terms:

Cash Investment: $32.4-67.5K
Total Investment: $72.4-107.5K
Minimum Net Worth: $250K
Fees: Franchise — $40K
 Royalty — 7%; Ad. — 1%
Earnings Claim Statement: No
Term of Contract (Years): 20/5
Avg. # Of Employees: 3-5 FT, 1-2 PT
Passive Ownership: Discouraged
Area Develop. Agreements: No
Sub-Franchising Contracts: No
Expand In Territory: Yes
Space Needs: 1,000 SF; Commercial Office Space

Support & Training Provided:

Site Selection Assistance: Yes
Lease Negotiation Assistance: Yes
Co-Operative Advertising: Yes
Franchisee Assoc./Member: Yes
Size Of Corporate Staff: 15
On-Going Support: A,B,C,D,E,F,G,H,I
Training: 2 Weeks Home Office, NY, NY: 5 Days Franchise Location.

Minority-Specific Programs: Although we support the objectives of the NMFI, we do not have any specific programs in place at this time.

Specific Expansion Plans:

US: All United States

HOME HELPERS

4010 Executive Park Dr., # 100
Cincinnati, OH 45241
Tel: (800) 216-4196 (513) 563-8339
Fax: (513) 563-2691
E-Mail: jbuckles@fuse.net
Web Site: www.homehelpers1.com
Ms. Julie Massey,

As America's population continues to age, there is a huge demand for non-medical, in-home companion care. There are over 33 million people in the US over 65 years old. Our franchise system is unique. At HOME HELPERS we provide non-medical, in-home companion care for the elderly, new mothers and those recuperating from illness. Our franchisees succeed due to our marketing expertise, market penetration and proven system. No experience or medical background needed.

Background:

Established: 1997; 1st Franchised: 1997
Franchised Units: 67
Company-Owned Units: 1
Total Units: 68
Minority-Owned Units:
 African-American: 10
 Asian-American: 0
 Hispanic: 0
 Native American: 0
 Other: 7
North America: 28 States
Density: NR

Financial/Terms:

Cash Investment: $7.5-11.5K
Total Investment: $19-39K
Minimum Net Worth: $N/A
Fees: Franchise — $13.9-23.9K
 Royalty — 4-7% Varies; Ad. — 3% Local
Earnings Claim Statement: No
Term of Contract (Years): 10/10/10
Avg. # Of Employees: N/A
Passive Ownership: Discouraged
Area Develop. Agreements: No
Sub-Franchising Contracts: No
Expand In Territory: N/A
Space Needs: N/A SF; HB

Support & Training Provided:

Site Selection Assistance: N/A
Lease Negotiation Assistance: N/A
Co-Operative Advertising: N/A
Franchisee Assoc./Member: No
Size Of Corporate Staff: 9
On-Going Support: B,C,D,G,H,I
Training: 5 Days Cincinnati, OH.

Minority-Specific Programs: Although we support the objectives of the NMFI, we do not have any specific programs in place at this time.

Specific Expansion Plans:

US: All United States

INITIAL STAFFING SERVICES

9703 Richmond Ave.
Houston, TX 77042
Tel: (800) 827-8733 (713) 789-1818
Fax: (713) 974-6507
E-Mail: judybishop@initial-staffing.com
Web Site: www.initial-staffing.com
Ms. Judy Bishop, VP Franchise Division

Initial

Talent Tree Staffing

Formerly Talent Tree Staffing Services. Full-service temporary, permanent and 'temp-to-hire' staffing franchise. We pioneered the on-site management concept and have expertise in placement of clerical, administrative, technical support and light industrial staff.

Background:

Established: 1976;	1st Franchised: 1991
Franchised Units:	15
Company-Owned Units:	<u>165</u>
Total Units:	180

Minority-Owned Units:
African-American:
Asian-American:
Hispanic:
Native American:
Other:

North America:	30 States
Density:	6 in GA, 3 in FL, 2 in TX

Financial/Terms:

Cash Investment:	$100-150K
Total Investment:	$120-170K
Minimum Net Worth:	$150-250K
Fees: Franchise —	$20K
Royalty — Scaled;	Ad. — 0
Earnings Claim Statement:	No
Term of Contract (Years):	5/5/5/5
Avg. # Of Employees:	4 FT, 1 PT
Passive Ownership:	Allowed
Area Develop. Agreements:	Yes
Sub-Franchising Contracts:	No
Expand In Territory:	Yes
Space Needs: 1,000 SF; Office Center	

Support & Training Provided:

Site Selection Assistance:	Yes
Lease Negotiation Assistance:	Yes
Co-Operative Advertising:	No
Franchisee Assoc./Member:	Yes/No
Size Of Corporate Staff:	110
On-Going Support:	A,B,C,D,E,G,h,I
Training: 3-4 Weeks in Houston, TX.	

Minority-Specific Programs: Although we support the objectives of the NMFI, we do not have any specific programs in place at this time.

Specific Expansion Plans:

US:	All United States

LABOR FINDERS INTERNATIONAL

3910 RCA Blvd., # 1001
Palm Beach Gardens, FL 33410
Tel: (800) 864-7749 (561) 627-6507
Fax: (561) 627-6556
E Mail: lfi@laborfinders.com
Web Site: www.laborfinders.com
Mr. Robert R. Gallagher, Vice President Marketing

LABOR FINDERS is a specialized labor staffing service that supplies highly productive skilled, semi-skilled and unskilled workers to companies in construction, industrial and commercial business segments.

Background:

Established: 1975;	1st Franchised: 1975
Franchised Units:	137
Company-Owned Units:	<u>4</u>
Total Units:	141

Minority-Owned Units:

African-American:	0
Asian-American:	0
Hispanic:	2.4%
Native American:	0
Other:	1%
North America:	23 States
Density:	41 in FL, 8 in AL, 1 in NC

Financial/Terms:

Cash Investment:	$45-75K
Total Investment:	$66.8-110.5K
Minimum Net Worth:	$500K
Fees: Franchise —	$10K
Royalty — % Billable Wages;	Ad. — 0%
Earnings Claim Statement:	No
Term of Contract (Years):	10/5/5
Avg. # Of Employees:	2 FT, 1 PT
Passive Ownership:	Discouraged
Area Develop. Agreements:	No
Sub-Franchising Contracts:	No
Expand In Territory:	Yes
Space Needs: 800-1,000 SF; FS, SF, SC	

Support & Training Provided:

Site Selection Assistance:	Yes
Lease Negotiation Assistance:	No
Co-Operative Advertising:	Yes
Franchisee Assoc./Member:	Yes/Yes
Size Of Corporate Staff:	15
On-Going Support:	C,D,E,G,h,I
Training: 2 Weeks Operating Unit, 2 Weeks	

On-Site, 1 Week Classroom.
Minority-Specific Programs: Although we support the objectives of the NMFI, we do not have any specific programs in place at this time.

Specific Expansion Plans:

US:	All United States

LAWCORPS LEGAL STAFFING

1819 L St., NW, 9th Fl.
Washington, DC 20036
Tel: (800) 437-8809 (202) 785-5996
Fax: (202) 785-1118
E-Mail:
Web Site: www.lawcorps.com
Mr. Bryce A. Arrowood, President

Temporary legal staffing: attorneys, law clerks, paralegals and support staff. LAWCORPS Franchise Corporation is the first and only exclusively legal temporary service to franchise. Join the fastest-growing segment of the fastest-growing industry.

Background:

Established: 1988;	1st Franchised: 1995
Franchised Units:	3
Company-Owned Units:	<u>4</u>
Total Units:	7

Minority-Owned Units:
African-American:
Asian-American:
Hispanic:
Native American:
Other:

North America:	NR
Density:	DC, NY, IL

Financial/Terms:

Cash Investment:	$88-110K
Total Investment:	$88-110K
Minimum Net Worth:	$N/A
Fees: Franchise —	$25K
Royalty — 8%;	Ad. — N/A
Earnings Claim Statement:	No
Term of Contract (Years):	7/7
Avg. # Of Employees:	2 FT, 1 PT
Passive Ownership:	Discouraged
Area Develop. Agreements:	No
Sub-Franchising Contracts:	No

Expand In Territory: No
Space Needs: 200-500 SF; Executive Suite

Support & Training Provided:
Site Selection Assistance: Yes
Lease Negotiation Assistance: No
Co-Operative Advertising: Yes
Franchisee Assoc./Member: No
Size Of Corporate Staff: 5
On-Going Support: a,b,C,D,E,g,H,I
Training: 2 Weeks Headquarters; 1 Week On-Site.
Minority-Specific Programs: Although we support the objectives of the NMFI, we do not have any specific programs in place at this time.

Specific Expansion Plans:
US: All United States

LINK STAFFING SERVICES
1800 Bering Dr., # 800
Houston, TX 77057-3129
Tel: (800) 848-5465 (713) 784-4400
Fax: (713) 784-4454
E-Mail: fran_dev@linkstaffing.com
Web Site: www.linkstaffing.com
Ms. Lana Peralta, Franchise Development Manager

In the staffing industry for 20 years, LINK is a temporary, temporary-to-hire personnel service emphasizing crafts and trades as well as general industrial labor placements. Link also serves as a full-service provider to its clients by offering Permanent recruiting, PEO opportunities, a call center division and productivity evaluation programs. We provide payroll funding, billing, accounts receivable processing, credit services and collections assistance.

Background:
Established: 1980; 1st Franchised: 1993
Franchised Units: 29
Company-Owned Units: 16
Total Units: 45
Minority-Owned Units:
  African-American: 2

Asian-American: 0
Hispanic: 3
Native American: 0
Other:
North America: 49 States
Density: 15 in TX, 10 in FL, 5 in CA

Financial/Terms:
Cash Investment: $25-35K
Total Investment: $95-159K
Minimum Net Worth: $N/A
Fees: Franchise — $15K
  Royalty — Varies; Ad. — 0.05%
Earnings Claim Statement: No
Term of Contract (Years): 10/5/5/5
Avg. # Of Employees: 2 FT
Passive Ownership: Discouraged
Area Develop. Agreements: No
Sub-Franchising Contracts: No
Expand In Territory: Yes
Space Needs: 1,200-1,800 SF; SF, SC, Industrial Office Park

Support & Training Provided:
Site Selection Assistance: Yes
Lease Negotiation Assistance: Yes
Co-Operative Advertising: Yes
Franchisee Assoc./Member: Yes/Yes
Size Of Corporate Staff: 42
On-Going Support: A,B,C,D,E,G,H,I
Training: 3-5 Days Existing Franchise; 5 Days (Sales), 5 Days (Operations) Support Center, TX.
Minority-Specific Programs: Although we support the objectives of the NMFI, we do not have any specific programs in place at this time.

Specific Expansion Plans:
US: All United States

MANAGEMENT RECRUITERS/ SALES CONSULTANTS
200 Public Sq., 31st Fl.
Cleveland, OH 44114-2301
Tel: (800) 875-4000 (216) 696-1122
Fax: (216) 696-6612
E-Mail: webmaster@brilliantpeople.com
Web Site: www.brilliantpeople.com
Mr. Robert A. Angell, VP Franchise Marketing

Complete range of recruitment and human resource services, including: permanent executive, mid-management, professional, marketing, sales management and sales

placement; temporary professional and sales staffing; video-conferencing; permanent and temporary office support personnel; with coverage on all continents. Franchises available ourside of North America through our wholly-owned subsidiary, the Humana Group International.

Background:
Established: 1957; 1st Franchised: 1965
Franchised Units: 791
Company-Owned Units: 39
Total Units: 830
Minority-Owned Units:
  African-American: 15
  Asian-American: 4
  Hispanic: 10
  Native American: 0
  Other:
North America: 48 States
Density: 64 in FL, 62 in CA,60 in NC

Financial/Terms:
Cash Investment: $110-145K
Total Investment: $110-145K
Minimum Net Worth: $N/A
Fees: Franchise — $72.5K
  Royalty — 7%; Ad. — 0.5%
Earnings Claim Statement: Yes
Term of Contract (Years): 5-20/10
Avg. # Of Employees: 3-4 FT
Passive Ownership: Discouraged
Area Develop. Agreements: No
Sub-Franchising Contracts: No
Expand In Territory: Yes
Space Needs: 600-1,000 SF; FS

Support & Training Provided:
Site Selection Assistance: Yes
Lease Negotiation Assistance: Yes
Co-Operative Advertising: N/A
Franchisee Assoc./Member: Yes
Size Of Corporate Staff: 91
On-Going Support: C,D,E,G,H,I
Training: 3 Weeks Headquarters, Cleveland, OH; 10 Days Franchisee's Location.
Minority-Specific Programs: Although we support the objectives of the NMFI, we do not have any specific programs in place at this time.

Specific Expansion Plans:
US: All United States

PMA FRANCHISE SYSTEMS
1950 Spectrum Circle, #B-310
Marietta, GA 30067
Tel: (800) 466-7822 (770) 916-1668
Fax: (770) 916-1429
E-Mail: jobs@pmasearch.com

Web Site: www.pmascarch.com
Mr. Bill Lins, CPC Director of Operations

National employment firm specializing in retail, restaurant and service management.

Background:

Established: 19NR;	1st Franchised: 1997
Franchised Units:	3
Company-Owned Units:	1
Total Units:	4
Minority-Owned Units:	
African-American:	
Asian-American:	
Hispanic:	
Native American:	
North America:	4 States
Density:	1 in OR, 1 in OK, 1 in GA

Financial/Terms:

Cash Investment:	$20K
Total Investment:	$30-40K
Minimum Net Worth:	$N/A
Fees: Franchise —	$20K
Royalty — 10%;	Ad. — 0%
Earnings Claim Statement:	
Term of Contract (Years):	5/5
Avg. # Of Employees:	2 FT
Passive Ownership:	Not Allowed
Area Develop. Agreements:	Yes/Varies
Sub-Franchising Contracts:	NR
Expand In Territory:	Yes
Space Needs: 150+ SF; NR	

Support & Training Provided:

Site Selection Assistance:	Yes
Lease Negotiation Assistance:	No
Co-Operative Advertising:	Yes
Franchisee Assoc./Member:	Yes/Yes
Size Of Corporate Staff:	12
On-Going Support:	A,C,E,G,h,I

Training: 4 Weeks Atlanta, GA.
Minority-Specific Programs: Although we support the objectives of the NMFI, we do not have any specific programs in place at this time.

Specific Expansion Plans:

US:	All United States

PRIDESTAFF

6780 N. West Ave., # 103
Fresno, CA 93711-1393
Tel: (800) 774-3316 (559) 432-7780
Fax: (559) 432-4371
E-Mail: rbladek@pridestaff.com
Web Site: www.pridestaff.com
Mr. Robert Bladek, Executive VP

We specialize in supplemental staffing (temporary help), outsourcing and full-time placement. PRIDESTAFF fills administrative, clerical, customer service, data entry, word processing and light industrial positions. The staffing industry is one of the fastest growing industries in the United States.

Background:

Established: 1974;	1st Franchised: 1994
Franchised Units:	26
Company-Owned Units:	8
Total Units:	34
Minority-Owned Units:	
African-American:	0
Asian-American:	0
Hispanic:	0
Native American:	0
Other:	75% Women
North America:	13 States
Density:	12 in CA, 4 in AZ, 4 in IL

Financial/Terms:

Cash Investment:	$75-100K
Total Investment:	$80.4-126.9K
Minimum Net Worth:	$N/A
Fees: Franchise —	$12.5K
Royalty — 65%Gross Margin;Ad. — N/A	
Earnings Claim Statement:	No
Term of Contract (Years):	10/5/5/5
Avg. # Of Employees:	2 FT
Passive Ownership:	Not Allowed
Area Develop. Agreements:	No
Sub-Franchising Contracts:	No
Expand In Territory:	Yes
Space Needs: 1,200 SF; Single story office building	

Support & Training Provided:

Site Selection Assistance:	Yes
Lease Negotiation Assistance:	Yes
Co-Operative Advertising:	N/A
Franchisee Assoc./Member:	No
Size Of Corporate Staff:	16
On-Going Support:	A,C,D,E,G,H,I

Training: 1 Week in Fresno, CA; 1 Week at Branch Office.
Minority-Specific Programs: We place advertisements in various minority publications. No assistance for potential minority franchisees. All franchisees are bound by a standard contract.

Specific Expansion Plans:

US:	All United States

SANFORD ROSE ASSOCIATES

3737 Embassy Dr., # 200
Akron, OH 44333-8369
Tel: (800) 731-7724 (330) 670-9797
Fax: (330) 670-9798
E-Mail: massrai@aol.com
Web Site: www.franchiseSRA.com
Mr. Mark A. Sweeterman, Director Franchise Development

Executive search is distinct within the SRA organization. We provide a highly-reliable service to fill critical openings with our corporate clients. Only the most qualified candidates are presented. Our adaptability allows us to work at virtually all professional levels, developing repeat business.

Background:

Established: 1959;	1st Franchised: 1970
Franchised Units:	53
Company-Owned Units:	0
Total Units:	53
Minority-Owned Units:	
African-American:	
Asian-American:	2
Hispanic:	
Native American:	
North America:	23 States
Density:	7 in OH, 7 in IL, 5 in CA

Financial/Terms:

Cash Investment:	$55-85K
Total Investment:	$55-85K
Minimum Net Worth:	$80K
Fees: Franchise —	$40K
Royalty — 7-3%;	Ad. — 0%
Earnings Claim Statement:	No
Term of Contract (Years):	7/1
Avg. # Of Employees:	10 FT, 1 PT
Passive Ownership:	Not Allowed
Area Develop. Agreements:	No
Sub-Franchising Contracts:	No
Expand In Territory:	No
Space Needs: 300-1,000 SF; Office Building	

Support & Training Provided:

Site Selection Assistance:	Yes
Lease Negotiation Assistance:	Yes
Co-Operative Advertising:	No
Franchisee Assoc./Member:	Yes/Yes
Size Of Corporate Staff:	6
On-Going Support:	C,G,H,I

Training: 10 Days National Headquarters; 5 Days On-Site.

Minority-Specific Programs: Although we support the objectives of the NMFI, we do not have any specific programs in place at this time.

Specific Expansion Plans:

US:	All United States

TECHSTAFF

11270 W. Park Pl., # 460
Milwaukee, WI 53224
Tel: (800) 515-4440 (414) 359-4444
Fax: (414) 359-4949
E-Mail: tom@techstaff.com
Web Site: www.techstaff.com
Mr. Thomas Montgomery, Franchise Director

Full-service employment firm, servicing the engineering and information technology niches. Long-term contract, contract to perm and permanent search. Computerized search and retrieval system. Funding of contract payroll. Marketing assistance, payroll, billing, funding, accounts receivable and all financial statements are provided. Large geographic availability, excellent franchise relations.

Background:

Established: 1985;	1st Franchised: 1987
Franchised Units:	9
Company-Owned Units:	3
Total Units:	12
Minority-Owned Units:	
African-American:	
Asian-American:	
Hispanic:	
Native American:	
Other:	
North America:	NR
Density:	3 in CA, 2 in WI, 2 in MI

Financial/Terms:

Cash Investment:	$75K
Total Investment:	$100-125K
Minimum Net Worth:	$100K
Fees: Franchise —	$25K
Royalty — 6.9-3.9%;	Ad. — N/A
Earnings Claim Statement:	No
Term of Contract (Years):	20/20
Avg. # Of Employees:	6 FT

Passive Ownership: Discouraged

Passive Ownership:	Discouraged
Area Develop. Agreements:	Yes/2-3
Sub-Franchising Contracts:	Yes
Expand In Territory:	Yes
Space Needs: 1,000 SF; SF, Office Building	

Support & Training Provided:

Site Selection Assistance:	Yes
Lease Negotiation Assistance:	Yes
Co-Operative Advertising:	N/A
Franchisee Assoc./Member:	No
Size Of Corporate Staff:	7
On-Going Support:	A,B,C,D,E,G,H

Training: 1 Week per Employee at Corporate Office; 10 Weeks in 1st Year Franchise Office.

Minority-Specific Programs: Although we support the objectives of the NMFI, we do not have any specific programs in place at this time.

Specific Expansion Plans:

US:	All United States

BETWEEN ROUNDS BAGEL DELI & BAKERY

19A John Fitch Blvd.
South Windsor, CT 06074
Tel: (860) 291-0323
Fax: (860) 289-2732
Mr. Jerry Puiia, President

Providing customers with more choices than just bagels, cream cheese and gourmet coffee, BETWEEN ROUNDS sells a wide variety of bakery and deli items, as well as offers extensive catering. BETWEEN ROUNDS BAGEL DELI & BAKERY is your competitive edge in the explosive bagel franchise field because, soon, selling bagels won't be enough!

Background:

Established: 1990;	1st Franchised: 1993
Franchised Units:	5
Company-Owned Units:	2
Total Units:	7
Minority-Owned Units:	
African-American:	
Asian-American:	
Hispanic:	
Native American:	
Other:	
North America:	3 States
Density:	4 in CT, 2 in MA, 1 in WV

Financial/Terms:

Cash Investment:	$50-80K
Total Investment:	$160-210K
Minimum Net Worth:	$100K
Fees: Franchise —	$18K
Royalty — 4%;	Ad. — 2%
Earnings Claim Statement:	Yes
Term of Contract (Years):	10/15
Avg. # Of Employees:	3 FT, 5 PT
Passive Ownership:	Discouraged
Area Develop. Agreements:	Yes
Sub-Franchising Contracts:	No
Expand In Territory:	Yes
Space Needs: 1,600 SF; SC	

Support & Training Provided:

Site Selection Assistance:	Yes
Lease Negotiation Assistance:	Yes
Co-Operative Advertising:	Yes
Franchisee Assoc./Member:	No
Size Of Corporate Staff:	3
On-Going Support:	a,C,D,E,F,G

Training: 2 Weeks Company Stores in CT; 1-2 Weeks Own Unit.
Minority Specific Programs: Although we support the objectives of the NMFI, we do not have any specific programs in place at this time.

Specific Expansion Plans:

US:	Mid-Atlantic and Northeast

BIG APPLE BAGELS

8501 W. Higgins Rd., # 320
Chicago, IL 60631
Tel: (800) 251-6101 (773) 380-6100
Fax: (773) 380-6183
E-Mail: hmarks@babholdings.com
Web Site: www.babholdings.com
Mr. Howard B. Marks, Dir. Franchise Development

Specialty bagel café, featuring fresh-from-scratch, proprietary recipes for bagels, cream cheeses, muffins and gourmet coffees. Our franchisees enjoy offering three of the hottest selling consumer concepts all under one roof. In addition, our franchise owners enjoy the right to develop "outside" wholesale business within their market.

Background:

Established: 1992;	1st Franchised: 1993
Franchised Units:	268
Company-Owned Units:	22
Total Units:	290
Minority-Owned Units:	
African-American:	
Asian-American:	
Hispanic:	
Native American:	
Other:	
North America:	32 States, 2 Provinces
Density:	48 in IL, 28 in NJ, 27 in WI

Financial/Terms:

Cash Investment:	$50K Minimum
Total Investment:	$250-300K
Minimum Net Worth:	$300K
Fees: Franchise —	$25K
Royalty — 5%;	Ad. — 2%
Earnings Claim Statement:	No

Term of Contract (Years):	10/Varies
Avg. # Of Employees:	2 FT, 10 PT
Passive Ownership:	Discouraged
Area Develop. Agreements:	Yes/Varies
Sub-Franchising Contracts:	No
Expand In Territory:	Yes
Space Needs: 500-2,000 SF; FS, SF, SC, RM	

Support & Training Provided:

Site Selection Assistance:	Yes
Lease Negotiation Assistance:	Yes
Co-Operative Advertising:	No
Franchisee Assoc./Member:	Yes/No
Size Of Corporate Staff:	34
On-Going Support:	B,C,D,E,F,G,H,I

Training: 2 Weeks Milwaukee, WI; Store Location 5 Days Prior to Opening

Minority-Specific Programs: Although we support the objectives of the NMFI, we do not have any specific programs in place at this time.

Specific Expansion Plans:

US:	All United States

BREADSMITH

418 E. Silver Spring Dr.
Whitefish Bay, WI 53217
Tel: (414) 962-1965
Fax: (414) 962-5888
E-Mail: marcc@breadsmith.com
Web Site: www.breadsmith.com
Mr. Marc L. Cayle, Director of Development

Award-winning, European, hearth-bread bakery, featuring fresh-from-scratch crusty breads, gourmet jams and coffee. Open kitchen concept reveals an eight-ton, stone hearth oven imported from France used to bake the hand-crafted loaves each morning. BREADSMITH has been ranked by Bon Appetit, Best of Philadelphia, Madison, WI, Orange Co., CA, Detroit, MI, Minneapolis, MN, Milwaukee, WI and Cleveland, OH as the best bread store in America.

Background:

Established: 1993;	1st Franchised: 1994
Franchised Units:	50
Company-Owned Units:	3
Total Units:	53

Minority-Owned Units:	
African-American:	
Asian-American:	
Hispanic:	
Native American:	
Other:	
North America:	15 States
Density:	8 in IL, 5 in WI, 4 in MN

Financial/Terms:

Cash Investment:	$200-260K
Total Investment:	$210.5-386K
Minimum Net Worth:	$350K
Fees: Franchise —	$25K
Royalty — 7%;	Ad. — 0%
Earnings Claim Statement:	No
Term of Contract (Years):	15/15
Avg. # Of Employees:	2 FT, 12 PT
Passive Ownership:	Not Allowed
Area Develop. Agreements:	No
Sub-Franchising Contracts:	No
Expand In Territory:	Yes
Space Needs: 1,500 SF; FS, SF, SC	

Support & Training Provided:

Site Selection Assistance:	Yes
Lease Negotiation Assistance:	Yes
Co-Operative Advertising:	No
Franchisee Assoc./Member:	Yes
Size Of Corporate Staff:	10
On-Going Support:	C,D,E,F,G,I

Training: 2 Weeks Corporate Store; 10 Days Franchisee Store.

Minority-Specific Programs: Although we support the objectives of the NMFI, we do not have any specific programs in place at this time.

Specific Expansion Plans:

US:	All United States

COOKIE BOUQUET/COOKIES BY DESIGN

1865 Summit Ave., # 605
Plano, TX 75074
Tel: (800) 945-2665 (972) 398-9536
Fax: (972) 398-9542
E-Mail: frandev@buz.net
Web Site: www.cookiebouquet.com
Mr. David Patterson, VP Franchise Dev.

Unique retail opportunity! Gift bakery, specializing in hand-decorated cookie arrangements and gourmet cookies, decorated for special events, holidays, centerpieces, etc. Clientele include both individual and corporate customers. A wonderfully delicious alternative to flowers or balloons.

Background:

Established: 1983;	1st Franchised: 1987
Franchised Units:	189
Company-Owned Units:	1
Total Units:	190
Minority-Owned Units:	
African-American:	7
Asian-American:	2
Hispanic:	2
Native American:	1
Other:	
North America:	39 States
Density:	27 in TX, 16 in FL, 15 in CA

Financial/Terms:

Cash Investment:	$80-140K
Total Investment:	$80-140K
Minimum Net Worth:	$NR
Fees: Franchise —	$20K
Royalty — 6%;	Ad. — 1%
Earnings Claim Statement:	No
Term of Contract (Years):	5/5
Avg. # Of Employees:	3 FT, 2 PT
Passive Ownership:	Discouraged
Area Develop. Agreements:	Yes
Sub-Franchising Contracts:	No
Expand In Territory:	Yes
Space Needs: 1,200-1,500 SF; SC	

Support & Training Provided:

Site Selection Assistance:	Yes
Lease Negotiation Assistance:	Yes
Co-Operative Advertising:	Yes
Franchisee Assoc./Member:	No
Size Of Corporate Staff:	12
On-Going Support:	C,d,e,G,h,I

Training: 2 Weeks Dallas, TX.

Minority-Specific Programs: Although we support the objectives of the NMFI, we do not have any specific programs in place at this time.

Specific Expansion Plans:

US:	All United States

GREAT AMERICAN COOKIES

2855 E. Cottonwood Pkwy., # 400
Salt Lake City, UT 84121
Tel: (800) 346-6311

Fax: (888) 867-7343
E-Mail: squireji@greatamcookie.com
Web Site: www.greatamericancookies.com
Franchise Development, Franchise
Development Manager

'Share the Fun of Cookies.' Established cookie concept with a great old family recipe, attractive retail price point, unique cookie cake program, available in combination store formats for traditional and non-traditional venues.

Background:
Established: 1977; 1st Franchised: 1977
Franchised Units: 206
Company-Owned Units: 101
Total Units: 307
Minority-Owned Units:
　African-American:
　Asian American:
　Hispanic:
　Native American:
North America: 39 States
Density: 47 in TX, 24 in GA, 24 in FL

Financial/Terms:
Cash Investment: $122-493K
Total Investment: $119.5-501K
Minimum Net Worth: $250K
Fees: Franchise — $25K
　Royalty — 7%; Ad. — N/A
Earnings Claim Statement: No
Term of Contract (Years): NR
Avg. # Of Employees: Varies
Passive Ownership: Allowed
Area Develop. Agreements: No
Sub-Franchising Contracts: No
Expand In Territory: Yes
Space Needs: 625 SF; RM

Support & Training Provided:
Site Selection Assistance: Yes
Lease Negotiation Assistance: Yes
Co-Operative Advertising: N/A
Franchisee Assoc./Member: Yes
Size Of Corporate Staff: 65
On Going Support: B,C,D,E,G,H,I
Training: 6 Days Atlanta, GA.
Minority-Specific Programs: Although we support the objectives of the NMFI, we do not have any specific programs in place at this time.

Specific Expansion Plans:
US: All United States

GREAT HARVEST BREAD CO.
28 S. Montana St.
Dillon, MT 59725-2434
Tel: (800) 442-0424 (406) 683-6842

Fax: (406) 683-5537
E-Mail: inquiry@greatharvest.com
Web Site: www.greatharvest.com
Ms. Lisa Wagner, Director of Franchise Growth

Neighborhood bread bakery, specializing in

whole wheat breads from scratch.

Background:
Established: 1976; 1st Franchised: 1978
Franchised Units: 137
Company-Owned Units: 2
Total Units: 139
Minority-Owned Units:
　African-American:
　Asian-American:
　Hispanic:
　Native American:
　Other:
North America: 35 States
Density: 10 in UT, 8 in OR, 8 in IL

Financial/Terms:
Cash Investment: $80K
Total Investment: $89-234K
Minimum Net Worth: $N/A
Fees: Franchise — $24K
　Royalty — 7/6/5%; Ad. — 0%
Earnings Claim Statement: Yes
Term of Contract (Years): 10
Avg. # Of Employees: 6 FT, 2 PT
Passive Ownership: Not Allowed
Area Develop. Agreements: Yes
Sub-Franchising Contracts: No
Expand In Territory: Yes
Space Needs: 1,800 SF; FS, SC

Support & Training Provided:
Site Selection Assistance: Yes
Lease Negotiation Assistance: Yes
Co-Operative Advertising: Yes
Franchisee Assoc./Member: Yes
Size Of Corporate Staff: 34
On-Going Support: B,C,D,E,G,H,I
Training: 2 Weeks Host Bakeries; 1 Week at Headquarters; 3 Trainers for Opening.
Minority-Specific Programs: Although we support the objectives of the NMFI, we do not have any specific programs in place at this time.

Specific Expansion Plans:
US: All United States, Canada

MMMARVELLOUS MMMUFFINS
16251 Dallas Pkwy.
Dallas, TX 75248
Tel: (972) 687-4091
Fax: (972) 687-4062
E-Mail: lboyd@richmont.com
Web Site: www.mmmuffins.com
Franchising Department,

Fresh, high-quality specialty baked goods including over 100 varieties of muffins as well as scones, cinnamon swirls, cookies and streusel cakes. In addition, we offer a selection of gourmet coffee, teas, and fruit juices.

Background:
Established: 1979; 1st Franchised: 1980
Franchised Units: 93
Company-Owned Units: 9
Total Units: 102
Minority-Owned Units:
　African American:
　Asian-American:
　Hispanic:
　Native American:
　Other:
North America: 8 Provinces
Density: 43 in ON, 26 in PQ, 13 in BC

Financial/Terms:
Cash Investment: $40-60K+
Total Investment: $160K
Minimum Net Worth: $200K
Fees: Franchise — $25K
　Royalty — 7%; Ad. — 1%
Earnings Claim Statement: No
Term of Contract (Years): 10/10
Avg. # Of Employees: 2-3 FT, 4-7 PT
Passive Ownership: Not Allowed
Area Develop. Agreements: Yes/(I'ntl)
Sub-Franchising Contracts: Yes
Expand In Territory: Yes
Space Needs: 300 SF; SF, SC, RM

Support & Training Provided:
Site Selection Assistance: Yes
Lease Negotiation Assistance: Yes
Co-Operative Advertising: Yes
Franchisee Assoc./Member: No
Size Of Corporate Staff: 35
On-Going Support: A,B,C,D,E,F,G,h
Training: 4 Weeks Toronto, ON.

Minority-Specific Programs: Although we support the objectives of the NMFI, we do not have any specific programs in place at this time.

Specific Expansion Plans:

US:	N/A

MRS. FIELDS COOKIES

2855 E. Cottonwood Pkwy., # 400
Salt Lake City, UT 84121
Tel: (800) 348-6311 (801) 736-5600
Fax: (888) 867-7343
E-Mail: timp@mrsfields.com
Web Site: www.mrsfields.com
Franchise Development, Franchise Development Manager

Premier retail cookie business with 'uncompromising quality,' 94% brand recognition, easy to operate, flexible designs and combination store options that operate in traditional and non-traditional venues.

Background:

Established: 1977;	1st Franchised: 1990
Franchised Units:	192
Company-Owned Units:	130
Total Units:	322

Minority-Owned Units:
  African-American:
  Asian-American:
  Hispanic:
  Native American:
  Other:

North America:	35 States, 1 Province
Density:	86 in CA, 27 in IL, 19 in NY

Financial/Terms:

Cash Investment:	$10-73.5K
Total Investment:	$146-245K
Minimum Net Worth:	$75K
Fees: Franchise —	$25K
Royalty — 6%;	Ad. — 0-2%
Earnings Claim Statement:	No
Term of Contract (Years):	7/5/5
Avg. # Of Employees:	3 FT, 4 PT
Passive Ownership:	Not Allowed
Area Develop. Agreements:	Yes
Sub-Franchising Contracts:	No
Expand In Territory:	Yes

Space Needs: 650-800 SF; RM, SC, SF, Stadium

Support & Training Provided:

Site Selection Assistance:	Yes
Lease Negotiation Assistance:	Yes
Co-Operative Advertising:	No
Franchisee Assoc./Member:	Yes/Yes
Size Of Corporate Staff:	60
On-Going Support:	A,B,C,D,E,F,G,H,I

Training: 10 Days Park City, UT; 5-10 Days Field Training.

Minority-Specific Programs: Although we support the objectives of the NMFI, we do not have any specific programs in place at this time.

Specific Expansion Plans:

US:	All United States

MY FAVORITE MUFFIN

8501 W. Higgins Rd., # 320
Chicago, IL 60631
Tel: (800) 251-6101 (773) 380-6100
Fax: (773) 380-6183
E-Mail: hmarks@babholdings.com
Web Site: www.babholdings.com
Mr. Howard Marks, Director Franchise Development

As a MY FAVORITE MUFFIN franchisee, you get to create and sell over 300 varieties of our special muffins in both regular and fat-free varieties. Where applicable, you can add BIG APPLE BAGELS and BREWSTER'S COFFEE to complement your wonderful muffins.

Background:

Established: 1987;	1st Franchised: 1988
Franchised Units:	63
Company-Owned Units:	8
Total Units:	71

Minority-Owned Units:
  African-American:
  Asian-American:
  Hispanic:
  Native American:

North America:	19 States
Density:	18 in NJ, 10 in PA, 8 in FL

Financial/Terms:

Cash Investment:	$NR
Total Investment:	$234-382.3K
Minimum Net Worth:	$50K Min.
Fees: Franchise —	$25K
Royalty — 5%;	Ad. — 2%
Earnings Claim Statement:	No
Term of Contract (Years):	10/10
Avg. # Of Employees:	3 FT, 15 PT
Passive Ownership:	Discouraged
Area Develop. Agreements:	Yes
Sub-Franchising Contracts:	No
Expand In Territory:	Yes

Space Needs: 1,800-2,200 SF; FS, SC, RM

Support & Training Provided:

Site Selection Assistance:	Yes
Lease Negotiation Assistance:	Yes
Co-Operative Advertising:	No
Franchisee Assoc./Member:	NR
Size Of Corporate Staff:	34
On-Going Support:	B,C,D,E,F,G,H,I

Training: 2 Weeks Milwaukee, WI; 5 Days Store Location Prior to Opening.

Minority-Specific Programs: Although we support the objectives of the NMFI, we do not have any specific programs in place at this time.

Specific Expansion Plans:

US:	All United States

ARABICA COFFEEHOUSE

ARABICA COFFEEHOUSE

5755 Granger Rd., # 200
Independence, OH 44131-1410
Tel: (800) 837-9599 (216) 351-1000
Fax: (216) 398-0707
E-Mail: mrhero@prodigy.net
Web Site:
Mr. Mitchell J. Winick, VP Business
Development

ARABICA COFFEEHOUSE is part of the community. An exciting place to own, to visit, to enjoy. Offering gourmet coffees, teas and specialty drinks with fresh and oversized muffins. A place where excellence is highly prized and friendships cherished.

Background:
Established: 1994;	1st Franchised: 1994
Franchised Units:	8
Company-Owned Units:	0
Total Units:	8
Minority-Owned Units:	
African-American:	
Asian-American:	
Hispanic:	
Native American:	
Other:	Women
North America:	1 State
Density:	8 in OH

Financial/Terms:
Cash Investment:	$30-50K
Total Investment:	$126-363K
Minimum Net Worth:	$230K
Fees: Franchise —	$22.5K
Royalty — 4%;	Ad. — 1.5%
Earnings Claim Statement:	No
Term of Contract (Years):	10/10
Avg. # Of Employees:	1 FT, 14 PT
Passive Ownership:	Allowed
Area Develop. Agreements:	Yes
Sub-Franchising Contracts:	No
Expand In Territory:	No
Space Needs: 2,400 SF; FS, SF, SC	

Support & Training Provided:
Site Selection Assistance:	Yes
Lease Negotiation Assistance:	Yes
Co-Operative Advertising:	N/A
Franchisee Assoc./Member:	No
Size Of Corporate Staff:	30
On-Going Support:	B,C,D,E,F,G,I
Training: 3 Weeks Cleveland, OH.	

Minority Specific Programs: Although we support the objectives of the NMFI, we do not have any specific programs in place at this time.

Specific Expansion Plans:
US:	MI, OH, PA, KY

✻

BREWSTER'S COFFEE

8501 W. Higgins Rd., # 320
Chicago, IL 60631
Tel: (800) 251-6101 (773) 380-6100
Fax: (773) 380-6183
E-Mail: hmarks@babholdings.com
Web Site: www.babholdings.com
Mr. Howard Marks, Franchise Director

Our BREWSTER'S COFFEE franchisees expertly prepare coffee and espresso beverages from the freshest coffee, roasted to the peak of flavor for each varietal and unique blend we offer. They also offer the same fresh coffee on a bulk basis for customers to enjoy at home. BREWSTER'S franchisees learn to consult with their customers and suggest the appropriate coffee to match any food or occasion.

Background:
Established: 1996;	1st Franchised: 1996
Franchised Units:	7
Company-Owned Units:	2
Total Units:	9
Minority-Owned Units:	
African-American:	
Asian-American:	
Hispanic:	
Native American:	
Other:	
North America:	3 States
Density:	7 in IL, 1 in OH

Financial/Terms:
Cash Investment:	$50K Min.
Total Investment:	$125.1-282.4K
Minimum Net Worth:	$Not Required
Fees: Franchise —	$25K
Royalty — 5%;	Ad. — 2%

Earnings Claim Statement: No
Term of Contract (Years): 10/10
Avg. # Of Employees: 5 FT, 10PT
Passive Ownership: Discouraged
Area Develop. Agreements: Yes/Varies
Sub-Franchising Contracts: No
Expand In Territory: Yes
Space Needs: 1,200-1,400 SF; FS, SF, SC

Support & Training Provided:

Site Selection Assistance: Yes
Lease Negotiation Assistance: Yes
Co-Operative Advertising: Yes
Franchisee Assoc./Member: No
Size Of Corporate Staff: 34
On-Going Support: B,C,D,E,F,G,H,I
Training: 2 Weeks Milwaukee, WI; 5 Days Store Location Prior to Opening.
Minority-Specific Programs: Although we support the objectives of the NMFI, we do not have any specific programs in place at this time.

Specific Expansion Plans:

US: All United States

COFFEE BEANERY, THE
3429 Pierson Place Rd.
Flushing, MI 48433
Tel: (800) 728-2326 (810) 728-2326
Fax: (810) 244-8151
E-Mail: franchiseinfo@CoffeeBeanery.com
Web Site: www.CoffeeBeanery.com
Mr. Kevin Shaw, VP Franchise Development

THE COFFEE BEANERY, LTD. offers a variety of investment levels with storefront cafes being the main growth vehicle in the future. The cornerstone and foundation of the business is the exceptional quality of its own hand-roasted coffee. Our customers enjoy the best coffee and assorted products available from a network of over 180 opened franchised and corporate locations. Our operations department and training are superb.

Background:
Established: 1976; 1st Franchised: 1985
Franchised Units: 159
Company-Owned Units: 27
Total Units: 186
Minority-Owned Units:
African-American: 3
Asian-American: 12
Hispanic: 1
Native American:
Other: 15
North America: 31 States
Density: 48 in MI, 19 in FL, 17 in NY

Financial/Terms:
Cash Investment: $50-80K
Total Investment: $140-250K
Minimum Net Worth: $250K
Fees: Franchise — $5-25K
Royalty — 6%; Ad. — 2%
Earnings Claim Statement: Yes
Term of Contract (Years): 5,10,15+
Avg. # Of Employees: 1 FT, 8-10 PT
Passive Ownership: Allowed
Area Develop. Agreements: Yes
Sub-Franchising Contracts: No
Expand In Territory: Yes
Space Needs: 2,000 SF; FS, SF, SC

Support & Training Provided:
Site Selection Assistance: Yes
Lease Negotiation Assistance: Yes
Co-Operative Advertising: Yes
Franchisee Assoc./Member: Yes/Yes
Size Of Corporate Staff: 100
On-Going Support: B,C,D,E,F,G,H,I
Training: 3.5 Days Corporate Office, Flushing, MI; 21 Days Flint.
Minority-Specific Programs: Although we support the objectives of the NMFI, we do not have any specific programs in place at this time.

Specific Expansion Plans:
US: All United States

JAVA DAVE'S COFFEE
6239 E. 15th St.
Tulsa, OK 74112
Tel: (800) 725-7315 (918) 836-5570
Fax: (918) 835-4348
E-Mail: davesbeans@aol.com
Web Site: www.javadavescoffee.com

Mr. Mike Blair, National Franchise Manager

The JAVA DAVE'S COFFEE House System is a thrifty franchise that allows the franchisee an opportunity to participate in the higher level retail purveyance of products which includes the world's finest arabic bean coffees, teas, cocoas and cappuccino mixes, as well as 200 other related products. The espresso and specialty drinks bar compliments the retail.

Background:
Established: 1982; 1st Franchised: 1993
Franchised Units: 11
Company-Owned Units: 3
Total Units: 14
Minority-Owned Units:
African-American:
Asian-American:
Hispanic:
Native American:
Other: 4 Women
North America: 1 State
Density: 14 in OK

Financial/Terms:
Cash Investment: $150K
Total Investment: $150K
Minimum Net Worth: $200K
Fees: Franchise — $17.5K
Royalty — 3%; Ad. — 2%
Earnings Claim Statement: No
Term of Contract (Years): 10/10
Avg. # Of Employees: 5-6 FT, 4-6 PT
Passive Ownership: Discouraged
Area Develop. Agreements: Yes/Varies
Sub-Franchising Contracts: Yes
Expand In Territory: Yes
Space Needs: 1,500-2,000 SF; SF, SC

Support & Training Provided:
Site Selection Assistance: Yes
Lease Negotiation Assistance: Yes
Co-Operative Advertising: Yes
Franchisee Assoc./Member: No
Size Of Corporate Staff: 65
On-Going Support: b,C,D,E,h,I
Training: 40-60 Hours in Tulsa, OK or On -Site.
Minority-Specific Programs: Although we support the objectives of the NMFI, we do not have any specific programs in place at this time.

Specific Expansion Plans:
US: Midwest, Southwest

JAVA'S BREWIN
95 Boston Rd.
North Bellerica, MA 01862
Tel: (800) 413-2376 (617) 924-7212

Fax: (617) 924-7202
E-Mail:
Web Site:
Mr. Chris Gregoris, President

Background:
Established: 1997;   1st Franchised: 1998
Franchised Units: 2
Company-Owned Units: <u>1</u>
Total Units: 3
Minority-Owned Units:
    African-American:
    Asian-American:
    Hispanic:
    Native American:
    Other:
North America: 1 State
Density: 3 in MA

Financial/Terms:
Cash Investment: $50-100K
Total Investment: $120-150K
Minimum Net Worth: $75K
Fees: Franchise — $17.5K
    Royalty — 5%;   Ad. — 2%
Earnings Claim Statement: No
Term of Contract (Years): 10/5/5
Avg. # Of Employees: 4 FT, 2 PT
Passive Ownership: Discouraged
Area Develop. Agreements: No
Sub-Franchising Contracts: No
Expand In Territory: Yes
Space Needs: 750-1,500 SF; FS, SF, SC

Support & Training Provided:
Site Selection Assistance: Yes
Lease Negotiation Assistance: Yes
Co-Operative Advertising: Yes
Franchisee Assoc./Member: No
Size Of Corporate Staff: 1
On-Going Support: B,C,D,E,F,H,I
Training: 2 Weeks in Company Store.
Minority-Specific Programs: Although we support the objectives of the NMFI, we do not have any specific programs in place at this time.

Specific Expansion Plans:
US: Northeast

KELLY'S COFFEE & FUDGE FACTORY

9100 Wilshire Blvd.
Beverly Hills, CA 90212
Tel: (310) 786-8600
Fax: (310) 786-8606
Web Site: www.kellyscoffee.com
Mr. Barry A. Ogawa, Director of Sales

Gourmet, upscale coffee house that caters to entire family by offering fresh baked products, sandwiches and salads. Treats for children. An exciting, fun business with high profit items and minimal inventories required. Coffee franchising is a booming industry.

Background:
Established: 1983;   1st Franchised: 1997
Franchised Units: 35
Company-Owned Units: <u>0</u>
Total Units: 35
Minority-Owned Units:
    African-American: 0
    Asian-American: 15
    Hispanic: 2
    Native American: 0
    Other: 2 Greek
North America: 3 States
Density: 32 in CA, 2 in AZ, 1 in MO

Financial/Terms:
Cash Investment: $30K
Total Investment: $120-180K
Minimum Net Worth: $250K
Fees: Franchise — $30K
    Royalty — 6%;   Ad. — 2%
Earnings Claim Statement: No
Term of Contract (Years): 10
Avg. # Of Employees: 2 FT, 4 PT
Passive Ownership: Discouraged
Area Develop. Agreements: Yes
Sub-Franchising Contracts: No
Expand In Territory: Yes
Space Needs: 1,000 SF; FS, SF, SC, RM

Support & Training Provided:
Site Selection Assistance: Yes
Lease Negotiation Assistance: Yes
Co-Operative Advertising: Yes
Franchisee Assoc./Member: Yes
Size Of Corporate Staff: 8
On-Going Support: A,B,C,D,E,F,H,I
Training: 1 Week - Location Varies.
Minority-Specific Programs: Financing -- working with Southern California partnership program for minorities in Los Angeles area.

Specific Expansion Plans:
US: All United States

MCBEANS

1560 Church Ave., # 6
Victoria, BC V8P 2H1 CANADA
Tel: (250) 721-2411
Fax: (250) 721-3213
Mr. Arne Andersson, President

Gourmet coffee stores in B. C. and Alberta, Canada that offer simply the finest in gourmet coffee by the cup, as well as lattes, cappuccino, espresso, a wide selection of beans (40 varieties), gourmet tea and the very best name-brand coffee-related merchandise. We offer our franchisees a well-researched and developed concept, lease negotiation, design and construction, and prime locations. We also provide continued and on-going support.

Background:
Established: 1983;   1st Franchised: 1985
Franchised Units: 16
Company-Owned Units: <u>1</u>
Total Units: 17
Minority-Owned Units:
    African-American:
    Asian-American: 12%
    Hispanic:
    Native American:
    Other:
North America: 2 Provinces
Density: 8 in BC, 9 in AB

Financial/Terms:
Cash Investment: $60K
Total Investment: $126-174K
Minimum Net Worth: $NR
Fees: Franchise — $25K
    Royalty — 7%;   Ad. — 0%
Earnings Claim Statement: No
Term of Contract (Years): Lease
Avg. # Of Employees: 1-3 FT, 3-5 PT
Passive Ownership: Allowed
Area Develop. Agreements: No
Sub-Franchising Contracts: No
Expand In Territory: Yes
Space Needs: 600 SF; SC, RM

Support & Training Provided:
Site Selection Assistance: Yes
Lease Negotiation Assistance: Yes
Co-Operative Advertising: N/A
Franchisee Assoc./Member: Yes/Yes
Size Of Corporate Staff: 5
On-Going Support: C,D,E,F
Training: 2 Weeks Corporate Training Center.
Minority-Specific Programs: Although we support the objectives of the NMFI, we do not have any specific programs in place at this time.

Specific Expansion Plans:
US: BC and Alberta

MOXIE JAVA

199 E. 52nd St.
Boise, ID 83714
Tel: (800) 659-6963 (208) 322-1166

Fax: (208) 322-6226
E-Mail:
Web Site: www.moxiejava.com
Mr. Lance Weibye, Concept Sales Manager

Espresso/specialty coffee cafes, carts, kiosks. No royalty fees. Fees for services selected. Seeking co-branding partners and multi-unit operators.

Background:
Established: 1987; 1st Franchised: 1989
Franchised Units: 84
Company-Owned Units: 0
Total Units: 84
Minority-Owned Units:
    African-American:
    Asian-American:
    Hispanic:
    Native American:
    Other:
North America: NR
Density: ID, ND, WI

Financial/Terms:
Cash Investment: $10-30K
Total Investment: $35--175K
Minimum Net Worth: $100
Fees: Franchise — $10K
    Royalty — 0%;   Ad. — 0
Earnings Claim Statement: Yes
Term of Contract (Years):   3/3/3
Avg. # Of Employees: 4 FT, 4 PT
Passive Ownership: Discouraged
Area Develop. Agreements: Yes
Sub-Franchising Contracts: No
Expand In Territory: Yes
Space Needs: 120-1,500 SF; FS, SF, SC, Co-Branding

Support & Training Provided:
Site Selection Assistance: Yes
Lease Negotiation Assistance: Yes
Co-Operative Advertising: Yes
Franchisee Assoc./Member: No
Size Of Corporate Staff: 50
On-Going Support: C,D,E,F,G,H,I
Training: 3-4 Days Boise, ID; 3-4 Days at Owner's Location.
Minority-Specific Programs: Although we support the objectives of the NMFI, we do not have any specific programs in place at this time.

Specific Expansion Plans:
US: All United States

BEN & JERRY'S

30 Community Dr.
South Burlington, VT 05403
Tel: (802) 846-1500
Fax: (802) 846-1538
E-Mail:
Web Site: www.benjerry.com
Ms. Sandy Julius, Franchise Selection

BEN & JERRY'S was started in 1978 in a renovated gas station in Burlington, VT, by childhood friends Ben Cohen and Jerry Greenfield. They soon became popular for their funky, chunky flavors, made from fresh Vermont milk and cream. The scoop shops feature a fun environment with a varied menu including cakes, gifts, baked goods and coffee drinks created from ice cream, frozen yogurt and sorbet flavors. Community involvement is an important element in being a successful BEN & JERRY'S franchisee.

Background:
Established: 1978;   1st Franchised: 1981
Franchised Units: 198
Company-Owned Units: <u>6</u>
Total Units: 204
Minority-Owned Units:
    African-American: 3
    Asian-American: 6
    Hispanic: 0
    Native American: 0
    Other:
North America: 28 States, 1 Province
Density: 39 in CA, 21 in NY, 12 in MA

Financial/Terms:
Cash Investment: $86K+
Total Investment: $150-253.5K
Minimum Net Worth: $150K
Fees: Franchise — $30K
    Royalty — 0%;   Ad. — 4%
Earnings Claim Statement: No
Term of Contract (Years):   10/10
Avg. # Of Employees: 2 FT, 10 PT
Passive Ownership: Not Allowed
Area Develop. Agreements: No
Sub-Franchising Contracts: No
Expand In Territory: No
Space Needs: Avg. 1,000 SF; FS, SF, SC, RM, KI

Support & Training Provided:
Site Selection Assistance: Yes
Lease Negotiation Assistance: No
Co-Operative Advertising: Yes
Franchisee Assoc./Member: No
Size Of Corporate Staff: 30
On-Going Support: C,D,E,F,G,H,I
Training: 10 Days in Vermont.
Minority-Specific Programs: Although we support the objectives of the NMFI, we do not have any specific programs in place at this time.

Specific Expansion Plans:
US: Various Markets

BRUSTER'S OLD-FASHIONED ICE CREAM & YOGURT

730 Mulberry St.
Bridgewater, PA 15009
Tel: (724) 774-4250
Fax: (724) 774-0666

Web Site: www.brustersicecream.com
Mr. David Guido, President

BRUSTER'S ICE CREAM features fresh, delicious homemade ice cream which is made fresh daily on-site at each of our stores. Quality products and exceptional customer service are our main goals. Our products feature only the best ingredients - whole nuts, cherries and the best caramels and fudges. Homemade waffle cones are a great complement to our homemade ice cream.

Background:
Established: 1989;   1st Franchised: 1993
Franchised Units: 37
Company-Owned Units: <u>3</u>
Total Units: 40
Minority-Owned Units:
    African-American: 0
    Asian-American: 4
    Hispanic: 0
    Native American: 0
    Other:
North America: 7 States
Density: 20 in PA, 13 in GA, 2 in OH

Financial/Terms:
Cash Investment: $150K
Total Investment: $150-761K
Minimum Net Worth: $None
Fees: Franchise — $30K
    Royalty — 5%;   Ad. — Up to 3%
Earnings Claim Statement: No
Term of Contract (Years):   10/10/10

Avg. # Of Employees:	2-3 FT, 25 PT
Passive Ownership:	Discouraged
Area Develop. Agreements:	Yes/Varies
Sub-Franchising Contracts:	No
Expand In Territory:	Yes
Space Needs: 988 SF; FS	

Support & Training Provided:

Site Selection Assistance:	Yes
Lease Negotiation Assistance:	Yes
Co-Operative Advertising:	Yes
Franchisee Assoc./Member:	No
Size Of Corporate Staff:	10
On-Going Support:	B,C,D,E,G,H

Training: 4 Weeks Western PA or Atlanta, GA.

Minority-Specific Programs: Although we support the objectives of the NMFI, we do not have any specific programs in place at this time.

Specific Expansion Plans:

US:	Eastern United States

EMACK & BOLIO'S ICE CREAM & YOGURT

P. O. Box 703
Brookline Village, MA 02447
Tel: (617) 739-7995
Fax: (617) 232-1102
E-Mail: ENBIC@aol.com
Web Site:
Mr. Robert Rook, President

Best Ice Cream NYC. 1998 — Best Buy in NYC 1999 Zagat Survey — Best Ice Cream Cape Cod — Best Ice Cream New Jersey — Best Ice Cream L.A. 1998 — We train in our Macy's NYC Store and give additional training in your store at opening. Manuals and videos provided, ad slicks. No fees or royalties. 25 years' experience.

Background:

Established: 1975;	1st Franchised: 1977
Franchised Units:	34
Company-Owned Units:	5
Total Units:	39
Minority-Owned Units:	
African-American:	0
Asian-American:	1
Hispanic:	0

Native American:	0
Other:	0
North America:	10 States
Density:	12 in MA, 5 in NJ, 4 in NY

Financial/Terms:

Cash Investment:	$60-90K
Total Investment:	$60-90K
Minimum Net Worth:	$N/A
Fees: Franchise —	$None
Royalty — 0%;	Ad. — 0%
Earnings Claim Statement:	No
Term of Contract (Years):	20/10
Avg. # Of Employees:	2 FT, 4-10 PT
Passive Ownership:	Discouraged
Area Develop. Agreements:	Yes/20
Sub-Franchising Contracts:	Yes
Expand In Territory:	Yes
Space Needs: 200-1,500 SF; SF	

Support & Training Provided:

Site Selection Assistance:	No
Lease Negotiation Assistance:	Yes
Co-Operative Advertising:	No
Franchisee Assoc./Member:	No
Size Of Corporate Staff:	3
On-Going Support:	B,C,D,E,F,G

Training: 1 Week Macy's NYC.

Minority-Specific Programs: Although we support the objectives of the NMFI, we do not have any specific programs in place at this time.

Specific Expansion Plans:

US:	All United States

GELATO AMARE

11504 Hyde Pl.
Raleigh, NC 27614
Tel: (919) 847-4435
Fax:
E-Mail: gamare@aol.com
Web Site:
Mr. John L. Franklin, President

GELATO AMARE stores feature super-premium, low-fat, homemade Italian ice cream and ices and all-natural, no-fat, no-cholesterol, sugar-free frozen yogurt, as well as smoothies, pastries, coffees, espresso, soups, salads and sandwiches.

Background:

Established: 1983;	1st Franchised: 1986
Franchised Units:	3
Company-Owned Units:	1
Total Units:	4
Minority-Owned Units:	
African-American:	50%
Asian-American:	

Hispanic:	
Native American:	
North America:	3 States
Density:	3 in NC

Financial/Terms:

Cash Investment:	$30-60K
Total Investment:	$90-225K
Minimum Net Worth:	$NR
Fees: Franchise —	$18.9K
Royalty — 5%;	Ad. — 2%
Earnings Claim Statement:	No
Term of Contract (Years):	10/5/5
Avg. # Of Employees:	1 FT, 6 PT
Passive Ownership:	Allowed
Area Develop. Agreements:	Yes
Sub-Franchising Contracts:	Yes
Expand In Territory:	Yes
Space Needs: 500-1,100 SF; SF, SC, RM	

Support & Training Provided:

Site Selection Assistance:	Yes
Lease Negotiation Assistance:	Yes
Co-Operative Advertising:	No
Franchisee Assoc./Member:	NR
Size Of Corporate Staff:	3
On-Going Support:	B,C,D,E,G,h

Training: 2 Weeks Headquarters; 3 Weeks in Store.

Minority-Specific Programs: Assistance in preparing loan documents.

Specific Expansion Plans:

US:	All United States

HAPPY & HEALTHY PRODUCTS

1600 S. Dixie Hwy., # 200
Boca Raton, FL 33432
Tel: (800) 764-6114 (561) 367-0739
Fax: (561) 368-5267
E-Mail: generalmanager@fruitfull.com
Web Site: www.fruitfull.com
Ms. Rosemary Harris, General Manager

A wholesale distributorship for the sale of frozen fruit bars, FRUITFULL, through dedicated freezers placed in retail locations or in retailer's own freezers. Super Grand, Grand and Standard wholesale franchisees will receive the services of an independent marketing consultant who will provide on-site training in identifying and negotiating agreements to place freezers. Training includes stocking, collection and route service procedures dealing with frozen storage supplies.

Background:

Established: 1991;	1st Franchised: 1993
Franchised Units:	113
Company-Owned Units:	0
Total Units:	113
Minority-Owned Units:	
African-American:	5
Asian-American:	5
Hispanic:	10
Native American:	1
Other:	
North America:	39 States
Density:	12 in CA, 11 in NJ, 9 in IL

Financial/Terms:

Cash Investment:	$23-54K
Total Investment:	$23-54K
Minimum Net Worth:	$23-54K
Fees: Franchise —	$17-24K
Royalty — 0%;	Ad. — 0%
Earnings Claim Statement:	No
Term of Contract (Years):	10/5
Avg. # Of Employees:	1 FT or 1 PT
Passive Ownership:	Discouraged
Area Develop. Agreements:	No
Sub-Franchising Contracts:	No
Expand In Territory:	Yes
Space Needs: N/A SF; N/A	

Support & Training Provided:

Site Selection Assistance:	N/A
Lease Negotiation Assistance:	N/A
Co-Operative Advertising:	N/A
Franchisee Assoc./Member:	No
Size Of Corporate Staff:	10
On-Going Support:	b,C,D,G,H

Training: 1 or 2 Weeks in Franchise MSA.
Minority-Specific Programs: Although we support the objectives of the NMFI, we do not have any specific programs in place at this time.

Specific Expansion Plans:

US:	All Except WA,LA,ND,ME

MAGGIEMOO'S INTERNATIONAL

10290 Old Columbia Rd.
Columbia, MD 21046

Tel: (800) 949-8114 (410) 309-6001
Fax: (410) 309-6006
E-Mail: maggiemoos@worldnet.att.net
Web Site: www.maggiemoos.com
Mr. Matt Cliney, Dir. Franchise Development

Unique and exciting retail shop, featuring homemade, super-premium ice cream, non-fat ice cream, sorbet, smoothies, homemade fudge, plus a line of specialty merchandise. We make our ice cream fresh in the store and serve it in fresh-baked waffle cones. Featuring over 40 mix-ins and folded in on a frozen granite slab to create 1,000s of great combos. Association with a marketable spokes character - MAGGIE MOO - in a fun, contemporary store design.

Background:

Established: 1996;	1st Franchised: 1996
Franchised Units:	25
Company-Owned Units:	2
Total Units:	27
Minority-Owned Units:	
African-American:	
Asian-American:	
Hispanic:	
Native American:	
Other:	
North America:	14 States
Density:	6 in KS, 5 in MD, 2 in VA

Financial/Terms:

Cash Investment:	$50-70K
Total Investment:	$148-228K
Minimum Net Worth:	$250K
Fees: Franchise —	$23K
Royalty — 5%;	Ad. — 2%
Earnings Claim Statement:	No
Term of Contract (Years):	10/5/5
Avg. # Of Employees:	3 FT, 8 PT
Passive Ownership:	Discouraged
Area Develop. Agreements:	Yes/3
Sub-Franchising Contracts:	No
Expand In Territory:	Yes
Space Needs: 900-1,400 SF; SC	

Support & Training Provided:

Site Selection Assistance:	Yes
Lease Negotiation Assistance:	Yes
Co-Operative Advertising:	Yes
Franchisee Assoc./Member:	No
Size Of Corporate Staff:	10
On-Going Support:	B,C,D,E,G,H,I

Training: 12 Days Alexandria, VA; 6 Days Grand Opening On-Site.
Minority-Specific Programs: Although we support the objectives of the NMFI, we do not have any specific programs in place at this time.

Specific Expansion Plans:

US:	All United States

MARBLE SLAB CREAMERY

3100 S. Gessner Dr., # 305
Houston, TX 77063
Tel: (713) 780-3601
Fax: (713) 780-0264
E-Mail: marbleslab@marbleslab.com
Web Site: www.marbleslab.com
Mr. Chris Dull, Franchise Development

Retail ice cream stores, featuring super-premium homemade ice cream, cones baked fresh daily, frozen yogurt, frozen pies and cakes, homemade cookies and brownies and specialty coffees. Ice cream is custom-designed for customer on frozen marble slab and made daily in the store.

Background:

Established: 1983;	1st Franchised: 1984
Franchised Units:	137
Company-Owned Units:	1
Total Units:	138
Minority-Owned Units:	
African-American:	
Asian-American:	
Hispanic:	
Native American:	
Other:	
North America:	15 States
Density:	80 in TX, 9 in LA, 6 in AZ

Financial/Terms:

Cash Investment:	$50-75K
Total Investment:	$165-247K
Minimum Net Worth:	$250K
Fees: Franchise —	$19K
Royalty — 6%;	Ad. — 2%
Earnings Claim Statement:	No
Term of Contract (Years):	10/10
Avg. # Of Employees:	2 FT, 8 PT
Passive Ownership:	Discouraged
Area Develop. Agreements:	Yes/Varies
Sub-Franchising Contracts:	No
Expand In Territory:	No
Space Needs: 500-1,800 SF; SC, RM	

Support & Training Provided:

Site Selection Assistance:	Yes
Lease Negotiation Assistance:	Yes
Co-Operative Advertising:	Yes
Franchisee Assoc./Member:	Yes/No
Size Of Corporate Staff:	10
On-Going Support:	B,C,D,E,H

Training: 10 Days Franchisor Location; 6 Days Franchisee Site.
Minority-Specific Programs: Although we support the objectives of the NMFI, we do not have any specific programs in place at this time.

Specific Expansion Plans:

US:	SW,S,SE,W and Midwest,East

MORRONE'S ITALIAN ICES & HOMEMADE ICE CREAM

117 S. 69th St.
Upper Darby, PA 19082
Tel: (800) 871-2975 (888) MORRONES
Fax: (610) 446-8381
E-Mail: italianices@compuserve.com
Web Site: www.italianices.com
Mr. Dennis Mason, Franchise Sales

Retail outlets selling Italian Ices and a special blend of homemade ice cream made right on the premises. Also offering walk-in, year-round operations - new for '99.

Background:

Established: 1910;	1st Franchised: 1995	
Franchised Units:		17
Company-Owned Units:		2
Total Units:		19
Minority-Owned Units:		
African-American:		2
Asian-American:		0
Hispanic:		1
Native American:		0
North America:		5 States
Density:	13 in PA, 2 in DC, 2 in DE	

Financial/Terms:

Cash Investment:	$52K
Total Investment:	$127.5-164.5K
Minimum Net Worth:	$100K
Fees: Franchise —	$20K
Royalty — 5%;	Ad. — 3%
Earnings Claim Statement:	No
Term of Contract (Years):	10/10
Avg. # Of Employees:	2 FT, 6 PT
Passive Ownership:	Discouraged
Area Develop. Agreements:	Yes/10
Sub-Franchising Contracts:	Yes
Expand In Territory:	Yes
Space Needs: 500-1,000 SF; FS, SF, SC, RM	

Support & Training Provided:

Site Selection Assistance:	Yes
Lease Negotiation Assistance:	Yes
Co-Operative Advertising:	Yes
Franchisee Assoc./Member:	No
Size Of Corporate Staff:	8
On-Going Support:	A,C,D,E,F,G,I

Training: 20-30 Hours Corporate Store; 40-100 Hours at Franchisee's Location.
Minority-Specific Programs: Although we support the objectives of the NMFI, we do not have any specific programs in place at this time.

Specific Expansion Plans:

US:	All United States

PETRUCCI'S ICE CREAM CO.

507 W. Corporate Dr.
Langhorne, PA 19047
Tel: (888) PETRUCCI (215) 860-4848
Fax: (215) 860-6123
E-Mail: mpmogul@aol.com
Web Site: www.petruccis.com
Mr. Mick Petrucci, President

Retailing '50' wild whirling flavors of soft ice cream, homemade fresh fruit Italian ices, frozen yogurt and premium hand-dipped ice cream. All shops feature custom decorated ice cream cakes and proprietary take home frozen novelties.

Background:

Established: 1983;	1st Franchised: 1996	
Franchised Units:		28
Company-Owned Units:		0
Total Units:		28
Minority-Owned Units:		
African-American:		0
Asian-American:		0
Hispanic:		0
Native American:		1
Other:		
North America:		5 States
Density:	18 in PA, 8 in NJ, 2 in MD	

Financial/Terms:

Cash Investment:	$20K
Total Investment:	$139.9-229.9K
Minimum Net Worth:	$150K
Fees: Franchise —	$20K
Royalty — 5%;	Ad. — 2%
Earnings Claim Statement:	No
Term of Contract (Years):	10/5
Avg. # Of Employees:	5 FT, 3 PT
Passive Ownership:	Discouraged
Area Develop. Agreements:	Yes/10
Sub-Franchising Contracts:	No
Expand In Territory:	Yes
Space Needs: 1,250 SF; FS, RM	

Support & Training Provided:

Site Selection Assistance:	Yes
Lease Negotiation Assistance:	Yes
Co-Operative Advertising:	Yes
Franchisee Assoc./Member:	Yes/Yes
Size Of Corporate Staff:	7
On-Going Support:	C,D,E,F,G,H

Training: 3 Days Langhorne, PA; 3 Days Local Shop Training; 3-4 Days at Your Location when Open.
Minority-Specific Programs: No program currenty exists -- "very" interested in establishing a minority program.

Specific Expansion Plans:

US:	NE, SE

A & W RESTAURANTS

One A & W Dr.
Farmington Hills, MI 48331
Tel: (888) 456-2929 (248) 669-2000
Fax: (248) 553-8728
E-Mail: PalmerL@awrestaurants.com
Web Site: www.awrestaurants.com
Mr. George Goulson, Exec. VP Franchise
Development

A & W has been a successful, all-American icon for more than 80 years. Since repositioning A & W as the home of 'All American Food' with a menu of hamburgers, hot dogs, coney dogs, french fires, onion rings, chicken strips, etc. and our signature A & W Root Beer and Root Beer floats, we have entered the ranks of the most rapidly-growing quick-service restaurants in the world. 'It is very simple - if our franchisees succeed, we succeed.' - Sidney Feltenstein, Chairman, CEO

Background:
Established: 1919;   1st Franchised: 1925
Franchised Units: 825
Company-Owned Units: 177
Total Units: 1002
Minority-Owned Units:
    African-American: 2
    Asian-American: 30
    Hispanic: 20

Native American: 3
    Other: 100, Arabic/Indian
North America: 48 States
Density: 79 in CA

Financial/Terms:
Cash Investment: $20% Turn-Key
Total Investment: $90-500K
Minimum Net Worth: $100K
Fees: Franchise — $10-20K
    Royalty — 4 6%;   Ad.   4%
Earnings Claim Statement: No
Term of Contract (Years):   20/10
Avg. # Of Employees: 50-60 FT & PT
Passive Ownership: Allowed
Area Develop. Agreements: Yes/Varies
Sub-Franchising Contracts: Yes
Expand In Territory: Yes
Space Needs: 600+ SF; FS, SF, SC, RM, Non-Tradit.

Support & Training Provided:
Site Selection Assistance: Yes
Lease Negotiation Assistance: Yes
Co-Operative Advertising: Yes
Franchisee Assoc./Member: Yes/Yes
Size Of Corporate Staff: 120
On-Going Support: B,C,D,E,F,G,H,I
Training: 18 Days Corp. Training Facility, Dearborn, MI; 3-5 Days Prior and 3-5 Days After Opening.
Minority-Specific Programs: Although we support the objectives of the NMFI, we do not have any specific programs in place at this time.

Specific Expansion Plans:
US: All United States

ANDERSON'S RESTAURANTS

6075 Main St.
Williamsville, NY 14221
Tel: (716) 633-2302
Fax: (716) 633-2671
E-Mail: info@andersonscustard.com
Web Site: www.andersonscustard.com
Mr. Kirk P. Wildermuth, President

A Western New York tradition, serving award-winning roast beef, BBQ, chicken and ham sandwiches. Also, we are famous for our one-of-a-kind frozen custard, plus homemade ice cream. We also specialize in ice cream cakes and pies. We are the Northeast's premium lunch, dinner and dessert fast casual concept.

Background:
Established: 1946,   1st Franchised: 1996
Franchised Units: 6
Company-Owned Units: 3
Total Units: 9
Minority-Owned Units:
    African-American:
    Asian-American:
    Hispanic:
    Native American:
    Other:
North America: 1 State
Density: 9 in NY

Financial/Terms:
Cash Investment: $100-200K
Total Investment: $900K-1.1MM

Minimum Net Worth:	$500K
Fees: Franchise —	$30K
Royalty — 4%;	Ad. — 2%
Earnings Claim Statement:	No
Term of Contract (Years):	20
Avg. # Of Employees:	10 FT, 25 PT
Passive Ownership:	Not Allowed
Area Develop. Agreements:	Yes/20
Sub-Franchising Contracts:	No
Expand In Territory:	Yes
Space Needs: 3,800 SF; FS, End Cap	

Support & Training Provided:

Site Selection Assistance:	Yes
Lease Negotiation Assistance:	Yes
Co-Operative Advertising:	Yes
Franchisee Assoc./Member:	No
Size Of Corporate Staff:	7
On-Going Support:	B,C,D,E,G

Training: 12-16 Weeks Buffalo, NY
Minority-Specific Programs: Although we support the objectives of the NMFI, we do not have any specific programs in place at this time.

Specific Expansion Plans:

US:	Ohio, New York, Penn

BACK YARD BURGERS

2768 Colony Park Dr.
Memphis, TN 30118
Tel: (800) 292-6939 (901) 367-0888
Fax: (901) 367-0999
E-Mail:
Web Site: www.backyardburgers.com
Mr. Ray Jones, Director of Franchise Dev.

BACK YARD BURGERS operates and franchises quick casual restaurants, serving 1/3 lb. gourmet hamburgers, boneless, skinless chicken fillet sandwiches, fresh lemonade, hand-dipped shakes and malts and other menu items. Our theme emphasizes charbroiled, fresh, great-tasting food as the customers would cook in their own back yard.

Background:

Established: 1987;	1st Franchised: 1988
Franchised Units:	51
Company-Owned Units:	37
Total Units:	88

Minority-Owned Units:

African-American:	0
Asian-American:	1
Hispanic:	0
Native American:	0
Other:	
North America:	16 States
Density:	32 in TN, 12 in AR, 8 in NC

Financial/Terms:

Cash Investment:	$200-300K
Total Investment:	$339-832K
Minimum Net Worth:	$300K
Fees: Franchise —	$25K
Royalty — 4%;	Ad. — 3%
Earnings Claim Statement:	No
Term of Contract (Years):	10/5
Avg. # Of Employees:	8 FT, 22 PT
Passive Ownership:	Discouraged
Area Develop. Agreements:	Yes/10
Sub-Franchising Contracts:	No
Expand In Territory:	Yes
Space Needs: 2,500 SF; FS	

Support & Training Provided:

Site Selection Assistance:	Yes
Lease Negotiation Assistance:	Yes
Co-Operative Advertising:	Yes
Franchisee Assoc./Member:	Yes/Yes
Size Of Corporate Staff:	30
On-Going Support:	B,C,D,E,F,G,H

Training: 8 Weeks Corporate Headquarters.
Minority-Specific Programs: Although we support the objectives of the NMFI, we do not have any specific programs in place at this time.

Specific Expansion Plans:

US:	SE, MW, Mid-Atlantic, SW

BALDINOS GIANT JERSEY SUBS

3823 Roswell Rd., # 204
Marietta, GA 30062
Tel: (770) 971-9441
Fax: (770) 977-1083
E-Mail:
Web Site:
Mr. Bill Baer, President/CEO

Quality submarine sandwiches with in-store bakery. All subs sliced fresh as ordered in full view of customer, served on freshly-baked rolls. Built for volume business at a 'fast-food' pace by use of multi-production lines. Variety of 20 hot and cold subs and freshly-baked gourmet cookies.

Background:

Established: 1975;	1st Franchised: 1984

Franchised Units:	13
Company-Owned Units:	6
Total Units:	19

Minority-Owned Units:

African-American:	8%
Asian-American:	8%
Hispanic:	
Native American:	
Other:	
North America:	3 States
Density:	13 in GA, 5 in NC, 1 in SC

Financial/Terms:

Cash Investment:	$NR
Total Investment:	$100-200K
Minimum Net Worth:	$NR
Fees: Franchise —	$10K
Royalty — 4.5%;	Ad. — .5%
Earnings Claim Statement:	No
Term of Contract (Years):	15/10
Avg. # Of Employees:	8 FT, 12 PT
Passive Ownership:	Not Allowed
Area Develop. Agreements:	Yes/15+
Sub-Franchising Contracts:	Yes
Expand In Territory:	Yes
Space Needs: 1,800-2,400 SF; FS	

Support & Training Provided:

Site Selection Assistance:	Yes
Lease Negotiation Assistance:	Yes
Co-Operative Advertising:	Yes
Franchisee Assoc./Member:	NR
Size Of Corporate Staff:	4
On-Going Support:	B,C,D,E,F,G,H,I

Training: 4 Weeks Headquarters.
Minority-Specific Programs: Although we support the objectives of the NMFI, we do not have any specific programs in place at this time.

Specific Expansion Plans:

US:	GA, SC, NC

BOJANGLES' FAMOUS CHICKEN 'N BISCUITS

P. O. Box 240239
Charlotte, NC 28224
Tel: (800) 366-9921 (704) 527-2675
Fax: (704) 523-6676
E-Mail: msandefer@bojangles.com
Web Site: www.bojangles.com
Mr. Mike Sandefer, Director Franchise Development

BOJANGLES OPERATES DURING ALL 3 DAY-PARTS. Breakfast items are available all day long. Our menu in unique, and flavorful, with chicken prepared either spicy or traditional Southern-style. Restaurants operate in traditional locations and non-traditional locations in convenience stores.

Background:

Established: 1977;	1st Franchised: 1979
Franchised Units:	112
Company-Owned Units:	158
Total Units:	270
Minority-Owned Units:	
African-American:	1
Asian-American:	2
Hispanic:	
Native American:	
Other:	
North America:	9 States
Density:	130 in NC, 55 in SC,18 in GA

Financial/Terms:

Cash Investment:	$225-350K
Total Investment:	$225K-1.2MM
Minimum Net Worth:	$500K
Fees: Franchise —	$12 or 20K
Royalty — 4%;	Ad. — 1%
Earnings Claim Statement:	No
Term of Contract (Years):	20/10
Avg. # Of Employees:	12 FT, 20 PT
Passive Ownership:	Discouraged
Area Develop. Agreements:	Yes/10
Sub-Franchising Contracts:	No
Expand In Territory:	Yes
Space Needs: 2,000+ SF; FS	

Support & Training Provided:

Site Selection Assistance:	Yes
Lease Negotiation Assistance:	No
Co-Operative Advertising:	Yes
Franchisee Assoc./Member:	Yes/Yes
Size Of Corporate Staff:	80
On-Going Support:	B,C,D,E,F,G,H,I

Training: 5 Weeks Training in Training Units.

Minority-Specific Programs: Although we support the objectives of the NMFI, we do not have any specific programs in place at this time.

Specific Expansion Plans:

US:	Southeast and Midwest

BREADEAUX PIZZA

P. O. Box 6158
St. Joseph, MO 64506
Tel: (800) 835-6534 (816) 364-1088
Fax: (816) 364-3739
E-Mail: scott@breadeauxpizza.com

Web Site: www.breadeauxpissa.com
Mr. Scott J. Henze, VP Sales & Marketing

BREADEAUX PIZZA is a growing regional chain, stressing quality and service. Our acclaimed pizza is made with a double raised crust that is chewy and sweet like fine french bread and our meat toppings have no fillers or additives. We also offer pastas, subs and salads to give customers plenty of variety. Our customers say 'Best Pizza in Town.'

Background:

Established: 1985;	1st Franchised: 1985
Franchised Units:	91
Company-Owned Units:	2
Total Units:	93
Minority-Owned Units:	
African-American:	
Asian-American:	
Hispanic:	
Native American:	
Other:	
North America:	7 States, 1 Province
Density:	43 in IA, 21 MO, 8 KS

Financial/Terms:

Cash Investment:	$30-80K
Total Investment:	$75-300K
Minimum Net Worth:	$50K
Fees: Franchise —	$15K
Royalty — 5%;	Ad. — 3%
Earnings Claim Statement:	Yes
Term of Contract (Years):	15/15
Avg. # Of Employees:	2 FT, 12 PT
Passive Ownership:	Discouraged
Area Develop. Agreements:	Yes/10
Sub-Franchising Contracts:	Yes
Expand In Territory:	Yes
Space Needs: 1,200-2,500 SF; FS, SF, SC, RM	

Support & Training Provided:

Site Selection Assistance:	Yes
Lease Negotiation Assistance:	Yes
Co-Operative Advertising:	Yes
Franchisee Assoc./Member:	Yes/Yes
Size Of Corporate Staff:	25
On-Going Support:	a,B,C,D,E,F,G,H,I

Training: 2 Weeks Corporate Headquarters; 1 Week Franchisee Location; On-Going As Needs.

Minority-Specific Programs: Although we support the objectives of the NMFI, we do not have any specific programs in place at this time.

Specific Expansion Plans:

US:	Midwest

BUMPERS DRIVE-IN

855 Pear Orchard, # 103
Ridgeland, MS 39157
Tel: (800) 467-0803 (601) 977-0803
Fax: (601) 977-9391
E-Mail: bumpers@netdoor.com
Web Site:
Ms. Monica Harrigill, President

Fast food drive-in system, which provides quality hamburgers, chicken, catfish, hot dogs, ice creams, shakes, french fries, potato pearls (tots), soft drinks, tea, coffee and desserts, namely apple pies, banana splits, short cakes with various toppings.

Background:

Established: 1985;	1st Franchised: 1995
Franchised Units:	4
Company-Owned Units:	28
Total Units:	32
Minority-Owned Units:	
African-American:	1
Asian-American:	1
Hispanic:	0
Native American:	0
Other:	
North America:	3 States
Density:	29 in MS, 2 in TN, 1 in AR

Financial/Terms:

Cash Investment:	$75-125K
Total Investment:	$350-425K
Minimum Net Worth:	$300K
Fees: Franchise —	$10K
Royalty — 3%;	Ad. — 6%
Earnings Claim Statement:	No
Term of Contract (Years):	10/10
Avg. # Of Employees:	8 FT, 12 PT
Passive Ownership:	Not Allowed
Area Develop. Agreements:	Yes/10
Sub-Franchising Contracts:	No
Expand In Territory:	Yes
Space Needs: 24,000 SF; FS	

Support & Training Provided:

Site Selection Assistance:	Yes

Lease Negotiation Assistance: Yes
Co-Operative Advertising: Yes
Franchisee Assoc./Member: No
Size Of Corporate Staff: 72
On-Going Support: A,B,C,D,E,F,G,H,I
Training: 6 Weeks at Bumpers of Pearl.
Minority-Specific Programs: We can provide all the assistance needed to be successful on requested basis.

Specific Expansion Plans:
US: MS, AR, TN, TX, MO, NC, SC

BURGER KING (CANADA)

401 The West Mall, 7th Fl.
Etobicoke, ON M9C 5J4 CANADA
Tel: (416) 626-7423
Fax: (416) 626-6691
E-Mail: gheos@whopper.com
Web Site: www.burgerking.com
Mr. George Heos, Franchise Devel. Manager

Second largest hamburger chain in the world. BURGER KING is currently recruiting franchisees qualified to develop multiple units in markets throughout Canada.

Background:
Established: 1954;   1st Franchised: 1969
Franchised Units: 190
Company-Owned Units: <u>110</u>
Total Units: 300
Minority-Owned Units:
  African-American:
  Asian-American:
  Hispanic:
  Native American:
  Other:
North America: 10 Provinces
Density: 143 in ON, 59 in PQ, 30 BC

Financial/Terms:
Cash Investment: $150-250K
Total Investment: $300K-1.1MM
Minimum Net Worth: $800K
Fees: Franchise — $55K
  Royalty — 4%;   Ad. — 4%

Earnings Claim Statement: Yes
Term of Contract (Years):   20/20
Avg. # Of Employees: 15 FT, 35 PT
Passive Ownership: Allowed
Area Develop. Agreements: Yes/1-5
Sub-Franchising Contracts: No
Expand In Territory: Yes
Space Needs: 3,000-3,800 SF; FS, SF, SC, RM

Support & Training Provided:
Site Selection Assistance: Yes
Lease Negotiation Assistance: Yes
Co-Operative Advertising: Yes
Franchisee Assoc./Member: Yes
Size Of Corporate Staff: 70
On-Going Support: B,C,D,E,F,H
Training: 15 Weeks Combined Classroom and Restaurant Training in Various Locations.
Minority-Specific Programs: Although we support the objectives of the NMFI, we do not have any specific programs in place at this time.

Specific Expansion Plans:
US: Throughout Canada

BW-3 BUFFALO WILD WINGS

600 S. Highway 169
1919 Interchange Tower
Minneapolis, MN 55426
Tel: (800) 499-9586 (612) 593-9943
Fax: (612) 593-9787
E-Mail: bill@bw3.com
Web Site: www.bw3.com
Mr. Bill McClintock, VP Franchise Development

BW-3 BUFFALO WILD WINGS has a sports-themed environment, complete with large-screen TV's, interactive games and memorabilia, with an inexpensive a la carte menu, concentrating buffalo wings, great sandwiches and 12 proprietary sauces.

Background:
Established: 1982;   1st Franchised: 1991
Franchised Units: 80
Company-Owned Units: <u>26</u>

Total Units: 106
Minority-Owned Units:
  African-American: 4
  Asian-American:
  Hispanic:
  Native American:
  Other:
North America: 18 States
Density: OH, MI, IN

Financial/Terms:
Cash Investment: $522-850K
Total Investment: $522-850K
Minimum Net Worth: $600K
Fees: Franchise — $25-30K
  Royalty — 5%;   Ad. — 3%
Earnings Claim Statement: Yes
Term of Contract (Years):   10/5/5
Avg. # Of Employees: Approx 50
Passive Ownership: Discouraged
Area Develop. Agreements: Yes
Sub-Franchising Contracts: No
Expand In Territory: Yes
Space Needs: 5,000-7,000 SF; FS, SF, SC, RM

Support & Training Provided:
Site Selection Assistance: Yes
Lease Negotiation Assistance: Yes
Co-Operative Advertising: Yes
Franchisee Assoc./Member: Yes
Size Of Corporate Staff: NR
On-Going Support: A,B,C,D,E,F,G,H,I
Training: 3 Weeks Training.
Minority-Specific Programs: We encourage anyone to apply who can meet financial and operational experience requirements.

Specific Expansion Plans:
US: All United States

CAPTAIN D'S SEAFOOD

1717 Elm Hill Pike, # A-10
Nashville, TN 37210
Tel: (800) 346-9637 (615) 231-2616
Fax: (615) 2312650
E-Mail: quentin_murray@captainds.com
Web Site: www.shoneys.com
Mr. Quentin Murray, Director of Franchising

Quick-service, sit-down/take-out seafood restaurant, serving broiled, baked and fried fish, shrimp and crab entrees, as well as chicken, specialty salads and a wide range of vegetables and desserts.

Background:
Established: 1969;   1st Franchised: 1969
Franchised Units: 207
Company-Owned Units: <u>365</u>

Total Units: 572
Minority-Owned Units:
  African-American: 2
  Asian-American: 6
  Hispanic: 0
  Native American: 0
North America: 22 States
Density: 96 in GA, 81 in TN, 65 AL

Financial/Terms:
Cash Investment: $150K
Total Investment: $884K-1.3MM
Minimum Net Worth: $300K
Fees: Franchise — $20K
  Royalty — 3%; Ad. — 5.25%
Earnings Claim Statement: Yes
Term of Contract (Years): 20/20
Avg. # Of Employees: 5 FT, 15 PT
Passive Ownership: Discouraged
Area Develop. Agreements: Yes/Varies
Sub-Franchising Contracts: No
Expand In Territory: Yes
Space Needs: 2,424-2,715 SF; FS, C-Store, Food Court

Support & Training Provided:
Site Selection Assistance: Yes
Lease Negotiation Assistance: No
Co-Operative Advertising: Yes
Franchisee Assoc./Member: Yes
Size Of Corporate Staff: NR
On-Going Support: C,D,e,G,h,I
Training: Approximately 6 Weeks Nashville, TN; Depends on Franchisee's Experience.
Minority-Specific Programs: Our assistance for minority franchisees encompasses fee deferral of the initial license fee and a royalty rate reduction for the first 3 years.

Specific Expansion Plans:
US: South and Southeast

CHICAGO'S PIZZA
1111 N. Broadway
Greenfield, IN 46140
Tel: (317) 462-9878
Fax: (317) 467-1877
E-Mail: colips@freewooeb.com
Mr. Robert L. McDonald, CEO

Franchise designed for owner/operator. Flexibility allowed to ensure success. Can be adapted to large and small operations. Inside dining/carry-out/delivery.

Background:
Established: 1979; 1st Franchised: 1981
Franchised Units: 10
Company-Owned Units: 0
Total Units: 10
Minority-Owned Units:
  African-American: 0
  Asian-American: 0
  Hispanic: 0
  Native American: 0
  Other: 0
North America: 4 States
Density: 8 in IN, 1 in OH, 1 in KY

Financial/Terms:
Cash Investment: $25-50K
Total Investment: $100-300K
Minimum Net Worth: $50K
Fees: Franchise — $10K
  Royalty — 4%; Ad. — 2%
Earnings Claim Statement: No
Term of Contract (Years): 10/10
Avg. # Of Employees: 3 FT, 12 PT
Passive Ownership: Not Allowed
Area Develop. Agreements: Yes/Open
Sub-Franchising Contracts: No
Expand In Territory: Yes
Space Needs: 1,800-3,000 SF; FS, SC

Support & Training Provided:
Site Selection Assistance: Yes
Lease Negotiation Assistance: Yes
Co-Operative Advertising: Yes
Franchisee Assoc./Member: No
Size Of Corporate Staff: 3
On-Going Support: C,D,E,F,H
Training: 2 Weeks at Existing Store.
Minority-Specific Programs: Although we support the objectives of the NMFI, we do not have any specific programs in place at this time.

Specific Expansion Plans:
US: IN, OH, MI, KY and IL

COUSINS SUBS
N83 W13400 Leon Rd.
Menomonee Falls, WI 53051
Tel: (800) 238-9736 (262) 253-7700
Fax: (262) 253-7705

E-Mail: dkilby@cousinssubs.com
Web Site: www.cousinssubs.com
Mr. David K. Kilby, Executive VP

COUSINS SUBS celebrates over 27 years as an exceptionally high-volume, fast service concept in up-scale, in-line, free-standing and non-traditional locations. # 1 sub sandwich chain for five years running (Income Opportunities Magazine). Midwest, Southwest and South development available for single, multiple and area developers.

Background:
Established: 1972; 1st Franchised: 1985
Franchised Units: 110
Company-Owned Units: 35
Total Units: 145
Minority-Owned Units:
  African-American: 3
  Asian-American: 0
  Hispanic: 1
  Native American: 0
  Other: 6 Indian
North America: NR
Density: 91in WI, 27 in AZ, 16 in MN

Financial/Terms:
Cash Investment: $47-76.6K
Total Investment: $165-253K
Minimum Net Worth: $200K
Fees: Franchise — $15K
  Royalty — 4-6%; Ad. — 2%
Earnings Claim Statement: Yes
Term of Contract (Years): 10/10
Avg. # Of Employees: 3 FT, 17 PT
Passive Ownership: Not Allowed
Area Develop. Agreements: Yes/10
Sub-Franchising Contracts: Yes
Expand In Territory: Yes
Space Needs: 1,800 SF; FS, SF, SC, C-Store

Support & Training Provided:
Site Selection Assistance: Yes
Lease Negotiation Assistance: Yes
Co-Operative Advertising: Yes
Franchisee Assoc./Member: Yes/Yes
Size Of Corporate Staff: 50
On-Going Support: B,C,D,E,F,G,H,I
Training: 1 Wk Corp. HQ;4 Wks Training Store;10 Days Franchisee's New Store;3 Field Visits/mo 1st yr
Minority-Specific Programs: Puerto Rico: 50 store development.

Specific Expansion Plans:
US: Midwest, Southwest, West

DAIRY BELLE FREEZE
780 Montague Expressway, # 702
San Jose, CA 95131

Tel: (408) 433-9337
Fax: (408) 433-9395
E-Mail: stone557@aol.com
Web Site: www.dairybelle.com
Ms. Patricia (Pat) Souza, Executive Vice
President

Locally-owned and operated since 1957, DAIRY BELLE restaurants have provided quality food that is cooked to order to ensure the satisfaction of each customer. Our menu has expanded from soft-serve cones, hamburgers, fries and soft drinks to now include specialty sandwiches, Mexican food and a variety of soft-serve desserts.

Background:
Established: 1957;	1st Franchised: 1981
Franchised Units:	13
Company-Owned Units:	0
Total Units:	13
Minority-Owned Units:	
African-American:	0
Asian-American:	11
Hispanic:	2
Native American:	0
Other:	
North America:	1 State
Density:	13 in CA

Financial/Terms:
Cash Investment:	$50-100K
Total Investment:	$50-200K
Minimum Net Worth:	$100K
Fees: Franchise —	$12.5K
Royalty — 4.5%/$600;	Ad. — 2%
Earnings Claim Statement:	Yes
Term of Contract (Years):	10/10
Avg. # Of Employees:	4 FT, 3-10 PT
Passive Ownership:	Not Allowed
Area Develop. Agreements:	No
Sub-Franchising Contracts:	No
Expand In Territory:	Yes
Space Needs: 1,500 SF; FS	

Support & Training Provided:
Site Selection Assistance:	Yes
Lease Negotiation Assistance:	Yes
Co-Operative Advertising:	Yes
Franchisee Assoc./Member:	No

Size Of Corporate Staff:	4
On-Going Support:	B,C,D,E,H

Training: 2-3 Weeks at Existing Franchisee's Restaurant; 2-3 Weeks at New Franchisee's Restaurant.
Minority-Specific Programs: Although we support the objectives of the NMFI, we do not have any specific programs in place at this time.

Specific Expansion Plans:
US:	Northern California

DIAMOND DAVE'S TACO COMPANY

201 S. Clinton St., # 281
Iowa City, IA 52240
Tel: (319) 337-7690
Fax: (319) 337-4707
E-Mail:
Web Site: www.diamonddaves.com
Mr. Stanley J. White, President

DIAMOND DAVE'S TACO COMPANY is a regional restaurant chain, featuring great family-priced Mexican/American cuisine. Opportunities include full-service restaurant/ bar concept. Locations available in enclosed regional malls, strip centers and free-standing units.

Background:
Established: 1980;	1st Franchised: 1981
Franchised Units:	29
Company-Owned Units:	2
Total Units:	31
Minority-Owned Units:	
African-American:	
Asian-American:	
Hispanic:	
Native American:	
Other:	
North America:	5 States
Density:	14 in IA, 9 in IL, 5 in WI

Financial/Terms:
Cash Investment:	$50-75K
Total Investment:	$150-250K
Minimum Net Worth:	$NR
Fees: Franchise —	$15K
Royalty — 4%;	Ad. — 1%
Earnings Claim Statement:	No
Term of Contract (Years):	10/10
Avg. # Of Employees:	5 FT, 15 PT

Passive Ownership:	Discouraged
Area Develop. Agreements:	Yes
Sub-Franchising Contracts:	No
Expand In Territory:	Yes
Space Needs: 2,000-3,000 SF; SC, RM	

Support & Training Provided:
Site Selection Assistance:	Yes
Lease Negotiation Assistance:	Yes
Co-Operative Advertising:	Yes
Franchisee Assoc./Member:	NR
Size Of Corporate Staff:	4
On-Going Support:	C,D,E,F,G,H

Training: 2-4 Weeks Local Restaurant.
Minority-Specific Programs: Although we support the objectives of the NMFI, we do not have any specific programs in place at this time.

Specific Expansion Plans:
US:	Midwest Only

EL POLLO LOCO

3333 Michelson Dr., # 550
Irvine, CA 92612
Tel: (800) 99-POLLO (949) 251-5031
Fax: (949) 251-5371
E-Mail: elpolloloco@hotmail.com
Web Site: www.elpollolocorestaurants.com
Mr. Stephen Dunn, Director Franchise Development

The nation's leading flame-broiled chicken, quick-service restaurant, specializing in great tasting Mexican food that offers customers a healthy alternative to traditional fast-food.

Background:
Established: 1975;	1st Franchised: 1983
Franchised Units:	161
Company-Owned Units:	100
Total Units:	261
Minority-Owned Units:	
African-American:	2%
Asian-American:	4%
Hispanic:	25%
Native American:	0%
Other:	25%
North America:	4 States
Density:	240 in CA, 7 in NV, 5 in AZ

Financial/Terms:

Cash Investment:	$300K minimum
Total Investment:	$315.5-645.5K
Minimum Net Worth:	$1MM
Fees: Franchise —	$35K
Royalty — 4%;	Ad. — 4%
Earnings Claim Statement:	No
Term of Contract (Years):	20
Avg. # Of Employees:	8 FT, 17 PT
Passive Ownership:	Discouraged
Area Develop. Agreements:	Yes/Varies
Sub-Franchising Contracts:	No
Expand In Territory:	Yes
Space Needs: 2,600 SF, FS, SF	

Support & Training Provided:

Site Selection Assistance:	Yes
Lease Negotiation Assistance:	Yes
Co-Operative Advertising:	Yes
Franchisee Assoc./Member:	Yes/Yes
Size Of Corporate Staff:	50
On-Going Support:	B,C,D,E,h,I
Training: 6 Weeks in Southern California.	

Minority-Specific Programs: Although we support the objectives of the NMFI, we do not have any specific programs in place at this time.

Specific Expansion Plans:

US:	CA, AZ, NV, TX

Since 1952
FATBURGER

1218 Third St. Promenade
Santa Monica, CA 90401-1308
Tel: (310) 319-1850
Fax: (310) 319-1863
E-Mail:
Web Site: www.fatburger.net
Mrs. Angelina Morse, Dir. Franchise Relations

The classic hamburger stand, serving cooked-to-order burgers at an open grill since 1952. Also serving grilled chicken-breast sandwiches, freshly-made onion rings and real milkshakes in a fun environment with a unique R & B jukebox.

Background:

Established: 1952;	1st Franchised: 1980
Franchised Units:	23
Company-Owned Units:	13
Total Units:	36
Minority-Owned Units:	
African-American:	30%
Asian-American:	
Hispanic:	
Native American:	
Other:	
North America:	3 States
Density:	28 in CA, 7 in NV

Financial/Terms:

Cash Investment:	$150-250K
Total Investment:	$370-730K
Minimum Net Worth:	$NR
Fees: Franchise —	$30K
Royalty — 5%;	Ad. — 2%
Earnings Claim Statement:	Yes
Term of Contract (Years):	15/10/10
Avg. # Of Employees:	16 - 40
Passive Ownership:	Allowed
Area Develop. Agreements:	Yes/5
Sub-Franchising Contracts:	No
Expand In Territory:	No
Space Needs: 1,800-2,000 SF; FS, SF, SC	

Support & Training Provided:

Site Selection Assistance:	Yes
Lease Negotiation Assistance:	No
Co-Operative Advertising:	No
Franchisee Assoc./Member:	No
Size Of Corporate Staff:	10
On-Going Support:	C,D,E,H
Training: 10 Weeks Orange County, CA; 7-10 Days On-Site.	

Minority-Specific Programs: Although we support the objectives of the NMFI, we do not have any specific programs in place at this time.

Specific Expansion Plans:

US:	All United States

FOX'S PIZZA DEN

3243 Old Frankstown Rd.
Pittsburgh, PA 15239
Tel: (800) 899-3697 (724) 733-7888
Fax: (724) 325-5479
E-Mail: foxs@alltel.net

Web Site: www.foxspizza.com
Mr. James R. Fox, President

FOX'S PIZZA DEN believes in one philosophy — you earned it, you keep it! FOX'S royalties are $200 a month — no percentages of sales. FOX'S PIZZA DENS offers the finest pizza, specialty sandwiches, salads and sides and our house special - the 'wedgie.'

Background:

Established: 1971;	1st Franchised: 1974
Franchised Units:	205
Company-Owned Units:	0
Total Units:	205
Minority-Owned Units:	
African-American:	
Asian-American:	
Hispanic:	
Native American:	
Other:	
North America:	19 States
Density:	105 in PA, 42 in WV, 12 OH

Financial/Terms:

Cash Investment:	$50-80K
Total Investment:	$50-80K
Minimum Net Worth:	$N/A
Fees: Franchise —	$8K
Royalty — $200/Mo.;	Ad. — 0%
Earnings Claim Statement:	No
Term of Contract (Years):	5/5
Avg. # Of Employees:	2-3 FT, 8-10 PT
Passive Ownership:	Discouraged
Area Develop. Agreements:	Yes
Sub-Franchising Contracts:	Yes
Expand In Territory:	Yes
Space Needs: 1,000-2,000 SF; FS, SF, SC	

Support & Training Provided:

Site Selection Assistance:	Yes
Lease Negotiation Assistance:	No
Co-Operative Advertising:	Yes
Franchisee Assoc./Member:	NR
Size Of Corporate Staff:	8
On-Going Support:	B,C,D,E,F,G,H,I
Training: 7 Days On-Site.	

Minority-Specific Programs: Although we support the objectives of the NMFI, we do not have any specific programs in place at this time.

Specific Expansion Plans:

US:	All United States

HARDEE'S FOOD SYSTEMS

1233 Hardee's Blvd.
Rocky Mount, NC 27804-2815
Tel: (800) 997-8435 (252) 977-2000
Fax: (252) 450-8655

Web Site: www.hardeesrestaurants.com
Mr. Don McLean, Franchise Manager
Fast food.

Background:

Established: 1960; 1st Franchised: 1961
Franchised Units: 1466
Company-Owned Units: 1418
Total Units: 2884
Minority-Owned Units:
  African-American: 7
  Asian-American:
  Hispanic:
  Native American:
  Other: 237
North America: 38 States
Density: 315 in NC, 207 in VA,186 SC

Financial/Terms:

Cash Investment: $300K
Total Investment: $1.19-1.25MM
Minimum Net Worth: $1MM
Fees: Franchise — $35K
  Royalty — 4%;   Ad. — 5%
Earnings Claim Statement: No
Term of Contract (Years):   20/5
Avg. # Of Employees: 40 Total
Passive Ownership: Allowed
Area Develop. Agreements: Yes/Varies
Sub-Franchising Contracts: No
Expand In Territory: Yes
Space Needs: 2,000 SF; FS, SC, RM, Univ.

Support & Training Provided:

Site Selection Assistance: Yes
Lease Negotiation Assistance: No
Co-Operative Advertising: Yes
Franchisee Assoc./Member: Yes/No
Size Of Corporate Staff: 300
On-Going Support: A,B,C,D,E,f,h,I
Training: 3 Days Local Restaurant
Orientation; 360 Hours Formal Training.
Minority-Specific Programs: Although we
support the objectives of the NMFI, we do
not have any specific programs in place at
this time.

Specific Expansion Plans:

US: Southeast and Midwest

HO-LEE-CHOW
658 Danforth Ave., # 201
Toronto, ON M4J 5B9 CANADA

Tel: (800)HO-LEE-CHOW (416) 778-6660
Fax: (416) 778-6818
E-Mail:
Web Site:
Mr. Jake Cappiello, President

Great Chinese food delivered fast and fresh.
Each entree in our restaurants is cooked-to-
order with no added MSG or preservatives.
Each order is delivered in under 45 minutes.
All locations are brightly lit and have our
open kitchen concept so customers can view
their food being cooked in the most pristine
kitchens.

Background:

Established: 1989;   1st Franchised: 1989
Franchised Units: 19
Company-Owned Units: 4
Total Units: 23
Minority-Owned Units:
  African-American:
  Asian-American:
  Hispanic:
  Native American:
North America: 1 State, 1 Provinces
Density: 22 in ON

Financial/Terms:

Cash Investment: $75-100K
Total Investment: $150-175K
Minimum Net Worth: $100K
Fees: Franchise — $Included
  Royalty — 6%;   Ad. — 3%
Earnings Claim Statement: Yes
Term of Contract (Years):   5/15
Avg. # Of Employees: 3 FT, 1 PT
Passive Ownership: Discouraged
Area Develop. Agreements: Yes/20
Sub-Franchising Contracts: Yes
Expand In Territory: Yes
Space Needs: 900 SF; FS, SF, SC

Support & Training Provided:

Site Selection Assistance: Yes
Lease Negotiation Assistance: Yes
Co-Operative Advertising: Yes
Franchisee Assoc./Member: Yes/Yes
Size Of Corporate Staff: 50+
On-Going Support: A,B,C,D,E,F,G,H,I
Training: 1 Week Head Office in Toronto,
ON; 4 Weeks On-Site.
Minority-Specific Programs: Although we
support the objectives of the NMFI, we do
not have any specific programs in place at
this time.

Specific Expansion Plans:

US: All United States

HUNGRY HOWIE'S PIZZA & SUBS
30300 Stephenson Highway, # 200
Madison Heights, MI 48071
Tel: (800) 624-8122 (248) 414-3300
Fax: (248) 414-3301
E-Mail: franchiseinfo@hungryhowies.com
Web Site: www.hungryhowies.com
Mr. Bob Cuffaro, Franchise Development

HUNGRY HOWIE'S, the innovator of the
award-winning Flavored-Crust Pizza, is the
nation's 9th largest carry-out / delivery pizza
company. Menu offerings include 8 varieties
of Flavored-Crust pizzas, delicious oven-
baked subs and fresh and crispy salads.

Background:

Established: 1973;   1st Franchised: 1982
Franchised Units: 425
Company-Owned Units: 0
Total Units: 425
Minority-Owned Units:
  African-American: 2
  Asian-American:
  Hispanic:
  Native American:
  Other:
North America: 19 States, 1 Province
Density: 180 in FL, 170 in MI, 15 CA

Financial/Terms:

Cash Investment: $50K
Total Investment: $85-125K
Minimum Net Worth: $150K
Fees: Franchise — $15K
  Royalty — 5%;   Ad. — 3%
Earnings Claim Statement: No
Term of Contract (Years):   20/20
Avg. # Of Employees: 4 FT, 8 PT
Passive Ownership: Discouraged
Area Develop. Agreements: Yes/20
Sub-Franchising Contracts: Yes
Expand In Territory: Yes
Space Needs: 1,200 SF; SC

Support & Training Provided:

Site Selection Assistance: Yes
Lease Negotiation Assistance: Yes
Co-Operative Advertising: Yes
Franchisee Assoc./Member: No
Size Of Corporate Staff: 20
On-Going Support: B,C,D,E,F,G,h

Training: 5 Weeks Madison Heights, MI.
Minority-Specific Programs: Although we support the objectives of the NMFI, we do not have any specific programs in place at this time.

Specific Expansion Plans:

US: All United States

JERSEY MIKE'S SUBMARINES & SALADS

1973 Hwy. 34, # E 21
Wall, NJ 07719
Tel: (800) 321-7676 (732) 282-2323
Fax: (732) 282-2244
E-Mail: jmikes@injersey.com
Web Site: www.jerseymikes.com
Mr. Victor F. Merlo, Vice President Sales

JERSEY MIKE'S is a submarine sandwich franchise company which prides itself on producing the freshest submarine sandwich in the industry. They bake bread daily in the store. Roast beefs are cooked on premises and meats and cheeses are sliced in front of the customer. Awards include 'Best Sub' in Nashville, Charlotte, RTP, Wilmington, Greenville and Ocean/Monmouth, NJ.

Background:

Established: 1956;	1st Franchised: 1986
Franchised Units:	125
Company-Owned Units:	6
Total Units:	131
Minority-Owned Units:	
African-American:	
Asian-American:	
Hispanic:	
Native American:	
Other:	5% Total
North America:	13 States
Density:	83 in NC, 25 in OH, 15 in TN

Financial/Terms:

Cash Investment:	$NR
Total Investment:	$150-200K
Minimum Net Worth:	$NR
Fees: Franchise —	$18.5K
Royalty — 5.5%;	Ad. — 3.5%
Earnings Claim Statement:	
Term of Contract (Years):	10/10
Avg. # Of Employees:	7 FT, 8 PT
Passive Ownership:	Discouraged
Area Develop. Agreements:	Yes/w0
Sub-Franchising Contracts:	No
Expand In Territory:	NR
Space Needs: 1,500 SF; FS, SC	

Support & Training Provided:

Site Selection Assistance:	Yes
Lease Negotiation Assistance:	Yes
Co-Operative Advertising:	Yes
Franchisee Assoc./Member:	No
Size Of Corporate Staff:	30
On-Going Support:	B,C,D,E,G,H,I
Training: 3-4 Weeks Nashville, TN.	

Minority-Specific Programs: Although we support the objectives of the NMFI, we do not have any specific programs in place at this time.

Specific Expansion Plans:

US: All United States

KFC

1441 Gardiner Ln.
Louisville, KY 40213
Tel: (502) 874-8300
Fax: (502) 874-8732
E-Mail:
Web Site: www.kfc.com
Mrs. Nikki Weis, Franchise Specialist

World's largest quick-service restaurant with a chicken-dominant menu. KFC offers full-service restaurants and non-traditional express units for captive markets.

Background:

Established: 1954;	1st Franchised: 1959
Franchised Units:	6663
Company-Owned Units:	2975
Total Units:	9638
Minority-Owned Units:	
African-American:	34
Asian-American:	43
Hispanic:	11
Native American:	0
Other:	
North America:	50 States,10 Provinces
Density:	CA, TX, IL

Financial/Terms:

Cash Investment:	$500K
Total Investment:	$700K-1.2MM
Minimum Net Worth:	$1MM
Fees: Franchise —	$25K
Royalty — 4%;	Ad. — 4.5%

Earnings Claim Statement: No
Term of Contract (Years): 20/10
Avg. # Of Employees: 2 FT, 22 PT
Passive Ownership: Not Allowed
Area Develop. Agreements: No
Sub-Franchising Contracts: No
Expand In Territory: Yes
Space Needs: 2,000-3,000 SF; FS

Support & Training Provided:

Site Selection Assistance:	Yes
Lease Negotiation Assistance:	No
Co-Operative Advertising:	Yes
Franchisee Assoc./Member:	Yes/Yes
Size Of Corporate Staff:	820
On-Going Support:	C,d,E,G,h,I
Training: 14 Weeks at Varied Sites.	

Minority-Specific Programs: Although we support the objectives of the NMFI, we do not have any specific programs in place at this time.

Specific Expansion Plans:

US: All United States

KOYA JAPAN

720 Broadway, # 207
Winnipeg, MB R3G 0X1 CANADA
Tel: (888) KOYA-USA (204) 783-4433
Fax: (204) 783-1749
E-Mail: koya-jp@pangea.ca
Web Site: www.koyajapan.com
Mr. Steve M. Sabbagh, President

Delicious Japanese food served fast from the freshest of ingredients and complimented by or unique sauce. What makes us successful is our cooking techniques, each meal is made to order in full view of the customer. Koya Japan -- where freshness sizzles before your eyes.

Background:

Established: 1985;	1st Franchised: 1986
Franchised Units:	19
Company-Owned Units:	0
Total Units:	19
Minority-Owned Units:	
African-American:	0
Asian-American:	16
Hispanic:	0
Native American:	0
Other:	
North America:	6 Provinces
Density:	5 in MB, 4 in ON, 4 in BC

Financial/Terms:

Cash Investment:	$50% of Total

Total Investment:	$135-250K
Minimum Net Worth:	$100K
Fees: Franchise —	$25K
Royalty — 6%;	Ad. — 2%
Earnings Claim Statement:	No
Term of Contract (Years):	Up to 10
Avg. # Of Employees:	3 FT, 1 PT
Passive Ownership:	Allowed
Area Develop. Agreements:	Yes/20
Sub-Franchising Contracts:	No
Expand In Territory:	Yes
Space Needs: 300-400 SF; RM	

Support & Training Provided:

Site Selection Assistance:	Yes
Lease Negotiation Assistance:	Yes
Co-Operative Advertising:	Yes
Franchisee Assoc./Member:	No
Size Of Corporate Staff:	3
On-Going Support:	C,d,E,I

Training: Up to 1 Month in Operating Location; up to 1 Month On-Site; 2-3 Days at Head Office.

Minority-Specific Programs: We currently have no specific programs in place to aid minorities. However, because of the style of the food we serve we have a franchisee base which is 90% Asian. We strongly encourage our franchisees to develop a network of support as well as provide administrative support through our head office.

Specific Expansion Plans:

US:	All United States

LE CROISSANT SHOP

LE CROISSANT SHOP
227 W. 40th St.
New York, NY 10018
Tel: (212) 719-5940
Fax: (212) 944-0269
E-Mail: franchise_info@lecroissantshop.com
Web Site: www.lecroissantshop.com
Mr. Arnaud Thieffry, Vice President

French bakery cafe - specialty croissants, bread, soups, french sandwiches and gourmet salads. Breakfast-Lunch-Dinner.

Background:

Established: 1981;	1st Franchised: 1984	
Franchised Units:		12
Company-Owned Units:		3
Total Units:		15
Minority-Owned Units:		
African-American:		0
Asian-American:		0
Hispanic:		8

Native American:		0
Other:		1
North America:		3 States
Density:	12 in NY, 1 in PA, 1 in FL	

Financial/Terms:

Cash Investment:	$1/3 Invest.
Total Investment:	$140-576K
Minimum Net Worth:	$NR
Fees: Franchise —	$22.5K
Royalty — 5%;	Ad. — NR
Earnings Claim Statement:	No
Term of Contract (Years):	10/5/5
Avg. # Of Employees:	10 FT
Passive Ownership:	Allowed
Area Develop. Agreements:	Yes/10
Sub-Franchising Contracts:	No
Expand In Territory:	Yes
Space Needs: 500-2,000 SF; FS, SF, SC, RM	

Support & Training Provided:

Site Selection Assistance:	Yes
Lease Negotiation Assistance:	Yes
Co-Operative Advertising:	N/A
Franchisee Assoc./Member:	No
Size Of Corporate Staff:	6
On-Going Support:	C,D,E

Training: 2 Weeks Headquarters in New York.

Minority-Specific Programs: Although we support the objectives of the NMFI, we do not have any specific programs in place at this time.

Specific Expansion Plans:

US:	East Coast

LEE'S FAMOUS RECIPE CHICKEN
6045 Barfield Rd.
Atlanta, GA 30328
Tel: (404) 459-5807
Fax: (404) 259-5797
E-Mail: kspencer@rtminc.com
Ms. Karen Spencer, VP Franchise Sales/Admin.

Quick-service restaurant - chicken segment. Winners International is a multi-category, multi-brand international growth company, focused on the quick, convenient distribution of food. Our vision is to place our products in the hands of people worldwide - 'Food Within Your Reach.'TM

Background:

Established: 1966;	1st Franchised: 1995	
Franchised Units:		154
Company-Owned Units:		18
Total Units:		172
Minority-Owned Units:		
African-American:		
Asian-American:		
Hispanic:		
Native American:		
Other:		
North America:	16 States, 1 Province	
Density:	54 in KY, 49 in OH, 20 in FL	

Financial/Terms:

Cash Investment:	$10K
Total Investment:	$410K-1.1MM
Minimum Net Worth:	$500K
Fees: Franchise —	$20K
Royalty — 4%;	Ad. — 2%
Earnings Claim Statement:	No
Term of Contract (Years):	20/20
Avg. # Of Employees:	8-10 FT, 30 PT
Passive Ownership:	Discouraged
Area Develop. Agreements:	Yes
Sub-Franchising Contracts:	No
Expand In Territory:	Yes
Space Needs: 1,800 SF; FS	

Support & Training Provided:

Site Selection Assistance:	Yes
Lease Negotiation Assistance:	No
Co-Operative Advertising:	Yes
Franchisee Assoc./Member:	Yes/Yes
Size Of Corporate Staff:	40
On-Going Support:	C,D,E,G,H

Training: 6 Weeks Certified Training Units.

Minority-Specific Programs: Although we support the objectives of the NMFI, we do not have any specific programs in place at this time.

Specific Expansion Plans:

US:	Southeast and Midwest

LONG JOHN SILVER'S
P. O. Box 11988
Lexington, KY 40579
Tel: (800) 545-8360 (606) 388-6000
Fax: (606) 388-6190
E-Mail: fsales@ljsilvers.com
Web Site: www.ljsilvers.com
Mr. John Ramsay, VP Franchise Development

LONG JOHN SILVER'S is the largest, quick-service seafood restaurant chain in the world. We continue to aggressively grow with new units and sales. Opportunities are available in new and existing markets.

Background:
Established: 1969; 1st Franchised: 1970
Franchised Units: 473
Company-Owned Units: 760
Total Units: 1233
Minority-Owned Units:
   African-American: 1
   Asian-American: 1
   Hispanic: 0
   Native American: 0
   Other:
North America: 38 States
Density: 185 in TX, 114 in OH, 101 IN

Financial/Terms:
Cash Investment: $NR
Total Investment: $500-800K
Minimum Net Worth: $300K
Fees: Franchise — $20K
   Royalty — 4%; Ad. — 5%
Earnings Claim Statement: NR
Term of Contract (Years): 15/5/5
Avg. # Of Employees: NR
Passive Ownership: NR
Area Develop. Agreements: Yes
Sub-Franchising Contracts: No
Expand In Territory: Yes
Space Needs: NR SF; FS, C-Store, Food Court

Support & Training Provided:
Site Selection Assistance: Yes
Lease Negotiation Assistance: NR
Co-Operative Advertising: NR
Franchisee Assoc./Member: Yes
Size Of Corporate Staff: 250
On-Going Support: C,D,E,G,h,I
Training: 5 Weeks Closest Training Shop to Franchisee.

Minority-Specific Programs: Although we support the objectives of the NMFI, we do not have any specific programs in place at this time.

Specific Expansion Plans:
US: All United States

MAGIC WOK
2060 Laskey Rd.
Toledo, OH 43613
Tel: (419) 471-0696
Fax: (419) 471-0405
E-Mail: tpipatjz@pop3.utoledo.edu

Mr. Tommy Pipatjarasgit, Vice President

Quick-service, made-to-order, hot oriental concept. Stand alone, mall, drive-thru, delivery, school lunch and other non-traditional operations. Low barrier to entry, high return on investment. Domestic and international.

Background:
Established: 1983; 1st Franchised: 1991
Franchised Units: 7
Company-Owned Units: 7
Total Units: 14
Minority-Owned Units:
   African-American:
   Asian-American: 14
   Hispanic:
   Native American:
   Other: 43, Mid-eastern
North America: 5 States
Density: 7 in OH, 3 in MI

Financial/Terms:
Cash Investment: $50K
Total Investment: $95-150K
Minimum Net Worth: $100K
Fees: Franchise — $12.5K
   Royalty — 5%; Ad. — 3%
Earnings Claim Statement: No
Term of Contract (Years): 10/10
Avg. # Of Employees: 2 FT, 8 PT
Passive Ownership: Discouraged
Area Develop. Agreements: Yes
Sub-Franchising Contracts: Yes
Expand In Territory: Yes
Space Needs: 1,600 SF; FS

Support & Training Provided:
Site Selection Assistance: Yes
Lease Negotiation Assistance: Yes
Co-Operative Advertising: Yes
Franchisee Assoc./Member: No
Size Of Corporate Staff: 7
On-Going Support: C,D,E,F,H,I
Training: 3-4 Weeks Toledo, OH.

Minority-Specific Programs: Although we support the objectives of the NMFI, we do not have any specific programs in place at this time.

Specific Expansion Plans:
US: Midwest

MANCHU WOK
816 S. Military Trail, Unit # 6
Deerfield Beach, FL 33442
Tel: (800) 423-4009 (954) 481-9555
Fax: (954) 481-9670
E-Mail: alechudson@manchuwok.com

Web Site: www.manchuwok.com/index2.html
Mr. Alec Hudson, Franchise Sales Manager

MANCHU WOK is one of the largest Chinese quick service franchises in North America. MANCHU WOK operates in over 225 food court locations in large regional malls. MANCHU WOK franchisees are enjoying profitable growth; many owning multiple locations.

Background:
Established: 1980; 1st Franchised: 1980
Franchised Units: 140
Company-Owned Units: 47
Total Units: 187
Minority-Owned Units:
   African-American: 1%
   Asian-American: 90%
   Hispanic: 2%
   Native American: 0%
   Other:
North America: 28 States, 10 Provinces
Density: 45 in ON, 14 in FL, 13 in IL

Financial/Terms:
Cash Investment: $100-150K
Total Investment: $260-306K
Minimum Net Worth: $100-150K
Fees: Franchise — $20K
   Royalty — 7%; Ad. — 1%
Earnings Claim Statement: Yes
Term of Contract (Years): 5/5
Avg. # Of Employees: 2-3 FT, 6-10 PT
Passive Ownership: Discouraged
Area Develop. Agreements: No
Sub-Franchising Contracts: No
Expand In Territory: Yes
Space Needs: 600 SF; RM

Support & Training Provided:
Site Selection Assistance: Yes
Lease Negotiation Assistance: Yes
Co-Operative Advertising: N/A
Franchisee Assoc./Member: No
Size Of Corporate Staff: 500
On-Going Support: B,C,D,E,F,G,H,I
Training: 3-4 Weeks at Corporate Site.

Minority-Specific Programs: Although we support the objectives of the NMFI, we do not have any specific programs in place at this time.

Specific Expansion Plans:
US: Northeast and Southeast

MAUI TACOS

1775 The Exchange, # 540
Atlanta, GA 30339
Tel: (888) 628-4822 (770) 226-8226
Fax: (770) 541-2300
E-Mail: normanw@mauitacos.com
Web Site: www.mauitacos.com
Mr. Norman D. Willden, VP Franchise Development

Fast-casual "Maui-Mex" restaurant featuring Mexican Foods created by internationally recognized chef Mark Ellmao, using pineapple and lime juice marinade with island spices. Char-grilled chicken, steak, and lean beef burritos topped with unique salsas is our mainstay. This food experience is like a vacation in Maui.

Background:
Established: 1993;	1st Franchised: 1998
Franchised Units:	13
Company-Owned Units:	1
Total Units:	14
Minority-Owned Units:	
African-American:	
Asian-American:	
Hispanic:	
Native American:	
Other:	
North America:	2 States
Density:	8 in HI, 3 in GA

Financial/Terms:
Cash Investment:	$60K-125K
Total Investment:	$180-375K
Minimum Net Worth:	$300K
Fees: Franchise —	$20K
Royalty — 6%;	Ad. — 4%
Earnings Claim Statement:	Yes
Term of Contract (Years):	20/20
Avg. # Of Employees:	4 FT, 10 PT

Passive Ownership:	Discouraged
Area Develop. Agreements:	Yes/50
Sub-Franchising Contracts:	Yes
Expand In Territory:	Yes
Space Needs: 2,000 SF; FS, SF,SC, RM, HB, open air	

Support & Training Provided:
Site Selection Assistance:	Yes
Lease Negotiation Assistance:	Yes
Co-Operative Advertising:	Yes
Franchisee Assoc./Member:	Yes/Yes
Size Of Corporate Staff:	6
On-Going Support:	A,B,C,D,E,F,G,h,I
Training: 160 Hours in Atlanta, GA.	

Minority-Specific Programs: Although we support the objectives of the NMFI, we do not have any specific programs in place at this time.

Specific Expansion Plans:
US: All United States

MCDONALD'S

One McDonald's Plaza, Kroc Dr.
Oak Brook, IL 60523
Tel: (630) 623-6196
Fax: (630) 623-5645
E-Mail:
Web Site: www.mcdonalds.com
Franchise Department,

Quick-service restaurant.

Background:
Established: 1955;	1st Franchised: 1956
Franchised Units:	19607
Company-Owned Units:	5729
Total Units:	25336
Minority-Owned Units:	
African-American:	
Asian-American:	
Hispanic:	
Native American:	
Other:	21% are Minority-Owned
North America:	50 States
Density:	1,180 in CA, 838 TX, 737 FL

Financial/Terms:
Cash Investment:	$100K+
Total Investment:	$433.8-1,361K
Minimum Net Worth:	$N/A
Fees: Franchise —	$45K

Royalty — 12.5%;	Ad. — 4%
Earnings Claim Statement:	No
Term of Contract (Years):	20/20
Avg. # Of Employees:	NR
Passive Ownership:	Not Allowed
Area Develop. Agreements:	No
Sub-Franchising Contracts:	No
Expand In Territory:	No
Space Needs: 2,000 SF; FS	

Support & Training Provided:
Site Selection Assistance:	N/A
Lease Negotiation Assistance:	N/A
Co-Operative Advertising:	Yes
Franchisee Assoc./Member:	Yes/Yes
Size Of Corporate Staff:	NR
On-Going Support:	b,C,d,E,G,h,I
Training: NR	

Minority-Specific Programs: Targeted marketing/advertising in minority publications and with minority organizations; Business Facilities Lease (BFL) program is a franchising tool which allows franchising to individuals who have all the necessary skills and competencies but lack the total needed equity injection*; Have a team of national and regional lenders who support streamlining the process for franchisees securing necessary financing*. *These programs are available to all franchisees.

Specific Expansion Plans:
US: All United States

MICHEL'S BAGUETTE

16251 Dallas Parkway
Dallas, TX 75248
Tel: (972) 687-4091
Fax: (972) 687-4062
E-Mail: lboyd@richmont.com
Web Site: www.mmmuffins.com
Ms. Lori Boyd, Project Coordinator

European bakery/café, featuring authentic European breads, rolls, and pastries. In addition, we offer gourmet soups, salads, sandwiches, and hot entrees. We also serve a variety of beverages including espresso, gourmet coffee, teas and fruit juices. In addition to our full store, we have a "grab 'n' go" version as well.

Background:
Established: 1980;	1st Franchised: 1984
Franchised Units:	13

Company-Owned Units: 4
Total Units: 17
Minority-Owned Units:
  African-American:
  Asian-American:
  Hispanic:
  Native American:
  Other:
North America: 3 Provinces
Density: 13 in ON, 3 in AB, 1 in BC

Financial/Terms:
Cash Investment: $300K+
Total Investment: $750-800K
Minimum Net Worth: $500K
Fees: Franchise — $40K
  Royalty — 6%; Ad. — 0.5%
Earnings Claim Statement: No
Term of Contract (Years): 10/10
Avg. # Of Employees: 10 FT, 8-12 PT
Passive Ownership: Not Allowed
Area Develop. Agreements: Yes/(Int'l)
Sub-Franchising Contracts: Yes
Expand In Territory: Yes
Space Needs: 4,000 SF; SF, SC, RM

Support & Training Provided:
Site Selection Assistance: Yes
Lease Negotiation Assistance: Yes
Co-Operative Advertising: Yes
Franchisee Assoc./Member: No
Size Of Corporate Staff: 35
On Going Support: A,B,C,D,E,F,G,h
Training: 3 Months Toronto, ON or Dallas, TX.
Minority-Specific Programs: Although we support the objectives of the NMFI, we do not have any specific programs in place at this time.

Specific Expansion Plans:
US: N/A

MR. GOODCENTS SUBS & PASTAS

16210 W. 110th St.
Lenexa, KS 66219
Tel: (800) 648-2368 (913) 888-9800
Fax: (913) 888-8477

E-Mail: frandev@mrgoodcents
Web Site: www.mrgoodcents.com
Ms. Margot A. Bubien, Dir. Fran. Dev.

Quick-service lunch and dinner restaurant, serving freshly-sliced submarine sandwiches served on bread baked daily on premises, hot pasta dishes, delicious soups and fresh salads, quick-service restaurant for dine-in, carry-out, delivery or catering. Continued business consultant support and in-house 30-day training period.

Background:
Established: 1989; 1st Franchised: 1990
Franchised Units: 127
Company-Owned Units: 12
Total Units: 139
Minority-Owned Units:
  African-American: 2
  Asian-American: 0
  Hispanic: 4
  Native American: 0
  Other: 7 East Indian
North America: 15 States
Density: 38 in KS, 35 in MO, 5 in AZ

Financial/Terms:
Cash Investment: $30-35K
Total Investment: $81.8-197.8K
Minimum Net Worth: $NR
Fees: Franchise — $12.5K
  Royalty — 5%; Ad. — 2.5%
Earnings Claim Statement: No
Term of Contract (Years): 10/10
Avg. # Of Employees: 1-3 FT, 10-20 PT
Passive Ownership: N/A
Area Develop. Agreements: No
Sub-Franchising Contracts: No
Expand In Territory: Yes
Space Needs: 1,700 SF; FS, SC

Support & Training Provided:
Site Selection Assistance: Yes
Lease Negotiation Assistance: Yes
Co-Operative Advertising: Yes
Franchisee Assoc./Member: No
Size Of Corporate Staff: 40
On-Going Support: I
Training: 30 Days Kansas City, MO.
Minority-Specific Programs: Although we support the objectives of the NMFI, we do not have any specific programs in place at this time.

Specific Expansion Plans:
US: All United States

MR. HERO

5755 Granger Rd., # 200
Independence, OH 44131-1410
Tel: (800) 837-9599 (216) 398-1101

Fax: (216) 398-0707
E-Mail: mrhero@prodigy.net
Web Site: www.mrhero.com
Mr. Mitchell J. Winick, VP Business Development

MR. HERO is home to the Romanburger, Grill Steak-Roma and Original Philly Cheesesteak sandwich, along with a wide menu offering a side of dishes such as pasta, poppers, Texas toothpicks and more. With the Romanburger, MR. HERO's unique signature sandwich, no one in the market can compete.

Background:
Established: 1969; 1st Franchised: 1969
Franchised Units: 120
Company-Owned Units: 13
Total Units: 133
Minority-Owned Units:
  African-American: 8%
  Asian-American: 5%
  Hispanic: 0%
  Native American: 0%
  Other: 35%
North America: 4 States
Density: 111 in OH, 5 in KY, 2 in VA

Financial/Terms:
Cash Investment: $20-30K
Total Investment: $111.1-265K
Minimum Net Worth: $200K
Fees: Franchise — $16.5K
  Royalty — 5.5%; Ad. — 4.5%
Earnings Claim Statement: Yes
Term of Contract (Years): 10/10
Avg. # Of Employees: 1 FT, 12 PT
Passive Ownership: Allowed
Area Develop. Agreements: Yes/3
Sub-Franchising Contracts: No
Expand In Territory: No
Space Needs: 1,200 SF; FS, SF, SC, RM

Support & Training Provided:
Site Selection Assistance: Yes
Lease Negotiation Assistance: Yes
Co-Operative Advertising: Yes
Franchisee Assoc./Member: Yes
Size Of Corporate Staff: 40
On-Going Support: B,C,D,E,F,G,H,I
Training: 4 Weeks Independence, OH.
Minority-Specific Programs: Although we support the objectives of the NMFI, we do not have any specific programs in place at this time.

Specific Expansion Plans:
US: Midwest, Mid-Atlantc, S. E.

MR. JIM'S PIZZA

4276 Kellway Circle
Addison, TX 75001
Tel: (800) 583-5960 (972) 267-5467
Fax: (972) 267-5463
E-Mail:
Web Site: www.mrjimspizza.net
Mr. Randall Wooley, Executive Director

Specializing in delivery and take-out operations. Low start-up cost of under $90,000, including franchise fee. Dallas, Ft. Worth's largest locally-owned pizza franchise.

Background:

Established: 1974;	1st Franchised: 1976
Franchised Units:	64
Company-Owned Units:	0
Total Units:	64
Minority-Owned Units:	
African-American:	1
Asian-American:	0
Hispanic:	0
Native American:	0
Other:	
North America:	NR
Density:	58 in TX, 2 in LA, 2 in VA

Financial/Terms:

Cash Investment:	$50K
Total Investment:	$56-108K
Minimum Net Worth:	$100K
Fees: Franchise —	$10K
Royalty — 5%;	Ad. — 0%
Earnings Claim Statement:	No
Term of Contract (Years):	15/15
Avg. # Of Employees:	5 FT, 15 PT
Passive Ownership:	Discouraged
Area Develop. Agreements:	Yes
Sub-Franchising Contracts:	No
Expand In Territory:	Yes
Space Needs: 1,100 SF; SC	

Support & Training Provided:

Site Selection Assistance:	Yes
Lease Negotiation Assistance:	Yes
Co-Operative Advertising:	Yes
Franchisee Assoc./Member:	No
Size Of Corporate Staff:	6
On-Going Support:	B,C,D,E,G,H

Training: 2 Months.
Minority-Specific Programs: Although we support the objectives of the NMFI, we do not have any specific programs in place at this time.

Specific Expansion Plans:
US: All Except FL, MI

MRS. WINNER'S CHICKEN & BISCUITS

6045 Barfield Rd.
Atlanta, GA 30328
Tel: (404) 459-5800
Fax: (404) 459-5797
E-Mail: kspencer@rtminc.com
Web Site: www.winners-international.com
Ms. Karen Spencer, VP Franchise Sales/ Admin.

Quick-service restaurant - chicken segment. Winners International is a multi-category, multi-brand international growth company, focused on the quick, convenient distribution of food. Our vision is to place our products in the hands of people worldwide - 'Food Within Your Reach.'TM

Background:

Established: 1977;	1st Franchised: 1989
Franchised Units:	46
Company-Owned Units:	145
Total Units:	191
Minority-Owned Units:	
African-American:	
Asian-American:	
Hispanic:	
Native American:	
Other:	
North America:	5 States
Density:	15 in AL, 15 in GA, 9 in TN

Financial/Terms:

Cash Investment:	$10K
Total Investment:	$410K-1.1MM
Minimum Net Worth:	$500K
Fees: Franchise —	$20K
Royalty — 4%;	Ad. — 2%
Earnings Claim Statement:	No
Term of Contract (Years):	20/20
Avg. # Of Employees:	8-10 FT, 30 PT
Passive Ownership:	Discouraged

Area Develop. Agreements:	Yes
Sub-Franchising Contracts:	No
Expand In Territory:	Yes
Space Needs: 1,800 SF; FS	

Support & Training Provided:

Site Selection Assistance:	Yes
Lease Negotiation Assistance:	No
Co-Operative Advertising:	Yes
Franchisee Assoc./Member:	Yes/Yes
Size Of Corporate Staff:	40
On-Going Support:	C,D,E,G,H

Training: 6 Weeks Certified Training Units.
Minority-Specific Programs: Although we support the objectives of the NMFI, we do not have any specific programs in place at this time.

Specific Expansion Plans:
US: Southeast and Midwest

MY FAMILY FOOD COURT

3331 Viking Way, Unit 7
Richmond, BC V6V 1X7 CANADA
Tel: (604) 270-2360
Fax: (604) 270-6560
E-Mail:
Web Site: www.edelweissdeli.com
Mr. Duncan Williams, President

We build food courts for one owner. We have six different franchisees. Customer can have one to four franchises in his location.

Background:

Established: 1973;	1st Franchised: 1989
Franchised Units:	20
Company-Owned Units:	0
Total Units:	20
Minority-Owned Units:	
African-American:	0
Asian-American:	6
Hispanic:	0
Native American:	0
North America:	1 Province
Density:	20 in BC

Financial/Terms:

Cash Investment:	$50K
Total Investment:	$50-500K
Minimum Net Worth:	$50K
Fees: Franchise —	$20K
Royalty — 6%/$600/Mo.;	Ad. — 2%
Earnings Claim Statement:	Yes
Term of Contract (Years):	20/20
Avg. # Of Employees:	3 FT, 3 PT
Passive Ownership:	Discouraged
Area Develop. Agreements:	Yes/20
Sub-Franchising Contracts:	Yes
Expand In Territory:	Yes
Space Needs: 1,000 SF; FS, SF, SC, RM, HB	

Support & Training Provided:

Site Selection Assistance:	Yes
Lease Negotiation Assistance:	Yes
Co-Operative Advertising:	Yes
Franchisee Assoc./Member:	Yes/Yes
Size Of Corporate Staff:	5
On-Going Support:	C,D,E,F,G

Training: 3 Weeks Richmond, BC; 2 Weeks Customer Location.

Minority-Specific Programs: We work with the Canadian government regarding franchises to bring people from other countries so they may become new Canadians. Must be able to speak English.

Specific Expansion Plans:

US:	Northwest

NATHAN'S FAMOUS

1400 Old Country Rd., # 400
Westbury, NY 11590
Tel: (800) NATHANS (516) 338-8500
Fax: (516) 338-7220
E-Mail: nfidevel@webspan.net
Web Site:
Mr. Carl Paley, Senior Vice President

Fast-food restaurant, featuring premium-quality, all beef hot dogs, fresh-cut fries, plus a large variety of menu items - 9 prototypes, ranging from carts, counter modules, food courts and full-service restaurants. Franchise license and area development opportunities available worldwide.

Background:

Established: 1916;	1st Franchised: 1979	
Franchised Units:		189
Company-Owned Units:		25
Total Units:		214

Minority-Owned Units:
  African-American:
  Asian-American:
  Hispanic:
  Native American:
  Other:

North America:	37 States
Density:	27 in NY, 19 in NJ, 17 in FL

Financial/Terms:

Cash Investment:		$50-250K
Total Investment:		$50-550K
Minimum Net Worth:		$400K
Fees: Franchise —		$15-30K
Royalty — 4.5%;	Ad. — 2.5%	
Earnings Claim Statement:		No
Term of Contract (Years):		20/15
Avg. # Of Employees:	6-7 FT, 10-15 PT	
Passive Ownership:		Discouraged
Area Develop. Agreements:		Yes/Varies

Sub-Franchising Contracts:	Yes
Expand In Territory:	Yes
Space Needs: 500-2,500 SF; SF, RM	

Support & Training Provided:

Site Selection Assistance:	Yes
Lease Negotiation Assistance:	Yes
Co-Operative Advertising:	Yes
Franchisee Assoc./Member:	No
Size Of Corporate Staff:	42
On-Going Support:	B,C,D,E,F,G,H,I

Training: 2-4 Weeks in Long Island, NY and in Store.

Minority-Specific Programs: Although we support the objectives of the NMFI, we do not have any specific programs in place at this time.

Specific Expansion Plans:

US:	All United States

NEW YORK BURRITO GOURMET WRAPS

955 E. Javelina Ave., # 106
Mesa, AZ 85204
Tel: (800) 711-4036 (480) 503-3363
Fax: (480) 503-1850
E-Mail: nybfoods@nybfoods.com
Web Site: www.newyorkburrito.com
Ms. Sharon Snyder,

Casual/up-scale, quick-serve restaurants serving multi-cultural gourmet wraps (burritos). Some restaurants feature breakfast, fruit smoothies, and/or beer and wine. Menu items prepared daily with the highest-quality and variety meats and veggies. Giant tortillas offered in a variety of flavors: tomato basil, whole wheat, spinach, jalapeno and white flour. Low start-up cost and ease of operation. Join the hottest new food trend of the 90s with the leader of the pack.

Background:

Established: 1995;	1st Franchised: 1996	
Franchised Units:		70
Company-Owned Units:		2
Total Units:		72

Minority-Owned Units:

African-American:	3
Asian-American:	12
Hispanic:	3
Native American:	0
Other:	
North America:	18 States
Density:	8 in CA, 8 in CO, 5 in UT

Financial/Terms:

Cash Investment:		$25-35K
Total Investment:		$65-100K
Minimum Net Worth:		$Varies
Fees: Franchise —		$12.5K
Royalty — 7%;	Ad. — 4%	
Earnings Claim Statement:		No
Term of Contract (Years):		Perpetual
Avg. # Of Employees:		Varies
Passive Ownership:		Discouraged
Area Develop. Agreements:		Yes
Sub-Franchising Contracts:		No
Expand In Territory:		Yes
Space Needs: 1,500-2,500 SF; FS, SC, RM		

Support & Training Provided:

Site Selection Assistance:	Yes
Lease Negotiation Assistance:	Yes
Co-Operative Advertising:	Yes
Franchisee Assoc./Member:	No
Size Of Corporate Staff:	9
On-Going Support:	A,B,C,D,E,F,G,H,I

Training: 5 Days at Headquarters/Training Center; 5 Days at Franchise Store.

Minority-Specific Programs: Training, financing and assistance in preparing loan documents are available to all minority franchisees.

Specific Expansion Plans:

US:	All United States

PASQUALE'S PIZZA & PASTA

983 Yeager Pkwy.
Pelham, AL 35124
Tel: (205) 664-1839
Mr. Millard Deason, President

PASQUALE'S specializes in the preparation and serving of oven-roasted Italian sandwiches, pizza and spaghetti. From day one, we are with you to help you succeed. Our mission is to build close alliances with franchisees that are dedicated to exceeding customer expectations by using the freshest ingredients, offering a uniquely diverse menu and unparalleled service.

Background:

Established: 1990;	1st Franchised: 1990	
Franchised Units:		32
Company-Owned Units:		0

Total Units: 32
Minority-Owned Units:
African-American: 0
Asian-American: 0
Hispanic: 0
Native American: 0
Other:
North America: 7 States
Density: 13 in AL, 6 in IN, 5 in KY

Financial/Terms:
Cash Investment: $80.3-208K
Total Investment: $115.3-293K
Minimum Net Worth: $100K
Fees: Franchise — $5K
Royalty — 5%/$150/Wk.;Ad. — 2%
Max.
Earnings Claim Statement: No
Term of Contract (Years): 10/10
Avg. # Of Employees: 4-6 FT, 6-8 PT
Passive Ownership: Not Allowed
Area Develop. Agreements: No
Sub-Franchising Contracts: No
Expand In Territory: Yes
Space Needs: 2,000 SF; FS, SF, SC

Support & Training Provided:
Site Selection Assistance: Yes
Lease Negotiation Assistance: Yes
Co-Operative Advertising: Yes
Franchisee Assoc./Member: No
Size Of Corporate Staff: 4
On-Going Support: a,B,C,D,E,F,I
Training: 1 Day Financial Seminar, Pelham, AL; 10 Working Days at Actual Restaurant Location.
Minority-Specific Programs: Although we support the objectives of the NMFI, we do not have any specific programs in place at this time.

Specific Expansion Plans:
US: AL, GA, MS, KY, IN, OH

**PAUL REVERE'S PIZZA
INTERNATIONAL**
1574 42nd St. NE
Cedar Rapids, IA 52402
Tel: (800) 995-9437 (319) 395-9113

Fax: (319) 395-9115
E-Mail: patrickroof@mcleodusa.net
Web Site: www.paulreverespizza.com
Mr. Patrick Roof, Franchise Development

PAUL REVERE'S PIZZA is a low investment, high quality franchise. Our concept is designed to utilize low square footage buildings or apaces. Low overhead equals larger bottomlines. High quality menu items, competitive pricing and excellent service make PAUL REVERE'S PIZZA a great buy for a customer ot prospective franchisee.

Background:
Established: 1975; 1st Franchised: 1982
Franchised Units: 48
Company-Owned Units: 0
Total Units: 48
Minority-Owned Units:
African-American:
Asian-American:
Hispanic:
Native American:
North America: 4 States
Density: 29 in IA; 15 in WI; 2 in MO

Financial/Terms:
Cash Investment: $25-75K
Total Investment: $110-210K
Minimum Net Worth: $70K
Fees: Franchise — $15K
Royalty — 4%; Ad. — 0%
Earnings Claim Statement: Yes
Term of Contract (Years): 10/10
Avg. # Of Employees: 6 FT, 8 PT
Passive Ownership: Discouraged
Area Develop. Agreements: Yes/10
Sub-Franchising Contracts: Yes
Expand In Territory: Yes
Space Needs: 1,100 SF; SF, SC

Support & Training Provided:
Site Selection Assistance: Yes
Lease Negotiation Assistance: Yes
Co-Operative Advertising: N/A
Franchisee Assoc./Member: No
Size Of Corporate Staff: 3
On-Going Support: B,C,D,d,E,F,G,H,I
Training: 10-14 Days in Cedar Rapids, IA.
Minority-Specific Programs: Although we support the objectives of the NMFI, we do not have any specific programs in place at this time.

Specific Expansion Plans:
US: IA,WI,IL,MN,MO,AR,NE,KS

PHILLY CONNECTION
120 Interstate N. Pkwy., E., # 112
Atlanta, GA 30339-2103

Tel: (800) 886-8826 (770) 952-6152
Fax: (770) 952-3168
E-Mail: phillycon@mindspring.com
Web Site: www.phillyconnection.com
Mr. John D. Pollock, SVP Franchise Development

Quick service restaurant and ice cream parlor. "The Cheesesteak Champion" serves fresh, high quality products prepared to order in front of customers. On premises, take out, drive though, delivery. May operate in strip shopping centers, convenience stores, freestanding buildings and "end cap" space. Franchisor helps in site location, lease negotiation, equipment purchasing, grand opening, initial and ongoing training, toll free helpline.

Background:
Established: 1984; 1st Franchised: 1987
Franchised Units: 83
Company-Owned Units: 2
Total Units: 85
Minority-Owned Units:
African-American: 4
Asian-American: 16
Hispanic: 1
Native American: 0
North America: 5 States
Density: 49 in GA, 13 in NC, 11 in FL

Financial/Terms:
Cash Investment: $30-80K
Total Investment: $130-231K
Minimum Net Worth: $110K
Fees: Franchise — $20K
Royalty — 5%; Ad. — 5%
Earnings Claim Statement: No
Term of Contract (Years): 10/5
Avg. # Of Employees: 2 FT, 10 PT
Passive Ownership: Discouraged
Area Develop. Agreements: Yes/3
Sub-Franchising Contracts: No
Expand In Territory: Yes
Space Needs: 1,000-1,600 SF; FS, SF, SC, "C" Stores

Support & Training Provided:
Site Selection Assistance: Yes

Lease Negotiation Assistance:	Yes
Co-Operative Advertising:	Yes
Franchisee Assoc./Member:	No
Size Of Corporate Staff:	14
On-Going Support:	a,B,C,D,E,F,G,H,I

Training: 2-6 Weeks Existing Restaurant; 1 Week Corporate Headquarters.

Minority-Specific Programs: Although we support the objectives of the NMFI, we do not have any specific programs in place at this time.

Specific Expansion Plans:

US:	Southeast

PIZZA MAN

6930 1/2 Tujunga Ave.
North Hollywood, CA 91605
Tel: (818) 766-4395
Fax: (818) 766-1496
Mr. Robert Ohanian, President

Pizza, chicken, ribs, Italian dishes. Delivery and fast food.

Background:

Established: 1964;	1st Franchised: 1973	
Franchised Units:		50
Company-Owned Units:		0
Total Units:		50
Minority-Owned Units:		
African-American:		1%
Asian-American:		30%
Hispanic:		1%
Native American:		1%
Other:		60% Middle Eastern
North America:		1 State
Density:		50 in CA

Financial/Terms:

Cash Investment:	$50K
Total Investment:	$100K
Minimum Net Worth:	$120K
Fees: Franchise —	$25K
Royalty — 4%/$140/Wk.;Ad. — 4%/$140/Wk.	
Earnings Claim Statement:	No
Term of Contract (Years):	1+/1+
Avg. # Of Employees:	3 FT, 2 PT
Passive Ownership:	Discouraged
Area Develop. Agreements:	Yes/2
Sub-Franchising Contracts:	No
Expand In Territory:	Yes
Space Needs: 1,000 SF; SF	

Support & Training Provided:

Site Selection Assistance:	Yes
Lease Negotiation Assistance:	Yes
Co-Operative Advertising:	Yes
Franchisee Assoc./Member:	No
Size Of Corporate Staff:	8
On-Going Support:	b,c,d,e,f

Training: 2 Weeks Los Angeles, CA.

Minority-Specific Programs: PIZZA MAN franchise is strongly supportive of the National Minority Franchising Initiative. We recruit and are highly visible in assisting potential minority franchisees. We finance the franchise fee and we assist in the preparation of the paperwork needed to obtain loans for equipment. We assist the franchisee to find and select site locations and also we assist with the negotiation of the lease. We provide all the necessary food and packaging items and guide the franchisee on advertising.

Specific Expansion Plans:

US:	All United States

Good Things, Everyday!

PIZZA RANCH, THE

1121 Main St., Box 823
Hull, IA 51239
Tel: (800) 321-3401 (712) 439-1150
Fax: (712) 439-1125
E-Mail: pizzar@mtcnet.net
Web Site: www.pizza-ranch.com
Mr. Lawrence Vander Esch, Co-Founder

THE PIZZA RANCH is a family restaurant, specializing in pizza, pasta and chicken.

Background:

Established: 1981;	1st Franchised: 1984	
Franchised Units:		76
Company-Owned Units:		6
Total Units:		82
Minority-Owned Units:		
African-American:		0
Asian-American:		0
Hispanic:		0
Native American:		1
Other:		
North America:		6 States
Density:	38 in IA, 20 in MN, 14 in SD	

Financial/Terms:

Cash Investment:	$20-50K

Total Investment:		$200-500K
Minimum Net Worth:		$25K
Fees: Franchise —		$10K
Royalty — 4%;	Ad. —	$1.7-2.2K
Earnings Claim Statement:		No
Term of Contract (Years):		10/10/10
Avg. # Of Employees:		2 FT, 20 PT
Passive Ownership:		Allowed
Area Develop. Agreements:		Yes
Sub-Franchising Contracts:		Yes
Expand In Territory:		Yes
Space Needs: 4,000 SF; Any		

Support & Training Provided:

Site Selection Assistance:	Yes
Lease Negotiation Assistance:	Yes
Co-Operative Advertising:	Yes
Franchisee Assoc./Member:	No
Size Of Corporate Staff:	13
On-Going Support:	C,D,E,F,G,H,I

Training: 2 Weeks Sioux Center, IA.; 1 Week On-Site.

Minority-Specific Programs: Although we support the objectives of the NMFI, we do not have any specific programs in place at this time.

Specific Expansion Plans:

US:	Midwest

PIZZA ROYALE

650 Graham Bell, # 217
Sainte-Foy, PQ G1N 4H5 CANADA
Tel: (418) 682-5744
Fax: (418) 682-2684
Mr. Rejean Samson, President

PIZZA ROYALE is a chain of Italian restaurants, specializing in pizza cooked in an open wood oven fire in the serving area. It also offers a salad bar and a pasta bar. Take-out orders and delivery are also available. Healthy food and warm atmosphere are the main features of a concept that has proven successful over the years.

Background:

Established: 1980;	1st Franchised: 1985	
Franchised Units:		7
Company-Owned Units:		5
Total Units:		12
Minority-Owned Units:		
African-American:		
Asian-American:		
Hispanic:		
Native American:		
Other:		1, European
North America:		1 Province
Density:		15 in PQ

Financial/Terms:

Cash Investment:	$100-125K
Total Investment:	$250-300K
Minimum Net Worth:	$NR
Fees: Franchise —	$30K
Royalty — 3%;	Ad. — 2%
Earnings Claim Statement:	NR
Term of Contract (Years):	10/10
Avg. # Of Employees:	20 FT, 5 PT
Passive Ownership:	Discouraged
Area Develop. Agreements:	Yes
Sub-Franchising Contracts:	No
Expand In Territory:	Yes
Space Needs: 3,500 SF; FS, SC, RM	

Support & Training Provided:

Site Selection Assistance:	Yes
Lease Negotiation Assistance:	Yes
Co-Operative Advertising:	Yes
Franchisee Assoc./Member:	NR
Size Of Corporate Staff:	8
On-Going Support:	B,C,d,E,F,H
Training: 2 Weeks Headquarters; 2 Weeks On-Site.	

Minority-Specific Programs: Although we support the objectives of the NMFI, we do not have any specific programs in place at this time.

Specific Expansion Plans:

US:	NW, Master Franchises Avail.

PUDGIE'S FAMOUS CHICKEN

5 Dakota Dr., # 302
Lake Success, NY 11042
Tel: (800) PUDGIES (516) 358-0600
Fax: (516) 358-5076
E-Mail: steven.gardner@pudgies.org
Web Site: www.pudgies.org
Mr. Steven R. Gardner, Dir. Franchise Dev.

Our secret is premium skinless chicken and proprietary breading. 25% less fat and cholestrol . Strong commitment to our franchise owners. Low start-up costs and low rent mean greater profits. Owners receive comprehensive training and extensive operational and marketing support.

Background:

Established: 1981;	1st Franchised: 1981
Franchised Units:	19
Company-Owned Units:	15
Total Units:	34

Minority-Owned Units:

African-American:	0
Asian-American:	5
Hispanic:	0
Native American:	0
Other:	
North America:	7 States
Density:	14 in NY, 2 in NJ, 2 in CT

Financial/Terms:

Cash Investment:	$60-75K
Total Investment:	$150-200K
Minimum Net Worth:	$100K
Fees: Franchise —	$30K
Royalty — 5%;	Ad. — 3%
Earnings Claim Statement:	No
Term of Contract (Years):	10/10
Avg. # Of Employees:	4 FT, 6 PT
Passive Ownership:	Discouraged
Area Develop. Agreements:	Yes
Sub-Franchising Contracts:	No
Expand In Territory:	Yes
Space Needs: 1,000 SF; SF SC	

Support & Training Provided:

Site Selection Assistance:	Yes
Lease Negotiation Assistance:	Yes
Co-Operative Advertising:	Yes
Franchisee Assoc./Member:	Yes/Yes
Size Of Corporate Staff:	200
On-Going Support:	A,B,C,D,e,F,G,H,I
Training: 1 Week-10 Days Long Island, NY.	

Minority-Specific Programs: Site location. Referall to SBA or other leasing and/or financing sources.

Specific Expansion Plans:

US:	Northeast and Southeast

RONZIO PIZZA

6 Blackstone Valley Place, Bldg. 202
Lincoln, RI 02865
Tel: (401) 334-9750
Fax: (401) 334-0030
E-Mail:
Web Site:
Mr. Julian Angelone, President

RONZIO PIZZA is a retail pizza and sub shop, with the main emphasis on delivery.

Background:

Established: 1987;	1st Franchised: 1992
Franchised Units:	15
Company-Owned Units:	0
Total Units:	15

Minority-Owned Units:

African-American:	0
Asian-American:	0
Hispanic:	0
Native American:	0
Other:	
North America:	1 State
Density:	15 in RI

Financial/Terms:

Cash Investment:	$25K Minimum
Total Investment:	$95-136K
Minimum Net Worth:	$100K
Fees: Franchise —	$10K
Royalty — 4%;	Ad. — 2%
Earnings Claim Statement:	No
Term of Contract (Years):	10/10
Avg. # Of Employees:	2 FT, 13 PT
Passive Ownership:	Allowed
Area Develop. Agreements:	Yes/10
Sub-Franchising Contracts:	No
Expand In Territory:	Yes
Space Needs: 1,000-1,400 SF; SF, SC	

Support & Training Provided:

Site Selection Assistance:	Yes
Lease Negotiation Assistance:	Yes
Co-Operative Advertising:	Yes
Franchisee Assoc./Member:	Yes
Size Of Corporate Staff:	2
On-Going Support:	B,C,D,E,F,G,H
Training: 2 Weeks in Cumberland, RI.	

Minority-Specific Programs: Although we support the objectives of the NMFI, we do not have any specific programs in place at this time.

Specific Expansion Plans:

US:	RI, CT, MA

SKYLINE CHILI

4180 Thunderbird Ln.
Fairfield, OH 45014
Tel: (800) 443-4371 (513) 874-1188
Fax: (513) 874-3591
Web Site: www.skylinechili.com
Mr. Rick C. Collamer, VP Restaurant/Fran. Operations

Fast-casual restaurant concept that delivers great Cincinnati style chili in the speed of fast food. Sit down unit with table service that is ideal for owner/operators. Concept has a fanatical following by consumers and is one of the simplest restaurant concepts to run.

Background:

Established: 1949; 1st Franchised: 1965
Franchised Units: 75
Company-Owned Units: 33
Total Units: 108
Minority-Owned Units:
  African-American: 0%
  Asian-American: 0%
  Hispanic: 0%
  Native American: 5%
  Other: 20%
North America: 5 States
Density: 94 in OH, 5 in KY, 5 in FL

Financial/Terms:

Cash Investment: $20%
Total Investment: $300K-1MM
Minimum Net Worth: $650K
Fees: Franchise — $20K
  Royalty — 4%; Ad. — 4%
Earnings Claim Statement: Yes
Term of Contract (Years): 20/20
Avg. # Of Employees: 15 FT, 20 PT
Passive Ownership: Allowed
Area Develop. Agreements: Yes/10
Sub Franchising Contracts: No
Expand In Territory: Yes
Space Needs: NR SF; FS, SF, SC, End Cap

Support & Training Provided:

Site Selection Assistance: Yes
Lease Negotiation Assistance: Yes
Co-Operative Advertising: Yes
Franchisee Assoc./Member: Yes/Yes
Size Of Corporate Staff: 40
On-Going Support: a,B,C,D,E,G,H,I
Training: 5 Weeks in Cincinnati
Minority-Specific Programs: Although we support the objectives of the NMFI, we do not have any specific programs in place at this time.

Specific Expansion Plans:

US: OH, KY, IN, FL

SNAPPY TOMATO PIZZA

7230 Turfway Rd.
Florence, KY 41042
Tel: (888) 463-7627 (606) 525-4680
Fax: (606) 525-4686
E-Mail: elliotst@bigplanet.com
Web Site: www.snappytomato.com
Mr. Jason Rummer, VP Franchising

We offer the best in pizza, subs and salads. We have a variety of concepts to offer to our franchisee. We are the pizza of choice in the new millennia.

Background:

Established: 1982; 1st Franchised: 1985
Franchised Units: 46
Company-Owned Units: 5
Total Units: 51
Minority-Owned Units:
  African-American: 0
  Asian-American: 0
  Hispanic: 0
  Native American: 0
North America: 7 States, 1 Province
Density: 17 in KY, 5 in FL, 5 in TN

Financial/Terms:

Cash Investment: $20-30K
Total Investment: $70-150K
Minimum Net Worth: $NR
Fees: Franchise — $15K
  Royalty — 5.5%/$200; Ad. — 2.5%
Earnings Claim Statement: Yes
Term of Contract (Years): 15/15
Avg. # Of Employees: 2 FT, 10 PT
Passive Ownership: Discouraged
Area Develop. Agreements: Yes/15
Sub-Franchising Contracts: Yes
Expand In Territory: Yes
Space Needs: 400-2,000 SF; FS, SF, SC, RM, C-Store

Support & Training Provided:

Site Selection Assistance: Yes
Lease Negotiation Assistance: Yes
Co-Operative Advertising: Yes
Franchisee Assoc./Member: No
Size Of Corporate Staff: 5
On-Going Support: A,B,C,D,E,G,H,I
Training: 3 Days-2 Weeks KY, TN or FL..
Minority-Specific Programs: Although we support the objectives of the NMFI, we do not have any specific programs in place at this time.

Specific Expansion Plans:

US: SE, SE, Mid-Atl., Midwest

SUBS PLUS

173 Queenston St.
St. Catharines, ON L2R 3A2 CANADA
Tel: (888) 549-7777 (905) 641-3696
Fax: (905) 641-3696
Mr. Robert Dumas, President

SUBS PLUS isn't just another fast food franchise. Cakes and pastries add extra delicious flavor to an already appetizing business opportunity. And no baking experience is necessary! We will train you in the skills required to successfully operate your own SUBS PLUS franchise.

Background:

Established: 1985; 1st Franchised: 1991
Franchised Units: 4
Company-Owned Units: 1
Total Units: 5
Minority-Owned Units:
  African-American:
  Asian-American:
  Hispanic:
  Native American:
  Other:
North America: 1 Province
Density: 5 in ON

Financial/Terms:

Cash Investment: $30-60K
Total Investment: $120-160K
Minimum Net Worth: $100K
Fees: Franchise — $15K
  Royalty — 4.5%; Ad. — 2%
Earnings Claim Statement: No
Term of Contract (Years): 10/10
Avg. # Of Employees: 1 FT, 6 PT
Passive Ownership: N/A
Area Develop. Agreements: Yes/10
Sub-Franchising Contracts: No
Expand In Territory: Yes
Space Needs: 1,500 SF; FS, SC, RM

Support & Training Provided:

Site Selection Assistance: Yes
Lease Negotiation Assistance: Yes
Co-Operative Advertising: Yes
Franchisee Assoc./Member: No
Size Of Corporate Staff: 2
On-Going Support: C,D,E,F,H
Training: 8 Weeks Head Office.
Minority-Specific Programs: Although we support the objectives of the NMFI, we do not have any specific programs in place at this time.

Specific Expansion Plans:

US: N/A

TACO MAKER, THE

4605 Harrison Blvd., 3rd Fl.
Ogden, UT 84403
Tel: (800) 207-5804 (801) 476-9780
Fax: (801) 476-9788
E-Mail: ttm@tacomaker.com
Web Site: www.tacomaker.com
Mr. Corey King, Dir. of Franchise
Licensing

International Mexican fast-food franchise, specializing in fast, friendly service and a complete menu with made-from-scratch and fresh ingredients. Centralized purchasing, corporate marketing and promotional support and progressive store design provide for the most comprehensive and fun investment opportunity. Available in free-standing, mall or strip center locations and also convenience stores, truck stops and co-branding opportunities.

Background:
Established: 1978;   1st Franchised: 1978
Franchised Units: 154
Company-Owned Units: 3
Total Units: 157
Minority-Owned Units:
   African-American:
   Asian-American:
   Hispanic:
   Native American:
   Other:
North America: 32 States
Density: 13 in UT, 10 in WA, 5 in NY

Financial/Terms:
Cash Investment: $20-140K
Total Investment: $75-650K
Minimum Net Worth: $NR
Fees: Franchise — $5-22.5K
   Royalty — 5-7%;   Ad. — 3%
Earnings Claim Statement: No
Term of Contract (Years):   15/15
Avg. # Of Employees: 2-6 FT, 5-20 PT
Passive Ownership: Discouraged
Area Develop. Agreements: Yes/15
Sub-Franchising Contracts: Yes
Expand In Territory: Yes
Space Needs: 200-3,000 SF; FS

Support & Training Provided:
Site Selection Assistance: Yes

Lease Negotiation Assistance: Yes
Co-Operative Advertising: Yes
Franchisee Assoc./Member: No
Size Of Corporate Staff: 30
On-Going Support: B,C,D,E,F,I
Training: 12-15 Days Utah.
Minority-Specific Programs: Although we support the objectives of the NMFI, we do not have any specific programs in place at this time.

Specific Expansion Plans:
US: All United States

TACO PALACE

814 E. Hwy. 60, P. O. Box 87
Monett, MO 65708
Tel: (417) 235-1150
Fax: (417) 235-1150
E-Mail: larry@tacopalace.com
Web Site: www.tacopalace.com
Mr. Larry Faria, President

No franchise fee; 1 year contract commitment; very low investment concept; low royalty fees; unlimited training at headquarters; franchise concept is targeted at people that normally cold not afford the cost and expense that other franchises require; Sunday closings.

Background:
Established: 1986;   1st Franchised: 1997
Franchised Units: 10
Company-Owned Units: 2
Total Units: 12
Minority-Owned Units:
   African-American: 0
   Asian-American: 0
   Hispanic: 0
   Native American: 0
   Other:
North America: 2 States
Density: 10 in MO, 2 in KS

Financial/Terms:
Cash Investment: $34-49K
Total Investment: $34-49K
Minimum Net Worth: $50K
Fees: Franchise — $None
   Royalty — 3-6%;   Ad. — 1%
Earnings Claim Statement: No
Term of Contract (Years):   1/1
Avg. # Of Employees: 3 FT, 5 PT
Passive Ownership: Discouraged
Area Develop. Agreements: No
Sub-Franchising Contracts: No
Expand In Territory: Yes
Space Needs: 1,000+ SF; FS, SF, SC, RM

Support & Training Provided:
Site Selection Assistance: Yes
Lease Negotiation Assistance: Yes
Co-Operative Advertising: Yes
Franchisee Assoc./Member: No
Size Of Corporate Staff: 2
On-Going Support: B,C,D,E,F,G,H
Training: 20 Days in Monett, MO; 20 Days with Trainers at Franchisee's Location.
Minority-Specific Programs: Although we support the objectives of the NMFI, we do not have any specific programs in place at this time.

Specific Expansion Plans:
US: MO,AR,TN,OK,KS,MS,KY,LA

TACO TIME

3880 W. 11th Ave.
Eugene, OR 97402
Tel: (800) 547-8907 (541) 687-8222
Fax: (541) 343-5208
E-Mail: bobn@tacotime.com
Web Site: www.tacotime.com
Mr. Bob Newton, Director of Franchise Devel.

TACO TIME continues to provide and improve our system for quick-service Mexican restaurants that have stood the test of time for 40 years. TACO TIME quality, focus on customer service, franchisee support and existing new products make us the innovative leader of high-quality Mexican food.

Background:
Established: 1959;   1st Franchised: 1960
Franchised Units: 313
Company-Owned Units: 4
Total Units: 317
Minority-Owned Units:
   African-American: 1
   Asian-American: 1
   Hispanic:
   Native American:
   Other:

North America: 14 States, 7 Provinces
Density: 74 in OR, 34 in BC, 42 in UT

Financial/Terms:

Cash Investment:	$100K
Total Investment:	$150-200K
Minimum Net Worth:	$300K
Fees: Franchise —	$25K
Royalty — 5%;	Ad. — 4%
Earnings Claim Statement:	No
Term of Contract (Years):	15/10
Avg. # Of Employees:	5 FT, 30 PT
Passive Ownership:	Not Allowed
Area Develop. Agreements:	Yes
Sub-Franchising Contracts:	Yes
Expand In Territory:	Yes
Space Needs: 1,500-2,160 SF; FS, RM	

Support & Training Provided:

Site Selection Assistance:	Yes
Lease Negotiation Assistance:	Yes
Co-Operative Advertising:	Yes
Franchisee Assoc./Member:	Yes/Yes
Size Of Corporate Staff:	25
On-Going Support:	B,C,D,E,F,G,h,I
Training: Up to 6 Weeks at Corporate Office.	

Minority-Specific Programs: Although we support the objectives of the NMFI, we do not have any specific programs in place at this time.

Specific Expansion Plans:

US:	All United States

TACO VILLA

3710 Chesswood Dr., # 220
North York, ON M3J 2W4 CANADA
Tel: (800) 608-8226 (416) 636-9348
Fax: (416) 636-9162
E-Mail:
Web Site:
Ms. Wendy J. MacKinnon, Franchise Director

TACO VILLA is a quick-service Mexican-food concept. With over 16 years' experience, we offer franchisees a dynamic design concept, full turn-key operation, proven menu and procedures, full training and marketing. We provide today's consumer with a high-quality, high-value food experience. TACO VILLA continues to expand.

Background:

Established: 1983;	1st Franchised: 1985
Franchised Units:	20
Company-Owned Units:	1
Total Units:	21
Minority-Owned Units:	
African-American:	0

Asian-American:	0
Hispanic:	0
Native American:	0
Other:	
North America:	1 Province
Density:	21 in ON

Financial/Terms:

Cash Investment:	$40-50K
Total Investment:	$140-150K
Minimum Net Worth:	$150K
Fees: Franchise —	$20K
Royalty — 6%;	Ad. — 2%
Earnings Claim Statement:	No
Term of Contract (Years):	10/10
Avg. # Of Employees:	3 FT, 5 PT
Passive Ownership:	Not Allowed
Area Develop. Agreements:	No
Sub-Franchising Contracts:	Yes
Expand In Territory:	Yes
Space Needs: 350-400 SF; RM	

Support & Training Provided:

Site Selection Assistance:	Yes
Lease Negotiation Assistance:	Yes
Co-Operative Advertising:	Yes
Franchisee Assoc./Member:	NR
Size Of Corporate Staff:	7
On-Going Support:	A,B,C,D,E,G,I
Training: 1 Week Head Office; 3 Weeks In Store.	

Minority-Specific Programs: We welcome all people to become a franchisee, should they qualify. We will assist all individuals with training and financing assistance through a lending institution. We will also assist with staff training and staff recruitment.

Specific Expansion Plans:

US:	Eastern Seaboard, New Eng.

TACONE WRAPS

4223 Glencoe Ave., # C-200
Marina Del Rey, CA 90292
Tel: (877) 482-2663 (310) 574-8177
Fax: (310) 574-8179
E-Mail: craig@tacone.com
Web Site: www.tacone.com
Mr. Craig Albert, President

Franchisor of quick-service restaurants serving fresh soups, sandwiches, salads, smoothies and catering.

Background:

Established: 1995;	1st Franchised: 1998
Franchised Units:	8
Company-Owned Units:	9
Total Units:	17
Minority-Owned Units:	
African-American:	

Asian-American:	
Hispanic:	
Native American:	
Other:	
North America:	6 States
Density:	9 in CA, 2 in MA, 1 in NJ

Financial/Terms:

Cash Investment:	$50K
Total Investment:	$125-300K
Minimum Net Worth:	$100K
Fees: Franchise —	$25K
Royalty — 6%/3K/Mo.;	Ad. — 2%
Earnings Claim Statement:	Yes
Term of Contract (Years):	10
Avg. # Of Employees:	1 FT, 5-7 PT
Passive Ownership:	Discouraged
Area Develop. Agreements:	Yes/10
Sub-Franchising Contracts:	Yes
Expand In Territory:	No
Space Needs: 400-1,500 SF; SF, SC, RM	

Support & Training Provided:

Site Selection Assistance:	Yes
Lease Negotiation Assistance:	Yes
Co-Operative Advertising:	Yes
Franchisee Assoc./Member:	No
Size Of Corporate Staff:	10
On-Going Support:	A,B,C,D,E,F,G,H,I
Training: 6 Weeks Los Angeles, CA.	

Minority-Specific Programs: We will do everything possible to aid the prospective franchisee.

Specific Expansion Plans:

US:	All United States

VILLA PIZZA/COZZOLI'S

17 Elm St.
Morristown, NJ 07960
Tel: (973) 285-4800
Fax: (973) 285-5252
E-Mail: atorine@villapizza.com
Web Site: www.villapizza.com
Mr. Adam Torine, Dir. Business Development

Quick-service pizza and Italian restaurant chain, primarily located in regional malls and outlet centers either in food courts or in-line locations. We use only the freshest cheeses, seasonings, vegetables, homemade sauces and other ingredients. Our large, tantalizing food display offers customers a wide variety of homemade dishes.

Background:

Established: 1964;	1st Franchised: 1995
Franchised Units:	70
Company-Owned Units:	120
Total Units:	190

Minority-Owned Units:

African-American:	5%
Asian-American:	0%
Hispanic:	30%
Native American:	0%
North America:	38 States
Density:	11 in TX, 10 in PA, 7 in VA

Financial/Terms:

Cash Investment:	$100-250K
Total Investment:	$190-400K
Minimum Net Worth:	$150K
Fees: Franchise —	$25K
Royalty — 5%;	Ad. — 0%
Earnings Claim Statement:	No
Term of Contract (Years):	10/10
Avg. # Of Employees:	2 FT, 4-7 PT
Passive Ownership:	Not Allowed
Area Develop. Agreements:	No
Sub-Franchising Contracts:	No
Expand In Territory:	Yes
Space Needs: 650 SF; RM, Non-Traditional	

Support & Training Provided:

Site Selection Assistance:	Yes
Lease Negotiation Assistance:	Yes
Co-Operative Advertising:	N/A
Franchisee Assoc./Member:	No
Size Of Corporate Staff:	25
On-Going Support:	B,C,D,E,F,G,I
Training: 2 Weeks.	

Minority-Specific Programs: Although we support the objectives of the NMFI, we do not have any specific programs in place at this time.

Specific Expansion Plans:

US:	All United States

WE'RE ROLLING PRETZEL COMPANY
2500 W. State St., P. O. Box 6106
Alliance, OH 44601
Tel: (888) 549-7655 (330) 823-0575
Fax: (330) 821-8908
E-Mail: kkrabill@wererolling.com
Web Site: www.wererolling.com
Mr. Kevin Krabill, President

A unique soft pretzel company designed for mall kiosks and in-line food service locations. Unique and innovative products and promotions. Featuring fresh-made pretzels, food products and beverages. Full corporate office training and support. Absentee owner permitted. Capitalize on the healthy aspect of pretzel snacks with your own WE'RE ROLLING PRETZEL COMPANY franchise.

Background:

Established: 1996;	1st Franchised: 1998
Franchised Units:	1
Company-Owned Units:	2
Total Units:	3

Minority-Owned Units:

African-American:	0
Asian-American:	0
Hispanic:	0
Native American:	0
Other:	0
North America:	1 State
Density:	2 in OH, 1 in SC

Financial/Terms:

Cash Investment:	$40-70K
Total Investment:	$55.5-109.2K
Minimum Net Worth:	$150K
Fees: Franchise —	$15K
Royalty — 5%;	Ad. — 1%
Earnings Claim Statement:	No
Term of Contract (Years):	5/5
Avg. # Of Employees:	3 FT, 3 PT
Passive Ownership:	Allowed
Area Develop. Agreements:	Yes/5
Sub-Franchising Contracts:	No
Expand In Territory:	Yes
Space Needs: 200-600 SF; RM, Non-Traditional	

Support & Training Provided:

Site Selection Assistance:	Yes
Lease Negotiation Assistance:	Yes
Co-Operative Advertising:	N/A
Franchisee Assoc./Member:	No
Size Of Corporate Staff:	5
On-Going Support:	B,C,D,E,F,G,H,I
Training: 5 Days Corporate Office; 3 Days Franchise Location.	

Minority-Specific Programs: Although we support the objectives of the NMFI, we do not have any specific programs in place at this time.

Specific Expansion Plans:

US:	All Exc. Registered States

WIENERSCHNITZEL
4440 Von Karman Ave., # 222
Newport Beach, CA 92660

Tel: (800) 764-9353 (949) 851-2609
Fax: (949) 851-2618
E-Mail: franks@wienerschnitzel.com
Web Site: www.wienerschnitzel.com
Mr. Frank R. Coyle, Franchise Sales Director

WIENERSCHNITZEL is the world's largest quick service hot dog restaurant chain with over 300 locations selling 70 million hot dogs annually. We are interested in developing new locations throughout California, the Southwest and Pacific Northwest.

Background:

Established: 1961;	1st Franchised: 1965
Franchised Units:	323
Company-Owned Units:	0
Total Units:	323

Minority-Owned Units:

African-American:	1%
Asian-American:	15%
Hispanic:	2%
Native American:	0%
Other:	20% Persian
North America:	11 States
Density:	220 in CA, 30 in TX, 7 in NM

Financial/Terms:

Cash Investment:	$100-250K
Total Investment:	$250K-1.2MM
Minimum Net Worth:	$100K
Fees: Franchise —	$20K
Royalty — 5%;	Ad. — 4-6%
Earnings Claim Statement:	No
Term of Contract (Years):	20/5
Avg. # Of Employees:	1-2 FT, 25-50 PT
Passive Ownership:	Discouraged
Area Develop. Agreements:	Yes/1
Sub-Franchising Contracts:	Yes
Expand In Territory:	Yes
Space Needs: 15,000-20,000 SF; FS, Anchored Centers	

Support & Training Provided:

Site Selection Assistance:	No
Lease Negotiation Assistance:	Yes
Co-Operative Advertising:	Yes
Franchisee Assoc./Member:	Yes/Yes
Size Of Corporate Staff:	40
On-Going Support:	A,B,C,d,E,F,G,h,I

Training: 2 Weeks Administration Corporate Office; 4 Weeks Store Level (Location Varies).

Minority-Specific Programs: Minority publications for awareness of our franchise offering. No special financing. All franchisees must meet minimum financial requirements and complete our 6 week training program, regardless of race.

Specific Expansion Plans:

US: West, SW, Pacific NW

WILLY DOG

120 Clarence St., # 1141
Kingston, ON K7L 4Y5 CANADA
Tel: (800) 915-4683 (613) 549-7366
Fax: (613) 549-4108
E-Mail:
Web Site:
Mr. Will R. Hodgekiss, President

A self-contained hot dog and fast-food cart that looks like a giant hot dog. All support, licensing, set-up and on-going support included. Unit has hot and cold running water, BBQ, ice box, etc. and runs from propane only. Fully towable behind any car. (We speak Spanish.)

Background:

Established: 1989;	1st Franchised: 1993
Franchised Units:	105
Company-Owned Units:	16
Total Units:	121
Minority-Owned Units:	
African-American:	0
Asian-American:	0
Hispanic:	2
Native American:	2
Other:	
North America:	2 States
Density:	5 in NY, 5 in VT

Financial/Terms:

Cash Investment:	$4.5K
Total Investment:	$4.5K
Minimum Net Worth:	$10K
Fees: Franchise —	$4.5K
Royalty — $500/Yr.;	Ad. — 0%
Earnings Claim Statement:	Yes
Term of Contract (Years):	10/10
Avg. # Of Employees:	1 FT, 1 PT
Passive Ownership:	Discouraged

Area Develop. Agreements:	Yes/10
Sub-Franchising Contracts:	Yes
Expand In Territory:	Yes
Space Needs: 30 SF; Outside, Self-Contained	

Support & Training Provided:

Site Selection Assistance:	Yes
Lease Negotiation Assistance:	Yes
Co-Operative Advertising:	Yes
Franchisee Assoc./Member:	No
Size Of Corporate Staff:	5
On-Going Support:	B,C,D,E,F,G,H,I
Training: On-Site As Needed.	

Minority-Specific Programs: Although we support the objectives of the NMFI, we do not have any specific programs in place at this time.

Specific Expansion Plans:

US: All United States

WING ZONE

1718 Peachtree St., NW, # 1070
Atlanta, GA 30309
Tel: (877) 333-9464 (404) 875-5045
Fax: (404) 875-6631
E-Mail: matt@wingzone.com
Web Site: www.wingzone.com
Mr. Matthew Friedman, Vice President of Operations

WING ZONE is a Buffalo-style chicken wing restaurant that offers 25 flavors of wings, salads, grilled sandwiches and appetizers. We offer take-out and delivery, and have anchored our stores around large college populations.

Background:

Established: 1993;	1st Franchised: 1999
Franchised Units:	2
Company-Owned Units:	6
Total Units:	8
Minority-Owned Units:	
African-American:	0
Asian-American:	1
Hispanic:	0
Native American:	0
North America:	4 States
Density:	3 in FL, 2 in GA, 1 in SC

Financial/Terms:

Cash Investment:	$40-75K
Total Investment:	$108-156K
Minimum Net Worth:	$125K

Fees: Franchise —	$20K
Royalty — 5%;	Ad. — 0.5%
Earnings Claim Statement:	No
Term of Contract (Years):	10/10
Avg. # Of Employees:	6 FT, 15 PT
Passive Ownership:	Discouraged
Area Develop. Agreements:	No
Sub-Franchising Contracts:	No
Expand In Territory:	Yes
Space Needs: 1,200-1,500 SF; SF, SC	

Support & Training Provided:

Site Selection Assistance:	Yes
Lease Negotiation Assistance:	Yes
Co-Operative Advertising:	Yes
Franchisee Assoc./Member:	No
Size Of Corporate Staff:	3
On-Going Support:	a,b,C,D,E,F,I

Training: 1 Week Home Office in Atlanta, GA; 1-2 Weeks Franchisee's Location.

Minority-Specific Programs: As a new franchisor, we do understand the importance of minority recruitment. Many of our top markets focus on a particular minority group, and having local people own and operate these units are vital. We do offer third party financing, and this company has minority SBA or conventional loans available. Our products appeal to many different ethnic groups and we feel minority ownership is one of the keys to our success. We recently sold a franchise in Austin, TX, to an African-American.

Specific Expansion Plans:

US: Southwest

WINGSTOP

1212 Northwest Hwy.
Garland, TX 75041
Tel: (972) 686-6500
Fax: (972) 686-6502
E-Mail: jimdeering@worldnet.att.net
Web Site: www.wingstop.com
Mr. James P. Deering, Director of Franchising

The Arlington Morning News wrote: ' With the somewhat rough-and-ready air of an early century barnstormers' aircraft hanger, WINGSTOP treads the line between neighborhood hang and a casual, laid-back dinner-snack spot. The place's signature chicken wings, however, are righteously

assertive, distinctive and anything but bland
. . ' WINGSTOP is fun! WINGSTOP is
focused! WINGSTOP is growing fast!

Background:

Established: 1994;   1st Franchised: 1997
Franchised Units: 16
Company-Owned Units: 1
Total Units: 17
Minority-Owned Units:
   African-American: 3
   Asian-American: 0
   Hispanic: 1
   Native American: 0
   Other: 3 Women-Owned
North America: 2 States
Density: 10 in TX, 1 in LA

Financial/Terms:

Cash Investment: $40-50K
Total Investment: $167.1-211.1K
Minimum Net Worth: $100K
Fees: Franchise — $20K
   Royalty — 5%;   Ad. — 2%
Earnings Claim Statement: Yes
Term of Contract (Years):   10/10
Avg. # Of Employees: 2 FT, 4 PT
Passive Ownership: Allowed
Area Develop. Agreements: Yes/Negot.
Sub-Franchising Contracts: No
Expand In Territory: Yes
Space Needs: 1,200-1,400 SF; SC

Support & Training Provided:

Site Selection Assistance: Yes
Lease Negotiation Assistance: Yes
Co-Operative Advertising: Yes
Franchisee Assoc./Member: No
Size Of Corporate Staff: 5
On-Going Support: A,B,C,D,E,H
Training: 2 Weeks Corporate Store; 1 Week
Franchise Store.
Minority-Specific Programs: Although we
support the objectives of the NMFI, we do
not have any specific programs in place at
this time.

Specific Expansion Plans:

US: All United States

ZERO'S SUBS
2106 Pacific Ave.
Virginia Beach, VA 23451
Tel: (800) 588-0782 (757) 425-8306
Fax: (757) 422-9157

E-Mail: zeros@norfolk.infi.net
Web Site: www.zeros.com
Mr. Charles J. McCotter, Executive Vice
President

Specializes in hot, oven-baked submarine
sandwiches made-to-order with quality
ingredients. We also serve pizzas, salads,
soups, kids meals, meal deals and desserts.
All priced for today's budget. Catering and
party subs complement any special event.
The uniqueness of ZERO'S SUBS will bring
customers back.

Background:

Established: 1969;   1st Franchised: 1990
Franchised Units: 45
Company-Owned Units: 6
Total Units: 51
Minority-Owned Units:
   African-American: 3
   Asian-American: 0
   Hispanic: 1
   Native American: 0
   Other: 7 Women
North America: 4 States
Density: 42 in VA, 7 in NC, 2 in AZ

Financial/Terms:

Cash Investment: $30-50K
Total Investment: $120-170K
Minimum Net Worth: $125K
Fees: Franchise — $15K
   Royalty — 6%;   Ad. — 2%
Earnings Claim Statement: Yes
Term of Contract (Years):   15/15
Avg. # Of Employees: 4 FT, 3 PT
Passive Ownership: Discouraged
Area Develop. Agreements: Yes/25
Sub-Franchising Contracts: Yes
Expand In Territory: Yes
Space Needs: 1,400 SF; FS, SC, RM,
Destination Center

Support & Training Provided:

Site Selection Assistance: Yes
Lease Negotiation Assistance: Yes
Co-Operative Advertising: Yes
Franchisee Assoc./Member: Yes/Yes
Size Of Corporate Staff: 10
On-Going Support: B,C,D,E,F,G,H,I
Training: 3-6 Weeks in Virginia Beach, VA.
Minority-Specific Programs: Although we
support the objectives of the NMFI, we do
not have any specific programs in place at
this time.

Specific Expansion Plans:

US: SE, NE, MW, Mid-Atl., AZ

BENNIGAN'S

6500 International Pkwy., # 1000
Plano, TX 75093
Tel: (800) 543-9670 (972) 588-5762
Fax: (972) 588-5806
E-Mail: lmckee@metrogroup.com
Web Site: www.bennigans.com
Ms. Lynette McKee, Dir. Dom. Fran. Dev.

BENNIGAN'S is a leading casual restaurant chain known for the warm hospitality of an Irish pub and the great taste of fun American foods. Established in 1976, BENNIGAN'S helped create the casual dining segment in the restaurant industry. BENNIGAN'S has expanded beyond its original tavern image to become more food-focused. Today, each restaurant serves a wide assortment of moderately-priced, quality food, as well as a wide selection of beverages.

Background:
Established: 1976; 1st Franchised: 1995
Franchised Units: 66
Company-Owned Units: 183
Total Units: 249
Minority-Owned Units:
  African-American:
  Asian-American:
  Hispanic:
  Native American:
North America: 29 States
Density: 47 in TX, 41 in FL, 14 in NJ

Financial/Terms:
Cash Investment: $750K
Total Investment: $1.1-2.1MM
Minimum Net Worth: $3MM
Fees: Franchise — $50K
  Royalty — 4%;   Ad. — 4%
Earnings Claim Statement: No
Term of Contract (Years):   20/20
Avg. # Of Employees: NR
Passive Ownership: Discouraged
Area Develop. Agreements: Yes
Sub-Franchising Contracts: No
Expand In Territory: Yes
Space Needs: 6,500 SF; FS

Support & Training Provided:
Site Selection Assistance: Yes
Lease Negotiation Assistance: No
Co-Operative Advertising: Yes
Franchisee Assoc./Member: Yes/No
Size Of Corporate Staff: 400
On Going Support: B,C,E,G,h
Training: Managers - 1 Week Home Office and 11 Weeks In Unit; Employees - 2-4 Weeks In Unit.
Minority-Specific Programs: Although we support the objectives of the NMFI, we do not have any specific programs in place at this time.

Specific Expansion Plans:
US: All United States

BOBBY RUBINO'S PLACE FOR RIBS

1990 E. Sunrise Blvd.
Fort Lauderdale, FL 33304
Tel: (800) 997-7427 (954) 763-9871
Fax: (954) 467-1192
E-Mail: rubinosusa@att.net
Web Site:
Ms. Kay Ferrara, Director Franchise Operations

Full-service, including full liquor service. Specializing in BBQ. BOBBY RUBINO'S PLACE FOR RIBS also has a large menu including steak, seafood, salads, etc. served in a casual atmosphere. A kiddie menu is available.

Background:
Established: 1978;   1st Franchised: 1982
Franchised Units: 10
Company-Owned Units: 0
Total Units: 10
Minority-Owned Units:
  African-American: 0
  Asian-American: 0
  Hispanic: 0
  Native American: 0
  Other: 0
North America: 5 States
Density: 4 in FL, 1 in CA, 1 in NY

Financial/Terms:
Cash Investment: $200K
Total Investment: $450-650K
Minimum Net Worth: $750K
Fees: Franchise — $50K
  Royalty — 4%;   Ad. — 3%

Earnings Claim Statement: No
Term of Contract (Years): 15/10
Avg. # Of Employees: 20 FT, 20 PT
Passive Ownership: Discouraged
Area Develop. Agreements: Yes/Negot.
Sub-Franchising Contracts: No
Expand In Territory: Yes
Space Needs: 6,000 SF; FS, SF, SC, RM

Support & Training Provided:
Site Selection Assistance: Yes
Lease Negotiation Assistance: Yes
Co-Operative Advertising: Yes
Franchisee Assoc./Member: No
Size Of Corporate Staff: 1
On-Going Support: a,C,d,E,F,h,I
Training: 6-8 Weeks Fort Lauderdale, FL.
Minority-Specific Programs: Although we support the objectives of the NMFI, we do not have any specific programs in place at this time.

Specific Expansion Plans:
US: All United States

BUFFALO'S CAFE
707 Whitlock Ave., SW., Bldg. H-13
Marietta, GA 30064
Tel: (800) 459-4647 (770) 420-1800
Fax: (770) 420-1811
E-Mail: kculkin@buffaloscafe.com
Web Site: www.buffaloscafe.com
Mr. Kevin Culkin, Director of Franchising

BUFFALO'S CAFE offers casual family dining in an 'Old West' cafe atmosphere. Menu is based on a fresh-food concept, featuring Buffalo-style chicken-wings, rotisserie chicken and other charbroiled specialties. Complete training is offered both initially and on-going.

Background:
Established: 1985; 1st Franchised: 1991
Franchised Units: 38
Company-Owned Units: 6
Total Units: 44
Minority-Owned Units:
  African-American:
  Asian-American: 1
  Hispanic:
  Native American:
  Other:
North America: 6 States/ Puerto Rico
Density: 32 in GA, 4 in SC, 2 in FL

Financial/Terms:
Cash Investment: $140K
Total Investment: $450K-1.5M
Minimum Net Worth: $500K
Fees: Franchise — $35K
  Royalty — 5%; Ad. — 2%
Earnings Claim Statement: No
Term of Contract (Years): 10/10/10
Avg. # Of Employees: 20 FT, 30 PT
Passive Ownership: Allowed
Area Develop. Agreements: Yes/Varies
Sub-Franchising Contracts: No
Expand In Territory: Yes
Space Needs: 4,000-5,000 SF; FS, SC

Support & Training Provided:
Site Selection Assistance: Yes
Lease Negotiation Assistance: Yes
Co-Operative Advertising: Yes
Franchisee Assoc./Member: Yes
Size Of Corporate Staff: 20
On-Going Support: B,C,D,E,F,G,H,I
Training: 30 Days Corporate Store; 2 Weeks Franchisee's Store - Pre & Post Opening.
Minority-Specific Programs: No specific programs, but we welcome minority ownership. We are currently workingwith an Asfrican-American franchise candidate.

Specific Expansion Plans:
US: All United States

CASEY'S BAR/GRILL
10 Kingsbridge Garden Circle, # 600
Mississauga, ON L5R 3K6 CANADA
Tel: (905) 568-0000
Fax: (905) 568-0080
E-Mail:
Web Site:
Mr. H. Ross R. Bain, VP Admin./Legal Counsel

Casual dining, grilled food, burgers, wraps.

Background:
Established: 1979; 1st Franchised: 1979
Franchised Units: 22
Company-Owned Units: 12
Total Units: 34
Minority-Owned Units:
  African-American:
  Asian-American:
  Hispanic:
  Native American:
  Other:
North America: 2 Provinces
Density: 28 in ON, 6 in PQ

Financial/Terms:
Cash Investment: $250-350K
Total Investment: $995K

Minimum Net Worth: $500K
Fees: Franchise — $40K
  Royalty — 5%; Ad. — 2%/2% Local
Earnings Claim Statement: No
Term of Contract (Years): 10/5
Avg. # Of Employees: 35 FT, 25 PT
Passive Ownership: Not Allowed
Area Develop. Agreements: Yes
Sub-Franchising Contracts: No
Expand In Territory: No
Space Needs: 5,168 SF; FS

Support & Training Provided:
Site Selection Assistance: Yes
Lease Negotiation Assistance: Yes
Co-Operative Advertising: Yes
Franchisee Assoc./Member: Yes/Yes
Size Of Corporate Staff: 100
On-Going Support: B,C,D,E,h
Training: 6 Weeks In-Store; 1 Week at Head Office.
Minority-Specific Programs: Although we support the objectives of the NMFI, we do not have any specific programs in place at this time.

Specific Expansion Plans:
US: Canada Only

CHARLEY'S STEAKERY
6610 Busch Blvd., # 100
Columbus, OH 43229
Tel: (800) 437-8325 (614) 847-8100
Fax: (614) 847-8110
E-Mail: franchising@charleyssteakery.com
Web Site: www.charleyssteakery.com
Mr. Richard A. Page, Vice President Development

CHARLEY'S STEAKERY is a progressive quick-service restaurant with over 100 locations across the United States and Canada. The heart of CHARLEY'S menu consists of freshly-grilled Steak and Chicken Subs, fresh-cut fries and freshly squeezed lemonade. CHARLEY'S open kitchen environment and freshly-prepared products are unique in the fast-food industry.

Background:

Established: 1986; 1st Franchised: 1991
Franchised Units: 92
Company-Owned Units: <u>10</u>
Total Units: 102
Minority-Owned Units:
 African-American: 3.3%
 Asian-American: 15.2%
 Hispanic: 3.3%
 Native American:
 Other:8.7% Women, 3.3% Indian, 3.3%
Mid-Eastern
North America: 27 States, 1 Province
Density: 15 in OH, 8 in FL,8 in ON

Financial/Terms:

Cash Investment: $NR
Total Investment: $124.5-294.5K
Minimum Net Worth: $200K
Fees: Franchise — $19.5K
 Royalty — 5% or $200/mon;Ad. —
.25%
Earnings Claim Statement: Yes
Term of Contract (Years): 10/10
Avg. # Of Employees: NR
Passive Ownership: Discouraged
Area Develop. Agreements: Yes/10
Sub-Franchising Contracts: Yes
Expand In Territory: Yes
Space Needs: NR SF; SC, RM

Support & Training Provided:

Site Selection Assistance: Yes
Lease Negotiation Assistance: Yes
Co-Operative Advertising: Yes
Franchisee Assoc./Member: Yes/Yes
Size Of Corporate Staff: 18
On-Going Support: B,C,D,e(required),G,h,I
Training: 3 Weeks at Columbus, OH.
Minority-Specific Programs: Although we support the objectives of the NMFI, we do not have any specific programs in place at this time.

Specific Expansion Plans:

US: All United States

DAMON'S INTERNATIONAL
4645 Executive Dr.
Columbus, OH 43220
Tel: (614) 442-7900
Fax: (614) 538-2521
E-Mail: kclark@damons.com
Web Site: www.damons.com
Mr. Ed Williams, VP of Development

DAMON'S... A dining event in a casual dining restaurant, dedicated to exceeding your expectations in all areas of operation. The 128-unit chain is famous for its award-winning BBQ ribs, prime rib and onion loaf. DAMON'S features 10' screens and is a state-of-the-art electronic sports/entertainment facility.

Background:

Established: 1979; 1st Franchised: 1982
Franchised Units: 114
Company-Owned Units: <u>21</u>
Total Units: 135
Minority-Owned Units:
 African-American: 2
 Asian-American: 0
 Hispanic: 0
 Native American: 0
 Other:
North America: NR
Density: 33 in OH, 11 in IN, 11 in MI

Financial/Terms:

Cash Investment: $300K Minimum
Total Investment: $940K-2.7MM
Minimum Net Worth: $1MM
Fees: Franchise — $50K
 Royalty — 4%; Ad. — .5%
Earnings Claim Statement: Yes
Term of Contract (Years): 10/3-5
Avg. # Of Employees: 30 FT, 50 PT
Passive Ownership: Discouraged
Area Develop. Agreements: Yes/Varies
Sub-Franchising Contracts: No
Expand In Territory: Yes
Space Needs: 6,500 Min. SF; FS, SC, RM, Hotel

Support & Training Provided:

Site Selection Assistance: Yes
Lease Negotiation Assistance: Yes
Co-Operative Advertising: Yes
Franchisee Assoc./Member: Yes
Size Of Corporate Staff: 53
On-Going Support: a,B,C,D,E,F,h
Training: 8 Weeks In-Restaurant Training.
Minority-Specific Programs: Although we support the objectives of the NMFI, we do not have any specific programs in place at this time.

Specific Expansion Plans:

US: Southwest, TX, CA, CO

DOGnSUDS®

DOG n SUDS DRIVE-IN RESTAURANTS
188 N. State Road 267, # 102-Avon N.
Avon, IN 46168
Tel: (800) DOGNSUDS (317) 272-1000
Fax: (317) 272-1002
E-Mail: dognsudscorp@juno.com
Web Site: www.DOGnSUDS.net
Mr. Richard T. Morath, President/CEO

Drive-in, curb service restaurant with carhops serving Coney dogs, fresh, char-grilled hamburgers and tenderloins made-to-order in 3 minutes or less. Features old-fashioned proprietary-brand root beer. The food is a 'cut above' fast food.

Background:

Established: 1953; 1st Franchised: 1954
Franchised Units: 12
Company-Owned Units: <u>7</u>
Total Units: 19
Minority-Owned Units:
 African-American: 0
 Asian-American: 0
 Hispanic: 0
 Native American: 0
 Other:
North America: 2 States
Density: 16 in IN, 2 in IL

Financial/Terms:

Cash Investment: $150K
Total Investment: $600K-1.2MM
Minimum Net Worth: $750K
Fees: Franchise — $25K
 Royalty — 3-5%; Ad. — 3%
Earnings Claim Statement: No
Term of Contract (Years): 15/5
Avg. # Of Employees: 10 FT, 25 PT
Passive Ownership: Allowed
Area Develop. Agreements: Yes
Sub-Franchising Contracts: No
Expand In Territory: Yes
Space Needs: 40,000 SF; NR

Support & Training Provided:

Site Selection Assistance: Yes
Lease Negotiation Assistance: Yes
Co-Operative Advertising: Yes
Franchisee Assoc./Member: No
Size Of Corporate Staff: 11
On-Going Support: b,C,D,E,F,H,I
Training: 6 Weeks Indianapolis, IN.
Minority-Specific Programs: We strongly support and would consider minority franchising initiatives. We also have an active

owner/operator program whereby a restaurant manager can own 20% of one of our restaurants at starting and can ultimately own 100% over a 60 month period. Please contact us for further information.

Specific Expansion Plans:
US: Midwest and Mid-South

EAST SIDE MARIO'S
10 Kingsbridge Garden Circle, # 600
Mississauga, ON L5R 3K6 CANADA
Tel: (800) 361-3111 (905) 568-0000
Fax: (905) 568-0080
E-Mail:
Web Site:
Mr. H. Ross R. Bain, VP Admin./Legal Counsel

American-Italian.

Background:

Established: 1979;	1st Franchised: 1989
Franchised Units:	67
Company-Owned Units:	8
Total Units:	75
Minority-Owned Units:	
African-American:	
Asian-American:	
Hispanic:	
Native American:	
Other:	
North America:	4 Provinces
Density:	58 in ON, 12 in PQ, 3 in NS

Financial/Terms:

Cash Investment:	$300-400K
Total Investment:	$1,080K
Minimum Net Worth:	$750K
Fees: Franchise —	$50K
Royalty — 5%;	Ad. — 3%/1% Local
Earnings Claim Statement:	No
Term of Contract (Years):	10/5
Avg. # Of Employees:	50 FT, 25 PT
Passive Ownership:	Not Allowed
Area Develop. Agreements:	Yes
Sub-Franchising Contracts:	No
Expand In Territory:	No
Space Needs: 5,314 SF; FS	

Support & Training Provided:

Site Selection Assistance:	Yes
Lease Negotiation Assistance:	Yes
Co-Operative Advertising:	Yes
Franchisee Assoc./Member:	Yes/Yes
Size Of Corporate Staff:	100
On-Going Support:	B,C,D,E,h

Training: 6 Weeks In-Store; 1 Week at Head Office.
Minority-Specific Programs: Although we support the objectives of the NMFI, we do not have any specific programs in place at this time.

Specific Expansion Plans:
US: Only Canada

EDO JAPAN
4838 32nd St.SE
Calgary, AB T2B 2S6 CANADA
Tel: (403) 215-8800
Fax: (403) 215-8801
E-Mail: edo@edojapan.com
Web Site: www.edojapan.com
Ms. Colleen Pickard, Manager, Legal Office

EDO JAPAN originated the concept of preparing Japanese Teppan Meals inexpensively through fast-food outlets more than 20 years ago. Since that time, EDO has maintained its popularity in the food courts due to EDO's menu placing emphasis on freshness, nutrition, service and very reasonable prices.

Background:

Established: 1977;	1st Franchised: 1986
Franchised Units:	88
Company-Owned Units:	11
Total Units:	99
Minority-Owned Units:	
African-American:	0
Asian-American:	73
Hispanic:	0
Native American:	0
Other:	
North America:	13 States, 5 Provinces
Density:	24 in AB, 14 in ON, 14 in CA

Financial/Terms:

Cash Investment:	$NR
Total Investment:	$160-250K
Minimum Net Worth:	$NR
Fees: Franchise —	$20K
Royalty — 6%;	Ad. — 2%
Earnings Claim Statement:	No
Term of Contract (Years):	5/5
Avg. # Of Employees:	3 FT, 3 PT
Passive Ownership:	Discouraged
Area Develop. Agreements:	Yes/NR
Sub-Franchising Contracts:	No
Expand In Territory:	Yes
Space Needs: 400-600 SF; RM	

Support & Training Provided:

Site Selection Assistance:	Yes
Lease Negotiation Assistance:	Yes
Co-Operative Advertising:	Yes
Franchisee Assoc./Member:	No
Size Of Corporate Staff:	29
On-Going Support:	B,C,D,E,F,G,H,I

Training: 2 Wks Calgary, AB (Cost);10 Days (No Cost) or Longer (cost) On-Site at Opening.
Minority-Specific Programs: Although we support the objectives of the NMFI, we do not have any specific programs in place at this time.

Specific Expansion Plans:
US: CA, TX, WA

FUDDRUCKERS
One Corporate Pl., 55 Ferncroft Rd.
Danvers, MA 01923-4001
Tel: (860) 651-4421
Fax: (860) 651-5218
E-Mail: craig.aherns@fuddruckers.com
Web Site: www.fuddruckers.com
Mr. Craig Aherns,

FUDDRUCKERS is a casual family restaurant, serving freshly-prepared 1/3 and 1/2 pound hamburgers, chicken, fish and steak sandwiches, hot dogs, salads, platters and beverages. On-premise bakery and butcher shop ensure freshness. Our full produce bar permits guests to prepare their own plate to their liking. Drink refills are free.

Background:

Established: 1980;	1st Franchised: 1983
Franchised Units:	93
Company-Owned Units:	108
Total Units:	201
Minority-Owned Units:	
African-American:	1
Asian-American:	0
Hispanic:	1
Native American:	0
North America:	33 States, 2 Provinces
Density:	37 in TX, 12 in VA, 12 in OH

Financial/Terms:

Cash Investment:	$300K
Total Investment:	$650K-1.28MM

Minimum Net Worth:	$1MM
Fees: Franchise —	$50K
Royalty — 5%;	Ad. — 0-3%
Earnings Claim Statement:	No
Term of Contract (Years):	20/20
Avg. # Of Employees:	15 FT, 30 PT
Passive Ownership:	Discouraged
Area Develop. Agreements:	Yes
Sub-Franchising Contracts:	No
Expand In Territory:	Yes
Space Needs: 7,000 SF; FS	

Support & Training Provided:

Site Selection Assistance:	No
Lease Negotiation Assistance:	Yes
Co-Operative Advertising:	N/A
Franchisee Assoc./Member:	No
Size Of Corporate Staff:	40
On-Going Support:	B,C,D,E,G,H,I

Training: 6 Weeks at Regional Training Locations.
Minority-Specific Programs: Although we support the objectives of the NMFI, we do not have any specific programs in place at this time.

Specific Expansion Plans:

US:	All United States

GOLDEN CORRAL FAMILY STEAKHOUSE

5151 Glenwood Ave., # 300
Raleigh, NC 27626-0502
Tel: (800) 284-5673 (919) 881-4647
Fax: (919) 881-5252
Web Site: www.goldencorralrest.com
Mr. Peter Charland, VP Franchise Dev.

We offer nearly 25 years of proven success in the family steakhouse market segment. The metromarket concept features in-store bakery, dessert bar and our Golden Choice Buffet, in addition to our up-dated core menu. The layout of our metro market restaurant, as well as our expanded food offering, enables each customer to define his own experience each time he visits a GOLDEN CORRAL.

Background:
Established: 1973;   1st Franchised: 1986

Franchised Units:	297
Company-Owned Units:	152
Total Units:	449
Minority-Owned Units:	
African-American:	1
Asian-American:	1
Hispanic:	2
Native American:	
Other:	4
North America:	38 States
Density:	TX, OK, NC

Financial/Terms:

Cash Investment:	$300K
Total Investment:	$1.2-3.3MM
Minimum Net Worth:	$1500K
Fees: Franchise —	$40K
Royalty — 4%;	Ad. — 2%
Earnings Claim Statement:	Yes
Term of Contract (Years):	15/5
Avg. # Of Employees:	80 FT, 40 PT
Passive Ownership:	Not Allowed
Area Develop. Agreements:	Yes/Varies
Sub-Franchising Contracts:	No
Expand In Territory:	Yes
Space Needs: 8,500-11,000 SF; FS	

Support & Training Provided:

Site Selection Assistance:	Yes
Lease Negotiation Assistance:	No
Co-Operative Advertising:	Yes
Franchisee Assoc./Member:	NR
Size Of Corporate Staff:	190
On-Going Support:	C,D,E,G

Training: 12 Weeks Headquarters and Field.
Minority-Specific Programs: Although we support the objectives of the NMFI, we do not have any specific programs in place at this time.

Specific Expansion Plans:

US:	All United States

GREAT STEAK & FRY COMPANY

222 High Street, # 300
Hamilton, OH 45011
Tel: (513) 896-9695
Fax: (513) 896-3750
E-Mail: franchiseinfo@thegreatsteak.com
Web Site: www.thegreatsteak.com

Mr. Nick Lanni, President

Signature items include genuine Philadelphia cheesesteak sandwiches, hand-cut French fries (cooked in peanut oil) and freshly-squeezed lemonade. Additional sandwich items include chicken, ham and vegetarian 'Philadelphias.' Other offerings include baked potatoes with toppings.

Background:

Established: 1983;	1st Franchised: 1984
Franchised Units:	200
Company-Owned Units:	20
Total Units:	220
Minority-Owned Units:	
African-American:	2
Asian-American:	15
Hispanic:	0
Native American:	0
North America:	31 States, 2 Provinces
Density:	28 in OH, 24 in IL, 17 in CA

Financial/Terms:

Cash Investment:	$50-100K
Total Investment:	$200-750K
Minimum Net Worth:	$150K
Fees: Franchise —	$20K
Royalty — 5%;	Ad. — 2%
Earnings Claim Statement:	No
Term of Contract (Years):	10/10
Avg. # Of Employees:	2 FT, 15 PT
Passive Ownership:	Allowed
Area Develop. Agreements:	Yes/10
Sub-Franchising Contracts:	Yes
Expand In Territory:	Yes
Space Needs: 600-2,000 SF; SC	

Support & Training Provided:

Site Selection Assistance:	Yes
Lease Negotiation Assistance:	Yes
Co-Operative Advertising:	Yes
Franchisee Assoc./Member:	No
Size Of Corporate Staff:	25
On-Going Support:	a,B,C,D,E,F,G

Training: 2 Weeks Cincinnati, OH.
Minority-Specific Programs: We employ a Korean consultant in California to help us reach the Asian community. We do not "change the rules" for any nationality and welcome all that are financially qualified. While not considered a minority, we do have over 30 franchisees from the Middle East.

Specific Expansion Plans:

US:	All United States

K-BOB'S STEAKHOUSES

3700 Rio Grande NW, # 6
Albuquerque, NM 87107
Tel: (800) 225-8403 (505) 242-8403

Fax: (505) 764-0492
Ms. Susan Rosulek, Director,
Administration

K-BOB'S caters to small, rural communities with populations of approximately 10,000 - 50,000 people. It concentrates on expanding with committed owner/operators in rural markets with good highway count and with the potential sales achievement of $900,000+ annually.

Background:

Established: 1966;   1st Franchised: 1992
Franchised Units: 27
Company-Owned Units: <u>6</u>
Total Units: 33
Minority-Owned Units:
   African-American: 0%
   Asian-American: 0%
   Hispanic: 3%
   Native American: 0%
   Other:
North America: 4 States
Density: 17 in TX, 11 in NM, 3 in CO

Financial/Terms:

Cash Investment: $62.5K
Total Investment: $170-973K
Minimum Net Worth: $NR
Fees: Franchise — $25K
   Royalty — 3%;   Ad. — 1%
Earnings Claim Statement: No
Term of Contract (Years):   20/10
Avg. # Of Employees: 4 FT, 30 PT
Passive Ownership: Not Allowed
Area Develop. Agreements: No
Sub-Franchising Contracts: No
Expand In Territory: Yes
Space Needs: 6,300 SF; FS

Support & Training Provided:

Site Selection Assistance: Yes
Lease Negotiation Assistance: No
Co-Operative Advertising: Yes
Franchisee Assoc./Member: NR
Size Of Corporate Staff: 12
On-Going Support: a,b,C,D,E,f,G,H,I
Training: 8 Weeks.
Minority-Specific Programs: Although we support the objectives of the NMFI, we do not have any specific programs in place at this time.

Specific Expansion Plans:

US: Southwest and Midwest

LE PEEP
4 W. Dry Creek Circle, # 201
Littleton, CO 80120
Tel: (303) 730-6300
Fax: (303) 730-7105
E-Mail: lepeep4w@ad.com
Web Site: www.lepeep.com
Ms. Allison Wilson, Licensing Manager

LE PEEP is a licenser of a breakfast, brunch and lunch concept, featuring an award-winning menu, decor and coffee and juice bar.

Background:

Established: 1992;   1st Franchised: 1981
Franchised Units: 64
Company-Owned Units: <u>8</u>
Total Units: 72
Minority-Owned Units:
   African-American:
   Asian-American:
   Hispanic:
   Native American:
   Other:
North America: 13 States
Density: 25 in CO, 8 in TX, 5 in GA

Financial/Terms:

Cash Investment: $100-350K
Total Investment: $100-550K
Minimum Net Worth: $100K
Fees: Franchise — $0
   Royalty — 3%;   Ad. — 1%
Earnings Claim Statement: Yes
Term of Contract (Years):   15/10
Avg. # Of Employees: 10 FT, 10 PT
Passive Ownership: N/A
Area Develop. Agreements: No
Sub-Franchising Contracts: No
Expand In Territory: Yes
Space Needs: 2,500-3,500 SF; FS, SF, SC

Support & Training Provided:

Site Selection Assistance: No
Lease Negotiation Assistance: No
Co-Operative Advertising: No
Franchisee Assoc./Member: No
Size Of Corporate Staff: 9
On-Going Support: b,c,d,e
Training: 8 Weeks in Denver, CO.
Minority-Specific Programs: Although we support the objectives of the NMFI, we do not have any specific programs in place at this time.

Specific Expansion Plans:

US: All United States

MAX & ERMA'S RESTAURANTS
4849 Evanswood Dr.
Columbus, OH 43229
Tel: (614) 431-5800
Fax: (614) 431-4111
E-Mail: rob@max-ermas.com
Web Site: www.max-ermas.com
Mr. Rob Lindeman, Director of Franchising

MAX & ERMA'S RESTAURANTS is famous for gourmet burgers, overstuffed sandwiches, homemade pasta dishes, chargrilled chicken specialties, super salads and taste-tempting munchies. Antiques artifacts and local paraphernalia make MAX & ERMA'S a fun, unique place to take friends and family. We work hard every day to help our guests enjoy their total dining experience so they can't wait to come back. And, we believe that experience starts with our food. We use only the freshest, highest-quality ingredients.

Background:

Established: 1972;   1st Franchised: 1997
Franchised Units: 4
Company-Owned Units: <u>53</u>
Total Units: 57
Minority-Owned Units:
   African-American:
   Asian-American:
   Hispanic:
   Native American:
   Other:
North America: 9 States
Density: 20 in OH, 8 in MI, 7 in IL

Financial/Terms:

Cash Investment: $400-500K
Total Investment: $800K-2.7MM

Minimum Net Worth:	$3MM
Fees: Franchise —	$40K
Royalty — 4%;	Ad. — 2%
Earnings Claim Statement:	No
Term of Contract (Years):	20/10
Avg. # Of Employees:	40 FT, 50 PT
Passive Ownership:	Allowed
Area Develop. Agreements:	Yes
Sub-Franchising Contracts:	No
Expand In Territory:	Yes
Space Needs: 5,000-6,900 SF; FS, RM	

Support & Training Provided:

Site Selection Assistance:	Yes
Lease Negotiation Assistance:	Yes
Co-Operative Advertising:	N/A
Franchisee Assoc./Member:	No
Size Of Corporate Staff:	55
On-Going Support:	B,C,D,E,F,G,H

Training: 14 Weeks Manager Training; 2-6 Weeks Staff Training; 2-3 weeks Opening Training.

Minority-Specific Programs: Although we support the objectives of the NMFI, we do not have any specific programs in place at this time.

Specific Expansion Plans:

US:	All United States

PEPE'S MEXICAN RESTAURANT

1325 W. 15th St.
Chicago, IL 60608
Tel: (312) 733-2500
Fax: (312) 733-2564
E-Mail:
Web Site:
Mr. Edwin A. Ptak, Corporate Counsel

A full-service Mexican restaurant, serving a complete line of Mexican food, with liquor, beer and wine. Complete training and help in remodeling, site selection, equipment purchasing and running the restaurant provided.

Background:

Established: 1967;	1st Franchised: 1968
Franchised Units:	56
Company-Owned Units:	1
Total Units:	57
Minority-Owned Units:	
African-American:	

Asian-American:	
Hispanic:	90%
Native American:	
Other:	
North America:	3 States
Density:	43 in IL, 13 in IN, 1 in VA

Financial/Terms:

Cash Investment:	$30-100K
Total Investment:	$75-300K
Minimum Net Worth:	$NR
Fees: Franchise —	$15K
Royalty — 4%;	Ad. — 3%
Earnings Claim Statement:	Yes
Term of Contract (Years):	20
Avg. # Of Employees:	8 FT, 5 PT
Passive Ownership:	Discouraged
Area Develop. Agreements:	Yes/Varies
Sub-Franchising Contracts:	No
Expand In Territory:	No
Space Needs: 3,000 SF; FS, SF, SC	

Support & Training Provided:

Site Selection Assistance:	Yes
Lease Negotiation Assistance:	Yes
Co-Operative Advertising:	Yes
Franchisee Assoc./Member:	NR
Size Of Corporate Staff:	15
On-Going Support:	B,C,D,E,F,G,H

Training: 4 Weeks Headquarters.

Minority-Specific Programs: Although we support the objectives of the NMFI, we do not have any specific programs in place at this time.

Specific Expansion Plans:

US:	Midwest

PERKINS RESTAURANT & BAKERY

6075 Poplar Ave., # 800
Memphis, TN 38119-4709
Tel: (800) 877-7375 (901) 766-6400
Fax: (901) 766-6482
E-Mail: franchise@perkinsrestaurants.com
Web Site: www.perkinsrestaurants.com
Mr. Robert J. Winters, VP Franchise Development

Full-service family-style restaurant, offering breakfast, lunch and dinner, along with proprietary bakery items at moderate prices.

Background:

Established: 1958;	1st Franchised: 1958

Franchised Units:	332
Company-Owned Units:	140
Total Units:	472
Minority-Owned Units:	
African-American:	
Asian-American:	
Hispanic:	
Native American:	
North America:	
35 States	
Density:	
73 in MN, 57 in OH,	
55 in FL	

Financial/Terms:

Cash Investment:	$100K-1.4MM
Total Investment:	$1.0-1.7MM
Minimum Net Worth:	$600K
Fees: Franchise —	$40K
Royalty — 4%;	Ad. — 3%
Earnings Claim Statement:	Yes
Term of Contract (Years):	20/10-20
Avg. # Of Employees:	20 FT, 40 PT
Passive Ownership:	Discouraged
Area Develop. Agreements:	Yes/3-8
Sub-Franchising Contracts:	No
Expand In Territory:	Yes
Space Needs: 5,000 SF; FS, SC	

Support & Training Provided:

Site Selection Assistance:	Yes
Lease Negotiation Assistance:	Yes
Co-Operative Advertising:	Yes
Franchisee Assoc./Member:	No
Size Of Corporate Staff:	224
On-Going Support:	a,B,C,D,E,F,G,H,I

Training: 8-12 Weeks Management Training at Various Locations.

Minority-Specific Programs: Although we support the objectives of the NMFI, we do not have any specific programs in place at this time.

Specific Expansion Plans:

US:	TX, MS, GA, AL, AR, IN

PIZZERIA UNO CHICAGO BAR & GRILL

100 Charles Park Rd.
Boston, MA 02132-4985
Tel: (800) 449-8667 (617) 323-9200
Fax: (617) 218-5376
E-Mail: randy.clifton@pizzeriauno.com
Web Site: www.pizzeriauno.com
Mr. Randy M. Clifton, VP Worldwide Franchising

A casual theme restaurant with a brand name signature product — UNO's Original Chicago Deep Dish Pizza. A full, varied menu with broad appeal and a flair for fun and comfortable decor in a facility that attracts guests of all ages.

Background:

Established: 1943;   1st Franchised: 1979
Franchised Units: 71
Company-Owned Units: 99
Total Units: 170
Minority-Owned Units:
  African-American: 2
  Asian-American: 3
  Hispanic: 5
  Native American: 0
  Other:
North America: 43 States
Density: 27 in MA, 10 in PA, 10 in CA

Financial/Terms:

Cash Investment: $500K
Total Investment: $900K-1.7MM
Minimum Net Worth: $1.5MM
Fees: Franchise — $35K
  Royalty — 5%;   Ad. — 1%
Earnings Claim Statement: Yes
Term of Contract (Years):   15/10
Avg. # Of Employees: 30 FT, 35 PT
Passive Ownership: Allowed
Area Develop. Agreements: Yes/Negot.
Sub-Franchising Contracts: No
Expand In Territory: Yes
Space Needs: 5,500 SF; FS, SC, RM

Support & Training Provided:

Site Selection Assistance: Yes
Lease Negotiation Assistance: Yes
Co-Operative Advertising: Yes
Franchisee Assoc./Member: Yes/Yes
Size Of Corporate Staff: 120
On-Going Support: a,B,C,D,E,F,G,H,I
Training: 8 Weeks in a Training Restaurant; 2 Weeks On-Site Staff Training
Minority-Specific Programs: Although we support the objectives of the NMFI, we do not have any specific programs in place at this time.

Specific Expansion Plans:

US: All United States

PONDEROSA/BONANZA STEAKHOUSES

6500 International Pkwy.
Plano, TX 75093
Tel: (800) 543-9670 (972) 588-5887
Fax: (972) 588-5806
E-Mail: franchise@metrogroup.com
Web Site: www.metromediarestaurants.com
Mr. Lawrence F. Stein, Director Franchise Development

PONDEROSA and BONANZA FAMILY STEAKHOUSES serve great-tasting, family-priced steaks and entrees, accompanied by a large variety of all-you-can-eat salad items, soups, appetizers, hot vegetables, breads, sundae and dessert bar and other tasty food. All steaks and entrees come with the salad bar, buffet and dessert bar at no extra cost.

Background:

Established: 1965;   1st Franchised: 1966
Franchised Units: 453
Company-Owned Units: 164
Total Units: 617
Minority-Owned Units:
  African-American: 7
  Asian-American:
  Hispanic:
  Native American:
  Other: Several
North America: 29 States
Density: 99 in OH, 53 in IN, 47 in NY

Financial/Terms:

Cash Investment: $300K Liquid
Total Investment: $810K-1.9MM
Minimum Net Worth: $1.0MM
Fees: Franchise — $40K
  Royalty — 4%;   Ad. — 4%
Earnings Claim Statement: No
Term of Contract (Years):   20
Avg. # Of Employees: Varies
Passive Ownership: Discouraged
Area Develop. Agreements: Yes/Varies
Sub-Franchising Contracts: No
Expand In Territory: Yes
Space Needs: 5,200-8,200 SF; FS, SC, RM

Support & Training Provided:

Site Selection Assistance: No
Lease Negotiation Assistance: Yes
Co-Operative Advertising: Yes
Franchisee Assoc./Member: Yes/No
Size Of Corporate Staff: 375
On-Going Support: C,D,E,F,G,H,I

Training: 9 Weeks Headquarters in Plano, TX and Restaurant in Field.
Minority-Specific Programs: Although we support the objectives of the NMFI, we do not have any specific programs in place at this time. We are in active communication with minority-oriented agancies such as L.I.S.C., as well as with the public affairs and emerging markets department at IFA, and we actively encourage minority applicants.

Specific Expansion Plans:

US: All United States

R. J. BOAR'S BBQ

3127 Brady St., # 3
Davenport, IA 52803
Tel: (319) 322-2627
Fax: (319) 322-1947
E-Mail:
Web Site: www.rjboars.com
Mr. Schuyler (Skip) Moore, Director of Franchise Sales

R. J. BOAR'S is awarding franchise opportunities in the Midwest to qualified individuals. We specialize in hickory-smoked ribs, chicken and beef. As a niche player in the casual theme restaurant category, we realized very early on that a broad and varied menu of popular items was a crucial factor in determining our formula. That's why R. J. BOAR'S has such a diverse menu, including signature appetizers, specialty salads, fresh fish, tender steaks and award-winning hickory-smoked BBQ.

Background:

Established: 1993;   1st Franchised: 1998
Franchised Units: 1
Company-Owned Units: 4
Total Units: 5
Minority-Owned Units:
  African-American:
  Asian-American:
  Hispanic:
  Native American:
  Other:
North America: 2 States
Density: 3 in IA, 2 in IL

Financial/Terms:

Cash Investment: $175-300K
Total Investment: $378-909K
Minimum Net Worth: $1.5MM
Fees: Franchise — $35K
  Royalty — 4%;   Ad. — 3%
Earnings Claim Statement: No
Term of Contract (Years):   10/5/5
Avg. # Of Employees: 10 FT, 60 PT

Passive Ownership: Not Allowed
Area Develop. Agreements: Yes/Varies
Sub-Franchising Contracts: No
Expand In Territory: Yes
Space Needs: 5,500 SF; FS

Support & Training Provided:
Site Selection Assistance: Yes
Lease Negotiation Assistance: No
Co-Operative Advertising: Yes
Franchisee Assoc./Member: No
Size Of Corporate Staff: 4
On-Going Support: B,C,D,E,f, h
Training: 8-10 Weeks Bettendorf, IA.
Minority Specific Programs: Although we support the objectives of the NMFI, we do not have any specific programs in place at this time.

Specific Expansion Plans:
US: Midwest

SANDELLA'S CAFÉ

9 Brookside Place
West Redding, CT 06896
Tel: (888) 544-9984 (203) 544-9984
Fax: (203) 544-7749
E-Mail: bmajor@sandellas.com
Web Site: www.sandellas.com
Mr. Bruce J. Major, Chief Development Officer

Positioned in the explosive wrap market, SANDELLA'S is carving a market niche in fresh, distinctive food at affordable prices. The SANDELLA'S concept combines the convenience and value of quick-service concepts with the quality, freshness and variety associated with up-scale, casual full-service dining.

Background:
Established: 1994; 1st Franchised: 1998
Franchised Units: 10
Company-Owned Units: 3
Total Units: 13
Minority-Owned Units:
African-American:
Asian-American:
Hispanic:
Native American:
North America: 5 States
Density: 5 in NY, 2 in TX, 2 in CT

Financial/Terms:
Cash Investment: $50-100K
Total Investment: $145-245K
Minimum Net Worth: $250K
Fees: Franchise — $20K
Royalty — 6%; Ad. — 3 + 1%
Earnings Claim Statement: No
Term of Contract (Years): 10/10
Avg. # Of Employees: 4 FT, 4 PT
Passive Ownership: Discouraged
Area Develop. Agreements: Yes/Varies
Sub-Franchising Contracts: Yes
Expand In Territory: Yes
Space Needs: 1,500 +/- SF; FS, SF, SC, RM

Support & Training Provided:
Site Selection Assistance: Yes
Lease Negotiation Assistance: Yes
Co-Operative Advertising: Yes
Franchisee Assoc./Member: No
Size Of Corporate Staff: 25
On-Going Support: A,B,C,D,E,F,G,H,I
Training: 6 Days Georgetown, CT; 10 Days in Store.
Minority-Specific Programs: SANDELLA'S CAFÉ is a member of Women in Franchising

Specific Expansion Plans:
US: All United States

SANDWICH TREE RESTAURANTS

535 Thurlow St., # 300
Vancouver, BC V6E 3L2 CANADA
Tel: (800) 663-8733 (604) 684-3314
Fax: (604) 684-2542
E-Mail:
Web Site: www.sandwichtree.ca
Mr. Tony Cardarelli, Director of Operations

Famous for our custom sandwiches, creative salads, hearty soups, catering and much more, SANDWICH TREE is a limited-hours operation located in shopping centres, commercial towers and industrial centres. Our quality food, served in our attractive surroundings, makes SANDWICH TREE a number one investment opportunity.

Background:
Established: 1978; 1st Franchised: 1979
Franchised Units: 31
Company-Owned Units: 0
Total Units: 31
Minority-Owned Units:
African-American:
Asian-American:
Hispanic:

Native American:
Other:
North America: 6 Provinces
Density: 19 in BC, 7 in NS, 5 in ON

Financial/Terms:
Cash Investment: $35-55K
Total Investment: $90-120K
Minimum Net Worth: $NR
Fees: Franchise — $10-17.5K
Royalty — 5%; Ad. — 3%
Earnings Claim Statement: Yes
Term of Contract (Years): 5/5
Avg. # Of Employees: 4 FT, 7 PT
Passive Ownership: Discouraged
Area Develop. Agreements: Yes/10
Sub-Franchising Contracts: Yes
Expand In Territory: Yes
Space Needs: 300+ SF; SF, RM, Ind. Park

Support & Training Provided:
Site Selection Assistance: Yes
Lease Negotiation Assistance: Yes
Co-Operative Advertising: Yes
Franchisee Assoc./Member: NR
Size Of Corporate Staff: 6
On-Going Support: a,B,C,D,E,F,G,H,I
Training: 2 Weeks Headquarters.
Minority-Specific Programs: Although we support the objectives of the NMFI, we do not have any specific programs in place at this time.

Specific Expansion Plans:
US: No

SBARRO

401 Broadhollow Rd.
Melville, NY 11747
Tel: (800) 766-4949 (516) 715-4100
Fax: (516) 715-4183
E-Mail: communications@sbarro.com
Web Site: www.sbarro.com
Ms. Meryl Jacovsky, Fran. Commun. Coord

The #1 quick-service Italian restaurant around the world. Family-owned and operated, SBARRO prides itself on its use of fresh ingredients, innovative recipes and a com-mitment to quality service known the world over.

Background:

Established: 1959; 1st Franchised: 1979
Franchised Units: 286
Company-Owned Units: <u>634</u>
Total Units: 920
Minority-Owned Units:
 African-American:
 Asian-American: 6
 Hispanic: 5
 Native American:
 Other: 5 Middle Eastern
North America: 30 States, 1 Province
Density: 25 in Il, 24 in NY, 16 in FL

Financial/Terms:

Cash Investment: $150K
Total Investment: $250-850K
Minimum Net Worth: $250K
Fees: Franchise — $45K
 Royalty — 6%; Ad. — 0%
Earnings Claim Statement: No
Term of Contract (Years): 10/10
Avg. # Of Employees: 8-10 FT, 10-15 PT
Passive Ownership: Not Allowed
Area Develop. Agreements: Yes/10
Sub-Franchising Contracts: No
Expand In Territory: Yes
Space Needs: 800-1,000 SF; RM

Support & Training Provided:

Site Selection Assistance: No
Lease Negotiation Assistance: No
Co-Operative Advertising: Yes
Franchisee Assoc./Member: Yes/Yes
Size Of Corporate Staff: 250
On-Going Support: A,B,C,E,G,I
Training: 3 Weeks Walt Whitman Mall, Huntington, NY.
Minority-Specific Programs: Although we support the objectives of the NMFI, we do not have any specific programs in place at this time.

Specific Expansion Plans:

US: NE, SE, Midwest, Southwest

STRAW HAT PIZZA

6400 Village Pkwy.
Dublin, CA 94568
Tel: (925) 829-1500
Fax: (925) 829-9533
E-Mail: info@strawhatpizza.com
Web Site: www.strawhatpizza.com
Mr. Ted Richman, Chief Operating Officer

STRAW HAT PIZZA is a cooperative owned by a membership made up of individual store owners. Royalty fees are very low and more than offset by purchasing, insurance and marketing advantages. Stores operate under a detailed system, yet are allowed a great deal of flexibility. Store owners participate in the operation of the parent company.

Background:

Established: 1987; 1st Franchised: 1987
Franchised Units: 60
Company-Owned Units: <u>0</u>
Total Units: 60
Minority-Owned Units:
 African-American:
 Asian-American:
 Hispanic:
 Native American:
North America: 2 States
Density: 47 in CA, 3 in NV

Financial/Terms:

Cash Investment: $50-100K
Total Investment: $100-400K
Minimum Net Worth: $100K
Fees: Franchise — $10K
 Royalty — 2%; Ad. — 0.75%
Earnings Claim Statement: No
Term of Contract (Years): 10/5
Avg. # Of Employees: 3-5 FT, 8-15 PT
Passive Ownership: Discouraged
Area Develop. Agreements: No
Sub-Franchising Contracts: No
Expand In Territory: Yes
Space Needs: 4,000 SF; SC

Support & Training Provided:

Site Selection Assistance: No
Lease Negotiation Assistance: No
Co-Operative Advertising: Yes
Franchisee Assoc./Member: No
Size Of Corporate Staff: 4
On-Going Support: B,C,d,E,F,G,H
Training: 4 Weeks in Long Beach, CA.
Minority-Specific Programs: Although we support the objectives of the NMFI, we do not have any specific programs in place at this time.

Specific Expansion Plans:

US: West and group of 5 all U.S.

VILLAGE INN RESTAURANTS

400 W. 48th Ave., P. O. Box 16601
Denver, CO 80216
Tel: (800) 891-9978 (303) 296-2121
Fax: (303) 672-2212
Web Site: www.vicorpinc.com
Ms. Maxine Crogle, Qualifications Specialist

Full-service, family-style restaurants, offering a variety of menu items and bi-monthly features, emphasizing our breakfast heritage in all dayparts.

Good Food ... Good Feelings®

Background:

Established: 1958; 1st Franchised: 1961
Franchised Units: 116
Company-Owned Units: <u>104</u>
Total Units: 220
Minority-Owned Units:
 African-American:
 Asian-American:
 Hispanic:
 Native American:
 Other:
North America: 21 States
Density: 45 in CO, 25 in FL, 23 AZ

Financial/Terms:

Cash Investment: $Varies
Total Investment: $512K-2.4MM
Minimum Net Worth: $750K
Fees: Franchise — $35K
 Royalty — 4%; Ad. — 0%
Earnings Claim Statement: No
Term of Contract (Years): 25/10
Avg. # Of Employees: 20 FT, 40 PT
Passive Ownership: Discouraged
Area Develop. Agreements: Yes/Varies
Sub-Franchising Contracts: No
Expand In Territory: Yes
Space Needs: 5,200 SF; FS, SC, RM

Support & Training Provided:

Site Selection Assistance: Yes
Lease Negotiation Assistance: No
Co-Operative Advertising: No
Franchisee Assoc./Member: No
Size Of Corporate Staff: 200
On-Going Support: C,d,E,F,G,h,I
Training: Approximately 10-12 Weeks Denver, CO.
Minority-Specific Programs: Although we support the objectives of the NMFI, we do not have any specific programs in place at this time.

Specific Expansion Plans:

US: Mid-Atlantic, Midwest,SE

152

WESTERN SIZZLIN'

317 Kimball Ave.
Roanoke, VA 24016
Tel: (800) 642-2157 (540) 345-3195
Fax: (540) 345-0831
E-Mail: wsinc@feist.com
Web Site: www.western-sizzlin.com
Mr. John Mash, Director Franchise
Development

WESTERN SIZZLIN' restaurants operate a full line of steak-chicken-seafood entrees, as well as a full expanded food bar, featuring proteins, vegetables and bakery items, along with an expanded salad bar. Our focus is on making a quality statement with excellent price/value. Also offering franchises for Great American Steak & Buffet and Austin's Steakhouse and Saloon.

Background:

Established. 1962,	1st Franchised. 1976
Franchised Units:	213
Company-Owned Units:	<u>26</u>
Total Units:	239

Minority-Owned Units:
   African-American:
   Asian-American:
   Hispanic:
   Native American:
   Other:

North America:	NR
Density:	31 in AR, 24 in VA, 21 in GA

Financial/Terms:

Cash Investment:	$NR
Total Investment:	$811K-2.3MM
Minimum Net Worth:	$NR
Fees: Franchise —	$30K
Royalty — 2% Gross; Ad. — 1% Gross	
Earnings Claim Statement:	No
Term of Contract (Years):	20/10
Avg. # Of Employees:	25 FT, 50 PT
Passive Ownership:	NR
Area Develop. Agreements:	Yes/Negot.
Sub-Franchising Contracts:	NR
Expand In Territory:	Yes
Space Needs: 7,500-8,500 SF; FS	

Support & Training Provided:

Site Selection Assistance:	Yes
Lease Negotiation Assistance:	No
Co-Operative Advertising:	No
Franchisee Assoc./Member:	Yes
Size Of Corporate Staff:	40
On-Going Support:	C,D,E,F,G,h,I

Training: 6 Weeks Training Center in Manassas, VA, Knoxville, TN, Little Rock, AR.

Minority-Specific Programs: Although we support the objectives of the NMFI, we do not have any specific programs in place at this time.

Specific Expansion Plans:

US:	All United States

AMERICANDY
1401 Lexington Rd.
Louisville, KY 40206-1928
Tel: (502) 583-1776
Fax: (502) 583-6627
E-Mail: omar@americandy.com
Web Site: www.americandy.com
Mr. Omar L. Tatum, President/Founder

A tour of America through candy. 50 state chocolates available by state, region or all 50 state chocolates in our signature collection. Retail store, kiosks, packing center.

Background:
Established: 1990;	1st Franchised: 1992
Franchised Units:	0
Company-Owned Units:	1
Total Units:	1
Minority-Owned Units:	
African-American:	0
Asian-American:	0
Hispanic:	0
Native American:	0
Other:	0
North America:	1 State
Density:	1 in KY

Financial/Terms:
Cash Investment:	$75-185K
Total Investment:	$75-100K
Minimum Net Worth:	$185K
Fees: Franchise —	$25K
Royalty — 6%;	Ad. — 2%
Earnings Claim Statement:	No
Term of Contract (Years):	5/5
Avg. # Of Employees:	2 FT, 4 PT

Passive Ownership:	Discouraged
Area Develop. Agreements:	Yes/10
Sub-Franchising Contracts:	Yes
Expand In Territory:	Yes
Space Needs: 1,200 SF; SF, SC, RM	

Support & Training Provided:
Site Selection Assistance:	Yes
Lease Negotiation Assistance:	Yes
Co-Operative Advertising:	N/A
Franchisee Assoc./Member:	No
Size Of Corporate Staff:	4
On-Going Support:	a,B,C,D,E,F,G,h
Training: 2 Weeks in Louisville, KY.	

Minority-Specific Programs: Although we support the objectives of the NMFI, we do not have any specific programs in place at this time.

Specific Expansion Plans:
US:	All United States

AUNTIE ANNE'S
160-A, Rt. 41, P. O. Box 529
Gap, PA 17527
Tel: (717) 442-4766
Fax: (717) 442-4139
Web Site: www.auntieannes.com
Ms. Terry Wisdo, VP Franchise Development

As the founder and leader of what Entrepreneur Magazine calls the pretzel retailing revolution, AUNTIE ANNE'S supports over 600 locations. Customers love to watch our pretzels being rolled, twisted and baked. They choose our pretzels not only for the variety and taste, but also for our commitment to providing a nutritious snack alternative to mall treats. Our innovative mall-based concept has made AUNTIE ANNE'S one of the most sought-after franchises in the industry today.

Background:
Established: 1988;	1st Franchised: 1989
Franchised Units:	561
Company-Owned Units:	18
Total Units:	579
Minority-Owned Units:	
African-American:	6
Asian-American:	27
Hispanic:	2
Native American:	0
Other:	2
North America:	42 States
Density:	81 in PA, 41 in CA, 40 in FL

Financial/Terms:
Cash Investment:	$156-252K
Total Investment:	$252K
Minimum Net Worth:	$300K
Fees: Franchise —	$30K
Royalty — 6%;	Ad. — 1%
Earnings Claim Statement:	No
Term of Contract (Years):	1-5/5
Avg. # Of Employees:	3 FT, 12 PT
Passive Ownership:	Discouraged
Area Develop. Agreements:	No
Sub-Franchising Contracts:	No
Expand In Territory:	Yes
Space Needs: 400-800 SF; RM	

Support & Training Provided:

Site Selection Assistance:	Yes
Lease Negotiation Assistance:	Yes
Co-Operative Advertising:	No
Franchisee Assoc./Member:	Yes/No
Size Of Corporate Staff:	135
On-Going Support:	A,B,C,D,E,G,h

Training: 7-14 Days Corporate Headquarters, Gap, PA.

Minority-Specific Programs: While AUNTIE ANNE'S, Inc. has been fortunate to receive numerous calls for franchise opportunities,we recently became involve with The Connections Program in Chicago. The program's goal is to increase minority business owners in the inner-city of Chicago. It serves as surrogate bringing potential minority franchisees together with franchises and lending institutions. Currently, we are in negotiations with our first possible store owner from the program.

Specific Expansion Plans:

US:	Parts of MW, SE, West. Regns

BEAVERTAILS PASTRY

112 Nelson St., Unit 101 C
Ottawa, ON K1N 7R5 CANADA
Tel: (800) 704-0351 (613) 789-4940
Fax: (613) 789-5158
E-Mail: info@beavertailsinc.com
Web Site: www.beavertailsinc.com
Mr. Robert Libbey, President/CEO

BEAVERTAILS are a unique, wholesome pastry cooked fresh at leisure sites. We offer low entry investment, interesting locations and excellent strategic support. We are interested in development opportunities at amusement parks, sports venues, tourist destinations and ski hills across North America.

Background:

Established: 1978;	1st Franchised: 1989
Franchised Units:	100
Company-Owned Units:	3
Total Units:	103
Minority-Owned Units:	
African-American:	
Asian-American:	
Hispanic:	
Native American:	
Other:	
North America:	4 States, 4 Provinces
Density:	1 in FL, 1 in CO, 1 in WV

Financial/Terms:

Cash Investment:	$30-50K
Total Investment:	$85-150K

Minimum Net Worth:	$50K
Fees: Franchise —	$20K
Royalty — 5%;	Ad. — 3%
Earnings Claim Statement:	Yes
Term of Contract (Years):	5/15
Avg. # Of Employees:	1 FT, 2-3 PT
Passive Ownership:	Discouraged
Area Develop. Agreements:	Yes
Sub-Franchising Contracts:	Yes
Expand In Territory:	Yes
Space Needs: 200-300 SF; FS, SF, RM, Amusement.Recr.	

Support & Training Provided:

Site Selection Assistance:	Yes
Lease Negotiation Assistance:	Yes
Co-Operative Advertising:	Yes
Franchisee Assoc./Member:	Yes/Yes
Size Of Corporate Staff:	10
On-Going Support:	A,B,C,D,E,F,G,I

Training: 14 Days Ottawa, ON; 3 Days On-Site.

Minority-Specific Programs: Although we support the objectives of the NMFI, we do not have any specific programs in place at this time.

Specific Expansion Plans:

US:	Southeast & Southwest

CANDY BOUQUET INTERNATIONAL, INC.

423 E. 3rd St.
Little Rock, AR 72201
Tel: (877) CANDY01 (501) 375-9990
Fax: (501) 375-9998
E-Mail: yumyum@candybouquet.com
Web Site: www.candybouquet.com
Mrs. Margaret M. McEntire, President/CEO

A CANDY BOUQUET is a full-scale candy store and a store of arrangements designed like flowers that is crafted from candies and the finest of chocolates. Each bouquet includes a burst of accessories, bright cellophane accents and unique containers. CANDY BOUQUETS are fun to give, fun to receive and fun to eat. They are perfect as corporate gifts and can be shipped anywhere.

Background:

Established: 1989;	1st Franchised: 1994
Franchised Units:	400
Company-Owned Units:	1
Total Units:	401
Minority-Owned Units:	
African-American:	7
Asian-American:	6
Hispanic:	10
Native American:	1
Other:	
North America:	47 States,10 Provinces
Density:	34 in AR, 26 in CA, 28 in TX

Financial/Terms:

Cash Investment:	$7.5-43K
Total Investment:	$7-43K
Minimum Net Worth:	$N/A
Fees: Franchise —	$3.5-25K
Royalty — 0%;	Ad. — 0%
Earnings Claim Statement:	No
Term of Contract (Years):	5/5
Avg. # Of Employees:	1 FT, 2 PT
Passive Ownership:	Not Allowed
Area Develop. Agreements:	Yes/10
Sub-Franchising Contracts:	Yes
Expand In Territory:	Yes
Space Needs: Appox. 1,000 SF; HB, SF	

Support & Training Provided:

Site Selection Assistance:	Yes
Lease Negotiation Assistance:	No
Co-Operative Advertising:	Yes
Franchisee Assoc./Member:	No
Size Of Corporate Staff:	27
On-Going Support:	b,c,d,D,e,G,h,I

Training: 5 Days Little Rock, AR.

Minority-Specific Programs: Although we support the objectives of the NMFI, we do not have any specific programs in place at this time.

Specific Expansion Plans:

US:	All United States

FROZEN FUSION FRUIT SMOOTHIES

8900 E. Chaparrel Rd., # 1000
Scottsdale, AZ 85250
Tel: (800) 385-3765 (480) 367-5600

Fax: (480) 367-5676
Web Site: www.frozenfusion.com
Mr. Michael A. Kiick, VP Franchise
Expansion

FROZEN FUSION is a tantalizing blend of fresh fruit and creamy non-fat yogurt. As a healthy snack or a satisfying meal, these fruit-based smoothies appeal to every taste. From the weight conscious, to the taste conscious, to the time conscious. There are a variety of tempting choices, including today's most popular nutritional supplements. They quench thirsts. They build energy. They even tame the sweetest tooth. FROZEN FUSION is perfect for any time of the day.

Background:
Established: 1995;	1st Franchised: 1996
Franchised Units:	20
Company-Owned Units:	4
Total Units:	24
Minority-Owned Units:	
African-American:	
Asian-American:	
Hispanic:	
Native American:	
North America:	9 States
Density:	5 in AZ, 4 in DC, 3 in CA

Financial/Terms:
Cash Investment:	$75K
Total Investment:	$180-250K
Minimum Net Worth:	$250K
Fees: Franchise —	$25-30K
Royalty — 5%;	Ad. — 1.5%
Earnings Claim Statement:	No
Term of Contract (Years):	10/10
Avg. # Of Employees:	4 FT, 10 PT
Passive Ownership:	Discouraged
Area Develop. Agreements:	Yes/10
Sub-Franchising Contracts:	No
Expand In Territory:	Yes
Space Needs: 500-1,000 SF; FS, SF, RM	

Support & Training Provided:
Site Selection Assistance:	Yes
Lease Negotiation Assistance:	Yes
Co-Operative Advertising:	Yes
Franchisee Assoc./Member:	No
Size Of Corporate Staff:	13
On-Going Support:	A,B,C,D,E,F,G,H,I

Training: 1 Week Headquarters in Scottsdale, AZ; 1 Week On-Site.
Minority-Specific Programs: The company is an enterprise of the Pima/Salt River Maricopa Tribe. We are an American Indian-owned enterprise.

Specific Expansion Plans:
US:	All United States

HARD TIMES CAFÉ
515 King St., # 440
Alexandria, VA 22314
Tel: (800) 422-2435 (703) 683-8545
Fax: (703) 683-7966
E-Mail: danr@hardtimes.com
Web Site: www.hardtimes.com
Mr. Dan A. Rowe, CEO

Authentic western-style chili parlor. Featuring chili, burgers and beer.

Background:
Established: 1980;	1st Franchised: 1992
Franchised Units:	10
Company-Owned Units:	4
Total Units:	14
Minority-Owned Units:	
African-American:	
Asian-American:	
Hispanic:	
Native American:	
North America:	3 States
Density:	6 in VA, 6 in MD, 2 in NC

Financial/Terms:
Cash Investment:	$100-200K
Total Investment:	$400-500K
Minimum Net Worth:	$250K
Fees: Franchise —	$30K
Royalty — 4%;	Ad. — 1%
Earnings Claim Statement:	No
Term of Contract (Years):	10/10
Avg. # Of Employees:	6 FT, 20 PT
Passive Ownership:	Not Allowed
Area Develop. Agreements:	Yes/20
Sub-Franchising Contracts:	Yes
Expand In Territory:	Yes
Space Needs: NR SF; FS, SC	

Support & Training Provided:
Site Selection Assistance:	Yes
Lease Negotiation Assistance:	Yes
Co-Operative Advertising:	Yes
Franchisee Assoc./Member:	No
Size Of Corporate Staff:	10
On-Going Support:	a,C,D,E,F,G,H,I

Training: 4 Weeks in Washington, DC Area.
Minority-Specific Programs: We will do

whatever we can to help each and every prospective franchisee become a successful franchisee.

Specific Expansion Plans:
US:	East Coast and Mid-Atlantic

MAUI WOWI SMOOTHIES
39 Viking Dr.
Englewood, CO 80110
Tel: (888) 862-8555 (303) 781-7800
Fax: (303) 781-2438
E-Mail: crm@concentric.net
Web Site: www.mauiwowi.com
Mr. Michael Haith, President

MAIU WOWI is a home-based business selling fresh-blended smoothies from carts at special events such as fairs, festivals, arenas, malls and airports. No royalties or financial reporting. Low investment and high income working when and where you want.

Background:
Established: 1983;	1st Franchised: 1997
Franchised Units:	46
Company-Owned Units:	3
Total Units:	49
Minority-Owned Units:	
African-American:	0
Asian-American:	0
Hispanic:	0
Native American:	0
Other:	90% Women
North America:	14 States
Density:	10 in CO, 6 in WA, 3 in UT

Financial/Terms:
Cash Investment:	$4.5-20K
Total Investment:	$24.5-54.7K
Minimum Net Worth:	$50K
Fees: Franchise —	$20K
Royalty — N/A;	Ad. — 5%
Earnings Claim Statement:	No
Term of Contract (Years):	5/5
Avg. # Of Employees:	2 PT
Passive Ownership:	Allowed
Area Develop. Agreements:	Yes/20
Sub-Franchising Contracts:	Yes
Expand In Territory:	Yes
Space Needs: 100 SF; HB	

Support & Training Provided:
Site Selection Assistance:	Yes
Lease Negotiation Assistance:	Yes

Co-Operative Advertising: Yes
Franchisee Assoc./Member: No
Size Of Corporate Staff: 5
On-Going Support: B,C,D,E,G,H,I
Training: 1.5 Days in Denver; 1.5 Days in Salt Lake City; 1.5 Days at Your Location.
Minority-Specific Programs: MAUI WOWI Provides assistance in acquiring MBE/ WBE/DBE status. In our particular non-traditional site locations such as airports, convention centers, stadiums and arenas, a minority status allows franchisees increased access in site acquisition and contracts. Minority status in our franchise is a giant benefit for fulfilling equal opportunity contracts in municipal and government facilities. Most franchisees work as couples with the wife owning a majority of the stock.

Specific Expansion Plans:
US: All United States

TAKE 'N' BAKE PIZZA

PAPA MURPHY'S
8000 NE Parkway Dr., # 350
Vancouver, WA 98662
Tel: (800) 257-7272 (360) 260-7272
Fax: (360) 260-0050
E Mail: bobc@papamurphys.com
Web Site: www.papamurphys.com
Franchise Department,

PAPA MURPHY'S produces a great pizza made from top quality ingredients. Letting customers bake it themselves is smart business. Put the 2 together and you get the largest, fastest-growing Take 'N' Bake franchise in the world. PAPA MURPHY'S now has 495 stores with another 175 stores expected to open in 2000.

Background:
Established: 1981;   1st Franchised: 1982
Franchised Units: 436
Company-Owned Units: 10
Total Units: 446
Minority-Owned Units:
  African-American:
  Asian-American: 10
  Hispanic: 5
  Native American:
  Other: Women-27

North America: 17 States
Density: 124 in CA, 79 in OR,98 in WA

Financial/Terms:
Cash Investment: $80K
Total Investment: $134-175K
Minimum Net Worth: $250K
Fees: Franchise — $25K
  Royalty — 5%; Ad. — 1%
Earnings Claim Statement: No
Term of Contract (Years): 10/5
Avg. # Of Employees: 2 FT, 8-10 PT
Passive Ownership: Not Allowed
Area Develop. Agreements: No
Sub-Franchising Contracts: No
Expand In Territory: Yes
Space Needs: 1,200 SF; FS, SF, SC

Support & Training Provided:
Site Selection Assistance: Yes
Lease Negotiation Assistance: Yes
Co-Operative Advertising: Yes
Franchisee Assoc./Member: Yes/No
Size Of Corporate Staff: 106
On-Going Support: B,C,D,E,G,H,I
Training: 6 Day/100 Hours Closest Training Store; 2 Weeks In-Store; 5 Days Corporate Office.
Minority-Specific Programs: PAPA MURPHY'S takes a proactive position in regard to minority recruitment. We have placed ads for franchisees in minority owned newspapers and attended Minority Business Symposiums in an attempt to attract new owners. Also, our Director of Franchise Sales, Bob Coltrane, is developing a Minority Recruitment Program. We hope to build an awareness and presence in the minority community prior to entering a burgeoning market and attract qualified owners while suburban and urban sites still exist.

Specific Expansion Plans:
US: Midwest

PIZZA NOVA
2247 Midland Ave.
Scarborough, ON M1P 4R1 CANADA
Tel: (416) 439-0051
Fax: (416) 299-3558
Mr. Frank Macri, Franchise Director

PIZZA NOVA specializes in traditional Italian pizza, pastas and chicken wings. All menu items are prepared fresh daily and are available for take-out or delivery. We pride ourselves on quality and service.

Background:
Established: 1963;   1st Franchised: 1969
Franchised Units: 85

Company-Owned Units: 2
Total Units: 87
Minority-Owned Units:
  African-American:
  Asian-American: 5%
  Hispanic:
  Native American:
  Other: 80%
North America: 1 State, 1 Provinces
Density: 80 in ON

Financial/Terms:
Cash Investment: $40K
Total Investment: $125-135K
Minimum Net Worth: $NR
Fees: Franchise — $N/A
  Royalty — 6%; Ad. — 4%
Earnings Claim Statement: Yes
Term of Contract (Years): 5/5
Avg. # Of Employees: 4 FT, 6 PT
Passive Ownership: Not Allowed
Area Develop. Agreements: No
Sub-Franchising Contracts: No
Expand In Territory: Yes
Space Needs: 800-1,100 SF; SF, SC, RM

Support & Training Provided:
Site Selection Assistance: Yes
Lease Negotiation Assistance: Yes
Co-Operative Advertising: Yes
Franchisee Assoc./Member: Yes
Size Of Corporate Staff: 18
On-Going Support: A,B,C,D,E,F,G,H
Training: 3 Weeks.
Minority-Specific Programs: Although we support the objectives of the NMFI, we do not have any specific programs in place at this time.

Specific Expansion Plans:
US: NR

"WORLD'S BEST SOFT PRETZEL"

PRETZEL MAKER
2855 E. Cottonwood Pkwy., # 400
Salt Lake City, UT 84121
Tel: (800) 348-6311 (801) 736-5600
Fax: (888) 867-7343
E-Mail:
Web Site:
Franchise Development, Franchise Development Manager

The 'World's Best Soft Pretzels,' hand-rolled and served hot with high consumer acceptance, precision portion control and available in combination store configurations. May be operated in both traditional and non-traditional venues.

Background:
Established: 1991;   1st Franchised: 1992
Franchised Units: 154
Company-Owned Units: 4
Total Units: 158
Minority-Owned Units:
    African-American:
    Asian-American:
    Hispanic:
    Native American:
    Other:
North America: 39 States, 9 Provinces
Density: 21 in CA, 13 in UT, 11 in CO

Financial/Terms:
Cash Investment: $10-30K
Total Investment: $90-160K
Minimum Net Worth: $150K
Fees: Franchise — $20K
    Royalty — 5%;   Ad. — 1.5%
Earnings Claim Statement: No
Term of Contract (Years):   10/10
Avg. # Of Employees: 5 FT, 7 PT
Passive Ownership: Discouraged
Area Develop. Agreements: Yes/3
Sub-Franchising Contracts: No
Expand In Territory: Yes
Space Needs: 500-700 SF; FS, SC, RM

Support & Training Provided:
Site Selection Assistance: Yes
Lease Negotiation Assistance: Yes
Co-Operative Advertising: Yes
Franchisee Assoc./Member: No
Size Of Corporate Staff: 37
On-Going Support: B,C,D,E,F,G,H
Training: 5 Days Denver, CO.
Minority-Specific Programs: Although we support the objectives of the NMFI, we do not have any specific programs in place at this time.

Specific Expansion Plans:
US: All United States

❈

PRETZEL TIME

PRETZEL TIME
2855 E. Cottonwood Pkwy., # 400
Salt Lake City, UT 84121
Tel: (800) 348-6311 (801) 736-5600
Fax: (888) 867-7343
E-Mail:
Web Site: www.pretzeltime.com

Franchise Development, Franchise Development Manager

'Freshness With A Twist.' Retail pretzel stores, offering a healthy snack alternative that is freshly mixed, rolled and baked. Unique combination store options are available for traditional and non-traditional venues.

Background:
Established: 1991;   1st Franchised: 1992
Franchised Units: 143
Company-Owned Units: 86
Total Units: 229
Minority-Owned Units:
    African-American:
    Asian-American:
    Hispanic:
    Native American:
    Other:
North America: 41 States, 2 Provinces
Density: 29 in CA, 20 in NY, 19 in TX

Financial/Terms:
Cash Investment: $175-250K
Total Investment: $175-250K
Minimum Net Worth: $250K
Fees: Franchise — $25K
    Royalty — 9%;   Ad. — 1%
Earnings Claim Statement: No
Term of Contract (Years):   20/5
Avg. # Of Employees: 3 FT, 9 PT
Passive Ownership: Allowed
Area Develop. Agreements: Yes
Sub-Franchising Contracts: No
Expand In Territory: Yes
Space Needs: 400-1,000 SF; RM

Support & Training Provided:
Site Selection Assistance: Yes
Lease Negotiation Assistance: Yes
Co-Operative Advertising: No
Franchisee Assoc./Member: No
Size Of Corporate Staff: 26
On-Going Support: B,C,D,E,F,G,H,I
Training: 5 Days Corporate Training Center; 5 Days On-Site.
Minority-Specific Programs: Although we support the objectives of the NMFI, we do not have any specific programs in place at this time.

Specific Expansion Plans:
US: All United States

❈

PRETZEL TWISTER, THE
2706 S. Horseshoe Dr., # 112
Naples, FL 34102
Tel: (888) 638-8806 (941) 643-2075
Fax: (941) 353-6479

E-Mail: keith@pretzeltwister.com
Web Site: www.pretzeltwister.com
Mr. Keith Johnson, President

THE PRETZEL TWISTER is a gourmet, hand-rolled soft pretzel franchise. Other products sold are fresh, hand-squeezed lemonade, frozen fruit smoothies and soft drinks. The pretzels are served fresh and hot and are available in a wide variety of flavors.

Background:
Established: 1992;   1st Franchised: 1993
Franchised Units: 30
Company-Owned Units: 0
Total Units: 30
Minority-Owned Units:
    African-American: 0%
    Asian-American: 9%
    Hispanic: 24%
    Native American:
    Other: 5 Mid-East
North America: 11 States, 4 Provinces
Density: 9 in FL, 7 in NC, 3 in SC

Financial/Terms:
Cash Investment: $NR
Total Investment: $82.7-140.2K
Minimum Net Worth: $NR
Fees: Franchise — $17.5K
    Royalty — 5%;   Ad. — .25-1%
Earnings Claim Statement: No
Term of Contract (Years):
Avg. # Of Employees: NR
Passive Ownership: Allowed
Area Develop. Agreements: No
Sub-Franchising Contracts: No
Expand In Territory: Yes
Space Needs: 300-900 SF; RN, Kiosk or In-Line

Support & Training Provided:
Site Selection Assistance: No
Lease Negotiation Assistance: Yes
Co-Operative Advertising: No
Franchisee Assoc./Member: NR
Size Of Corporate Staff: NR
On-Going Support: C,D,E,G,h,I
Training: NR
Minority-Specific Programs: Although we support the objectives of the NMFI, we do not have any specific programs in place at this time.

Specific Expansion Plans:
US: All United States

❈

PRETZELS PLUS
639 Frederick St.
Hanover, PA 17331
Tel: (800) 559-7927 (717) 633-7927

Fax: (717) 633-5078
E-Mail: pretzelsplus@pretzelsplus.com
Web Site: www.pretzelsplus.com
Mr. Alan Harbaugh, Director of
Franchising

"HOME OF THE BUTTER DIPPED SOFT PRETZEL"

PRETZELS PLUS stores sell soft, hand-rolled pretzels, soups and hearty sandwiches made on our famous pretzel dough rolls. Our mall-based stores provide ample seating for about twenty people in the cafe-styled environment. With our sandwich menu along with our pretzels, we're definitely a twist above the competition.

Background:
Established: 1990;	1st Franchised: 1991
Franchised Units:	25
Company-Owned Units:	0
Total Units:	25
Minority-Owned Units:	
African-American:	
Asian-American:	4%
Hispanic:	
Native American:	
North America:	9 States
Density:	9 in PA, 5 in VA, 3 in NC

Financial/Terms:
Cash Investment:	$70-90K
Total Investment:	$70-90K
Minimum Net Worth:	$N/A
Fees: Franchise —	$12K
Royalty — 4%;	Ad. — 0%
Earnings Claim Statement:	No
Term of Contract (Years):	10/10
Avg. # Of Employees:	5 FT, 4 PT
Passive Ownership:	Allowed
Area Develop. Agreements:	No
Sub-Franchising Contracts:	No
Expand In Territory:	Yes
Space Needs: 1,000 SF; RM	

Support & Training Provided:
Site Selection Assistance:	Yes
Lease Negotiation Assistance:	No
Co-Operative Advertising:	No
Franchisee Assoc./Member:	No

Size Of Corporate Staff:	3
On-Going Support:	B,D,E,I
Training: 3 Days Before Opening; 7 Days After.	

Minority-Specific Programs: Although we support the objectives of the NMFI, we do not have any specific programs in place at this time.

Specific Expansion Plans:
US:	Eastern United States

CLASSIC SUBS

QUIZNO'S CLASSIC SUBS
1099 18th St. # 2850
Denver, CO 80202-9275
Tel: (800) 335-4782 (303) 291-0999
Fax: (303) 291-0909
E-Mail:
Web Site: www.quiznos.com
Ms. Patricia Meyer, Director Franchise Sales

QUIZNO'S CLASSIC SUBS is an up-scale, Italian-theme sub sandwich restaurant that features 'the best sandwich you will ever eat.' QUIZNO'S subs are oven-baked and made with our special recipe bread, QUIZNO'S special dressing and the highest-quality meats and cheeses. With 600 units open across the U. S., Canada and Puerto Rico, our success will continue as we double the number of units open in the coming year. Franchisees are supported at both the corporate level and by one of our 100 area owners.

Background:
Established: 1981;	1st Franchised: 1984
Franchised Units:	584
Company-Owned Units:	28
Total Units:	612
Minority-Owned Units:	
African-American:	
Asian-American:	
Hispanic:	
Native American:	
North America:	NR
Density:	CO, IL, TX

Financial/Terms:
Cash Investment:	$50K
Total Investment:	$129-199K
Minimum Net Worth:	$150K
Fees: Franchise —	$20K
Royalty — 6%;	Ad. — 1%
Earnings Claim Statement:	No
Term of Contract (Years):	15

Avg. # Of Employees:	2 FT, 6 PT
Passive Ownership:	Discouraged
Area Develop. Agreements:	Yes/10
Sub-Franchising Contracts:	Yes
Expand In Territory:	Yes
Space Needs: 1,200 SF; SC, RM	

Support & Training Provided:
Site Selection Assistance:	Yes
Lease Negotiation Assistance:	Yes
Co-Operative Advertising:	Yes
Franchisee Assoc./Member:	No
Size Of Corporate Staff:	46
On-Going Support:	C,D,E,F,G,H,I
Training: 11 Days Regional Market; 11 Days Corporate Office Denver, CO.	

Minority-Specific Programs: Although we support the objectives of the NMFI, we do not have any specific programs in place at this time.

Specific Expansion Plans:
US:	All United States

SCHAKOLAD CHOCOLATE FACTORY
509 S. Semoran Blvd.
Winter Park, FL 32792
Tel: (407) 677-4114
Fax: (407) 677-4118
E-Mail:
Web Site: www.schakolad.com
Mr. Edgar Schaked, CEO

Hand-made, fine chocolates made on premises for customers to watch. Over 30 years experience in chocolate making. Our goal is to become the premiere high quality chocolatier in the U.S. and international markets.

Background:
Established: 1995;	1st Franchised: 1999
Franchised Units:	0
Company-Owned Units:	4
Total Units:	4
Minority-Owned Units:	
African-American:	
Asian-American:	
Hispanic:	2
Native American:	
Other:	
North America:	2 States
Density:	2 in FL, 1 in TN

Financial/Terms:
Cash Investment:	$80-110K
Total Investment:	$80-110K
Minimum Net Worth:	$200K
Fees: Franchise —	$30K

Royalty — 4%;   Ad. — 1%

Earnings Claim Statement:	No
Term of Contract (Years):	10/10
Avg. # Of Employees:	3 FT
Passive Ownership:	Not Allowed
Area Develop. Agreements:	No
Sub-Franchising Contracts:	No
Expand In Territory:	Yes
Space Needs: 800-1,400 SF; SC, RM	

Support & Training Provided:

Site Selection Assistance:	Yes
Lease Negotiation Assistance:	Yes
Co-Operative Advertising:	Yes
Franchisee Assoc./Member:	No
Size Of Corporate Staff:	2
On-Going Support:	C,D,E

Training: 1-2 Weeks in Orlando, FL
Minority-Specific Programs: We are working with Banco Popular to create an easy loan application process for minority franchises.

Specific Expansion Plans:

US:	Eastern U.S.

... the sweetest place on earth

SWEETS FROM HEAVEN

1830 Forbes Ave.
Pittsburgh, PA 15219-5836
Tel: (412) 434-6711
Fax: (412) 434-6718
E-Mail: sfheaven@aol.com
Web Site: www.sweetsfromheaven.com
Mr. Mark R. Lando, President

Self-serve candy stores with unique selection of international candies. Part of an international chain of over 300 stores.

Background:

Established: 1992;	1st Franchised: 1993
Franchised Units:	287
Company-Owned Units:	<u>16</u>
Total Units:	303
Minority-Owned Units:	
African-American:	0
Asian-American:	8
Hispanic:	0
Native American:	0
Other:	
North America:	16 States
Density:	6 in TX, 5 in FL, 6 in PA

Financial/Terms:

Cash Investment:	$50K
Total Investment:	$125-232K
Minimum Net Worth:	$125K
Fees: Franchise —	$30K
Royalty — 6%;	Ad. — 0%
Earnings Claim Statement:	No
Term of Contract (Years):	10/5
Avg. # Of Employees:	4 FT, 3 PT
Passive Ownership:	Allowed
Area Develop. Agreements:	Yes/10
Sub-Franchising Contracts:	Yes
Expand In Territory:	Yes
Space Needs: 800-1,000 SF; SF, RM, Tourist Areas	

Support & Training Provided:

Site Selection Assistance:	Yes
Lease Negotiation Assistance:	Yes
Co-Operative Advertising:	No
Franchisee Assoc./Member:	No
Size Of Corporate Staff:	13
On-Going Support:	B,C,D,E,F,G

Training: 1 Week Corporate Office; 1 Week Company Store; 1 Week Franchisee's Store.
Minority-Specific Programs: Although we support the objectives of the NMFI, we do not have any specific programs in place at this time.

Specific Expansion Plans:

US:	All United States

WINE NOT INTERNATIONAL

15 Heritage Rd., Unit 1
Markham, ON L3P 3T1 CANADA
Tel: (888) 946-3668 (905) 294-6121
Fax: (905) 294-7772
E-Mail: global@winenot.com
Web Site: www.winenot.com
Mr. Kerry Baskey, VP Sales and Marketing

Turn-key commercial custom wineries and u-vint operations in which we provide equipment and supplies for the on-premises winemaker and provide wine pub services for restaurants and hotels.

Background:

Established: 1993;	1st Franchised: 1993
Franchised Units:	37
Company-Owned Units:	<u>0</u>
Total Units:	37
Minority-Owned Units:	

African-American:	0
Asian-American:	0
Hispanic:	0
Native American:	0
Other:	0
North America:	11 Province
Density:	36 in ON

Financial/Terms:

Cash Investment:	$60-150K
Total Investment:	$110-375K
Minimum Net Worth:	$60K-1MM
Fees: Franchise —	$35-40K
Royalty — 5%;	Ad. — 2%
Earnings Claim Statement:	No
Term of Contract (Years):	5/5/5
Avg. # Of Employees:	2 FT, 2 PT
Passive Ownership:	Not Allowed
Area Develop. Agreements:	Yes
Sub-Franchising Contracts:	Yes
Expand In Territory:	Yes
Space Needs: 1,200-3,000 SF; FS, SF	

Support & Training Provided:

Site Selection Assistance:	Yes
Lease Negotiation Assistance:	Yes
Co-Operative Advertising:	Yes
Franchisee Assoc./Member:	Yes/Yes
Size Of Corporate Staff:	10
On-Going Support:	A,B,C,D,E,F,G,H,I

Training: 2 Weeks Home Study; 6 Days Head Office; 1-2 Week On Location.
Minority-Specific Programs: We are actively working with Native American groups, i.e. the establishment of Wine Making facilities in their properties.

Specific Expansion Plans:

US:	All United States

COST CUTTERS® (FAMILY HAIR CARE)

We're your style:

COST CUTTERS FAMILY HAIR CARE

7201 Metro Blvd.
Minneapolis, MN 55439
Tel: (800) 858-2266 (612) 947-7328
Fax: (612) 947-7301
E-Mail: jcook@regiscorp.com
Web Site: www.costcutters.com
Ms. Jen Cook, Franchise Development
Coord.

COST CUTTERS FAMILY HAIR CARE is a value-priced, family hair salon chain with over 850 locations in 45 states. COST CUTTERS offers its customers high-quality hair care services and products in an attractive atmosphere and at affordable prices.

Background:

Established: 1968;	1st Franchised: 1982
Franchised Units:	774
Company-Owned Units:	31
Total Units:	805
Minority-Owned Units:	
African-American:	1
Asian-American:	3
Hispanic:	5
Native American:	0
Other:	
North America:	45 States
Density:	114 in WI, 81 in MN, 79 CO

Financial/Terms:

Cash Investment:	$75K
Total Investment:	$67.7K-123.8K
Minimum Net Worth:	$250K
Fees: Franchise —	$19.5/12.5K
Royalty — 6%/4%-Yr. 1;	Ad. — 5%
Earnings Claim Statement:	Yes
Term of Contract (Years):	15/15
Avg. # Of Employees:	6 FT, 3 PT
Passive Ownership:	Discouraged
Area Develop. Agreements:	Yes/Varies
Sub-Franchising Contracts:	No
Expand In Territory:	Yes
Space Needs: 1,000 SF; SC	

Support & Training Provided:

Site Selection Assistance:	Yes
Lease Negotiation Assistance:	Yes
Co-Operative Advertising:	Yes
Franchisee Assoc./Member:	No
Size Of Corporate Staff:	55
On-Going Support:	C,D,E,G,h,I

Training: 1 Week at National HQ; 1 Week On-Site; Several On-Site Visits Prior to Opening.

Minority-Specific Programs: Although we support the objectives of the NMFI, we do not have any specific programs in place at this time.

Specific Expansion Plans:

US:	All United States

✳

Fantastic Sams

FANTASTIC SAMS

1400 N. Kellogg, # E
Anaheim, CA 92807
Tel: (800) 441-6588 (714) 701-3471
Fax: (714) 779-3422
E-Mail: franchise@fantasticsams.com
Web Site: www.fantasticsams.com
Mr. Terry Cooper, VP Franchising/
Licensing

FANTASTIC SAMS is the world's largest hair care franchise, with over 1,300 salons represented throughout 5 countries. Our full service salons offer quality hair care services for the entire family, including cuts, perms and color. When you join the FANTASTIC SAMS family of franchisees, you'll receive both local and national support through on-going management training, educational programs and national conferences, as well as advertising and other benefits. No hair care experience required.

Background:

Established: 1974;	1st Franchised: 1976
Franchised Units:	1323
Company-Owned Units:	5
Total Units:	1328
Minority-Owned Units:	
African-American:	0.5%
Asian-American:	3%
Hispanic:	0.5%
Native American:	0
Other:	
North America:	42 States, 4 Provinces
Density:	212 in CA, 131 in FL, 96 MI

Financial/Terms:

Cash Investment:	$20-30K
Total Investment:	$75-165K
Minimum Net Worth:	$Varies
Fees: Franchise —	$20-30K
Royalty — $200/Wk.;	Ad. — $100/Wk.
Earnings Claim Statement:	No
Term of Contract (Years):	10/10
Avg. # Of Employees:	8 FT
Passive Ownership:	Allowed

Area Develop. Agreements:	Yes/10
Sub-Franchising Contracts:	Yes
Expand In Territory:	Yes
Space Needs: 1,200 SF; SC	

Support & Training Provided:

Site Selection Assistance:	Yes
Lease Negotiation Assistance:	Yes
Co-Operative Advertising:	Yes
Franchisee Assoc./Member:	No
Size Of Corporate Staff:	42
On-Going Support:	C,d,E,G,h

Training: 6 Days in Anaheim, CA; On-Going Within Region.

Minority-Specific Programs: Although we support the objectives of the NMFI, we do not have any specific programs in place at this time.

Specific Expansion Plans:

US:	All United States

LEMON TREE — A UNISEX HAIRCUTTING EST.

3301 Hempstead Tnpk.
Levittown, NY 11756
Tel: (800) 345-9156 (516) 735-2828
Fax: (516) 735-1851
E-Mail: lemontree@lemontree.com
Web Site: www.lemontree.com
Mr. Glen Yaris, Vice President Sales

LEMON TREE serves the haircare needs of all people, offering the entire family affordable prices and quality service. Lemon Tree uses only name brand quality products. Lemon Tree is open from early morning to late evening, 7 days per week. We provide a strong, hands-on training program to each franchisee.

Background:

Established: 1975;	1st Franchised: 1975
Franchised Units:	73
Company-Owned Units:	0
Total Units:	73
Minority-Owned Units:	
African-American:	
Asian-American:	X
Hispanic:	X
Native American:	
Other:	
North America:	5 States
Density:	65 in NY, 3 in CT, 2 in PA

Financial/Terms:

Cash Investment:	$25-30K

Total Investment:	$42.5-75K
Minimum Net Worth:	$40K
Fees: Franchise —	$15K
Royalty — 6%;	Ad. — $400/Mo.
Earnings Claim Statement:	No
Term of Contract (Years):	15/15
Avg. # Of Employees:	4-6 FT, 3 PT
Passive Ownership:	Discouraged
Area Develop. Agreements:	Yes/Varies
Sub-Franchising Contracts:	No
Expand In Territory:	Yes
Space Needs: 800-1,200 SF; FS, SF, SC, RM	

Support & Training Provided:

Site Selection Assistance:	Yes
Lease Negotiation Assistance:	Yes
Co-Operative Advertising:	Yes
Franchisee Assoc./Member:	No
Size Of Corporate Staff:	8
On-Going Support:	C,D,E,F,G,H,I

Training: 1 Week at Headquarters, 1 Week plus whatever needed at Store Location.

Minority-Specific Programs: LEMON TREE supports the inclusion of minority franchisee's. We have specific seminars at minority beauty schools, specifically geared for recruiting not only staff for own locations, but for influencing their lives by the possibility of them owning their own business, controlling their own future and destiny. Lemon Tree provides assistance through house financing to an approved franchisee, with hands-on assistance in site selection, and a personal training program to meet the needs of each franchisee.

Specific Expansion Plans:

US:	East Coast

SNIP N' CLIP HAIRCUT SHOPS

7910 Quivira Rd.
Lenexa, KS 66215
Tel: (800) 944-7182 (913) 438-1200
Fax: (913) 438-3456
E-Mail:
Web Site:
Mr. Steve Lidskin, VP, Franchise Director

Family haircut shops. Fast service, low price, no appointments. Strip mall shopping centers. Least expensive cpt. turn key

Background:

Established: 1976;	1st Franchised: 1986
Franchised Units:	51
Company-Owned Units:	55

Total Units:	106
Minority-Owned Units:	
African-American:	0
Asian-American:	0
Hispanic:	0
Native American:	0
Other:	
North America:	16 States
Density:	36 in KS, 27 in MO, 6 in AR

Financial/Terms:

Cash Investment:	$51.8K
Total Investment:	$60-80K
Minimum Net Worth:	$100K
Fees: Franchise —	$10K
Royalty — 5%;	Ad. — 0%
Earnings Claim Statement:	No
Term of Contract (Years):	5/5
Avg. # Of Employees:	4 FT, 2 PT
Passive Ownership:	Allowed
Area Develop. Agreements:	Yes
Sub-Franchising Contracts:	No
Expand In Territory:	Yes
Space Needs: 1,000 SF; SF, SC	

Support & Training Provided:

Site Selection Assistance:	Yes
Lease Negotiation Assistance:	Yes
Co-Operative Advertising:	N/A
Franchisee Assoc./Member:	Yes
Size Of Corporate Staff:	10
On-Going Support:	C,D,E,G,H,I

Training: 5 Days On-Site.

Minority-Specific Programs: We wish to recruit and assist anyone interested in SNIP 'N' CLIP that has the desire and financial wherewithall to do so.

Specific Expansion Plans:

US:	Midwest, West, Southwest

SPORT CLIPS

PMB 266, P. O. Box 3000
Georgetown, TX 78627-3000
Tel: (800) 872-4247 (512) 869-1201
Fax: (512) 869-0366
E-Mail: bjboecker@aol.com
Web Site: www.sportclips.com
Ms. Beth Boecker, Market Development Coord.

Sports-themed haircutting salons, appealing primarily to men and boys. Unique design, proprietary haircutting system and complete support at the unit level. Retail sale of Paul Mitchell hair care products, sports apparel and memorabilia.

Background:

Established: 1995; 1st Franchised: 1995
Franchised Units: 28
Company-Owned Units: 4
Total Units: 32
Minority-Owned Units:
  African-American:
  Asian-American:
  Hispanic:
  Native American:
  Other:
North America: 2 States
Density: 27 in TX, 5 in NY, CO

Financial/Terms:

Cash Investment: $30-50K
Total Investment: $100-150K
Minimum Net Worth: $250K
Fees: Franchise — $15K
  Royalty — 6%; Ad. — $250/Wk.
Earnings Claim Statement: Yes
Term of Contract (Years): 5/5
Avg. # Of Employees: 8 FT, 4 PT
Passive Ownership: Allowed
Area Develop. Agreements: Yes
Sub-Franchising Contracts: No
Expand In Territory: Yes
Space Needs: 1,200 SF; SC

Support & Training Provided:

Site Selection Assistance: Yes
Lease Negotiation Assistance: Yes
Co-Operative Advertising: Yes
Franchisee Assoc./Member: No
Size Of Corporate Staff: 12
On-Going Support: B,C,D,E,F,G,H,I
Training: 3 Days in Georgetown, TX for Franchisee; 2 Wks. in Austin, TX for Manager; 2 Wks. Locally.
Minority-Specific Programs: Although we support the objectives of the NMFI, we do not have any specific programs in place at this time.

Specific Expansion Plans:

US: Texas, Utah, Colorado

Web Site: www.supercuts.com
Ms. Jen Cook, Franchise Development Coord.

Top quality, affordable haircare salons.

Background:

Established: 1975; 1st Franchised: 1977
Franchised Units: 821
Company-Owned Units: 517
Total Units: 1338
Minority-Owned Units:
  African-American: 12
  Asian-American: 5
  Hispanic: 11
  Native American: 0
  Other:
North America: 50
Density: NR

Financial/Terms:

Cash Investment: $75K
Total Investment: $90.0-164.1K
Minimum Net Worth: $250K
Fees: Franchise — $12.5-22.5K
  Royalty — 6%/4% Yr. 1; Ad. — 5%
Earnings Claim Statement: No
Term of Contract (Years): Evergreen
Avg. # Of Employees: 6 FT, 4 PT
Passive Ownership: Discouraged
Area Develop. Agreements: Yes
Sub-Franchising Contracts: No
Expand In Territory: Yes
Space Needs: 1,200 SF; SC

Support & Training Provided:

Site Selection Assistance: Yes
Lease Negotiation Assistance: Yes
Co-Operative Advertising: Yes
Franchisee Assoc./Member: Yes/Yes
Size Of Corporate Staff: 50
On-Going Support: B,C,D,E,G,H
Training: 4 Days Minneapolis, MN.
Minority-Specific Programs: Although we support the objectives of the NMFI, we do not have any specific programs in place at this time.

Specific Expansion Plans:

US: All United States

SUPERCUTS

7201 Metro Blvd.
Minneapolis, MN 55439
Tel: (888) 888-7008 (612) 947-7328
Fax: (612) 947-7301
E-Mail: jcook@regiscorp.com

DIET CENTER

395 Springside Dr.
Akron, OH 44333-2496
Tel: (800) 656-3294 (330) 666-7952
Fax: (330) 666-2197
E-Mail: info@dietcenterworldwide.com
Web Site: www.dietcenterworldwide.com
Mr. Kenneth M. Massey, Director Franchise
Development

DIET CENTER offers innovative weight
management programs.

Background:
Established: 1972;   1st Franchised: 1972
Franchised Units: 250
Company-Owned Units: 0
Total Units: 250
Minority-Owned Units:
   African-American:
   Asian-American:
   Hispanic:
   Native American:
   Other:
North America: 44 States, 4 Provinces
Density: 28 in NY, 19 in NC, 18 in CA

Financial/Terms:
Cash Investment: $16.4-34.9K
Total Investment: $16.4-34.9K
Minimum Net Worth: $50-75K

Fees: Franchise — $15K
   Royalty — 8%/$100/Wk.;Ad.   —
8%/$500/Mo.
Earnings Claim Statement: No
Term of Contract (Years):   5/5
Avg. # Of Employees: 2 FT, 1 PT
Passive Ownership: Discouraged
Area Develop. Agreements: No
Sub-Franchising Contracts: No
Expand In Territory: Yes
Space Needs: 700-1,200 SF; FS, SF, SC

Support & Training Provided:
Site Selection Assistance: Yes
Lease Negotiation Assistance: Yes
Co-Operative Advertising: No
Franchisee Assoc./Member: No
Size Of Corporate Staff: 40
On-Going Support: C,D,E,G,H,I
Training: 3 Weeks in Akron, OH.
Minority-Specific Programs: Although we
support the objectives of the NMFI, we do
not have any specific programs in place at
this time.

Specific Expansion Plans:
US: All United States

FIT AMERICA
401 Fairway Dr., # 200
Deerfield Beach, FL 33441
Tel: (800) 221-1186 (954) 570-3211
Fax: (954) 570-8608
E-Mail: fitstores@aol.com
Web Site: www.fitamerica.com
Mr. Jack Farland, Dir. Franchise
Development

Retail store operation offering the finest

all-natural herbal products, comprehensive
education and training, and unparalleled, free
customer service, as well as motivation to
help people lose weight.

Background:
Established: 1992;   1st Franchised: 1996
Franchised Units: 72
Company-Owned Units: 0
Total Units: 72
Minority-Owned Units:
   African-American:
   Asian-American: 1
   Hispanic: 3
   Native American:
   Other:
North America: 13 States
Density: 18 in NJ, 12 in FL, 12 in NY

Financial/Terms:
Cash Investment: $25-45K
Total Investment: $25-45K
Minimum Net Worth: $N/A
Fees: Franchise — $8.4K
   Royalty — $400/Mo.;   Ad. — $165/Mo.
Earnings Claim Statement: No
Term of Contract (Years):   2/2
Avg. # Of Employees: 3 FT
Passive Ownership: Discouraged

Area Develop. Agreements:	No
Sub-Franchising Contracts:	No
Expand In Territory:	Yes
Space Needs: 800-1,200 SF; SC	

Support & Training Provided:

Site Selection Assistance:	Yes
Lease Negotiation Assistance:	Yes
Co-Operative Advertising:	Yes
Franchisee Assoc./Member:	Yes/Yes
Size Of Corporate Staff:	32
On-Going Support:	A,B,C,D,E,F,G,h,I

Training: 3 Days Corporate Headquarters; 1 Week at Already Existing Site; 2 Weeks Franchisee's Store

Minority-Specific Programs: Although we support the objectives of the NMFI, we do not have any specific programs in place at this time.

Specific Expansion Plans:

US:	All United States

LADY OF AMERICA

2400 E. Commercial Blvd., # 808
Fort Lauderdale, FL 33308
Tel: (800) 833-5239 (954) 492-1201
Fax: (954) 492-1187
E-Mail: landman1@gate.net
Web Site: www.ladyofamerica.com
Mr. Chuck Cououto, Sales Director

Ladies-only health club, specializing in aerobics, weight training, personal training and the sales of related products and services.

Background:

Established: 1984;	1st Franchised: 1985
Franchised Units:	193
Company-Owned Units:	0
Total Units:	193
Minority-Owned Units:	
African-American:	4
Asian-American:	2
Hispanic:	25
Native American:	0
Other:	
North America:	25 States, 4 Countries
Density:	46 in FL, 25 in TX, 15 in PA

Financial/Terms:

Cash Investment:	$20-30K
Total Investment:	$40-75K
Minimum Net Worth:	$50K

Fees: Franchise —	$12.5K
Royalty — 10%;	Ad. — 0%
Earnings Claim Statement:	No
Term of Contract (Years):	10/5
Avg. # Of Employees:	2 FT, 6 PT
Passive Ownership:	Allowed
Area Develop. Agreements:	Yes/10
Sub-Franchising Contracts:	Yes
Expand In Territory:	Yes
Space Needs: 4,500 SF; SC	

Support & Training Provided:

Site Selection Assistance:	Yes
Lease Negotiation Assistance:	Yes
Co-Operative Advertising:	Yes
Franchisee Assoc./Member:	Yes/No
Size Of Corporate Staff:	25
On-Going Support:	A,B,C,D,E,F,G,H,I

Training: 2-3 Weeks On-Site; 1-2 Weeks at Corporate Headquarters.

Minority-Specific Programs: Franchisor actively assists in the preparation of business plans, financial pro formas and the breakdown of the use of funds for the security of loans and/or equipment leases.

Specific Expansion Plans:

US:	All United States

OUR WEIGH

3637 Park Ave., # 201
Memphis, TN 38111-5614
Tel: (901) 458-7546
Fax:
E-Mail:
Web Site:
Ms. Helen K. Seale, President

A unique weight control group, consisting of 30-minute meetings, behavior modification exercise and, most importantly, a nutritional diet that allows members to eat what they like and not have to eat foods that they don't like. First in the field to introduce food rewards and free weekly weigh-in upon reaching desired weight.

Background:

Established: 1974;	1st Franchised: 1974
Franchised Units:	0
Company-Owned Units:	3
Total Units:	3
Minority-Owned Units:	
African-American:	0
Asian-American:	0
Hispanic:	0
Native American:	0
Other:	0
North America:	1 States
Density:	3 in TN

Financial/Terms:

Cash Investment:	$0K
Total Investment:	$0K
Minimum Net Worth:	$0K
Fees: Franchise —	$5K
Royalty — 0%;	Ad. — 0%
Earnings Claim Statement:	No
Term of Contract (Years):	NR
Avg. # Of Employees:	1 FT, 4 PT
Passive Ownership:	Not Allowed
Area Develop. Agreements:	No
Sub-Franchising Contracts:	No
Expand In Territory:	Yes
Space Needs: 1,500 SF; Varies	

Support & Training Provided:

Site Selection Assistance:	No
Lease Negotiation Assistance:	No
Co-Operative Advertising:	No
Franchisee Assoc./Member:	No
Size Of Corporate Staff:	1
On-Going Support:	N/A

Training: None.

Minority-Specific Programs: Although we support the objectives of the NMFI, we do not have any specific programs in place at this time.

Specific Expansion Plans:

US:	All United States

PHYSICIANS WEIGHT LOSS CENTERS OF AMERICA

395 Springside Dr.
Akron, OH 44333-2496
Tel: (800) 205-7887 (330) 666-7952
Fax: (330) 666 2197
E-Mail: info@pwlc.com
Web Site: www.pwlc.com
Mr. Kenneth M. Massey, Director Franchise Development

Supervised weight reduction business, offering the customer a comprehensive program, utilizing individual treatment, personal care, counseling and weight management.

Background:

Established: 1979;	1st Franchised: 1980
Franchised Units:	54
Company-Owned Units:	2
Total Units:	56

Minority-Owned Units:
African-American:
Asian-American:
Hispanic:
Native American:
Other:
North America: 12 States
Density: 20 in OH, 10 in SC, 4 in NC

Financial/Terms:
Cash Investment: $21.04-52.1K
Total Investment: $38-70K
Minimum Net Worth: $100K
Fees: Franchise — $20K
    Royalty — 5.5%/$115/Wk.;Ad. —
7%/$600/Wk.
Earnings Claim Statement: No
Term of Contract (Years): 5/5/5
Avg. # Of Employees: 2 FT, 2 PT
Passive Ownership: Not Allowed
Area Develop. Agreements: No
Sub-Franchising Contracts: No
Expand In Territory: Yes
Space Needs: 1,200 SF; SC

Support & Training Provided:
Site Selection Assistance: Yes
Lease Negotiation Assistance: Yes
Co-Operative Advertising: Yes
Franchisee Assoc./Member: No
Size Of Corporate Staff: 45
On-Going Support: A,B,c,d,E,G,H,I
Training: 3 Weeks Akron, OH; 1-3 Days
On-Site.
Minority-Specific Programs: Although we
support the objectives of the NMFI, we do
not have any specific programs in place at
this time.

Specific Expansion Plans:
US: All United States

SANGSTER'S HEALTH CENTRES

2218 Hanselman Ave.
Saskatoon, SK S7L 6A4 CANADA
Tel: (306) 653-4481
Fax: (306) 653-4688
E-Mail: sangsters@sangsters.com
Web Site: www.sangsters.com
Ms. Wendy Sangster, Franchise
Representative

SANGSTER'S HEALTH CENTRES offer
their own brand of quality vitamins, herbs
and natural cosmetics, along with those of
most major companies. Increased buying
power gives maximum profits.

Background:
Established: 1971; 1st Franchised: 1978
Franchised Units: 46
Company-Owned Units: 3
Total Units: 49
Minority-Owned Units:
African-American:
Asian-American:
Hispanic:
Native American:
Other: Brazilian, Indian
North America: 7 Provinces
Density: 15 in SK, 11 in ON, 8 in AB

Financial/Terms:
Cash Investment: $30K
Total Investment: $118-125K
Minimum Net Worth: $50K
Fees: Franchise — $25K
    Royalty — 5%; Ad. — 1%
Earnings Claim Statement: No
Term of Contract (Years): 5/5
Avg. # Of Employees: 1 FT, 2 PT
Passive Ownership: Discouraged
Area Develop. Agreements: Yes
Sub-Franchising Contracts: Yes
Expand In Territory: Yes
Space Needs: 600-800 SF; RM

Support & Training Provided:
Site Selection Assistance: Yes
Lease Negotiation Assistance: Yes
Co-Operative Advertising: Yes
Franchisee Assoc./Member: No
Size Of Corporate Staff: 11
On-Going Support: D,E,G,h
Training: 7-10 Days in Saskatoon, SK; 5-10
Days Franchisee Location.
Minority-Specific Programs: Although we
support the objectives of the NMFI, we do
not have any specific programs in place at
this time.

Specific Expansion Plans:
US: All United States

JIM'S MOWING

210 Lark Ln.
Euless, TX 76039
Tel: (817) 684-0192
Fax:
E-Mail: jmhstn@swbell.net
Web Site: www.jims.com.au
Mr. Peter Barley, Regional Franchisor

JIM'S MOWING is the worlds largest lawn and garden care franchisor with over 1500 units in 4 countries. We offer full office support in training, marketing, live call answering and automated paging system.

Background:

Established: 1982;	1st Franchised: 1989
Franchised Units:	4
Company-Owned Units:	2
Total Units:	6
Minority-Owned Units:	
African American:	25%
Asian-American:	
Hispanic:	
Native American:	
Other:	
North America:	1 State
Density:	6 in TX

Financial/Terms:

Cash Investment:	$12-16K
Total Investment:	$12-20K
Minimum Net Worth:	$N/A
Fees: Franchise —	$8K
Royalty — 6%;	Ad. — $30/Mo.
Earnings Claim Statement:	No
Term of Contract (Years):	10/10
Avg. # Of Employees:	2 FT
Passive Ownership:	Discouraged
Area Develop. Agreements:	No
Sub-Franchising Contracts:	No
Expand In Territory:	Yes
Space Needs: N/A SF; N/A	

Support & Training Provided:

Site Selection Assistance:	N/A
Lease Negotiation Assistance:	N/A
Co-Operative Advertising:	Yes
Franchisee Assoc./Member:	Yes/Yes
Size Of Corporate Staff:	37
On-Going Support:	A,B,C,D,G,H,I
Training: 3 Days on Site; 2 Days Office	

Minority-Specific Programs: JIM'S MOWING is an equal opportunity employer/organization. We do not currently have programs in place to assist only minority franchisee, although we do offer financing options and our one minority franchisee has taken advantage of that. We welcome any suggestions or programsyou may have in place elsewhere. Please send any details to bove address.

Specific Expansion Plans:

US:	Texas only

THE LEADER IN ORGANIC-BASED LAWN CARE®
www.nl-amer.com

NATURALAWN OF AMERICA

1 E. Church St.
Frederick, MD 21701
Tel: (800) 989-5444 (301) 694-5440
Fax: (301) 846-0320
E-Mail: natlawn@erols.com
Web Site: www.nl-amer.com
Mr. Randy Loeb, VP Franchise Dev.

NATURALAWN of America is the only nationwide lawn care franchise offering an environmentally friendly lawn care service incorporating natural, organic-based fertilizers and biological controls. Our franchise owners provide residential and commercial customers with fertilization, weed control, insect control, disease control and lawn diagnosis services using safer and healthier products, eliminating the need for harsh chemicals and pesticides.

Background:

Established: 1987;	1st Franchised: 1989
Franchised Units:	46
Company-Owned Units:	2
Total Units:	48
Minority-Owned Units:	
African-American:	0
Asian-American:	0
Hispanic:	0
Native American:	0
Other:	0
North America:	19 States
Density:	6 in MD, 5 in PA, 5 in VA

Financial/Terms:

Cash Investment:	$30K
Total Investment:	$50-125K
Minimum Net Worth:	$125K
Fees: Franchise —	$29.5K
Royalty — 7-9%;	Ad. — 0%
Earnings Claim Statement:	Yes
Term of Contract (Years):	5/10
Avg. # Of Employees:	2 FT, 4-6 PT
Passive Ownership:	Discouraged
Area Develop. Agreements:	No
Sub-Franchising Contracts:	No
Expand In Territory:	Yes
Space Needs: 1,200-1,500 SF; Warehouse	

Support & Training Provided:

Site Selection Assistance:	N/A
Lease Negotiation Assistance:	Yes
Co-Operative Advertising:	N/A
Franchisee Assoc./Member:	No
Size Of Corporate Staff:	14
On-Going Support:	B,C,D,E,F,G,H,I

Training: 1 Week + 3 Days + 3 Days Corporate Headquarters; 2 Days Regionally 3-4 Times Per Year.

Minority-Specific Programs: NATURALAWN OF AMERICA's franchisees are eligible for streamlined financing through the SBA, including the minority programs the SBA has available. As part of this process NATURALAWN OF AMERICA will provide assistance in the development of a business plan that a minority franchisee can submit to an SBA certified or preferred lender.

Specific Expansion Plans:

US:	All United States

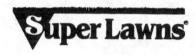

SUPER LAWNS

15901 Derwood Rd., P. O. Box 5677
Rockville, MD 20855
Tel: (800) 44-LAWN1 (301) 948-8181
Fax: (301) 948-8461
E-Mail:
Web Site: www.superlawns.com
Mr. Ron Miller, Vice President

Our system is a modern, profitable approach to lawn care. One person or many, depending upon your desire to succeed. We offer complete training and constant assistance in all areas of business. We'll try to keep you 'One step ahead of the competition.'

Background:

Established: 1975;	1st Franchised: 1979
Franchised Units:	22
Company-Owned Units:	1
Total Units:	23

Minority-Owned Units:

African-American:	1
Asian-American:	
Hispanic:	
Native American:	
Other:	
North America:	5 States
Density:	8 in MD, 5 in VA, 3 in DE

Financial/Terms:

Cash Investment:	$30K

Total Investment:	$60-70K
Minimum Net Worth:	$60K
Fees: Franchise —	$17.5K
Royalty — 10% Decreasing;	Ad. — 0%
Earnings Claim Statement:	No
Term of Contract (Years):	20/5
Avg. # Of Employees:	1 FT
Passive Ownership:	Discouraged
Area Develop. Agreements:	No
Sub-Franchising Contracts:	No
Expand In Territory:	Yes
Space Needs: N/A SF; N/A	

Support & Training Provided:

Site Selection Assistance:	N/A
Lease Negotiation Assistance:	N/A
Co-Operative Advertising:	Yes
Franchisee Assoc./Member:	No
Size Of Corporate Staff:	3
On-Going Support:	B,C,D,F,I

Training: 7-10 Days Rockville, MD or Elkton, MD and As Needed.

Minority-Specific Programs: We will work with hungry, aggressive individuals as long as it takes.

Specific Expansion Plans:

US:	East of Mississippi

U. S. LAWNS

4777 Old Winter Garden Rd.
Orlando, FL 33211
Tel: (800) US-LAWNS (407) 522-1630
Fax: (407) 522-1669
E-Mail:
Web Site: www.uslawns.com
Mr. Kenneth Hutcheson, Director of Development

Train and support franchisees in a commercial landscape market.

Background:

Established: 1986;	1st Franchised: 1987
Franchised Units:	47
Company-Owned Units:	4
Total Units:	51

Minority-Owned Units:

African-American:	5
Asian-American:	0
Hispanic:	0
Native American:	0
Other:	2 Woman-Owned
North America:	14 States
Density:	FL, MD, CA

Financial/Terms:

Cash Investment:	$10-40K
Total Investment:	$40-70K
Minimum Net Worth:	$50K
Fees: Franchise —	$29K
Royalty — 3-4%;	Ad. — 1%
Earnings Claim Statement:	No
Term of Contract (Years):	5/5
Avg. # Of Employees:	8-10 FT
Passive Ownership:	Discouraged
Area Develop. Agreements:	Yes
Sub-Franchising Contracts:	No
Expand In Territory:	Yes
Space Needs: NR SF; N/A	

Support & Training Provided:

Site Selection Assistance:	Yes
Lease Negotiation Assistance:	Yes
Co-Operative Advertising:	Yes
Franchisee Assoc./Member:	Yes/Yes
Size Of Corporate Staff:	14
On-Going Support:	A,b,C,D,G,H,I

Training: 5 Days in Florida; 5 Days at Your Location.

Minority-Specific Programs: Although we support the objectives of the NMFI, we do not have any specific programs in place at this time.

Specific Expansion Plans:

US:	PA,NJ,CT,NY,MA,FL,CA,NC,SC

AMERICINN INTERNATIONAL

18202 Minnetonka Blvd.
Deephaven, MN 55391
Tel: (612) 476-9020
Fax: (612) 476-7601
E-Mail: franchise@americinn.com
Web Site: www.americinn.com
Mr. Jon D Kennedy, VP Mktg./Franchise Develop.

AMERICINN is an up-scale, limited-service, value-oriented chain. Currently, AMERICINN has over 170 franchises and continues to grow. Typically, the motels are located along major highways in cities with populations of between 10,000 and 300,000. AMERICINN has been successful with both travelers and vacationers because of their up-scale amenities and economy rates.

Background:
Established: 1984;   1st Franchised: 1984
Franchised Units: 166
Company-Owned Units: 4
Total Units: 170
Minority-Owned Units:
   African-American: 0
   Asian-American: 4
   Hispanic: 0
   Native American: 1
   Other:

North America: 17 States
Density: 64 in MN, 35 in WI,16 in IA

Financial/Terms:
Cash Investment: $25% Budget
Total Investment: $1.83MM
Minimum Net Worth: $1MM
Fees: Franchise — $30K
   Royalty — 5%;   Ad. — 2%
Earnings Claim Statement: No
Term of Contract (Years):   20
Avg. # Of Employees: 20 FT, 9 PT
Passive Ownership: Allowed
Area Develop. Agreements: No
Sub-Franchising Contracts: No
Expand In Territory: Yes
Space Needs: 60,000 SF; FS

Support & Training Provided:
Site Selection Assistance: Yes
Lease Negotiation Assistance: Yes
Co-Operative Advertising: Yes
Franchisee Assoc./Member: Yes/Yes
Size Of Corporate Staff: 50
On-Going Support: a,b,C,D,E,G,H,I
Training: 3 Different Properties, 1 Week at Each.

Minority-Specific Programs: Although we support the objectives of the National Minority Franchising Initiative, we do not have any specific programs in place at this time. AMERICINN INTERNATIONAL, LLC provides outstanding development and support services to all franchisees on a non-discriminating basis.

Specific Expansion Plans:
US: All United States

BASS HOTELS & RESORTS

3 Ravinia Dr., # 2900
Atlanta, GA 30346
Tel: (770) 604-2166
Fax: (770) 604-2107
E-Mail: hifranchise@basshotels.com
Web Site: www.basshotels.com
Mr. Brown Kessler, VP Franchise Sales

BASS HOTELS & RESORTS, the hotel business of Bass PLC of the United Kingdom, operates or franchises more than 2,700 hotels and 450,000 guest rooms in more than 90 countries and territories. Franchisor of Holiday Inn, Holiday Inn Express, Crowne Plaza, STAYBRIDGE SUITES and INTER-CONTINENTAL HOTELS.

Background:
Established: 1952;   1st Franchised: 1952
Franchised Units: 2465
Company-Owned Units: 266
Total Units: 2731
Minority-Owned Units:
   African-American:
   Asian-American:
   Hispanic:
   Native American:
   Other:
North America: 50 States
Density: 156 in CA,151 in FL,147 TX

Financial/Terms:
Cash Investment: $1-20MM
Total Investment: $40-150K/Room

Minimum Net Worth:	$Varies
Fees: Franchise —	$500/Rm,40Kmin
Royalty — 5%;	Ad. — 2.5-3%
Earnings Claim Statement:	Yes
Term of Contract (Years):	10
Avg. # Of Employees:	Varies
Passive Ownership:	Allowed
Area Develop. Agreements:	No
Sub-Franchising Contracts:	No
Expand In Territory:	Yes
Space Needs: NR SF; FS	

Support & Training Provided:

Site Selection Assistance:	No
Lease Negotiation Assistance:	Yes
Co-Operative Advertising:	Yes
Franchisee Assoc./Member:	Yes
Size Of Corporate Staff:	1,000
On-Going Support:	B,c,d,e,g,h

Training: Varying fees required. Programs supported by franchisor.

Minority-Specific Programs: Although we support the objectives of the NMFI, we do not have any specific programs in place at this time.

Specific Expansion Plans:

US:	All United States

BAYMONT INNS & SUITES

250 E. Wisconsin Ave., # 1750
Milwaukee, WI 53202-1750
Tel: (414) 905-1382
Fax: (414) 905-2496
E-Mail: gilsimon@baymontinns.com
Web Site: www.baymontinns.com
Mr. Gilbert S. Simon, Natl. Director
Franchise Sales

BAYMONT INNS AND SUITES is positioned to appeal to both business and leisure travelers offering many amenities - frequent travelers' rewards, complimentary breakfast, voice mail, coffee makers and much more for $45.00 - 65.00.

Background:

Established: 1935;	1st Franchised: 1986	
Franchised Units:		76
Company-Owned Units:		96
Total Units:		172
Minority-Owned Units:		
African-American:		
Asian-American:		20%

Hispanic:	
Native American:	
Other:	
North America:	30 States
Density:	20 in MI, 18 in IL, 17 in WI

Financial/Terms:

Cash Investment:	$70%
Total Investment:	$3MM+
Minimum Net Worth:	$3MM
Fees: Franchise —	$35K
Royalty — 5%;	Ad. — 2%
Earnings Claim Statement:	Yes
Term of Contract (Years):	20/10
Avg. # Of Employees:	4 FT, 12-18 PT
Passive Ownership:	Allowed
Area Develop. Agreements:	No
Sub-Franchising Contracts:	No
Expand In Territory:	No
Space Needs: 2 Acres SF; FS	

Support & Training Provided:

Site Selection Assistance:	Yes
Lease Negotiation Assistance:	No
Co-Operative Advertising:	Yes
Franchisee Assoc./Member:	Yes/Yes
Size Of Corporate Staff:	76
On-Going Support:	C,D,E,G,H,I

Training: 1-2 Weeks Milwaukee, WI, Based on Experience.

Minority-Specific Programs: Our current franchise development and support services are provided on a nondiscriminatory basis to all franchisees, regardless of race, national origin or sex. While those services do not include reduction or deferment of franchise fees or financing, we do provide assistance in locating sources of financing and facilitate loan processing by working with the proposed lenders.

Specific Expansion Plans:

US:	All United States

Where Value Stays

CANDLEWOOD SUITES/ CAMBRIDGE SUITES

8621 E. 21st St. N., # 200
Wichita, KS 67206
Tel: (316) 631-1300
Fax: (316) 631-1333
E-Mail: bgordon@candlewoodsuites.com
Web Site: www.candlewoodsuites.com

Ms. Becky Gordon, Franchise Sales Specialist

CANDLEWOOD SUITES is a unique, high-quality, mid-priced hotel brand designed to deliver exceptional value to both owners and guests. CAMBRIDGE SUITES by CANDLEWOOD, established in 1998, is another tremendous opportunity to build or convert an existing hotel into the newest concept in lodging for the up-scale traveler.

Background:

Established: 1995;	1st Franchised: 1996	
Franchised Units:		11
Company-Owned Units:		66
Total Units:		77
Minority-Owned Units:		
African-American:		0
Asian-American:		1
Hispanic:		0
Native American:		0
Other:		
North America:		30 States
Density:	14 in TX, 6 in IL, 6 in CA	

Financial/Terms:

Cash Investment:	$700K-2MM
Total Investment:	$3-7MM
Minimum Net Worth:	$N/A
Fees: Franchise —	$$400/Key/40K
Royalty — 4-5%RR;	Ad. — 1.5%RR
Earnings Claim Statement:	Yes
Term of Contract (Years):	20
Avg. # Of Employees:	6-13 FT
Passive Ownership:	Allowed
Area Develop. Agreements:	No
Sub-Franchising Contracts:	No
Expand In Territory:	Yes
Space Needs: 56,628-108,90 SF; FS	

Support & Training Provided:

Site Selection Assistance:	No
Lease Negotiation Assistance:	Yes
Co-Operative Advertising:	No
Franchisee Assoc./Member:	Yes/Yes
Size Of Corporate Staff:	100
On-Going Support:	C,D,G,H,I

Training: Extensive Training Program.

Minority-Specific Programs: We are members of the AAHOA and participate in AAHOA trade shows to actively solicit the Asian-American hoteliers as franchisees. Additionally, we continue to pursue business relationships with all minority groups through daily personal and phone solicitation.

Specific Expansion Plans:

US:	All United States

A cozy stay at a comfortable price®

COUNTRY INNS & SUITES BY CARLSON

P. O. Box 59159, Carlson Pkwy.
Minneapolis, MN 55459-8203
Tel: (800) 456-4000 (612) 212-2525
Fax: (612) 212-1338
E-Mail: njohnson@countryinns.com
Web Site: www.countryinns.com
Ms. Nancy Johnson, SVP - .Development

COUNTRY INNS & SUITES locations feature traditional architecture and sophisticated residential interior design with hardwood flooring and decorative ceiling borders. Each hotel welcomes guests with traditional funishings that blend rich woods and elegant patterned fabrics. The brand is known for its consistently high-quality accomodations and personal, warm hospitality.

Background:
Established: 1987;   1st Franchised: 1987
Franchised Units: 175
Company-Owned Units: 4
Total Units: 179
Minority-Owned Units:
  African-American:
  Asian-American: 35%
  Hispanic: .5%
  Native American:
  Other:
North America: 31 States, 4 Provinces
Density: 36 in MN, 21 in WI, 13 in GA

Financial/Terms:
Cash Investment: $720K-1.3MM
Total Investment: $2.8-4.9MM
Minimum Net Worth: $500K
Fees: Franchise — $40K
  Royalty — 3-4%;   Ad. — 2-3%
Earnings Claim Statement: Yes
Term of Contract (Years):   15/0
Avg. # Of Employees: 10 FT, 6 PT
Passive Ownership: Allowed
Area Develop. Agreements: No
Sub-Franchising Contracts: No
Expand In Territory: No
Space Needs: 87,000 SF; FS

Support & Training Provided:
Site Selection Assistance: No
Lease Negotiation Assistance: Yes
Co-Operative Advertising: Yes

Franchisee Assoc./Member: No
Size Of Corporate Staff: 39
On-Going Support: B,C,d,E,G,h,I
Training: 1 Week Minneapolis, MN. (Brand Orientation); 3 Days Opening On-Site; 3 Days New Franchisee
Minority-Specific Programs: Although we support the objectives of the NMFI, we do not have any specific programs in place at this time.

Specific Expansion Plans:
US: All United States

EMBASSY SUITES

755 Crossover Ln.
Memphis, TN 38117
Tel: (901) 374-5000
Fax: (901) 374-5008
E-Mail:
Web Site: www.embassy-suites.com
Mr. Mickey Powell, SVP Franchise Development

Promus Hotel Corporation is the franchisor/operator of the DOUBLETREE HOTELS, EMBASSY SUITES, HAMPTON INN & SUITES, HOMEWOOD SUITES, DOUBLETREE CLUB, RED LION HOTELS. The company franchises, operates or owns hotels throughout the United States, Canada, Mexico and Latin America. Promus is headquartered in Memphis, Tennessee and has approximately 40,000 employees.

Background:
Established: 1983;   1st Franchised: 1983
Franchised Units: 63
Company-Owned Units: 85
Total Units: 148
Minority-Owned Units:
  African-American:
  Asian-American:
  Hispanic:
  Native American:
  Other:
North America: 38 States
Density: 32 in CA, 26 in TX, 23 in FL

Financial/Terms:
Cash Investment: $3MM
Total Investment: $15-30MM
Minimum Net Worth: $3MM
Fees: Franchise — $100K Min.
  Royalty — 4% Gross Rm. Rev;Ad. —
3.5% Rm.Rev
Earnings Claim Statement: No
Term of Contract (Years):   20
Avg. # Of Employees: 75 FT
Passive Ownership: Allowed

Area Develop. Agreements: No
Sub-Franchising Contracts: No
Expand In Territory: Yes
Space Needs: 153,000 SF; NR

Support & Training Provided:
Site Selection Assistance: No
Lease Negotiation Assistance: Yes
Co-Operative Advertising: Yes
Franchisee Assoc./Member: No
Size Of Corporate Staff: 850
On-Going Support: A,b,C,D,E,G,h
Training: 2 Weeks in Memphis, TN.
Minority-Specific Programs: Although we support the objectives of the NMFI, we do not have any specific programs in place at this time.

Specific Expansion Plans:
US: All United States

One of the few nice places still around."

HAMPTON INN

755 Crossover Ln.
Memphis, TN 38117
Tel: (800) HAMPTON (901) 374-5000
Fax: (901) 374-5008
E-Mail:
Web Site: www.hampton-inn.com
Mr. Mickey Powell, SVP Franchise Development

Promus Hotel Corporation is the franchisor/operator of the DOUBLETREE HOTELS, EMBASSY SUITES, HAMPTON INN & SUITES, HOMEWOOD SUITES, DOUBLETREE CLUB, RED LION HOTELS. The company franchises, operates or owns hotels throughout the United States, Canada, Mexico and Latin America. Promus is headquartered in Memphis, Tennessee and has approximately 40,000 employees.

Background:
Established: 1983;   1st Franchised: 1983
Franchised Units: 844
Company-Owned Units: 17
Total Units: 861
Minority-Owned Units:
  African-American:
  Asian-American:
  Hispanic:

Native American:

North America:	48 States
Density:	110 in FL, 88 in TX, 78 in NC

Financial/Terms:

Cash Investment:	$750K
Total Investment:	$3-5MM
Minimum Net Worth:	$1.5 MM
Fees: Franchise —	$45K Min.
Royalty — 4% Gross Rm. Rev;Ad. — 4% Rm. Rev.	
Earnings Claim Statement:	No
Term of Contract (Years):	20
Avg. # Of Employees:	20 FT
Passive Ownership:	Allowed
Area Develop. Agreements:	No
Sub-Franchising Contracts:	No
Expand In Territory:	Yes
Space Needs: 110 SF; NR	

Support & Training Provided:

Site Selection Assistance:	No
Lease Negotiation Assistance:	Yes
Co-Operative Advertising:	Yes
Franchisee Assoc./Member:	No
Size Of Corporate Staff:	850
On-Going Support:	A,b,C,D,E,G,h
Training: 2 Weeks Memphis, TN.	

Minority-Specific Programs: Although we support the objectives of the NMFI, we do not have any specific programs in place at this time.

Specific Expansion Plans:

US:	All United States

HOMEWOOD SUITES

755 Crossover Ln.
Memphis, TN 38117
Tel: (901) 374-5000
Fax: (901) 374-5008
Web Site: www.homewood-suites.com
Mr. Mickey Powell, SVP Franchise Development

Promus Hotel Corporation is the franchisor/operator of the DOUBLETREE HOTELS, EMBASSY SUITES, HAMPTON INN & SUITES, HOMEWOOD SUITES, DOUBLETREE CLUB, RED LION

HOTELS. The company franchises, operates or owns hotels throughout the United States, Canada, Mexico and Latin America. Promus is headquartered in Memphis, Tennessee and has approximately 40,000 employees.

Background:

Established: 1988;	1st Franchised: 1988
Franchised Units:	57
Company-Owned Units:	26
Total Units:	83

Minority-Owned Units:

African-American:	
Asian-American:	
Hispanic:	
Native American:	
North America:	29 States
Density:	25 in TX, 13 in NC, 11 in FL

Financial/Terms:

Cash Investment:	$1.5MM
Total Investment:	$6-12MM
Minimum Net Worth:	$1.5MM
Fees: Franchise —	$45K Min.
Royalty — 4% Gross Rm. Rev;Ad. — 4% Rm. Rev.	
Earnings Claim Statement:	No
Term of Contract (Years):	20
Avg. # Of Employees:	25 FT
Passive Ownership:	Allowed
Area Develop. Agreements:	No
Sub-Franchising Contracts:	No
Expand In Territory:	Yes
Space Needs: 110,000 SF; NR	

Support & Training Provided:

Site Selection Assistance:	No
Lease Negotiation Assistance:	Yes
Co-Operative Advertising:	Yes
Franchisee Assoc./Member:	No
Size Of Corporate Staff:	850
On-Going Support:	A,b,C,D,E,G,h
Training: 2 Weeks in Memphis, TN.	

Minority-Specific Programs: Although we support the objectives of the NMFI, we do not have any specific programs in place at this time.

Specific Expansion Plans:

US:	All United States

HOSPITALITY INTERNATIONAL

1726 Montreal Circle
Tucker, GA 30084
Tel: (800) 892-8405 (770) 270-1180
Fax: (770) 270-1077
E-Mail: hospitality@reservahost.com
Web Site: www.reservahost.com
Ms. Dimple Patel, Franchise Dev. Coord.

Hotel franchisor of MASTER HOSTS INNS AND RESORTS, RED CARPET INNS, SCOTTISH INNS, PASSPORT INNS, DOWNTOWNER INNS and SUNDOWNER INNS, with over 250 franchised properties. HOSPITALITY INTERNATIONAL is proud of the fact that approximately 75% of its current franchisees are minorities. The company is actively pursuing the addition of new minority-owned franchises in all of the U.S.

Background:

Established: 1982;	1st Franchised: 1982
Franchised Units:	222
Company-Owned Units:	0
Total Units:	222

Minority-Owned Units:

African-American:	
Asian-American:	75%
Hispanic:	
Native American:	
Other:	5%
North America:	34 States
Density:	34 in FL, 40 in GA, 16 in TN

Financial/Terms:

Cash Investment:	$70-200K
Total Investment:	$1.0-5.0MM
Minimum Net Worth:	$Varies
Fees: Franchise —	$1K
Royalty — 3.5-2%;	Ad. — 2%
Earnings Claim Statement:	No
Term of Contract (Years):	5/1
Avg. # Of Employees:	6 FT, 3 PT
Passive Ownership:	Allowed
Area Develop. Agreements:	No
Sub-Franchising Contracts:	No
Expand In Territory:	N/A
Space Needs: 288/Guest SF; N/A	

Support & Training Provided:

Site Selection Assistance:	Yes
Lease Negotiation Assistance:	Yes
Co-Operative Advertising:	Yes
Franchisee Assoc./Member:	Yes/Yes
Size Of Corporate Staff:	26
On-Going Support:	B,C,D,E,G,H,I
Training: 1.5 Days in Tucker, GA.	

Minority-Specific Programs: We have one in place because we do not own or operate our hotels

Specific Expansion Plans:

US:	All United States

MOTEL 6

14651 Dallas Pkwy., # 500
Dallas, TX 75240
Tel: (888) 842-2942 (972) 702-6951
Fax: (972) 386-4107
E-Mail: arcioto@airmail.net
Web Site: www.motel6.com
Mr. Dean Savas, Vice President Franchise

Quality product, proven operational results, easy to operate. Many open motels available. Well-established brand. Part of Accor organization, largest owner/operator of economy lodging in the U.S.

Background:

Established: 1962;	1st Franchised: 1996
Franchised Units:	134
Company-Owned Units:	722
Total Units:	856
Minority-Owned Units:	
African-American:	0
Asian-American:	64%
Hispanic:	0
Native American:	0
North America:	48 States
Density:	172 in CA, 95 in TX, 44 AZ

Financial/Terms:

Cash Investment:	$100-500K
Total Investment:	$1-3MM
Minimum Net Worth:	$N/A
Fees: Franchise —	$25K
Royalty — 4%;	Ad. — 3.5%
Earnings Claim Statement:	Yes
Term of Contract (Years):	10-15/10
Avg. # Of Employees:	2-4 FT, 4-10 PT
Passive Ownership:	Allowed
Area Develop. Agreements:	Yes/2-5
Sub-Franchising Contracts:	No
Expand In Territory:	No
Space Needs: 69,000 SF; FS	

Support & Training Provided:

Site Selection Assistance:	No
Lease Negotiation Assistance:	No
Co-Operative Advertising:	N/A
Franchisee Assoc./Member:	Yes/No
Size Of Corporate Staff:	500

On-Going Support:	B,C,D,G,I

Training: 1.5 Weeks Dallas, TX for Owners and Managers.

Minority-Specific Programs: We have sponsored minority African-American organizations which undertake to provide access to qualified minority franchisee candidates. These organizations include AAHOA, NEHBA, Rainbow, PUSH, as well as Emerging Markets Program of the IFA. We expect to continue sponsorship of those organizations that prove effective in recruiting qualified candidates.

Specific Expansion Plans:

US:	All U. S. - Emphasis on East

RADISSON HOTELS WORLDWIDE

P. O. Box 59159, Carlson Parkway
Minneapolis, MN 55459-8204
Tel: (800) 333-3333 (612) 212-5526
Fax: (612) 212-3400
E-Mail: abender@carlson.com
Web Site: www.radisson.com
Ms. Amy Bender, Administrative Assistant

RADISSON HOTELS WORLDWIDE is a leader in the hotel industry which operates, manages and franchises nearly 400 up-scale hotels and resorts in 52 countries.

Background:

Established: 1962;	1st Franchised: 1987
Franchised Units:	391
Company-Owned Units:	7
Total Units:	398
Minority-Owned Units:	
African-American:	
Asian-American:	
Hispanic:	
Native American:	
North America:	45 States
Density:	30 in CA, 35 in FL, 17 in TX

Financial/Terms:

Cash Investment:	$50K
Total Investment:	$22-44MM
Minimum Net Worth:	$Varies
Fees: Franchise —	$50K
Royalty — 4%;	Ad. — 3.75%
Earnings Claim Statement:	Yes
Term of Contract (Years):	15/0

Avg. # Of Employees:	Varies
Passive Ownership:	NR
Area Develop. Agreements:	No
Sub-Franchising Contracts:	No
Expand In Territory:	Yes
Space Needs: 150,000 SF; Hotel	

Support & Training Provided:

Site Selection Assistance:	No
Lease Negotiation Assistance:	No
Co-Operative Advertising:	No
Franchisee Assoc./Member:	No
Size Of Corporate Staff:	72
On-Going Support:	b,C,D,E,G,h,I

Training: GM Certification, Yes I Can Training.

Minority-Specific Programs: Although we support the objectives of the NMFI, we do not have any specific programs in place at this time.

Specific Expansion Plans:

US:	All United States

RED ROOF INNS

14651 Dallas Pkwy., # 500
Dallas, TX 75240
Tel: (888) 842-2942 (972) 702-5963
Fax: (972) 702-3610
E-Mail: arcinfo@airmail.net
Web Site: www.redroofinns.com
Mr. Dean Savas, VP Franchise

RED ROOF is a strong, proven brand, delivering excellent results. Now a part of Accor, the world's leading owner/operator in economy lodging. Through franchising, this brand offers many opportunities to interested entrepreneurs in open markets throughout the U.S.

Background:

Established: 1972;	1st Franchised: 1996
Franchised Units:	70
Company-Owned Units:	258
Total Units:	328
Minority-Owned Units:	
African-American:	0

Asian-American:	60%
Hispanic:	0
Native American:	0
North America:	39 States
Density:	35 in OH, 29 in TX, 23 in MI

Financial/Terms:

Cash Investment:	$100-500K
Total Investment:	$2.6-5.0MM
Minimum Net Worth:	$N/A
Fees: Franchise —	$30K
Royalty — 4.5%;	Ad. — 4%
Earnings Claim Statement:	Yes
Term of Contract (Years):	20/10
Avg. # Of Employees:	2-4 FT, 4-10 PT
Passive Ownership:	Allowed
Area Develop. Agreements:	Yes
Sub-Franchising Contracts:	No
Expand In Territory:	No
Space Needs: 93,000+ SF; Hotel	

Support & Training Provided:

Site Selection Assistance:	N/A
Lease Negotiation Assistance:	N/A
Co-Operative Advertising:	N/A
Franchisee Assoc./Member:	Yes/Yes
Size Of Corporate Staff:	500
On-Going Support:	B,C,D,e,g,H,I

Training: 1.5 Weeks for Owners and Managers in Dallas, TX.

Minority-Specific Programs: We have sponsored minority African-American organizations which undertake to provide access to qualified minority franchisee candidates. These organizations include AAHOA, NEHBA, Rainbow, PUSH, as well as Emerging Markets Program of the IFA. We expect to continue sponsorship of those organizations that prove effective in recruiting qualified candidates.

Specific Expansion Plans:

US:	All United States

U. S. FRANCHISE SYSTEMS

13 Corporate Square, # 250
Atlanta, GA 30329
Tel: (404) 321-4045

Fax: (404) 235-7460
E-Mail: steve.romaniello@usfsi.com
Web Site: www.usfsi.com
Mr. Steve Romaniello, EVP Franchise Sales/Admin.

Hotel franchisor of MICROTEL INNS & SUITES, BEST INNS & SUITES and HAWTHORN SUITES brands. MICRO-TEL — all new construction, budget. BEST INNS — middle level limited service. HAWTHORN — upscale, suite-oriented brand. USFS is known as the "fair franchisor" with the most 2-sided agreement, lower than average fee structure, and no-hidden fees. Brands range from low-capital requirements (MICROTEL) to high (HAWTHORN).

Background:

Established: 1995;		1st Franchised: 1995
Franchised Units:		350
Company-Owned Units:		0
Total Units:		350
Minority-Owned Units:		
African-American:		5-10
Asian-American:		100+
Hispanic:		2-3
Native American:		1-2
North America:		49 States
Density:		NR

Financial/Terms:

Cash Investment:	$300K-2MM
Total Investment:	$1.2-7MM
Minimum Net Worth:	$N/A
Fees: Franchise —	$35-40K
Royalty — 5-6%;	Ad. — 2.5%
Earnings Claim Statement:	Yes
Term of Contract (Years):	20/10
Avg. # Of Employees:	10-25 FT
Passive Ownership:	Allowed
Area Develop. Agreements:	No
Sub-Franchising Contracts:	No
Expand In Territory:	Yes
Space Needs: 45,000 SF; FS, Raw land for development	

Support & Training Provided:

Site Selection Assistance:	No
Lease Negotiation Assistance:	Yes
Co-Operative Advertising:	No
Franchisee Assoc./Member:	Yes
Size Of Corporate Staff:	150
On-Going Support:	B,C,D,E,G,H,I

Training: 3-4 Days Atlanta, GA; On-Site as Needed.

Minority-Specific Programs: Although we support the objectives of the NMFI, we do not have any specific programs in place at this time.

Specific Expansion Plans:

US:	All United States

YOGI BEAR JELLYSTONE PARK CAMP-RESORTS

6201 Kellogg Ave.
Cincinnati, OH 45228-1118
Tel: (800) 626-3720 (513) 232-6800
Fax: (513) 231-1191
vWeb Site: www.campjellystone.com
Mr. Robert E. Schutter, Jr., President/COO

A unique recreation camp-resort for the entire family. YOGI and friends offer daily activities with a full amenity package, clean restrooms and YOGI souvenirs. Each camp-resort is independently owned and operated and maintains system standards.

Background:

Established: 1969;		1st Franchised: 1969
Franchised Units:		71
Company-Owned Units:		0
Total Units:		71
Minority-Owned Units:		
African-American:		0
Asian-American:		1
Hispanic:		1
Native American:		0
North America:		25 States, 2 Provinces
Density:		8 in IN, 7 in MI, 7 in WI

Financial/Terms:

Cash Investment:	$28K+
Total Investment:	$28K+
Minimum Net Worth:	$NR
Fees: Franchise —	$18-28K
Royalty — 6%;	Ad. — 1%
Earnings Claim Statement:	NR
Term of Contract (Years):	5-20/5-10
Avg. # Of Employees:	3 FT, 25 PT
Passive Ownership:	Discouraged
Area Develop. Agreements:	No
Sub-Franchising Contracts:	No
Expand In Territory:	No
Space Needs: NR SF; NR	

Support & Training Provided:

Site Selection Assistance:	Yes
Lease Negotiation Assistance:	Yes
Co-Operative Advertising:	Yes
Franchisee Assoc./Member:	NR
Size Of Corporate Staff:	6
On-Going Support:	B,C,D,E,G,H,I

Training: 2-3 Days Site; 3-4 Days Headquarters; 1-3 Days/Year On-Site.

Minority-Specific Programs: Although we support the objectives of the NMFI, we do not have any specific programs in place at this time.

Specific Expansion Plans:

US:	All United States

CLASSY MAIDS USA

P. O. Box 8552
Madison, WI 53708
Tel: (800) 445-5238 (608) 242-8943
Fax: (608) 242-1788
E-Mail: franchiseguy@cwix.com
Web Site:
Mr. William D. Olday, Vice President
Franchising

Multi-service cleaning franchise. Choose one or all of the following services: maid service, light janitorial, carpet cleaning, window washing, move-in/move-out. One week training program (your location or ours). Special conversion program available ($250 fee). Financing assistance and more.

Background:
Established: 1980; 1st Franchised: 1985
Franchised Units: 8
Company-Owned Units: 0
Total Units: 8
Minority-Owned Units:
  African-American:
  Asian-American:
  Hispanic:
  Native American:
  Other:
North America: 5 States
Density: 2 in MN, 2 in WI, 2 in FL

Financial/Terms:
Cash Investment: $7K

Total Investment: $12K
Minimum Net Worth: $15K
Fees: Franchise — $9.9K
  Royalty — 6%; Ad. — 0%
Earnings Claim Statement: No
Term of Contract (Years): 10/10
Avg. # Of Employees: 1 FT, 5-8 PT
Passive Ownership: Not Allowed
Area Develop. Agreements: No
Sub-Franchising Contracts: No
Expand In Territory: Yes
Space Needs: NR SF; HB

Support & Training Provided:
Site Selection Assistance: N/A
Lease Negotiation Assistance: N/A
Co-Operative Advertising: Yes
Franchisee Assoc./Member: No
Size Of Corporate Staff: 3
On-Going Support: a,b,c,d,e,G,h,I
Training: 3-5 Days Madison, WI, or 3-5 Days at Franchisee Location ($1,200).

Minority-Specific Programs: Although we support the objectives of the NMFI, we do not have any specific programs in place at this time.

Specific Expansion Plans:
US: All United States

CLEANING AUTHORITY, THE

9017 Red Branch Rd., # G
Columbia, MD 21045
Tel: (800) 783-6243 (410) 740-1900
Fax: (410) 740-1906
E-Mail: tim@thecleaningauthority.com
Web Site: www.thecleaningauthority.com
Mr. Tim Evankovich, Chief Operating Officer

THE CLEANING AUTHORITY offers franchisees new and innovative methods in developing a successful maid service. Our unique, high-response marketing, coupled with our state-of-the-art proprietary software system, sets us far above the competition in supporting the franchisee. Join us to make your future more successful. Member Platinum 200.

Background:
Established: 1978; 1st Franchised: 1996
Franchised Units: 35
Company-Owned Units: 1
Total Units: 36
Minority-Owned Units:
  African-American: 15%
  Asian-American:
  Hispanic:
  Native American:
  Other:
North America: 15 States
Density: 6 in MD, 5 in FL, 4 in TX

Financial/Terms:
Cash Investment: $15-25K
Total Investment: $40-60K
Minimum Net Worth: $50K
Fees: Franchise — $18-28K
  Royalty — 6-5-4%; Ad. — 2%
Earnings Claim Statement: No
Term of Contract (Years): 10/5
Avg. # Of Employees: Varies
Passive Ownership: Not Allowed
Area Develop. Agreements: No

Sub-Franchising Contracts: No
Expand In Territory: Yes
Space Needs: 800-1,200 SF; Industrial

Support & Training Provided:
Site Selection Assistance: Yes
Lease Negotiation Assistance: No
Co-Operative Advertising: Yes
Franchisee Assoc./Member: Yes/Yes
Size Of Corporate Staff: 8
On-Going Support: b,C,D,G,H,I
Training: 2 Weeks Corporate Office in Columbia, MD
Minority-Specific Programs: Although we support the objectives of the NMFI, we do not have any specific programs in place at this time.

Specific Expansion Plans:
US: All United States

DIAMOND HOME CLEANING SERVICES

4887 E. La Palma Ave., # 708
Anaheim, CA 92807
Tel: (800) 393-6243 (714) 701-9771
Fax: (714) 693-8106
E-Mail: mtgi@maintenanceinc.com
Web Site: www.maintenanceinc.com
Mr. Tom Devlin, President

3 franchise concepts - 1 franchise fee when you join the DIAMOND HOME CLEANING SERVICES franchise system. After completion of our extensive training program, you will be an expert in maid services, carpet cleaning and window cleaning services. Benefits include explosive 20% annual customer growth demand; home-based business; no weekends (have a life!); low investment of $25-60K, including start-up/working capital; and prime territories available.

Background:
Established: 1993;   1st Franchised: 1997
Franchised Units: 3
Company-Owned Units: 10
Total Units: 13
Minority-Owned Units:
  African-American: 0
  Asian-American: 0
  Hispanic: 0
  Native American: 0

North America: 1 State
Density: 13 in CA
Financial/Terms:
Cash Investment: $25K
Total Investment: $25-61K
Minimum Net Worth: $100K
Fees: Franchise — $5K
  Royalty — 4-6%; Ad. — 0%
Earnings Claim Statement: No
Term of Contract (Years): 10/5
Avg. # Of Employees: 3 FT, 24 PT
Passive Ownership: Discouraged
Area Develop. Agreements: No
Sub-Franchising Contracts: No
Expand In Territory: Yes
Space Needs: 500 SF; HB

Support & Training Provided:
Site Selection Assistance: Yes
Lease Negotiation Assistance: Yes
Co-Operative Advertising: No
Franchisee Assoc./Member: No
Size Of Corporate Staff: 6
On-Going Support: B,C,D,E,F,G,H,I
Training: 1 Week Anaheim, CA.
Minority-Specific Programs: Although we support the objectives of the NMFI, we do not have any specific programs in place at this time.

Specific Expansion Plans:
US: Southwest

HOME CLEANING CENTERS OF AMERICA

P. O. Box 11427
Overland Park, KS 66207-1427
Tel: (800) 767-1118 (913) 327-5227
Fax: (913) 327-5272
E-Mail: mcalhoon@aol.com
Web Site: www.homecleaninginc.com
Mr. Mike Calhoon, President

Very large franchise zones. Quality Quality Quality. Owners do not clean houses. Every corporate policy is made by the franchise owners. Each and every owner is hand picked - having money is not enough. Corporate "Mission Statement" is to have the largest grossing, highest-quality offices in the industry.

Background:
Established: 1981;   1st Franchised: 1984
Franchised Units: 25
Company-Owned Units: 0
Total Units: 25

Minority-Owned Units:
  African-American: 0
  Asian-American: 0
  Hispanic: 1
  Native American: 0
  Other:
North America: 9 States
Density: 7 in MO, 4 in KS, 4 in CO

Financial/Terms:
Cash Investment: $20-30K
Total Investment: $30-50K
Minimum Net Worth: $N/A
Fees: Franchise — $9.5K
  Royalty — 4.5-5%; Ad. — 0%
Earnings Claim Statement: Yes
Term of Contract (Years): 10/10
Avg. # Of Employees: 12 FT
Passive Ownership: Discouraged
Area Develop. Agreements: No
Sub-Franchising Contracts: No
Expand In Territory: Yes
Space Needs: 500 SF; Non-Retail

Support & Training Provided:
Site Selection Assistance: Yes
Lease Negotiation Assistance: Yes
Co-Operative Advertising: No
Franchisee Assoc./Member: Yes/Yes
Size Of Corporate Staff: 2
On-Going Support: b,C,D,E,F,G,H,I
Training: 5 Days Denver, CO or 5 days at St. Louis, MO.
Minority-Specific Programs: We give every potential franchisee the same help!

Specific Expansion Plans:
US: All United States

MAID BRIGADE SERVICES

Four Concourse Pkwy., # 200
Atlanta, GA 30328
Tel: (800) 722-6243 (770) 551-9630
Fax: (770) 391-9092
E-Mail: chay@maidbrigade.com
Web Site: www.maidbrigade.com
Ms. Cathy Hay, VP Franchise Development

MAID BRIGADE offers the largest territory size with an all-inclusive franchise fee (i.e. territory, equipment and supplies, software, etc.). Lifelong franchise support, plus carefully-designed systems provide the opportunity to develop a large house cleaning business. Franchisee profitability is at the heart of everything we do. Master franchises available outside the USA.

Background:

Established: 1979;	1st Franchised: 1984
Franchised Units:	253
Company-Owned Units:	3
Total Units:	256
Minority-Owned Units:	
African-American:	
Asian-American:	
Hispanic:	
Native American:	
Other:	
North America:	28 States,10 Provinces
Density:	VA, TX, WA

Financial/Terms:

Cash Investment:	$35-50K
Total Investment:	$50-60K
Minimum Net Worth:	$100K
Fees: Franchise —	$16.9K
Royalty — 7-3%;	Ad. — 2%
Earnings Claim Statement:	Yes
Term of Contract (Years):	10/10
Avg. # Of Employees:	15 FT
Passive Ownership:	Not Allowed
Area Develop. Agreements:	Yes/5
Sub-Franchising Contracts:	Yes
Expand In Territory:	Yes
Space Needs: 500-1,000 SF; HB, SF, SC	

Support & Training Provided:

Site Selection Assistance:	Yes
Lease Negotiation Assistance:	Yes
Co-Operative Advertising:	No
Franchisee Assoc./Member:	Yes/Yes
Size Of Corporate Staff:	9
On-Going Support:	A,B,C,D,E,F,G,H,I

Training: 5 Days Atlanta, GA; 8 Days On-Site Week of Opening. Training Videos/ Manuals.

Minority-Specific Programs: Although we support the objectives of the NMFI, we do not have any specific programs in place at this time.

Specific Expansion Plans:

US:	All United States

MAID SERVICES OF AMERICA

475 E. Main St., # 151
Cartersville, GA 30121
Tel: (800) 289-8642 (770) 387-2455
Fax: (770) 387-2454
E-Mail: maidmoney@aol.com
Web Site:
Ms. Tammy Spivey, Sales Manager

You own it! You name it! You keep the profits! We show you how to operate a successful cleaning service that includes: residential, new construction, property management, window washing and floor care. Consulting and unlimited support is provided through- out your first year of business.

Background:

Established: 1977;	1st Franchised: 1981
Franchised Units:	216
Company-Owned Units:	1
Total Units:	217
Minority-Owned Units:	
African-American:	15%
Asian-American:	5%
Hispanic:	0%
Native American:	0%
Other:	
North America:	47 States
Density:	33 in CA, 32 in TX, 27 in FL

Financial/Terms:

Cash Investment:	$1.5-2.5K
Total Investment:	$4.5-12.5K
Minimum Net Worth:	$N/A
Fees: Franchise —	$2-7K
Royalty — 0%;	Ad. — 0%
Earnings Claim Statement:	Yes
Term of Contract (Years):	5
Avg. # Of Employees:	1 FT, 7-10 PT
Passive Ownership:	Allowed
Area Develop. Agreements:	Yes/1
Sub-Franchising Contracts:	Yes
Expand In Territory:	Yes
Space Needs: NR SF; HB	

Support & Training Provided:

Site Selection Assistance:	N/A
Lease Negotiation Assistance:	N/A
Co-Operative Advertising:	N/A
Franchisee Assoc./Member:	No
Size Of Corporate Staff:	7
On-Going Support:	D,e,G,H,I

Training: 5 Days Atlanta, GA.

Minority-Specific Programs: Minority ownership is encouraged by offering a 25% reduction in franchise fee and allowing the business owner 3 months before their first loan payment is due. Also no qualifying financing. Example: $6,990 fee (Plan B) - 1,747 (25% discount) = $5,243 - 2,621.50 (50% down payment) = $2,621.50. Payments divided over 18 months at 10%, no payments for 90 days.

Specific Expansion Plans:

US:	All United States

MAID TO PERFECTION

7133 Rutherford Rd., # 105
Baltimore, MD 21244
Tel: (800) 648-6243 (410) 944-6466
Fax: (410) 944-6469
E-Mail: maidsvc@aol.com
Web Site: www.maidtoperfectioncorp.com
Ms. Gloria Goldstraw, Vice President Marketing

MAID TO PERFECTION (r) is the only major cleaning franchise that provides access to every residential and commercial service dollar, within an exclusive territory. Ranked #1 for franchisee support/satisfaction in Success, April, 1999; cited as one of only 15 Great, Low-Investment franchises by Black Enterprise, September, 1999.

Background:

Established: 1980;	1st Franchised: 1990
Franchised Units:	175
Company-Owned Units:	0
Total Units:	175
Minority-Owned Units:	
African-American:	7
Asian-American:	10
Hispanic:	13
Native American:	0
Other:	
North America:	18 States, 2 Provinces
Density:	50 in MD, 33 in PA, 20 in CA

Financial/Terms:

Cash Investment:	$15-20K
Total Investment:	$35-40K
Minimum Net Worth:	$80K
Fees: Franchise —	$9K
Royalty — 5-7%;	Ad. — 0%
Earnings Claim Statement:	No
Term of Contract (Years):	5/5
Avg. # Of Employees:	15 FT, 5 PT
Passive Ownership:	Discouraged
Area Develop. Agreements:	Yes/5
Sub-Franchising Contracts:	No
Expand In Territory:	Yes
Space Needs: 400-500 SF; FS, HB, Non-Retail	

Support & Training Provided:

Site Selection Assistance:	Yes
Lease Negotiation Assistance:	Yes
Co-Operative Advertising:	No
Franchisee Assoc./Member:	Yes/No
Size Of Corporate Staff:	7
On-Going Support:	C,D,E,G,H,I

Training: 1 Week at Corporate Headquarters; 1 Week On-Site.

Minority-Specific Programs: Our Minority Ownership Initiative is available to anyone of a racial minority. We discount our initial farnchise fee by 10% and offer full financing on all additional units at an interest rate of 8%, as opposed to our regular 9 1/4% rate. Our industry employs many minority employees and we'd like that reflected in the make-up of our owners as well. We'd like to double minority ownership by mid-2000.

Specific Expansion Plans:

US:	All United States

MAIDPRO

180 Canal St.
Boston, MA 02114
Tel: (888) MAIDPRO (617) 742-8787
Fax: (617) 720-0700
E-Mail: maidpro@aol.com
Web Site: www.maidpro.com
Mr. Richard Sparacio, Director Franchise Development

MAIDPRO is setting the trend in the home and office cleaning industry. MAIDPRO has a contemporary approach to this high-growth service. With unmatched graphic design and marketing, a completely paperless office and the ability for clients to request service on the Internet, MAIDPRO's franchisees have become successful in running a larger business.

Background:

Established: 1991;	1st Franchised: 1997	
Franchised Units:		13
Company-Owned Units:		2
Total Units:		15
Minority-Owned Units:		
African-American:		2
Asian-American:		1
Hispanic:		0
Native American:		0
Other:		
North America:		9 States

Density:	8 in MA, 1 in FL, 1 in CT

Financial/Terms:

Cash Investment:	$10-15K
Total Investment:	$24.4-42.4K
Minimum Net Worth:	$N/A
Fees: Franchise —	$7.9K
Royalty — 3-6%;	Ad. — N/A
Earnings Claim Statement:	No
Term of Contract (Years):	10/5
Avg. # Of Employees:	15 FT, 3 PT
Passive Ownership:	Not Allowed
Area Develop. Agreements:	No
Sub-Franchising Contracts:	No
Expand In Territory:	Yes
Space Needs: 500-1,500 SF; SF, Office Building	

Support & Training Provided:

Site Selection Assistance:	Yes
Lease Negotiation Assistance:	Yes
Co-Operative Advertising:	Yes
Franchisee Assoc./Member:	No
Size Of Corporate Staff:	5
On-Going Support:	C,d,E,G,h,I

Training: 2 Weeks in Boston, MA.

Minority-Specific Programs: Although we support the objectives of the NMFI, we do not have any specific programs in place at this time.

Specific Expansion Plans:

US:	All United States

MAIDS, THE

4820 Dodge St.
Omaha, NE 68132-4820
Tel: (800) 843-6243 (402) 558-5555
Fax: (402) 558-4112
E-Mail: jbasden@navix.net
Web Site: www.maids.com
Mr. Michael P. Fagen, Executive Vice President

AMERICA'S MAID SERVICE - THE MAIDS is the premier residential cleaning franchise. Our cleaning system is the most thorough in the industry and sets us ahead of all competition. We offer low investment, comprehensive training and on-going support that set the industry standard. Call THE MAIDS today and discover why we are AMERICA'S MAID SERVICE.

Background:

Established: 1979;	1st Franchised: 1980

Franchised Units:	378
Company-Owned Units:	50
Total Units:	428
Minority-Owned Units:	
African-American:	2
Asian-American:	3
Hispanic:	2
Native American:	
Other:	
North America:	40 States, 5 Provinces
Density:	34 in CA, 23 in NY, 20 in IL

Financial/Terms:

Cash Investment:	$14-61K
Total Investment:	$56-245K
Minimum Net Worth:	$180-350K
Fees: Franchise —	$17.5K
Royalty — 3.3-7%;	Ad. — 1%
Earnings Claim Statement:	Yes
Term of Contract (Years):	20/20
Avg. # Of Employees:	1-2 FT, 8-12 PT
Passive Ownership:	Discouraged
Area Develop. Agreements:	No
Sub-Franchising Contracts:	Yes
Expand In Territory:	Yes
Space Needs: 200 SF; FS, SC, SF	

Support & Training Provided:

Site Selection Assistance:	Yes
Lease Negotiation Assistance:	No
Co-Operative Advertising:	Yes
Franchisee Assoc./Member:	Yes/Yes
Size Of Corporate Staff:	35
On-Going Support:	A,B,C,D,G,H,I

Training: 8 Days Each in Both Managerial and Technical Training at Headquarters; 90 Days On-Site.

Minority-Specific Programs: Residential cleanin is a booming industry and we encourage anyone to look into buying a THE MAIDS franchise. The staff at THE MAIDS INTERNATIONAL has always been available to assist all prospective franchisees and answer any questions they may have. TMI also provides all training materials in Spanish, as well as English. Our monthly newsletter, The Sweeper, is also translated into Spanish.

Specific Expansion Plans:

US:	All United States

AEROWEST & WESTAIR SANITATION SERVICES

3882 Del Amo Blvd., # 602
Torrance, CA 90503
Tel: (310) 793-4242
Fax: (310) 793-4250
E-Mail: westsaninc@aol.com
Web Site: www.members.aol.com/
westsaninc
Mr. Chris Ratay, Franchise Manager

WEST provides unique odor counteractant dispensers and fluids at cost to franchisees for their service work in the 'high end' market, including hospitals, offices, government and municipal buildings, etc. Administrative support is performed by WEST on behalf of the franchisee, including billings and collections (gross franchise income is advanced at time of billing), allowing franchisees to concentrate on sales and service.

Background:

Established: 1983;   1st Franchised: 1983
Franchised Units: 46
Company-Owned Units: 29
Total Units: 75
Minority-Owned Units:

African-American:	7
Asian-American:	1
Hispanic:	3
Native American:	0
Other:	
North America:	30 States
Density:	13 in CA, 9 in NY, 7 in IL

Financial/Terms:

Cash Investment:	$3-10K
Total Investment:	$3-40K
Minimum Net Worth:	$NR
Fees: Franchise —	$2K
Royalty — 35%;	Ad. — 0%
Earnings Claim Statement:	No
Term of Contract (Years):	5/1
Avg. # Of Employees:	1 FT
Passive Ownership:	Discouraged
Area Develop. Agreements:	N/A
Sub-Franchising Contracts:	No
Expand In Territory:	Yes
Space Needs: N/A SF; HB	

Support & Training Provided:

Site Selection Assistance:	N/A
Lease Negotiation Assistance:	N/A
Co-Operative Advertising:	N/A
Franchisee Assoc./Member:	No
Size Of Corporate Staff:	12
On-Going Support:	A,B,C,D,G,H,I

Training: 1-2 Weeks Local, Near Franchisee's Home.

Minority-Specific Programs: Although we support the objectives of the NMFI, we do not have any specific programs in place at this time.

Specific Expansion Plans:

US: All United States

AIRE-MASTER OF AMERICA

P. O. Box 2310, 1821 N. Highway CC,
Nixa, MO 65714
Tel: (800) 525-0957 (417) 725-2691
Fax: (417) 725-5737
E-Mail: aire@airemaster.com
Web Site: www.airemaster.com
Mr. Jim M. Roudenis, Franchise Director

AIRE-MASTER is a unique system of odor control and restroom fixture cleaning. Unlike the majority of 'air-fresheners' on the market, AIRE-MASTER deodorizers and deodorant products actually eliminate odors by oxidation. You don't need prior experience in the odor control/sanitary supply industry to qualify for an AIRE-MASTER franchise. Customer base is built by making sales calls and providing good customer service. Complete training.

Background:

Established: 1958;   1st Franchised: 1977
Franchised Units: 42
Company-Owned Units: 4
Total Units: 46
Minority-Owned Units:
  African-American:

Asian-American:
Hispanic:
Native American: 1
North America: 33 States, 1 Province
Density: 4 in MO, 3 in CA, 3 in NJ

Financial/Terms:
Cash Investment: $25K
Total Investment: $25-75K
Minimum Net Worth: $NR
Fees: Franchise — $17K
Royalty — 5%; Ad. — 0%
Earnings Claim Statement: No
Term of Contract (Years): 20/3
Avg. # Of Employees: 2-3 FT
Passive Ownership: Discouraged
Area Develop. Agreements: No
Sub-Franchising Contracts: No
Expand In Territory: N/A
Space Needs: N/A SF; HB

Support & Training Provided:
Site Selection Assistance: N/A
Lease Negotiation Assistance: Yes
Co-Operative Advertising: Yes
Franchisee Assoc./Member: Yes/Yes
Size Of Corporate Staff: 66
On-Going Support: a,B,C,D,E,G,h,I
Training: 5 Days Headquarters, Nixa MO; 5 Days Franchisee's Location.
Minority-Specific Programs: Although we support the objectives of the NMFI, we do not have any specific programs in place at this time.

Specific Expansion Plans:
US: All United States

AMERICAN LEAK DETECTION

888 Research Dr., # 100, P. O. Box 1701
Palm Springs, CA 92263
Tel: (800) 755-6697 (760) 320-9991
Fax: (760) 320-1288
E-Mail: sbangs@ leakbusters.com
Web Site: www.leakbusters.com
Ms. Sheila T. Bangs, Director of Franchise Sales

Electronic detection of water, drain, waste, sewer and gas leaks under concrete slabs of homes, commercial buildings, pools, spas, fountains, etc. with equipment commissioned/ manufactured by company.

Background:
Established: 1974; 1st Franchised: 1985

Franchised Units: 303
Company-Owned Units: 2
Total Units: 305
Minority-Owned Units:
African-American: 9
Asian-American: 0
Hispanic: 2
Native American: 0
Other:
North America: 38 States, 3 Provinces
Density: 63 in CA, 29 in FL, 17 in TX

Financial/Terms:
Cash Investment: $45-120K
Total Investment: $75-150K
Minimum Net Worth: $Varies
Fees: Franchise — $49.5K+
Royalty — 8-10%; Ad. — N/A
Earnings Claim Statement: No
Term of Contract (Years): 10/10
Avg. # Of Employees: 1-4 FT, 2 PT
Passive Ownership: Discouraged
Area Develop. Agreements: No
Sub-Franchising Contracts: No
Expand In Territory: Yes
Space Needs: NR SF; NR

Support & Training Provided:
Site Selection Assistance: N/A
Lease Negotiation Assistance: N/A
Co-Operative Advertising: Yes
Franchisee Assoc./Member: Yes/Yes
Size Of Corporate Staff: 42
On-Going Support: a,B,C,D,f,G,H,I
Training: 6-10 Weeks Palm Springs, CA.
Minority-Specific Programs: We do support the overall objectives, but, in an effort to treat everyone in a fair and positive manner, we do not have any programs specifically targeted to any minority group.

Specific Expansion Plans:
US: Northeast, Midwest

BONUS BUILDING CARE

4950 Keller Springs, # 190
Addison, TX 75001
Tel: (800) 931-1102 (972) 931-1100
Fax: (972) 789-9399
E-Mail: bonusinc@aol.com
Web Site: www.bonusbuildingcare.com
Mrs. Margaret A. Masterson,

Commercial cleaning. Turn-key operation, with customers, training, operations

assistance, equipment, business insurance and clerical support. Best cleaning franchise on the market today because of lower fees, personalized support, less restrictions and quicker start-up. We're not the biggest, but we are the best. Master franchises available. IFA Member.

Background:
Established: 1999; 1st Franchised: 1999
Franchised Units: 118
Company-Owned Units: 4
Total Units: 122
Minority-Owned Units:
African-American:
Asian-American:
Hispanic:
Native American:
Other:
North America: 4 States
Density: TN, MO, TX

Financial/Terms:
Cash Investment: $Varies
Total Investment: $Varies
Minimum Net Worth: $N/A
Fees: Franchise — $6.5K
Royalty — 10%; Ad. — 0%
Earnings Claim Statement: No
Term of Contract (Years): 20/20
Avg. # Of Employees: Variesz
Passive Ownership: Discouraged
Area Develop. Agreements: No
Sub-Franchising Contracts: Yes
Expand In Territory: No
Space Needs: N/A SF; BH

Support & Training Provided:
Site Selection Assistance: N/A
Lease Negotiation Assistance: N/A
Co-Operative Advertising: N/A
Franchisee Assoc./Member: Yes/No
Size Of Corporate Staff: 6
On-Going Support: B,C,D,I
Training: Min. 20 Hours On-Site; Min 10 Hours Classroom; As Needed Self-Study.
Minority-Specific Programs: Although we support the objectives of the NMFI, we do not have any specific programs in place at this time.

Specific Expansion Plans:
US: All United States

CHEM-DRY CARPET & UPHOLSTERY CLEANING

1530 North 1000 West
Logan, UT 84321
Tel: (877) 307-8233 (435) 755-0099
Fax: (435) 755-0021

E-Mail: charlie@chemdry.com
Web Site: www.chemdry.com
Mr. Mark S. Coon, National Franchise
Director

We have over 20 years of experience, state-of-the-art, patented equipment, on-going research and development and technical support. CHEM-DRY lets you offer a unique, patented, hot carbonating carpet and upholstery cleaning service that is second-to-none! Entrepreneur Magazine has rated us #1 in our field for the past 10 years.

Background:

Established: 1977;   1st Franchised: 1978
Franchised Units: 3876
Company-Owned Units: 0
Total Units: 3876
Minority-Owned Units:
   African-American:
   Asian-American:
   Hispanic:
   Native American:
North America: 50 States, 11Provinces
Density: 424 in CA, 166 in TX, 165 FL

Financial/Terms:

Cash Investment: $6K Down Pay.
Total Investment: $6.9-27.6K
Minimum Net Worth: $N/A
Fees: Franchise — $18.9K
   Royalty — $193/Mo.;   Ad. — 0%
Earnings Claim Statement: No
Term of Contract (Years):   5/5
Avg. # Of Employees: 3 FT
Passive Ownership: Allowed
Area Develop. Agreements: No
Sub-Franchising Contracts: No
Expand In Territory: No
Space Needs: N/A SF; N/A

Support & Training Provided:

Site Selection Assistance: N/A
Lease Negotiation Assistance: N/A
Co-Operative Advertising: Yes
Franchisee Assoc./Member: Yes/No
Size Of Corporate Staff: 60
On-Going Support: B,C,D,G,H,I
Training: 5 Days Logan, UT; 8 Hour Home Study With Video.

Minority-Specific Programs: Although we support the objectives of the NMFI, we do not have any specific programs in place at this time.

Specific Expansion Plans:

US: All United States

CHEMSTATION INTERNATIONAL

3400 Encrete Ln.
Dayton, OH 45439
Tel: (877) 999-8265 (937) 294-8265
Fax: (937) 534-0426
E-Mail: customerservice@chemstation.com
Web Site: www.chemstation.com
Mr. John D. Shafer, Director New Business Develop.

CHEMSTATION is an affiliation of manufacturing centers which offer their customers the unique service of custom manufactured cleaning chemicals delivered in bulk to refillable containers that eliminate the waste and inefficiencies of drums.

Background:

Established: 1983;   1st Franchised: 1984
Franchised Units: 33
Company-Owned Units: 7
Total Units: 40
Minority-Owned Units:
   African-American: 1
   Asian-American:
   Hispanic:
   Native American:
   Other:
North America.   27 States
Density: 5 in OH, 3 in MI, 3 in IN

Financial/Terms:

Cash Investment: $150-300K
Total Investment: $500K
Minimum Net Worth: $NR
Fees: Franchise — $45K
   Royalty — 4%;   Ad. — 2%
Earnings Claim Statement: No
Term of Contract (Years):   10/5
Avg. # Of Employees: 6 FT
Passive Ownership: Discouraged
Area Develop. Agreements: No
Sub-Franchising Contracts: No
Expand In Territory: Yes
Space Needs: 6,000 SF; Commercial/Industrial

Support & Training Provided:

Site Selection Assistance: Yes
Lease Negotiation Assistance: Yes
Co-Operative Advertising: Yes
Franchisee Assoc./Member: Yes
Size Of Corporate Staff: 35
On-Going Support: A,B,C,D,E,F,G,H,I
Training: 1 Week Dayton, OH and On-Going.

Minority-Specific Programs: Although we support the objectives of the NMFI, we do not have any specific programs in place at this time.

Specific Expansion Plans:

US: West, NY, Northeast

CLEANNET USA

9861 Broken Land Pkwy., # 208
Columbia, MD 21046
Tel: (800) 735-8838 (410) 720-6444
Fax: (410) 720-5307
E-Mail:
Web Site: www.cleannetusa.com
Mr. Dennis M. Urner, Executive Vice President

Full-service, turn-key commercial office cleaning franchise, offering guaranteed customer accounts, training equipment, supplies, local office support, quality control backup, billing/invoicing and guaranteed payment for services provided. Company also sells master licenses for markets with metropolitan populations of 500,000 and up.

Background:

Established: 1987;   1st Franchised: 1988
Franchised Units: 1718
Company-Owned Units: 7
Total Units: 1725
Minority-Owned Units:
   African-American: 60%
   Asian-American: 5%
   Hispanic: 20%
   Native American:
   Other:
North America: 13 States
Density: 366 in MD, 308 in NJ, 195 PA

Financial/Terms:

Cash Investment: $0-25K
Total Investment: $2.9-35.7K
Minimum Net Worth: $0-100K
Fees: Franchise — $2-255K
   Royalty — 3%;   Ad. — 0%
Earnings Claim Statement: No

Term of Contract (Years): 20/20
Avg. # Of Employees: 2 FT, 10 PT
Passive Ownership: Discouraged
Area Develop. Agreements: Yes/20
Sub-Franchising Contracts: Yes
Expand In Territory: Yes
Space Needs: 2,000 SF; Multi-Tenant

Support & Training Provided:
Site Selection Assistance: Yes
Lease Negotiation Assistance: Yes
Co-Operative Advertising: No
Franchisee Assoc./Member: No
Size Of Corporate Staff: 75
On-Going Support: A,B,C,D,E,G,H,I
Training: 8 Days - 2 Weeks Company Offices;
4 Days - 3 Weeks Job Site or Master Offices.
Minority-Specific Programs: Although we support the objectives of the NMFI, we do not have any specific programs in place at this time.

Specific Expansion Plans:
US: All United States

COIT SERVICES
897 Hinckley Rd.
Burlingame, CA 94010
Tel: (800) 243-8797 (650) 697-5471
Fax: (650) 697-6117
E-Mail: craig@coit.com
Web Site: www.coit.com
Mr. Craig Ratkovich, Director Franchise Sales

Granting large, exclusive territories, COIT SERVICES provides a proven opportunity in the carpet, upholstery, drapery, area rug and air-duct cleaning business. COIT franchisees enjoy use of a universal 800# (1-800-FORCOIT), along with successful marketing and management programs that have been proven in place for 50 years.

Background:
Established: 1950; 1st Franchised: 1963
Franchised Units: 57
Company-Owned Units: 12
Total Units: 69
Minority-Owned Units:
  African-American: 0
  Asian-American: 1
  Hispanic: 2
  Native American: 0

Other: Arab, Egyptian
North America: 26 States, 2 Provinces
Density: 16 in CA, 4 in WA, 4 in OH

Financial/Terms:
Cash Investment: $40-60K
Total Investment: $100K
Minimum Net Worth: $No Minimum
Fees: Franchise — $25K
  Royalty — 2-6%; Ad. — 0%
Earnings Claim Statement: Yes
Term of Contract (Years): 10/10
Avg. # Of Employees: 2 FT, 1 PT
Passive Ownership: Discouraged
Area Develop. Agreements: No
Sub-Franchising Contracts: No
Expand In Territory: Yes
Space Needs: 1,000 SF; Industrial

Support & Training Provided:
Site Selection Assistance: Yes
Lease Negotiation Assistance: Yes
Co-Operative Advertising: Yes
Franchisee Assoc./Member: Yes/Yes
Size Of Corporate Staff: 19
On-Going Support: A,a,B,C,D,E,G,H,I
Training: 7 Days Corporate Headquarters;
1-2 Weeks in Field.
Minority-Specific Programs: Although we support the objectives of the NMFI, we do not have any specific programs in place at this time.

Specific Expansion Plans:
US: Northeast, Southeast, Midwest

COVERALL CLEANING CONCEPTS
500 W. Cypress Creek Rd., # 580
Fort Lauderdale, FL 33309
Tel: (800) 537-3371 (954) 351-1110
Fax: (954) 492-5044
E-Mail: info@coverall.com
Web Site: www.coverall.com
Mr. Jack Caughey, VP Franchise Dev.

Comprehensive janitorial franchise which includes state-of-the-art training, franchise development, equipment and supplies, billing and collection services, as well as customer assistance services. Additional training, bulk volume-buying power, insurance and benefit packages also available. Master franchises also available. Master insurance plans offered.

Background:
Established: 1985; 1st Franchised: 1985

Franchised Units: 4546
Company-Owned Units: 26
Total Units: 4572
Minority-Owned Units:
  African-American:
  Asian-American:
  Hispanic:
  Native American:
  Other:
North America: 31 States, 1 Province
Density: 620 in FL, 333 in VA, 443 CA

Financial/Terms:
Cash Investment: $1.5K+
Total Investment: $5.3-35.9K
Minimum Net Worth: $2K
Fees: Franchise — $5-32.2K
  Royalty — 5%; Ad. — 2%
Earnings Claim Statement: No
Term of Contract (Years): 20
Avg. # Of Employees: 3-5 PT
Passive Ownership: Allowed
Area Develop. Agreements: No
Sub-Franchising Contracts: Yes
Expand In Territory: Yes
Space Needs: N/A SF; N/A

Support & Training Provided:
Site Selection Assistance: No
Lease Negotiation Assistance: No
Co-Operative Advertising: Yes
Franchisee Assoc./Member: Yes/Yes
Size Of Corporate Staff: 450
On-Going Support: A,B,C,D,G,H,I
Training: Approximately 40 Hours at Local Regional Office.
Minority-Specific Programs: Although we support the objectives of the NMFI, we do not have any specific programs in place at this time.

Specific Expansion Plans:
US: All United States

DURACLEAN INTERNATIONAL
220 Campus Dr.
Arlington Heights, IL 60006
Tel: (800) 251-7070 (847) 704-7100
Fax: (847) 704-7101

E-Mail: mhiggins@duraclean.com
Web Site: www.duraclean.com
Mr. Michael Higgins, VP Global Expansion

DURACLEAN offers distinct services, markets and revenue center packages to fit your needs for independence and growth. Carpet cleaning, ceiling and wall cleaning, upholstery and drapery cleaning, fire/smoke/water restoration, janitorial, pressure washing, hard surface floor care, duct cleaning and ultrasonic cleaning are all services that we offer. We are the most diversified cleaning franchise in the world.

Background:

Established: 1930;	1st Franchised: 1945
Franchised Units:	347
Company-Owned Units:	1
Total Units:	348
Minority-Owned Units:	
African-American:	15
Asian-American:	5
Hispanic:	15
Native American:	
Other:	
North America:	50 States
Density:	38 in FL, 34 in IL, 30 in CA

Financial/Terms:

Cash Investment:	$25K
Total Investment:	$54-70K
Minimum Net Worth:	$N/A
Fees: Franchise —	$10K
Royalty — 6-8%,	Ad. — 0%
Earnings Claim Statement:	No
Term of Contract (Years):	5/5
Avg. # Of Employees:	2 FT, 1 PT
Passive Ownership:	Discouraged
Area Develop. Agreements:	No
Sub-Franchising Contracts:	No
Expand In Territory:	Yes
Space Needs: N/A SF; HB	

Support & Training Provided:

Site Selection Assistance:	N/A
Lease Negotiation Assistance:	N/A
Co-Operative Advertising:	No
Franchisee Assoc./Member:	Yes/No
Size Of Corporate Staff:	25
On-Going Support:	C,D,G,H,I

Training: 6 Days Success Institute, Corp. Office; 2 Days On-Site Cleaning; Home Study Program.
Minority-Specific Programs: Although we support the objectives of the NMFI, we do not have any specific programs in place at this time.

Specific Expansion Plans:

US:	All United States

E. P. I. C. SYSTEMS
402 East Maryland
Evansville, IN 47711
Tel: (800) 230-3742 (812) 428-7750
Fax: (812) 428-4162
E-Mail:
Web Site:
Mr. Jeffrey R. Schaperjohn, President

Complete janitorial service franchising master and individual units. Single unit initial franchise fee is $6,500, master franchise is $25,000 per million population.

Background:

Established: 1993;	1st Franchised: 1994
Franchised Units:	9
Company-Owned Units:	0
Total Units:	9
Minority-Owned Units:	
African-American:	2%
Asian-American:	0%
Hispanic:	0%
Native American:	0%
Other:	1
North America:	2 States
Density:	6 in KY, 3 in IN

Financial/Terms:

Cash Investment:	$6.5-28.5K
Total Investment:	$6.5-60K
Minimum Net Worth:	$10.2-28.5K
Fees: Franchise —	$6.5K
Royalty — 4-10%;	Ad. — N/A
Earnings Claim Statement:	No
Term of Contract (Years):	10/10
Avg. # Of Employees:	1 FT, 5 PT
Passive Ownership:	Discouraged
Area Develop. Agreements:	Yes/10
Sub-Franchising Contracts:	Yes
Expand In Territory:	Yes
Space Needs: 250-700 SF; HB, Office	

Support & Training Provided:

Site Selection Assistance:	Yes
Lease Negotiation Assistance:	No
Co-Operative Advertising:	No
Franchisee Assoc./Member:	No
Size Of Corporate Staff:	4
On-Going Support:	c,D,I

Training: 2 Weeks at Headquarters.
Minority-Specific Programs: Although we support the objectives of the NMFI, we do not have any specific programs in place at this time.

Specific Expansion Plans:

US:	Midwest

HEAVEN'S BEST CARPET/ UPHOLST. CLEANING
247 N. 1st E., P. O. Box 607
Rexburg, ID 83440
Tel: (800) 359-2095 (208) 359-1106
Fax: (208) 359-1236
E-Mail:
Web Site: www.heavensbest.com
Mr. Cody Howard, Chief Executive Officer

Unique low moisture cleaning process. There is no better franchise opportunity than this. Our franchisees are happy, our customers are happy. Our franchise is very affordable. Call for our free video.

Background:

Established: 1983;	1st Franchised: 1983
Franchised Units:	380
Company-Owned Units:	0
Total Units:	380
Minority-Owned Units:	
African-American:	4
Asian-American:	8
Hispanic:	
Native American:	
Other:	3 Women
North America:	28 States
Density:	48 in CA, 46 in ID, 25 in CO

Financial/Terms:

Cash Investment:	$7.5-20K
Total Investment:	$16-40K
Minimum Net Worth:	$10K
Fees: Franchise —	$2.9K
Royalty — $80/Mo.;	Ad. — NR
Earnings Claim Statement:	No
Term of Contract (Years):	5/5
Avg. # Of Employees:	1 FT
Passive Ownership:	Allowed
Area Develop. Agreements:	No
Sub-Franchising Contracts:	Yes
Expand In Territory:	Yes
Space Needs: N/A SF; N/A	

Support & Training Provided:

Site Selection Assistance:	N/A
Lease Negotiation Assistance:	N/A
Co-Operative Advertising:	Yes
Franchisee Assoc./Member:	Yes/Yes
Size Of Corporate Staff:	5

On-Going Support: A,B,F,G,H,I
Training: 4 days Rexburg, IA.
Minority-Specific Programs: Although we support the objectives of the NMFI, we do not have any specific programs in place at this time.

Specific Expansion Plans:
US: All United States

JAN-PRO CLEANING SYSTEMS
383 Strand Industrial Dr.
Little River, SC 29566
Tel: (800) 668-1001 (843) 399-9895
Fax: (843) 399-9890
E-Mail: janpro1@aol.com
Web Site: www.jan-pro.com
Ms. Carol McLennan, Vice President

JAN-PRO has built a solid reputatioon as a quality franchise orgranization within the commercial cleaning industry. We have been highly ranked in magazines such as Entrepreneur, Income Opportunities, Home Business and Business Start-Up. JAN-PRO franchise owners are in business for themselves, but not by themselves.

Background:
Established: 1991; 1st Franchised: 1992
Franchised Units: 570
Company-Owned Units: 100
Total Units: 570
Minority-Owned Units:
  African-American: 30%
  Asian-American: 10%
  Hispanic: 15%
  Native American:
  Other: 5%
North America: 16 States
Density: 75 in NJ, 55 in GA, 45 in IL

Financial/Terms:
Cash Investment: $1-35K
Total Investment: $2.8-44K
Minimum Net Worth: $3K
Fees: Franchise — $1-35K
  Royalty — 8%; Ad. — 0%
Earnings Claim Statement: No
Term of Contract (Years): 10/20
Avg. # Of Employees: 2 FT, 2 PT
Passive Ownership: Allowed
Area Develop. Agreements: No
Sub-Franchising Contracts: Yes
Expand In Territory: Yes
Space Needs: NR SF; HB

Support & Training Provided:
Site Selection Assistance: N/A
Lease Negotiation Assistance: N/A
Co-Operative Advertising: N/A

Franchisee Assoc./Member: No
Size Of Corporate Staff:
On-Going Support: A,B,C,D,G,H
Training: 5 On-Site Training Sessions.
Minority-Specific Programs: Our presentation material is provided in their native language

Specific Expansion Plans:
US: All United States

MAXCARE PROFESSIONAL CLEANING SYSTEMS
210 Town Park Dr.
Kennesaw, GA 30144
Tel: (800) 707-4332 (678) 355-4407
Fax: (678) 355-4977
E-Mail: kkaplan@maximgp.com
Web Site: www.maxcarecleaning.com
Mr. Ken Kaplan, VP Franchise Development

All surfaces floor maintenance featuring state-of-the-art equipment, such as "dust free" wook refinishing, and interior powerwashing of tile surfaces with no overspray. Many pre-established relationships with insurance companies, retailers, home improvement centers and real estate companies.

Background:
Established: 1997; 1st Franchised: 1997
Franchised Units: 85
Company-Owned Units: 0
Total Units: 85
Minority-Owned Units:
  African-American: 2
  Asian-American: 0
  Hispanic: 0
  Native American: 0
  Other: 1
North America: 34 States
Density: 11 in FL, 8 in TX, 6 in IL

Financial/Terms:
Cash Investment: $NR
Total Investment: $12.5-50K
Minimum Net Worth: $50K
Fees: Franchise — $8.7K

Royalty — 6%; Ad. — 2%
Earnings Claim Statement: No
Term of Contract (Years): 10/10
Avg. # Of Employees: 3 FT
Passive Ownership: Allowed
Area Develop. Agreements: No
Sub-Franchising Contracts: No
Expand In Territory: Yes
Space Needs: NR SF; HB

Support & Training Provided:
Site Selection Assistance: N/A
Lease Negotiation Assistance: N/A
Co-Operative Advertising: N/A
Franchisee Assoc./Member: No
Size Of Corporate Staff: 12
On-Going Support: B,C,D,E,G,H,I
Training: 10-16 Days Atlanta, GA.
Minority-Specific Programs: We will provide in-house financing of franchise fees and guarantees of equipment leases for credit worthy minority applicants who may not credit qualify through traditional sources.

Specific Expansion Plans:
US: All United States

MILLICARE ENVIRONMENTAL SERVICES
201 Lukken Industrial Dr., W.
LaGrange, GA 30240
Tel: (888) 88M-CARE (706) 880-3377
Fax: (706) 880-3279
E-Mail: millicare@millicare.com
Web Site: www.millicare.com
Mr. Pete Franetovich, Director Franchise Recruiting

Buy into experience and professionalism. MILLICARE(r) ENVIRONMENTAL SERVICES is currently seeking to select people to become franchisees worldwide. The MILLICARE (r) system includes a variety of services provided to commercial facility managers including carpet maintenance, carpet recycling, panel and upholstery cleaning, hard surface maintenance and entryway systems. Franchisees receive world-class training, sales and marketing programs from a strong, experienced global franchisor.

Background:

Established: 1984;   1st Franchised: 1996
Franchised Units: 73
Company-Owned Units: 0
Total Units: 73
Minority-Owned Units:
    African-American: 0
    Asian-American: 2
    Hispanic: 2
    Native American: 0
    Other:
North America: NR
Density: NR

Financial/Terms:

Cash Investment: $30-50K
Total Investment: $70-170K
Minimum Net Worth: $100K
Fees: Franchise — $18K
    Royalty — 6%;   Ad. — 2%
Earnings Claim Statement: No
Term of Contract (Years):   5/5
Avg. # Of Employees: 6 FT
Passive Ownership: Allowed
Area Develop. Agreements: No
Sub-Franchising Contracts: No
Expand In Territory: Poss.
Space Needs: 1,000 SF; Warehouse

Support & Training Provided:

Site Selection Assistance: No
Lease Negotiation Assistance: N/A
Co-Operative Advertising: Yes
Franchisee Assoc./Member: Yes
Size Of Corporate Staff: 20
On-Going Support: C,D,E,G,H,I
Training: 3 Days La Grange, GA; 3 Days Model Franchise Location, DE; 2 Days Franchisee's Location
Minority-Specific Programs: Although we support the objectives of the NMFI, we do not have any specific programs in place at this time.

Specific Expansion Plans:
US: All Major Metropolitan Areas

O.P.E.N. CLEANING SYSTEMS

2777 E. Camelback Rd., # 350
Phoenix, AZ 85016
Tel: (800) 777-6736 (602) 224-0440
Fax: (602) 468-3788
E-Mail: info@opencs.com
Web Site: www.opencs.com
Mr. Rich Stark, Dir. Franchising & Marketing

O.P.E.N. CLEANING SYSTEMS

O.P.E.N. has been granting commercial cleaning franchises since 1983. Our program is centered around on-going training and support in addition to guaranteed initial customers. All franchises include a customer base, equipment and advanced business training. We also offer Master Franchises on an exclusive basis for certain metropolitan areas.

Background:

Established: 1983;   1st Franchised: 1983
Franchised Units: 387
Company-Owned Units: 3
Total Units: 390
Minority-Owned Units:
    African-American: 40
    Asian-American: 25
    Hispanic: 95
    Native American: 0
North America: 3 States
Density: 187 in AZ, 125 in WA, 75 CA

Financial/Terms:

Cash Investment: $1.9-150K
Total Investment: $7-90K
Minimum Net Worth: $10-500K
Fees: Franchise — $6-45K
    Royalty — 10%;   Ad. — N/A
Earnings Claim Statement: No
Term of Contract (Years):   10/10
Avg. # Of Employees: 3+ FT
Passive Ownership: Discouraged
Area Develop. Agreements: Yes/20
Sub-Franchising Contracts: Yes
Expand In Territory: Yes
Space Needs: 3,000(master) SF; Master

Support & Training Provided:

Site Selection Assistance: No
Lease Negotiation Assistance: Yes
Co-Operative Advertising: N/A
Franchisee Assoc./Member: No
Size Of Corporate Staff: 36
On-Going Support: A,B,C,D,E,G,H,I
Training: 2 Wks. Regional Office (Janitorial); 4 Wks. Regional Off. & 3 Wks. Master's Off. (Master).

Minority-Specific Programs: Involving franchisees in local Hispanic/Black/Asian Chambers of Commerce; promoting franchisees to gain certification as minority vendors.

Specific Expansion Plans:
US: All United States

P.E.S.T. MACHINE TEAM, THE

3616 Lake Rd.
Ponca City, OK 74604-5100
Tel: (800) 654-4541 (580) 762-6614
Fax: (580) 765-4613
E-Mail: parke1@hit.net
Web Site:
Mr. Brad Parker, President

Using patented P.E.S.T. (r) Machine, treat homes for cockroaches one time with a one year guarantee. Other clients include apartment complexes (especially low rent), restaurants and health care facilities. Can also offer all other aspects of pest control.

Background:

Established: 1963;   1st Franchised: 1987
Franchised Units: 3
Company-Owned Units: 6
Total Units: 9
Minority-Owned Units:
    African-American: 0
    Asian-American: 0
    Hispanic: 0
    Native American: 0
    Other:
North America: 3 States
Density: 1 in OK, 1 in KS, 1 in CA

Financial/Terms:

Cash Investment: $N/A
Total Investment: $25-75K
Minimum Net Worth: $NR
Fees: Franchise — $25K
    Royalty — 8%/150/Mo.;   Ad. — N/A
Earnings Claim Statement: No
Term of Contract (Years):   5/5
Avg. # Of Employees: 1 FT
Passive Ownership: Discouraged
Area Develop. Agreements: No
Sub-Franchising Contracts: No
Expand In Territory: Yes
Space Needs: NR SF; HB

Support & Training Provided:

Site Selection Assistance: N/A
Lease Negotiation Assistance: N/A
Co-Operative Advertising: No
Franchisee Assoc./Member: No
Size Of Corporate Staff: 15
On-Going Support: A,a,B,C,c,D,d,E,F,G,I

185

Training: 3 Weeks in Ponca City, OK; 1 Week at Franchisee's Location.
Minority-Specific Programs: We have no programs set up currently; however, minority and disadvantaged corporations are given preferential (10% leeway) on gov't. bids and this would be great treatment for business!

Specific Expansion Plans:

US: All United States

A Total Franchise System

PROFESSIONAL POLISH

5450 East Loop, 820 South
Fort Worth, TX 76119
Tel: (800) 255-0488 (817) 572-7353
Fax: (817) 561-6193
E-Mail: info@professionalpolish.com
Web Site:
Mr. Carren Cavanaugh, President

Janitorial, lawn and building repair. Alto distributor.

Background:

Established: 1981;	1st Franchised: 1986
Franchised Units:	30
Company-Owned Units:	2
Total Units:	32
Minority-Owned Units:	
African-American:	5%
Asian-American:	0%
Hispanic:	95%
Native American:	0%
Other:	
North America:	3 States
Density:	30 in TX, 1 in NC, 1 in AL

Financial/Terms:

Cash Investment:	$6K
Total Investment:	$14.5K
Minimum Net Worth:	$6K
Fees: Franchise —	$5K
Royalty — 15%;	Ad. — 0%
Earnings Claim Statement:	Yes
Term of Contract (Years):	25/25
Avg. # Of Employees:	5 FT, 3 PT
Passive Ownership:	Not Allowed
Area Develop. Agreements:	Yes/25
Sub-Franchising Contracts:	No
Expand In Territory:	Yes
Space Needs: 1,000 SF; Office Building	

Support & Training Provided:

Site Selection Assistance:	Yes
Lease Negotiation Assistance:	Yes
Co-Operative Advertising:	Yes
Franchisee Assoc./Member:	No

Size Of Corporate Staff:	8
On-Going Support:	A,B,C,D,E,F,G,H,I
Training: 10 Days Fort Worth, TX; 30 Days Franchise City.	

Minority-Specific Programs: We put minority families into the janitorial business. We cannot find African-American families who want to be in janitorial business. We have Hispanics waiting in line. However most are not self-employable.

Specific Expansion Plans:

US: Southwest and Southeast

RACS™
INTERNATIONAL

RACS INTERNATIONAL

9302 N. Meridian St., # 355
Indianapolis, IN 46290
Tel: (800) 949-7227 (317) 844-8152
Fax: (317) 844-2270
E-Mail:
Web Site: www.racsclean.com
Mr. Chuck Morrison, President

RACS INTERNATIONAL is a name known for quality, integrity and outstanding service, with over 20 years of commercial cleaning experience. RACS is listed in Entrepreneur Magazine and ranked as one of '15 Great Franchises You Can Afford' in Black Enterprise Magazine. Currently, it is among the top 20 new franchises in the country and is listed as one of the top 20 in terms of low investment start-up costs. RACS has developed a highly-trained network of commercial cleaning franchises with excellent ratings.

Background:

Established: 1989;	1st Franchised: 1991
Franchised Units:	8
Company-Owned Units:	9
Total Units:	178
Minority-Owned Units:	
African-American:	9
Asian-American:	1
Hispanic:	2
Native American:	1
Other:	
North America:	2 States
Density:	23 in FL, 11 in IN

Financial/Terms:

Cash Investment:	$1.5-28K
Total Investment:	$4.4-43.1K

Minimum Net Worth:	$N/A
Fees: Franchise —	$3-31.5K
Royalty — 5%;	Ad. — 1%
Earnings Claim Statement:	No
Term of Contract (Years):	20/20
Avg. # Of Employees:	5 FT
Passive Ownership:	Not Allowed
Area Develop. Agreements:	Yes/10
Sub-Franchising Contracts:	Yes
Expand In Territory:	Yes
Space Needs: 1,500 SF; HB, Other	

Support & Training Provided:

Site Selection Assistance:	Yes
Lease Negotiation Assistance:	Yes
Co-Operative Advertising:	Yes
Franchisee Assoc./Member:	No
Size Of Corporate Staff:	11
On-Going Support:	A,b,C,D,G,I
Training: 18 Hours RACS Office; 12 Hours On-The-Job.	

Minority-Specific Programs: RAC'S International, Inc. does not have any programs or strategic initiatives geared to recruiting and/or assisting potential minority franchisees. As a minority franchisor, the company is sensitive to the needs of minorities, as we are in the business of

Specific Expansion Plans:

US: All United States

ServiceMASTER
Clean
The clean you expect.
The service you deserve.

SERVICEMASTER
RESIDENTIAL/COMMERCIAL

860 Ridge Lake Blvd..
Memphis, TN 38120-9792
Tel: (800) 230-2360 (901) 684-7500
Fax: (901) 684-7600
E-Mail: dcoopwco@amrescom.com
Web Site: www.ownafranchise.com
Mr. Dan Kellow, Vice President

SERVICEMASTER provides heavy-duty cleaning services to both residential and commercial customers. Services include carpet, upholstery, window, drapery, disaster restoration and janitorial cleaning that is recognized around the world. With 50 years experience, SERVICEMASTER offers state-of-the-art equipment, research and development, continuous training, cross-selling promotions with our partner companies and a strong franchise relations base.

Background:
Established: 1947;   1st Franchised: 1952
Franchised Units: 4389
Company-Owned Units: 0
Total Units: 4389
Minority-Owned Units:
    African-American:
    Asian-American:
    Hispanic:
    Native American:
    Other:
North America: 50 States, 9 Provinces
Density: 212 in IL, 168 in CA, 150 OH

Financial/Terms:
Cash Investment: $10-20K
Total Investment: $21.9-72.1K
Minimum Net Worth: $100K
Fees: Franchise — $12.5-26.5K
    Royalty — 4-10%;   Ad. — 0.5-1%
Earnings Claim Statement: No
Term of Contract (Years):   5/5
Avg. # Of Employees: 3 FT, 2 PT
Passive Ownership: Discouraged
Area Develop. Agreements: No
Sub-Franchising Contracts: Yes
Expand In Territory: Yes
Space Needs: N/A SF; N/A

Support & Training Provided:
Site Selection Assistance: No
Lease Negotiation Assistance: No
Co-Operative Advertising: Yes
Franchisee Assoc./Member: Yes/Yes
Size Of Corporate Staff: 200
On-Going Support: A,B,C,D,F,G,H,I
Training: 2 Weeks Memphis, TN; 1 Week
On Location.
Minority-Specific Programs: SERVICE
MASTER has estimated that about 5% of
franchises are owned by minorities in the
U.S. An estimated 30% of total franchises
are owned internationally. We offer minority
discount off liscense fee from 2,000 to 4,000.
In-house financing of 80% is available to
minorities. SERVICE MASTER also has
a minority on their collateral material and
video that goes out to prospective franchise
owners. This minority, Charles Horton,
is available for minority function speeches,
consultations and advisory.

Specific Expansion Plans:
US: All United States

SPARKLE WASH
26851 Richmond Rd.
Bedford Heights, OH 44146
Tel: (800) 321-0770 (216) 464-4212

Fax: (216) 464-8869
E-Mail: pfunku@en.com
Web Site: www.sparklewash.com
Mr. Hans G. Funk, President

SPARKLE WASH provides mobile
power-cleaning and restoration, providing
broad market opportunities to our
franchisees for the commercial, industrial,
residential and fleet markets. SPARKLE
WASH franchisees can also provide special
services, including wood restoration, all using
our environmentally-friendly products.

Background:
Established: 1965;   1st Franchised: 1967
Franchised Units: 171
Company-Owned Units: 1
Total Units: 172
Minority-Owned Units:
    African-American: 0
    Asian-American: 0
    Hispanic: 0
    Native American: 0
    Other:
North America: 32 States
Density: 13 in OH, 13 in PA, 8 in NY

Financial/Terms:
Cash Investment: $19.3-21.3K
Total Investment: $50K
Minimum Net Worth: $60K
Fees: Franchise — $15K
    Royalty — 3-5%;   Ad. — 0%
Earnings Claim Statement: Yes
Term of Contract (Years):   Continual
Avg. # Of Employees: 2 FT, 2 PT
Passive Ownership: Allowed
Area Develop. Agreements: No
Sub-Franchising Contracts: No
Expand In Territory: Yes
Space Needs: NR SF; N/A

Support & Training Provided:
Site Selection Assistance: N/A
Lease Negotiation Assistance: N/A
Co-Operative Advertising: No
Franchisee Assoc./Member: Yes/Yes
Size Of Corporate Staff: 15
On-Going Support: B,C,D,G,H,I
Training: 1 Week Headquarters; 3 Days
Franchisee Location; 3 Days National/
Regional Meetings.
Minority-Specific Programs: Although we
support the objectives of the NMFI, we do
not have any specific programs in place at
this time.

Specific Expansion Plans:
US: All United States

**VANGUARD CLEANING
SYSTEMS**
3 Twin Dolphin, # 295
Redwood City, CA 94065
Tel: (800) 654-6422 (650) 594-1500
Fax: (650) 591-1545
E-Mail: rlee@vanguardcleaning.com
Web Site: www.vanguardcleaning.com
Mr. Raymond C. Lee, President

VANGUARD CLEANING SYSTEMS has
been successfully franchising in the
commercial cleaning industry since 1984.
VANGUARD is currently seeking unit and
master franchisees in the United States.
A VANGUARD Master has 2 key
responsibilities: recruiting individual unit
franchisees and securing commercial cleaning
accounts for them.

Background:
Established: 1984;   1st Franchised: 1984
Franchised Units: 179
Company-Owned Units: 2
Total Units: 181
Minority-Owned Units:
    African-American: 6%
    Asian-American: 38%
    Hispanic: 29%
    Native American: 0%
    Other:
North America: 1 State
Density: 181 in CA

Financial/Terms:
Cash Investment: $37.5K(Master)
Total Investment: $100-470K(M)
Minimum Net Worth: $100K (Master)
Fees: Franchise — $75K (Master)
    Royalty — 4% (Master); Ad. — 1.5%(M)
Earnings Claim Statement: No
Term of Contract (Years):   20/10
Avg. # Of Employees: 5 Ft, 2 PT
Passive Ownership: Discouraged

Area Develop. Agreements: No
Sub-Franchising Contracts: Yes
Expand In Territory: Yes
Space Needs: N/A SF; N/A

Support & Training Provided:
Site Selection Assistance: N/A
Lease Negotiation Assistance: N/A
Co-Operative Advertising: N/A
Franchisee Assoc./Member: No
Size Of Corporate Staff: 14
On-Going Support: A,b,C,D,G,I
Training: 3 Weeks+ Redwood City, CA.
Minority-Specific Programs: Although we support the objectives of the NMFI, we do not have any specific programs in place at this time.

Specific Expansion Plans:
US: All United States

WINDOW BUTLER
6355 E. Kemper Rd., # 250
Cincinnati, OH 45241
Tel: (800) 808-6470 (513) 489-4000
Fax: (513) 469-2226
E-Mail: wbutler@one.net
Web Site: www.windowbutler.com
Mr. Bill Blair, President

Home services are in demand! A WINDOW BUTLER franchise provides busy homeowners with window cleaning and all the maintenance services they need. It is a business built around managing people, not doing the work yourself. Our complete package was developed by the founders of 2 highly successful service-related franchises with over 450 units collectively.

Background:
Established: 1997;   1st Franchised: 1997
Franchised Units: 19
Company-Owned Units: 0
Total Units: 19
Minority-Owned Units:
    African-American: 0

Asian-American: 0
Hispanic: 0
Native American: 2
Other:
North America: 10 States
Density: 4 in OH, 2 in KS, 2 in TN

Financial/Terms:
Cash Investment: $10-20K
Total Investment: $17.5-35K
Minimum Net Worth: $10K
Fees: Franchise — $7.9-22.9K
    Royalty — 6%;   Ad. — 3%
Earnings Claim Statement: No
Term of Contract (Years): 10/10/10
Avg. # Of Employees: 3 FT
Passive Ownership: Discouraged
Area Develop. Agreements: No
Sub-Franchising Contracts: No
Expand In Territory: No
Space Needs: N/A SF; HB

Support & Training Provided:
Site Selection Assistance: Yes
Lease Negotiation Assistance: N/A
Co-Operative Advertising: N/A
Franchisee Assoc./Member: No
Size Of Corporate Staff: 5
On-Going Support: C,D,E,G,H,I
Training: 1 Week Cincinnati, OH.
Minority-Specific Programs: We do finance up to 50% of the franchise fee.

Specific Expansion Plans:
US: All United States

WINDOW GANG
6509 Aviation Pkwy.
Morrisville, NC 27560
Tel: (800) 849-2308 (252) 728-7444
Fax: (252) 728-4246
E-Mail: gang@mail.clis.com
Web Site: www.windowgang.com
Mr. Tim McCullen, President

Residential/commercial window, gutter, pressure and blind cleaning company. Large, extensive markets

Background:
Established: 1986;   1st Franchised: 1996
Franchised Units: 42
Company-Owned Units: 10
Total Units: 52
Minority-Owned Units:
    African-American:
    Asian-American:
    Hispanic: 5%
    Native American:

North America: 4
Density: 34 in NC, 14 in SC, 4 in VA

Financial/Terms:
Cash Investment: $50K
Total Investment: $50K
Minimum Net Worth: $50K
Fees: Franchise — $20K
    Royalty — 6%;   Ad. — 0%
Earnings Claim Statement: No
Term of Contract (Years): 10/10
Avg. # Of Employees: 4 FT
Passive Ownership: Discouraged
Area Develop. Agreements: NR
Sub-Franchising Contracts: No
Expand In Territory: Yes
Space Needs: NR SF; HB, Warehouse

Support & Training Provided:
Site Selection Assistance: Yes
Lease Negotiation Assistance: Yes
Co-Operative Advertising: No
Franchisee Assoc./Member: No
Size Of Corporate Staff:
On-Going Support: B,C,D,e,G,H,I
Training: 5-10 Days Morrisville, NC.
Minority-Specific Programs: Although we support the objectives of the NMFI, we do not have any specific programs in place at this time.

Specific Expansion Plans:
US: All United States

WINDOW GENIE
700 W. Pete Rose Way, Longworth Hall
Cincinnati, OH 45203
Tel: (800) 700-0022 (513) 241-8443
Fax: (513) 412-7760
E-Mail: squegeepro@aol.com
Web Site: www.windowgenie.com
Mr. Richard Nonelle, President

Residential window cleaning and pressure washing business.

Background:
Established: 1994;   1st Franchised: 1998
Franchised Units: 13
Company-Owned Units: 1
Total Units: 14
Minority-Owned Units:
    African-American: 0
    Asian-American: 0
    Hispanic: 0

Native American:	0
Other:	0
North America:	6 States
Density:	6 in OH, 1 in KY, 1 in PA

Financial/Terms:

Cash Investment:	$10-15K
Total Investment:	$28-42K
Minimum Net Worth:	$Varies
Fees: Franchise —	$15K
Royalty — 6%;	Ad. — 1%
Earnings Claim Statement:	No
Term of Contract (Years):	10/5
Avg. # Of Employees:	2 FT, 2 PT
Passive Ownership:	Discouraged
Area Develop. Agreements:	No
Sub-Franchising Contracts:	No
Expand In Territory:	Yes
Space Needs: N/A SF; N/A	

Support & Training Provided:

Site Selection Assistance:	N/A
Lease Negotiation Assistance:	N/A
Co-Operative Advertising:	N/A
Franchisee Assoc./Member:	No
Size Of Corporate Staff:	3
On-Going Support:	B,C,D,E,F,G,H,I

Training: 5 Days Corporate, Cincinnati, OH; 5 Days On-Site.

Minority-Specific Programs: Although we do not have any specific programs in place, as a new franchisee our main concern is the attraction of truly qualified candidates, regardless of race. We are currently working closely with several minorities who fit the exact profile we look for. For the time being we will continue our general advertising, but give aggressive attention to whomever qualifies.

Specific Expansion Plans:

US:	All United States

HEMORRHOID CLINIC, THE

P. O. Box 12488
Oakland, CA 94604
Tel: (510) 839-5471
Fax: (510) 547-3245
E-Mail:
Web Site:
Dr. Bobby C. Anning, President

Highly efficient and automated out-patient clinics for hemorrhoid and related rectal procedures. Proprietary laser techniques developed by Dr. Anning insure painless, 20-minute procedure and minimal recuperative discomfort. Lucrative business that takes advantage of the fact that 1 in 8 adults requires rectal surgery. 12 week training at headquarters clinic. All procedures on video. Excellent opportunity to work with the best!

Background:
Established: 1987; 1st Franchised: 1988
Franchised Units: 32
Company-Owned Units: 1
Total Units: 33
Minority-Owned Units:
  African-American: 2
  Asian-American: 2
  Hispanic: 1
  Native American: 0
  Other:
North America: 10 States, 2 Provinces
Density: 5 in OH, 2 in KY, 2 in MS

Financial/Terms:
Cash Investment: $80-125K
Total Investment: $140-225K
Minimum Net Worth: $NR
Fees: Franchise — $25K
  Royalty — 6%; Ad. — 1%

Earnings Claim Statement: Yes
Term of Contract (Years): 10/10
Avg. # Of Employees: 3 FT, 4 PT
Passive Ownership: Not Allowed
Area Develop. Agreements: Yes/10
Sub-Franchising Contracts: Yes
Expand In Territory: Yes
Space Needs: 1,500-2,000 SF; FS, SF

Support & Training Provided:
Site Selection Assistance: Yes
Lease Negotiation Assistance: Yes
Co-Operative Advertising: Yes
Franchisee Assoc./Member: NR
Size Of Corporate Staff: 12
On-Going Support: C,D,E,G,H,I
Training: 12 Weeks Anning Clinic; 3 Weeks On-Site; On-Going Video Training Procedures.
Minority-Specific Programs: Although we support the objectives of the NMFI, we do not have any specific programs in place at this time.

Specific Expansion Plans:
US: All United States

STERLING OPTICAL

1500 Hempstead Turnpike
East Meadow, NY 11554
Tel: (800) 332-6302 (516) 390-2100
Fax: (516) 390-2111
E-Mail: sterlopt@aol.com
Web Site: www.sterlingoptical.net
Mr. Jerry Darnel, Dir. Franchise Dev.

STERLING OPTICAL offers full-service, retail optical franchises to qualified individuals. Opportunities include the opening of a new location, the conversion of an existing company store to a franchise or the conversion of an independent optical location to a franchised STERLING OPTICAL CENTER.

Background:
Established: 1914; 1st Franchised: 1992
Franchised Units: 270
Company-Owned Units: 47
Total Units: 317
Minority-Owned Units:
  African-American: 4
  Asian-American: 3
  Hispanic: 3
  Native American: 0
  Other:
North America: 33 States, 1 Province
Density: NY, CA, WI

Financial/Terms:
Cash Investment: $50K
Total Investment: $50-172K
Minimum Net Worth: $250K
Fees: Franchise — $8-15K
  Royalty — 8%; Ad. — 6%
Earnings Claim Statement: No
Term of Contract (Years): 10
Avg. # Of Employees: 5 FT, 5 PT
Passive Ownership: Discouraged
Area Develop. Agreements: Yes
Sub-Franchising Contracts: No
Expand In Territory: Yes
Space Needs: 1,200-1,400 SF; FS, SF, SC, RM, C-Store/Serv.

Support & Training Provided:
Site Selection Assistance: Yes

Lease Negotiation Assistance: Yes
Co-Operative Advertising: Yes
Franchisee Assoc./Member: No
Size Of Corporate Staff: 17
On-Going Support: C,D,E,G,H,I
Training: 5 Days Headquarters; 3 Weeks Training Store; 1 Week On-Site Opening.
Minority-Specific Programs: LISC, CDC -- working areas with CDCS.

Specific Expansion Plans:
US: All United States

TOTAL MEDICAL COMPLIANCE

633 NE 167th St., # 1002
North Miami, FL 33169
Tel: (800) 840-6742 (305) 690-9890
Fax: (305) 690-9992
E-Mail: tmcfran@aol.com
Web Site: www.centercourt.com/tmc
Mr. Chuck Weiss, President

TOTAL MEDICAL COMPLIANCE franchisees work in the growing health care industry, providing consultant services to health care providers such as doctors, dentists and clinics. Every health care provider must comply with federal and state health related laws. The TMC system allows you to provide this consulting service even if you do not have a medical background.

Background:
Established: 1993; 1st Franchised: 1995
Franchised Units: 5
Company-Owned Units: 2
Total Units: 7
Minority-Owned Units:
 African-American:
 Asian-American:
 Hispanic:
 Native American:
 Other:
North America: 7 States
Density: 4 in FL, 2 in TX, 1 in NC

Financial/Terms:
Cash Investment: $35-80K
Total Investment: $50-100K
Minimum Net Worth: $200K
Fees: Franchise — $35-80K
 Royalty — 2%; Ad. — 0.25%
Earnings Claim Statement: Yes
Term of Contract (Years): 5/5
Avg. # Of Employees: 2 FT, 1 PT
Passive Ownership: Allowed
Area Develop. Agreements: No
Sub-Franchising Contracts: No
Expand In Territory: Yes

Space Needs: NR SF; N/A
Support & Training Provided:
Site Selection Assistance: N/A
Lease Negotiation Assistance: N/A
Co-Operative Advertising: N/A
Franchisee Assoc./Member: No
Size Of Corporate Staff: 5
On-Going Support: b,C,D,G,h,I
Training: 1 Week Home Office; 1 Week Franchisee Territory.
Minority-Specific Programs: Although we support the objectives of the NMFI, we do not have any specific programs in place at this time.

Specific Expansion Plans:
US: All United States

WOMEN'S HEALTH BOUTIQUE

12715 Telge Rd.
Cypress, TX 77429
Tel: (888) 280-2053 (281) 256-4100
Fax: (281) 256-4178
E-Mail: w-h-bsales@w-h-b.com
Web Site: www.w-h-b.com
Mr. Bob Dolan, VP Franchise Sales

One-stop shopping for women with special needs in a tasteful environment, attended by knowledgeable, highly trained, compassionate saleswomen. Real products and services for post breast surgery, pre- and post-natal, post-mastectomy, compression therapy, hair loss, incontinence, skin care, wigs and turbans and personal care.

Background:
Established: 1988; 1st Franchised: 1993
Franchised Units: 15
Company-Owned Units: 3
Total Units: 18
Minority-Owned Units:
 African-American:
 Asian-American:
 Hispanic:
 Native American:
 Other:
North America: 10 States
Density: 5 in TX, 3 in MI, 2 in GA
Financial/Terms:
Cash Investment: $55K
Total Investment: $214.7-234.7K

Minimum Net Worth: $200K
Fees: Franchise — $20.8K
 Royalty — 4-7%; Ad. — 0%
Earnings Claim Statement: No
Term of Contract (Years): 10/10
Avg. # Of Employees: 2-3 FT
Passive Ownership: Not Allowed
Area Develop. Agreements: No
Sub-Franchising Contracts: No
Expand In Territory: Yes
Space Needs: 1,500 SF; SC, Medical Center

Support & Training Provided:
Site Selection Assistance: Yes
Lease Negotiation Assistance: Yes
Co-Operative Advertising: No
Franchisee Assoc./Member: Yes/Yes
Size Of Corporate Staff: NR
On-Going Support: C,D,E,G,H,I
Training: Approximately 5 Weeks.
Minority-Specific Programs: Interest-free financing of the franchise fee offered to all new owners. Prospective owners are eligible for streamlined and expedited SBA loan processing through our inclusion in the franchise registry. See www.franchiseregistry.com for more information.

Specific Expansion Plans:
US: All United States

AIM MAIL CENTERS

20381 Lake Forest Dr., # B-2
Lake Forest, CA 92630
Tel: (800) 669-4246 (949) 837-4151
Fax: (949) 837-4537
E-Mail: mherrera@aimmailcenters.com
Web Site: www.aimmailcenters.com
Mr. Michael R. Herrera, VP of Franchise
Development

AIM MAIL CENTERS take care of all
business service needs. AIM's services
include renting mailboxes, buying stamps,
sending faxes, notary, making copies and
passport photos. AIM is also an authorized
UPS and FedEx Shipping Outlet. It's like
having a post office, office supply store, gift
shop, and copy shop all rolled into one. We
are so confident of our franchise program
that we offer a money-back guarantee.

Background:
Established: 1985;   1st Franchised: 1989
Franchised Units: 58
Company-Owned Units: 0
Total Units: 58
Minority-Owned Units:
   African-American:
   Asian-American:
   Hispanic:
   Native American:

North America: 7 States
Density: 46 in CA, 2 in WA, 2 in AZ

Financial/Terms:
Cash Investment: $30K
Total Investment: $75-95K
Minimum Net Worth: $125K
Fees: Franchise — $23.9K
   Royalty — 5%;   Ad. — 2%
Earnings Claim Statement: Yes
Term of Contract (Years):   15
Avg. # Of Employees: 1 FT, 2 PT
Passive Ownership: Discouraged
Area Develop. Agreements: Yes/5
Sub-Franchising Contracts: No
Expand In Territory: Yes
Space Needs: 1,000 SF; SF, SC, Anchored
Center

Support & Training Provided:
Site Selection Assistance: Yes
Lease Negotiation Assistance: Yes
Co-Operative Advertising: Yes
Franchisee Assoc./Member: Yes
Size Of Corporate Staff: 10
On-Going Support: C,D,E,G,H,I
Training: 2 Weeks Corporate Headquarters;
3 Days In Store.
Minority-Specific Programs: Although we
support the objectives of the NMFI, we do
not have any specific programs in place at
this time.

Specific Expansion Plans:
US: All United States

CRATERS & FREIGHTERS

7000 E. 47th Ave. Dr., # 100
Denver, CO 80216

Tel: (800) 949-9931 (303) 399-8190
Fax: (303) 393-7644
E-Mail:
Franchising@CratersAndFreighters.com
Web Site: www.CratersAndFreighters.com
Mr. Bob Molnar, Dir. of Franchise
Development

As specialty freight handlers, CRATERS &
FREIGHTERS is the best-niched concept
in the industry. We're the exclusive source
for reliable, affordable specialty shipping
services for pieces that are too big for UPS
and too small for movers. We provide high-
demand crating and shipping with iron-clad
insurance to an up-scale clientele. Serve your
large territory from low overhead warehouse
space.

Background:
Established: 1990;   1st Franchised: 1991
Franchised Units: 58
Company-Owned Units: 0
Total Units: 58
Minority-Owned Units:
   African-American: 1
   Asian-American: 0
   Hispanic: 0
   Native American: 0
   Other: 1
North America: 29 States
Density: 6 in CA, 5 in FL, 5 in TX

Financial/Terms:
Cash Investment: $NR
Total Investment: $54-77K

Minimum Net Worth:	$100K
Fees: Franchise —	$24.8K
Royalty — 5%;	Ad. — 1%
Earnings Claim Statement:	No
Term of Contract (Years):	10/10
Avg. # Of Employees:	3 FT
Passive Ownership:	Discouraged
Area Develop. Agreements:	No
Sub-Franchising Contracts:	No
Expand In Territory:	Yes
Space Needs: 1,800-2,000 SF; Warehouse	

Support & Training Provided:

Site Selection Assistance:	Yes
Lease Negotiation Assistance:	Yes
Co-Operative Advertising:	Yes
Franchisee Assoc./Member:	Yes/No
Size Of Corporate Staff:	12
On-Going Support:	A,B,C,D,E,G,h,I

Training: 7 Days Home Office in Denver, CO.

Minority-Specific Programs: Standard operating procedure applies.

Specific Expansion Plans:

US:	All United States

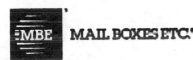

MAIL BOXES ETC.

6060 Cornerstone Court West
San Diego, CA 92121-3795
Tel: (800) 280-9229 (858) 455-8800
Fax: (858) 546-7488
E-Mail: fransale@mbe.com
Web Site: www.mbe.com
Mr. John Dring, Dir. Domestic Franchise Sales

MAIL BOXES ETC. (MBE) is the world's largest franchisor of independently-owned and operated business, communication and postal service centers. MBE Centers serve a large customer group of small and home-based businesses and general consumers. Products and services include: mailbox services, copies, faxes, U. S. Postal services, shipping (FedEx, UPS, etc.), freight shipping, packaging, office and mailing supplies, printing services and more.

Background:

Established: 1980;	1st Franchised: 1980
Franchised Units:	4074
Company-Owned Units:	0
Total Units:	4074
Minority-Owned Units:	

African-American:	
Asian-American:	
Hispanic:	
Native American:	
Other:	
North America:	50 States,10 Provinces
Density:	505 in CA, 263 in FL, 166 TX

Financial/Terms:

Cash Investment:	$45K
Total Investment:	$118-199K
Minimum Net Worth:	$150K
Fees: Franchise —	$29.9K
Royalty — 5%;	Ad. — 3.5%
Earnings Claim Statement:	No
Term of Contract (Years):	10/10
Avg. # Of Employees:	2 Minimum
Passive Ownership:	Allowed
Area Develop. Agreements:	Yes/10
Sub-Franchising Contracts:	No
Expand In Territory:	Yes
Space Needs: 1,200-1,800 SF; FS, SF, SC, RM, Non-Tradit.	

Support & Training Provided:

Site Selection Assistance:	No
Lease Negotiation Assistance:	Yes
Co-Operative Advertising:	Yes
Franchisee Assoc./Member:	Yes/Yes
Size Of Corporate Staff:	260
On-Going Support:	B,C,D,E,G,H,I

Training: 5 Days Local Market; 2 Weeks San Diego, CA; 5 Days Local Market.

Minority-Specific Programs: Although we support the objectives of the NMFI, we do not have any specific programs in place at this time.

Specific Expansion Plans:

US:	All United States

PACKAGING AND SHIPPING SPECIALIST

5211 85th St., # 104
Lubbock, TX 79424
Tel: (800) 877-8884 (806) 794-9996
Fax: (806) 794-9997

E-Mail: packship@arn.net
Web Site: www.packship.com
Mr. Mike Gallagher, President

We are the only company that does not charge royalties and one of the most affordable and knowledgable companies in this industry. A complete copy center and mail center with an array of related retail items for the consumer.

Background:

Established: 1981;	1st Franchised: 1988
Franchised Units:	471
Company-Owned Units:	6
Total Units:	477
Minority-Owned Units:	
African-American:	25%
Asian-American:	10%
Hispanic:	15%
Native American:	0%
Other:	
North America:	37 States,10 Provinces
Density:	75 in TX, 20 in NY, 12 in IL

Financial/Terms:

Cash Investment:	$10-20K
Total Investment:	$56-85K
Minimum Net Worth:	$100K
Fees: Franchise —	$24.5K
Royalty — 0%;	Ad. — 0%
Earnings Claim Statement:	No
Term of Contract (Years):	5/5
Avg. # Of Employees:	2 FT, 2 PT
Passive Ownership:	Allowed
Area Develop. Agreements:	Yes/10
Sub-Franchising Contracts:	No
Expand In Territory:	Yes
Space Needs: 1,000-2,000 SF; SF, SC	

Support & Training Provided:

Site Selection Assistance:	Yes
Lease Negotiation Assistance:	Yes
Co-Operative Advertising:	No
Franchisee Assoc./Member:	No
Size Of Corporate Staff:	20
On-Going Support:	B,C,D,E,G,h,I

Training: 10-14 Days in Raleigh, NC; 10-14 in Dallas, TX.

Minority-Specific Programs: Assistance in preparing loan documents; deferment of franchise fees; assistance in financing.

Specific Expansion Plans:

US:	All United States

PAK MAIL

7173 S. Havana St., # 600
Englewood, CO 80112
Tel: (800) 833-2821 (303) 957-1000
Fax: (800) 336-7363

E-Mail: sales@pakmail.com
Web Site: www.pakmail.com
Mr. Chuck Prentner, Licensing Manager

PAK MAIL is a convenient center for packaging, shipping and business support services, offering both residential and commercial customers air, ground, and ocean carriers, custom packaging and crating, private mailbox rental, mail services, packaging and moving supplies, copy and fax service and internet access and related services. We ship anything, anywhere.

Background:

Established: 1983;	1st Franchised: 1984
Franchised Units:	400
Company-Owned Units:	0
Total Units:	400
Minority-Owned Units:	
African-American:	15
Asian-American:	10
Hispanic:	45
Native American:	2
Other:	
North America:	42 States
Density:	91 in FL, 41 in GA, 22 in CA

Financial/Terms:

Cash Investment:	$30-108K
Total Investment:	$70-115K
Minimum Net Worth:	$100K
Fees: Franchise —	$28K
Royalty — 5% Sliding;	Ad. — 2%
Earnings Claim Statement:	Yes
Term of Contract (Years):	10/10
Avg. # Of Employees:	1 FT, 1 PT
Passive Ownership:	Discouraged
Area Develop. Agreements:	Yes/5
Sub-Franchising Contracts:	No
Expand In Territory:	Yes
Space Needs: 1,200 SF; SC	

Support & Training Provided:

Site Selection Assistance:	Yes
Lease Negotiation Assistance:	Yes
Co-Operative Advertising:	Yes
Franchisee Assoc./Member:	Yes/Yes
Size Of Corporate Staff:	22
On-Going Support:	B,C,D,E,F,G,H,I

Training: 10 Days in Englewood, CO; 3 Days in Existing Center; 3 Days In New Center at Opening.
Minority-Specific Programs: Although we support the objectives of the NMFI, we do not have any specific programs in place at this time.

Specific Expansion Plans:

US:	All United States

POSTNET POSTAL & BUSINESS CENTERS

2501 N. Green Valley Pkwy., # 101
Henderson, NV 89014
Tel: (800) 841-7171 (702) 792-7100
Fax: (702) 792-7115
E-Mail: info@postnet.net
Web Site: www.postnet.net
Mr. Ken Ross, VP Global Franchise Dev't.

Become a POSTNET Pro! POSTNET's franchise opportunity offers a proven method of marketing products and services, which consumers need on a daily basis. The opportunity to get in on the ground floor of a rapidly expanding business is a rarity -- PostNet's domestic and international franchisees have the opportunity to tap into the world market, offering personal and business services including UPS and FedEx Shipping, B/W and color copy services, private mail boxes, fax, printing and much more.

Background:

Established: 1985;	1st Franchised: 1993
Franchised Units:	632
Company-Owned Units:	0
Total Units:	632
Minority-Owned Units:	
African-American:	
Asian-American:	
Hispanic:	
Native American:	
North America:	38 States, 4 Provinces
Density:	17 in CA, 14 in IL, 11 in FL

Financial/Terms:

Cash Investment:	$35-50K
Total Investment:	$91-122K
Minimum Net Worth:	$150K
Fees: Franchise —	$26.9K
Royalty — 4%;	Ad. — 1%
Earnings Claim Statement:	No
Term of Contract (Years):	10/10
Avg. # Of Employees:	2 FT, 1 PT
Passive Ownership:	Not Allowed
Area Develop. Agreements:	Yes/10
Sub-Franchising Contracts:	No
Expand In Territory:	Yes
Space Needs: 1,200 SF; SC	

Support & Training Provided:

Site Selection Assistance:	Yes
Lease Negotiation Assistance:	Yes
Co-Operative Advertising:	No
Franchisee Assoc./Member:	Yes
Size Of Corporate Staff:	30
On-Going Support:	C,D,E,G,H,I

Training: 1 Week Henderson, NV; 1 Week at Store Opening; 2-3 Days Follow-Up.
Minority-Specific Programs: Although we support the objectives of the NMFI, we do not have any specific programs in place at this time.

Specific Expansion Plans:

US:	All United States

AMERICAN WHOLESALE THERMOGRAPHERS / AWT

12715 Telge Rd.
Cypress, TX 77429 0777
Tel: (888) 280-2053 (281) 256-4100
Fax: (281) 256-4178
E-Mail: awtsales@awt.com
Web Site: www.awt.com
Mr. Bob Dolan, VP Franchise Sales

Wholesale printing, providing next-day raised-letter printed materials to retail printers, copy centers and business service centers. Products include quality business cards, stationery, announcements and invitations.

Background:
Established: 1980;   1st Franchised: 1981
Franchised Units: 20
Company-Owned Units: 0
Total Units: 20
Minority-Owned Units:
  African-American:
  Asian-American:
  Hispanic:
  Native American:
  Other:
North America: 14 States, 2 Provinces
Density: 3 in ON, 2 in OK, 2 in CA

Financial/Terms:
Cash Investment: $90K
Total Investment: $340-352K
Minimum Net Worth: $250K
Fees: Franchise — $30K
  Royalty — 5%;   Ad. — NR

Earnings Claim Statement: Yes
Term of Contract (Years):   25/25
Avg. # Of Employees: 9 FT, 4 PT
Passive Ownership: Not Allowed
Area Develop. Agreements: No
Sub-Franchising Contracts: No
Expand In Territory: Yes
Space Needs: 2,500-3,000 SF; Business Park, Warehouse

Support & Training Provided:
Site Selection Assistance: Yes
Lease Negotiation Assistance: Yes
Co-Operative Advertising: Yes
Franchisee Assoc./Member: Yes/Yes
Size Of Corporate Staff: NR
On-Going Support: B,C,D,E,G,h,I
Training: 2 Weeks Headquarters; 2 Weeks Operating Store; 2 Weeks On-Site.
Minority-Specific Programs: Interest-free financing of the franchise fee offered to all new owners. Prospective owners are eligible for streamlined and expedited SBA loan processing through our inclusion in the franchise registry. See www.franchiseregistry.com for more information.

Specific Expansion Plans:
US: All United States

BCT
3000 N.E. 30th Place, 5th Floor
Fort Lauderdale, FL 33306
Tel: (800) 627-9998 (954) 563-1224
Fax: (954) 565-0742

E-Mail: rsa@herald.infi.net
Web Site: www.bct-net.com
Mr. Robert S. Anderson, Franchise Development Director

Join the 24-year old industry-leading wholesale, manufacturing franchise with the competitive advantage. We are recession-resistant, high-volume, quick-turn around, wholesale only manufacturers, specializing in next-day delivery of thermographed and offset-printed products and rubber stamps to retail printers, mailing centers, office supply stores and other retailers. Comprehensive training, excellent support and nationally praised.

Background:
Established: 1975;   1st Franchised: 1977
Franchised Units: 92
Company-Owned Units: 1
Total Units: 93
Minority-Owned Units:
  African-American: 0
  Asian-American: 1
  Hispanic: 4
  Native American: 0
  Other: 2
North America: 38 States, 4 Provinces
Density: 16 in CA, 7 in FL, 5 in NY

Financial/Terms:
Cash Investment: $115-151K
Total Investment: $354-441K
Minimum Net Worth: $250K
Fees: Franchise — $35K
  Royalty — 6%;   Ad. — N/A
Earnings Claim Statement: No
Term of Contract (Years):   25/10
Avg. # Of Employees: 10 FT, 6 PT
Passive Ownership: Not Allowed

Area Develop. Agreements: No
Sub-Franchising Contracts: No
Expand In Territory: No
Space Needs: 4,000+ SF; FS, SC, Commercial Park

Support & Training Provided:
Site Selection Assistance: Yes
Lease Negotiation Assistance: Yes
Co-Operative Advertising: No
Franchisee Assoc./Member: Yes
Size Of Corporate Staff: 32
On-Going Support: a,B,C,d,E,G,h,I
Training: 2 Weeks Ft. Lauderdale, FL; 1 Week Pre-Opening at New-Site; 2 Weeks After and Ongoing.
Minority-Specific Programs: We have no special programs to recruit minorities. Many of our better operations are headed by women or jointly owned by women. Since our capital requirements are high, it is difficult to obtain financing for anyone with a net worth of less than $250,000 - which leaves out lots of people.

Specific Expansion Plans:
US: NJ, NE

COPY CLUB

12715 Telge Rd.
Cypress, TX 77429-0777
Tel: (888) 280-2053 (281) 256-4100
Fax: (281) 256-4178
E-Mail: ccsales@copyclub.com
Web Site: www.copyclub.com
Mr. Bob Dolan, VP Franchise Sales

High-visibility, high-traffic digital imaging and copying and business/communications center, open 24 hours a day. Dynamic retail environment. Also offering self-service copying and computer rental.

Background:
Established: 1992; 1st Franchised: 1994
Franchised Units: 14
Company-Owned Units: 0
Total Units: 14
Minority-Owned Units:
  African-American:
  Asian-American:
  Hispanic:
  Native American:
  Other:

North America: 4 States
Density: TX, CA, GA

Financial/Terms:
Cash Investment: $95K
Total Investment: $361.6-495.4K
Minimum Net Worth: $500K
Fees: Franchise — $30K
  Royalty — 7%; Ad. — 0%
Earnings Claim Statement: Yes
Term of Contract (Years): 25/25
Avg. # Of Employees: 8 FT, 5 PT
Passive Ownership: Allowed
Area Develop. Agreements: Yes/10
Sub-Franchising Contracts: Yes
Expand In Territory: Yes
Space Needs: 4,000 SF; FS

Support & Training Provided:
Site Selection Assistance: Yes
Lease Negotiation Assistance: Yes
Co-Operative Advertising: No
Franchisee Assoc./Member: Yes/Yes
Size Of Corporate Staff: NR
On-Going Support: C,D,E,G,h,I
Training: 3 Weeks in Classroom; 2 Weeks On-Site.
Minority-Specific Programs: Interest-free financing of the franchise fee offered to all new owners. Prospective owners are eligible for streamlined and expedited SBA loan processing through our inclusion in the franchise registry. See www.franchiseregistry.com for more information.

Specific Expansion Plans:
US: All United States

FRANKLIN'S SYSTEMS

12715 Telge Rd.
Cypress, TX 77429
Tel: (888) 280-2053 (281) 256-4100
Fax: (281) 256-4178
E-Mail: fgsales@franklin's-printing.com
Web Site: www.franklins-printing.com
Mr. Bob Dolan, VP Franchise Sales

Part of the ICED family of franchises, now in our 30th year, with over 1,000 franchises in 21 countries. We maintain a position of leadership in our traditional printing and digital publishing, including Webpage design and maintenance, as well as legendary outside sales consultant training. Your corporate management skills are transferable in our business-to-business environment.

Background:
Established: 1971; 1st Franchised: 1977
Franchised Units: 66
Company-Owned Units: 0
Total Units: 66
Minority-Owned Units:
  African-American:
  Asian-American:
  Hispanic:
  Native American:
North America: 14 States
Density: 22 in GA, 11 in FL, 7 in TN

Financial/Terms:
Cash Investment: $84K
Total Investment: $296.4-359.8K
Minimum Net Worth: $250K
Fees: Franchise — $25K
  Royalty — 4-8%; Ad. — 0%
Earnings Claim Statement: No
Term of Contract (Years): 25/25
Avg. # Of Employees: 3-7 FT, 1 PT
Passive Ownership: Not Allowed
Area Develop. Agreements: No
Sub-Franchising Contracts: No
Expand In Territory: Yes
Space Needs: 1,500-2,000 SF; SC, SF, Business Park

Support & Training Provided:
Site Selection Assistance: Yes
Lease Negotiation Assistance: Yes
Co-Operative Advertising: No
Franchisee Assoc./Member: Yes/Yes
Size Of Corporate Staff: NR
On-Going Support: B,C,D,E,G,h,I
Training: 5 Weeks Training. (Lodging and Airfare Included.)
Minority-Specific Programs: Interest-free financing of the franchise fee offered to all new owners. Prospective owners are eligible for streamlined and expedited SBA loan processing through our inclusion in the franchise registry. See www.franchiseregistry.com for more information.

Specific Expansion Plans:
US: All United States

INK WELL, THE

12715 Telge Rd.
Cypress, TX 77429
Tel: (888) 280-2053 (281) 256-4100
Fax: (281) 256-4178
E-Mail: iwsales@iwa.com
Web Site: www.iwa.com
Mr. Bob Dolan, VP Franchise Sales

We're serious about printing.

THE INK WELL printing centers are positioned to provide high-quality, full-service printing and copying, typesetting and design services to the business community.

Background:

Established: 1972;   1st Franchised: 1981
Franchised Units: 40
Company-Owned Units: 0
Total Units: 40
Minority-Owned Units:
 African-American:
 Asian-American:
 Hispanic:
 Native American:
North America: 8 States
Density: 24 in OH, 5 in IL, 3 in FL

Financial/Terms:

Cash Investment: $84K
Total Investment: $296.4-357.8K
Minimum Net Worth: $250K
Fees: Franchise — $25K
 Royalty — 4-6%;   Ad. — 2%
Earnings Claim Statement: No
Term of Contract (Years):   25/25
Avg. # Of Employees: 4-6 FT, 1 PT
Passive Ownership: Not Allowed
Area Develop. Agreements: No
Sub-Franchising Contracts: No
Expand In Territory: Yes
Space Needs: 1,500-2,000 SF; SC, SC, Business Park

Support & Training Provided:

Site Selection Assistance: Yes
Lease Negotiation Assistance: Yes
Co-Operative Advertising: Yes
Franchisee Assoc./Member: Yes/Yes
Size Of Corporate Staff: NR
On-Going Support: B,C,D,E,G,h,I
Training: 5 Weeks Headquarters; 1 Week In Field; 8 Days On-Site.
Minority-Specific Programs: Interest-free financing of the franchise fee offered to all new owners. Prospective owners are eligible for streamlined and expedited SBA loan processing through our inclusion in the franchise registry. See www.franchiseregistry.com for more information.

Specific Expansion Plans:

US: All United States

KWIK-KOPY PRINTING

12715 Telge Rd.
Cypress, TX 77429
Tel: (888) 280-2053 (281) 256-4100
Fax: (281) 256-4178
E-Mail: kksales@kwikkopy.com
Web Site: www.kwikkopy.com
Mr. Bob Dolan, VP Franchise Sales

Part of the ICED family of franchises, now in our 30th year, with over 1,000 franchises in 21 countries. As a member of the ICED family of franchises, we maintain a position of leadership with our traditional printing and digital publishing, including Website design and maintenance, as well as legendary outside sales consultant training. Your corporate management skills are transferable in our business-to-business environment.

Background:

Established: 1967;   1st Franchised: 1967
Franchised Units: 773
Company-Owned Units: 0
Total Units: 773
Minority-Owned Units:
 African-American:
 Asian-American:
 Hispanic:
 Native American:
 Other:
North America: 39 States, 6 Provinces
Density: 147 in TX, 32 in IL, 27 CA

Financial/Terms:

Cash Investment: $84K
Total Investment: $296.4-357.8K
Minimum Net Worth: $250K
Fees: Franchise — $25K
 Royalty — 4-8%;   Ad. — 0%
Earnings Claim Statement: Yes
Term of Contract (Years):   25/25
Avg. # Of Employees: 3-7 FT, 1 PT
Passive Ownership: Not Allowed
Area Develop. Agreements: No
Sub-Franchising Contracts: No
Expand In Territory: Yes
Space Needs: 1,500-2,000 SF; SC, SF, Business Park

Support & Training Provided:

Site Selection Assistance: Yes
Lease Negotiation Assistance: Yes
Co-Operative Advertising: No
Franchisee Assoc./Member: Yes/Yes
Size Of Corporate Staff: NR
On-Going Support: B,C,D,E,G,h,I
Training: 5 Weeks for 2 People, Lodging Included. $1,500 Allowance for Meals/Airfare. Other Credits.
Minority-Specific Programs: Interest-free financing of the franchise fee offered to all new owners. Prospective owners are eligible for streamlined and expedited SBA loan processing through our inclusion in the franchise registry. See www.franchiseregistry.com for more information.

Specific Expansion Plans:

US: All United States

LAZERQUICK

27375 SW Parkway Ave., # 200
Wilsonville, OR 97070
Tel: (800) 477-2679 (503) 682-1322
Fax: (503) 682-7816
E-Mail: mhart@lazerquick.com
Web Site: www.lazerquick.com
Mr. Michael Hart, Vice President of Franchising

LAZERQUICK centers are complete, one-stop printing and copying centers. All centers feature state-of-the-art electronic publishing, digital graphics and imaging services that support our range of quality, fast-service offset printing, high-speed copying and related bindery and finishing services. The LAZERQUICK franchise is based on value and performance. Affiliates benefit from our unique and innovative programs.

Background:

Established: 1968;   1st Franchised: 1990
Franchised Units: 29
Company-Owned Units: 23
Total Units: 52
Minority-Owned Units:
 African-American: 0
 Asian-American: 3
 Hispanic: 0
 Native American: 0
 Other: 1 Asian-Canadian

North America:	7 States
Density:	31 in OR, 14 in WA, 2 in CA

Financial/Terms:

Cash Investment:	$51.8-82.5K
Total Investment:	$172.5-275K
Minimum Net Worth:	$N/A
Fees: Franchise —	$25K
Royalty — 5-3%;	Ad. — 1.5%/$250
Earnings Claim Statement:	Yes
Term of Contract (Years):	7/7/7
Avg. # Of Employees:	2 FT, 2 PT
Passive Ownership:	Not Allowed
Area Develop. Agreements:	Yes/Varies
Sub-Franchising Contracts:	No
Expand In Territory:	No
Space Needs: 1,400-1,800 SF; SC	

Support & Training Provided:

Site Selection Assistance:	Yes
Lease Negotiation Assistance:	Yes
Co-Operative Advertising:	N/A
Franchisee Assoc./Member:	No
Size Of Corporate Staff:	40
On-Going Support:	C,D,E,G,I

Training: 5-7 Weeks at Corporate Headquarters.

Minority-Specific Programs: Although we support the objectives of the NMFI, we do not have any specific programs in place at this time.

Specific Expansion Plans:

US:	All United States

SCREEN PRINTING USA

534 W. Shawnee Ave.
Plymouth, PA 18651-2009
Tel:
Fax:
E-Mail:
Web Site:
Mr. Russell Owens, President

Full-service silk screen printing. Hats, shirts, jackets, signs, posters, decals. Full ASI services. Computer artwork and design.

Background:

Established: 1988;	1st Franchised: 1988
Franchised Units:	32
Company-Owned Units:	0
Total Units:	32
Minority-Owned Units:	
African-American:	
Asian-American:	
Hispanic:	
Native American:	
Other:	
North America:	5 States, 1 Province
Density:	PA, NY

Financial/Terms:

Cash Investment:	$10K
Total Investment:	$40-60K
Minimum Net Worth:	$NR
Fees: Franchise —	$25K
Royalty — 6%;	Ad. — 2%
Earnings Claim Statement:	No
Term of Contract (Years):	10/10
Avg. # Of Employees:	2 FT, 1 PT
Passive Ownership:	Discouraged
Area Develop. Agreements:	Yes/10
Sub-Franchising Contracts:	Yes
Expand In Territory:	Yes
Space Needs: 1,500 SF; FS, SF, HB	

Support & Training Provided:

Site Selection Assistance:	Yes
Lease Negotiation Assistance:	Yes
Co-Operative Advertising:	Yes
Franchisee Assoc./Member:	Yes/Yes
Size Of Corporate Staff:	4
On-Going Support:	B,C,D,E,G,H

Training: 2 Weeks Plymouth, PA.

Minority-Specific Programs: Up to 100% financiing to minority owners

Specific Expansion Plans:

US:	All United States

SIR SPEEDY

26722 Plaza Dr.
Mission Viejo, CA 92672
Tel: (800) 854-3321 (949) 348-5000
Fax: (949) 348-5068
E-Mail: fdelucia@sirspeedy.com
Web Site: www.sirspeedy.com
Mr. Frank A. de Lucia, VP Franchise Development

A Monday through Friday business-to-business service, it provides copying, printing, digital communication and graphic design for a diverse range of corporate clients. It's global digital link facilitates instantaneous communication and transfer of material between all centers in the group.

Background:

Established: 1968;	1st Franchised: 1968
Franchised Units:	755
Company-Owned Units:	17
Total Units:	772
Minority-Owned Units:	
African-American:	4
Asian-American:	13
Hispanic:	8

Native American:	0
Other:	22
North America:	47 States, 1 Province
Density:	86 in CA, 72 in FL, 41 in IL

Financial/Terms:

Cash Investment:	$100-150K
Total Investment:	$316-391K
Minimum Net Worth:	$300K
Fees: Franchise —	$20K
Royalty — 4-6%;	Ad. — 1-2%
Earnings Claim Statement:	Yes
Term of Contract (Years):	20/10
Avg. # Of Employees:	5+ FT
Passive Ownership:	Discouraged
Area Develop. Agreements:	No
Sub-Franchising Contracts:	No
Expand In Territory:	Yes
Space Needs: 2,000-12,000 SF; FS, SC	

Support & Training Provided:

Site Selection Assistance:	Yes
Lease Negotiation Assistance:	Yes
Co-Operative Advertising:	No
Franchisee Assoc./Member:	No
Size Of Corporate Staff:	50
On-Going Support:	B,C,D,E,F,G,H,I

Training: 3 Weeks in Mission Viejo, CA; 6 Weeks at franchisee's site.

Minority-Specific Programs: Although we support the objectives of the NMFI, we do not have any specific programs in place at this time.

Specific Expansion Plans:

US:	All United States

North America's Bingo & Gaming Newspaper

BINGO BUGLE NEWSPAPER

P. O. Box 527
Vashon Island, WA 98070
Tel: (800) 327-6437 (206) 463-5656
Fax: (206) 463-5630
E-Mail: roger@bingobugle.com
Web Site: www.bingobugle.com
Mr. Roger Snowden, President

THE BINGO BUGLE is North America's largest network of newspapers devoted to bingo & gaming. Circulation over 1 million copies monthly. Listed in Entrepreneur's Annual Franchise 500 as one of the lowest cost franchise opportunities. Franchise fees range from $1,500 to $7,000. Complete training and support. Modest investment. Call 1-800-327-6437 for details.

Background:

Established: 1981;	1st Franchised: 1983	
Franchised Units:		71
Company-Owned Units:		0
Total Units:		71

Minority-Owned Units:
   African-American:
   Asian-American:
   Hispanic:
   Native American:
   Other:

North America:	30 States, 2 Provinces
Density:	12 in CA, 6 in NY, 5 in FL

Financial/Terms:

Cash Investment:	$1.5-6K
Total Investment:	$1.5-10K
Minimum Net Worth:	$NR
Fees: Franchise —	$1.5-10K
Royalty — 10%;	Ad. — 0%
Earnings Claim Statement:	No
Term of Contract (Years):	5/5
Avg. # Of Employees:	0
Passive Ownership:	Allowed
Area Develop. Agreements:	No
Sub-Franchising Contracts:	No
Expand In Territory:	No
Space Needs: N/A SF; N/A	

Support & Training Provided:

Site Selection Assistance:	N/A
Lease Negotiation Assistance:	No
Co-Operative Advertising:	No
Franchisee Assoc./Member:	Yes/Yes
Size Of Corporate Staff:	2
On-Going Support:	NR
Training: 2.5 Days Seattle, WA.	

Minority Specific Programs: Although we support the objectives of the NMFI, we do not have any specific programs in place at this time.

Specific Expansion Plans:

US:	Northeast & Central US, NC

 Coffee News

COFFEE NEWS

P. O. Box 8444
Bangor, ME 04402-8444
Tel: (207) 941-0860
Fax: (207) 941-0860
E-Mail: bill@coffeednewsusa.com
Web Site: www.coffeenewsusa.com
Mr. William A. Buckley, President

COFFEE NEWS is an international, fun-filled weekly publication produced and delivered free of charge by local franchisors to restaurants, coffee shops and the hospitality industry. Each issue contains short stories, trivia, horoscopes, interesting facts and jokes, plus a local event section edited by the franchisee. Income is derived from the sale of ads to small businesses in each community.

Background:

Established: 1994;	1st Franchised: 1996	
Franchised Units:		266
Company-Owned Units:		3
Total Units:		269

Minority-Owned Units:
   African-American:
   Asian-American:
   Hispanic:
   Native American:
   Other:

North America:	NR
Density:	31 in BC, 29 ME, 23 ON

Financial/Terms:

Cash Investment:	$950
Total Investment:	$1K
Minimum Net Worth:	$None
Fees: Franchise —	$495
Royalty — $20-75/Wk.;	Ad. — 0%
Earnings Claim Statement:	No
Term of Contract (Years):	4/4
Avg. # Of Employees:	1 FT, 1 PT
Passive Ownership:	Discouraged
Area Develop. Agreements:	No
Sub-Franchising Contracts:	No

Expand In Territory: Yes
Space Needs: N/A SF; HB

Support & Training Provided:
Site Selection Assistance: Yes
Lease Negotiation Assistance: No
Co-Operative Advertising: N/A
Franchisee Assoc./Member: No
Size Of Corporate Staff: 5
On-Going Support: d,G,H,h
Training: Quarterly Sales Meetings in Various States
Minority-Specific Programs: Although we support the objectives of the NMFI, we do not have any specific programs in place at this time.

Specific Expansion Plans:
US: All United States

FINDERBINDER / SOURCEBOOK DIRECTORIES
8546 Chevy Chase Dr.
La Mesa, CA 91941-5325
Tel: (800) 255-2575 (619) 463-5050
Fax: (619) 463-5097
E-Mail:
Web Site: www.marketing-tactics.com
Mr. Gary Beals, President

The FINDERBINDER News Media Directory and the SOURCEBOOK Directory of Clubs and Associations are locally-produced reference books created by existing communications firms, such as an advertising agency or public relations consultants. It is an added profit center that builds public awareness for the local company.

Background:
Established: 1974; 1st Franchised: 1978
Franchised Units: 18
Company-Owned Units: 1
Total Units: 19
Minority-Owned Units:
  African-American: 0
  Asian-American: 0
  Hispanic: 0
  Native American: 0
  Other:
North America: 15 States
Density: 4 in CA

Financial/Terms:
Cash Investment: $NR
Total Investment: $10-15K
Minimum Net Worth: $30K
Fees: Franchise — $1K
  Royalty — 5-10%; Ad. — N/A
Earnings Claim Statement: No

Term of Contract (Years): Open
Avg. # Of Employees: 2 FT, 1 PT
Passive Ownership: Discouraged
Area Develop. Agreements: No
Sub-Franchising Contracts: No
Expand In Territory: Yes
Space Needs: N/A SF; N/A

Support & Training Provided:
Site Selection Assistance: N/A
Lease Negotiation Assistance: N/A
Co-Operative Advertising: Yes
Franchisee Assoc./Member: No
Size Of Corporate Staff: 3
On-Going Support: C,D,E,G,H,I
Training: 1 Day in San Diego.
Minority-Specific Programs: Although we support the objectives of the NMFI, we do not have any specific programs in place at this time.

Specific Expansion Plans:
US: All United States

PERFECT WEDDING GUIDE, THE
1206 N C.R. 427
Longwood, FL 32750
Tel: (888) 22-BRIDE (407) 331-6212
Fax: (407) 331-5004
E-Mail:
orlando@perfectweddingguide.com
Web Site: www.perfectweddingguide.com
Mr. Patrick J. McGroder, President

THE PERFECT WEDDING GUIDE is a comprehensive buyers' guide to wedding and honeymoon products and services. As the owner of a PERFECT WEDDING GUIDE, you will publish a magazine that thousands of people will read every day. With the guidance of the nation's premier wedding magazine publisher, you will own and manage your own business!

Background:
Established: 1991; 1st Franchised: 1998
Franchised Units: 19
Company-Owned Units: 3

Total Units: 22
Minority-Owned Units:
  African-American:
  Asian-American:
  Hispanic:
  Native American:
  Other:
North America: 6 States
Density: 4 in FL, 2 in TX

Financial/Terms:
Cash Investment: $30-50K
Total Investment: $35-50K
Minimum Net Worth: $50K
Fees: Franchise — $25-35K
  Royalty — 6%; Ad. — 1%
Earnings Claim Statement: No
Term of Contract (Years): 10/10
Avg. # Of Employees: 2 FT
Passive Ownership: Discouraged
Area Develop. Agreements: No
Sub-Franchising Contracts: No
Expand In Territory: Yes
Space Needs: N/A SF; HB

Support & Training Provided:
Site Selection Assistance: N/A
Lease Negotiation Assistance: N/A
Co-Operative Advertising: No
Franchisee Assoc./Member: No
Size Of Corporate Staff: 7
On-Going Support: a,b,C,d,G,h,I
Training: 5 Days Longwood, FL; 5 Days Franchise Territory.
Minority-Specific Programs: Although we support the objectives of the NMFI, we do not have any specific programs in place at this time.

Specific Expansion Plans:
US: All United States

AMERISPEC HOME INSPECTION SERVICE

860 Ridge Lake Blvd., 3rd Fl.
Memphis, TN 38120
Tel: (800) 426-2270 (901) 820-8509
Fax: (901) 820-8520
E-Mail: amerispec@worldnet.att.net
Web Site: www.amerispecfranchise.com
Mr. Thomas Jeffries, Fran. Sales Manager

AMERISPEC delivers productivity enhancing tools to our owners like AMERISPEC HOME INSPECTOR (R), proprietary home inspection software loaded on an affordable hand-held computer and our E&O Insurance policy, which protects real estate agents against negligent referral claims. A private intranet permits two-way communication with and among our owners. Consider our extensive training, the acclaimed and recognized 'AMERISPEC report,' our ongoing educational support and the package is complete.

Background:

Established: 1987;	1st Franchised: 1988
Franchised Units:	345
Company-Owned Units:	1
Total Units:	346
Minority-Owned Units:	
African-American:	1
Asian-American:	1
Hispanic:	3
Native American:	0
Other:	2 Women
North America:	48 States, 8 Provinces
Density:	23 in CA, 15 in FL, 11 in IL

Financial/Terms:

Cash Investment:	$10-15K
Total Investment:	$18.9-59.5K
Minimum Net Worth:	$25K
Fees: Franchise —	$13.9-23.9K
Royalty — 7%;	Ad. — 3%
Earnings Claim Statement:	No
Term of Contract (Years):	5/5
Avg. # Of Employees:	1 FT, 2 PT
Passive Ownership:	Allowed
Area Develop. Agreements:	No
Sub-Franchising Contracts:	No
Expand In Territory:	Yes
Space Needs: N/A SF; HB	

Support & Training Provided:

Site Selection Assistance:	N/A
Lease Negotiation Assistance:	N/A
Co-Operative Advertising:	N/A
Franchisee Assoc./Member:	No
Size Of Corporate Staff:	30
On-Going Support:	C,D,E,G,h,I

Training: 2 Weeks Memphis, TN.
Minority-Specific Programs: Although we support the objectives of the NMFI, we do not have any specific programs in place at this time.

Specific Expansion Plans:

US:	All United States

ASSIST-2-SELL

535 E. Plumb Ln., # 102
Reno, NV 89502
Tel: (800) 528-7816 (775) 688-6060
Fax: (775) 688-6069
E-Mail: assist@assist2sell.com
Web Site: www.assist2sell.com
Mr. Lyle Martin, Vice President

America's 'full service for less' discount real estate franchise. Real estate license required. The future of real estate will focus around a 'menu of services' concept. Lower commissions will be the norm. Don't be left behind: catch our vision and step into the future.

Background:

Established: 1987;	1st Franchised: 1994
Franchised Units:	75
Company-Owned Units:	0
Total Units:	75
Minority-Owned Units:	
African-American:	0
Asian-American:	3
Hispanic:	1
Native American:	0
North America:	28 States
Density:	12 in CO, 9 in CA, 5 in MA

Financial/Terms:

Cash Investment:	$15.5-49.5K
Total Investment:	$15.5-49.5K
Minimum Net Worth:	$N/A
Fees: Franchise —	$7K
Royalty — 5%;	Ad. — 0%
Earnings Claim Statement:	No
Term of Contract (Years):	7/7
Avg. # Of Employees:	3 FT
Passive Ownership:	Discouraged
Area Develop. Agreements:	No
Sub-Franchising Contracts:	No
Expand In Territory:	Yes
Space Needs: 500 SF; Office Building	

Support & Training Provided:

Site Selection Assistance:	Yes
Lease Negotiation Assistance:	Yes
Co-Operative Advertising:	No
Franchisee Assoc./Member:	No
Size Of Corporate Staff:	6
On-Going Support:	G,H,I

Training: 4 Days Reno, NV.
Minority-Specific Programs: Although we support the objectives of the NMFI, we do not have any specific programs in place at this time.

Specific Expansion Plans:

US:	All United States

Each office is independently owned and operated.

BETTER HOMES REALTY

1777 Botelho Dr., # 390
Walnut Creek, CA 94596
Tel: (800) 642-4428 (925) 937-9001
Fax: (925) 988-2770
E-Mail: flo@bhrcorp.com
Web Site: www.bhr.com
Ms. Florence Stevens, Vice President

Established identity, legal hot line support, no institutional advertising fee, franchise cap each calendar year, excellent corporate support, free DRE renewal, corporate advertising, hands-on regional support.

Background:

Established: 1964;	1st Franchised: 1969	
Franchised Units:		39
Company-Owned Units:		0
Total Units:		39
Minority-Owned Units:		
African-American:		10%
Asian-American:		
Hispanic:		
Native American:		
Other:		20%
North America:		1 State
Density:		39 in CA

Financial/Terms:

Cash Investment:	$10-60K
Total Investment:	$N/A
Minimum Net Worth:	$N/A
Fees: Franchise —	$9.95K

Royalty — 6% w/Cap/4.5%; Ad. — 0%

Earnings Claim Statement:	Yes
Term of Contract (Years):	5/5
Avg. # Of Employees:	N/A
Passive Ownership:	Allowed
Area Develop. Agreements:	NR
Sub-Franchising Contracts:	Yes
Expand In Territory:	Yes

Space Needs: N/A SF; N/A

Support & Training Provided:

Site Selection Assistance:	N/A
Lease Negotiation Assistance:	N/A
Co-Operative Advertising:	Yes
Franchisee Assoc./Member:	No
Size Of Corporate Staff:	7
On-Going Support:	b,C,D,G,H,I

Training: Varies. 1/2 to Full Day.
Minority-Specific Programs: Although we support the objectives of the NMFI, we do not have any specific programs in place at this time.

Specific Expansion Plans:

US:	West

BUYER'S AGENT, THE

1255 A Lynnfield Rd., # 273
Memphis, TN 38119
Tel: (800) 766-8728 (901) 767-1077
Fax: (901) 767-3577
E-Mail: rebuyragt@aol.com
Web Site: www.forbuyers.com
Mr. Tom Hathaway, President

The nation's oldest and largest real estate franchise in the business of exclusive buyer representation.

Background:

Established: 1988;	1st Franchised: 1988	
Franchised Units:		70
Company-Owned Units:		0
Total Units:		70
Minority-Owned Units:		
African-American:		2%
Asian-American:		2%
Hispanic:		4%
Native American:		0
Other:		30% Women

North America:		28 States
Density:	8 in FL, 8 in CA, 5 in TN	

Financial/Terms:

Cash Investment:	$20-30K
Total Investment:	$25-50K
Minimum Net Worth:	$50K
Fees: Franchise —	$14.9K
Royalty — 5%;	Ad. — 1%
Earnings Claim Statement:	No
Term of Contract (Years):	5/5
Avg. # Of Employees:	5-15 FT
Passive Ownership:	Discouraged
Area Develop. Agreements:	Consider
Sub-Franchising Contracts:	No
Expand In Territory:	Yes

Space Needs: 2,000 SF; FS, SF, SC

Support & Training Provided:

Site Selection Assistance:	Yes
Lease Negotiation Assistance:	Yes
Co-Operative Advertising:	Yes
Franchisee Assoc./Member:	No
Size Of Corporate Staff:	12
On-Going Support:	A,B,C,D,E,G,H,I

Training: 5 Days Memphis, TN.
Minority-Specific Programs: Short-term financing is available for those who qualify. As with all franchise opportunities, the franchisee's success is entirely dependent on that person's willingness to work hard, work smart and follow the instructions of the franchisor to the letter.

Specific Expansion Plans:

US:	All United States

CASTLES UNLIMITED

837 Beacon St.
Newton Centre, MA 02159
Tel: (617) 964-3300
Fax: (617) 244-5847
E-Mail: franchise@castlesunltd.com
Web Site: www.castlesunltd.com
Mr. James D. Lowenstern, President

CASTLES UNLIMITED is the originator of the 100% Plus Commission Marketing Program which accelerates real estate broker production and competitiveness. The company also encourages brokers in Massachusetts to call to investigate special alliances.

Background:

Established: 1985;	1st Franchised: 1990	
Franchised Units:		4
Company-Owned Units:		1
Total Units:		5
Minority-Owned Units:		
African-American:		

Asian-American:
Hispanic:
Native American:
Other:
North America: 1 State
Density: 5 in MA

Financial/Terms:
Cash Investment: $10-25K
Total Investment: $15-30K
Minimum Net Worth: $100K
Fees: Franchise — $11K
Royalty — 4.5%; Ad. — 1%
Earnings Claim Statement: No
Term of Contract (Years): 10/10
Avg. # Of Employees: 10 FT, 5 PT
Passive Ownership: Discouraged
Area Develop. Agreements: Yes
Sub-Franchising Contracts: Yes
Expand In Territory: Yes
Space Needs: 1,500 SF; SF

Support & Training Provided:
Site Selection Assistance: Yes
Lease Negotiation Assistance: Yes
Co-Operative Advertising: Yes
Franchisee Assoc./Member: Yes
Size Of Corporate Staff: 2
On-Going Support: b,C,d,e,f,G,H,I
Training: 2 Days at Newton, MA.
Minority-Specific Programs: Although we support the objectives of the NMFI, we do not have any specific programs in place at this time.

Specific Expansion Plans:
US: New England

COMMISSION EXPRESS

8300 Arlington Blvd., Unit E-3
Fairfax, VA 22031
Tel: (888) 560-5501 (703) 560-5500
Fax: (703) 560-5502
E-Mail: manager@commissionexpress.com
Web Site: www.commissionexpress.com
Mr. John L. Stedman, President

We are a true 'white collar' franchise. We offer 'exclusive' territories with professional customers. 9 to 5, no holidays or late nights, a normal life. High profit margin per transaction and a high 80% repeat factor.

Background:
Established: 1992; 1st Franchised: 1996
Franchised Units: 13
Company-Owned Units: 1
Total Units: 14

Minority-Owned Units:
African-American: 1
Asian-American: 1
Hispanic: 0
Native American: 0
Other:
North America: 5 States
Density: 4 in VA, 3 in GA, 2 in MD

Financial/Terms:
Cash Investment: $34.4-43.7K
Total Investment: $80-150K
Minimum Net Worth: $100K
Fees: Franchise — $10-20K
Royalty — 4.5 9%; Ad. — 1%
Earnings Claim Statement: Yes
Term of Contract (Years): 10/5
Avg. # Of Employees: 1 FT, 0 PT
Passive Ownership: Discouraged
Area Develop. Agreements: No
Sub-Franchising Contracts: No
Expand In Territory: Yes
Space Needs: 400 SF; NR

Support & Training Provided:
Site Selection Assistance: Yes
Lease Negotiation Assistance: No
Co-Operative Advertising: Yes
Franchisee Assoc./Member: No
Size Of Corporate Staff: 3
On-Going Support: C,D,G,H,I
Training: 5 Days Fairfax, VA.
Minority-Specific Programs: Our minority owners are some of our best!

Specific Expansion Plans:
US: All United States

HOMETEAM INSPECTION SERVICE, THE

6355 E. Kemper Rd., # 250
Cincinnati, OH 45241
Tel: (800) 598-5297 (513) 469-2100
Fax: (513) 469-2226
E-Mail: hometean@one.net
Web Site: www.hmteam.com
Mr. James H. Young, President

Ranked #1 fastest-growing home inspection franchise in 48 States and Canada. Unique and field-proven marketing system that produces leads and appointments. Exclusive, protected territory. Extensive and continuous training. Sales hotline to build your business. Financing provided.

Background:
Established: 1992; 1st Franchised: 1992
Franchised Units: 293
Company-Owned Units: 0
Total Units: 293
Minority-Owned Units:
African-American: 3
Asian-American: 1
Hispanic: 0
Native American: 0
Other: 2 Eastern Indians, 9 Women
North America: 48 States, 1 Province
Density: 25 in FL, 16 in MI, 20 in OH

Financial/Terms:
Cash Investment: $6.5-15.7K
Total Investment: $17.5-44.6K
Minimum Net Worth: $N/A
Fees: Franchise — $10.9-28.9K
Royalty — 6%; Ad. — 3%
Earnings Claim Statement: No
Term of Contract (Years): 10/10
Avg. # Of Employees: 1 FT
Passive Ownership: Discouraged
Area Develop. Agreements: No
Sub-Franchising Contracts: No
Expand In Territory: Yes
Space Needs: N/A SF; N/A

Support & Training Provided:
Site Selection Assistance: N/A
Lease Negotiation Assistance: N/A
Co-Operative Advertising: N/A
Franchisee Assoc./Member: Yes/Yes
Size Of Corporate Staff: 20
On-Going Support: A,B,C,D,G,H,I
Training: 2 Weeks Corporate Headquarters, Cincinnati, OH
Minority-Specific Programs: We will finance up to 50% of franchise fee.

Specific Expansion Plans:
US: All United States

HOMEVESTORS OF AMERICA

11910 Greenville Ave., # 300
Dallas, TX 75243
Tel: (888) 701-3888 (972) 761-0046
Fax: (972) 761-9022
E-Mail: hvmarketing@homevestors.com
Web Site: www.homevestors.com
Mr. L. T. Jasper, VP Franchise Development

HOMEVESTORS specializes in purchasing houses that are undervalued and selling them quickly. Franchisees use mass advertising, such as billboards and TV advertising for homeowners willing to trade a full market price for an immediate cash sale. Experts estimated the market for undervalued real estate at $10 billion. After remodeling houses, HOMEVESTORS has a finance program to sell properties quickly to credit-injured buyers with a minimum down payment.

Background:
Established: 1989; 1st Franchised: 1996
Franchised Units: 30
Company-Owned Units: 0
Total Units: 30
Minority-Owned Units:
   African-American:
   Asian-American:
   Hispanic:
   Native American:
North America: 5 States
Density: 20 in TX, 4 in FL, 3 in MO

Financial/Terms:
Cash Investment: $30-40K
Total Investment: $60-250KK
Minimum Net Worth: $150K
Fees: Franchise — $35K
   Royalty — $775/Property;Ad. —
$175/Prop.
Earnings Claim Statement: No
Term of Contract (Years): 5/5
Avg. # Of Employees: 2-5 FT
Passive Ownership: Discouraged
Area Develop. Agreements: No
Sub-Franchising Contracts: No
Expand In Territory: N/A
Space Needs: 500 SF; SF, SC

Support & Training Provided:
Site Selection Assistance: Yes
Lease Negotiation Assistance: N/A
Co-Operative Advertising: Yes
Franchisee Assoc./Member: Yes
Size Of Corporate Staff: 13
On-Going Support: C,D,G,H
Training: 5 Days in Dallas, TX.
Minority-Specific Programs: Although we support the objectives of the NMFI, we do not have any specific programs in place at this time.

Specific Expansion Plans:
US: TX,OK,KS,MO,FL,NM, GA

RE/MAX INTERNATIONAL
P. O. Box 3907
Englewood, CO 80155-3907
Tel: (800) 525-7452 (303) 770-5531
Fax: (303) 796-3599
E-Mail: echols@remax.net
Web Site: www.remax.com
Mr. Bill Echols, VP, Public Relations

The RE/MAX real estate franchise network, celebrating its 26th year of consecutive growth, is a global system of more than 3,000 independently-owned and operated offices in 32 countries, engaging 56,000 members. RE/MAX sales associates lead the industry in professional designations, experience and production while providing real estate services in residential, commercial, referral, relocation and asset management. RE/MAX lists and sells more real estate than any other real estate network in the world.

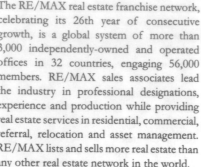
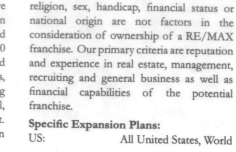

Background:
Established: 1973; 1st Franchised: 1975
Franchised Units: 3349
Company-Owned Units: 0
Total Units: 3349
Minority-Owned Units:
   African-American:
   Asian-American:
   Hispanic:
   Native American:
   Other:
North America: 50 States,12 Provinces
Density: 250 in CA, 200 in ON, 131 FL

Financial/Terms:
Cash Investment: $15-200K
Total Investment: $20-150K
Minimum Net Worth: $15K
Fees: Franchise — $7.5-25K
   Royalty — Varies; Ad. — Varies
Earnings Claim Statement: No
Term of Contract (Years): 5/5
Avg. # Of Employees: 2-4 FT, 1 PT
Passive Ownership: Discouraged
Area Develop. Agreements: No
Sub-Franchising Contracts: Yes
Expand In Territory: Varies
Space Needs: Varies SF; FS, SF, SC, RM

Support & Training Provided:
Site Selection Assistance: Yes
Lease Negotiation Assistance: Yes
Co-Operative Advertising: N/A
Franchisee Assoc./Member: No
Size Of Corporate Staff: 250
On-Going Support: C,D,G,h,I
Training: 40+ Hours at headquarters in Englewood, CO.

Minority-Specific Programs: Race, color, religion, sex, handicap, financial status or national origin are not factors in the consideration of ownership of a RE/MAX franchise. Our primary criteria are reputation and experience in real estate, management, recruiting and general business as well as financial capabilities of the potential franchise.

Specific Expansion Plans:
US: All United States, World

AMERICAN POOLPLAYERS ASSOCIATION

1000 Lake St. Louis Blvd., # 325
Lake Saint Louis, MO 63367
Tel: (800) 3-RACKEM (636) 625-8611
Fax: (636) 625-2975
E-Mail: khinkebein@poolplayers.com
Web Site: www.poolplayers.com
Franchise Development Manager,

APA franchisees operate recreational pool leagues utilizing "The Equalizer", a unique handicap system that equalizes play. The League, previously known as the Bud Light Pool League or the Camel pool League and now known nationally as the "APA Pool League", currently consists of over 170,000 members who compete in year-round weekly play. Franchisees receive customized software, technical updates, complete training, marketing support and networking opportunities at the annual convention.

Background:

Established: 1980; 1st Franchised: 1982
Franchised Units: 225
Company-Owned Units: 1
Total Units: 226
Minority-Owned Units:
   African-American: 2

Asian-American: 2
Hispanic: 1
Native American: 0
North America: 46 States, 5 Provinces
Density: 14 in IL, 16 in FL, 13 in CA

Financial/Terms:

Cash Investment: $4.3-6.2K
Total Investment: $4.3-6.2K
Minimum Net Worth: $N/A
Fees: Franchise — $Varies
   Royalty — 20%; Ad. — N/A
Earnings Claim Statement: No
Term of Contract (Years): 2/5/10
Avg. # Of Employees: Varies
Passive Ownership: Not Allowed
Area Develop. Agreements: No
Sub-Franchising Contracts: No
Expand In Territory: N/A
Space Needs: N/A SF; HB

Support & Training Provided:

Site Selection Assistance: Yes
Lease Negotiation Assistance: N/A
Co-Operative Advertising: Yes
Franchisee Assoc./Member: Yes/No
Size Of Corporate Staff: 40+
On-Going Support: A,D,G,H
Training: 6 Days APA Home Office.
Minority-Specific Programs: The APA is an organization dedicated to providing recreational billiards to all segments of society. As a result, we want our franchise network to reflect the broad diversity that has helped to make the United States the "land of opportunity" and the "economic wonder of the free world." Any and all qualified applicants are welcome. We expect only that our franchisee's be motivated, have integrity and, most importantly, have the desire to set their own financial limits.

Specific Expansion Plans:

US: All United States

CALCULATED COUPLES

4839 E. Greenway Rd., PMB # 183
Scottsdale, AZ 85254
Tel: (800) 44-MATCH (602) 230-4172
Fax: (602) 765-0076
E-Mail: sales@cupidhelp.com
Web Site: www.cupidhelp.com
Mr. David E. Gorman, President

Singles matchmaking party service. Copyrighted system matches hundreds of singles each week at CALCULATED COUPLES matchmaking parties. Replaces dating services. Fun, unique, part-time, all cash singles business.

Background:

Established: 1983; 1st Franchised: 1987
Franchised Units: 9
Company-Owned Units: 6
Total Units: 15
Minority-Owned Units:
   African-American: 0
   Asian-American: 0
   Hispanic: 0
   Native American: 0
   Other:
North America: 9 States
Density: 5 in NY, 1 in AZ, 1 in NE

Financial/Terms:

Cash Investment: $5K
Total Investment: $5K
Minimum Net Worth: $NR
Fees: Franchise — $5K
   Royalty — 0%; Ad. — 0%

Earnings Claim Statement: No
Term of Contract (Years): 2/2
Avg. # Of Employees: 4 PT
Passive Ownership: Allowed
Area Develop. Agreements: Yes/2
Sub-Franchising Contracts: No
Expand In Territory: Yes
Space Needs: NR SF; NR

Support & Training Provided:
Site Selection Assistance: Yes
Lease Negotiation Assistance: N/A
Co-Operative Advertising: Yes
Franchisee Assoc./Member: No
Size Of Corporate Staff: 2
On-Going Support: b,c,d,e,G,h,I
Training: Video Training With Manuals.
Minority-Specific Programs: Although we support the objectives of the NMFI, we do not have any specific programs in place at this time.

Specific Expansion Plans:
US: All United States

7270 ROSWELL ROAD • (770) 395-0724

CINEMA GRILL

P. O. Box 28467
Atlanta, GA 30358
Tel: (404) 250-9536
Fax: (404) 256-1569
E-Mail: cinegrill@aol.com
Web Site: www.cinemagrill.com
Mr. John J. Duffy, Vice President

A unique entertainment concept that combines movie viewing and restaurant dining. Patrons enjoy current film releases on the giant screen while enjoying beer, wine, fresh-dough pizza, burgers, sandwiches and desserts.

Background:
Established: 1995; 1st Franchised: 1995
Franchised Units: 29
Company-Owned Units: 1
Total Units: 30
Minority-Owned Units:
 African-American: 1
 Asian-American:
 Hispanic:
 Native American: 1
 Other:
North America: 9 States
Density: 3 in VA, 3 in MD, 2 in NC

Financial/Terms:
Cash Investment: $75-100K
Total Investment: $400-500K
Minimum Net Worth: $100K
Fees: Franchise — $20K
 Royalty — 3%; Ad. — 0%
Earnings Claim Statement: Yes
Term of Contract (Years): 10/10
Avg. # Of Employees: 40 FT
Passive Ownership: Discouraged
Area Develop. Agreements: Yes/10
Sub-Franchising Contracts: No
Expand In Territory: Yes
Space Needs: 10,000 SF; FS, SC, RM

Support & Training Provided:
Site Selection Assistance: Yes
Lease Negotiation Assistance: Yes
Co-Operative Advertising: N/A
Franchisee Assoc./Member: Yes/Yes
Size Of Corporate Staff: 7
On-Going Support: C,D,F,G,h,i
Training: 2 Weeks Site.
Minority-Specific Programs: Although we support the objectives of the NMFI, we do not have any specific programs in place at this time.

Specific Expansion Plans:
US: All United States

HOOP MOUNTAIN

130 Centre St., # 7
Danvers, MA 01923
Tel: (800) 819-8445
Fax: (978) 774-8628
Mr. Steven Gibbs, President

Basketball camp. Manage tournaments. Manage all-star games. Manage exposure events.

Background:
Established: 1985; 1st Franchised: 1996
Franchised Units: 8
Company-Owned Units: 1
Total Units: 9
Minority-Owned Units:
 African-American:
 Asian-American:
 Hispanic:
 Native American:
North America: 14 States
Density: 2 in MA, 2 in CT, 2 in RI

Financial/Terms:
Cash Investment: $10K
Total Investment: $10-20K
Minimum Net Worth: $50K
Fees: Franchise — $10K
 Royalty — 8%; Ad. — N/A

Earnings Claim Statement: Yes
Term of Contract (Years): 10/10
Avg. # Of Employees: 1 FT or 1 PT
Passive Ownership: Not Allowed
Area Develop. Agreements: Yes
Sub-Franchising Contracts: Yes
Expand In Territory: Yes
Space Needs: N/A SF; N/A

Support & Training Provided:
Site Selection Assistance: Yes
Lease Negotiation Assistance: Yes
Co-Operative Advertising: No
Franchisee Assoc./Member: No
Size Of Corporate Staff: 1
On-Going Support: A,B,C,D,F,I
Training: 2 Weeks in Boston, MA.
Minority-Specific Programs: Although we support the objectives of the NMFI, we do not have any specific programs in place at this time.

Specific Expansion Plans:
US: NR

PUTT-PUTT GOLF COURSES OF AMERICA

3007 Ft. Bragg Rd.
Fayetteville, NC 28303-0237
Tel: (910) 485-7131
Fax: (910) 485-1122
Web Site: www.putt-putt.com
Mr. Scott Anderson, National Franchise Director

PUTT-PUTT GOLF is now in its 44th year of operation. It is the oldest and largest operator/franchisor of miniature golf and family entertainment centers in the world. PUTT-PUTT GOLF operates in 28 states and in 8 foreign countries and specializes in the development of PUTT-PUTT GOLF, gamerooms, batting cages, bumpercars, go-carts, laser tag and total play.

Background:
Established: 1954; 1st Franchised: 1955
Franchised Units: 201
Company-Owned Units: 6
Total Units: 207
Minority-Owned Units:
 African-American: 1
 Asian-American: 2

Hispanic:	2
Native American:	0
North America:	28 States, 1 Province
Density:	28 in TX, 25 in NC, 21 in OH

Financial/Terms:

Cash Investment:	$30K-1MM
Total Investment:	$100K-5MM
Minimum Net Worth:	$100K
Fees: Franchise —	$5-30K
Royalty — 5%;	Ad. — 2%
Earnings Claim Statement:	No
Term of Contract (Years):	40
Avg. # Of Employees:	NR
Passive Ownership:	Allowed
Area Develop. Agreements:	No
Sub-Franchising Contracts:	No
Expand In Territory:	No
Space Needs: 3-7 acres SF; N/A	

Support & Training Provided:

Site Selection Assistance:	Yes
Lease Negotiation Assistance:	Yes
Co-Operative Advertising:	No
Franchisee Assoc./Member:	No
Size Of Corporate Staff:	24
On-Going Support:	C,D,G,H,I

Training: 1 Week in Fayetteville, NC; 3-7 Days at Franchisee's Location.

Minority-Specific Programs: Currently we assist in the completion of loan documentation and the development of the business plan. We are evaluating ways to advertise more directly to the minority community. We feel our current training program meets the needs of all our franchisees.

Specific Expansion Plans:

US:	All United States

THEMED MINIATURE GOLF COURSES

P. O. Box 2435
Myrtle Beach, SC 29578-2435
Tel: (843) 236-4733
Fax: (843) 249-2118
E-Mail: chgrove@sccoast.net
Mr. Charles H. Grove, President

Themed, contoured adventure-type miniature golf courses with lakes, streambeds and waterfalls. Lush landscaping and the very finest designed, unique, playable holes that invite repeat participation. We also design and build complete family entertainment centers.

Background:

Established: 1977;	1st Franchised: 1985
Franchised Units:	12
Company-Owned Units:	4
Total Units:	16
Minority-Owned Units:	
African-American:	
Asian-American:	1
Hispanic:	
Native American:	
North America:	10 States
Density:	SC, FL, TX

Financial/Terms:

Cash Investment:	$62.5K-100K
Total Investment:	$250-400K
Minimum Net Worth:	$N/A
Fees: Franchise —	$N/A
Royalty — N/A;	Ad. — N/A
Earnings Claim Statement:	No
Term of Contract (Years):	Unlimited
Avg. # Of Employees:	2 FT, 2 PT
Passive Ownership:	Allowed
Area Develop. Agreements:	No
Sub-Franchising Contracts:	No
Expand In Territory:	Yes
Space Needs: 30,000 SF; FS	

Support & Training Provided:

Site Selection Assistance:	Yes
Lease Negotiation Assistance:	Yes
Co-Operative Advertising:	No
Franchisee Assoc./Member:	Yes/Yes
Size Of Corporate Staff:	5
On-Going Support:	B,C,D
Training: NR	

Minority-Specific Programs: Although we support the objectives of the NMFI, we do not have any specific programs in place at this time.

Specific Expansion Plans:

US:	All United States

WORLD GYM

2210 Main St.
Santa Monica, CA 90405
Tel: (800) 544-7441 (310) 450-0080
Fax: (310) 450-3455
E-Mail: info@worldgym.com
Web Site: www.worldgym.com
Mr. Mike Uretz, Chief Executive Officer

The franchise originally started with hard-core bodybuilding gyms and has evolved into fitness centers. We encourage franchisees to purchase state-of-the-art equipment catering to all types of members — from individual members, to families, to corporate memberships. The business involves the sale of gym memberships, clothing, accessories and food and vitamin supplements.

Background:

Established: 1977;	1st Franchised: 1985
Franchised Units:	264
Company-Owned Units:	0
Total Units:	264
Minority-Owned Units:	
African-American:	
Asian-American:	
Hispanic:	
Native American:	
North America:	36 States, 2 Provinces
Density:	34 in FL, 23 in CA, 19 in NY

Financial/Terms:

Cash Investment:	$221.3K
Total Investment:	$221.3-632K
Minimum Net Worth:	$300K
Fees: Franchise —	$12.75K
Royalty — $6.5K/Yr.;	Ad. — 0%
Earnings Claim Statement:	No
Term of Contract (Years):	5/5
Avg. # Of Employees:	3-5 FT, 3 PT
Passive Ownership:	Allowed
Area Develop. Agreements:	Yes/6
Sub-Franchising Contracts:	Yes
Expand In Territory:	Yes
Space Needs: 10,000-15,000 SF; SC, RM	

Support & Training Provided:

Site Selection Assistance:	Yes
Lease Negotiation Assistance:	Yes
Co-Operative Advertising:	No
Franchisee Assoc./Member:	No
Size Of Corporate Staff:	4
On-Going Support:	d,G,H,I
Training: NR	

Minority-Specific Programs: Although we support the objectives of the NMFI, we do not have any specific programs in place at this time.

Specific Expansion Plans:

US:	All United States

GINGISS FORMALWEAR

2101 Executive Dr.
Addison, IL 60101-1482
Tel: (800) 621-7125 (630) 620-9050
Fax: (630) 620-8840
E-Mail: gingiss@gingiss.com
Web Site: www.gingiss.com
Mr. Tom Ryan, VP of Franchise
Development

GINGISS FORMALWEAR specializes in the rental and sale of men's and boys' tuxedos and related accessories. GINGISS is the leader in the formalwear wedding industry that does not go out of style, and is the only national formalwear chain that can coordinate groomsmen from coast to coast. GINGISS manufactures its own proprietary lines of formalwear, including exclusive designers such as Oleg Cassini.

Background:

Established: 1936;   1st Franchised: 1968
Franchised Units: 189
Company-Owned Units: 49
Total Units: 238
Minority-Owned Units:
    African-American:
    Asian-American:
    Hispanic:
    Native American:
    Other:
North America: 30 States

Density: 38 in TX, 38 in IL, 33 in CA

Financial/Terms:

Cash Investment:	$59-107K
Total Investment:	$98.7-242.7K
Minimum Net Worth:	$NR
Fees: Franchise —	$15K
Royalty — 6%;	Ad. — 2%
Earnings Claim Statement:	Yes
Term of Contract (Years):	10/10
Avg. # Of Employees:	2 FT, 4 PT
Passive Ownership:	Discouraged
Area Develop. Agreements:	Yes
Sub-Franchising Contracts:	No
Expand In Territory:	Yes
Space Needs: 1,100-1,200 SF; FS, SF, SC, RM	

Support & Training Provided:

Site Selection Assistance:	Yes
Lease Negotiation Assistance:	Yes
Co-Operative Advertising:	Yes
Franchisee Assoc./Member:	Yes/Yes
Size Of Corporate Staff:	50
On-Going Support:	B,C,D,E,F,G,H

Training: 1 Week Corporate Heaquarters; 1 Week Company Operated Store; On-Going on Location.

Minority-Specific Programs: Although we support the objectives of the NMFI, we do not have any specific programs in place at this time.

Specific Expansion Plans:

US: All United States

JOE RENT ALL/LOUE TOUT

28 Vanier St.
Chateauguay, PQ J6J 3W8 CANADA
Tel: (800) 361-2020 (450) 692-6268
Fax: (450) 692-2848
E-Mail: mrjoe@cam.org
Web Site: www.joelouetout.ca
Mr. Ray Bellerose, Network Development

Equipment rental in 3 different options: tools, recreational vehicles, special events, motorcycles. Full operating support, including school. Buying group with central billing. Specific insurance plans. Own computer program.

Background:

Established: 1979;   1st Franchised: 1982
Franchised Units: 85
Company-Owned Units: 0
Total Units: 85
Minority-Owned Units:
    African-American:
    Asian-American:
    Hispanic:
    Native American:
North America: 5 Provinces
Density: 66 in PQ, 15 in ON, 4 in NB

Financial/Terms:

Cash Investment:	$25K

Total Investment: $100-500K
Minimum Net Worth: $50K
Fees: Franchise — $20K
    Royalty — 4%;   Ad. — 0%
Earnings Claim Statement: Yes
Term of Contract (Years):   5/5
Avg. # Of Employees: 2 FT, 2 PT
Passive Ownership: Discouraged
Area Develop. Agreements: No
Sub-Franchising Contracts: No
Expand In Territory: Yes
Space Needs: 2,500 SF; FS, SF

Support & Training Provided:
Site Selection Assistance: Yes
Lease Negotiation Assistance: No
Co-Operative Advertising: No
Franchisee Assoc./Member: Yes/Yes
Size Of Corporate Staff: 5
On-Going Support: B,C,D,E,F,H,I
Training: 1 Full Week Head Office School; 1 Week with Existing Successful Operator.
Minority-Specific Programs: Although we support the objectives of the NMFI, we do not have any specific programs in place at this time.

Specific Expansion Plans:
US: N/A

COLOR ME MINE

14721 Califa St.
Van Nuys, CA 91411
Tel: (888) 265-6764 (818) 989-8404
Fax: (818) 780-1442
E-Mail: maria@colormemine.com
Web Site: www.colormemine.com
Ms. Maria Baker, Director of Franchise
Sales

COLOR ME MINE is the world's leader in contemporary ceramics and crafts studios. Our comprehensive training and support system includes glazing, firing and design techniques, construction marketing, accounting services and manufacturing plants to ensure consistency and supply.

Background:

Established: 1992;	1st Franchised: 1996
Franchised Units:	44
Company-Owned Units:	4
Total Units:	48
Minority-Owned Units:	
African-American:	0
Asian-American:	5
Hispanic:	0
Native American:	0
North America:	10 States
Density:	22 in CA, 5 in PA, 4 in NJ

Financial/Terms:

Cash Investment:	$50K
Total Investment:	$125-165K
Minimum Net Worth:	$150K
Fees: Franchise —	$20K
Royalty — 5%;	Ad. — 1%
Earnings Claim Statement:	No
Term of Contract (Years):	5/5
Avg. # Of Employees:	2 FT, 4 PT
Passive Ownership:	Discouraged
Area Develop. Agreements:	No
Sub-Franchising Contracts:	No
Expand In Territory:	Yes

Space Needs: 1,300-2,000 SF; SF, SC, RM, Entertainment Cent

Support & Training Provided:

Site Selection Assistance:	Yes
Lease Negotiation Assistance:	Yes
Co-Operative Advertising:	No
Franchisee Assoc./Member:	No
Size Of Corporate Staff:	48
On-Going Support:	A,B,C,D,E,F,G,H,I

Training: 2 Weeks at Home Office in Van Nuys, CA; 5-7 days at franchised location.
Minority-Specific Programs: COLOR ME MINE welcomes applications from minority franchisees and supports the objectives of the Initiative.

Specific Expansion Plans:

US:	All United States

DECK THE WALLS
Expressive Art and Custom Framing

DECK THE WALLS

100 Glenborough Dr., 14th Fl.
Houston, TX 77067
Tel: (800) 543-3325 (281) 775-5200
Fax: (281) 775-5250
E-Mail: ann@deckthewalls.com
Web Site: www.deckthewalls.com
Ms. Ann Nance, Franchise Recruitment
Manager

The nation's largest retailer specializing in art and custom framing. DECK THE WALLS has tailored the art gallery concept to meet the needs of mall shoppers. Stores feature prints, posters and frames that complement current decorating styles. Inviting decor and emphasis on skilled personal service make shopping at DECK THE WALLS a quality experience.

Background:

Established: 1979;	1st Franchised: 1981
Franchised Units:	190
Company-Owned Units:	1
Total Units:	191
Minority-Owned Units:	
African-American:	0
Asian-American:	2
Hispanic:	0
Native American:	0
Other:	2
North America:	38 States
Density:	26 in TX, 16 in PE, 14 in FL

Financial/Terms:

Cash Investment:	$75K
Total Investment:	$184-236K
Minimum Net Worth:	$250K
Fees: Franchise —	$35K
Royalty — 6%;	Ad. — 1%
Earnings Claim Statement:	No
Term of Contract (Years):	10/10
Avg. # Of Employees:	3 FT, 2 PT
Passive Ownership:	Not Allowed
Area Develop. Agreements:	No
Sub-Franchising Contracts:	No

Expand In Territory: Yes
Space Needs: 1,800 SF; RM

Support & Training Provided:

Site Selection Assistance: Yes
Lease Negotiation Assistance: Yes
Co-Operative Advertising: Yes
Franchisee Assoc./Member: Yes/Yes
Size Of Corporate Staff: 50
On-Going Support: A,B,C,D,E,F,G,H,I
Training: 2 Weeks in Houston, Texas.
Minority-Specific Programs: Although we support the objectives of the NMFI, we do not have any specific programs in place at this time.

Specific Expansion Plans:

US: All United States

The Great Frame Up

YOU MAKE IT OR WE MAKE IT.
THAT'S WHAT MAKES IT GREAT.

GREAT FRAME UP, THE

P. O. Box 1187
Houston, TX 77251-1187
Tel: (800) 543-3325 (281) 775-5262
Fax: (281) 775-5250
E-Mail: annn@franchiseconceptsinc.com
Web Site: www.thegreatframeup.com
Ms. Ann Nance, Franchise Recruitment Manager

THE GREAT FRAME UP stores provide customers with immediate, quality framing services. Located in friendly, neighborhood shopping centers, the stores specialize in custom-framing and provide create-it-yourself framing facilities. National buying power, marketing programs, training, site selection assistance, insurance, retirement programs and more.

Background:

Established: 1971;   1st Franchised: 1975
Franchised Units: 122
Company-Owned Units: 0
Total Units: 122
Minority-Owned Units:
   African-American: 0
   Asian-American: 1
   Hispanic: 0
   Native American: 0
   Other: 1 Middle Eastern
North America: 26 States
Density: 25 in IL, 15 in CA, 15 in GA

Financial/Terms:

Cash Investment: $100K
Total Investment: $97.2-138.2K
Minimum Net Worth: $300K

Fees: Franchise — $25K
   Royalty — 6%;   Ad. — 1.5%
Earnings Claim Statement: No
Term of Contract (Years):   10/10
Avg. # Of Employees: 3 FT, 2 PT
Passive Ownership: Allowed
Area Develop. Agreements: No
Sub-Franchising Contracts: No
Expand In Territory: Yes
Space Needs: 1,800 SF; SC

Support & Training Provided:

Site Selection Assistance: Yes
Lease Negotiation Assistance: Yes
Co-Operative Advertising: Yes
Franchisee Assoc./Member: Yes/Yes
Size Of Corporate Staff: 38
On-Going Support: B,C,D,E,F,G,H,I
Training: 2 Weeks in Houston, Texas.
Minority-Specific Programs: Although we support the objectives of the NMFI, we do not have any specific programs in place at this time.

Specific Expansion Plans:

US: All United States

ATHLETE'S FOOT, THE
1950 Vaughn Rd.
Kennesaw, GA 30144
Tel: (800) 524-6444 (770) 514-4721
Fax: (770) 514-4903
E-Mail: rsmith@theathletesfoot.com
Web Site: www.theathletesfoot.com
Mr. Russell A. Smith, Director Franchise Sales

THE ATHLETE'S FOOT, with more than 650 stores, is the leading international franchisor of name-brand athletic footwear. As a franchisee, you will benefit from headquarters' support, including training, advertising, product selection, special vendor discount programs, continual footwear research at our exclusive-wear test center and much more.

Background:
Established: 1971;   1st Franchised: 1972
Franchised Units: 462
Company-Owned Units: <u>279</u>
Total Units: 741
Minority-Owned Units:
   African-American:
   Asian-American:
   Hispanic:
   Native American:
   Other:
North America: 49 States, 1 Province
Density: NR

Financial/Terms:
Cash Investment: $75-125K
Total Investment: $175-350K
Minimum Net Worth: $100K
Fees: Franchise — $25K
   Royalty — 5%;   Ad. — 0.6%
Earnings Claim Statement: No
Term of Contract (Years):   10/5
Avg. # Of Employees: 2 FT, 6 PT
Passive Ownership: Discouraged
Area Develop. Agreements: Yes/10
Sub-Franchising Contracts: No
Expand In Territory: Yes
Space Needs: 1,200 SF; FS, SF, SC, RM

Support & Training Provided:
Site Selection Assistance: Yes
Lease Negotiation Assistance: Yes
Co-Operative Advertising: No
Franchisee Assoc./Member: Yes/Yes
Size Of Corporate Staff: 180
On-Going Support: B,C,D,E,f,G,H,I
Training: 1 Wk. at Headquarters in Atlanta; 1 Wk. Prior To and During Opening On Location; On-Going.
Minority-Specific Programs: Although we support the objectives of the NMFI, we do not have any specific programs in place at this time.

Specific Expansion Plans:
US: All United States

FAN-A-MANIA SPORTS AND ENTERTAINMENT
3855 S. 500 W., # R
Salt Lake City, UT 84115
Tel: (800) 770-9120 (801) 288-9120
Fax: (801) 288-9210
E-Mail: Fanaman1@hotmail.com
Web Site: www.fanamania.com
Mr. Mark Helean, VP Franchise Operations

Largest sport and entertainment retail franchise, great look, exciting hot products: NFL, MLB, NASCAR, NBA, NHL, WWF, Disney, Warner Brothers, Pooh, Sesame Street, Marvel Comics, Star Wars, Star Trek, Teletubies and Rugrats apparel, novelty items and memorabilia. Malls love us and customers flock to our stores.

Background:
Established: 1993;   1st Franchised: 1994
Franchised Units: 16
Company-Owned Units: <u>5</u>
Total Units: 21
Minority-Owned Units:
   African-American: 1
   Asian-American: 1
   Hispanic:
   Native American:
   Other: 1 Woman
North America: 8 States, 2 Provinces
Density: 4 in OR, 3 in PA, 2 in TX

Financial/Terms:
Cash Investment: $40K
Total Investment: $120-160K
Minimum Net Worth: $250K
Fees: Franchise — $19.5K
   Royalty — 3.5%;   Ad. — 2%

Earnings Claim Statement:	No
Term of Contract (Years):	10/10
Avg. # Of Employees:	2 FT, 4 PT
Passive Ownership:	Discouraged
Area Develop. Agreements:	Yes/10
Sub-Franchising Contracts:	No
Expand In Territory:	Yes
Space Needs: 2,000 SF; RM, Outlet Center	

Support & Training Provided:

Site Selection Assistance:	Yes
Lease Negotiation Assistance:	Yes
Co-Operative Advertising:	N/A
Franchisee Assoc./Member:	No
Size Of Corporate Staff:	7
On-Going Support:	b,C,D,E,f,G,H,I
Training: 4 Days Salt Lake City, UT; 7 Days Franchise Locations	

Minority-Specific Programs: Presently,19% of the FAN-A-MANIA franchises are owned by minorities. We actively seek qualified individuals to become franchisees regardless of race or gender. Although we support the objectives of the Natioal Minority Franchising Initiative, we do not have any specific programs in place at this time.

Specific Expansion Plans:

US:	All United States

GOLF ETC. OF AMERICA

710 E. Hwy. 337 East
Granbury, TX 76048
Tel: (800) 806-8633 (817) 279-7888
Fax: (817) 279-9882
E-Mail: sales@golfetc.com
Web Site: www.golfetc.com
Mr. Shane Hunt, Chief Executive Officer

Total turn-key golf pro shop franchise. Retail center for golf equipment, accessories, gift items and furniture. Service center built inside for precision custom fitting and repair of golf clubs. Exciting and fun sports and entertainment industry.

Background:

Established: 1992;	1st Franchised: 1996
Franchised Units:	29
Company-Owned Units:	1
Total Units:	30
Minority-Owned Units:	
African-American:	

Asian-American:	
Hispanic:	
Native American:	
Other:	
North America:	18 States
Density:	10 in TX, 5 in FL, 4 in NC

Financial/Terms:

Cash Investment:	$25-40K
Total Investment:	$130-145K
Minimum Net Worth:	$130-145K
Fees: Franchise —	$NR
Royalty — NR;	Ad. — N/A
Earnings Claim Statement:	No
Term of Contract (Years):	NR
Avg. # Of Employees:	1 FT, 2 PT
Passive Ownership:	Allowed
Area Develop. Agreements:	NR
Sub-Franchising Contracts:	No
Expand In Territory:	NR
Space Needs: 2,000-2,500 SF; SF, SC, RM	

Support & Training Provided:

Site Selection Assistance:	Yes
Lease Negotiation Assistance:	Yes
Co-Operative Advertising:	No
Franchisee Assoc./Member:	No
Size Of Corporate Staff:	11
On-Going Support:	b,D,E,G,H,I
Training: 1 Week Granbury, TX.	

Minority-Specific Programs: 1 week training program in Granbury, TX. On-going training, newsletters and our curtomer relations representatives. We currently advertise for recruiting on the Internet @ www.golfetc.com.

Specific Expansion Plans:

US:	All United States

LAS VEGAS GOLF & TENNIS

2701 Crimson Canyon Dr.
Las Vegas, NV 89128
Tel: (800) 873-5110 (702) 798-5500
Fax: (702) 798-6847
E-Mail: franchise@lvgtcorp.com
Web Site: www.lvgolf.com
Ms. Staci Behnke, Franchise Development Admin.

Country club atmosphere at the off-course price. Our retail stores specialize in a wide variety of name brand pro-line golf and tennis equipment and apparel, as well as our present Vision line and merchandise.

Our operational staff, store development department, in-house advertising agency, computerization system and 2-week training course, along with the on-going support proves to be well above the rest.

Background:

Established: 1974;	1st Franchised: 1984
Franchised Units:	35
Company-Owned Units:	10
Total Units:	45
Minority-Owned Units:	
African-American:	
Asian-American:	
Hispanic:	
Native American:	
Other:	
North America:	17 States
Density:	12 in CA, 5 in MI, 4 in AZ

Financial/Terms:

Cash Investment:	$250K
Total Investment:	$538-798K
Minimum Net Worth:	$750K
Fees: Franchise —	$45K
Royalty — 3%;	Ad. — 2%
Earnings Claim Statement:	Yes
Term of Contract (Years):	15/15
Avg. # Of Employees:	5 FT, 2-3 PT
Passive Ownership:	Discouraged
Area Develop. Agreements:	Yes
Sub-Franchising Contracts:	No
Expand In Territory:	Yes
Space Needs: 6,000-10,000 SF; FS, SF, SC, RM, End Cap	

Support & Training Provided:

Site Selection Assistance:	Yes
Lease Negotiation Assistance:	Yes
Co-Operative Advertising:	Yes
Franchisee Assoc./Member:	No
Size Of Corporate Staff:	36
On-Going Support:	A,B,C,D,e,F,G,h,I
Training: 2 Weeks Corporate Headquarters in Las Vegas, NV.	

Minority-Specific Programs: Although we support the objectives of the NMFI, we do not have any specific programs in place at this time.

Specific Expansion Plans:

US:	All United States

THE SPORT SHOE

SPORT SHOE, THE

1770 Corporate Dr., # 500
Norcross, GA 30093
Tel: (800) 944-7463 (770) 279-7494

Fax: (770) 279-7180
E-Mail: franchise@thesportshoe.com
Web Site: www.thesportshoe.com
Mrs. Jan Judd, Director of Franchising

For over 25 years, THE SPORT SHOE has been one of America's premier athletic shoe stores and sports-related activewear. THE SPORT SHOE offers continuing professional support, including site selection, lease negotiation, in-store operation and product knowledge, marketing and merchandising assistance, in-store set up and grand opening assistance.

Background:

Established: 1974; 1st Franchised: 1989

Franchised Units:	7
Company-Owned Units:	<u>25</u>
Total Units:	32
Minority-Owned Units:	
African-American:	0
Asian-American:	0
Hispanic:	0
Native American:	0
Other:	
North America:	4 States
Density:	4 in GA, 1 in NC, 1 in AL

Financial/Terms:

Cash Investment:	$150K
Total Investment:	$300K+
Minimum Net Worth:	$300K
Fees: Franchise —	$25K
Royalty — 4%;	Ad. — N/A
Earnings Claim Statement:	No
Term of Contract (Years):	10/5/5
Avg. # Of Employees:	2-4 FT, 6-8 PT
Passive Ownership:	Allowed
Area Develop. Agreements:	Yes
Sub-Franchising Contracts:	No
Expand In Territory:	Yes

Space Needs: 3,000 SF; FS, SC

Support & Training Provided:

Site Selection Assistance:	Yes
Lease Negotiation Assistance:	Yes
Co-Operative Advertising:	Yes
Franchisee Assoc./Member:	No
Size Of Corporate Staff:	60
On-Going Support:	C,D,E,H,I

Training: 6-8 Weeks Corporate Office and Store.

Minority-Specific Programs: Although we support the objectives of the NMFI, we do not have any specific programs in place at this time.

Specific Expansion Plans:

US:	All United States

7-ELEVEN, INC.

2711 N. Haskell Ave., Box 711
Dallas, TX 75204
Tel: (800) 255-0711 (214) 841-6800
Fax: (214) 841-6776
E-Mail:
Web Site: www.7-eleven.com
Ms. Joanne Webb-Joyce, National Franchise
Manager

7-ELEVEN stores were born from the simple concept of giving people 'what they want, when and where they want it.' This idea gave rise to the entire convenience store industry. While this formula still works today, customers' needs are changing at an accelerating pace. We are meeting this challenge with an infrastructure of daily distribution of fresh perishables, regional production of fresh foods and pastries and an information system that greatly improves ordering and merchandising decisions.

Background:
Established: 1927;   1st Franchised: 1964
Franchised Units: 15572
Company-Owned Units: 2666
Total Units: 18238
Minority-Owned Units:
   African-American:

Asian-American:
Hispanic:
Native American:
Other:
North America: 36 States, 5 Provinces
Density: 1,172 in CA, 604 VA, 452 FL

Financial/Terms:
Cash Investment: $76K Avg.
Total Investment: $Varies
Minimum Net Worth: $10K
Fees: Franchise — $54K Avg.
   Royalty — N/A;   Ad. — N/A
Earnings Claim Statement: No
Term of Contract (Years):   10
Avg. # Of Employees: 4 FT, 4 PT
Passive Ownership: Not Allowed
Area Develop. Agreements: No
Sub-Franchising Contracts: No
Expand In Territory: No
Space Needs: 2,400 SF; FS, SC

Support & Training Provided:
Site Selection Assistance: N/A
Lease Negotiation Assistance: N/A
Co-Operative Advertising: No
Franchisee Assoc./Member: Yes/No
Size Of Corporate Staff: 1000
On-Going Support: A,B,C,D,E,F,G,H,I
Training: 6 Weeks at Various Training Stores
Throughout the US.
Minority-Specific Programs: Although we support the objectives of the NMFI, we do not have any specific programs in place at this time.

Specific Expansion Plans:
US: NW, SW, MW, NE, Great Lakes

We'll always make time for you.

MEDICAP PHARMACY

4700 Westown Pkwy, # 300
West Des Moines, IA 50266-6730
Tel. (800) 445-2244 (515) 224-8400
Fax: (515) 224-8415
E-Mail:
Web Site: www.medicapRX.com
Mr. Calvin C. James, VP Franchise
Development

MEDICAP PHARMACY - convenient, low-cost, professional pharmacies. The stores operate in an average of 1,500 square feet. We average 90% RX and the remaining 10% over-the-counter products, including MEDICAP-brand private label. We specialize in starting new stores and converting existing full-line drug stores and independent pharmacies to the MEDICAP concept. We teach independent pharmacists how to survive in today's marketplace.

Background:
Established: 1971;   1st Franchised: 1974
Franchised Units: 172
Company-Owned Units: 15
Total Units: 187
Minority-Owned Units:
   African-American:
   Asian-American:
   Hispanic:
   Native American:
North America: 38 States
Density: 50 in IA, 11 in SC, 10 in IL

Financial/Terms:

Cash Investment:	$10K-45K
Total Investment:	$20-300.5K
Minimum Net Worth:	$NR
Fees: Franchise —	$8.5-15K
Royalty — 2/4%;	Ad. — 1%
Earnings Claim Statement:	Yes
Term of Contract (Years):	20/20
Avg. # Of Employees:	2 FT
Passive Ownership:	Allowed
Area Develop. Agreements:	No
Sub-Franchising Contracts:	No
Expand In Territory:	Yes
Space Needs: 1,500 SF; FS, SF, SC	

Support & Training Provided:

Site Selection Assistance:	Yes
Lease Negotiation Assistance:	Yes
Co-Operative Advertising:	N/A
Franchisee Assoc./Member:	NR
Size Of Corporate Staff:	52
On-Going Support:	B,C,D,E,F,G,H,I
Training: 5 Days Headquarters; 3 Days On-Site; 3 Days Computer.	

Minority-Specific Programs: Although we support the objectives of the NMFI, we do not have any specific programs in place at this time.

Specific Expansion Plans:

US:	All United States

STAR MART

10445 W. Office Dr.
Houston, TX 77042
Tel: (888) 629-6919
Fax: (713) 952-3830
E-Mail: rbgoodyear@equiva.com
Web Site: www.starmart@equiva.com
Mr. Bob Goodyear, Manager Franchise Development

STAR MART is a convenience store franchise that is combined with the well-recognized Texaco gasoline brand to give our customers an unparalleled service experience.

Background:

Established: 1902;	1st Franchised: 1992
Franchised Units:	116
Company-Owned Units:	322
Total Units:	438
Minority-Owned Units:	

African-American:	6%
Asian-American:	0%
Hispanic:	0%
Native American:	0%
North America:	11 States
Density:	84 in CA, 62 in AZ, 57 in WA

Financial/Terms:

Cash Investment:	$20%/300K
Total Investment:	$70K-2.75MM
Minimum Net Worth:	$600K
Fees: Franchise —	$25K
Royalty — 4%;	Ad. — 2%
Earnings Claim Statement:	No
Term of Contract (Years):	3
Avg. # Of Employees:	5 FT, 6 PT
Passive Ownership:	Discouraged
Area Develop. Agreements:	No
Sub-Franchising Contracts:	No
Expand In Territory:	Yes
Space Needs: NR SF; FS	

Support & Training Provided:

Site Selection Assistance:	No
Lease Negotiation Assistance:	Yes
Co-Operative Advertising:	No
Franchisee Assoc./Member:	Yes
Size Of Corporate Staff:	15
On-Going Support:	C,D,E,G,H
Training: 3 Weeks Orange County, CA.	

Minority-Specific Programs: No specific program. Third party financing available to all qualified applicants.

Specific Expansion Plans:

US:	Our target markets only.

UNCLESAM'S CONVENIENT STORE

P. O. Box 870
Elsa, TX 78543-0870
Tel: (888) 786-7373 (956) 262-7273
Fax: (956) 262-7290
E-Mail: uscs12@aol.com
Web Site: www.unclesamscstore.com
Mr. Jackie L. Thomas, Executive Vice President

A turn-key convenience store franchise program available in 31 states. Affiliated with major fuel and merchandise suppliers. Attractive financing available to qualified candidates. Training, site evaluation, store design, operations manual, software package, advertising, promotions, security systems, deli, car wash and many more benefits.

Background:

Established: 1970;	1st Franchised: 1997
Franchised Units:	1
Company-Owned Units:	52
Total Units:	53
Minority-Owned Units:	
African-American:	0
Asian-American:	0
Hispanic:	0
Native American:	0
Other:	0
North America:	1 State
Density:	52 in TX

Financial/Terms:

Cash Investment:	$100K+
Total Investment:	$800K+
Minimum Net Worth:	$300K
Fees: Franchise —	$25K
Royalty — 5%;	Ad. — 1%
Earnings Claim Statement:	No
Term of Contract (Years):	5/5/5/5/5
Avg. # Of Employees:	6 FT, 2 PT
Passive Ownership:	Discouraged
Area Develop. Agreements:	Yes/5
Sub-Franchising Contracts:	No
Expand In Territory:	Yes
Space Needs: 2,500+ SF; FS	

Support & Training Provided:

Site Selection Assistance:	Yes
Lease Negotiation Assistance:	Yes
Co-Operative Advertising:	Yes
Franchisee Assoc./Member:	Yes/No
Size Of Corporate Staff:	6
On-Going Support:	a,B,C,d,E,F,I
Training: 4 Weeks at Corporate Headquarters.	

Minority-Specific Programs: We support and encourage minority ownership of UNCLESAM'S CONVENIENT STORES. At the present time we do not have minority classified franchisees. But, we are in serious discussions with some.

Specific Expansion Plans:

US:	South, SW, SE, East, West

WHITE HEN PANTRY

660 Industrial Dr.
Elmhurst, IL 60126
Tel: (800) PANTRY-1 (630) 833-3100
Fax: (630) 833-0292
E-Mail:

Web Site:

Ms. Gail M. Bosch, Franchising Manager

WHITE HEN PANTRY is a neighborhood convenience store, specializing in fresh-brewed coffee, full-service deli, custom-made sandwiches and salads, fresh produce and a bakery.

Background:

Established: 1965;	1st Franchised: 1965
Franchised Units:	298
Company-Owned Units:	2
Total Units:	300

Minority-Owned Units:

African-American:

Asian-American:

Hispanic:

Native American:

Other:

North America:	4 States
Density:	238 in IL, 56 in MA, 6 in IN

Financial/Terms:

Cash Investment:	$56.8K+
Total Investment:	$Flexible
Minimum Net Worth:	$N/A
Fees: Franchise —	$25K
Royalty — 7%+;	Ad. — Included
Earnings Claim Statement:	Yes
Term of Contract (Years):	10/10
Avg. # Of Employees:	2 FT, 12 PT
Passive Ownership:	Not Allowed
Area Develop. Agreements:	No
Sub-Franchising Contracts:	No
Expand In Territory:	No

Space Needs: 2,500 SF; SC

Support & Training Provided:

Site Selection Assistance:	Yes
Lease Negotiation Assistance:	Yes
Co-Operative Advertising:	N/A
Franchisee Assoc./Member:	Yes
Size Of Corporate Staff:	260
On-Going Support:	A,C,D,E,F,G,H,I

Training: 1 Week Corporate Office; 2 Weeks On-Site.

Minority-Specific Programs: While our programs are not specifically geared only to the minority candidate, we offer full support in all of the areas listed above to include a flexible down payment, financing, deferred fees for select locations and on-going support to all of our franchisees.

Specific Expansion Plans:

US:	IL, IN, MA, NH Only

CARPET NETWORK

109 Gaither Dr., # 302
Mount Laurel, NJ 08054
Tel: (800) 428-1067 (856) 273-9393
Fax: (856) 273-0160
E-Mail: CPTNetwork@aol.com
Web Site: www.carpetnetwork.com
Mr. Leonard Rankin, President

'The Traveling Floor and Window Store.' A mobile business offering carpet, area rugs, laminate, wood, vinyl flooring and window treatments in the convenience of the consumer's home or business. Over 4,000 selections from leading manufacturers, serving today's 'time starved' consumer. Large exclusive territories, marketing strategy - training - 24-hour support and much more.

Background:

Established: 1991;	1st Franchised: 1992
Franchised Units:	42
Company-Owned Units:	1
Total Units:	43
Minority-Owned Units:	
African-American:	0
Asian-American:	0
Hispanic:	0
Native American:	0
Other:	
North America:	19 States
Density:	PA, NY, NJ

Financial/Terms:

Cash Investment:	$20-30K
Total Investment:	$20-30K

Minimum Net Worth:	$20K
Fees: Franchise —	$15.5K
Royalty — 5%;	Ad. — 0%
Earnings Claim Statement:	No
Term of Contract (Years):	10/10
Avg. # Of Employees:	1 FT
Passive Ownership:	Discouraged
Area Develop. Agreements:	Yes/10
Sub-Franchising Contracts:	No
Expand In Territory:	Yes
Space Needs: NR SF; HB	

Support & Training Provided:

Site Selection Assistance:	Yes
Lease Negotiation Assistance:	N/A
Co-Operative Advertising:	N/A
Franchisee Assoc./Member:	Yes/Yes
Size Of Corporate Staff:	5
On-Going Support:	G,h,I

Training: 6 Days at Corporate Office, Mt. Laurel, NJ.
Minority-Specific Programs: Although we support the objectives of the NMFI, we do not have any specific programs in place at this time.

Specific Expansion Plans:

US:	All United States

DECOR-AT-YOUR-DOOR INTERNATIONAL

P. O. Box 2290
Pollock Pines, CA 95726
Tel: (800) 936-3326 (530) 644-6056
Fax: (530) 644-3326
E-Mail:
Web Site:
Mr. Steven L. McGee, President/CEO

One of the best franchises in America, selling national-brand carpet, blinds and wallpaper direct to the home-owner from a custom mobile showcase. We train you, no experience necessary, to work part- or full-time. No quotas, no transfer or renewal charge. Royalty only $100 or 3% per month. Expanded selling area, order-processing available. Very low product cost, just sell carpet and blinds at great prices. CHECK US OUT!

Background:

Established: 1983;	1st Franchised: 1995
Franchised Units:	31
Company-Owned Units:	7
Total Units:	38
Minority-Owned Units:	
African-American:	
Asian-American:	
Hispanic:	
Native American:	
Other:	
North America:	17 States
Density:	6 in CA, 2 in TX, 2 in HI

Financial/Terms:

Cash Investment:	$5K

Total Investment:	$5K
Minimum Net Worth:	$5K
Fees: Franchise —	$4K
Royalty — 1%;	Ad. — 1%
Earnings Claim Statement:	No
Term of Contract (Years):	7
Avg. # Of Employees:	1 PT
Passive Ownership:	Allowed
Area Develop. Agreements:	No
Sub-Franchising Contracts:	No
Expand In Territory:	No
Space Needs: N/A SF; Mobile	

Support & Training Provided:

Site Selection Assistance:	N/A
Lease Negotiation Assistance:	N/A
Co-Operative Advertising:	No
Franchisee Assoc./Member:	No
Size Of Corporate Staff:	5
On-Going Support:	A,b,C,E,F,G,h

Training: 1 Week Corporate Office or In-Field.

Minority-Specific Programs: Although we support the objectives of the NMFI, we do not have any specific programs in place at this time.

Specific Expansion Plans:

US:	All United States

**FLOOR COVERINGS
INTERNATIONAL**

5182B Old Dixie Hwy.
Forest Park, GA 30297
Tel: (800) 955-4324 (404) 361-5047
Fax: (404) 366-4606
E-Mail: jsmith@carpetvan.com
Web Site: www.carpetvan.com
Ms. Janice Hall, Director of Development

FLOOR COVERINGS INTERNATIONAL is the 'Flooring Store at youir Door.' FCI is the first and leading mobile "shop at home" flooring store. Customers can select from over 3,000 styles and colors of flooring right in their own home! All the right ingredients are there to simplify a buying decision. We offer all the brand names you and your customers will be familiar with. We carry all types of flooring, as well as window blinds.

Background:

Established: 1988;	1st Franchised: 1989	
Franchised Units:		249
Company-Owned Units:		0
Total Units:		249
Minority-Owned Units:		
African-American:		
Asian-American:		
Hispanic:		
Native American:		
Other:		
North America:	43 States, 5 Provinces	
Density:	15 in PA, 11 in OH, 9 in IL	

Financial/Terms:

Cash Investment:	$25K
Total Investment:	$21.9K
Minimum Net Worth:	$25K
Fees: Franchise —	$16K
Royalty — 5%/$45/Wk.;Ad.	—
2%/$15/Wk.	
Earnings Claim Statement:	No
Term of Contract (Years):	10/10
Avg. # Of Employees:	1 FT
Passive Ownership:	Discouraged
Area Develop. Agreements:	No
Sub-Franchising Contracts:	No
Expand In Territory:	Yes
Space Needs: NR SF; Mobile Van	

Support & Training Provided:

Site Selection Assistance:	Yes
Lease Negotiation Assistance:	N/A
Co-Operative Advertising:	Yes
Franchisee Assoc./Member:	No
Size Of Corporate Staff:	14
On-Going Support:	C,D,G,H,I

Training: 2 Weeks Home Study; 2 Weeks Atlanta, GA.

Minority-Specific Programs: Although we support the objectives of the NMFI, we do not have any specific programs in place at this time.

Specific Expansion Plans:

US:	All United States

NAKED FURNITURE

1157 Lackawanna Trail, P. O. Box F
Clarks Summit, PA 18411
Tel: (800) 352-2522 (570) 587-7800
Fax: (570) 586-8587
E-Mail: nkdfurn@epix.net
Web Site: www.nakedfurniture.com
Mr. Bruce C. MacGowan, President

NAKED FURNITURE is the nation's largest retailer of custom-finished and ready-to-finish solid wood home furnishings. We offer a wide range of innovative and affordable choices. We serve our markets with attractive, professionally-run stores and a diverse selection of quality furniture and accessories that allow our store owners to maintain their leadership position in the rapidly-growing specialty furniture market.

Background:

Established: 1972;	1st Franchised: 1979	
Franchised Units:		34
Company-Owned Units:		3
Total Units:		37
Minority-Owned Units:		
African-American:		0
Asian-American:		1
Hispanic:		0
Native American:		0
Other:		
North America:		12 States
Density:	9 in MI, 8 in IL, 5 in PA	

Financial/Terms:

Cash Investment:	$72-123K
Total Investment:	$143-245K
Minimum Net Worth:	$NR
Fees: Franchise —	$19.5K
Royalty — 4%;	Ad. — 1%
Earnings Claim Statement:	No
Term of Contract (Years):	10/10
Avg. # Of Employees:	3 FT, 2 PT
Passive Ownership:	Allowed
Area Develop. Agreements:	Yes
Sub-Franchising Contracts:	No
Expand In Territory:	Yes
Space Needs: 6,500+ SF; FS, SF, SC, RM	

Support & Training Provided:

Site Selection Assistance:	Yes
Lease Negotiation Assistance:	Yes
Co-Operative Advertising:	No
Franchisee Assoc./Member:	Yes/Yes
Size Of Corporate Staff:	19
On-Going Support:	a,B,C,D,E,F,G,h,I

Training: 1 Week Headquarters; 1 Week On-Site.

Minority-Specific Programs: Although we support the objectives of the NMFI, we do not have any specific programs in place at this time.

Specific Expansion Plans:

US:	All United States

**VERLO MATTRESS FACTORY
STORES**

P. O. Box 298; W3130 Route 4 Hwy 59
Whitewater, WI 53190
Tel: (800) 229-8957 (414) 473-8957
Fax: (414) 473-4623
E-Mail:
Web Site: www.verlo.com
Mr. James M. Young, Director of Franchise
Awards

VERLO MATTRESS FACTORY STORES
(R) is the nation's largest CRAFTSMAN
DIRECT (R) retailer. Each franchise
assembles hand-crafted mattresses to the
customer's specifics. With unparalleled
support and an operating system in place
to take us into the next century, this is an
opportunity you will need to investigate.

Background:
Established: 1958;   1st Franchised: 1981
Franchised Units: 65
Company-Owned Units: 2
Total Units: 67
Minority-Owned Units:
   African-American:
   Asian-American:
   Hispanic:
   Native American:
   Other: 5 Units Minority-Owned
North America: 8 States
Density: 26 in IL, 21 in WI, 5 in MO

Financial/Terms:
Cash Investment: $100-150K
Total Investment: $100-150K
Minimum Net Worth: $400K
Fees: Franchise — $30K
   Royalty — 5%;   Ad. — $300/Mo.
Earnings Claim Statement: No
Term of Contract (Years):   5/5
Avg. # Of Employees: 3+ FT
Passive Ownership: Allowed
Area Develop. Agreements: Yes/Varies
Sub-Franchising Contracts: No
Expand In Territory: Yes
Space Needs: 3,000-10,000 SF; FS, SF, Store
Within a Store

Support & Training Provided:
Site Selection Assistance: Yes
Lease Negotiation Assistance: Yes
Co-Operative Advertising: No
Franchisee Assoc./Member: Yes/Yes

Size Of Corporate Staff: 20
On-Going Support: B,C,D,E,G,H,i
Training: 12 Days Corporate Office; 7 Days
On-Site; On-Going.
Minority-Specific Programs: We are
registered through the Small Business
Administration franchise registry program.
Franchisees of the VERLO MATTRESS
FACTORY STORES are eligible for
expedited SBA loan processing through SBA
franchise registry program.

Specific Expansion Plans:
US: All United States

ASHLEY AVERY'S COLLECTABLES

100 Glenborough Dr., 14th Fl.
Houston, TX 77067
Tel: (800) 543-3325 (281) 775-5290
Fax: (281) 775-5250
Web Site: www.ashleyaverys.com
Ms. Ann Nance, Franchise Recruitment
Manager

At ASHLEY AVERY'S COLLECTABLES you will find up-scale, proven products from the best-known names in the collectables industry. Our stores are located in high-traffic regional malls. Our concept offers both an attractive, free-standing boutique, or an elegant, in-line store.

Background:
Established: 1981;	1st Franchised: 1990
Franchised Units:	35
Company-Owned Units:	1
Total Units:	36
Minority-Owned Units:	
African-American:	0
Asian-American:	0
Hispanic:	0
Native American:	0
North America:	13 States
Density:	17 in TX, 4 in FL, 2 in GA

Financial/Terms:
Cash Investment:	$125K
Total Investment:	$262.8-366.8K
Minimum Net Worth:	$300K
Fees: Franchise —	$30K
Royalty — 6%;	Ad. — 2%
Earnings Claim Statement:	No
Term of Contract (Years):	10
Avg. # Of Employees:	2 FT, 2 PT
Passive Ownership:	Allowed
Area Develop. Agreements:	Yes
Sub-Franchising Contracts:	No
Expand In Territory:	Yes
Space Needs: 200-1,800 SF; RM	

Support & Training Provided:
Site Selection Assistance:	Yes
Lease Negotiation Assistance:	Yes
Co-Operative Advertising:	Yes
Franchisee Assoc./Member:	Yes/Yes
Size Of Corporate Staff:	6
On-Going Support:	A,B,C,D,E,F,G,H,I
Training: 7 Days Houston, TX.	

Minority-Specific Programs: Although we support the objectives of the NMFI, we do not have any specific programs in place at this time.

Specific Expansion Plans:
US:	All United States

※

CAR PHONE STORE, THE

2608 Berlin Turnpike
Newington, CT 06109
Tel: (860) 571-7600
Fax: (860) 257-1818
E-Mail: info@thecarphonestore.com
Web Site: www.thecarphonestore.com
Mr. Keith Sinclair, President

THE CAR PHONE STORE/WIRELESS ZONE is a retail store chain dedicated to the sale of cellular phones, accessories and other wireless products. Volume discounted merchandise from a full-service warehouse, training, on-going support and advertising are available, enabling franchisees to concentrate on selling product and taking advantage of the wireless industry's continuing fast growth.

Background:
Established: 1988;	1st Franchised: 1988
Franchised Units:	83
Company-Owned Units:	2
Total Units:	85
Minority-Owned Units:	
African-American:	1
Asian-American:	1
Hispanic:	2
Native American:	
Other:	
North America:	11 States
Density:	29 in MA, 28 in CT, 9 in MD

Financial/Terms:
Cash Investment:	$N/A
Total Investment:	$22.9-125.8K
Minimum Net Worth:	$N/A
Fees: Franchise —	$7.5-25K
Royalty — 10-20%;	Ad. — Varies
Earnings Claim Statement:	
Term of Contract (Years):	7/7
Avg. # Of Employees:	2 FT, 1 PT
Passive Ownership:	Discouraged
Area Develop. Agreements:	No
Sub-Franchising Contracts:	Yes
Expand In Territory:	Yes
Space Needs: 1,200-2000 SF; SC	

Support & Training Provided:
Site Selection Assistance:	Yes
Lease Negotiation Assistance:	Yes

Co-Operative Advertising: Yes
Franchisee Assoc./Member: No
Size Of Corporate Staff: 41
On-Going Support: b,C,D,E,G,H
Training: 5 Days Newington, CT or 5 Days Columbia, MD.
Minority-Specific Programs: Although we support the objectives of the NMFI, we do not have any specific programs in place at this time.

Specific Expansion Plans:
US: Northeast and Mid-Atlantic

CHRISTMAS DECOR

206 23rd St., P. O. Box 5946
Lubbock, TX 79404
Tel: (800) 687-9551 (806) 772-1225
Fax: (806) 722-9627
E-Mail:
Web Site: www.christmasdecor.net
Mr. Blake K. Smith, President

Holiday and event decorating services provided to homes and businesses. Fun, high-margin business that offers annual income by working only 4-6 months of the year. Also, an excellent add-on business for landscape, pool and spa, electrical and other seasonal service contractors. Landscape lighting franchise available also to create year round business.

Background:
Established: 1986; 1st Franchised: 1996
Franchised Units: 210
Company-Owned Units: 0
Total Units: 210
Minority-Owned Units:
  African-American: 5%
  Asian-American: 0%
  Hispanic: 10%
  Native American: 0%
  Other:
North America: 44 States, 2 Provinces
Density: 23 in TX, 14 in OH, 13 in MI

Financial/Terms:
Cash Investment: $6.6-9.5K
Total Investment: $15.9-31.9K
Minimum Net Worth: $N/A
Fees: Franchise — $9.5-15.9K
  Royalty — 2-4.5%; Ad. — $180/Yr.
Earnings Claim Statement: No
Term of Contract (Years): 5/5
Avg. # Of Employees: 2-4 FT, 3-20 PT

Passive Ownership: Discouraged
Area Develop. Agreements: No
Sub-Franchising Contracts: No
Expand In Territory: No
Space Needs: Varies SF; HB, Many Add-On Businesses

Support & Training Provided:
Site Selection Assistance: Yes
Lease Negotiation Assistance: No
Co-Operative Advertising: No
Franchisee Assoc./Member: Yes/Yes
Size Of Corporate Staff: 18
On-Going Support: A,B,D,G,h,I
Training: 3 Days Major Cities in US; 2 Days of Continuing Education in Major Cities.
Minority-Specific Programs: Although we support the objectives of the NMFI, we do not have any specific programs in place at this time.

Specific Expansion Plans:
US: All United States

"America's Computer Service Store"

COMPUTER DOCTOR

12 2nd Ave. SW
Aberdeen, SD 57401
Tel: (888) 297-2292 (605) 225-4122
Fax: (605) 225-5176
E-Mail: sales @cdfs.com
Web Site: www.cdfs.com
Ms. Lisa Hinz, Director Franchise Devel.

COMPUTER DOCTOR retail stores buy, trade-in, resell used computer parts and systems, sell new computer parts, systems, printers, and components, sell computer supplies, cables, and adapters, combined with mobile on-site or in-store computer and printer repair services and upgrades. A multiple profit center in one franchise with unlimited market potential.

Background:
Established: 1992; 1st Franchised: 1996
Franchised Units: 101
Company-Owned Units: 1
Total Units: 102
Minority-Owned Units:
  African-American: 0
  Asian-American: 0
  Hispanic: 0
  Native American: 0
North America: 10 States
Density: 6 in IA, 5 in SD, 4 in ND

Financial/Terms:
Cash Investment: $15-50K
Total Investment: $38.9-170.7
Minimum Net Worth: $100K
Fees: Franchise — $10-20K
  Royalty — 3%; Ad. — 0%
Earnings Claim Statement: No
Term of Contract (Years): 5/5
Avg. # Of Employees: 1-3 ft
Passive Ownership: Discouraged
Area Develop. Agreements: Yes/10
Sub-Franchising Contracts: Yes
Expand In Territory: Yes
Space Needs: 300-1,500 SF; FS, SF, SC

Support & Training Provided:
Site Selection Assistance: Yes
Lease Negotiation Assistance: Yes
Co-Operative Advertising: No
Franchisee Assoc./Member: No
Size Of Corporate Staff: 10
On-Going Support: B,C,D,E,F,G,H,I
Training: 2 Weeks Aberdeen, SD.
Minority-Specific Programs: Although we support the objectives of the NMFI, we do not have any specific programs in place at this time.

Specific Expansion Plans:
US: All United States

CONNOISSEUR, THE

201 Torrance Blvd.
Redondo Beach, CA 90277
Tel: (310) 374-9768
Fax: (310) 372-9097
E-Mail: info@giftsofwine.com
Web Site: www.giftsofwine.com
Mr. Sandy French, President

Personalized gifts of fine wines, champagnes, gourmet, crystal and special occasion items.

Background:
Established: 1975; 1st Franchised: 1989
Franchised Units: 6
Company-Owned Units: 1
Total Units: 7
Minority-Owned Units:
  African-American: 0
  Asian-American: 0
  Hispanic: 0
  Native American: 0
  Other:
North America: 5 States
Density: 2 in CO, 2 in CA, 1 in IL

Financial/Terms:
Cash Investment: $175K
Total Investment: $175K
Minimum Net Worth: $NR

Fees: Franchise — $29.5K
    Royalty — 6%;   Ad. — 1%
Earnings Claim Statement: No
Term of Contract (Years): 10/10
Avg. # Of Employees: 1 FT, 2 PT
Passive Ownership: Discouraged
Area Develop. Agreements: Yes/10/10
Sub-Franchising Contracts: Yes
Expand In Territory: Yes
Space Needs: 2,000 SF; FS, SC, RM

Support & Training Provided:

Site Selection Assistance: Yes
Lease Negotiation Assistance: Yes
Co-Operative Advertising: No
Franchisee Assoc./Member: NR
Size Of Corporate Staff: 4
On-Going Support: A,B,C,D,E,F,H
Training: 1 Week Headquarters.
Minority-Specific Programs: Although we support the objectives of the NMFI, we do not have any specific programs in place at this time.

Specific Expansion Plans:
US: All United States

ELEPHANT HOUSE

3007 Longhorn Blvd., # 101
Austin, TX 78758
Tel: (800) 729-2273 (512) 339-3004
Fax: (512) 339-7990
E-Mail: jscott@elephanthouse.com
Web Site: www.elephanthouse.com
Ms. Julia Scott, National Sales Director

THE ELEPHANT HOUSE system is a proven, home-based greeting card franchise, where you can be your own boss. Independent retail stores are your clients, and we teach you our successful method of obtaining these clients and keeping them happy. The investment is inventory-based and includes all fees. Training is provided at your home.

Background:
Established: 1991;   1st Franchised: 1995
Franchised Units: 47
Company-Owned Units: 1
Total Units: 48
Minority-Owned Units:
   African-American: 1
   Asian-American: 0
   Hispanic: 0
   Native American: 0
   Other:
North America: NR
Density: 7 in CA, 5 in FL, 5 in TX

Financial/Terms:
Cash Investment: $Total
Total Investment: $16-26.5K
Minimum Net Worth: $50K
Fees: Franchise — $5K
    Royalty — 0%;   Ad. — 0%
Earnings Claim Statement: No
Term of Contract (Years): 7/7
Avg. # Of Employees: 1 FT
Passive Ownership: Allowed
Area Develop. Agreements: No
Sub-Franchising Contracts: No
Expand In Territory: N/A
Space Needs: NR SF; N/A

Support & Training Provided:
Site Selection Assistance: N/A
Lease Negotiation Assistance: N/A
Co-Operative Advertising: N/A
Franchisee Assoc./Member: No
Size Of Corporate Staff: 5
On-Going Support: C,D,E,G,I
Training: 5 Days in Franchisee's Territory.
Minority-Specific Programs: ELEPHANT HOUSE, INC. assists potential franchisees in preparing loan documents by providing a detailed business plan. Our home office support does not end at training, rather, our toll free line is manned 8:30 AM to 5:30 PM CST and franchisees are strongly encouraged to take advantage of our expertise. Monthly newsletters and special incentive plans are available to every franchisee who wants to grow the business.

Specific Expansion Plans:
US: All United States

FAST-FIX JEWELRY REPAIRS

1750 N. Florida Mango Rd. # 103
West Palm Beach, FL 33409
Tel: (800) 359-0407 (561) 478-5292
Fax: (561) 478-5291
E-Mail: fastfix@bellsouth.net
Web Site: www.fastfix.com
Mr. Mark Goldstein, VP Franchise Development

FAST-FIX JEWELRY REPAIRS (r) is a proven business with a 15 year track record in the multi-billion dollar jewelry and watch repair industry. FAST-FIX stores operate only in major regional malls, which guarantees high visibility and traffic. Most repairs can be completed within an hour while customers watch or enjoy shopping. FAST-FIX JEWELRY REPAIRS (r) has more than 95 franchise locations nationwide. The chain's innovative and complete training program is conducted at the site of each new store.

Background:
Established: 1984;   1st Franchised: 1987
Franchised Units: 95
Company-Owned Units: 0
Total Units: 95
Minority-Owned Units:
   African-American: 2
   Asian-American: 10
   Hispanic: 12
   Native American: 0
North America: NR
Density: 16 in FL, 16 in TX, 12 in CA

Financial/Terms:
Cash Investment: $35-50K
Total Investment: $102-170K
Minimum Net Worth: $N/A
Fees: Franchise — $25K
    Royalty — 5%;   Ad. — 0%
Earnings Claim Statement: No
Term of Contract (Years): 10/10
Avg. # Of Employees: 2 FT, 2 PT
Passive Ownership: Discouraged
Area Develop. Agreements: Yes/10
Sub-Franchising Contracts: No
Expand In Territory: Yes
Space Needs: 150-700 SF; RM

Support & Training Provided:
Site Selection Assistance: Yes
Lease Negotiation Assistance: Yes
Co-Operative Advertising: N/A
Franchisee Assoc./Member: Yes/Yes
Size Of Corporate Staff: 8
On-Going Support: B,C,D,E,G,H,I
Training: 6 Days On-Site.
Minority-Specific Programs: Although we support the objectives of the NMFI, we do not have any specific programs in place at this time.

Specific Expansion Plans:
US: All United States

FLAG SHOP, THE

1755 West 4th Ave.
Vancouver, BC V6J 1M2 CANADA

Tel: (800) 663-8681 (604) 736-8161
Fax: (604) 736-6439
E-Mail: doreenb@flagshop.ca
Web Site: www.flagshop.com
Ms. Doreen Braverman, President

Flags and banners, retail and custom-designed, flagpole, flag hardware, pins, crests, books, charts, windsocks--everything flag-related. We sell from catalogues, through dealers and our retail shops.

Background:
Established: 1974;   1st Franchised: 1988
Franchised Units: 8
Company-Owned Units: 2
Total Units: 10
Minority-Owned Units:
  African-American: 1
  Asian-American:
  Hispanic:
  Native American: 1
North America: 7 Provinces
Density: 2 in BC, 2 in AB, 2 in ON

Financial/Terms:
Cash Investment: $80K
Total Investment: $70-90K
Minimum Net Worth: $250K
Fees: Franchise — $25K
  Royalty — 4%;   Ad. — 2%
Earnings Claim Statement: Yes
Term of Contract (Years):   10/10
Avg. # Of Employees: 3 FT, 1 PT
Passive Ownership: Allowed
Area Develop. Agreements: No
Sub-Franchising Contracts: Yes
Expand In Territory: Yes
Space Needs: 1,200+ SF; FS, SF, SC

Support & Training Provided:
Site Selection Assistance: Yes
Lease Negotiation Assistance: Yes
Co-Operative Advertising: No
Franchisee Assoc./Member: No
Size Of Corporate Staff: 27
On-Going Support: A,B,C,D,e,G,h
Training: 3 Weeks Vancouver, BC; 1 Week Franchise Location.
Minority-Specific Programs: We do not discriminate on the basis of race or religion. We seek the best regardless.

Specific Expansion Plans:
US: No

GENERAL NUTRITION CENTERS

300 Sixth Ave.
Pittsburgh, PA 15222
Tel: (800) 766-7099 (412) 288-2043

Fax: (412) 288-2033
E-Mail: franchising@gnc-hq.com
Web Site: www.gncfranchising.com
Director of Franchising,

GNC is the leading national specialty retailer of vitamins, minerals, herbs and sports nutrition supplements and is uniquely positioned to capitalize on the accelerating self-care trend. As the leading provider of products and information for personal health enhancement, the company holds the largest specialty-retail share of the nutritional supplement market. GNC was ranked America's #1 retail franchise in 1998/1999 by Entrepreneur International.

Background:
Established: 1935;   1st Franchised: 1988
Franchised Units: 1563
Company-Owned Units: 2825
Total Units: 4388
Minority-Owned Units:
  African-American: 38
  Asian-American: 63
  Hispanic: 76
  Native American: 0
  Other: 178 Other, 88 Unknown
North America: 50 States, 1 Province
Density: 408 in CA, 340 in FL, 293 TX

Financial/Terms:
Cash Investment: $32.5-60K
Total Investment: $118.2-173.0K
Minimum Net Worth: $60K
Fees: Franchise — $32.5K
  Royalty — 6%;   Ad. — 3%
Earnings Claim Statement: Yes
Term of Contract (Years):   10/5
Avg. # Of Employees: 1 FT, 3-5 PT
Passive Ownership: Not Allowed
Area Develop. Agreements: Yes/Varies
Sub-Franchising Contracts: No
Expand In Territory: Yes
Space Needs: 1,402 (avg.) SF; SC, RM

Support & Training Provided:
Site Selection Assistance: Yes
Lease Negotiation Assistance: Yes
Co-Operative Advertising: Yes
Franchisee Assoc./Member: Yes/Yes
Size Of Corporate Staff: 574
On-Going Support: A,B,C,D,E,F,G,H,I
Training: 1 Wk. On-Site in Local Corporate Store; 1 Wk. in Pittsburgh, PA; 1 Wk. opening assistance.
Minority-Specific Programs: GNC Directors of Financing promote minority assistance

programs including the Local Initiative Support Corporation and programs associated with the International Franchise Association. Minorities also have the opportunity to utilize GNC's special Expansion Market financing.

Specific Expansion Plans:
US: All United States

LATEX CITY

1814 Franklin St., # 820
Oakland, CA 94612
Tel: (510) 839-5462
Fax: (510) 839-2104
E-Mail:
Web Site:
Dr. David C. Brown, President

Unique ground-floor specialty retailing opportunity in booming latex novelty aid business. Complete line of proprietary products. Turn-key package includes lease negotiation, fully-stocked inventory, in-store merchandising/display. On-going support. LATEX CITY is ideal for aggressive couples. This is not smut - but a highly profitable, high-margin, fully legal business.

Background:
Established: 1972;   1st Franchised: 1986
Franchised Units: 26
Company-Owned Units: 4
Total Units: 30
Minority-Owned Units:
  African-American: 2
  Asian-American: 4
  Hispanic: 2
  Native American: 0
  Other:
North America: 17 States, 1 Province
Density: 3 in CA, 3 in NY, 2 in OR

Financial/Terms:
Cash Investment: $65K
Total Investment: $85-235K
Minimum Net Worth: $NR
Fees: Franchise — $15K
  Royalty — 6%;   Ad. — 2%
Earnings Claim Statement: Yes
Term of Contract (Years):   10/10
Avg. # Of Employees: 2 FT
Passive Ownership: Discouraged
Area Develop. Agreements: Yes/5
Sub-Franchising Contracts: No
Expand In Territory: No
Space Needs: 1,000-1,400 SF; FS, SF, SC, RM

Support & Training Provided:
Site Selection Assistance: Yes

Lease Negotiation Assistance: Yes
Co-Operative Advertising: Yes
Franchisee Assoc./Member: NR
Size Of Corporate Staff: 6
On-Going Support: A,B,C,D,G,H
Training: 3 Weeks Headquarters; 1 Week
Plant; 2 Weeks On-Site.
Minority-Specific Programs: Although we
support the objectives of the NMFI, we do
not have any specific programs in place at
this time.

Specific Expansion Plans:
US: All United States

LITTLE PROFESSOR BOOK CENTERS

405 Little Lake Dr., # C
Ann Arbor, MI 48103
Tel: (800) 899-6232 (734) 994-1212
Fax: (734) 994-9009
E-Mail: lpbchome@aol.com
Web Site: www.littleprofessor.com
Ms. Christi M. Shaw, Franchise
Development Manager

Full-line, full-service, community-oriented
general bookstore.

Background:
Established: 1964;   1st Franchised: 1969
Franchised Units: 65
Company-Owned Units: 0
Total Units: 65
Minority-Owned Units:
   African-American:
   Asian-American:
   Hispanic:
   Native American:
   Other: 25 Women
North America: 29 States
Density: 12 in OH, 8 in WI, 8 in MI

Financial/Terms:
Cash Investment: $100-500K
Total Investment: $300K-1.5MM
Minimum Net Worth: $250K
Fees: Franchise — $37K
   Royalty — 3%;   Ad. — 0.5%
Earnings Claim Statement: Yes
Term of Contract (Years):   10/10
Avg. # Of Employees: 2 FT, 6 PT
Passive Ownership: Discouraged
Area Develop. Agreements: No
Sub-Franchising Contracts: No
Expand In Territory: Yes
Space Needs: 3,000-15,000 SF; FS, SF, SC

Support & Training Provided:
Site Selection Assistance: Yes
Lease Negotiation Assistance: Yes
Co-Operative Advertising: Yes
Franchisee Assoc./Member: Yes/Yes
Size Of Corporate Staff: 10
On-Going Support: A,b,C,d,E,F,G,H,h,I
Training: 1 Week Ann Arbor, MI (Home
Office), 1-2 Weeks On-Site, LPBC
Coventions Once a Year
Minority-Specific Programs: Although we
support the objectives of the NMFI, we do
not have any specific programs in place at
this time.

Specific Expansion Plans:
US: Midwest

MUSIC-GO-ROUND

4200 Dahlberg Dr.
Minneapolis, MN 55422-4837
Tel: (800) 645-7298 (612) 520-8419
Fax: (612) 520-84501
E-Mail: jschwitzer@growbiz.com
Web Site: www.musicgoround.com
Mr. Jim Schwitzer, National Franchise
Development

MUSIC GO ROUND is a franchised, retail
music store that buys, sells, trades and
consigns used and new musical instruments,
gear and equipment. Our success formula is
based on buying and selling used products,
aggressive marketing, retail site selection and
support of franchises.

Background:
Established: 1986;   1st Franchised: 1994
Franchised Units: 72
Company-Owned Units: 8
Total Units: 80
Minority-Owned Units:
   African-American: 1
   Asian-American: 2
   Hispanic: 0
   Native American: 1
   Other:
North America: 30 States
Density: 12 in MN, 9 in IL, 4 in WI

Financial/Terms:
Cash Investment: $45-60K
Total Investment: $186.4-254.9K
Minimum Net Worth: $200K Appx.
Fees: Franchise — $20K
   Royalty — 3%;   Ad. — $500/Yr.

Earnings Claim Statement: Yes
Term of Contract (Years):   10/10
Avg. # Of Employees: 2 FT, 2 PT
Passive Ownership: Discouraged
Area Develop. Agreements: Yes/3
Sub-Franchising Contracts: No
Expand In Territory: Yes
Space Needs: 2,500 SF; SC

Support & Training Provided:
Site Selection Assistance: Yes
Lease Negotiation Assistance: Yes
Co-Operative Advertising: Yes
Franchisee Assoc./Member: No
Size Of Corporate Staff: 175
On-Going Support: A,C,D,E,F,G,h,I
Training: 11 Days at Home Office.
Minority-Specific Programs: Although we
support the objectives of the NMFI, we do
not have any specific programs in place at
this time.

Specific Expansion Plans:
US: All United States

PAPER WAREHOUSE/PARTY UNIVERSE

7630 Excelsior Blvd.
Minneapolis, MN 55426-4504
Tel: (800) 229-1792 (612) 936-1000
Fax: (612) 936-9800
E-Mail:
mikeanderson@paperwarehouse.com
Web Site: www.paperwarehouse.com
Mr. Mike Anderson, Vice President of
Franchising

PARTY UNIVERSE is a specialty retailer,
featuring party supplies, balloons and
greeting cards at everyday discount prices.
Single and multiple unit markets are available.
PARTY UNIVERSE provides the following
support: site selection and leasing, store
planning, classroom and in-store training,
store set-up, pre-opening team, extensive
merchandise selection with factory direct
purchasing, comprehensive print, direct mail
and electronic advertising programs.

Background:
Established: 1985;   1st Franchised: 1987
Franchised Units: 46
Company-Owned Units: 97

Total Units: 143
Minority-Owned Units:
  African-American:
  Asian-American:
  Hispanic:
  Native American:
  Other:
North America: 23 States
Density: 29 in MN, 21 in KS, 19 in CO

Financial/Terms:
Cash Investment: $54.6-132K
Total Investment: $165.4-430K
Minimum Net Worth: $250K+
Fees: Franchise — $19-25K
  Royalty — 4%; Ad. — N/A
Earnings Claim Statement: No
Term of Contract (Years): 10/10
Avg. # Of Employees: 2 FT, 4 PT
Passive Ownership: Allowed
Area Develop. Agreements: Yes/5
Sub-Franchising Contracts: No
Expand In Territory: Yes
Space Needs: 4,000-8,500 SF; FS, SC

Support & Training Provided:
Site Selection Assistance: Yes
Lease Negotiation Assistance: Yes
Co-Operative Advertising: No
Franchisee Assoc./Member: No
Size Of Corporate Staff: 59
On-Going Support: C,D,E,F,G,H,I
Training: 4 Nights, 5 Days in Minneapolis, MN.
Minority-Specific Programs: We do support the initiative and would love to have some minority franchisees. We would help them in any way possible.

Specific Expansion Plans:
US: All United States and Canada

PARTY LAND

5215 Militia Hill Rd.
Plymouth Meeting, PA 19462-1216
Tel: (800) 778-9563 (610) 941-6200
Fax: (610) 941-6301
E-Mail: jbarry@partyland.com
Web Site: www.partyland.com
Mr. John L. Barry, VP Franchise Sales

World's largest international retail party supply franchise, specializing in service, selection and savings. The official party store for the 'new millennium.'

Background:
Established: 1986; 1st Franchised: 1988

Franchised Units: 102
Company-Owned Units: 5
Total Units: 107
Minority-Owned Units:
  African-American: 5
  Asian-American: 5
  Hispanic: 5
  Native American:
  Other:
North America: 23 States, 3 Provinces
Density: 20 in PA, 8 in TX, 3 in CO

Financial/Terms:
Cash Investment: $80K
Total Investment: $249-329K
Minimum Net Worth: $250K
Fees: Franchise — $35K
  Royalty — 5%; Ad. — 4%
Earnings Claim Statement: No
Term of Contract (Years): 20/10
Avg. # Of Employees: 2 FT, 6 PT
Passive Ownership: Allowed
Area Develop. Agreements: Yes/5
Sub-Franchising Contracts: Yes
Expand In Territory: No
Space Needs: NR SF; FS, SF, SC

Support & Training Provided:
Site Selection Assistance: Yes
Lease Negotiation Assistance: Yes
Co-Operative Advertising: Yes
Franchisee Assoc./Member: Yes/Yes
Size Of Corporate Staff: 30+
On-Going Support: A,B,C,D,E,F,G,H,I
Training: 1 Week Party Land University.
Minority-Specific Programs: PARTY LAND currently has a multi-unit regional development program for minorities.

Specific Expansion Plans:
US: All United States

TFM

10333 - 174 St.
Edmonton, AB T5S 1H1 CANADA
Tel: (780) 483-3217
Fax: (780) 486-7528
E-Mail: tfm@istar.ca
Web Site:
Mr. A. J. Herfst, President

Retail sales of pre-recorded music, including

compact discs, cassettes, videos and DVD, as well as related accessories and other paraphernalia. Franchisor provides full turn-key operation, inventory controls and full operational guidance.

Background:
Established: 1974; 1st Franchised: 1985
Franchised Units: 14
Company-Owned Units: 3
Total Units: 17
Minority-Owned Units:
  African-American: 0
  Asian-American: 0
  Hispanic: 0
  Native American: 0
  Other: 3
North America: 7 Provinces
Density: 7 in AB, 5 in SK, 3 in BC

Financial/Terms:
Cash Investment: $40-80K
Total Investment: $125-200K
Minimum Net Worth: $N/A
Fees: Franchise — $15K
  Royalty — 5%; Ad. — 1%
Earnings Claim Statement: No
Term of Contract (Years): 5/5
Avg. # Of Employees: 2 FT, 4 PT
Passive Ownership: Allowed
Area Develop. Agreements: No
Sub-Franchising Contracts: No
Expand In Territory: Yes
Space Needs: 1,400 SF; RM

Support & Training Provided:
Site Selection Assistance: Yes
Lease Negotiation Assistance: Yes
Co-Operative Advertising: Yes
Franchisee Assoc./Member: No
Size Of Corporate Staff: 5
On-Going Support: B,C,D,E,F,H
Training: 1 Week Headquarters; 1 Week In Store; 2 Day Refresher On-Site.
Minority-Specific Programs: Although we support the objectives of the NMFI, we do not have any specific programs in place at this time.

Specific Expansion Plans:
US: Canada only

TINDER BOX INTERNATIONAL

Three Bala Plaza East, # 102
Bala Cynwyd, PA 19004
Tel: (800) 846-3372 (610) 668-4220
Fax: (610) 668-4266
E-Mail: tbiltd@ix.netcom.com
Web Site: www.tinderbox.com

Mr. Fred Haas, Director Franchise
Development

The world's largest and oldest chain of premium cigar, tobacco, smoking accessory and gift stores, with 70 years' experience as the undisputed industry leader.

Background:

Established: 1928;   1st Franchised: 1965

Franchised Units:	128
Company-Owned Units:	<u>3</u>
Total Units:	131
Minority-Owned Units:	
African-American:	0%
Asian-American:	12%
Hispanic:	1%
Native American:	0%
North America:	50 States
Density:	17 in CA, 9 in IL, 9 in OH

Financial/Terms:

Cash Investment:	$75-100K
Total Investment:	$175-250K
Minimum Net Worth:	$250-300K
Fees: Franchise —	$30K
Royalty — 4-5%;	Ad. — 3%
Earnings Claim Statement:	Yes
Term of Contract (Years):	10/5
Avg. # Of Employees:	1-2 FT, 2-3 PT
Passive Ownership:	Allowed
Area Develop. Agreements:	Yes/5
Sub-Franchising Contracts:	No
Expand In Territory:	Yes

Space Needs: 800-1,500 SF; FS, SF, SC, RM

Support & Training Provided:

Site Selection Assistance:	Yes
Lease Negotiation Assistance:	Yes
Co-Operative Advertising:	Yes
Franchisee Assoc./Member:	No
Size Of Corporate Staff:	10
On-Going Support:	a,C,D,E,F,G,H,I

Training: 5 Days Home Office; 3-5 Days at Franchisee's Store; Follow-Up Store Visit within 30 Days

Minority-Specific Programs: Although we support the objectives of the NMFI, we do not have any specific programs in place at this time.

Specific Expansion Plans:

US:	All United States

CD WAREHOUSE

1204 Sovereign Row
Oklahoma City, OK 73108
Tel: (800) 641-9394 (405) 949-2422
Fax: (405) 949-2566
E-Mail: cdwhome@cdwarehouse.co
Web Site: www.cdwarehouse.com
Ms. Vicky L. Sugg, Franchise Sales Manager

CD WAREHOUSE is a rapidly-growing franchise, specializing in the sale of pre-owned CDs. Our stores also buy and trade used CD's, sell Top 100 new CDs, and sell other music-related items. Our proprietary software makes it easy to buy and sell pre-owned CDs, even without prior music knowledge.

Background:

Established: 1992;	1st Franchised: 1992
Franchised Units:	262
Company-Owned Units:	71
Total Units:	333
Minority-Owned Units:	
African-American:	1
Asian-American:	
Hispanic:	
Native American:	
North America:	41 States, 4 Provinces
Density:	50 in TX, 22 in FL, 11 in OH

Financial/Terms:

Cash Investment:	$30-40K
Total Investment:	$123-151K
Minimum Net Worth:	$150K
Fees: Franchise —	$15K
Royalty — 5%;	Ad. — 1.75%+0.50%
Earnings Claim Statement:	No
Term of Contract (Years):	10/10

Avg. # Of Employees:	1-3 FT 3-4 PT
Passive Ownership:	Discouraged
Area Develop. Agreements:	Yes
Sub-Franchising Contracts:	No
Expand In Territory:	Yes
Space Needs: 1,500-2,000 SF; SC	

Support & Training Provided:

Site Selection Assistance:	Yes
Lease Negotiation Assistance:	Yes
Co-Operative Advertising:	Yes
Franchisee Assoc./Member:	No
Size Of Corporate Staff:	67
On-Going Support:	A,B,C,D,E,G,H,I

Training: 5 days at Oklahoma City, OK. 4-5 days at store location.
Minority-Specific Programs: Although we support the objectives of the NMFI, we do not have any specific programs in place at this time.

Specific Expansion Plans:

US:	All United States

RADIO SHACK SELECT

300 W. 3rd St., # 1600
Fort Worth, TX 76102
Tel: (817) 415-3499
Fax: (817) 415-8651
E-Mail: pcrump1@tandy.com
Web Site: www.radioshack.com
Mr. Paul Crump, Marketing Director

RADIO SHACK is a consumer electronics retailer.

Background:

Established: 1921;	1st Franchised: 1969
Franchised Units:	2154
Company-Owned Units:	5033
Total Units:	7187
Minority-Owned Units:	
African-American:	4
Asian-American:	4
Hispanic:	10
Native American:	6
Other:	4 Middle Eastern
North America:	48 States
Density:	CA, NY, IL

Financial/Terms:

Cash Investment:	$20% Down
Total Investment:	$60K
Minimum Net Worth:	$N/A
Fees: Franchise —	$25K
Royalty — 0%;	Ad. — 0%
Earnings Claim Statement:	No
Term of Contract (Years):	10/Annual
Avg. # Of Employees:	NR
Passive Ownership:	Discouraged
Area Develop. Agreements:	No
Sub-Franchising Contracts:	No
Expand In Territory:	Yes
Space Needs: 500 SF; FS, SF, SC, RM	

Support & Training Provided:

Site Selection Assistance:	No
Lease Negotiation Assistance:	No
Co-Operative Advertising:	Yes
Franchisee Assoc./Member:	Yes/Yes
Size Of Corporate Staff:	150
On-Going Support:	A,B,C,D,E,F,G,H,I

Training: 5 Days On-Site.
Minority-Specific Programs: Although we support the objectives of the NMFI, we do not have any specific programs in place at this time.

Specific Expansion Plans:

US:	All States Except Hawaii

CASH CONVERTERS

1450 E. American Ln., # 1350
Schaumburg, IL 60173-6083
Tel: (888) 910-2274 (847) 330-1122
Fax: (847) 330-1660
E-Mail: inquiries@cashconverters.com
Web Site: www.cashconverters.com
Mr. Roger A. Hunt, President/CEO

We are an up-scale retail business specializing in the buying and selling of pre-owned consumer goods, i.e. computers, televisions, stereos, jewelry, sporting goods, VCRs, power tools, etc. We buy and sell within the community. We have 50% gross margins. Our stores are beautifully organized and operated by well-trained individuals such as yourself.

Background:
Established: 1995;   1st Franchised: 1995
Franchised Units: 16
Company-Owned Units: 2
Total Units: 18
Minority-Owned Units:
   African-American:
   Asian-American: 1
   Hispanic:
   Native American:
North America: 9 States, 7 Provinces
Density: 3 in IL, 3 in MA, 2 in PA

Financial/Terms:
Cash Investment: $70-100K

Total Investment:	$270-400K
Minimum Net Worth:	$100K
Fees: Franchise —	$50K
Royalty — $400/Wk.; Ad. — $2000/Mo.	
Earnings Claim Statement:	No
Term of Contract (Years):	10/10
Avg. # Of Employees:	8 FT, 7 PT
Passive Ownership:	Allowed
Area Develop. Agreements:	Yes/10
Sub-Franchising Contracts:	Yes
Expand In Territory:	Yes
Space Needs: 4,000-6,000 SF; SF, SC, RM	

Support & Training Provided:
Site Selection Assistance:	Yes
Lease Negotiation Assistance:	Yes
Co-Operative Advertising:	No
Franchisee Assoc./Member:	No
Size Of Corporate Staff:	7
On-Going Support:	A,C,D,E,F,G,h,I

Training: 3 Weeks Corporate Training and In-Store Training; 1 Week Initial Opening Training
Minority-Specific Programs: Although we support the objectives of the NMFI, we do not have any specific programs in place at this time.

Specific Expansion Plans:
US:	All United States

FEATHER RIVER WOOD & GLASS

2365 Forest Ave.
Chico, CA 95928
Tel: (800) 395-3667 (530) 895-0762
Fax: (530) 895-9207
E-Mail:

Web Site: www.featherdoor.com
Mr. Paul Wolfe, VP Franchise Development

FEATHER RIVER is the premier manufacturer of hardwood doors and entry systems. FEATHER RIVER offers a unique store concept that is tailored to the top 8% of homeowners in the country. Please contact us for an analysis of your proposed franchise location.

Background:
Established: 1971;   1st Franchised: 1999
Franchised Units: 2
Company-Owned Units: 1
Total Units: 3
Minority-Owned Units:
   African-American: 0
   Asian-American: 0
   Hispanic: 0
   Native American: 0
   Other: 0
North America: 3 States
Density: 1 in NV, 1 in CA, 1 in PA

Financial/Terms:
Cash Investment:	$100-180K
Total Investment:	$150-190K
Minimum Net Worth:	$NR
Fees: Franchise —	$37K
Royalty — 6%;	Ad. — 3%

Earnings Claim Statement:	No
Term of Contract (Years):	10/10
Avg. # Of Employees:	1 FT, 1 PT
Passive Ownership:	Allowed
Area Develop. Agreements:	No
Sub-Franchising Contracts:	No
Expand In Territory:	Yes
Space Needs: 1,200-2,000 SF; FS, SF, SC	

Support & Training Provided:

Site Selection Assistance:	No
Lease Negotiation Assistance:	Yes
Co-Operative Advertising:	Yes
Franchisee Assoc./Member:	No
Size Of Corporate Staff:	160
On-Going Support:	C,D,E,G,h,I
Training: 2 Weeks Corporate Headquarters, Chico, CA.	

Minority-Specific Programs: Franchise financing is available.

Specific Expansion Plans:

US:	All United States

GLAMOUR SHOTS

1300 Metropolitan Ave.
Oklahoma City, OK 73108
Tel: (800) 336-4550 (405) 947-8747
Fax: (405) 951-7343
E-Mail: reesa@glamourshots.com
Web Site: www.glamourshots.com
Ms. Kim McElroy, Dir. of Franchise Development

GLAMOUR SHOTS is more than you ever pictured. We are the industry leader in high-fashion photography. We provide pre-opening assistance, comprehensive training, operational training and systems and regional field consultants, as well as solid, on-going support. Come join the leader!

Background:

Established: 1988;	1st Franchised: 1992
Franchised Units:	156
Company-Owned Units:	2
Total Units:	158
Minority-Owned Units:	
African-American:	
Asian-American:	
Hispanic:	
Native American:	
North America:	42 States, 1 Province
Density:	25 in TX, 21 in FL, 14 in CA

Financial/Terms:

Cash Investment:	$15K

Total Investment:	$150K
Minimum Net Worth:	$200K
Fees: Franchise —	$15K
Royalty — 0%;	Ad. — $357/Mo.
Earnings Claim Statement:	No
Term of Contract (Years):	10/10
Avg. # Of Employees:	NR
Passive Ownership:	Not Allowed
Area Develop. Agreements:	Yes
Sub-Franchising Contracts:	No
Expand In Territory:	Yes
Space Needs: 800-1,200 SF; RM	

Support & Training Provided:

Site Selection Assistance:	Yes
Lease Negotiation Assistance:	Yes
Co-Operative Advertising:	Yes
Franchisee Assoc./Member:	Yes
Size Of Corporate Staff:	NR
On-Going Support:	A,B,C,D,E,G,H
Training: 1 Week at National Training Center; 4 Wks. at Training Store; As Needed at Your Location.	

Minority-Specific Programs: Although we support the objectives of the NMFI, we do not have any specific programs in place at this time.

Specific Expansion Plans:

US:	All United States

GATEWAY NEWSTANDS

30 E. Beaver Creek Rd., # 206
Richmond Hill, ON L4B 1J2 CANADA
Tel: (800) 942-5351 (905) 886-8900
Fax: (905) 886-8904
E-Mail:
Web Site: www.gatewaynewstands.com
Mr. David Goldman, President

Newsstand, candy, lotto and limited food. Service locations in high-rise office towers, shopping centers and transit locations throughout the United States.

Background:

Established: 1983;	1st Franchised: 1983
Franchised Units:	282
Company-Owned Units:	0
Total Units:	282
Minority-Owned Units:	
African-American:	
Asian-American:	150
Hispanic:	25
Native American:	
Other:	
North America:	NR
Density:	193 in ON, 19 in IL, 16 NY

Financial/Terms:

Cash Investment:	$40-150K

Total Investment:	$50-200K
Minimum Net Worth:	$NR
Fees: Franchise —	$Varies
Royalty — 3%;	Ad. — 0%
Earnings Claim Statement:	No
Term of Contract (Years):	5-10/5
Avg. # Of Employees:	1 FT, 2 PT
Passive Ownership:	Not Allowed
Area Develop. Agreements:	No
Sub-Franchising Contracts:	Yes
Expand In Territory:	Yes
Space Needs: 100-1,000 SF; SF, RM, Transit Location	

Support & Training Provided:

Site Selection Assistance:	Yes
Lease Negotiation Assistance:	Yes
Co-Operative Advertising:	Yes
Franchisee Assoc./Member:	No
Size Of Corporate Staff:	11
On-Going Support:	C,D,E,F,I
Training: 2 Days to 2 Weeks in Store.	

Minority-Specific Programs: Training and some financing is available

Specific Expansion Plans:

US:	All United States

HEEL QUIK!

1730 Cumberland Point Dr., # 5
Marietta, GA 30067
Tel: (800) 255-8145 (770) 951-9440
Fax: (770) 933-8268
E-Mail: hqcorp@bellsouth.net
Web Site: www.aquik.com
Mr. Raymond J. Margiano, President/CEO

World's largest and #1 ranked service business franchise, ranked by Black Enterprise last 3 years Top 15 Low Cost Franchise Opportunities, we specialize in personal services: shoe repair, clothing alterations, dry cleaning, orthotics and custom shoes. We are a basic service needed by everyone!

Background:

Established: 1984;	1st Franchised: 1985
Franchised Units:	732
Company-Owned Units:	2
Total Units:	734
Minority-Owned Units:	
African-American:	7
Asian-American:	14
Hispanic:	36
Native American:	0

Other:
North America:	23 States, 1 Province
Density:	18 in GA, 14 in FL, 13 in TX

Financial/Terms:
Cash Investment:	$10-50K
Total Investment:	$15-140K
Minimum Net Worth:	$15K
Fees: Franchise —	$7.5-17.5K
Royalty — 4%;	Ad. — 2%
Earnings Claim Statement:	No
Term of Contract (Years):	20/10
Avg. # Of Employees:	2 FT, 1 PT
Passive Ownership:	Discouraged
Area Develop. Agreements:	Yes/10/10
Sub-Franchising Contracts:	No
Expand In Territory:	Yes
Space Needs:	150-1,000 SF;

FS,SF,SC,RM,HB,inside business

Support & Training Provided:
Site Selection Assistance:	Yes
Lease Negotiation Assistance:	Yes
Co-Operative Advertising:	No
Franchisee Assoc./Member:	Yes/Yes
Size Of Corporate Staff:	18
On-Going Support:	B,C,D,E,F,G,H,I

Training: 2 Weeks Atlanta, GA; 2 Weeks Regional.

Minority-Specific Programs: We have extended our support and willingness to work with inner city groups in New York, Chicago and Philadelphia. We have offered additional training, both technical and business, at no additional cost. If there are special circumstances we have agreed in some cases to work on an out-of-pocket cost basis.

Specific Expansion Plans:
US:	All United States

MAINSTREAM FASHIONS
13877 Elkhart Rd.
Apple Valley, MN 55124
Tel: (612) 423-6254
Fax: (612) 322-1923
E-Mail:

nick.denicola@mainstreamfashions.com
Web Site: www.mainstreamfashions.com
Mr. Nick DeNicola, VP Franchise Development

MAINSTREAM FASHIONS is a home-based business which markets contemporary women's and children's clothing through home and office shows. We're looking for entrepreneur-minded individuals with some business experience and a passion for fashion. Must be motivated to succeed in a fun, flexible and rewarding business environment.

Background:
Established: 1991;	1st Franchised: 1998
Franchised Units:	4
Company-Owned Units:	15
Total Units:	19
Minority Owned Units:	
African-American:	0
Asian-American:	0
Hispanic:	0
Native American:	0
Other:	0
North America:	4 States
Density:	15 in MN, 2 in IA, 1 in WI

Financial/Terms:
Cash Investment:	$31.5-40.3K
Total Investment:	$31.5-40.3K
Minimum Net Worth:	$40K
Fees: Franchise —	$15K
Royalty — 8%;	Ad. — 0-2%
Earnings Claim Statement:	Yes
Term of Contract (Years):	10/10
Avg. # Of Employees:	1 FT
Passive Ownership:	Discouraged
Area Develop. Agreements:	No
Sub-Franchising Contracts:	No
Expand In Territory:	Yes
Space Needs: N/A SF; HB	

Support & Training Provided:
Site Selection Assistance:	N/A
Lease Negotiation Assistance:	N/A
Co-Operative Advertising:	N/A
Franchisee Assoc./Member:	No
Size Of Corporate Staff:	3
On-Going Support:	B,C,D,E,G,H

Training: Approximately 3 Days Apple Valley, MN; 2-3 Days in Territory.

Minority-Specific Programs: Although we support the objectives of the NMFI, we do not have any specific programs in place at this time.

Specific Expansion Plans:
US:	Most States

MOTOPHOTO™

MOTOPHOTO (SM)
4444 Lake Center Dr.
Dayton, OH 45426-0096
Tel: (800) 733-6686 (937) 854-6686
Fax: (937) 854-0140
E-Mail: franchise@motophoto.com
Web Site: www.motophoto.com
Mr. Paul Pieschel, SVP Franchise Development

MOTOPHOTO(SM) is an up-scale specialty retailer in the $14 billion and still-growing photo processing and portrait industries. MOTOPHOTO (SM) stores feature on-site processing, portrait studios, select merchandise and digital applications. This is a happy, clean and up-scale business, operating with a small, professional staff and requiring a modest inventory investment with strong profit potential. Ranked #1 in category by Entrepreneur Magazine and # 15 in Success Franchise Gold 100.

Background:
Established: 1981;	1st Franchised: 1982
Franchised Units:	377
Company-Owned Units:	37
Total Units:	414
Minority-Owned Units:	
African-American:	1
Asian American:	25
Hispanic:	2
Native American:	
Other:	
North America:	27 States, 1 Province
Density:	44 in ON, 49 in NJ, 27 in IL

Financial/Terms:
Cash Investment:	$60K
Total Investment:	$280K
Minimum Net Worth:	$150K
Fees: Franchise —	$15K
Royalty — 6%;	Ad. — 0.5%
Earnings Claim Statement:	Yes
Term of Contract (Years):	10/10
Avg. # Of Employees:	3 FT, 3 PT
Passive Ownership:	Allowed
Area Develop. Agreements:	Yes/5/5/5/5
Sub-Franchising Contracts:	No
Expand In Territory:	Yes
Space Needs: 1,200-1,400 SF; FS, SF, SC, RM	

Support & Training Provided:
Site Selection Assistance:	Yes
Lease Negotiation Assistance:	Yes
Co-Operative Advertising:	Yes
Franchisee Assoc./Member:	No
Size Of Corporate Staff:	80

On-Going Support: B,C,D,E,G,H,I
Training: 3 Weeks Dayton, OH; 3 Weeks Local Market.
Minority-Specific Programs: No special programs for minorities, but we do have a special financing program for all franchisees who qualify.

Specific Expansion Plans:
US: All United States

PET VALU INTERNATIONAL
2 Devon Square, # 200, 744 W. Lancaster Ave.
Wayne, PA 19087
Tel: (888) 564-6784 (610) 225-0800
Fax: (610) 225-0822
E-Mail: petvalu@aol.com
Web Site: www.petvalu.com
Mr. David J. Wheat, VP Franchise Development

Discount retailer of pet foods and supplies. 'Your Neighborhood Store With Superstore Prices.'

Background:
Established: 1976; 1st Franchised: 1987
Franchised Units: 333
Company-Owned Units: 95
Total Units: 428
Minority-Owned Units:
  African-American:
  Asian-American:
  Hispanic:
  Native American:
  Other:
North America: 5 States, 2 Provinces
Density: 227 in ON, 30 in PA,26 in NJ

Financial/Terms:
Cash Investment: $15-95K
Total Investment: $85.4-207.9K
Minimum Net Worth: $40-160KK
Fees: Franchise — $20K
  Royalty — N/A; Ad. — N/A
Earnings Claim Statement: No
Term of Contract (Years): 10/5/5
Avg. # Of Employees: 2 FT, 2 PT
Passive Ownership: Not Allowed
Area Develop. Agreements: No
Sub-Franchising Contracts: No
Expand In Territory: No
Space Needs: 2,000-3,000 SF; SC

Support & Training Provided:
Site Selection Assistance: N/A
Lease Negotiation Assistance: Yes
Co-Operative Advertising: Yes
Franchisee Assoc./Member: Yes
Size Of Corporate Staff: 59
On-Going Support: A,C,E,F,I
Training: 1 Day at Head Office, Wayne, PA; 3 Weeks at Head Office and Operating Store.
Minority-Specific Programs: Although we support the objectives of the NMFI, we do not have any specific programs in place at this time.

Specific Expansion Plans:
US: Northeast

STREET CORNER NEWS
2945 SW Wanamaker Dr.
Topeka, KS 66614
Tel: (800) 789-NEWS (785) 272-8529
Fax: (785) 272-2384
E-Mail: peter@streetcornernews.com
Web Site: www.streetcornernews.com
Mr. Peter LaColla, Chief Executive Officer

STREET CORNER NEWS is a convenience store serving the needs of the customers and employees of a regional shopping center. Locations are either in kiosks or in-line stores. Merchandise selection includes newspapers, magazines, sodas and other beverages, tobacco products, office supplies, gift items and sundries.

Background:
Established: 1988; 1st Franchised: 1995
Franchised Units: 19
Company-Owned Units: 1
Total Units: 20
Minority-Owned Units:
  African-American: 0
  Asian-American: 7
  Hispanic: 0
  Native American: 0

North America: 11 States
Density: 5 in TN, 4 in NY, 4 in KS

Financial/Terms:
Cash Investment: $35K
Total Investment: $90-150K
Minimum Net Worth: $150K
Fees: Franchise — $19.9K
  Royalty — 4.5%; Ad. — 0%
Earnings Claim Statement: No
Term of Contract (Years): 7/7
Avg. # Of Employees: 1 FT, 3 PT
Passive Ownership: Discouraged
Area Develop. Agreements: No
Sub-Franchising Contracts: No
Expand In Territory: Yes
Space Needs: 300 SF; RM

Support & Training Provided:
Site Selection Assistance: Yes
Lease Negotiation Assistance: Yes
Co-Operative Advertising: No
Franchisee Assoc./Member: No
Size Of Corporate Staff: 5
On-Going Support: A,C,d,E,F,G,h,I
Training: 1 Week On-Site.
Minority-Specific Programs: Although we support the objectives of the NMFI, we do not have any specific programs in place at this time.

Specific Expansion Plans:
US: All United States

FIRE DEFENSE CENTERS

6120-10 Powers, # 144
Jacksonville, FL 32217
Tel: (800) 554-3028 (904) 731-1833
Fax:
E-Mail:
Web Site:
Ms. I. A. La Russo, President

Dealing with national accounts on servicing of fire extinguishers, automatic restaurant hood systems, municipal supplies and first aid kits. Warranty on equipment sold to business and guaranteed fire code compliance to business. Provide consultation for businesses to comply with city and state governments.

Background:

Established: 1973,	1st Franchised: 1986
Franchised Units:	17
Company-Owned Units:	44
Total Units:	61
Minority-Owned Units:	
African-American:	2%
Asian-American:	0%
Hispanic:	0%
Native American:	0%
Other:	
North America:	15 States
Density:	20 in FL

Financial/Terms:

Cash Investment:	$36K
Total Investment:	$42.5K

Minimum Net Worth:	$NR
Fees: Franchise —	$19.5K
Royalty — 10%;	Ad. — 2%
Earnings Claim Statement:	No
Term of Contract (Years):	10/10
Avg. # Of Employees:	2 FT
Passive Ownership:	Allowed
Area Develop. Agreements:	No
Sub-Franchising Contracts:	No
Expand In Territory:	Yes
Space Needs: 1,500 SF; Warehouse	

Support & Training Provided:

Site Selection Assistance:	Yes
Lease Negotiation Assistance:	Yes
Co-Operative Advertising:	Yes
Franchisee Assoc./Member:	NR
Size Of Corporate Staff:	16
On-Going Support:	A,B,C,D,E,F,G,H,I
Training: 2 Weeks Headquarters.	

Minority-Specific Programs: We do not specifically recruit minorities, but we do not refuse any qualified person regardless of race, color or creed. We are more interested in qualified people.

Specific Expansion Plans:

US:	All United States

ROLL-A-WAY

10601 Oak St., N.E.
St. Petersburg, FL 33716
Tel: (888) 765-5292 (727) 576-6044
Fax: (727) 579-9410
E-Mail:

Web Site: www.roll-a-way.com
Mr. Bill Salin, VP Franchise Development

ROLL-A-WAY manufactures rolling-security and storm shutters for residential and commercial applications. We are the largest and oldest manufacturer in the U. S. The franchise consists of training in sales, marketing and installation of the shutter system. The franchisee purchases directly from the manufacturer, and the business is very profitable and gaining in popularity every day. The shutters are excellent for saving money on utilities.

Background:

Established: 1955;	1st Franchised: 1994	
Franchised Units:		35
Company-Owned Units:		4
Total Units:		39
Minority-Owned Units:		
African-American:		
Asian-American:		1
Hispanic:		2
Native American:		
Other:		1 Bahamian
North America:		15 States
Density:	2 in NY, 3 in NC, 2 in CA	

Financial/Terms:

Cash Investment:	$15.8-40K
Total Investment:	$35-65K
Minimum Net Worth:	$250K
Fees: Franchise —	$7.9-21.7K
Royalty — 0%;	Ad. — 0%
Earnings Claim Statement:	No
Term of Contract (Years):	10/5/5
Avg. # Of Employees:	2 FT, 2 PT
Passive Ownership:	Discouraged
Area Develop. Agreements:	No
Sub-Franchising Contracts:	No

Expand In Territory: Yes
Space Needs: NR SF; N/A

Support & Training Provided:
Site Selection Assistance: N/A
Lease Negotiation Assistance: No
Co-Operative Advertising: No
Franchisee Assoc./Member: No
Size Of Corporate Staff: 30
On-Going Support: B,C,D,F,h
Training: 2 Weeks Corporate Office, St. Petersburg, FL.
Minority-Specific Programs: Although we support the objectives of the NMFI, we do not have any specific programs in place at this time.

Specific Expansion Plans:
US: All United States

FASTSIGNS

FASTSIGNS

2550 Midway Rd., # 150
Carrollton, TX 75006
Tel: (800) 827-7446 (972) 447-0777
Fax: (972) 248-8201
E-Mail: Larry.Lane@fastsigns.com
Web Site: www.fastsigns.com
Mr. Larry Lane, VP of Franchise Devopment

Computer generate signs and graphics. FASTSIGNS is the acknowledged leader of the quick sign industry. Rated #7 in Success Magazine's Franchisee Satisfaction Survey. Quality systems included comprehensive 3 week training, on-going support, unique marketing materials and National Accounts program. Site selection assistance and the latest industry equipment.

Background:
Established: 1985;   1st Franchised: 1986
Franchised Units: 426
Company-Owned Units: 0
Total Units: 426
Minority-Owned Units:
   African-American: 2
   Asian-American: 3
   Hispanic: 6
   Native American: 0
   Other:
North America: 41 States, 2 Provinces
Density: 47 in TX, 34 in CA, 20 in IL

Financial/Terms:
Cash Investment: $50-75K
Total Investment: $144.5-207.5K
Minimum Net Worth: $150K
Fees: Franchise — $20K

Royalty — 6%;   Ad. — 2%
Earnings Claim Statement: Yes
Term of Contract (Years):   20/10
Avg. # Of Employees: 6 FT
Passive Ownership: Not Allowed
Area Develop. Agreements: No
Sub-Franchising Contracts: Yes
Expand In Territory: Yes
Space Needs: 1,400 SF; SC

Support & Training Provided:
Site Selection Assistance: Yes
Lease Negotiation Assistance: Yes
Co-Operative Advertising: Yes
Franchisee Assoc./Member: No
Size Of Corporate Staff: 75
On-Going Support: C,D,E,G,H,I
Training: 3 Weeks in Dallas, TX.

Minority-Specific Programs: Although we support the objectives of the NMFI, we do not have any specific programs in place at this time.

Specific Expansion Plans:
US: All United States

SIGN-A-RAMA

1601 Belvedere Rd., # 501 S.
West Palm Beach, FL 33406
Tel: (800) 776-8105 (561) 640-5570
Fax: (561) 478-4340
E-Mail: signinfo@sign-a-rama.com
Web Site: www.sign-a-rama.com
Mr. Tony Foley, International Director

SIGN-A-RAMA is the world's largest sign franchise with approximately 500 stores worldwide. Being a full-service sign center allows us to do everything a quick-stop shop does but also to get deeply involved in the commercial aspects of the industry. Utilizing the very latest in computer technology, SIGN-A-RAMA is unmatched in franchise supported innovation.

Background:
Established: 1986;   1st Franchised: 1987
Franchised Units: 515
Company-Owned Units: 0
Total Units: 515
Minority-Owned Units:
   African-American: 8
   Asian-American: 7
   Hispanic: 18
   Native American: 5
   Other:
North America: 44 States
Density: 50 in CA, 45 in IL, 35 in NJ

Financial/Terms:
Cash Investment: $45-55K
Total Investment: $103K
Minimum Net Worth: $NR
Fees: Franchise — $37.5K
   Royalty — 6% w/ Cap;   Ad. — 0%
Earnings Claim Statement: No
Term of Contract (Years):   35/35
Avg. # Of Employees: 3 FT
Passive Ownership: Discouraged
Area Develop. Agreements: No
Sub-Franchising Contracts: No

Expand In Territory: Yes
Space Needs: 1,200 SF; SF, SC

Support & Training Provided:
Site Selection Assistance: Yes
Lease Negotiation Assistance: Yes
Co-Operative Advertising: Yes
Franchisee Assoc./Member: Yes/Yes
Size Of Corporate Staff: 85
On-Going Support: C,D,E,F,G,H,I
Training: 2 Weeks West Palm Beach, FL; 2 Weeks On-Site. Master License Training - 1 Week FL.

Minority-Specific Programs: As a company we are actively pursuing minority owned franchises and will be very creative in assisting the candidates to get started in a fantastic franchise opportunity. Our goal is to give minorities the chance to own their own Sign-A-Rama so we work with the individual to achieve their goals.

Specific Expansion Plans:
US: All United States

SIGNS FIRST
813 Ridge Lake Blvd., # 390
Memphis, TN 38120
Tel: (800) 852-2163 (901) 682-2264
Fax: (901) 682-2475
E-Mail: signsfirst@earthlink.net
Web Site: www.signsfirst.com
Ms. Peggy Cahoon, Office Manager

SIGNS FIRST is the only franchise with over 25 years sign industry experience. We specialize in computer-generated, one-day temporary and permanent signs for retail, professional and commercial businesses on a cash and carry basis. Franchisee support is unparalleled wth comprehensive training, on-going technological support and marketing assistance.

Background:
Established: 1966; 1st Franchised: 1989
Franchised Units: 36
Company-Owned Units: 0
Total Units: 36
Minority-Owned Units:
  African-American: 0
  Asian-American: 0
  Hispanic: 0
  Native American: 0
North America: 17 States
Density: 13 in TN, 12 in MS, 3 in CO

Financial/Terms:
Cash Investment: $20K
Total Investment: $20-65K
Minimum Net Worth: $250K
Fees: Franchise — $10-15K
  Royalty — 6%; Ad. — 0%
Earnings Claim Statement: No
Term of Contract (Years): 10/10
Avg. # Of Employees: 2 FT
Passive Ownership: Discouraged
Area Develop. Agreements: Yes/10
Sub-Franchising Contracts: No
Expand In Territory: Yes
Space Needs: 1,500 SF; FS, SF, SC, RM

Support & Training Provided:
Site Selection Assistance: Yes
Lease Negotiation Assistance: Yes
Co-Operative Advertising: No
Franchisee Assoc./Member: No
Size Of Corporate Staff: 6
On-Going Support: B,C,D,E,F,G,I
Training: 2 Weeks Memphis, TN; 1 Week + Follow-Up Visit in Store.

Minority-Specific Programs: Although we support the objectives of the NMFI, we do not have any specific programs in place at this time.

Specific Expansion Plans:
US: All United States

CRUISE LINES RESERVATION CENTER

9229 Kaufman Place
Brooklyn, NY 11236
Tel: (718) 763-4259
Fax:
E-Mail: y2ktravel@aol.com
Web Site: www.members.aol.com/y2ktravel/ home/page.htm
Mr. Bernard Korn, President

Travel agency business that can be operated full time or part time from home, office or store. The perfect home-based business, utilizing the internet. No experience required. Easy to start and run.

Background:

Established: 1989;	1st Franchised: 1990
Franchised Units:	24
Company-Owned Units:	1
Total Units:	25
Minority-Owned Units:	
African-American:	
Asian-American:	
Hispanic:	
Native American:	
Other:	
North America:	50 States
Density:	NR

Financial/Terms:

Cash Investment:	$1-2K
Total Investment:	$2-3K
Minimum Net Worth:	$NR
Fees: Franchise —	$None
Royalty — 1%;	Ad. — 0%
Earnings Claim Statement:	No
Term of Contract (Years):	10/10
Avg. # Of Employees:	1 FT
Passive Ownership:	Allowed

Area Develop. Agreements:	Yes/20
Sub-Franchising Contracts:	Yes
Expand In Territory:	Yes
Space Needs: 100 SF; HB	

Support & Training Provided:

Site Selection Assistance:	Yes
Lease Negotiation Assistance:	Yes
Co-Operative Advertising:	Yes
Franchisee Assoc./Member:	NR
Size Of Corporate Staff:	10
On-Going Support:	a,b,c,d,e,f,g,h,i

Training: Internet Training On-Going.
Minority-Specific Programs: No initial franchise fees. I would be very interested in helping individuals start their own franchise company and become franchisors. This is a vital area that needs to be addressed.

Specific Expansion Plans:

US:	All United States

#1 In Cruising Nationwide

CRUISEONE

10 Fairway Dr., # 200
Deerfield Beach, FL 33441-1802
Tel: (800) 892-3928 (954) 480-9265
Fax: (954) 428-6588

E-Mail: franchise@cruiseone.com
Web Site: www.cruiseone.com
Mr. Anthony Persico, President

CRUISEONE is a nationwide, home-based cruise-only franchise company representing all major cruise lines. Franchisees are professionally trained in a 7-day extensive program. How to close the sale and service the client, on-board ship inspections, sales and marketing techniques and customized software use are just the beginning. National Account Status offers consumers cruises for the lowest possible price and pays highest commissions in the industry. 1997 sales exceeded $80 million. Low start-up costs.

Background:

Established: 1992;	1st Franchised: 1993
Franchised Units:	430
Company-Owned Units:	0
Total Units:	420
Minority-Owned Units:	
African-American:	
Asian-American:	
Hispanic:	
Native American:	
Other:	
North America:	45 States
Density:	40 in FL, 39 in CA, 33 in TX

Financial/Terms:

Cash Investment:	$10-22K
Total Investment:	$10-22K
Minimum Net Worth:	$N/A
Fees: Franchise —	$9.8K
Royalty — 4%;	Ad. — 0%
Earnings Claim Statement:	No
Term of Contract (Years):	1
Avg. # Of Employees:	1 FT
Passive Ownership:	Not Allowed

Area Develop. Agreements: No
Sub-Franchising Contracts: No
Expand In Territory: Yes
Space Needs: N/A SF; HB

Support & Training Provided:
Site Selection Assistance: N/A
Lease Negotiation Assistance: N/A
Co-Operative Advertising: Yes
Franchisee Assoc./Member: No
Size Of Corporate Staff: 42
On-Going Support: A,B,C,D,F,g,h,I
Training: 6 Days Ft. Lauderdale, FL.
Minority-Specific Programs: Although we support the objectives of the NMFI, we do not have any specific programs in place at this time.

Specific Expansion Plans:
US: All United States

TRAVEL NETWORK

560 Sylvan Ave.
Englewood Cliffs, NJ 07632
Tel: (800) 669-9000 (201) 567-8500
Fax: (201) 567-4405
E-Mail: info@travnet.com
Web Site: www.travnet.com
Ms. Stephanie Abrams, Executive Vice President

Join the exciting travel industry with the leading travel franchisor as the owner of a TRAVEL NETWORK full-service travel agency catering to the business and leisure traveler. A TRAVEL NETWORK VACATION CENTRAL agency focuses solely on the lucrative leisure travel markets, or, as the owner of a full-service agency, catering to the business traveler as well as the leisure traveler. Our program includes complete start-up assistance, site selection and more.

Background:
Established: 1982; 1st Franchised: 1983
Franchised Units: 507
Company-Owned Units: 1
Total Units: 508
Minority-Owned Units:
  African-American:
  Asian-American:
  Hispanic:
  Native American:
  Other:

North America: 35 States, 1 Province
Density: 65 in NY, 32 in NJ, 26 in CA

Financial/Terms:
Cash Investment: $5-50K
Total Investment: $10-100K
Minimum Net Worth: $150K
Fees: Franchise — $5-30K
  Royalty — $350-750/Mo;Ad. — $200/Mo.
Earnings Claim Statement: No
Term of Contract (Years): 15/15
Avg. # Of Employees: 2 FT, 1 PT
Passive Ownership: Discouraged
Area Develop. Agreements: Yes/20
Sub-Franchising Contracts: Yes
Expand In Territory: Yes
Space Needs: 800-1,000 SF; FS, SF, SC, RM, HB

Support & Training Provided:
Site Selection Assistance: Yes
Lease Negotiation Assistance: Yes
Co-Operative Advertising: Yes
Franchisee Assoc./Member: Yes
Size Of Corporate Staff: 25
On-Going Support: A,B,C,D,E,F,G,H,I
Training: 1 Week in NJ; 1 Week in Orlando, FL; 1 Week in Houston, TX; 1 Week On-Site at Store.
Minority-Specific Programs: Although we support the objectives of the NMFI, we do not have any specific programs in place at this time.

Specific Expansion Plans:
US: All United States

UNIGLOBE TRAVEL

3223 Crow Canyon Rd. #240
San Ramon, CA 94583
Tel: (800) 590-4111
Fax: (925) 242-0203
E-Mail: dperkins@uniglobe.com
Web Site: www.uniglobe.com
Mr. Douglas T. Perkins, Natl. Dir., US Franchise Sales

Entrepreneur has consistently awarded UNIGLOBE TRAVEL the #1 company in travel-agency franchising. All UNIGLOBE travel agency franchisees benefit from programs and systems designed to handle the needs of both the corporate and leisure client. UNIGLOBE franchisees benefit from

money-saving automation agreements and top-notch incentive commission programs with major airline, hotel, car rental, tour and cruise-line companies.

Background:
Established: 1979; 1st Franchised: 1980
Franchised Units: 1100
Company-Owned Units: 0
Total Units: 1100
Minority-Owned Units:
  African-American: 10
  Asian-American: 15
  Hispanic: 5
  Native American: 1
  Other:
North America: 50 States, 9 Provinces
Density: 109 in CA,45 in IL,41 in OH

Financial/Terms:
Cash Investment: $10-35K
Total Investment: $60-120K
Minimum Net Worth: $60K
Fees: Franchise — $35K
  Royalty — Fixed; Ad. — $550
Earnings Claim Statement: No
Term of Contract (Years): 10/5
Avg. # Of Employees: 3 FT, 1 PT
Passive Ownership: Discouraged
Area Develop. Agreements: Yes/5
Sub-Franchising Contracts: Yes
Expand In Territory: Yes
Space Needs: 1,200 SF; FS, SF, SC, RM, HB

Support & Training Provided:
Site Selection Assistance: Yes
Lease Negotiation Assistance: Yes
Co-Operative Advertising: Yes
Franchisee Assoc./Member: Yes/No
Size Of Corporate Staff: 85
On-Going Support: B,C,D,e,G,h,I
Training: 1 Week in Vancouver, BC, Canada; 3 Days in Huntington Beach, CA; in agency.
Minority-Specific Programs: Although we support the objectives of the NMFI, we do not have any specific programs in place at this time.

Specific Expansion Plans:
US: All United States

A QUIK SERVICES

1730 Cumberland Point Dr., #5
Marietta, GA 30067
Tel: (800) 255-8145 (770) 951-9440
Fax: (770) 933-8268
E-Mail: fnrjm@bellsouth.net
Web Site: www.aquik.com
Mr. Raymond J. Margiano, President

A QUIK SERVICES has over 30 different service business franchise opportunities, including dry cleaning, sign stores, printing, hair salon, cleaning, etc. A large range of opportunities from $2,500 to $200,000. Home-based, business to business, service, retail, we will help you find the right business opportunity for you.

Background:

Established: 1998;   1st Franchised: 1999
Franchised Units: 30
Company-Owned Units: 3
Total Units: 33
Minority-Owned Units:
    African-American: 1
    Asian-American: 1
    Hispanic: 3
    Native American: 0
    Other:
North America: 1 State
Density: 3 in GA, 30 international

Financial/Terms:

Cash Investment: $2.5-75K
Total Investment: $2.5-200K
Minimum Net Worth: $2.5K
Fees: Franchise — $2.5-17.5K
    Royalty — 4%;   Ad. — 2%
Earnings Claim Statement: No
Term of Contract (Years):   20/10
Avg. # Of Employees: 1-5 FT

Passive Ownership: Allowed
Area Develop. Agreements: Yes/10/10
Sub-Franchising Contracts: No
Expand In Territory: Yes
Space Needs: Varies SF; FS, SF, SC, RM, HB

Support & Training Provided:

Site Selection Assistance: Yes
Lease Negotiation Assistance: Yes
Co-Operative Advertising: No
Franchisee Assoc./Member: No
Size Of Corporate Staff: 10
On-Going Support: B,C,D,e,F,G,H,I
Training: 20 Weeks in Atlanta, GA; 2 Weeks Regional; Home Town.
Minority-Specific Programs: We have established a range of franchise business opportunities, our objective is to function as a coach or mentor to help a person not only through the business evaluation process, but on an on-going basis to assure their success. Our job is to fit the person to the right opportunity.

Specific Expansion Plans:

US: All United States

APARTMENT MOVERS ETC.

4048 Ashley Phosphate Rd.
North Charleston, SC 29418
Tel: (800) 847-2861 (843) 767-0073

Fax: (843) 767-1440
E-Mail:
apartmentmovers@mindsprings.com
Web Site:
Ms. Kim Swanson, President/CEO

The mission of APARTMENT MOVERS ETC. is to quickly gain brand name awareness, providing the best moving services for the best price. Our exclusive software enables us to give guaranteed price quotes right over the phone. Finally the move it yourself-ers have an affordable, local, professional moving company! APARTMENT MOVERS ETC. is truly the franchise to buy.

Background:

Established: 1995;   1st Franchised: 1998
Franchised Units: 0
Company-Owned Units: 3
Total Units: 3
Minority-Owned Units:
    African-American:
    Asian-American:
    Hispanic:
    Native American:
    Other: Woman-owned
North America: 1 State
Density: 3 in SC

Financial/Terms:

Cash Investment: $19.9K
Total Investment: $64-134K
Minimum Net Worth: $50K
Fees: Franchise — $19.9K
    Royalty — 5%;   Ad. — 1%
Earnings Claim Statement: No
Term of Contract (Years):   10/10
Avg. # Of Employees: 3 FT 1 PT
Passive Ownership: Discouraged

Area Develop. Agreements: No
Sub-Franchising Contracts: No
Expand In Territory: Yes
Space Needs: Minimal SF; Parking for Vehicles.

Support & Training Provided:
Site Selection Assistance: N/A
Lease Negotiation Assistance: Yes
Co-Operative Advertising: NR
Franchisee Assoc./Member: No
Size Of Corporate Staff: 4
On-Going Support: B,C,D,E,G,H,I
Training: 1 Week Charleston, SC.
Minority-Specific Programs: Although we support the objectives of the NMFI, we do not have any specific programs in place at this time.

Specific Expansion Plans:
US: All United States

ATLANTIC MOWER PARTS & SUPPLIES

13421 S.W. 14th Pl.
Fort Lauderdale, FL 33325
Tel: (954) 474-4942
Fax: (954) 475-0414
E-Mail:
Web Site:
Mr. Robert J. Bettelli, President

Lawn mower replacement after-market. Parts for national brands (Snapper, Toro, MTD, Murray, etc.).

Background:
Established: 1978; 1st Franchised: 1988
Franchised Units: 14
Company-Owned Units: 1
Total Units: 15
Minority-Owned Units:
African-American:
Asian-American:
Hispanic:
Native American:
Other:
North America: 3 States
Density: 12 in FL, 2 in MI, 1 in CT

Financial/Terms:
Cash Investment: $~45K
Total Investment: $~45K
Minimum Net Worth: $NR
Fees: Franchise — $15.9K
   Royalty — 5%; Ad. — .5%
Earnings Claim Statement: No
Term of Contract (Years): 10/10
Avg. # Of Employees: 1 FT
Passive Ownership: Allowed

Area Develop. Agreements: Yes/1
Sub-Franchising Contracts: Yes
Expand In Territory: Yes
Space Needs: 250 SF; Warehouse

Support & Training Provided:
Site Selection Assistance: Yes
Lease Negotiation Assistance: Yes
Co-Operative Advertising: Yes
Franchisee Assoc./Member: NR
Size Of Corporate Staff: 3
On-Going Support: B,C,D,E
Training: 5 Days Headquarters; 5 Days On-Site.
Minority-Specific Programs: Although we support the objectives of the NMFI, we do not have any specific programs in place at this time.

Specific Expansion Plans:
US: All United States

AWC COMMERCIAL WINDOW COVERINGS

825 W. Williamson
Fullerton, CA 92832
Tel: (800) 252-2280 (714) 879-3880
Fax: (714) 879-8419
E-Mail:
Web Site: www.ibos.com/pub/ibos/awc
Mr. Leland B. Daniels, President

Mobile non-toxic drapery dry cleaning services provided on location for commercial customers; as well as sales, installation & repairs of all types of window coverings at competitive prices through centralized buying. Nation-wide accounts will be serviced by the franchisees as they are established. Utilizing the customer base, references and reputation of the franchisor, developed over the past 37 years makes this an exceptional opportunity with endless possibilities and immediate credibility.

Background:
Established: 1963; 1st Franchised: 1992
Franchised Units: 10
Company-Owned Units: 4
Total Units: 14
Minority-Owned Units:
African-American:
Asian-American:
Hispanic:

Native American:
Other:
North America: 5 States
Density: 6 in CA, 1 in MD, 1 in NV

Financial/Terms:
Cash Investment: $25-50K
Total Investment: $112.5-181.4K
Minimum Net Worth: $N/A
Fees: Franchise — $25K
   Royalty — 5-12.5%; Ad. — 2.5%
Earnings Claim Statement: No
Term of Contract (Years): 10/10
Avg. # Of Employees: 1 FT, PT As Needed
Passive Ownership: Not Allowed
Area Develop. Agreements: Yes
Sub-Franchising Contracts: No
Expand In Territory: Yes
Space Needs: N/A SF; HB

Support & Training Provided:
Site Selection Assistance: N/A
Lease Negotiation Assistance: Yes
Co-Operative Advertising: Yes
Franchisee Assoc./Member: No
Size Of Corporate Staff: 8
On-Going Support: A,B,C,D,F,h,I
Training: 2 Weeks at Plant and On-Site; On-Going.
Minority-Specific Programs: Although we support the objectives of the NMFI, we do not have any specific programs in place at this time.

Specific Expansion Plans:
US: All United States

BEVINCO

250 Consumers Rd., # 1103
Toronto, ON M2J 4V6 CANADA
Tel: (888) 238-4626 (416) 490-6266
Fax: (416) 490-6899
E-Mail: info@bevinco.com
Web Site: www.bevinco.com
Mr. Barry Driedger, President

Liquor inventory auditing and control service for bars and restaurants. Utilizing our computerized weighing system, franchisees will identify and resolve the shrinkage problems associated with the bar business. On-going weekly accounts make for an excellent executive income.

Background:
Established: 1987; 1st Franchised: 1990
Franchised Units: 166
Company-Owned Units: 1

Total Units: 167
Minority-Owned Units:
  African-American:
  Asian-American:
  Hispanic: 1%
  Native American:
  Other:
North America: 40 States, 7 Provinces
Density: 9 in CA, 8 in OH, 6 in TX

Financial/Terms:
Cash Investment: $30K
Total Investment: $25-35K
Minimum Net Worth: $40K
Fees: Franchise — $22.5K
  Royalty — $12/Audit; Ad. — $2/Audit
Earnings Claim Statement: No
Term of Contract (Years): 5/5
Avg. # Of Employees: 1-3 FT, 1-3 PT
Passive Ownership: Not Allowed
Area Develop. Agreements: Yes/5
Sub-Franchising Contracts: No
Expand In Territory: N/A
Space Needs: NR SF; N/A

Support & Training Provided:
Site Selection Assistance: N/A
Lease Negotiation Assistance: N/A
Co-Operative Advertising: N/A
Franchisee Assoc./Member: Yes/Yes
Size Of Corporate Staff: 4
On-Going Support: A,h,D,G,H,I
Training: 5 Days at Head Office in Toronto;
5 Days Franchisee's Location.
Minority-Specific Programs: Although we support the objectives of the NMFI, we do not have any specific programs in place at this time.

Specific Expansion Plans:
US: All United States

HOUSE DOCTORS HANDYMAN SERVICE
6355 E. Kemper Rd., # 250
Cincinnati, OH 45241
Tel: (800) 319-3359 (513) 469-2443
Fax: (513) 469-2226

E-Mail: housedr@one.net
Web Site: www.housedoctors.com
Mr. Steve Cohen, President

There's big money in house calls. Millions of dollars are being spent every day on those odd jobs around the house that people don't have the time or skill to do. You don't need a screwdriver or hammer to own this franchise. Financing and training provided.

Background:
Established: 1994; 1st Franchised: 1995
Franchised Units: 225
Company-Owned Units: 0
Total Units: 225
Minority-Owned Units:
  African-American: 3
  Asian-American: 0
  Hispanic: 1
  Native American: 0
  Other:
North America: 41 States
Density: 11 in OH, 8 in IN, 7 in IL

Financial/Terms:
Cash Investment: $12-23K
Total Investment: $18-39K
Minimum Net Worth: $10K
Fees: Franchise — $9-22K
  Royalty — 6%; Ad. — 3%
Earnings Claim Statement: No
Term of Contract (Years): 10/10/10
Avg. # Of Employees: 3 FT, 2 PT
Passive Ownership: Discouraged
Area Develop. Agreements: Yes/10
Sub-Franchising Contracts: No
Expand In Territory: No
Space Needs: N/A SF; N/A

Support & Training Provided:
Site Selection Assistance: N/A
Lease Negotiation Assistance: N/A
Co-Operative Advertising: N/A
Franchisee Assoc./Member: No
Size Of Corporate Staff: 12
On-Going Support: A,B,C,D,E,G,H,I
Training: 1 Week Cincinnati, OH.
Minority-Specific Programs: Although we support the objectives of the NMFI, we do not have any specific programs in place at this time.

Specific Expansion Plans:
US: All United States

MAGIS FUND RAISING SPECIALISTS
845 Heathermoor Ln.
Perrysburg, OH 43551-2933

Tel: (419) 874-4459
Fax: (419) 874-4459
Dr. Richard W. Waring, President

Conducts annual giving, endowment, capital campaigns, feasibility studies, fund raising audits, personnel searches, corporate solicitations, etc. Presents seminars, designs brochures, presentations, etc. for churches, schools, hospitals, etc. 30 years of fund raising experience. Contract with small- to medium-sized charities who cannot afford full-time development directors. The first fund raising franchise with a guarantee in the U. S. and Canada. $150 million raised.

Background:
Established: 1991; 1st Franchised: 1991
Franchised Units: 6
Company-Owned Units: 3
Total Units: 9
Minority-Owned Units:
  African-American: 6
  Asian-American: 4
  Hispanic: 0
  Native American: 0
  Other: 2
North America: 2 States, 1 Province
Density: 3 in MI, 3 in OH, 3 in ON

Financial/Terms:
Cash Investment: $17K
Total Investment: $28.5K
Minimum Net Worth: $100K
Fees: Franchise — $7.5K
  Royalty — 8%; Ad. — 2%
Earnings Claim Statement: No
Term of Contract (Years): 5/5
Avg. # Of Employees: 2 FT, 4 PT
Passive Ownership: Not Allowed
Area Develop. Agreements: Yes
Sub-Franchising Contracts: Yes
Expand In Territory: Yes
Space Needs: 500 SF; HB

Support & Training Provided:
Site Selection Assistance: N/A
Lease Negotiation Assistance: N/A
Co-Operative Advertising: Yes
Franchisee Assoc./Member: No
Size Of Corporate Staff: 2
On-Going Support: a,B,c,d,E,G,h
Training: 1 Week Home Study; 1 Week Support Service Center; 1 Week On-Site.
Minority-Specific Programs: Our expanded use of the Internet has provided much more of an opportunity for minorities to learn about us. During this year, we have also advertised in Black Enterprise Magazine.

Specific Expansion Plans:
US: All United States

PURE WATER, INC.

3725 Touzalin Ave.
Lincoln, NE 68501
Tel: (800) 875-5915 (402) 467-9300
Fax: (402) 467-9393
E-Mail: JHarrington@purewaterinc.com
Web Site: www.purewaterinc.com
Mr. Jason Harrington, Dir. of International Sales

The PURE WATER ULTIMA franchise puts you in business providing the freshest, highest-quality drinking water to your clients, using the state-of-the-art PURE WATER ULTIMA 888, which purifies the water and dispenses it exactly as your client desires. The PURE WATER ULTIMA 888 purification unit, which removes up to 99.9% of impurities from tapwater, replaces the five gallon bottle on a conventional cooler/dispenser.

Background:

Established: 1968; 1st Franchised: 1995	
Franchised Units:	13
Company-Owned Units:	0
Total Units:	13
Minority-Owned Units:	
African-American:	
Asian-American:	
Hispanic:	
Native American:	
North America:	None
Density:	N/A

Financial/Terms:

Cash Investment:	$100-175K
Total Investment:	$NR
Minimum Net Worth:	$N/A
Fees: Franchise —	$None
Royalty — 0%;	Ad. — 0%
Earnings Claim Statement:	No
Term of Contract (Years):	5/5
Avg. # Of Employees:	7 FT + Sales
Passive Ownership:	Discouraged
Area Develop. Agreements:	No
Sub-Franchising Contracts:	Yes
Expand In Territory:	Yes
Space Needs: 4,500 SF; N/A	

Support & Training Provided:

Site Selection Assistance:	No
Lease Negotiation Assistance:	No
Co-Operative Advertising:	No
Franchisee Assoc./Member:	No
Size Of Corporate Staff:	10
On-Going Support:	C,D,G,H,I
Training: 1 Week — International.	

Minority-Specific Programs: All franchises in countries outside United States.

Specific Expansion Plans:

US:	International only

PURIFIED WATER TO GO

5160 S. Valley View Blvd., # 110
Las Vegas, NV 89118-1778
Tel: (800) 976-9283 (702) 895-9350
Fax: (702) 895-9306
E-Mail: www.WaterToGo.com
Web Site: www.WaterToGo.com
Mr. Jim Heller, Franchise Marketing

PURIFIED WATER TO GO, recently featured on NBC nightly news, is a full-service or express retail outlet, selling purified water by the gallon, purified ice and related products. As the leader in water store franchises, PURIFIED WATER TO GO answers today's need for superior quality drinking water. Water is purified on store premises, and customers are drawn to the appeal of our sparkling clean, blue and white interior design.

Background:

Established: 1992; 1st Franchised: 1995	
Franchised Units:	44
Company-Owned Units:	0
Total Units:	44
Minority-Owned Units:	
African-American:	1
Asian-American:	2
Hispanic:	6
Native American:	
Other:	
North America:	12 States
Density:	12 in WA, 5 in NV, 4 in CA

Financial/Terms:

Cash Investment:	$25-50K
Total Investment:	$39-85K
Minimum Net Worth:	$75K
Fees: Franchise —	$10-19.5K
Royalty — 4-7.5%;	Ad. — $150-200/Mo
Earnings Claim Statement:	No
Term of Contract (Years):	10/10
Avg. # Of Employees:	1 FT, 1 PT
Passive Ownership:	Discouraged
Area Develop. Agreements:	Yes/10
Sub-Franchising Contracts:	No
Expand In Territory:	Yes
Space Needs: 500-1,000 SF; SF, SC	

Support & Training Provided:

Site Selection Assistance:	Yes
Lease Negotiation Assistance:	Yes
Co-Operative Advertising:	Yes
Franchisee Assoc./Member:	Yes
Size Of Corporate Staff:	9
On-Going Support:	B,C,D,E,F,G,H,I
Training: 5 Days Corporate Office in Las Vegas, NV.	

Minority-Specific Programs: Although we support the objectives of the NMFI, we do not have any specific programs in place at this time.

Specific Expansion Plans:

US:	All United States

RIBBON XCHANGE

8566 Fraser St., # 200
Vancouver, BC V5X 3Y3 CANADA
Tel: (800) 796-5377 (604) 322-9421
Fax: (604) 322-1658
E-Mail: rynker@dowco.com
Web Site: www.ribbon-xchange.com
Mr. J. Peter Benson, President

RIBBON XCHANGE is a service promoted to the small and medium size business community, specifically for the recycling of print media cartridges eg. Lasers, inksets and ribbons for computer printers, copiers and fax machines.

Background:

Established: 1989; 1st Franchised: 1994	
Franchised Units:	26
Company-Owned Units:	2
Total Units:	28
Minority-Owned Units:	
African-American:	
Asian-American:	
Hispanic:	
Native American:	
North America:	4 Provinces
Density:	19 in BC, 4 in AB, 6 in ON

Financial/Terms:

Cash Investment:	$65K
Total Investment:	$85K
Minimum Net Worth:	$NR
Fees: Franchise —	$25K
Royalty — $600/Mo;	Ad. — 1%
Earnings Claim Statement:	No
Term of Contract (Years):	5/5
Avg. # Of Employees:	2 FT
Passive Ownership:	Allowed
Area Develop. Agreements:	No
Sub-Franchising Contracts:	No
Expand In Territory:	Yes
Space Needs: NR SF; HB	

Support & Training Provided:

Site Selection Assistance:	NR

Lease Negotiation Assistance: NR
Co-Operative Advertising: Yes
Franchisee Assoc./Member: Yes/No
Size Of Corporate Staff: 9
On-Going Support: D,G,H,I
Training: 5 Days in Vancouver, 5 Days On-Site.
Minority-Specific Programs: Although we support the objectives of the NMFI, we do not have any specific programs in place at this time.

Specific Expansion Plans:
US: All United States

❋

SHRED-IT

2794 S. Sheridan Way
Oakville, ON L6J 7T4 CANADA
Tel: (905) 829-2794
Fax: (905) 829-1999
E-Mail: info@shredit.com
Web Site: www.shredit.com
Mr. Jeff Kish, Director Franchise Operations

Business service, offering mobile paper shredding and recycling, serving Fortune 1,000 companies, hospitals, medical facilities, banks, financial institutions, investment and professional firms and the government.

Background:
Established: 1988; 1st Franchised: 1992
Franchised Units: 52
Company-Owned Units: 19
Total Units: 71
Minority-Owned Units:
  African-American:
  Asian-American:
  Hispanic:
  Native American:
  Other:
North America: 27 States, 7 Provinces
Density: 6 in CA, 5 in FL, 3 in OH

Financial/Terms:
Cash Investment: $70-140K
Total Investment: $350-450K
Minimum Net Worth: $350K
Fees: Franchise — $55K
  Royalty — 5%; Ad. — 1.5%
Earnings Claim Statement: No
Term of Contract (Years): 10/10/10
Avg. # Of Employees: 6 FT
Passive Ownership: Not Allowed
Area Develop. Agreements: Yes/10/10
Sub-Franchising Contracts: No
Expand In Territory: Yes
Space Needs: 1,500 SF; Industrial Flex Space

Support & Training Provided:
Site Selection Assistance: Yes
Lease Negotiation Assistance: Yes
Co-Operative Advertising: N/A
Franchisee Assoc./Member: Yes/Yes
Size Of Corporate Staff: 40
On-Going Support: B,C,D,E,G,H,I
Training: 2 Weeks in Oakville, ON.
Minority-Specific Programs: Although we support the objectives of the NMFI, we do not have any specific programs in place at this time.

Specific Expansion Plans:
US: All United States

❋

UNITED STATES BASKETBALL LEAGUE

46 Quirk Rd.
Milford, CT 06460
Tel: (800) THE USBL (203) 877-9508
Fax: (203) 878-8109
E-Mail: usbl96@aol.com
Web Site: www.usbl.com
Mr. Daniel Meisenheimer, III, President

The USBL is the first and only sports league structured as a franchisor and the only publicly-traded sports league (OTCBB: USBL). The USBL is 14 years old with 13 teams and 126 USBL players have made the NBA. Visit the USBL Website at www.usbl.com.

Background:
Established: 1985; 1st Franchised: 1990
Franchised Units: 12
Company-Owned Units: 0
Total Units: 12
Minority-Owned Units:
  African-American: 2
  Asian-American:
  Hispanic:
  Native American:
  Other:
North America: 9 States
Density: 2 in NY, 2 in FL, 2 in NJ

Financial/Terms:
Cash Investment: $500K
Total Investment: $500-750K
Minimum Net Worth: $1MM
Fees: Franchise — $300K
  Royalty — 5%/$20K; Ad. — 1%/$3K
Earnings Claim Statement: No
Term of Contract (Years): 10/10
Avg. # Of Employees: 4 FT, 15 PT
Passive Ownership: Discouraged
Area Develop. Agreements: Yes/10
Sub-Franchising Contracts: Yes
Expand In Territory: Yes
Space Needs: N/A SF; N/A

Support & Training Provided:
Site Selection Assistance: Yes
Lease Negotiation Assistance: Yes
Co-Operative Advertising: Yes
Franchisee Assoc./Member: No
Size Of Corporate Staff: 8
On-Going Support: A,B,C,D,E,F,G,H,I
Training: 2 Weeks Connecticut or Pennsylvania.
Minority-Specific Programs: The USBL will provide some financing for qualified minority franchisees. The USBL will also assist in recruiting and training.

Specific Expansion Plans:
US: All US - Focus East of Miss.

Resources for minority investors

Government Assistance for Minorities and Women

Office of Minority Enterprise Development
409 Third St., SW
Washington, DC 20416
(202) 205 6410
www.sba.gov/MED/
MED's main objective is to foster business ownership by individuals who are socially and economically disadvantaged. Some of the programs and services offered are management and technical assistance, federal procurement opportunities, and Section 8(a) Business Development Program certification.

Office of Women's Business Ownership (OWBO)
409 Third St., SW
Washington, DC 20416
(202) 205-6673
www.sba.gov/womeninbusiness/
OWBO is the primary advocate for the interests of potential or existing women business owners. Some of the programs and services offered to women entrepreneurs are access to capital, Women's Prequalification Loan Program, long-term training, counseling, networking and mentoring.

Minority Business Development Agency (MBDA)
14th St. between Constitution Ave. & E St., NW
Washington, DC 20230
(202) 482-5061
www.mbda.gov/

MBDA funds a nationwide network of Minority Business Development Centers that assist with the start-up, expansion and acquisition of competitive minority owned-firms.

Office of Small and Disadvantaged Business Utilization (OSDBU)
www.sba.gov/gc/osdbu.html
OSDBU ensures that an equitable share of the total prime contracts and subcontracts awarded by major federal departments and agencies are given to small businesses, small disadvantaged businesses and women-owned businesses.

Government Assistance for Small Businesses

Small Business Administration
409 Third St., SW
Washington, DC 20416
(800) 827-5722
www.sba.gov/

U.S. Department of Commerce
14th St. and Constitution Ave., NW
Washington, DC 20230
(202) 482-2000
www.doc.gov

Minority and Women Small Business Associations

Asian American Association
9550 Flair Dr., 4th Fl.
El Monte, CA 91731

(800) 777-2582
www.aan.net
AAA is a national organtization that provides
an array of benefits and services. Some of the
services provide for small businesses are collection,
business loan, management consulting and free
in-language directory assistance.

National Association of Investment Companies
(NAIC)
1111 14th St., NW, #700
Washington, DC 20005
(202) 289-4336
NAIC is an association of investment companies
combining their financial resources to promote
and invest in an ethnically and socially diverse
marketplace. Some of the services they provide
are professional development seminars and
opportunities for alliances with other professionals
through NAIC's affiliate member program.

National Association of Minority Contractors
(NAMC)
666 11th St., NW, #520
Washington, DC 20001
(202) 347-8259
http://namc.org
NAMC is a trade association that addresses the
concerns and needs of minority contractors. They
put on educational and training seminars, as
well as present main issues concerning minority
contractors to all levels of government.

National Association of Women Business Owners
(NAWBO)
1100 Wayne Ave., #830
Silver Spring, MD 20910
(301) 608-2590
www.nawbo.org
NAWBO is a national organization that represents
the interests of all women entrepreneurs in all
types of businesses. In looking after the interest
of their members, NAWBO helps build strategic
alliances, transform public policy and promote economic development.

National Foundation for Women Business Owners
(NFWBO)
1100 Wayne Ave., #830
Silver Spring, MD 20910-5603

phone: (301) 495-4975
fax: (301) 495-4979
NFWBO@worldnet.att.net
www.nfwbo.org
NFWBO is a non-profit research organization that
supports the growth of women business owners
and their enterprises by conducting research,
sharing information and increasing knowledge.

National Association for Female Executives
(NAFE)
135 W. 50th St., 16th Fl.
New York, NY 10020
(212) 445-6235
www.nafe.com
NAFE is the largest business women's organization
in the nation committed to advancing women
in the workplace. Education and networking
programs are provided to give women the
techniques and resources needed to succeed in the
competitive business world.

The National Black Chamber of Commerce
(NBCC)
2000 L St., NW, #200
Washington, DC 20036
(202) 416-1622
NBCC's main objective is to provide technical
assistance and advocate economic empowerment
within Black communities through entrepreneurship and an understanding of capitalism. Some
of the industries NBCC focuses on are high
technology, construction, health care, finance,
manufacturing and policy information.

National Minority Supplier Development Council
(NMSDC)
15 West 39th St., 9th Fl.
New York, NY 10018
(212) 944-2430
NMSC1@aol.com
www.trainingforum.com/ASN/NMSDC
NMSDC aims to link corporate America with
minority-owned businesses of all sizes and to
increase business opportunities through various
services and programs.

U.S. Hispanic Chamber of Commerce
1030 15th St., NW, #206
Washington, DC 20005

(202) 842-1212
www.ushcc.com
The U.S. Hispanic Chamber of Commerce's primary goal is to represent the interests of over 1.3 million Hispanic-owned businesses in the U.S. and Puerto Rico. Some of the programs and services offered are internet consulting and multimedia solutions for the Spanish-speaking, networking and business opportunities with the Federal Government and corporate America.

Business and Trade Associations

Alliance of Independent Store Owners and Professionals (ASIOP)
P.O. Box 2014 Loop Station
Minneapolis, MN 55402
(612) 340-1568

Chamber of Commerce of the United States
1615 H St., NW
Washington, DC 20062
(202) 659-6000
www.uschamber.org

International Franchise Association
1350 New York Ave., NW, #900
Washington, DC 20005-4709
(202) 628-8000
www.franchise.org

National Association of Manufacturers (NAM)
1331 Pennsylvania Ave., NW, #600
Washington, DC 20004-1790
(202) 637-3000
www.nam.org

National Association for the Self-Employed (NASE)
2121 Precinct Line Rd.
Hurst, TX 76054
(800) 232-6273
www.selfemployed.nase.org/NASE

National Business Association
5151 Beltline Rd., #1150
Dallas, TX 75240
(800) 456-0440
www.nationalbusiness.org

National Federation of Independent Business (NFIB)
53 Century Blvd., #3000
Nashville, TN 37214
(800) 634-2669

600 Maryland Ave., SW, #700
Washington, DC 20024
(800) 552-6342
www.nfibonline.com

National Small Business United (NSBU)
1156 15th St., NW, #1100
Washington, DC 20005
(800) 345-6728, (202) 293-8830
www.nsbu.org

Arizona Small Business Association
1500 E. Bethany Home Rd., #140
Phoenix, AZ 85014
(602) 265-4563

Association of Small Business Development Centers
3108 Columbia Pike, #300
Arlington, VA 22204
(703) 271-8700

California Small Business Association
6101 W. Centinela Ave., #342
Culver City, CA 90230-6349
(310) 642-0838

Colorado Small Business United
3635 Holland Ct.
Wheatridge, CO 80033
(303) 420-2253

Council of Smaller Enterprise (COSE)
Greater Cleveland Growth Association
200 Tower City Center
50 Public Square
Cleveland, OH 44113
(216) 621-3300

Council of Small Business Executives
756 N. Milwaukee St., #400
Milwaukee, WI 53202
(414) 287-4100

Indiana Chamber of Commerce
One North Capital Ave., #200
Indianapolis, IN 46204
(317) 264-6892

Missouri Merchants and Manufacturers
Association
16100 Chesterfield Pkwy., W, #210
Chesterfield, MO 63017
(314) 537-1360

National Association of Government Guaranteed
Lenders, Inc.
424 South Squires, #130
Stillwater, OK 74075
(405) 377-4022

National Association of Small Business Investment
Companies
666 11th St., #750
Washington, DC 20001
(202) 628-5055

Nebraska Small Business United
14523 Grant St.
Omaha, NE 60116
(402) 498-5702

Retail Confectioners International
1807 Glenview Rd.
Glenview, IL 60025
(847) 724-6120

SMC—The Voice of Smaller Business
1400 S. Braddock Ave.
Pittsburgh, PA 15218
(412) 371-1500

Small Business Association of Michigan (SBAM)
222 N. Washington Sq., #100
Lansing, MI 48933
(517) 482-8788

The Smaller Business Association of New England
(SBANE)
204 Second Ave.
Waltham, MA 02451
(781) 890-9070

Small Business United of Texas
1011 West Eleventh St., #A
Austin, TX 78703
(512) 476-1707

Internet Resources

SmallbizNet
www.lowe.org

BankWeb
www.bankweb.com

Business Funding Directory
www.businessfinance.com
Corporate Finance Network
www.corpfinet.com/

EntrepreNet
www.enterprise.org/enet/index.html

MasterCard
www.mastercard.com/business

Small Business Credit Process
www.ny.frb.org/pihome.addpub/credit.html

Venture Capital Resource Library
www.vfinance.com

U.S. Business Advisor
www.business.gov

SBA On-Line
www.sba.gov/

ACE-Net
www.ace-net.sr.unh.edu/pub

STAT-USA/Internet (DOC)
(800) 782-8872
stat-usa@doc.gove
WWW (subscriber): www.stat-usa.gov
Guest User: www.stat.gov/inqsample.htm

FedWorld
www.fedworld.gov

State Programs for Small Businesses

ALABAMA
Alabama Development Office
401 Adams Ave
Montgomery, AL 36104
(800) 248-0033
(334) 242-0400
www.ado.state.al.us

Minority/Women's Opportunities:
Office of Minority Business Enterprise
(334) 242-2220

ALASKA
Department of Commerce and Economic Development
State Office Building, 9th Fl.
333 Willoughby Ave.
P.O. Box 110800
Juneau, AK 99811-0800
(907) 465-2500
www.state.ak.us/local/business.htm

Minority/Women's Opportunities:
Alaska Business Development Center
(800) 478-3474
(907) 562-0335

Alaska Village Initiatives
(907) 274-5400

ARIZONA
Arizona Business Assistance Center
Arizona Department of Commerce
3800 N. Central Ave., Bldg. D
Phoenix, Arizona 85012
(800) 542-5684
(602) 280-1480
www.state.az.us/ep/

Minority/Women's Opportunities:
Business Assistance Center
(800) 542-5684
(602) 280-1480

ARKANSAS
Arkansas Economic Development Commission
One State Capitol Mall

Little Rock, AR 72201
(501) 682-1121
www.aedc.state.ar.us

Minority/Women's Opportunities:
Small & Minority Business Development
(501) 682-1060

CALIFORNIA
California Office of Small Business
California Trade and Commerce Agency
801 K St., #1700
Sacramento, CA 95814
(916) 324-1295
www.commerce.ca.gov

Minority/Women's Opportunities:
Office of Small and Minority Business
(916) 322-5060

COLORADO
Office of Business Development
1625 Broadway, #1710
Denver, CO 80202
(303) 892-3840
www.state.co.us/gov_dir/obd/obd.htm

Minority/Women's Opportunities:
Minority Business Office
(303) 892-3764

Women's Business Office
(303) 892-3763

CONNECTICUT
Connecticut Economic Resource Center, Inc.
805 Brook St., Bldg. 4
Rocky Hill, CT 06067-3405
(800) 392-2122
www.cerc.com/cerc/cercweb.nsf/frmHome

Minority/Women's Opportunities:
Connecticut Economic Resource Center, Inc
(800) 392-2122

DELAWARE
Delaware Economic Development Office
99 Kings Highway
Dover, DE 19903

(302) 739-4271
www.state.de.us/dedo/

DISTRICT OF COLUMBIA
Office of the Assistant City Administrator for
Economic Development
441 4th St., NW, #1140
Washington, DC 20001
(202) 727-6365
www.ci.washingtondc.us/

Minority/Women's Opportunities:
D.C. Department of Human Rights and Minority
Business Development
(202) 724-1385

FLORIDA
Enterprise Florida
390 N. Orange Ave., #1300
Orlando, FL 32801
(407) 316-4600
www.floridabusiness.com/

Minority/Women's Opportunities:
Minority Business Development Programs
(305) 377-8766

Black Business Investment Board
(904) 487-4850

GEORGIA
Georgia Department of Industry, Trade and
Tourism
P.O. Box 1776
Atlanta, GA 30301
(404) 656-3545
www.georgia.org

Minority/Women's Opportunities:
Office of Small and Minority Business
(404) 656-6315

HAWAII
Business Action Center
1130 N. Nimitz Hwy., #A-254
Honolulu, HI 96817-4580
(808) 586-2545
www.hawaii.gov/dbedt/

IDAHO
Department of Commerce
700 West State St., P.O. Box 83720
Boise, ID 83720-0093
(208) 334-2470
www.idoc.state.id.us/Pages/DEPTPAGE.htm

ILLINOIS
Department of Commerce and Community Affairs
620 E. Adams St., 3rd Fl
Springfield, IL 62701
(217) 524-5856
www.commerce.state.il.us

Minority/Women's Opportunities:
Office of Minority Business Development
(312) 814-3540

Women's Business Advocacy
(312) 814-7170

INDIANA
State Information Center
402 W. Washington St., Rm. W160
Indianapolis, IN 46204
(800) 457-8283 in-state
(317) 233-0800
www.ai.org/bdev/index.html

Minority/Women's Opportunities:
ISBD Corp. Women & Minority Business
Assistance Program
(317) 264-2820

Minority Business Development Division,
Department of Administration
(317) 232-3061

IOWA
Department of Economic Development
200 E. Grand Ave.
Des Moines, IA 50309
(515) 242-4700
www.state.ia.us/government/ided

Minority/Women's Opportunities:
Targeted Small Business Financial Assistance
Program
(515) 242-4813

Targeted Small Business Program
(515) 242-4721

KANSAS
Department of Commerce and Housing
700 S.W. Harrison St., #1300
Topeka, KS 66603-3712
(785) 296-3481
www.kansascommerce.com

Minority/Women's Opportunities:
Office of Minority & Women's Business
Development
(785) 296-5298

KENTUCKY
Kentucky Cabinet for Economic Development
2300 Capital Plaza Tower
Frankfurt, KY 40601
(800) 626-2930
(502) 564-7670
www.thinkkentucky.com

Minority/Women's Opportunities:
Kentucky Cabinet for Economic Development
(502) 564-4320 ext. 5

Small and Minority Business Division
(502) 564-2064

LOUISIANA
Department of Economic Development
P.O. Box 94185
Baton Rouge, LA 70804-9185
(504) 342-3000
www.lded.state.la.us

Minority/Women's Opportunities:
Economically Disadvantaged Business
Development Office
(225) 342-5373

Louisiana Economic Development Corporation
(225) 342-5673
MAINE
Department of Economic and Community
Development
State House Station #59
Augusta, ME 04333-0059

(800) 541-5872
(800) 872-3838 in-state
www.econdevmaine.com/

MARYLAND
Department of Business and Economic
Development
Redwood Tower
217 E. Redwood St.
Baltimore, MD 21202
(410) 767-6300
www.dbed.state.md.us/

Minority/Women's Opportunities:
Office of Minority Affairs
(410) 767-8232

MASSACHUSETTS
Department of Economic Development
One Ashburton Pl., Rm. 2101
Boston, MA 02108
(617) 727-8380
www.state.ma.us/mobd

Minority/Women's Opportunities:
State Office of Minority and Women Business
Assistance
(617) 973-8692

MICHIGAN
Michigan Jobs Commission
Victor Office Center, 4th Fl
201 N. Washington Square
Lansing, MI 48913
(517) 373-9808
www.state.mi.us/mjc/ceo

Minority/Women's Opportunities:
Michigan Jobs Commission
(517) 373-9808

MINNESOTA
Small Business Assistance Office
500 Metro Square
121 7th Pl., E
St. Paul, MN 55101-2146
(800) 657-3858
(612) 282-2103
www.dted.state.mn.us/busasst/busasst.html

MISSISSIPPI
Mississippi Department of Economic and
Community Development
P.O. Box 849
Jackson, MS 39205-0849
(601) 359-3449
www.mississippi.org

Minority/Women's Opportunities:
Minority Business Enterprise
(601) 359-3448

MISSOURI
Missouri Department of Economic Development
Truman State Office Building
301 W. High St., Rm. 680
P.O. Box 1157
Jefferson City, MO 65102
(800) 523-1434
(573) 751-4962
www.ecodev.state.mo.us

Minority/Women's Opportunities:
Missouri Dept. of Economic Development,
Minority Business
(800) 523-1434 ext. 4

Minority Business Assistance Office
(573) 751-3237

Women's Council
(573) 751-0810

MONTANA
Department of Commerce
1424 Ninth Ave.
Helena, MT 59620-0501
(406) 444-3494
www.commerce.mt.gov/

NEBRASKA
Nebraska Department of Economic Development
P.O. Box 94666
301 Centennial Mall South
Lincoln, NE 68509-4666
(800) 426-6505
www.ded.state.ne.us

Minority/Women's Opportunities:
Nebraska Department of Economic Development
(402) 471-3758

NEVADA
Nevada State Development Corporation
350 S. Center St., #310
Reno, NV 89501
(702) 323-3625
www.state.nv.us

Minority/Women's Opportunities:
Nevada Department of Business and Industry
(702) 486-4335

Nevada Minority Purchasing Council
(702) 894-4477

NEW HAMPSHIRE
Business Finance Authority
New Hampshire Industrial Development Authority
14 Dixon Ave., #101
Concord NH 03301-4954
(603) 271-2391
www.state.nh.us/bfa/bfa.htm

NEW JERSEY
New Jersey Department of Commerce and
Economic Development
20 W. State St., CN 835
Trenton, NJ 08625
(609) 292-2444
www.njeda.com/

Minority/Women's Opportunities:
Certification Program
(888) 239-1288

Community Development and Small Business
Lending
(609) 292-1890

New Jersey Commerce and Economic Growth
Commission
(609) 292-3860

NEW MEXICO
Economic Development Department
P.O. Box 20003

Santa Fe, NM 87504-5003
(505) 827-0300
www.edd.state.nm.us/

Minority/Women's Opportunities:
Governor's Commission on the Status of Women
(505) 841-8920

NEW YORK
Empire State Development
633 Third Ave.
New York, NY 10017
(212) 803-2319
www.empire.state.ny.us/

Minority/Women's Opportunities:
Minority and Women's Business Development
(212) 803-2410

New York State Division for Women
(212) 681-4547

NORTH CAROLINA
North Carolina Small Business and Technology
Development Center
333 Fayetteville Street Mall, #1150
Raleigh, NC 27601
(919) 715-7272
www.sbtdc.org

Minority/Women's Opportunities:
Minority Business Enterprise Development
(919) 715-7272

NORTH DAKOTA
Department of Economic Development and
Finance (ED&F)
1833 E. Bismarck Expressway
Bismarck, ND 58504-6708
(701) 328-5300
www.growingnd.com/

Minority/Women's Opportunities:
Economic Development and Finance
(701) 328-5300

OHIO
Office of Small and Developing Business
Ohio Department of Development

77 S. High St.
P.O. Box 1001
Columbus, OH 43216-1001
(614) 466-2718
www.odod.ohio.gov/

Minority/Women's Opportunities:
Office of Minority Financial Incentives
(614) 644-7708

Women's Business Resource Program
(614) 466-4945

Minority Business Development Program
(614) 466-5700

OKLAHOMA
Oklahoma Department of Commerce
900 N. Stiles
P.O. Box 26980
Oklahoma City, OK 73126-0980
(800) 879-6552
(405) 815-6552
www.odoc.state.ok.us

Minority/Women's Opportunities:
Minority Business Assistance
(405) 815-5227

Tribal Government Assistance
(405) 815-5111

Women-Owned Business Certification
(405) 815-5143

OREGON
Economic Development Office
775 Summer St., NE
Salem, OR 97310
(503) 986-0123
www.econ.state.or.us

Minority/Women's Opportunities:
Oregon Department of Transportation, Office of
Civil Rights
(503) 986-4355

Department of Consumer and Business Affairs;
Office of Minority, Women & Emerging Small
Businesses
(503) 947-7976

PENNSYLVANIA
Small Business Resource Center
Department of Community and Economic
Development
374 Forum Building
Harrisburg, PA 17120
(800) 280 3801
www.teampa.com

Minority/Women's Opportunity:
Women's Business Development
(717) 787-3339

Minority Business Development
(717) 787-9147

Small Business First
(717) 783-5046

PUERTO RICO
Economic Development Administration
355 F.D. Roosevelt Ave.,
Hato Rey, PR 00918-2318
(787) 758-4747
www.pr-eda.com/econ-dev.html

RHODE ISLAND
Rhode Island Economic Development   ·
Corporation
One West Exchange St.
Providence, RI 02903
(401) 222-2601
www.riedc.com

Minority/Women's Opportunities:
Office of Minority Business Assistance
(401) 222-6670

Minority Investment Development Commission
(401) 351-2999

SOUTH CAROLINA
Enterprise Development, Inc.
P.O. Box 1149

Columbia, SC 29202
(803) 252-8806
www.state.sc.us/commerce/

Minority/Women's Opportunities:
Office of Small and Minority Business Assistance
(803) 734-0657

SOUTH DAKOTA
Governor's Office of Economic Development
711 East Wells Ave.
Pierre, SD 57501 3369
(800) 872-6190
www.state.sd.us/goed

TENNESSEE
Department of Economic and Community
Development
320 Sixth Ave, N
Nashville, TN 37243
(800) 251-8594 out-of-state
(800) 342-8470 in-state
(800) 872-7201 in-state
www.tnedc.org/

Minority/Women's Opportunities:
Business Development
(615) 741-2545

Minority Business Development Center
(615) 255-0432

TEXAS
Texas Department of Economic Development
1700 N. Congress Ave., P.O. Box 12728
Austin, TX 78711
(512) 936-0100
www.tded.state.tx.us

Minority/Women's Opportunities:
Business Finance, Office of Business Services
(512) 936-0260

UTAH
Division of Business and Economic Development
324 S. State St., #500
Salt Lake City, UT 84111
(801) 538-8700
www.ce.ex.state.ut.us/dbed/welcome.htm

Minority Opportunities:
Office of Asian Affairs
(801) 538-8612

Office of Black Affairs
(801) 538-8815

Office of Hispanic Affairs
(801) 538-8755

Office of Indian Affairs
(801) 538-8808

Office of Polynesian Affairs
(801) 538-8617

VERMONT
Business Development, Expansion and
Recruitment
Vermont Department of Economic Development
109 State St.
Montpelier, VT 05602
(802) 828-3211
www.thinkvermont.com

Minority/Women's Opportunities:
Government Assistance Program
(802) 828-5237

VIRGINIA
Virginia Department of Business Assistance
P.O. Box 446
Richmond, VA 23218-0446
(804) 371-8200
www.dba.state.va.us/

Minority/Women's Opportunities:
Dept. of Minority Business Enterprise
(800) 223-0671
(804) 786-5560

Virginia Department of Transportation, Equal
Opportunity Division
(804) 371-8254

WASHINGTON
Business Assistance Center
Department of Community, Trade and Economic
Development

906 Columbia St., SW
P.O. Box 48300
Olympia, WA 98504-8300
(360) 753-4900
www.wa.gov/cted/

Minority/Women's Opportunities:
Minority and Women Business Development
(206) 956-3164

Office of Minority and Women Business
Enterprises
(360) 753-9693

WEST VIRGINIA
West Virginia Development Office
West Virginia Economic Development Authority
1018 Kanawha Blvd., E, #501
Charleston, WV 25301
(304) 558-3650
www.wvdo.org

WISCONSIN
Department of Development
201 W. Washington Ave.
P.O. Box 7970
Madison, WI 53703
(800) 435-7287
(608) 266-1018
www.commerce.state.wi.us/index.html

Minority/Women's Opportunities:
Bureau of Minority Business Development—
Madison
(608) 267-9550

Wisconsin Women's Business Initiatives Corp.:
Madison
(608) 267-7409
Milwaukee
(414) 372-2070
Wisconsin Housing and Economic Development
Authority
(800) 642-6474 in-state

WYOMING
Division of Economic and Community
Development
Herschler Bldg. 1EW

122 W. 25th St.
Cheyenne, WY 82002
(307) 777-7284
www.wyomingbusiness.org

Minority/Women's Opportunities:
Wyoming Department of Transportation
Disadvantaged Business Assistance
(307) 777-4574

Sources of Financing — Organized by State

ALABAMA
Mr. Frank L. Collazo, President
FJC Growth Capital Corporation
200 West Court Square, #750
Huntsville, AL 35801
(205) 922-2918
(205) 922-2909

Mr. Robert K. Dobbs, Vice President
Compass Bank
Business Banking
15 S. 20th St.
Birmingham, AL 35233
(205) 933-3638
(205) 715-7607
rd1@compassbank.com

ARIZONA
Ms. Cheryl A. Chepeus-Miller, Director
US West Communications
Association Marketing
6350 South Maple Ave., #116
Tempe, AZ 85283
(602) 831-4790
(602) 831-4947

CALIFORNIA
Mr. Michael Ford, Vice President, Region Manager
QuesTech Financial
63 Fletcher Court
Bay Point, CA 94565
(925) 709-5015
(925) 709-5017
suntca@ix.netcom.com

Mr. C. Robert Kemp, CEO
Los Angeles Community Development Bank
5312A S. Vermont Ave.

Los Angeles, CA 90037
(213) 759-7759
(213) 759-7750

Mr. Mike Mantle, President
Bank of America, FSB
Community Development
1500 Newell Ave., #308
Walnut Creek, CA 94596
(510) 988-4819

Ms. Linda Smith, Microloan Project Manager
FAME Renaissance
2241 S. Hobart Blvd.
Los Angeles, CA 90018
(218) 730-9194
(213) 737-5717

Mr. Daryl W. Sweeney
Regional Comm. Dev. Manager
Home Savings of America
4900 Rivergrade Road, #2160
Irwindale, CA 91706
(626) 814-7870
(626) 814-7319

Mr. Bruce E. Wilson, Regional Vice President
Tokai Bank of California
South Bay Regional Office
21201 Hawthorne Blvd.
Torrance, CA 90503
(310) 543-3146
(310) 543-5347

CONNECTICUT
Mr. Henry Price, Senior Vice President
Business Lenders LLC
National Franchise Lending
15 Lewis St.
Hartford, CT O6103
(800) 646-7689
(860) 244-9303
hprice@businesslenders.com

Mr. Warren Smith, Senior Vice President
Fleet Bank
Mail Stop: CT OP 0111
70 Farmington Ave., 1st Fl.
Hartford, CT 06105

(860) 986-3055
(860) 986-3062

DELAWARE
Mr. William Allen
Vice President, Sales & Client Services
The Faneuil Group
42-C Read's Way
New Castle Corp. Commons
New Castle, DE 19720
(302) 324-5661
(302) 323-8015

Mr. J. Nathan Hill, President/General Manager
Green Wood Trust Company
Novus
12 Read's Way
New Castle, DE 19720
(302) 323-7688
(302) 323-7527

DISTRICT OF COLUMBIA
Mr. Lloyd M. Arrington, Jr., President
Neighborhood Economic Development Corp.
1660 L St., NW, #308
Washington, DC 20036
(202) 775-8815
(202) 223-0544

Mr. Edward L. Cleveland
The Capstone Capital Group
1210 Constitution Ave., NE
Washington, DC 20002
(202) 543-0515
(202) 328-7846

Ms. Jacqueline C. Fleming
MED Nat. Training Coordinator
U.S. Small Business Administration
Office of Minority Enterprise
Development
409 Third St., SW, #8000
Washington, DC 20416
(202) 205-6177
(202) 205-7135
jacqueline.fleming@sba.gov

Ms. Paulette Hicks
Sr. Vice President & Area Director

Citibank F.S.B.
1101 Pennsylvania Ave., NW, 11th Fl.
Washington, DC 20004
(202) 879-6834
(202) 879-6888
paulette.hicks@citicorp.com

Ms. Marie A. Mann, Vice President
Crestar
Community Development
1445 New York Ave., NW
Washington, DC 20005
(202) 879-6413

Ms. Jacqueline Daughtry Miller, Vice President
Independence Federal Savings Bank
Student Loan Department
1900 L St., NW, #700
Washington, DC 20036
(202) 626-0473
(202) 775-4553
jdaughtry2@aol.com

Mr. Deric A. Mims, Vice President
Crestar
Small Business Resource Center
1445 New York Ave., NW
Washington, DC 20005
(202) 879-6349
(202) 879-6088

Ms. Joyce Schwartz
The Adams National Bank
1627 K St., NW
Washington, DC 20006
(202) 466-4090

Ms. Leslie S. Shapiro, President
Padgett Business Services Foundation
1200 G St., NW, #800
Washington, DC 20005
(202) 434-8743
(202) 628-3497

Mr. Lance Withers Slaughter
Asst. Vice President & Financial Consultant
Merrill Lynch
1850 K St., NW, #700
Washington, DC 20006

(202) 659-7264
(202) 659-3079
Lance_Slaughter@ML.com

Mr. Charles A. Watson, Jr.
Business Banking Officer
NationsBank
730 15th St., NW, 5th Fl.
Washington, DC 20005
(202) 624-5190
(202) 624-5181

Mr. Randy Wilkins, Managing Principal
Waterford Global Ventures, LLC
1718 M St., NW, #130
Washington, DC 20036
(202) 298-9731
(202) 217-3519

Ms. Abigail M. Williams, Partner
Bert Smith & Co.
1401 New York Ave., NW, #540
Washington, DC 20005
(202) 393-8682
(202) 393-5608

Mr. George S. Willie, Managing Partner
Bert Smith & Co.
1401 New York Ave., NW, #540
Washington, DC 20005
(202) 393-5600
(202) 393-5608

FLORIDA
Mr. Jim Gleason
Sr. Vice President, Sr. Credit Officer
Jefferson Bank of Florida
301-41st St.
Arthur Godfrey Rd.
Miami Beach, FL 33140
(305) 535-9200
(305) 531-4747

Mr. Lucious T. Harris
Executive Vice President & CFO
Capital Bank
1221 Brickell Ave.
Miami, FL 33131
(305) 536-1677

Ms. Judy R. Jones
J.R. Jones & Associates
5409 DeFoors Ferry Rd.
Tallahassee, FL 32308
(850) 668-3316
(850) 668-0089

Mr. Kelsey R. Dorsett, President
Alliance Development Group
13780 S.W. 56 St., #222, Miller Square
Miami, FL 33175
(305) 387-6964
(305) 387-3710

Ms. Deloris Coleman
Community Development Officer
American Savings of Florida
Administrative Offices/Mail Stop
OC220, 17801 N.W. 2nd Ave.
Miami, FL 33169
(305) 770-2572
(305) 770-2073

Mr. James E. Tisdale, Senior Vice President
Jefferson Bank of Florida
Retail Banking
301-41st St.
Miami Beach, FL 33140
(305) 535-9300

GEORGIA
Cordova Capital Partners, LP
2500 Northwinds
Northwinds Pkwy., #475
Alpharetta, GA 30004
(678) 942-0300

ILLINOIS
Ms. Jacqueline C. Brown, Personal Banker
Firstar Bank Illinois
Oak Park Office
104 North Oak Park Ave.
Oak Park, IL 60301
(708) 445-4567
(708) 383-4854

Mr. Lawrence C. Manson, Jr.
General Partner
PENMAN Partners

333 West Wacker Dr., #700
Chicago, IL 60606
(312) 444-2763
(312) 750-4676

Mr. Xcylur R. Stoakley, Principal
Ark Capital Management
150 N. Wacker Dr., #2650
Chicago, IL 60606
(312) 541-0330
(312) 541-0335

Mr. Tyrone Wideman, Vice President
The Northern Trust Company
181 West Madison St.
Chicago, IL 60675
(312) 630-6000

IOWA
Mr. Robert A. Comey, Executive Vice President
Invest America Venture Group, Inc.
101 Second St., SE, #800
Cedar Rapids, IA 52401
(319) 363-8249
(319) 363-9683

KENTUCKY
Ms. Christie J. McCravy
Vice President
National City
Cash Management Sales
P.O. Box 36000
Louisville, KY 40233
(502) 581-7803
(502) 581-4075

MARYLAND
Mr. William L. Green
Commercial Loan Officer
MD Dept. of Economic & Employment Dev.
Trade Finance
401 E. Pratt St., 7th Fl.
Baltimore, MD 21202
(410) 333-8189
(410) 333-4453

MASSACHUSETTS
Mr. Milton J. Benjamin, Jr., President
CDFC

MA Community Dev. Finance
10 Post Office Square, #1090
Boston, MA 02109
(617) 482-9141
(617) 482-7129

Mr. Grady Hedgespeth, President
Bank of Boston
100 Federal St.
P.O. Box 2016
Boston, MA 02110
(617) 434-9040
(617) 434-0351

MICHIGAN
Mr. Lawrence Jones, Director, Greater Michigan
Michigan National Bank
Commercial Financial Servies
27777 Inkster Rd.
P.O. Box 9065
Farmington Hills, MI 48333
(810) 473-3248
(810) 473-5889

MISSISSIPPI
Mr. Michael D. Booker
Senior Vice President/Manager Commercial Lend.
Bank of Mississippi
P.O. Box 1605
Jackson, MS 39215
(601) 944-3509
(601) 354-4500

MISSOURI
Mr. David B. Harper, President/CEO
New Age Financial, Inc.
3855 Lucas & Hunt Road, #223
St. Louis, MO 63121
(314) 381-6499
(314) 381-6576

Mr. Robert J. Lee
Vice President, Comm. Dev. Director
Mercantile Mortgage
12680 Olive Blvd.
St. Louis, MO 63141
(314) 523-2410
(314) 579-2215

NEBRASKA
Ms. Wanda Nesbitt
International Banking Officer
First National Bank of Omaha
One First National Center
Omaha, NE 68102
(402) 341-0500
(402) 633-3554

NEW JERSEY
Mr. Michael A. Rambert, Senior Advisor
New Jersey Commerce & Economic
Growth Commission
Venture Finance
20 West State St., P.O. Box 838
Trenton, NJ 8625
ccvramb@commerce.state.nj.us

Mr. Albert A. Sturdivant, Chairman, CIO
Sturdivant & Co.
223 Gibbsboro Rd.
Clementon, NJ 08021
(609) 627-4500
(609) 627-9487

NEW YORK
Mr. David D. Cutting, Senior Vice President
Standard Chartered Bank
Retailers & Wholesalers Unit
7 World Trade Center
New York, NY 10048
(212) 667-0469
(212) 667-0225

Mr. Gabriel P. Caprio, President/CEO
Amalgamated Bank of New York
11-15 Union Square
New York, NY 10003
(212) 620-8627

Mr. Publio E. Teurbe-Tolon, Senior Vice President
Amalgamated Bank of New York
11-15 Union Square
New York, NY 10003
(212) 620-8652

Ms. Bernell K. Grier, Vice President
NatWest Bank
Community Development
175 Water St., 25th Fl.

New York, NY 10038
(212) 602-2926
(212) 602-1109

NORTH CAROLINA
Mr. Chester A. Williams, Sr.
Senior Vice President/Director of CRA
BB&T
Community Development
200 S. College St.
Charlotte, NC 28202
(704) 954 1100
(704) 954-1105

OHIO
Mr. Paul G. Anderson, President & CEO
The Columbus Personal Business Monitor
5684 Bisbywoods Ct., #C
Columbus, OH 43232
(614) 860-9388

Mr. Samuel E. McDaniel
Redwood Development Center
815 E. Mound St., Columbus, OH 43205
(614) 252-0057
(614) 252-3186

Ms. Vivian Parkes, Planning Consultant
1st Cleveland Financial Services
23220 Chagrin Blvd., #207
Beachwood, OH 44122
(216) 595-9000
(216) 595-2329
stocks@1stcleveland.com

Mr. Edgar A. Pressley, Jr., Vice President
KeyBank
Community Finance
525 Vine St.
Cincinnati, OH 45202
(513) 762-8383
(513) 762-8408

Mr. Andre L. Reynolds
Relationship Officer, Central Region
The Huntington National Bank
7933 Euclid Ave.
Cleveland, OH 44103
(216) 515-0313
(216) 515-0141

Ms. Alicia B. Townsend, Branch Manager
Star Bank
Elmwood Place Office
5655 Vine St., ML 1416
Cincinnati, OH 45216
(513) 632-4862
(513) 242-5208

Mr. William K. Willis, Jr., Vice President/Director
Society National Bank
Govt. and Community Affairs
88 East Broad St.
Columbus, OH 43215
(614) 460-3417
(614) 365-3313

PENNSYLVANIA
Mr. Tony C. Leonard
Client Relations Representative
Philadelphia Industrial Dev. Corp.
1500 Market St.
Philadelphia, PA 19102 2126
(215) 496-8109
(215) 977-9618

Mr. Steven D. Tolbert
GS Capital L.P.
Safeguard Corp. Campus
435 Devon Park Dr., #201
Wayne, PA 19087
(610) 293-9151
(610) 293-1979
stolbert@safeguard.comWinternet

TEXAS
Mr. Charles English, President
Dallas Business Finance Corporation
1402 Corinth St., #1150
Dallas, TX 75215
(214) 428-7332
(214) 426-6847

Mr. Eric Kern
Comerical Bank
P.O. Box 4167
Mail Code 6629
Houston, TX 77210
(800) 715-5838
(713) 888-2674

VIRGINIA
Mr. Larry J. Daniely
Senior Vice President/Senior Credit Officer
First Union National Bank of VA
1751 Pinnacle Dr., 3rd Fl.
McLean, VA 22102
(703) 760-5918
(703) 760-6230

Ms. Sylvesta L. Jennings, President
First State Bank
P.O. Box 640
201 N. Union St.
Danville, VA 24543
(804) 793-4611

Mr. Hugh C. Long II, Capital Area President
First Union National Bank
P.O. Box 7606
McLean, VA 22106
(703) 760-6940
(703) 760-5779

Ms. Karen Smaw, Director
Fairfax County Economic Development Authority
Small & Minority Business Development
8300 Boone Blvd., #450
Vienna, VA 22182
(703) 790-0600
(703) 893-1269
Ksmaw@mindspring.com

WASHINGTON
Ms. Cheryl A. LeMelle, Assistant Vice President
Seafirst Bank
Human Resources
10500 N.E. Eighth St., #400
Bellevue, WA 98004
(206) 585-6293
(206) 585-6297

CANADA
Mr. Harvey Robinson, Investment Analyst
Goodman & Company
55th Floor, Scotia Plaza
40 King St. West
Toronto, CANADA
(416) 365-2414
(416) 863-0021

National Minority Franchising Initiative
Bond's Minority Franchising Guide

YES, our Company would like to participate in the National Minority Franchising Initiative. We enthusiastically welcome this opportunity to encourage minority ownership in our system. Our response to this survey clarifies our commitment to increasing minority representation. Our **profile data will be published <u>at no cost</u> in both the new publication *Minority Franchising Guide*** and on the Website www.minorityfranchising.com.

1. Name of Franchise (i.e. DBA): _____

2. Address: _____
   City: _____ State/Province: _____ Zip/Postal Code: _____
   Telephone: (800) _____ or (   ) _____
   Fax Number: (   ) _____ ; E-Mail Address: _____
   Internet: www._____

3. Contact: _____ Position: _____

4. Description of Business: (Use the full space available to set yourself apart from other franchising opportunities, i.e. sell the potential franchisee, keeping in mind that the audience is the prospective minority franchisee.) Please limit the description to 50 words.

   _____
   _____
   _____
   _____
   _____

5. Company was founded in 19 _____ .   First year as franchisor was 19 _____ .

6. Actual number of **Franchised Units** as of **6/1/1999**   _____ Units

7. Actual number of **Company-Owned** Units as of **6/1/1999**   _____ Units

   Total Operating Units as of **6/1/1999**   _____ Units

8. Do you provide potential franchisees with an **<u>Earnings Claim Statement</u>**?   ❏ Yes   ❏ No

9. In how many States do you have operating units?   _____ States

10. What 3 States have the largest number of operating units?

    Top 3 States   # Units in Each

    1. _____   _____

    2. _____   _____

    3. _____   _____

11. What is the **minimum net worth** required of the franchisee? $ _____

12. Even though the cash investment may vary substantially by individual unit, what is the **range of equity capital** (up-front cash) required? $ _____

13. What is the <u>range of **total investment**</u> required? $_____

14. How much is the **initial franchise fee** for a new franchisee? $_____

15. How much is the **on-going royalty fee**?   _____ % or _____

16. How much is the **on-going advertising fee**?   _____ % or _____

17. What is the **term of the original franchise agreement**? _____ Years   Renewal period? _____ Years

18. Do you have **Area Development Agreements**? ❑ Yes ❑ No; If Yes, for what period? _____ Years

19. Do you have **Sub-Franchisor Contracts** covering specified territories?   ❑ Yes   ❑ No

20. Can the franchisee establish **additional outlets** within his area?   ❑ Yes   ❑ No

21. Is **passive ownership** of the initial unit: ❑ Allowed   ❑ Allowed, But Discouraged   ❑ Not Allowed

22. What **square footage and types of sites** do most of your franchise units require? _____ SF
    - ❑ Free-Standing Building
    - ❑ Storefront
    - ❑ Strip Center
    - ❑ Regional Mall
    - ❑ Home-Based
    - ❑ Other _____
    - ❑ Not Applicable

23. Do you assist the franchisee in **site selection**?   ❑ Yes   ❑ No   ❑ Not Applicable

24. Do you assist the franchisee in **lease negotiations**?   ❑ Yes   ❑ No   ❑ Not Applicable

25. Do you participate in **co-operative advertising**?   ❑ Yes   ❑ No   ❑ Not Applicable

26. <u>Including the owner/operator, **how many employees**</u> are recommended to properly staff the <u>average</u> franchised unit? _____ Full-Time _____ Part-Time

27. How many **full-time, paid personnel** are currently on your corporate staff? _____

28. What are the location and duration of any **initial training sessions** included in the franchise fee?

    Location   Duration

    A. _____   _____

    B. _____   _____

    C. _____   _____

29. Does your system have a **franchisee association**? ❑ Yes   ❑ No;
    If Yes, are you a member? ❑ Yes   ❑ No

30. In which specific regions of the U.S. are you actively seeking new franchisees? For example: All U.S., or NW & SW, or NJ Only. _____

31. Which of the following <u>on-going</u> services do you provide to the franchisee?

Service	Included in Fees	At Additional Cost	N.A.
Central Data Processing	A. ❑	a. ❑	❑
Central Purchasing	B. ❑	b. ❑	❑
Field Operations Evaluation	C. ❑	c. ❑	❑
Field Training	D ❑	d. ❑	❑
Initial Store Opening	E. ❑	e. ❑	❑
Inventory Control	F. ❑	f. ❑	❑
Franchisee Newsletter	G. ❑	g. ❑	❑
Regional or National Meetings	H. ❑	h. ❑	❑
800 Telephone Hotline	I. ❑	i. ❑	❑

32. Of the Total Franchised Units noted in Question 6 above, approximately how many units (or what percentage) are owned (50% or greater minority ownership) by:

_____ African-Americans.   _____ Asian-Americans.

_____ Hispanics.   _____ Native Americans.

Other Minorities _____ .

33. Please use the space below to describe any programs that are specifically geared for recruiting and/or assisting poten-tial minority franchisees. Such programs could involve recruiting, training, financing, the deferment of franchise fees, assistance in preparing loan documents, etc. As the vast majority of franchisors do not have specific programs in place, please know that the absence of any particular program(s) in no way indicates that you do not support the inclusion of minority franchisees. What is important is that you support the overall objectives of the Initiative. If you do not wish to use this open-ended space to respond, we will include the following response — *"Although we support the objectives of the National Minority Franchising Initiative, we do not have any specific programs in place at this time."*

_____
_____
_____
_____
_____
_____
_____
_____

Name of Respondent: _____ Telephone No: (   ) _____

Thank you very much for your time and prompt attention. Please return to:

Source Book Publications
P.O. Box 12488, Oakland, CA 94604
(510) 839-5471 v Fax (510) 839-2104

Alphabetical listing of franchisors

DEFINITIVE FRANCHISOR DATA BASE AVAILABLE FOR RENT

SAMPLE FRANCHISOR PROFILE

Name of Franchise:	**AARON'S RENTAL PURCHASE**
Address:	309 East Paces Ferry Rd., N. E.
City/State/Zip/Postal Code:	Atlanta, GA 30305-2377
Country:	U. S. A.
800 Telephone #:	(800) 551-6015
Local Telephone #:	(404) 237-4016
Alternate Telephone #:	
Fax #:	(404) 240-6540
E-Mail:	billwilson@aaronsfranchise.com
Internet Address:	www.aaronsfranchise.com
# Franchised Units:	136
# Company-Owned Units:	<u>199</u>
# Total Units:	335
Company Contact:	Mr. Todd Evans
Contact Title/Position:	VP Franchise Development
Contact Salutation:	Mr. Evans
President:	Mr. R. Charles Loudermilk, Sr.
President Title:	Chairman/Chief Executive Officer
President Salutation:	Mr. Loudermilk
Industry Category (of 45):	37 / Rental Services
IFA Member:	International Franchise Association
CFA Member:	

KEY FEATURES

- Number of Active North American Franchisors — ~ 2,150
  - % US — ~85%
  - % Canadian — ~15%
- Data Fields (See Above) — 23
- Industry Categories — 45
- % With Toll-Free Telephone Numbers — 67%
- % With Fax Numbers — 97%
- % With Name of Preferred Contact — 99%
- % With Name of President — 97%
- % With Number of Total Operating Units — 95%
- Guaranteed Accuracy - $.50 Rebate/Returned Bad Address
- Converted to Any Popular Data Base or Contact Management Program
- Initial Front-End Cost — $550
- Quarterly Up-Dates — $75
- Mailing Labels Only - One-Time Use — $350

For More Information, Please Contact
Source Book Publications
1814 Franklin Street, Suite 820, Oakland, California 94612
(800) 841-0873 ❖ (510) 839-5471 ❖ FAX (510) 839-2104

THE DEFINITIVE ANNUAL GUIDE OF INTERNATIONAL FRANCHISING

THE 1999 INTERNATIONAL HERALD TRIBUNE
INTERNATIONAL FRANCHISE GUIDE

Key Features:

- The Most Comprehensive and Up-To-Date Directory of Committed International Franchisors.

- Profiles Are the Result of an Exhaustive 60-Point Questionnaire.

- 32 Distinct Business Categories.

- Listing of International Franchise Consultants, Attorneys and Service Providers.

- 192 Pages.

- Direct Comparability Between Franchise Listings.

Yes, I want to order ___ copy(ies) of the 1999 IHT *International Franchise Guide* at US$34.95 each, shipping included.

Name _____ Title _____

Company _____ Telephone No. (_____) _____

Address _____

City _____ State/Prov. _____ Zip _____

❑ Check Enclosed or

Charge my: ❑ MasterCard ❑ Visa

Card #: _____ Expiration Date: _____

Signature: _____

Please send to:
Source Book Publications
P.O. Box 12488, Oakland, CA 94604

Satisfaction Guaranteed. If not fully satisfied, return for a prompt, 100% refund.

For faster service, call (800) 841-0873 or (510) 839-5471 or fax us at (510) 839-2104.
Also check us out on the Internet at <u>www.franchiseintl.com</u>.

TIPS & TRAPS WHEN BUYING A FRANCHISE

2nd Edition (Completely revised in 1999)

By Mary Tomzack, President of FranchiseHelp, Inc., an international information and research company servicing the franchising industry.

Key Features:

- Completely updated version of the 1994 reader-acclaimed classic on franchising, with the same practical advice, non-textbook approach.

- Provides an insightful crash course on selecting, negotiating and financing the right franchise, and turning it into a lucrative, satisfying business.

- How to select the best franchise for your personal finances and lifestyle; navigate the legal maze; and finance your investment.

- Reveals the hottest franchise opportunities for the 21st Century and discusses co-branding. Provides advice on building a business empire through franchising.

- "This book is the bible for anyone who is considering a franchise investment."

- 236 Pages.

Yes, I want to order ____ copy(ies) of *Tips & Traps When Buying a Franchise (2nd Edition)* at US$19.95 each, plus US$4 for shipping & handling (international shipments at actual cost).

Name _____ Title _____

Company _____ Telephone No. (_____) _____

Address _____

City _____ State/Prov. _____ Zip _____

☐ Check Enclosed or
Charge my: ☐ MasterCard ☐ Visa

Card #: _____ Expiration Date: _____

Signature: _____

Please send to:
Source Book Publications
P.O. Box 12488, Oakland, CA 94604

Satisfaction Guaranteed. If not fully satisfied, return for a prompt, 100% refund.

For faster service, call (800) 841-0873 or (510) 839-5471 or fax us at (510) 839-2104.
Also check us out on the Internet at www.franchiseintl.com.